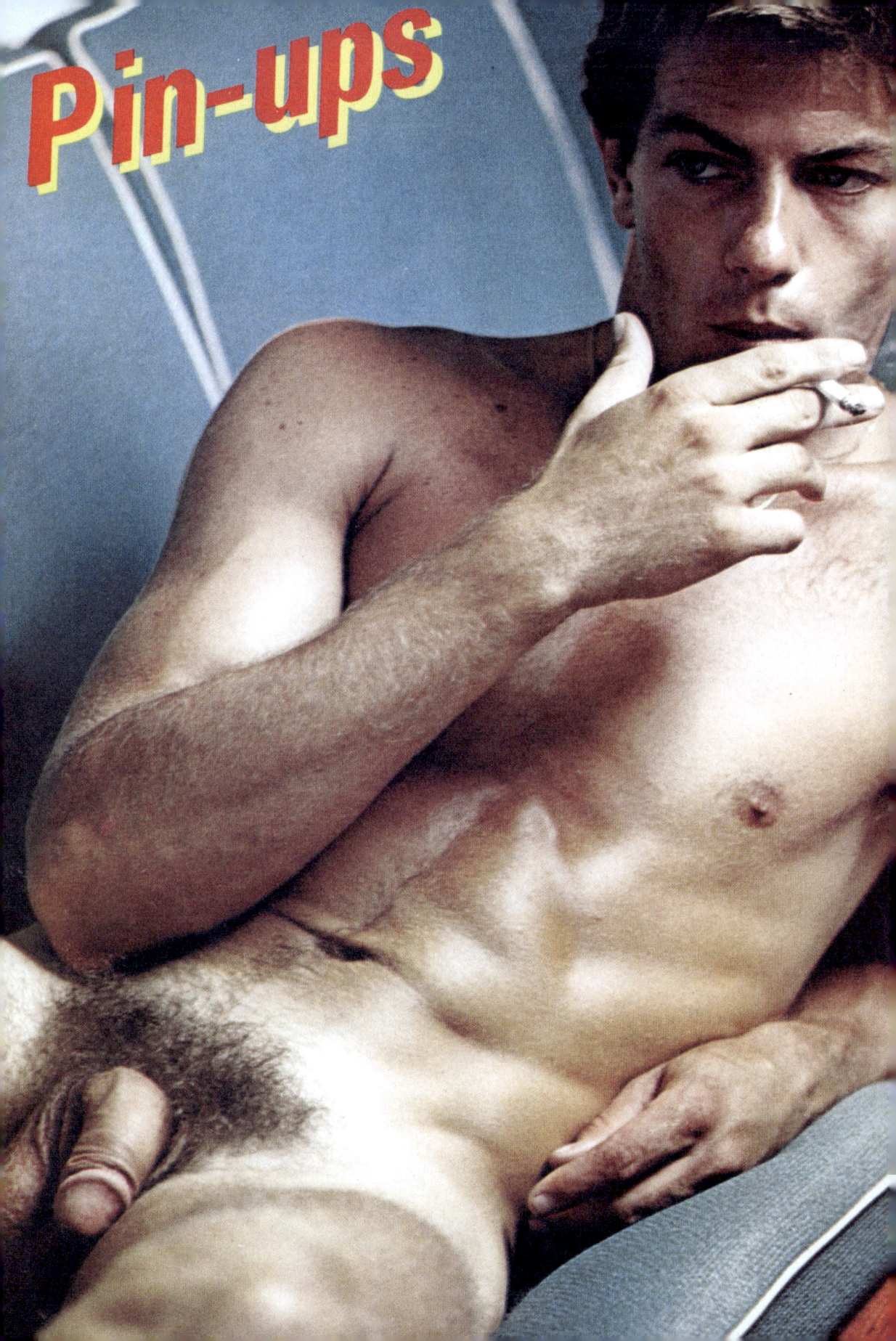

Pin-ups

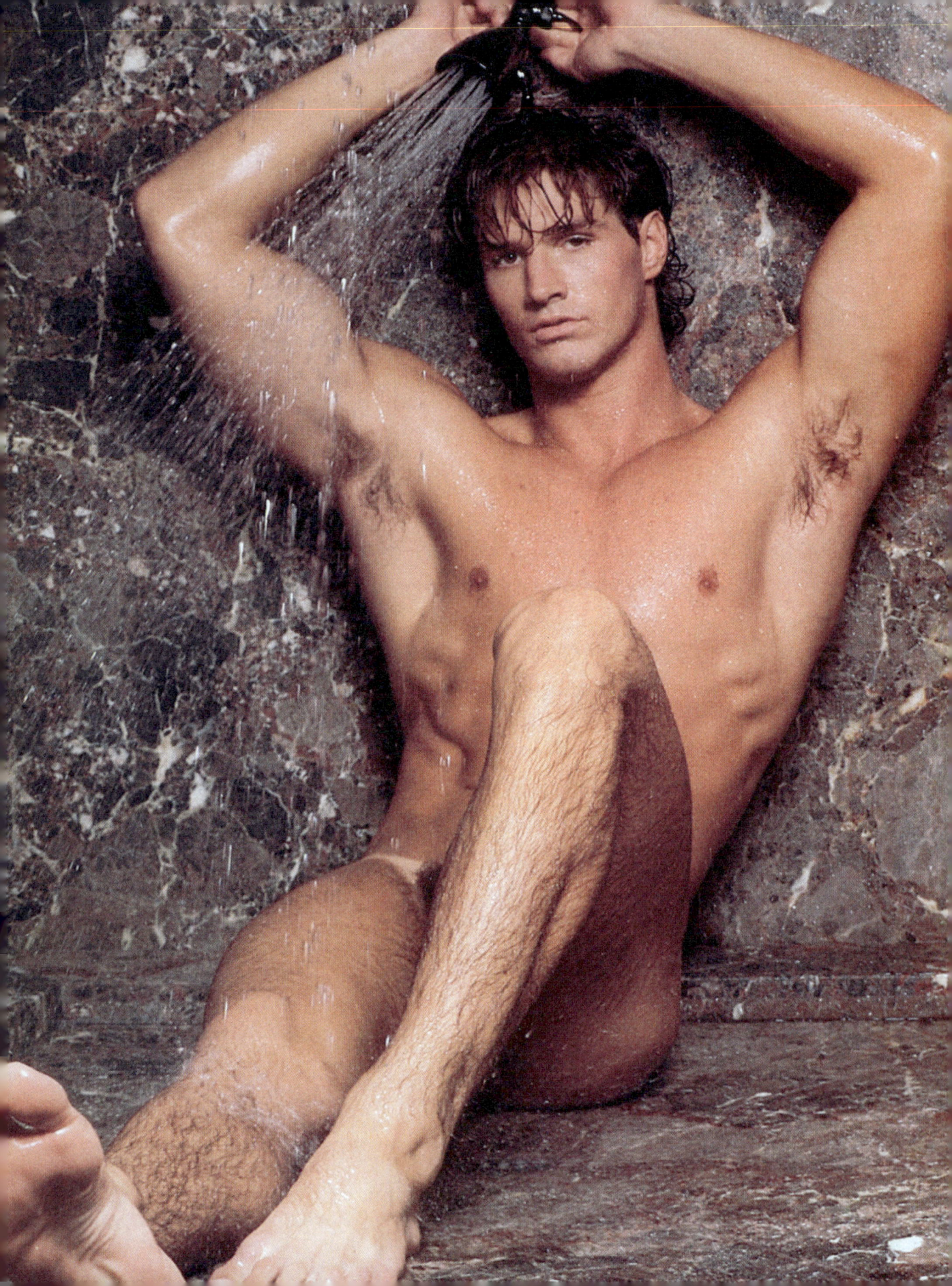

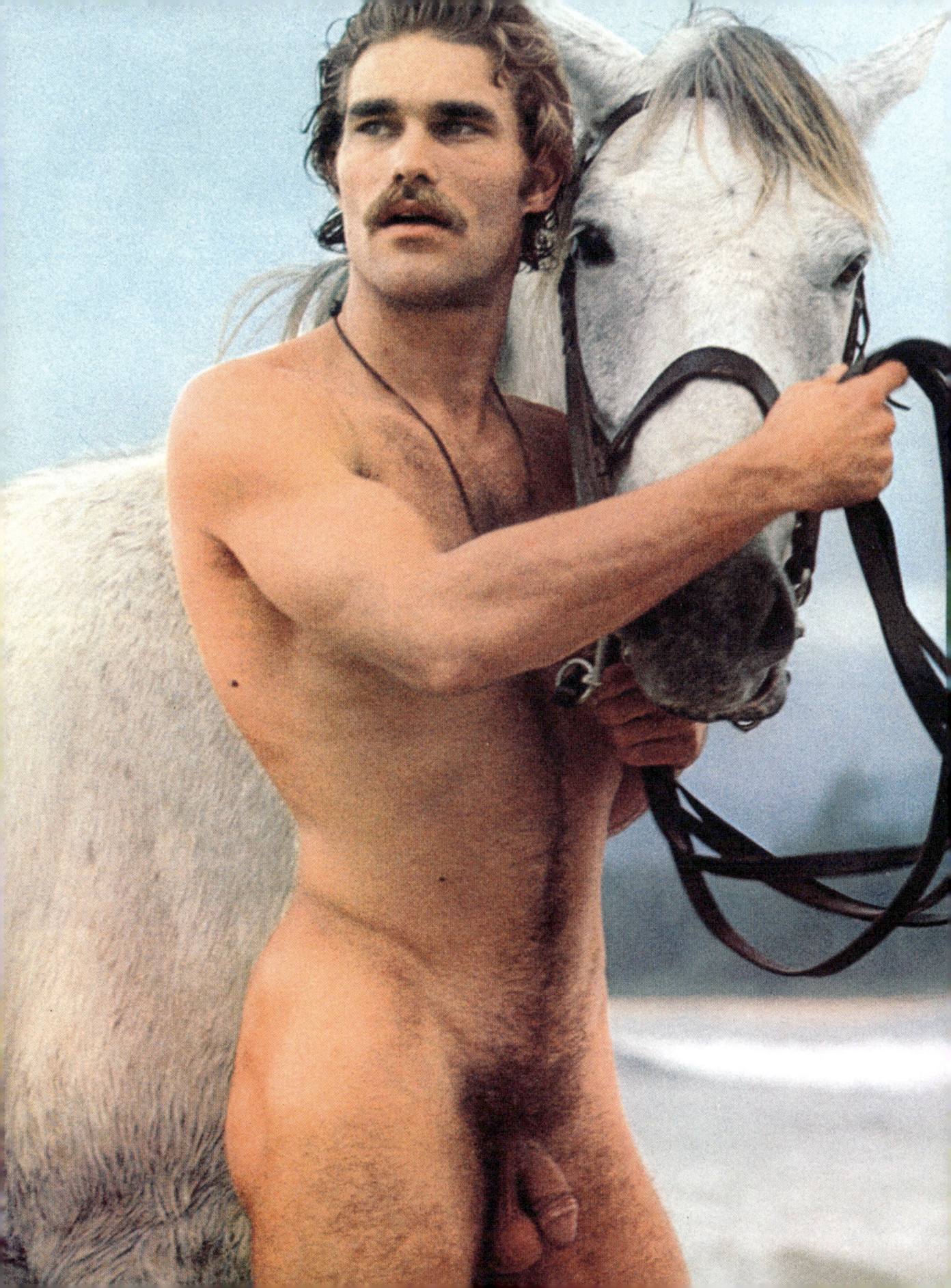

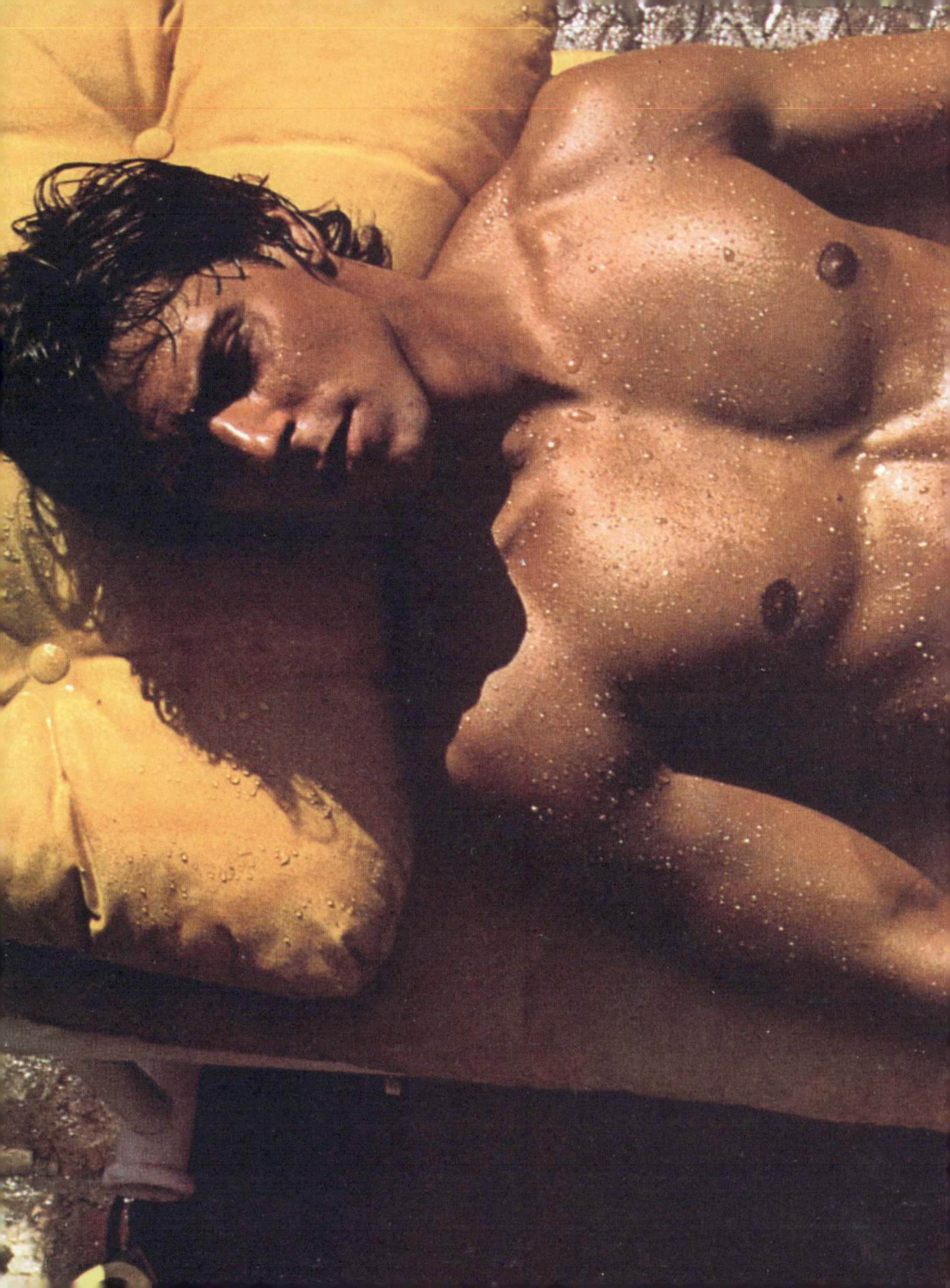

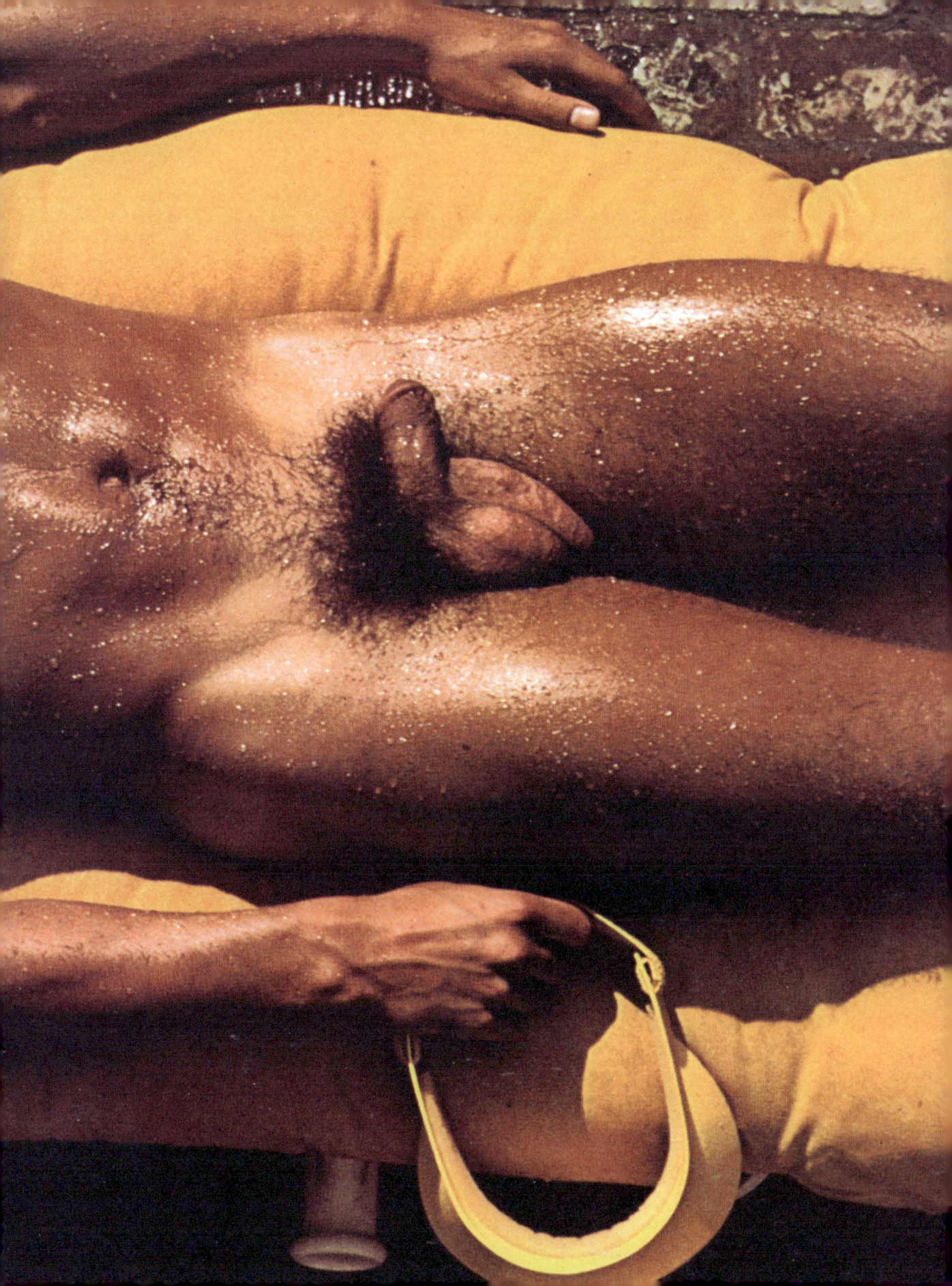

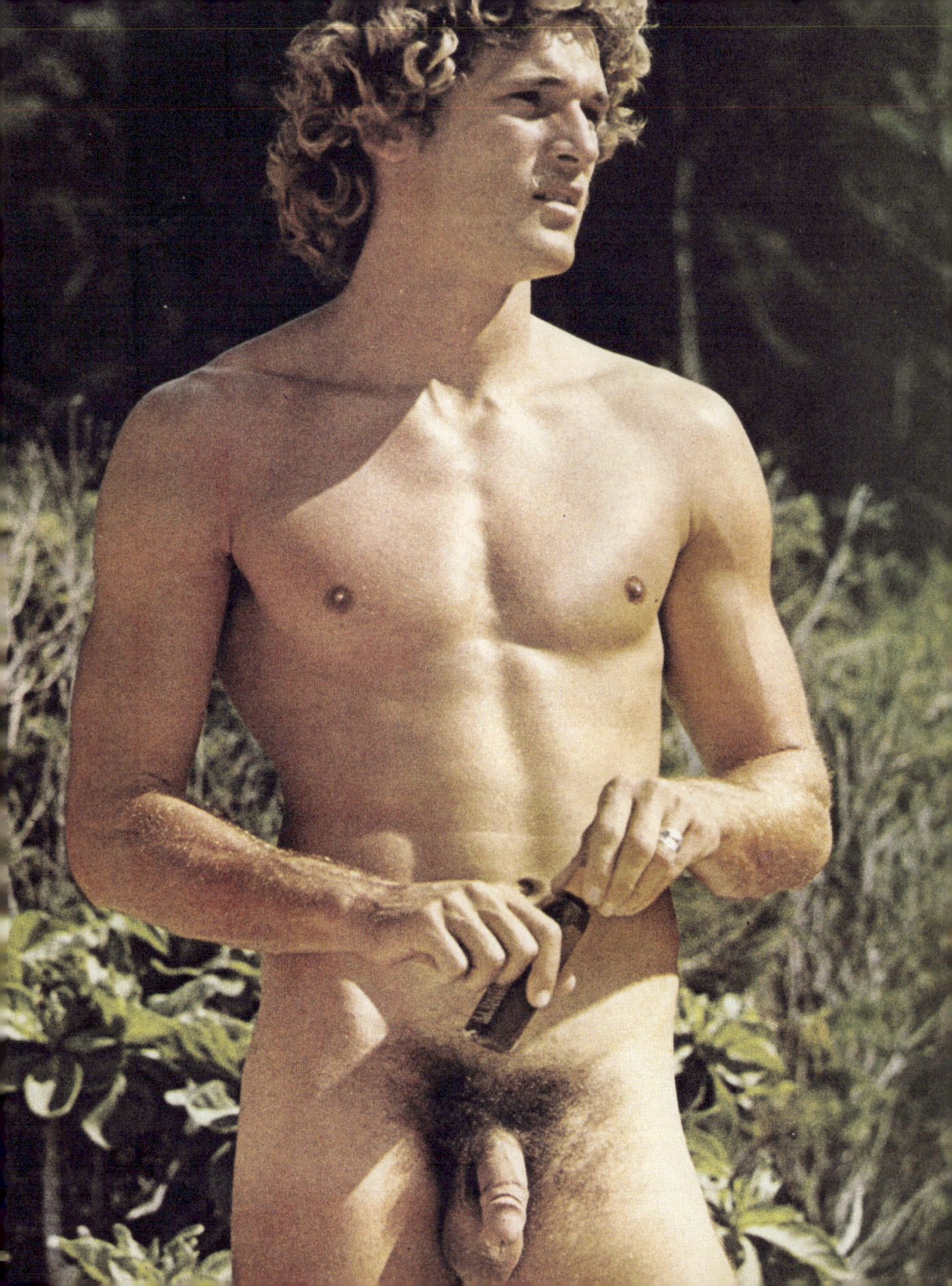

Playgirl

The Official History
of a Cult Magazine

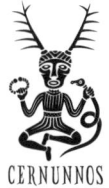

CERNUNNOS

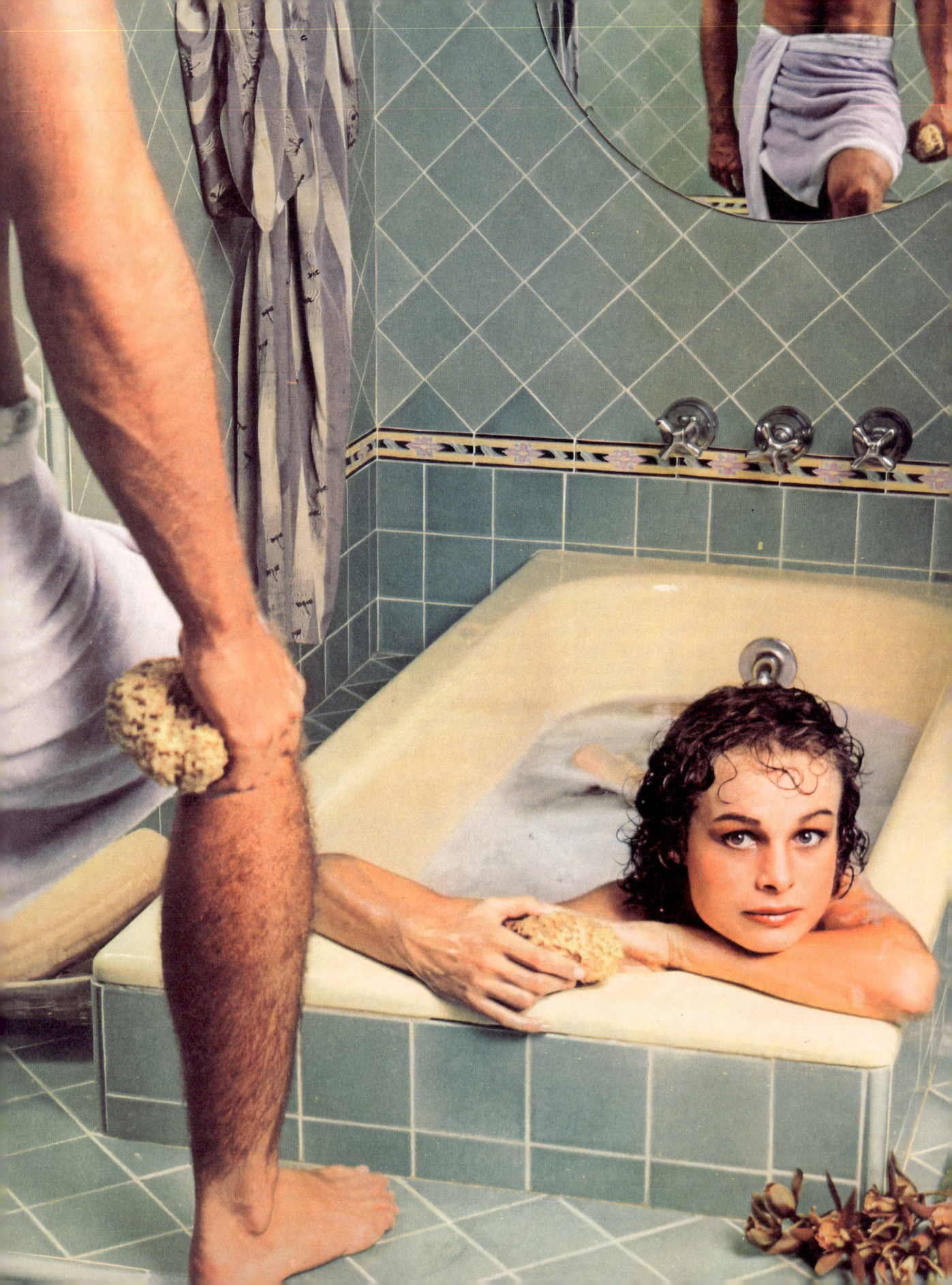

CONTENTS

10 **FOREWORD**
Bruce LaBruce

13 MY INTRODUCTION TO *PLAYGIRL*
Daniel McKernan

17 FIFTY YEARS OF *PLAYGIRL*:
THE LEGACY OF AN ICON
Nicole Caldwell

21 THE SYMBIOTIC RELATIONSHIP
OF FEMINISM AND *PLAYGIRL*
Michele Zipp

25 *PLAYGIRL* MADE ME GAY
Mickey Boardman

30 **COVERS**

44 **ARTICLES**

47 ARE FEMINISTS HUMORLESS?
Maya Angelou

48 I SLEPT WITH A MALE PROSTITUTE
Tracy Cabot

52 EROTICISM IN WOMEN
Anaïs Nin

56 A USER-FRIENDLY GUIDE TO THE PENIS
S. W. Westcott

59 I WAS AN X-RATED NOVELIST
Yona Zeldis McDonough

63 WIENERS
Heather Fink

65 A CAUTIOUS USER'S GUIDE
TO DRUGS AND SEX
Jack Owen Jardine

72 COUPLING IN THE YEAR 2000
Richard Meltzer

76 **PICTORIALS**

90 **INTERVIEWS**

92 Grace Jones
Dolly Parton

94 Larry Flynt

99 Anne Rice

100 Sandra Bernhard
Shirley Manson

101 Bette Midler
Duran Duran

103 John Travolta
Burt Reynolds

104 Gloria Steinem

105 Alan Cumming

107 Joan Rivers

109 Beastie Boys

110 Jane Fonda

113 Joan Collins

115 Sylvester Stallone

117 Cher
Margaret Cho

118 **CENTERFOLDS**

144 **BEST OF THE 1970s**

156 **BEST OF THE 1980s**

168 **BEST OF THE 1990s**

180 **BEST OF THE 2000s**

192 ***PLAYGIRL* FUNNIES**

205 **SEX TALK**

212 **MISCELLANEOUS**

224 ***PLAYGIRL* TODAY**

233 **ACKNOWLEDGMENTS**

FOREWORD

BRUCE LaBRUCE

It would be easy (and foolish) to dismiss the publication of a book on the history of *Playgirl* magazine as mere brazen nostalgia or camp fetish for our favorite lampoonable decades of the twentieth century: the seventies—the decade of the magazine's debut (in 1973)—fraught with pornstaches, kaftans, wood-paneled basements, key parties, and quaaludes; and the eighties—the decade of the magazine's popular ascendancy—evoking padded shoulders, Jheri curls (or curly bangs), big hair, AIDS, and *The Cosby Show*. What really matters about the advent of *Playgirl*—a feisty feminist corrective to those big-titted juggernauts *Playboy* and *Penthouse*, whose outsize popularity seemed to imply that only men could get their rocks off by perusing the nude human form—is that feminists finally got to eat their cake, so to speak, and have it.

In a famous episode of the popular seventies sitcom *The Mary Tyler Moore Show* entitled "Not Just Another Pretty Face," which aired in September 1974, not long after *Playgirl* hit the stands, Mary, a single workingwoman in her thirties, has a dilemma: in a department store, she meets a tall, beautiful, and slightly vapid male ski instructor named Paul, whom she begins to date (and have sex with: that she fucks her dates in the series is always understood but never overtly stated) purely for his looks. When her neighbor Phyllis (played by Cloris Leachman, interviewed in the very first issue of *Playgirl*!) expresses surprise that she let herself be picked up, Mary says slyly, "Don't be silly. I wouldn't let a man pick me up. I picked him up." This notion in America at this historical moment was pretty heady

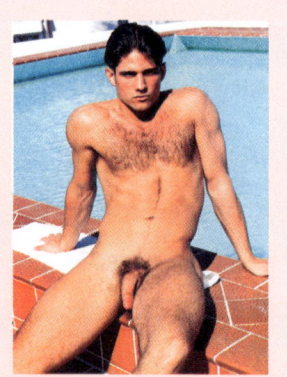

10

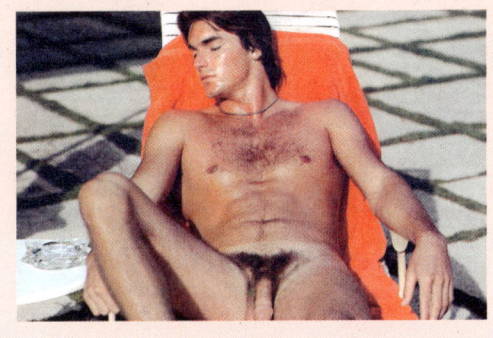

stuff for TV—a woman picking up a man in broad daylight and starting to have sex with him solely on the basis of physical attraction. The episode hammers home the point: Mary's boss tells her, reproachfully, "I hate to tell you, but he's prettier than you are!" and Mary's always horny coworker Sue Ann Nivens blurts out to Paul, "Incidentally you are the most gorgeous hunk of flesh I have ever seen." Housewives may have clutched their pearls, but this episode nailed the nascent zeitgeist: female sexual empowerment, the objectification of the male body, and the female appropriation of the male gaze were not only possible but somehow long overdue. Phyllis's teenage daughter, Bess, gives the sentiment its full feminist expression in a pep talk to Mary: "So what if you just go out with him because he's attractive? Men go out with women just because they're attractive. Nobody seems to think there's anything wrong with that. I mean, for thousands of years men have been using women, and I think it's about time we started using them back!" (It took the spirited teenager on the show to identify using men as playthings as a feminist revenge fantasy!) I don't think Mary was ever shown reading an issue of *Playgirl*, but she and every other female character on the show—Phyllis, Rhoda, Sue Ann, young Bess, even Georgette—certainly would have.

Of course, gay men, who have never had a problem sexually objectifying the hell out of one another, were quick to jump on the *Playgirl* bandwagon. As a young teenager in the late seventies, I used both furtively purchased copies of *Playgirl* and the porn-adjacent *GQ* magazine of the era to jerk off to when no one was home. But it was *Playgirl*, with its trenchant columns ("Are Feminists Humorless?" by Maya Angelou? Priceless!), its incisive interviews (Sandra Bernhard: "Pornography is an absolute necessity. I don't condemn it in any way at all. I actively condone it. I think it's very healthy and actually helps a lot of people come to terms with their own sexuality." Hallelujah!), and its free and open discussion of sexuality ("A Cautious User's Guide to Drugs and Sex." Essential!), that proved to be a worthy and equal companion to *Playboy*, giving as good as it got—and without resorting to a female variation of Hef's hokey smoking-jacket routine. Long live *Playgirl*! I look forward to its continued sexcess!

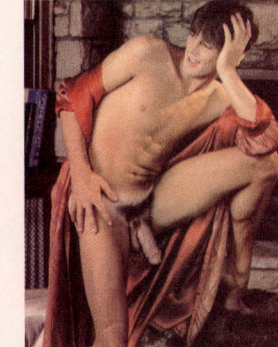

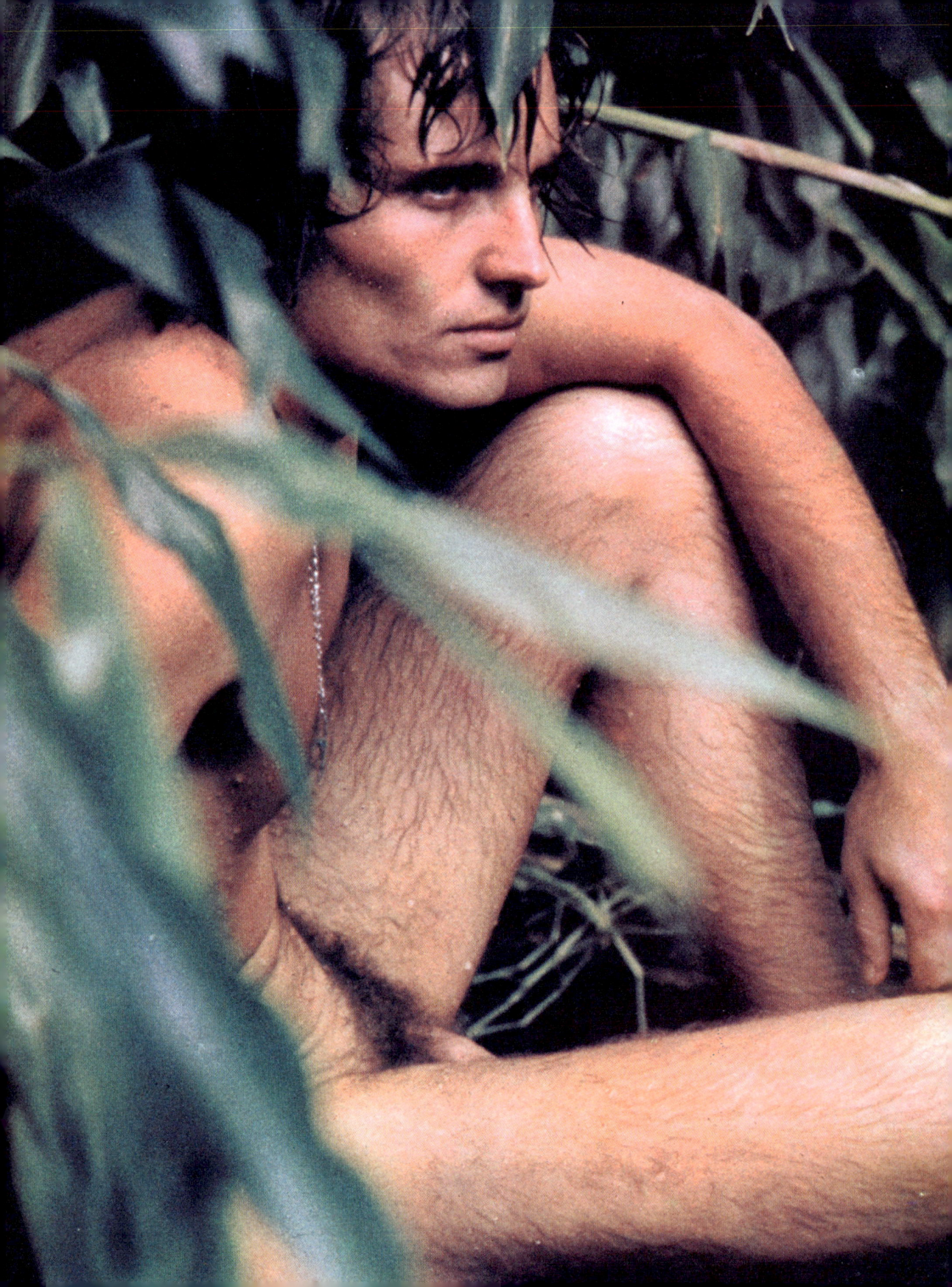

MY INTRODUCTION TO *PLAYGIRL*

DANIEL McKERNAN

I n 2007, I came upon an ad with the headline: "Gay Video Editor Needed." Ignoring the choice of words, I thought: *I could do that*. I got the job. Little did I know it would send me on a journey that would dominate the next decade and a half of my life—it was *Playgirl*.

It turned out most of the editors at *Playgirl TV* (our VOD/broadcast division) were straight men who didn't mind editing the couples scenes but had zero interest in the solo footage that had piled up before they hired me. The magazine existed on a separate floor at 801 Second Avenue, and we at *Playgirl TV* seldom mingled with the magazine editors, whom we referred to as "the girls on the ninth floor." A year after being hired, I was tasked with producing my first cover shoot for the magazine (April 2008's "Beach Bodies on Fire," shot on Fire Island), which was perhaps the first time I met then editor in chief Nicole Caldwell.

I was also unaware that the company had had a tumultuous past: the magazine rights have fallen into numerous hands over the years. At some point the *Playgirl* trademark landed in my lap, and it was my job—my cultural responsibility and civic duty, even—to carry it to safety and to greener horizons (rather than blue ones). In many ways, it has carried me through life as much as I have carried it.

Despite the magazine's iconic status as a legacy brand and a cultural institution, I hid the job from my family for a decade before finally "coming out" to them. What was I ashamed of? My desire to "elevate" the brand back into the mainstream from the fag rag it had become was always there in my mind: it had been done in the seventies (when our peak monthly readership was more than fourteen million in 1974) and eighties (before becoming a "flaccid failure," as described online). Regardless, is pornography a world from which there is no return? Only a few "adult" magazines can be resold on eBay, among them *Playboy*, *Penthouse*, *Hustler*, and *Playgirl*. Certainly there is a way to normalize an esteem of getting nude for money: no one judges the many celebrities who show all in films and on TV.

I've always thought of *Playgirl* as the gateway drug: celebrities and first-time models who wouldn't show their cocks to anyone else would show them to *Playgirl*. At the start of the magazine, the editors preferred celebrity men as our centerfolds. Jenny Lambert—magazine cofounder with her husband, Douglas Lambert—says in *A Teardrop on a Rose*, their collaborative tell-all story: "We felt that men, especially those with a healthy sense of humor, would be more interesting to women when the ladies already watched these 'hunks' in movies or on TV."

I must also address the elephant dong in the room: the cheesiness that permeates the nineties and aughts era of the magazine (the mimbo years). Of course, it's there: *Playgirl* is the butt (pun intended) of so many jokes throughout pop culture, be they on *SNL* or *30 Rock*. Our storylines and narratives over those years, as well as the styling and captions, were oftentimes as camp as they come.

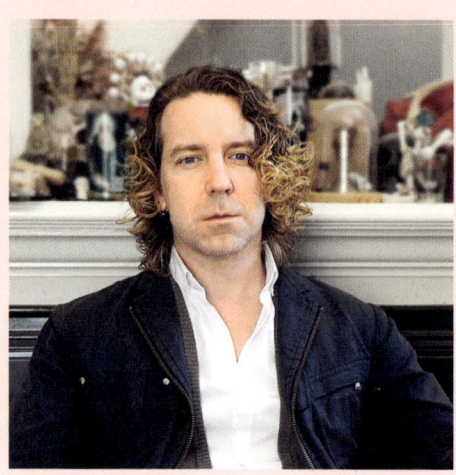

To many a gay, it is a coming-of-age experience—an introduction to their sexuality—to find a stack of *Playgirls* under a bed. Plenty have told me they'd stolen a *Playgirl* magazine as a teenager because they weren't old enough to buy it or because they were too embarrassed to be seen purchasing it. Men still email me asking how to log in to PlaygirlPlus.com because their "wife cannot figure out her password" and they are allegedly writing on her behalf.

One fun fact about the brand is that it started out as a go-go girl and live-music nightclub for men and women alike to congregate and let loose. The dancers were all women, and this acted as a social lubricant for the patrons to feel more comfortable around one another. Douglas Lambert wrote:

> "Playgirl" conjured up what females wanted in today's world: independence, freedom from the old mores, fun, options, playfulness, and personal decisions based on their terms. For guys, the name told them that when they walked through our doors, they would find girls who, to put it bluntly, might (or might not) be considering a sexual experience—but on their terms. The message was that females were in the lead. Being female was a great thing, and males were poised to enjoy the benefits of these new attitudes.

Furthermore, did you know that *Playgirl* has *never* been related to *Playboy*? In truth, Hugh Hefner sued and lost more than once over the years. I met Hefner's son, the heir to *Playboy*, at the Playboy Club in New York, and as he shook my hand he quipped: "Ahh, the impostors."

When people find out what I do, the first thing they usually ask is, "*Playgirl*? Does that still exist? Is that still around?" And I say yes.

"Can I ask you something?" they ask (unironically), with a look in their eyes that is so familiar to me, as if they think they've thought of something no one else has ever asked me: "Is *Playgirl* for women or men?" And I say yes.

DANIEL McKERNAN

Daniel McKernan (born New Orleans, 1981) is an artist, musician, and curator. His video work has appeared on screens at the Museum of Modern Art, Andy Warhol Museum, Brooklyn Academy of Music, Queen Elizabeth Hall, Yerba Buena Center for the Arts, and HAU1 (Berlin). He has collaborated on videos and performances with Coil, Sophia Lamar, Anohni, Cyclobe, Little Annie, Amanda Lepore, Thighpaulsandra, Genesis Breyer P-Orridge, and Psychic TV, and he has released his own music on ten-inch vinyl as PROTECTION via his label Formlessness Press. His artwork, interviews, and editorials have been featured in *Playgirl*, *V* magazine, *VMan*, and *The Wire*. He holds a BFA in electronic multimedia from Loyola University New Orleans (2003) and an MFA in computer art from New York's School of Visual Arts (2005). He has been producing content for *Playgirl* since 2007 (under the pseudonym Danny McKaren) and recently began digitizing the magazine for the first time in its history, with this book being the result. He currently lives in Hollywood.

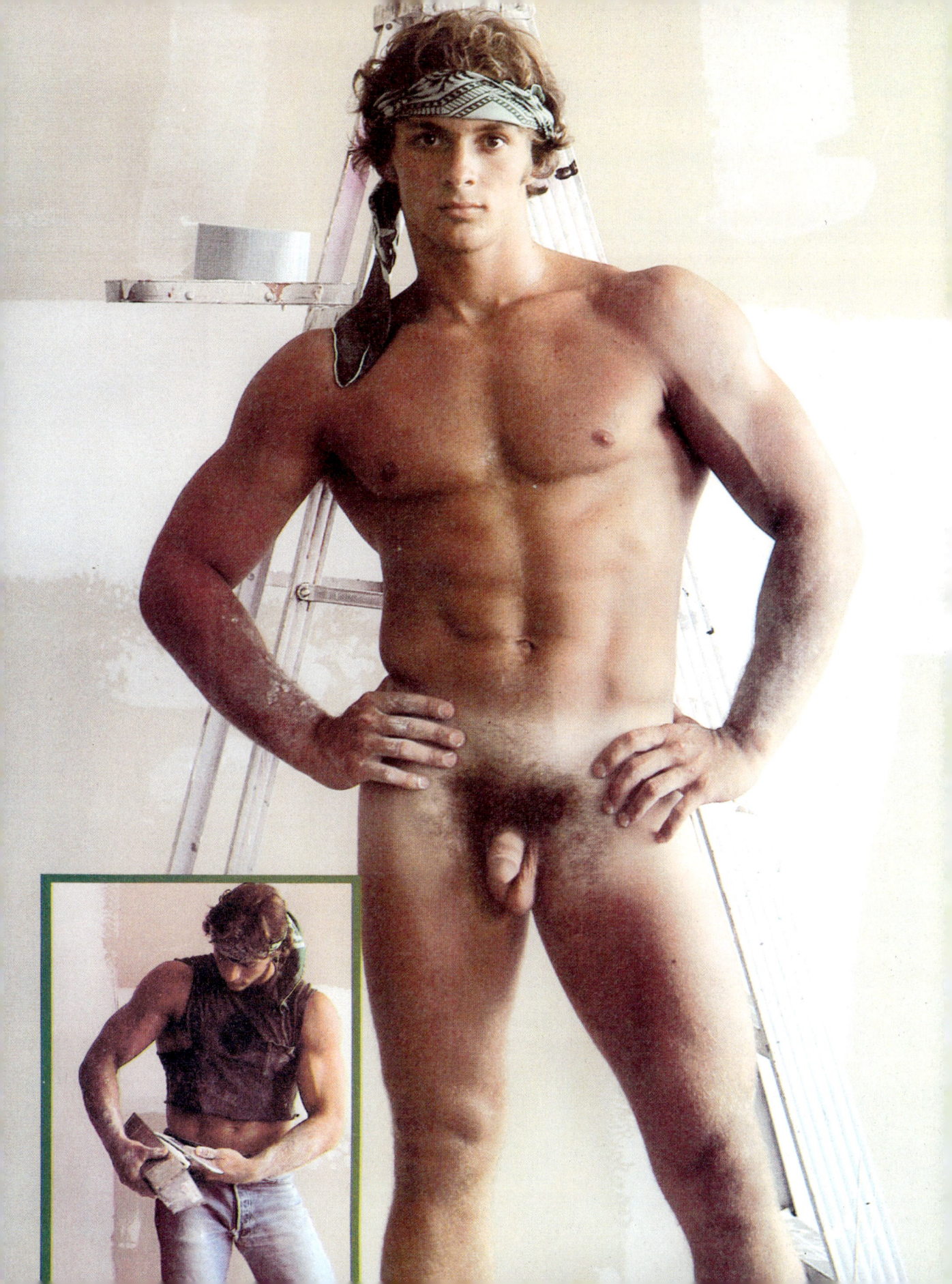

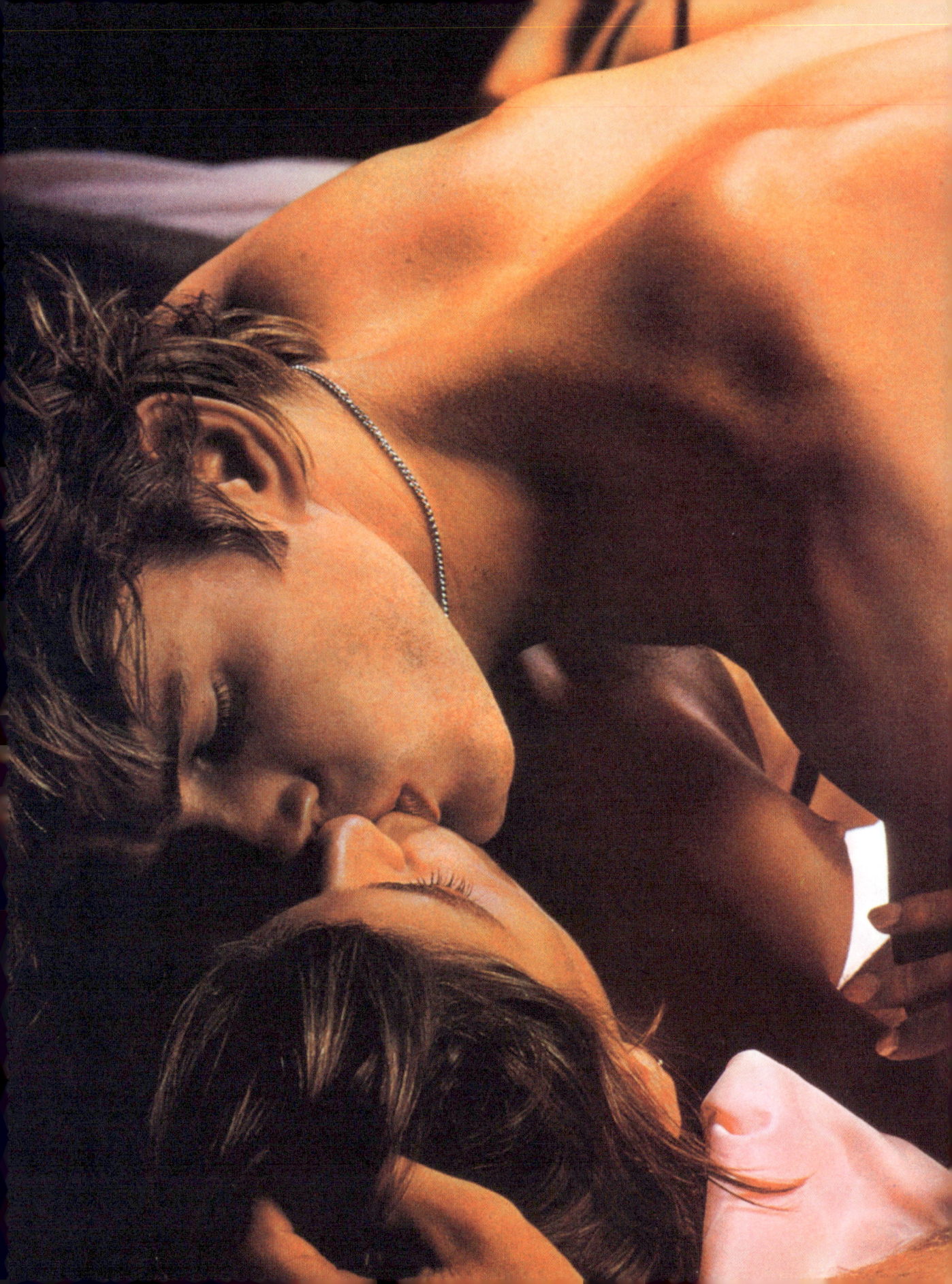

FIFTY YEARS OF *PLAYGIRL:* THE LEGACY OF AN ICON

NICOLE CALDWELL, EDITOR IN CHIEF, 2006–2016

We wanted a revolution. We got a whole lot of mimbos along the way.

Playgirl magazine roared into existence in 1973—the same year as the Supreme Court's ruling in *Roe v. Wade*, the first American oil crisis, and the signing of the Paris Peace Accords. Feminism was in full swing coming off the tumultuous sixties.

Bringing the glossy to life was a California nightclub owner named Douglas Lambert, who topped his new magazine's masthead with a woman, Marin Scott Milam, and the brand wasted no time establishing itself as a lightning rod of controversy. *Playgirl*'s first official issue, dated June 1973, neglected to show full-frontal nudity of centerfold Lyle Waggoner (costar of *The Carol Burnett Show*), making it less an explosive, revolutionary entrance than a close mimicry of *Cosmopolitan*'s cheeky 1972 photo shoot featuring a nude (yet carefully covered) Burt Reynolds splayed across a bear rug. Still, the first-issue run of six hundred thousand *Playgirl* copies immediately sold out. "*Playgirl* from all appearances has made it," the *New York Times* reported in 1974, adding that the magazine was selling 1.7 million magazines per issue in the United States, Canada, and Europe.

As for the lack of full-frontal? *Playgirl* quickly corrected course, delivering an entirely—and quite visibly—nude George Maharis (*Route 66, The Most Deadly Game*) in the very next issue.

As a blueprint, turning *Playboy* inside out was straightforward enough. But *Playgirl* wanted—or at least some of the magazine's employees wanted—more. The country was in the throes of a cultural inflection point, primed for a touchstone somewhere in American media that spoke directly to women's sexual desires. A huge component of that lay in who was doing the looking and who was being looked at. *Playgirl* was birthed on the heels of John Berger's groundbreaking BBC series and eventual book *Ways of Seeing*, which examines the power of the gaze and how the act of seeing—and being seen—impacts social perceptions and influences the way art is made.

Feminists latched on to Berger's exploration of male voyeurism in traditionally Western art and media, in which nude women are presented as disempowered subjects of male desire. Enter *Playgirl*, inviting women (and, winkingly at first, gay men) to look—and in so doing, to flip the antiquated script on who is beholding and who is being beheld.

However slowly, the proverbial needle was moving. *Time* gave its 1975 "Man of the Year" nod to "American women." 1977's massive National Women's Conference brought together thousands of people to discuss the problems facing women—and sparked a counterprotest that drove a wedge still evident in the postfeminist movement. The world was changing, and rapidly. And *Playgirl*, although wildly imperfect and exceedingly narrow in its presentation of "empowered" straight white woman sexuality, was here for it.

Against the glittering tapestry of 1970s American history, *Playgirl* paired coverage of very serious politics in its articles with utter silliness in its photographs. Centerfolds were neither shy nor short on body hair; the popular "Guys Next Door" feature, highlighting "normal" American men who submitted amateur photos, introduced eventual porn star Ron Jeremy to the world in 1978.

Of course, what women want isn't singular. Women's sexuality, as it turns out (I hope unsurprisingly), is many different things—infinitely nuanced, along a wonderfully wide and varied spectrum—and it's a shame that only one women's magazine ever attempted to truly explore female desire so brazenly.

And let's not ignore the big, gay elephant in the room. From the jump, *Playgirl* offered broad appeal to gay men, for whom being "out" wasn't particularly popular or safe at the time. And as the years went on, the glossy's gay readership grew while the heterosexual female demographic shrank. *Playgirl* arrived the same year the American Psychiatric Association issued a long-overdue resolution stating that homosexuality was not a mental illness. While *Playgirl* purported to offer women the opportunity to be voyeurs, it also granted a massive gay audience the opportunity to have a sneak peek into women's heteronormative fantasies and indulge in more than a few themselves. This dance of overtly courting women while more quietly nodding to gay men lasted throughout *Playgirl*'s entire run. As the United States charged through hard-fought milestones in LGBTQ+ history, experienced the devastating AIDS epidemic, and witnessed the meteoric rise of a marketing industry all too happy to vie for the money of gay men, *Playgirl* offered a safe and welcoming harbor.

In 1977, Lambert sold the brand to Ira Ritter—another man—who took over as publisher. *Playgirl* was sold again and again over the years, with each sale eroding some element of that original energy, always lobbing the purported "Entertainment for Women" back and forth between male hands. Each regime change caused the bubbling up of a tired refrain: that women might not actually be interested in or attracted to the naked male form. This notion was played out decade after decade, in *Playgirl* conference rooms and in the glossy itself (and, let's be honest, across American media), up to and through

my tenure with the magazine—and often by the men at the very top. You can see it in 1987 when the higher-ups (temporarily!) took away *Playgirl*'s male nudity altogether, or during the early beefcake years when nary a woman could be found ogling any of the models.

Unlike *Playboy*, which regularly featured nude photo shoots of the most famous female celebrities of the day, *Playgirl* had a harder time appealing to mainstream male stars. Most of the biggest names came by way of licensed paparazzi images that were splashed across many covers throughout the eighties and nineties. The magazine did land a few big names over the years for actual photo shoots, such as Christopher Atkins (*The Blue Lagoon*, *Dallas*) in 1983 and Keith Urban in 2001. When celebrities did pose, they stayed modest like Lyle Waggoner before them. Other photo shoots within *Playgirl* issues did what the staff considered to be the next best thing: celebrity look-alikes, as well as blonder and hunkier nude models with far less body hair, who featured prominently.

As *Playgirl* evolved as a brand and became increasingly shocking—*Playgirl* models of the eighties suddenly possessed erections—an important conversation was being had over women's roles in society. Could they be feminine *and* businesswomen? Was taking care of the house and kids while climbing the corporate ladder actually indicative of "having it all," or were we finally pushing women too far? How could women compete with men in the workplace, anyway, when the former's hourly wages in 1980 were only 67 percent of the latter's?

Playgirl couldn't possibly be all things to all women, just as one woman couldn't be all things to her boss, children, and husband. The divide played out across the country: there was a very widely held perception at the time that we were living in a postfeminist world. Women had successfully challenged gender roles, infiltrating previously all-male institutions like the US Army and NASA. Gender discrimination was now technically illegal. Hadn't women already made it?

We collectively worked our way through the Reagan era, in which the president remained entrenched in a prehistoric worldview of male and female identity and *Playgirl* pushed harder to align with feminism as an exact inverse of the machismo so many feminists at the time railed against. Photo sets were increasingly vivid, with less left up to shadow or the imagination.

The eighties also quietly—yet knowingly—redefined the "Playgirl" as a reliable consumer. Women in this decade could have credit cards in their name, and advertisers, along with *Playgirl*'s owners, knew it. *Playgirl*'s ad space continued to toe the line between the erotic and the mainstream, while the magazine itself sought to commodify women's sexual empowerment by equating it with product consumption. Gone were the think pieces that had graced the glossy's pages along with feature interviews with strong women from Gloria Steinem to Maya Angelou. In its tunneled emphasis on the material world and physical form, *Playgirl* neglected to fully embrace the reality that the cure for lingering inequalities called for serious policy and cultural changes—not simply, or at least not solely, a great vibrator or a bit of branded gear.

Then the nineties came, bringing new *Playgirl* ownership yet again and a dramatic rise in "anonymous beefcake" content. It was a much more explicit nod to the magazine's gay audience—an ironic move, as sexual content for the gay market was exploding while similar content for straight women was nearly impossible to find. *Playgirl*'s marketing still addressed women, but more and more its advertising content seemed not to.

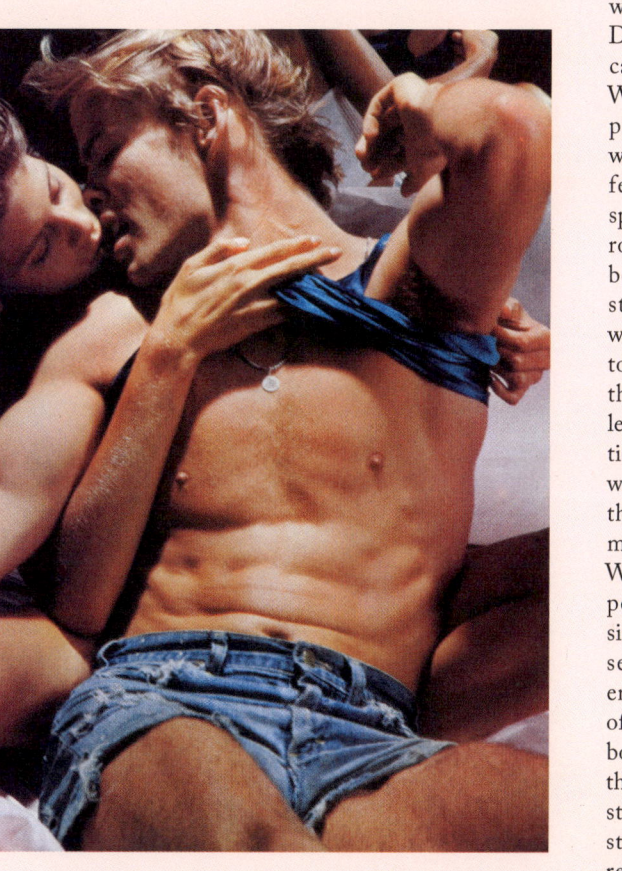

As *Playgirl* shed much of its female readership, some of the magazine's earliest tropes pierced the wall of American culture. The nineties played up "girl power" and women's empowerment in exciting new ways, to be sure. But portrayals of strong women on shows like *Sex and the City* followed a problematic script *Playgirl* had written decades earlier: where sexually empowered women simply acted like badly behaving straight men.

But you can't blame a girl for trying, and like in all eras of political or social movements, change is constant. As *Playgirl*'s circulation shrank in the 2000s and mainstream ads—including those targeting women—dropped off almost completely between issues, women were changing too. The first use of the phrase "Me Too" came in 2006, with the hashtag (and every important thing that came with it) arriving a decade later. LGBTQ+ rights expanded, with essential activists continuing to battle for a wider lens through which we could view our bodies, ourselves, and our sexuality.

My first day working for *Playgirl* came in September 2006, just four months after I had finished graduate school. I was twenty-four. Over the course of the next decade, my female coworkers and I did what we could to push the needle again, bringing back relevant feature articles about women's issues and interviews with celebrities we admired (nabbing Dolly Parton was a career favorite for me). We fought for more provocative photo sets with better lighting and fewer beefcakes. We spoke up in conference rooms with our male bosses, insisting that straight and bisexual women were attracted to the male form and that they shouldn't be left out of the conversation. We believed there was some way to do things right again—or maybe for the first time. We believed in our purported feminist mission and took it deadly seriously while still embracing the hilarity of it all: the glossary of body parts and sex acts that served as *Playgirl*'s style guide, the steady stream of sex toys for review, the blow-up dolls bandied about the office, and the issue-release parties, just to name a few.

It was a magnificent time to be young and alive and a woman in New York City, and to work so unselfconsciously toward a more complete picture of women's sexuality. And even as the magazine rose and fell, tried and failed, and in some ways took spectacular strides and made admirable wins, so too did the story of women evolve and expand.

No single magazine could have ever hoped to capture so much of an era or leave such a significant legacy. Yet *Playgirl*, in its own very raunchy, outspoken, and at times misguided way, did just that.

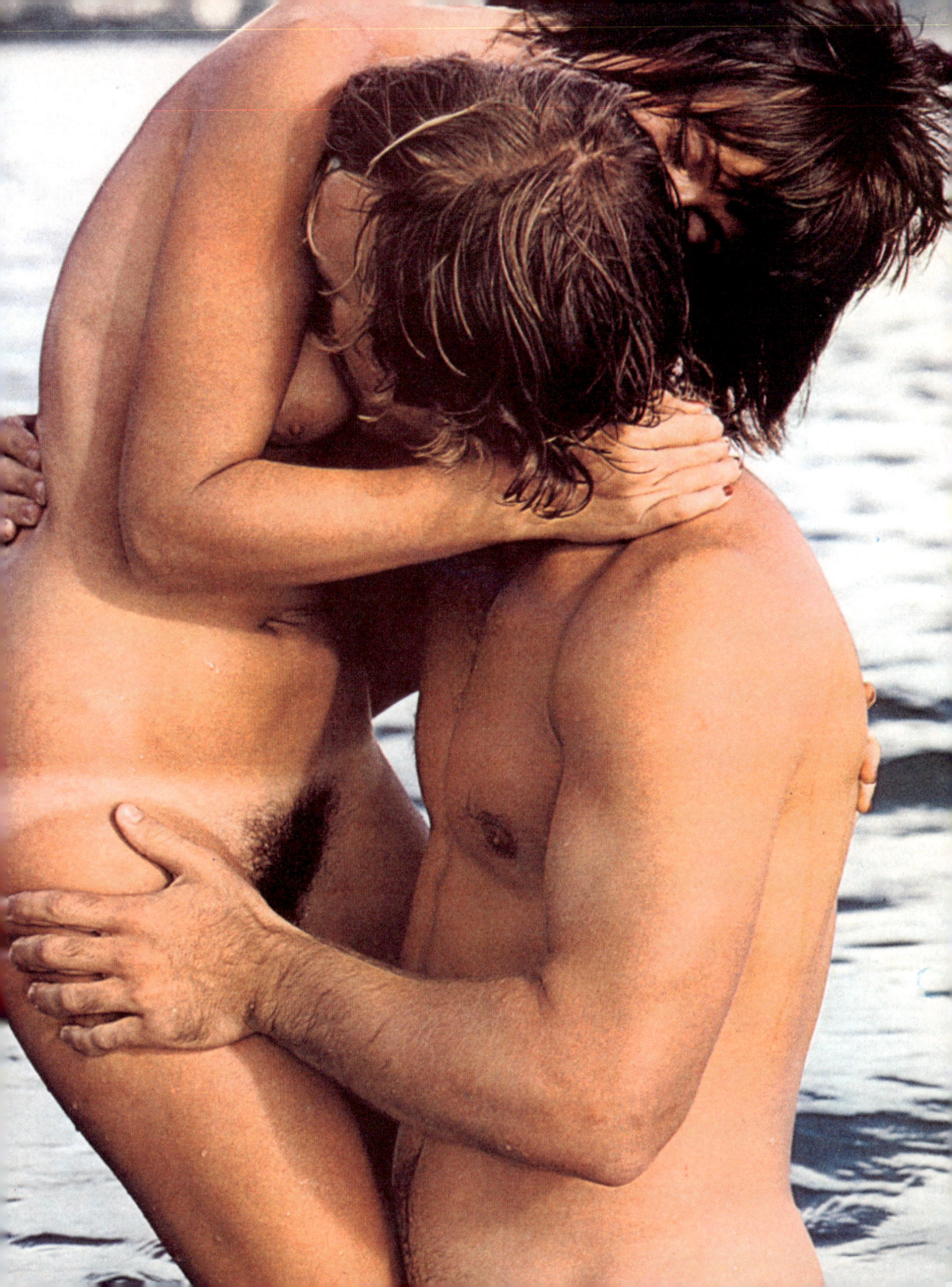

THE SYMBIOTIC RELATIONSHIP OF FEMINISM AND *PLAYGIRL*

MICHELE ZIPP, EDITOR IN CHIEF, 2000–2005

W hen *Playgirl* was born in 1973, women were empowered to embark on the feminist movement. At the time, women had had the right to vote for only fifty-three years. It was two years prior, in 1971, that the Supreme Court had deemed it illegal for private companies to discriminate against hiring women with school-aged children. And it was also in 1973 that *Roe v. Wade* protected a person's reproductive rights. Basic human rights were denied, and continue to be denied. Feminism was beginning to solidify its definition, with *Playgirl* playing an integral part.

At its core, feminism advocates for two kinds of women's freedoms: those that are legal and those involving self-expression across the spectrum of gender. When it comes to sex, men alone have historically been granted permission to fully and unapologetically express themselves—sometimes at the expense and exploitation of women. It's the double standard we've come to expect, a notion as old as time: men can be viewed as dominant and lead healthy and active sex lives, while women should be more submissive and, even chaste.

These views continue to plague society. That's precisely why *Playgirl*—its beginnings and its history—remains vital in the narrative of sexual expression and equality.

Playgirl, I believe, was much more than a simple counterpart to what men already enjoyed in strip clubs and nudie mags. The magazine and mission felt different, revolutionary, an assertion of a sexuality that had, until then, been denied. In that very first issue, published in June 1973 for one dollar, a Playgirl was described as "independent. Self-confident. Sensuous. Aware. Involved. Ambitious. Sensitive. Loving. Giving. Alive. Liberated. Free." She was the full expression of liberation without holding back. *Almost.*

There were high-profile mainstream ads by Maybelline, Pall Mall, Kahlúa, and Excedrin. Writers who graced the pages included Cameron Crowe, Gloria Steinem, and Maya Angelou. And men were photographed nude in the first issue, but there wasn't one image of a penis. Instead, Ryan Macdonald and Lyle Waggoner bared their bodies in coy poses or shielded by bubbles in a tub. It was sexy, subtle, and very seventies, and that first issue should be celebrated. However, all this restraint played directly into the dominant patriarchal attitudes of the time, with the magazine posturing as if women didn't want to see it all, feel it all, experience it all. It failed to take Playgirls to the climax. And thankfully, readers voiced their desires to take the foreplay further. The publishers listened.

21

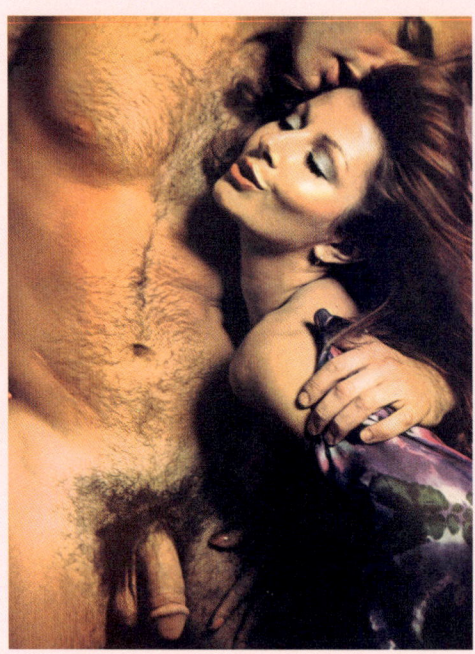

Issue two delivered with George Maharis in all his full-frontal glory. As *Playgirl* learned the desires of its readers, it found its voice—and one that ended up being rather gender inclusive at that. It was sex-positive and naughty, fiercely smart and exploratory.

The magazine didn't always perfectly maintain its original mission. It wavered and experimented, working out kinks and trying on new visions. Each and every woman who worked there imprinted her brand of feminism, her voice, her desires, all in the spirit of representing the vast intricacies and passions we possess. And just like in society at large, the women at the helm of the magazine over the years faced injustices and resistance both in daily life and on the job. However, their commitment to uphold the only magazine of its kind—*Playgirl*'s tagline *is* "Entertainment for Women," after all—never wavered. We'd be remiss without acknowledging all the people who contributed to *Playgirl* over the years: to each of the women in the editorial and art departments who held fast to the magazine's feminist roots, and to all the freelancers, columnists, and photographers who upheld the mission—thank you! It's a testament to these folks that the values of *Playgirl* continue to thrive. The work is fueled by those who believe in the full power of women's sexuality and also the full spectrum of men's sexuality, and that any reader can delight in the words and images that *Playgirl* delivers.

Still, a "Playgirl" can be anyone. That's one ideal of feminism: to allow us all, no matter our gender, to express our sensuality, our sexuality. What matters is our right to exist and express. Playgirls want to be bold but also subtle; we want nuance and diversity. We want to feel empowered, to be tantalized by intrigue. Some of us love bright, show-it-all photo shoots, while others prefer them moody and dimly lit. *Playgirl* has always dared to bare and share what no one else has. It wasn't going to cower from what was considered taboo. And for that, we should be proud. From the magazine's very inception, the mission took many meandering forms, but it's still going strong. To look back on our bold beginnings is to be inspired again, to remember what was overcome and what work still needed to be done. In some ways, feminism has progressed, but in others, there is still so much to do.

In the early 2000s, when I was editor in chief, we adhered to the expression "Playgirls always come first." We even had those words printed on underwear. We didn't want women to fake an orgasm or yield to men as if theirs was the only pleasure that mattered. We wanted to boldly say that it was our time as well—our time for all the firsts, to break all the glass ceilings. Society *needs* fully liberated Playgirls. It's been a gift to feminism, and one that should keep on giving.

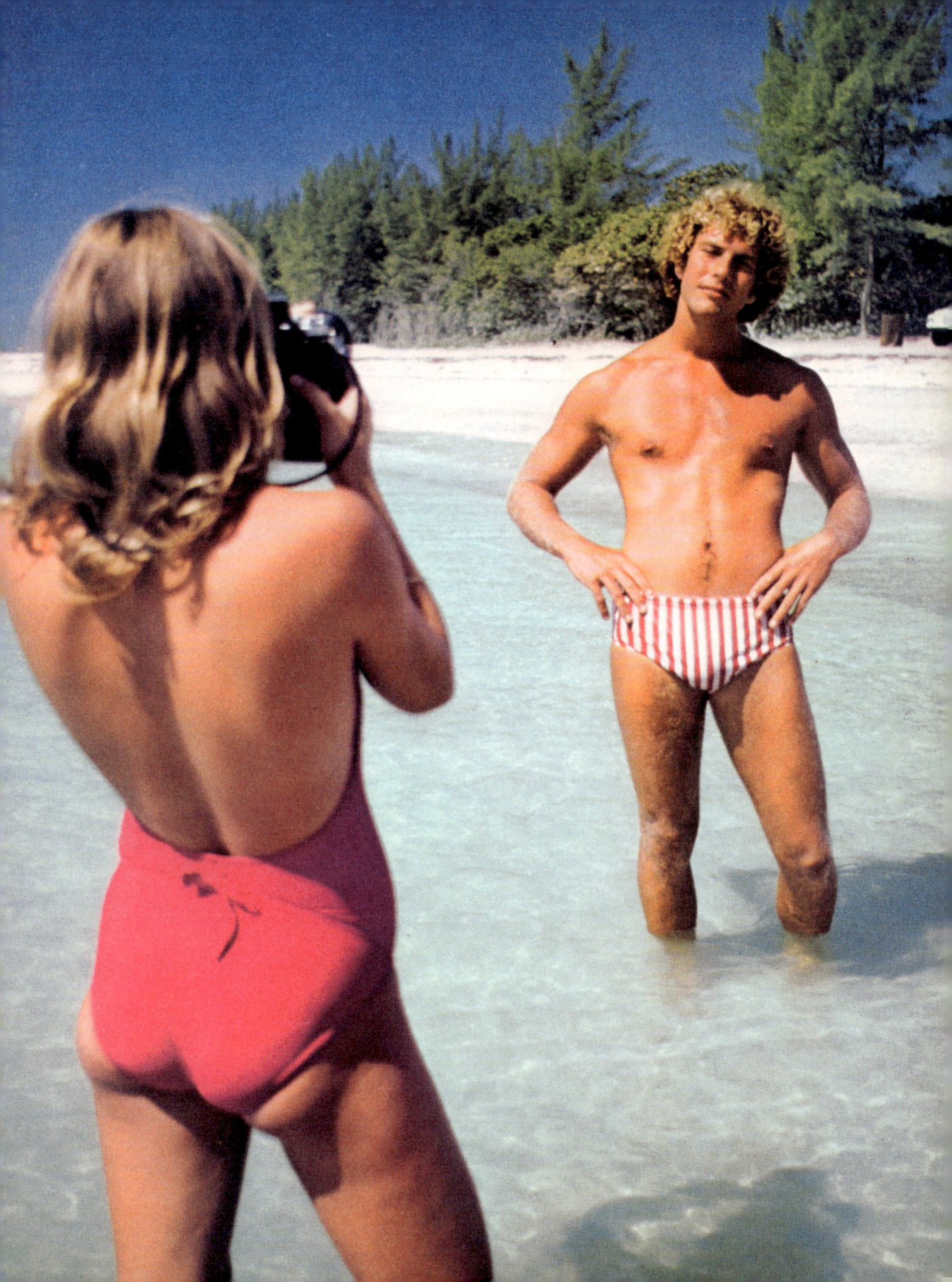

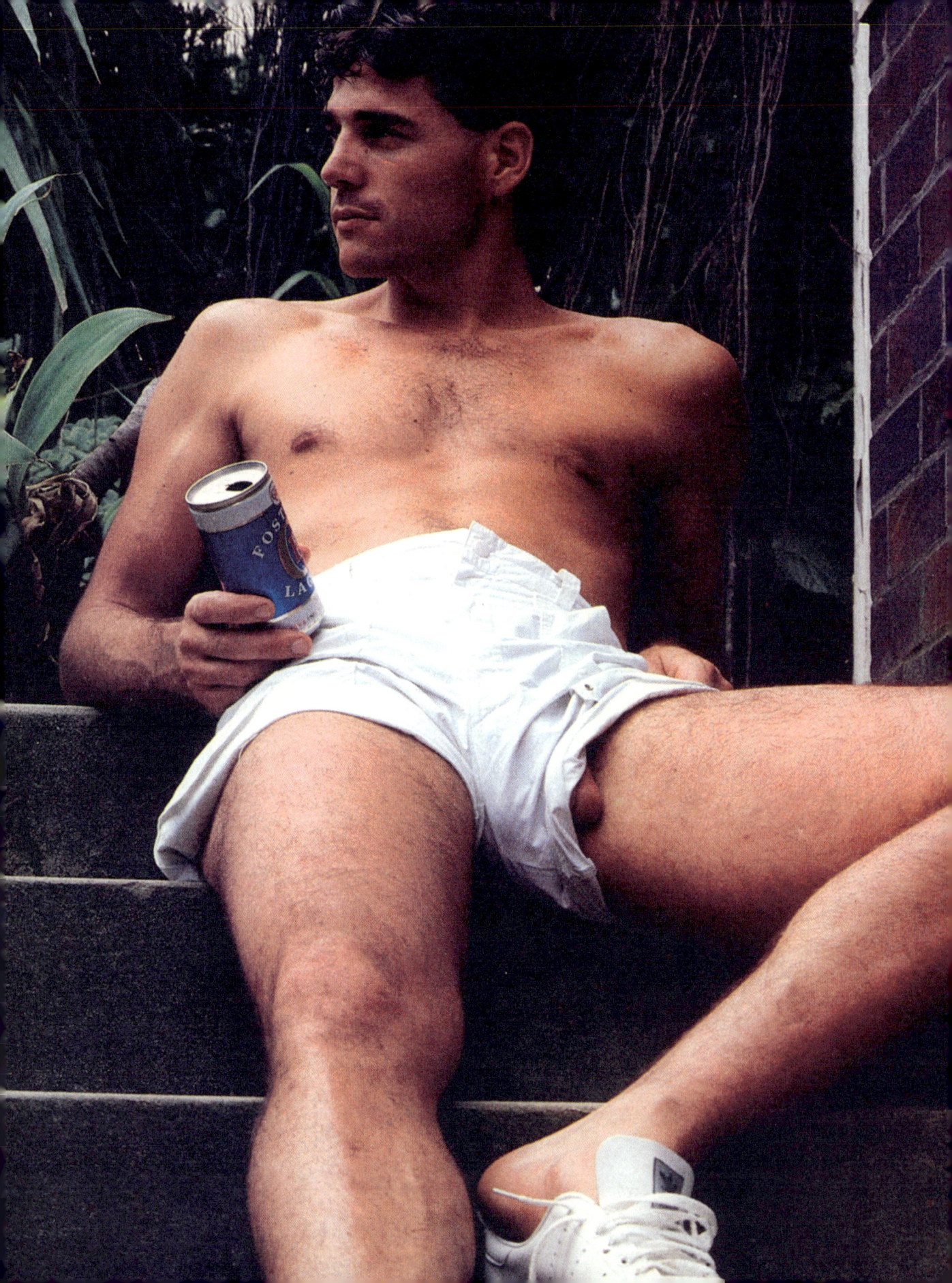

PLAYGIRL MADE ME GAY

MICKEY BOARDMAN

As a closeted gay growing up in the suburbs of Chicago during the seventies and eighties, I was thrilled anytime I stumbled across a gorgeous male physique. Seeing hunky actor Lee Majors show off his hairy chest on *The Six Million Dollar Man* made my heart race. The summer Olympics was a chance to see runners in short-shorts and swimmers in skimpy Speedos. Of course, I always had to act like I was interested in the sporting event or TV show and not the hot men.

Then one day at the 7-Eleven, I fell in love with *Playgirl*. It was displayed behind the cash register with the other sexy magazines such as *Penthouse* and *Hustler*, but this one was different: it unashamedly celebrated hot men. There were sexy celebrities such as Lyle Waggoner (yes, that hairy chest!) and football hero Jim Brown. Muscly dudes, guys next door, and more. Yes, *Playgirl* was meant for modern women, but I certainly related more to its sexually liberated female readers than I did to the horny straight guys who bought *Playboy*. For an adolescent gay-in-the-making like me, *Playgirl* was a godsend.

It offered me the sexiness I craved in such a celebratory, nonjudgmental way, plus so much more. The magazine showcased amazing folks such as Gloria Steinem, Jane Fonda, Truman Capote, and Dolly Parton. It featured respected writers such as Joyce Carol Oates and William S. Burroughs. One of my all-time favorite *Playgirl* moments didn't even involve a naked man. Studly, bearded Beverly Hills hairstylist to the stars Jon Peters was allegedly the inspiration for Warren Beatty's character in *Shampoo*. More importantly to little gay me, he was the boyfriend of Barbra Streisand. In summer of 1973, *Playgirl* took actress Florence Henderson—yes,

the mom from *The Brady Bunch*—to Peters's salon for a makeover. It was a great pop-culture moment, and it helped that Jon was sexy. Talk about checking all the boxes for a fashion- and pop-culture-crazed young gay!

In society at the time, women were usually disrespected like gays were, so it was nice to see them treated well and catered to by a popular publication. And it was a treat to see hot men presented in a sex-positive way. These guys were happy to show off their physiques and be celebrated by readers. They had worked hard to develop great bodies and were proud of them.

To this day, fifty years after the magazine launched in 1973, you can just say the word "Playgirl" and people know you mean sex positivity, empowering women, and celebrating hot, sexy men: men such as Sam J. Jones, star of *Flash Gordon*; Steve Bond of *General Hospital*; and Christopher Atkins from *The Blue Lagoon*. So many of our pop-culture icons stand on the shoulders of *Playgirl*—the proudly sexual stars of *Sex and the City* grew up in the residual glow of the magazine's heyday. Everyone I know, male or female, knows the *Playgirl* brand.

While the magazine has traditionally been produced by and for women, naturally it developed a loyal following of gay men like me, who were excited to have a place to find gorgeous men showcased and celebrated. Our sexually liberated sisters shared their toys with the gays. And now, in 2024, even with gay publications that publish nude male pictorials, *Playgirl* is the OG. Surrounded by OnlyFans creators and thirsty Instagram fitness models, *Playgirl*'s Man of the Month feels special.

As I was growing up, the man who truly represented all *Playgirl* stood for was 1985 Man of the Year,

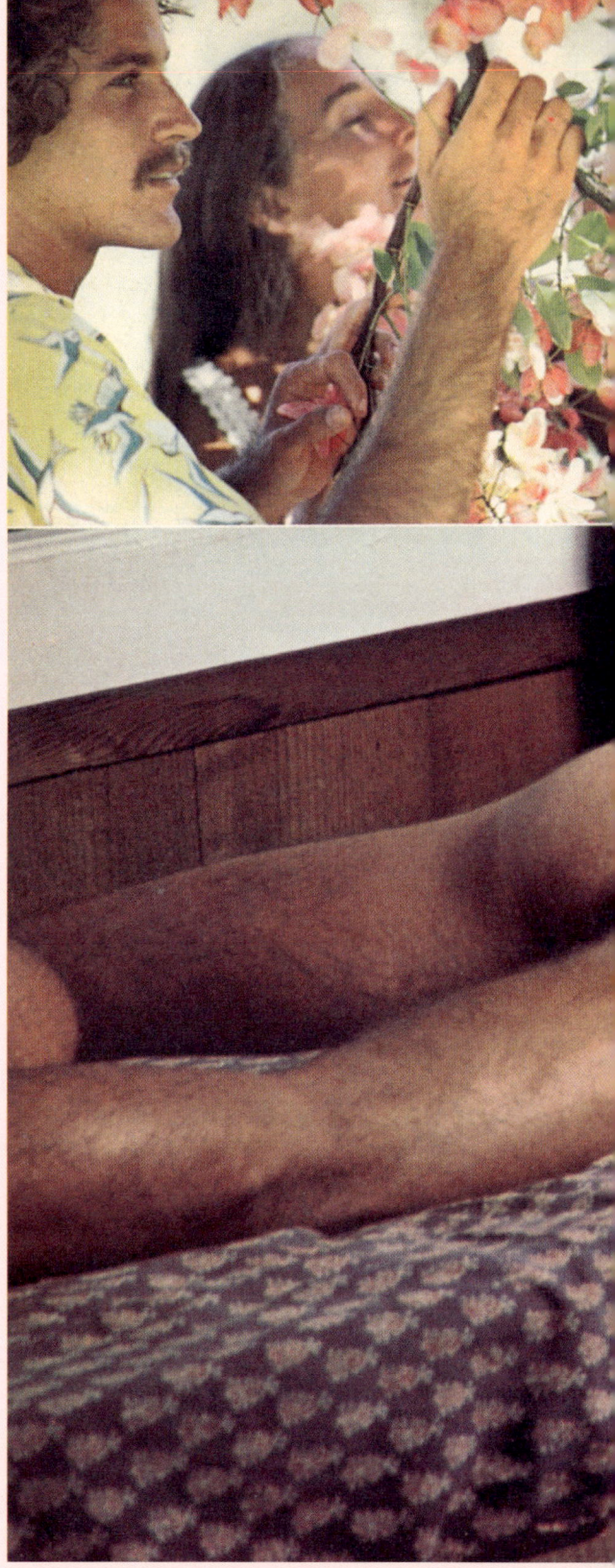

Brian Buzzini. He was a hunky Italian who modeled for Versace ads shot by the iconic photographer Richard Avedon, as well as the campy and fun International Male catalog, another publication sought out by the gays for the scantily clad male models who posed in barely their underwear. That's a high-low combo never matched in fashion! Buzzini was stunning and fit, a true dreamboat. My *Playgirl* fan fantasies came true more than twenty years later, when Buzzini and I became Facebook friends.

When I was an editor at *Paper* magazine in 1994, a publicist pitched me a story on Darren Fox, *Playgirl*'s Man of the Decade. Fox was described as "a man of steel made of flesh and pure heaven." And was he ever! You can imagine how hot Fox was to be named Man of the Decade. He had become famous as a Chippendales dancer and, like Brian Buzzini before him, combined movie-star good looks with the mouthwatering physique of an Adonis. When we photographed Fox, I asked if he'd mind showing a little skin, and not surprisingly, before I knew it, he was almost nude and showing off his signature tattoo, a little devil curling barbells. The men of *Playgirl* looked great and had fun showing it off.

As *Playgirl* celebrates a historic fifty years, I salute them for celebrating five decades of hot men. I thank them for showing women (and gays like me) that nudity and sex are natural, fun, and to be celebrated. And to the cavalcade of *Playgirl* men I've enjoyed over the years, thank you for the memories!

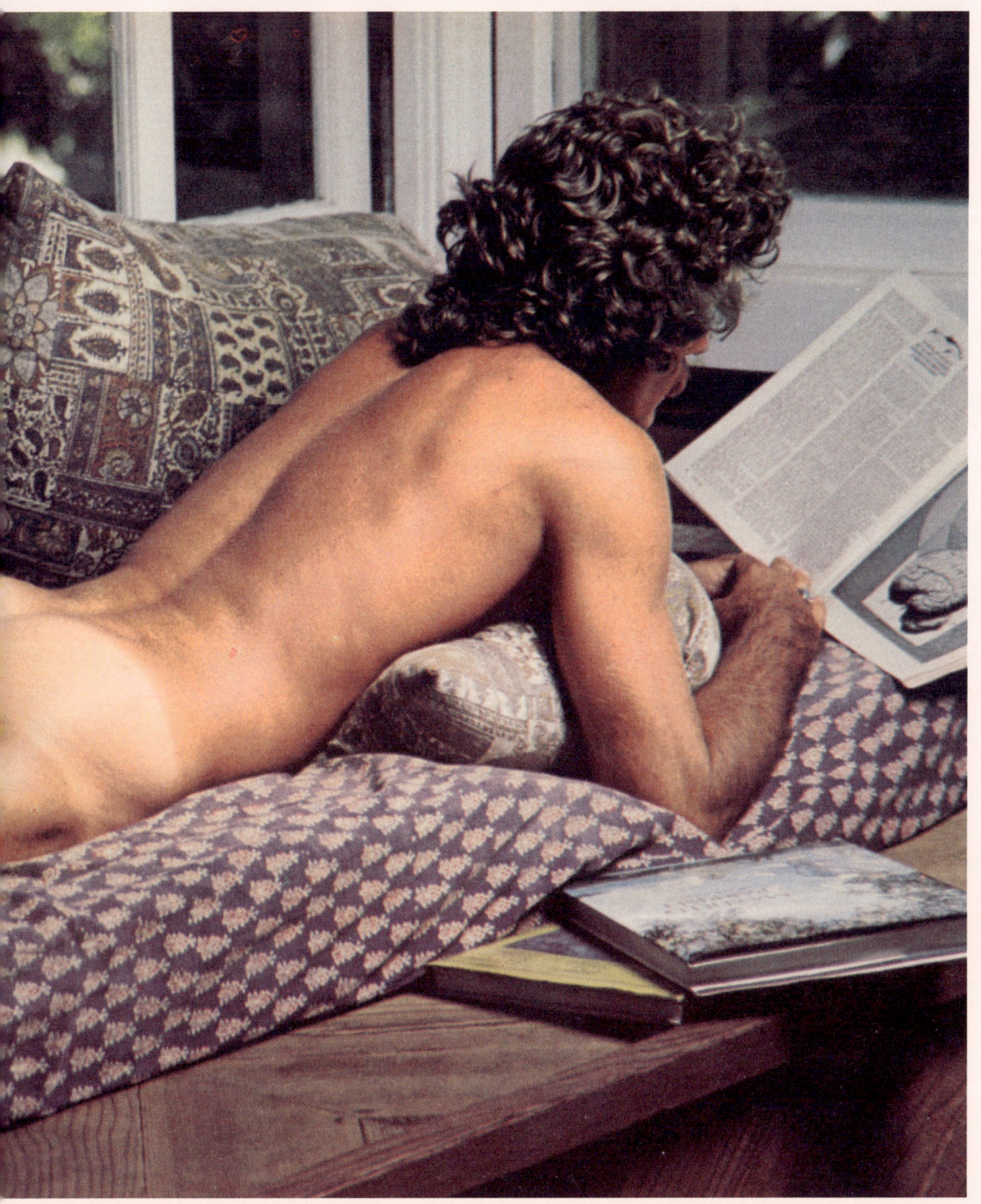

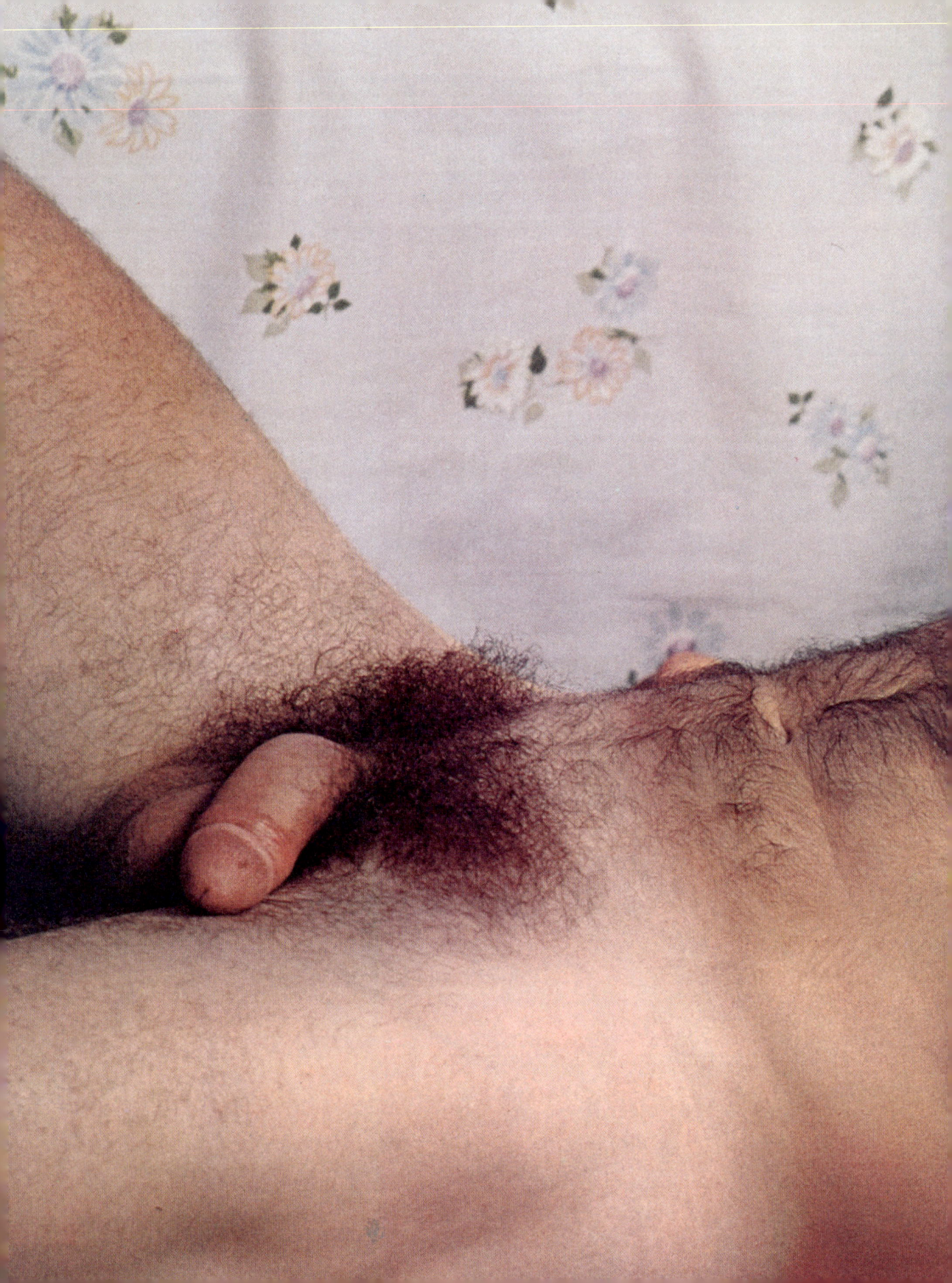

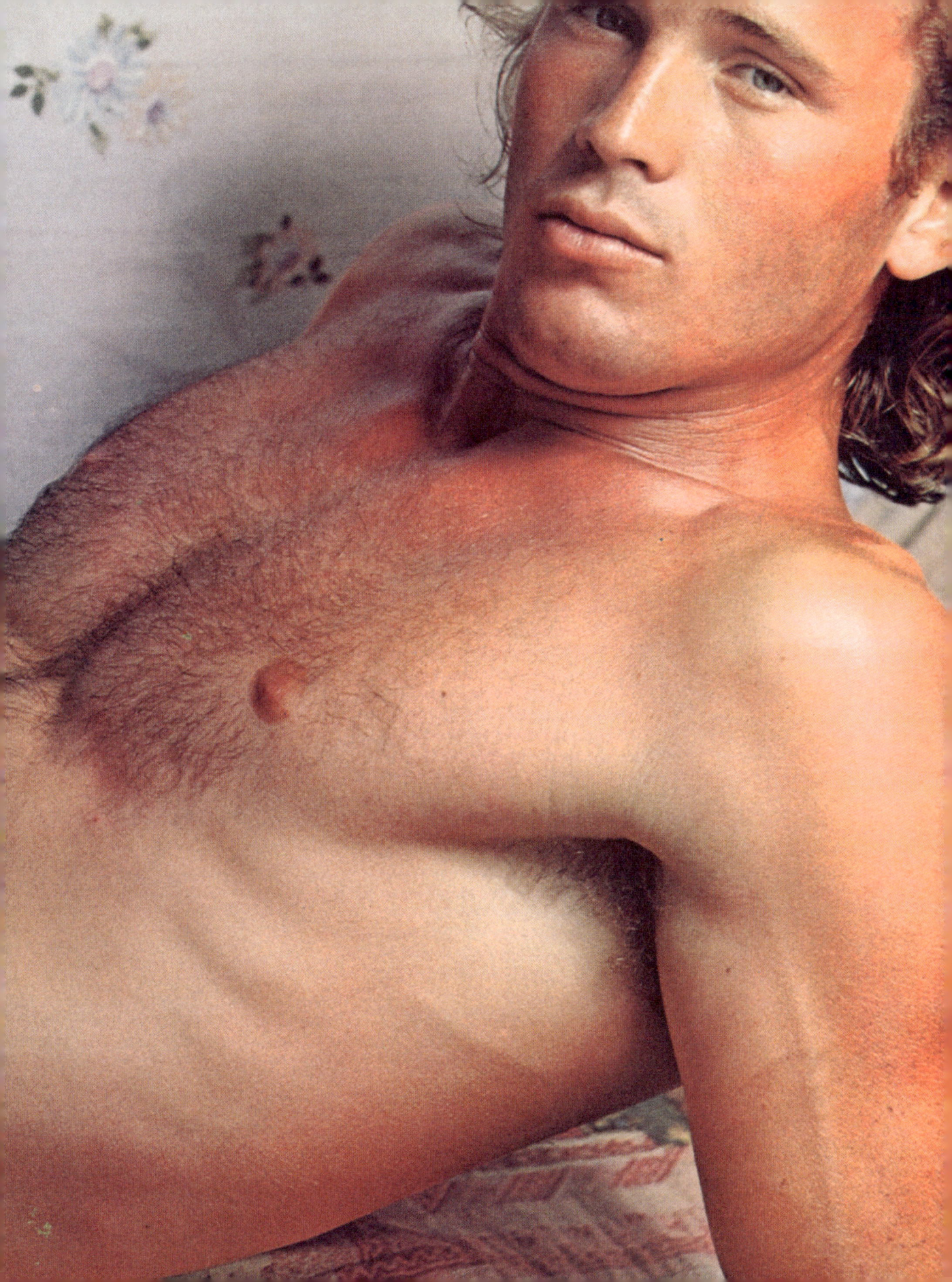

CHAPTER 1

COVERS

Over the past fifty years, *Playgirl* magazine has established itself in the pop-culture lexicon as revolutionary and iconic. Founded in 1973, it evolved over the decades into a legacy brand that quickly became a household name. This progression can be seen in the timeline of magazine covers showcasing *Playgirl*'s shifting aesthetic, logo makeovers, and style trends of yesteryear. These covers were shot by renowned photographers, including Annie Leibovitz, Greg Gorman, Herb Ritts, and Robert Mapplethorpe and spotlighted such classic Hollywood hunks as Robert Redford, Jack Nicholson, Burt Reynolds, Warren Beatty, James Caan, and Sylvester Stallone, as well as rock stars like Mick Jagger and Paul McCartney. In keeping with the publication's tagline "Entertainment for Women," they also feature many fierce female megastars like Jane Fonda, Sally Field, Joan Collins, Liza Minnelli, Goldie Hawn, "the freshest face in Hollywood" Meryl Streep (November 1979), and Hollywood on-screen duos like Jamie Lee Curtis and John Travolta. As the years progressed, A-lister covers gave way to our so-called "mimbos." And the less said about a certain August 1997 issue featuring Brad Pitt, the better.

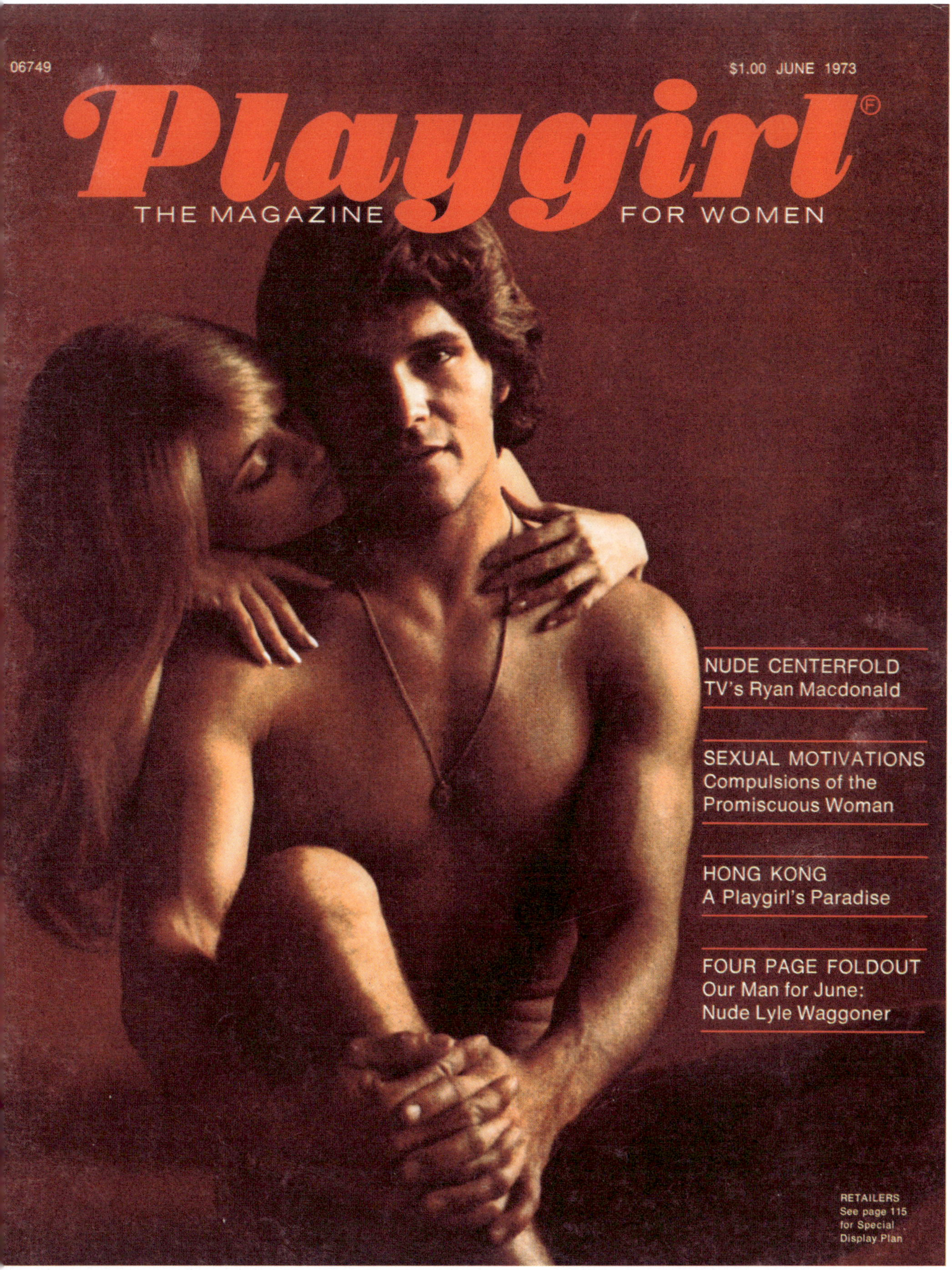

06749

$1.00 JUNE 1973

Playgirl

THE MAGAZINE ——— FOR WOMEN

®

NUDE CENTERFOLD
TV's Ryan Macdonald

SEXUAL MOTIVATIONS
Compulsions of the
Promiscuous Woman

HONG KONG
A Playgirl's Paradise

FOUR PAGE FOLDOUT
Our Man for June:
Nude Lyle Waggoner

RETAILERS
See page 115
for Special
Display Plan

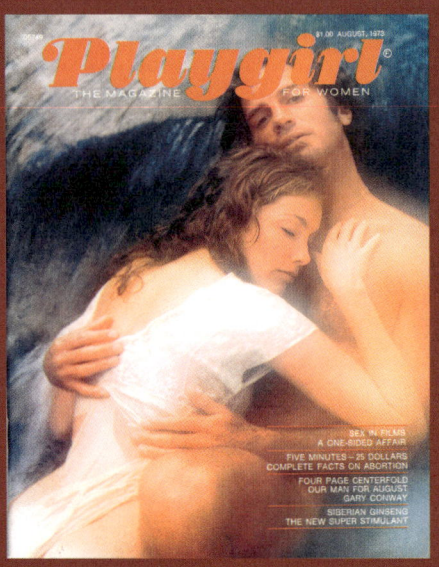

Playgirl
THE MAGAZINE FOR WOMEN
$1.00 AUGUST, 1973

SEX IN FILMS
A ONE-SIDED AFFAIR

FIVE MINUTES—25 DOLLARS
COMPLETE FACTS ON ABORTION

FOUR PAGE CENTERFOLD
OUR MAN FOR AUGUST
GARY CONWAY

SIBERIAN GINSENG
THE NEW SUPER STIMULANT

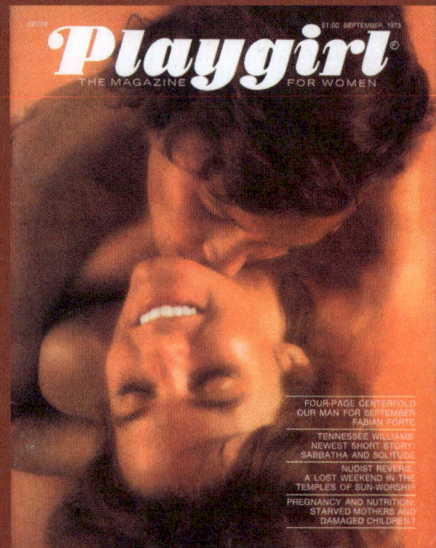

Playgirl
THE MAGAZINE FOR WOMEN
$1.00 SEPTEMBER, 1973

FOUR-PAGE CENTERFOLD
OUR MAN FOR SEPTEMBER
FABIAN FORTE

TENNESSEE WILLIAMS
NEWEST SHORT STORY
SABBATHA AND SOLITUDE

NUDIST REVERIE
A LOST WEEKEND IN THE
TEMPLES OF SUN-WORSHIP

PREGNANCY AND NUTRITION
STARVED MOTHERS AND
DAMAGED CHILDREN?

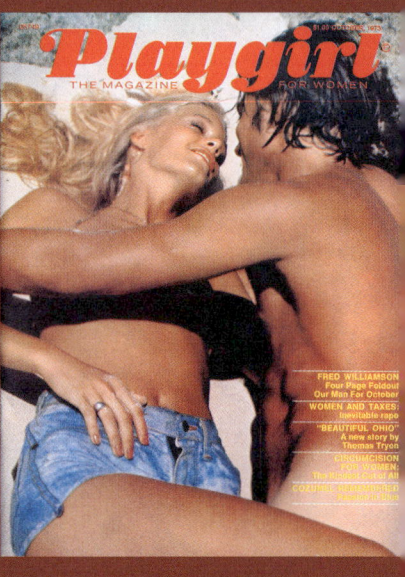

Playgirl
THE MAGAZINE FOR WOMEN

FRED WILLIAMSON
Four Page Foldout
Our Man For October

WOMEN AND TAXES:
Inevitable rape

"BEAUTIFUL OHIO"
A new story by
Thomas Tryon

CIRCUMCISION
Pro Women

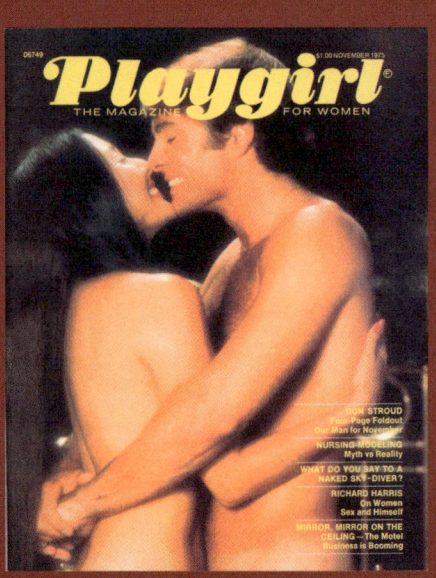

Playgirl
THE MAGAZINE FOR WOMEN
$1.00 NOVEMBER, 1973

DON STROUD
Four-Page Foldout
Our Man for November

NURSING-MODELING
Myth vs Reality

WHAT DO YOU SAY TO A
NAKED SKY-DIVER?

RICHARD HARRIS
On Women
Sex and Himself

MIRROR, MIRROR ON THE
CEILING—The Motel
Business is Booming

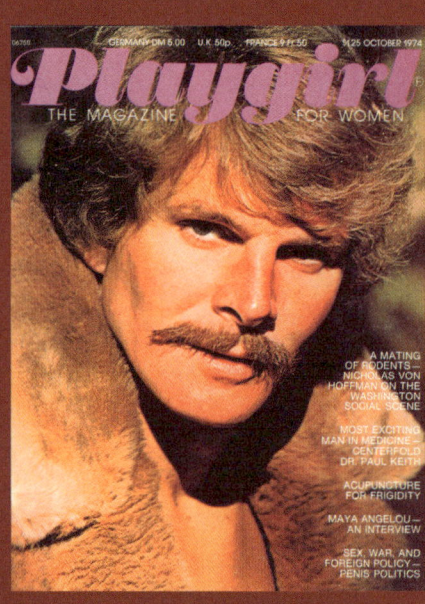

Playgirl
THE MAGAZINE FOR WOMEN
GERMANY DM 6.00   U.K. 50p   FRANCE 4 Fr.50 $1.25 OCTOBER 1974

A MATING
OF RODENTS—
NICHOLAS VON
HOFFMAN ON THE
WASHINGTON
SOCIAL SCENE

MOST EXCITING
MAN IN MEDICINE—
CENTERFOLD
DR. PAUL KEITH

ACUPUNCTURE
FOR FRIGIDITY

MAYA ANGELOU—
AN INTERVIEW

SEX, WAR, AND
FOREIGN POLICY—
PENIS POLITICS

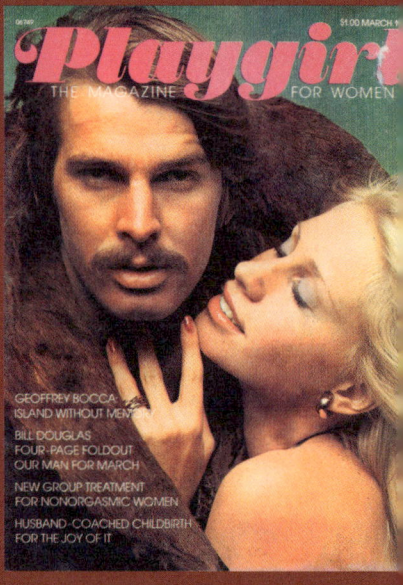

Playgirl
THE MAGAZINE FOR WOMEN
$1.00 MARCH

GEOFFREY BOCCA
ISLAND WITHOUT MEN

BILL DOUGLAS
FOUR-PAGE FOLDOUT
OUR MAN FOR MARCH

NEW GROUP TREATMENT
FOR NONORGASMIC WOMEN

HUSBAND-COACHED CHILDBIRTH
FOR THE JOY OF IT

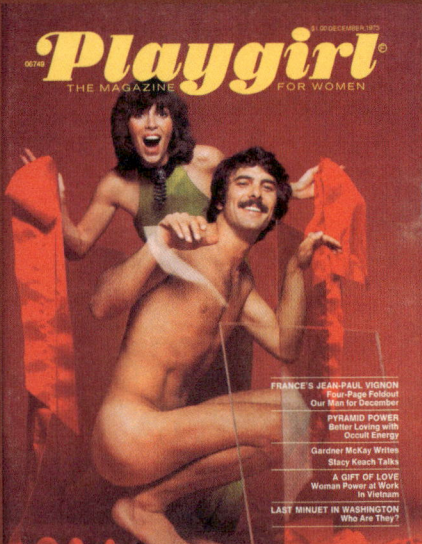

Playgirl
THE MAGAZINE FOR WOMEN
$1.00 DECEMBER, 1973

FRANCE'S JEAN-PAUL VIGNON
Four-Page Foldout
Our Man for December

PYRAMID POWER
Better Loving with
Occult Energy

Gardner McKay Writes
Stacy Keach Talks

A GIFT OF LOVE
Woman Power at Work
in Vietnam

LAST MINUET IN WASHINGTON
Who Are They?

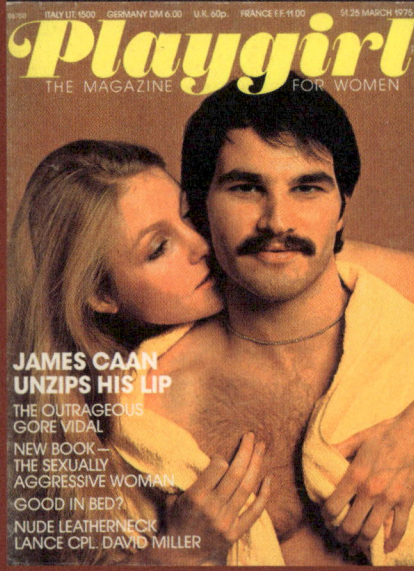

Playgirl
THE MAGAZINE FOR WOMEN
ITALY LIT 1500   GERMANY DM 6.00   U.K. 60p   FRANCE F.F. 11.00 $1.25 MARCH 1975

JAMES CAAN
UNZIPS HIS LIP

THE OUTRAGEOUS
GORE VIDAL

NEW BOOK—
THE SEXUALLY
AGGRESSIVE WOMAN

GOOD IN BED?

NUDE LEATHERNECK
LANCE CPL. DAVID MILLER

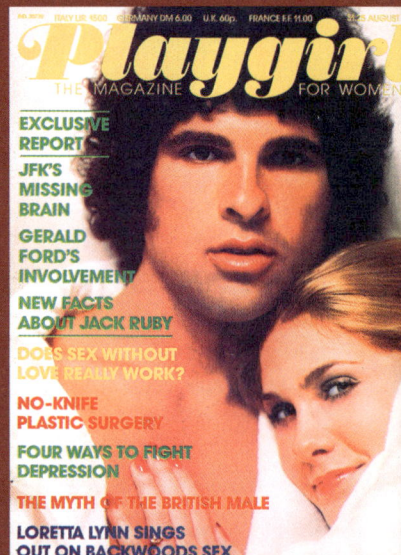

Playgirl
THE MAGAZINE FOR WOMEN
ITALY LIT 1500   GERMANY DM 6.00   U.K. 60p   FRANCE F.F. 11.00

EXCLUSIVE
REPORT

JFK'S
MISSING
BRAIN

GERALD
FORD'S
INVOLVEMENT

NEW FACTS
ABOUT JACK RUBY

DOES SEX WITHOUT
LOVE REALLY WORK?

NO-KNIFE
PLASTIC SURGERY

FOUR WAYS TO FIGHT
DEPRESSION

THE MYTH OF THE BRITISH MALE

LORETTA LYNN SINGS
OUT ON BACKWOODS SEX

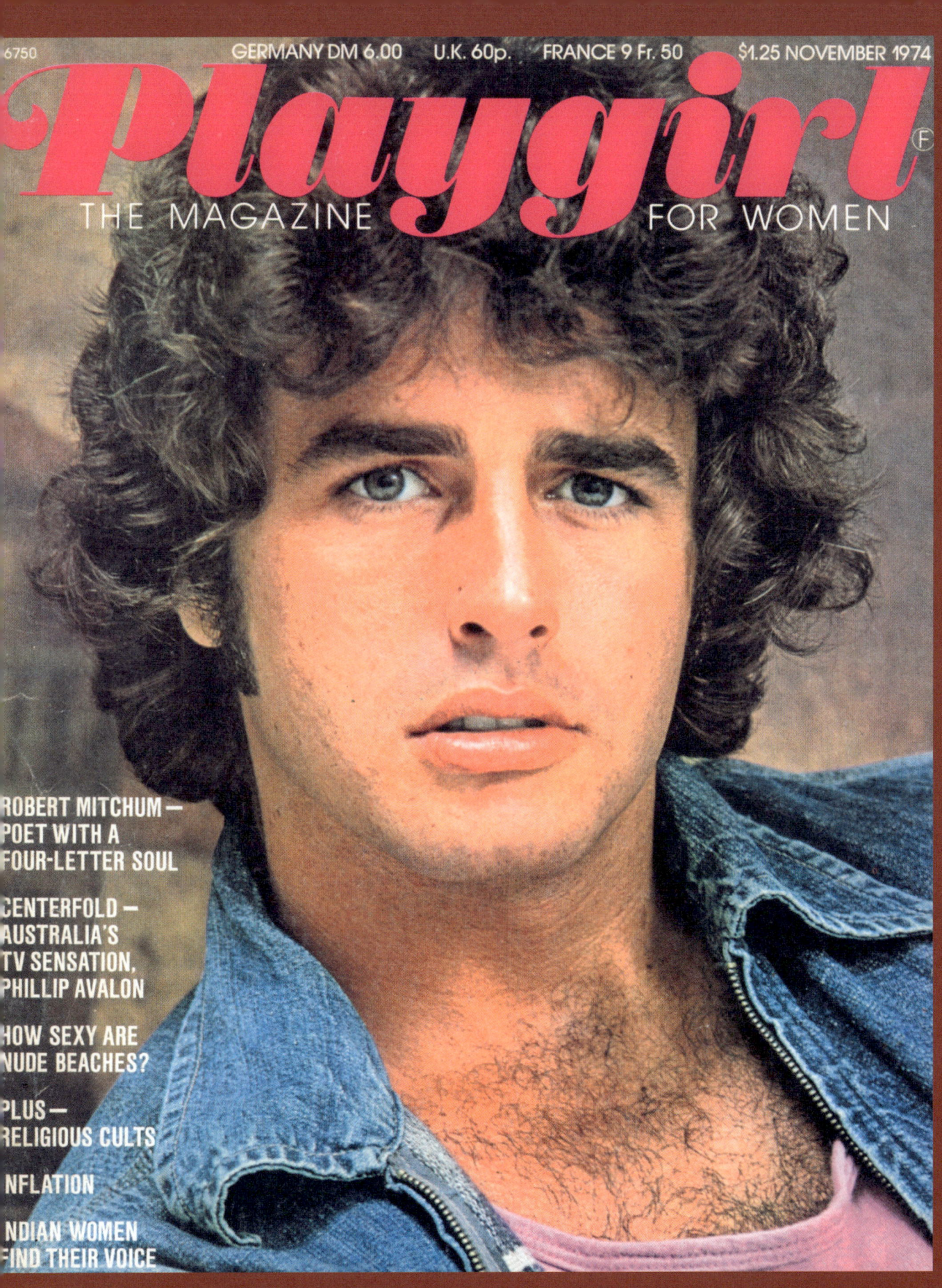

6750

GERMANY DM 6.00   U.K. 60p.   FRANCE 9 Fr. 50 $1.25 NOVEMBER 1974

Playgirl

THE MAGAZINE   FOR WOMEN

ROBERT MITCHUM —
POET WITH A
FOUR-LETTER SOUL

CENTERFOLD —
AUSTRALIA'S
TV SENSATION,
PHILLIP AVALON

HOW SEXY ARE
NUDE BEACHES?

PLUS —
RELIGIOUS CULTS

INFLATION

INDIAN WOMEN
FIND THEIR VOICE

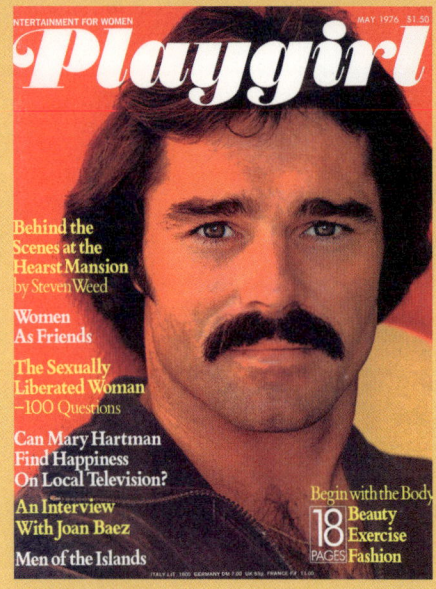

ENTERTAINMENT FOR WOMEN

Playgirl

MAY 1976 $1.50

Behind the
Scenes at the
Hearst Mansion
by Steven Weed

Women
As Friends

The Sexually
Liberated Woman
—100 Questions

Can Mary Hartman
Find Happiness
On Local Television?

An Interview
With Joan Baez

Men of the Islands

Begin with the Body

18 PAGES
Beauty
Exercise
Fashion

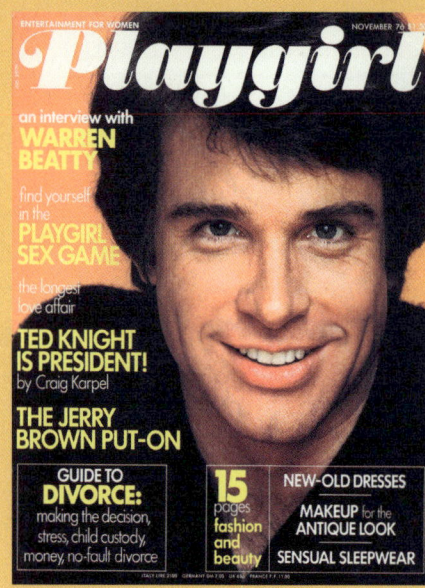

ENTERTAINMENT FOR WOMEN

Playgirl

NOVEMBER 76 $1.50

an interview with
WARREN
BEATTY

find yourself
in the
PLAYGIRL
SEX GAME

the longest
love affair

TED KNIGHT
IS PRESIDENT!
by Craig Karpel

THE JERRY
BROWN PUT-ON

GUIDE to
DIVORCE:
making the decision,
stress, child custody,
money, no-fault divorce

15 pages
fashion
and
beauty

NEW-OLD DRESSES

MAKEUP for the
ANTIQUE LOOK

SENSUAL SLEEPWEAR

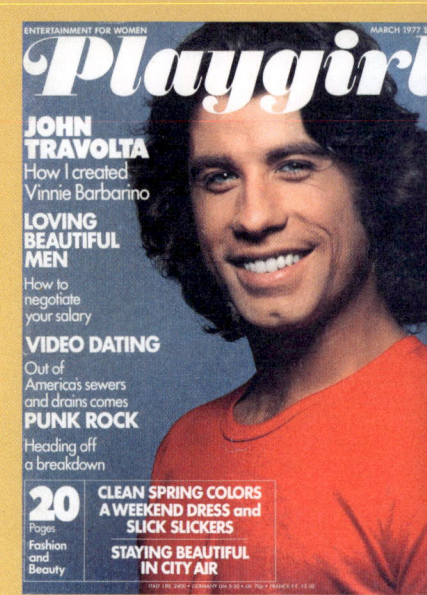

ENTERTAINMENT FOR WOMEN

Playgirl

MARCH 1977

JOHN
TRAVOLTA
How I created
Vinnie Barbarino

LOVING
BEAUTIFUL
MEN
How to
negotiate
your salary

VIDEO DATING
Out of
America's sewers
and drains comes
PUNK ROCK

Heading off
a breakdown

20 Pages
Fashion
and
Beauty

CLEAN SPRING COLORS
A WEEKEND DRESS and
SLICK SLICKERS

STAYING BEAUTIFUL
IN CITY AIR

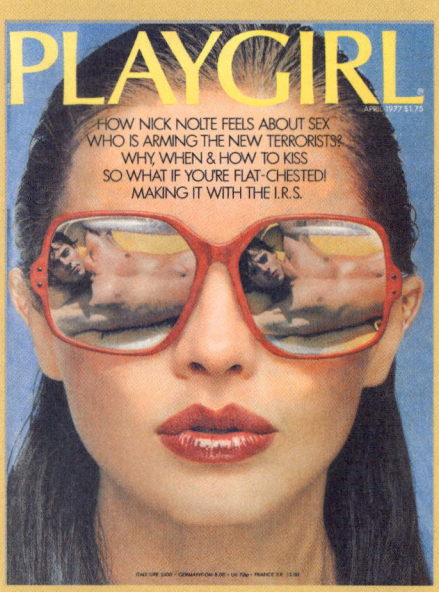

PLAYGIRL

APRIL 1977 $1.75

HOW NICK NOLTE FEELS ABOUT SEX
WHO IS ARMING THE NEW TERRORISTS?
WHY, WHEN & HOW to KISS
SO WHAT IF YOU'RE FLAT-CHESTED!
MAKING IT WITH THE I.R.S.

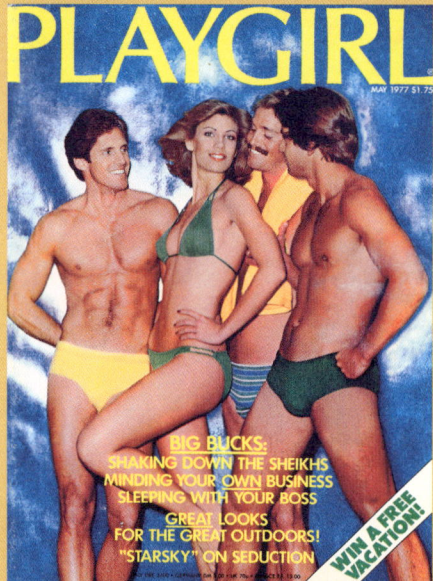

PLAYGIRL

MAY 1977 $1.75

BIG BUCKS:
SHAKING DOWN THE SHEIKHS
MINDING YOUR OWN BUSINESS
SLEEPING WITH YOUR BOSS

GREAT LOOKS
FOR THE GREAT OUTDOORS!

"STARSKY" ON SEDUCTION

WIN A FREE
VACATION!

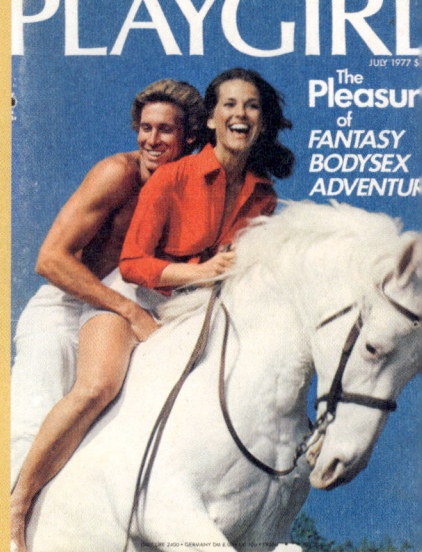

PLAYGIRL

JULY 1977 $

The
Pleasur
of
FANTASY
BODYSEX
ADVENTUR

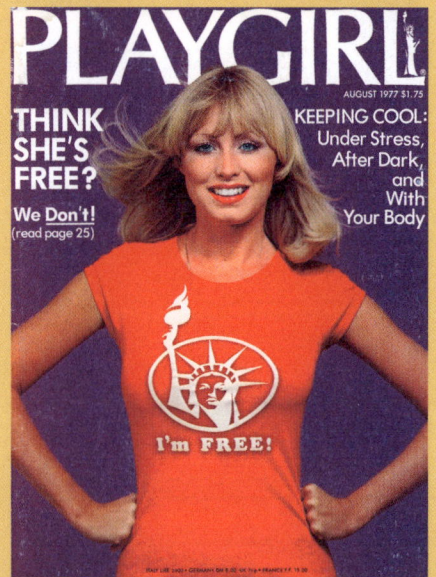

PLAYGIRL

AUGUST 1977 $1.75

THINK
SHE'S
FREE?

We Don't!
(read page 25)

KEEPING COOL:
Under Stress,
After Dark,
and
With
Your Body

I'm FREE!

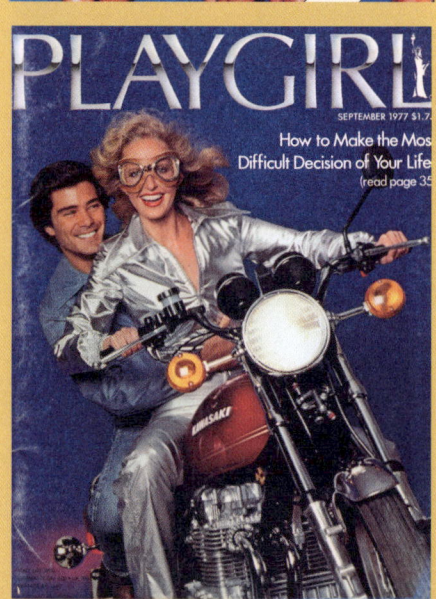

PLAYGIRL

SEPTEMBER 1977 $1.7

How to Make the Mos
Difficult Decision of Your Life
(read page 35

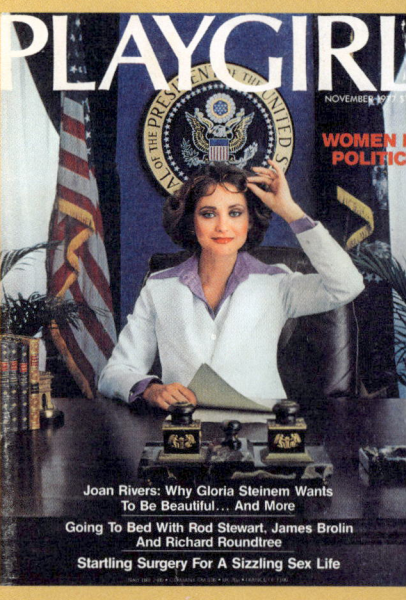

PLAYGIRL

NOVEMBER 1977 $

WOMEN
POLITIC

Joan Rivers: Why Gloria Steinem Wants
To Be Beautiful... And More

Going To Bed With Rod Stewart, James Brolin
And Richard Roundtree

Startling Surgery For A Sizzling Sex Life

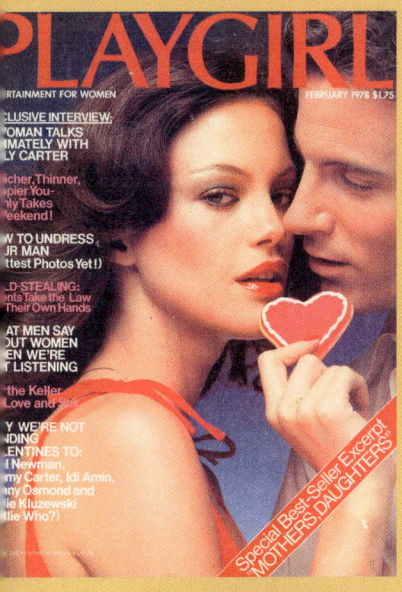

PLAYGIRL

ENTERTAINMENT FOR WOMEN

FEBRUARY 1978 $1.75

XCLUSIVE INTERVIEW:
ROMAN TALKS
MATELY WITH
LY CARTER

Richer, Thinner,
pier You—
ly Takes
Weekend!

HOW TO UNDRESS
UR MAN
ttest Photos Yet!)

LD-STEALING:
nts Take the Law
Their Own Hands

AT MEN SAY
UT WOMEN
EN WE'RE
T LISTENING

the Keller
Love and

Y WE'RE NOT
NDING
ALENTINES?

Special Best-Seller Excerpt
MOTHERS DAUGHTERS!

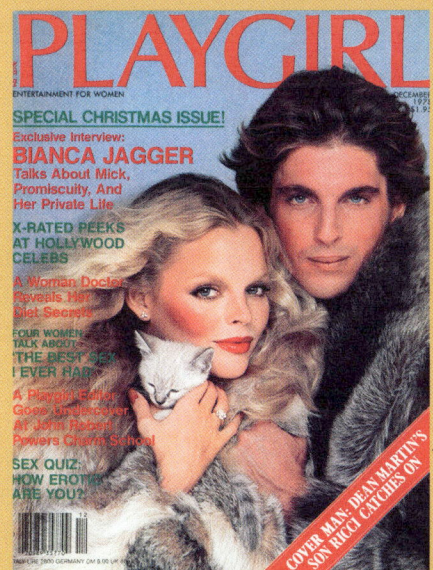

PLAYGIRL

ENTERTAINMENT FOR WOMEN

DECEMBER

SPECIAL CHRISTMAS ISSUE!

Exclusive Interview:
BIANCA JAGGER
Talks About Mick,
Promiscuity, And
Her Private Life

X-RATED PEEKS
AT HOLLYWOOD
CELEBS

A Woman Doctor
Reveals Hot
Diet Secrets

FOUR WOMEN
TALK ABOUT
'THE BEST SEX
I EVER HAD'

A Playgirl Party
Goes Undercover
At John Robert
Powers Charm School

SEX QUIZ:
HOW EROTIC
ARE YOU?

COVER MAN: DEAN MARTIN'S
SON RICCI CATCHES ON

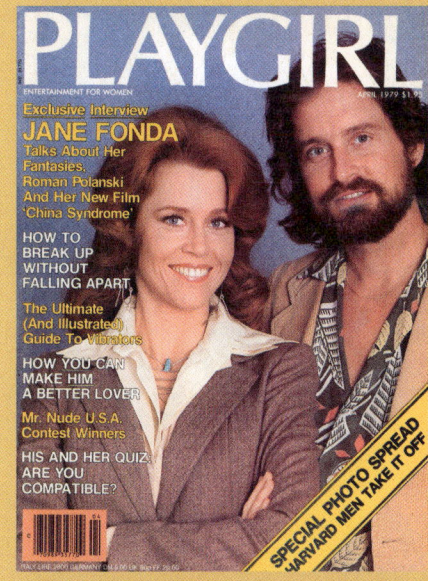

PLAYGIRL

ENTERTAINMENT FOR WOMEN

APRIL 1979 $1.95

Exclusive Interview
JANE FONDA
Talks About Her
Fantasies,
Roman Polanski
And Her New Film
'China Syndrome'

HOW TO
BREAK UP
WITHOUT
FALLING APART

The Ultimate
(And Illustrated)
Guide To Vibrators

HOW YOU CAN
MAKE HIM
A BETTER LOVER

Mr. Nude U.S.A.
Contest Winners

HIS AND HER QUIZ
ARE YOU
COMPATIBLE?

SPECIAL PHOTO SPREAD
HARVARD MEN TAKE IT OFF

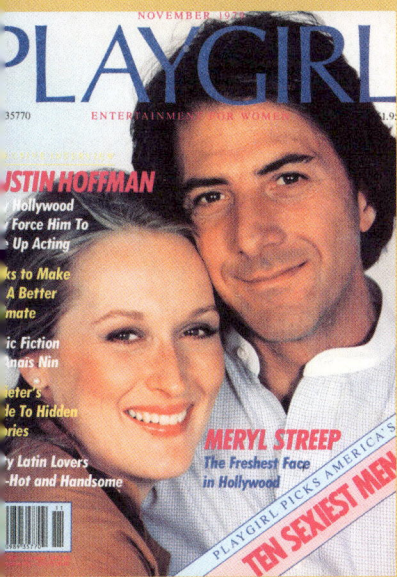

PLAYGIRL

ENTERTAINMENT FOR WOMEN

NOVEMBER 1979

$1.95

USTIN HOFFMAN
y Hollywood
Force Him To
Up Acting

ks to Make
A Better
mate

ic Fiction
nais Nin

ter's
e To Hidden
ries

y Latin Lovers
Hot and Handsome

MERYL STREEP
The Freshest Face
in Hollywood

PLAYGIRL PICKS AMERICA'S
TEN SEXIEST MEN

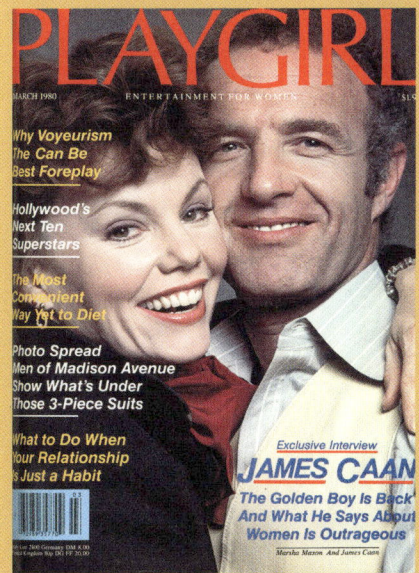

PLAYGIRL

ENTERTAINMENT FOR WOMEN

MARCH 1980

$1.95

Why Voyeurism
The Can Be
Best Foreplay

Hollywood's
Next Ten
Superstars

The Most
Convenient
Way Yet to Diet

Photo Spread
Men of Madison
Avenue
Show What's Under
Those 3-Piece Suits

What to Do When
Your Relationship
Is Just a Habit

Exclusive Interview
JAMES CAAN
The Golden Boy Is Back
And What He Says About
Women Is Outrageous

Marsha Mason and James Caan

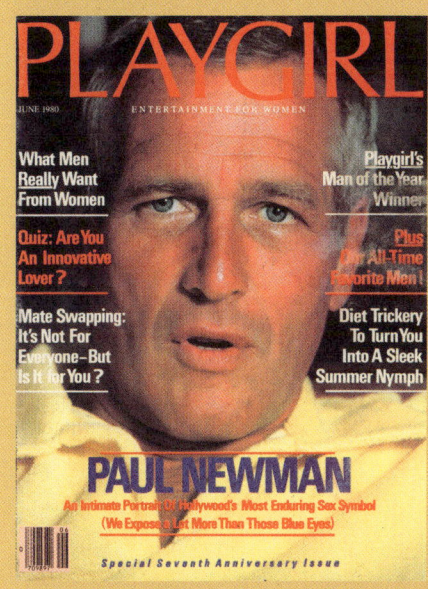

PLAYGIRL

ENTERTAINMENT FOR WOMEN

JUNE 1980

What Men
Really Want
From Women

Quiz: Are You
An Innovative
Lover?

Mate Swapping:
It's Not For
Everyone–But
Is It for You?

Playgirl's
Man of the Year
Winner

Plus
Our All-Time
Favorite Men

Diet Trickery
To Turn You
Into A Sleek
Summer Nymph

PAUL NEWMAN
An Intimate Portrait Of Hollywood's Most Enduring Sex Symbol
(We Expose A Lot More Than Those Blue Eyes)

Special Seventh Anniversary Issue

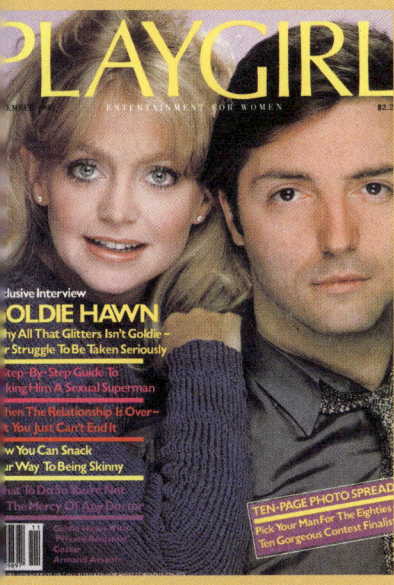

PLAYGIRL

ENTERTAINMENT FOR WOMEN

$2.25

clusive Interview
OLDIE HAWN
y All That Glitters Isn't Goldie -
r Struggle To Be Taken Seriously

tep-By-Step Guide To
ing Him A Sexual Superman

hen The Relationship Is Over—
You Just Can't End It

w You Can Snack
ur Way To Being Skinny

at To Do So You Won't Play
The Mercy Of Any Doctor

TEN-PAGE PHOTO SPREAD
Pick Your Man For The Eighties
Ten Gorgeous Contest Finalists

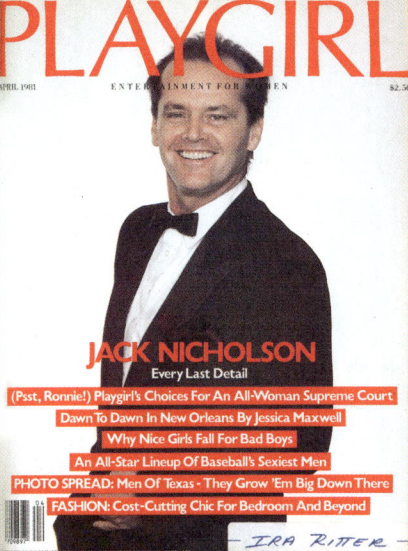

PLAYGIRL

ENTERTAINMENT FOR WOMEN

APRIL 1981

$2.50

JACK NICHOLSON
Every Last Detail

(Psst, Ronnie!) Playgirl's Choices For An All-Woman Supreme Court

Dawn To Dawn In New Orleans By Jessica Maxwell

Why Nice Girls Fall For Bad Boys

An All-Star Lineup Of Baseball's Sexiest Men

PHOTO SPREAD: Men Of Texas - They Grow 'Em Big Down There

FASHION: Cost-Cutting Chic For Bedroom And Beyond

Ira Ritter

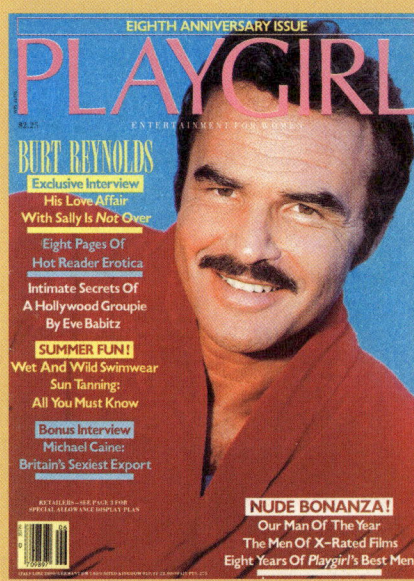

EIGHTH ANNIVERSARY ISSUE

PLAYGIRL

ENTERTAINMENT FOR WOMEN

$2.25

BURT REYNOLDS
Exclusive Interview
His Love Affair
With Sally Is Not Over

Eight Pages Of
Hot Reader Erotica

Intimate Secrets Of
A Hollywood Groupie
By Eve Babitz

SUMMER FUN!
Wet And Wild Swimwear
Sun Tanning:
All You Must Know

Bonus Interview
Michael Caine:
Britain's Sexiest Export

NUDE BONANZA!
Our Man Of The Year
The Men Of X-Rated Films
Eight Years Of Playgirl's Best Men

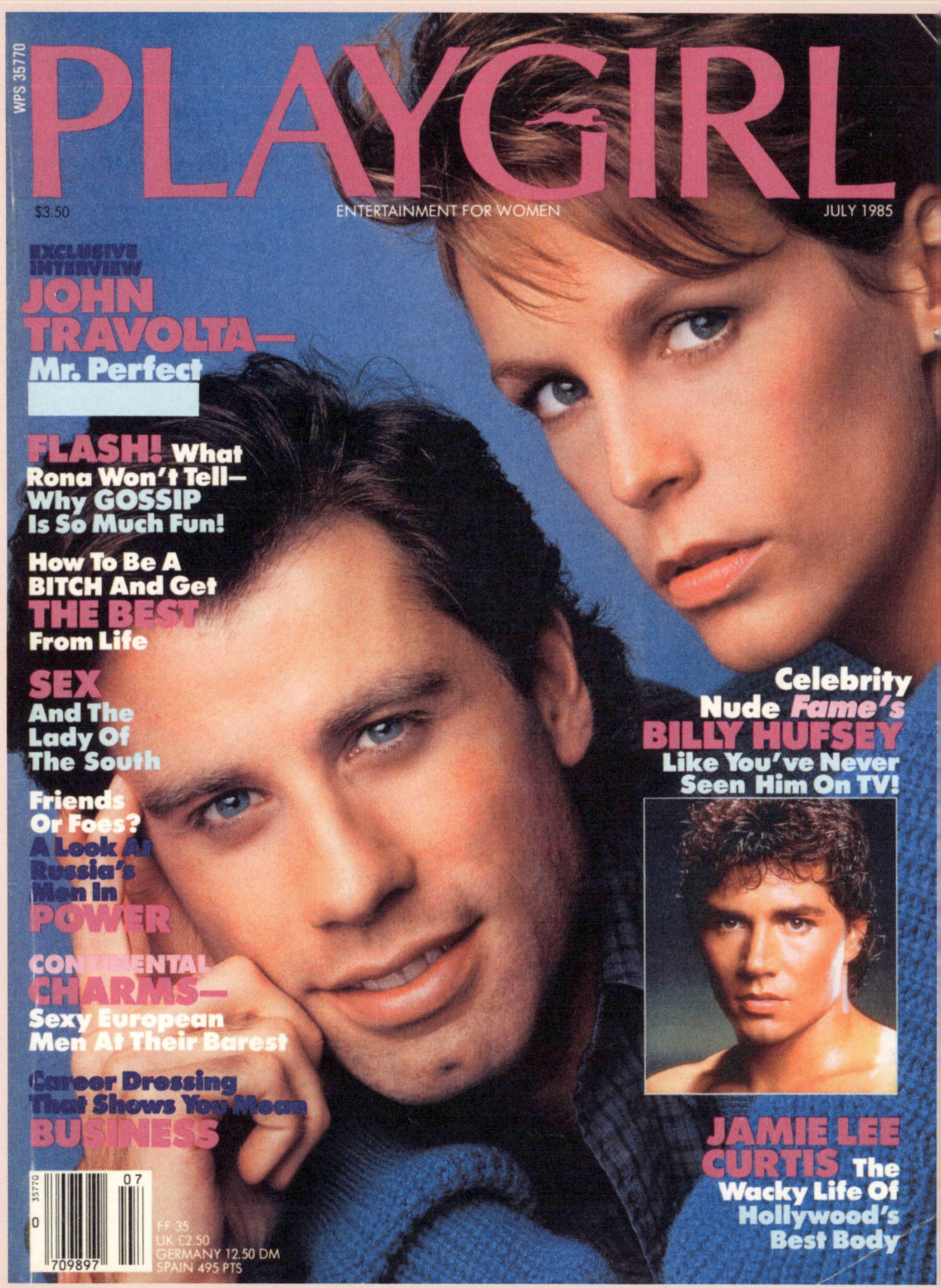

WPS 35770

PLAYGIRL

ENTERTAINMENT FOR WOMEN

$3.50

JULY 1985

EXCLUSIVE INTERVIEW
JOHN TRAVOLTA—
Mr. Perfect

FLASH! What Rona Won't Tell— Why **GOSSIP** Is So Much Fun!

How To Be A **BITCH** And Get **THE BEST** From Life

SEX And The Lady Of The South

Friends Or Foes? **A Look At Russia's Men In POWER**

CONTINENTAL CHARMS— Sexy European Men At Their Barest

Career Dressing That Shows You Mean **BUSINESS**

Celebrity **Nude** *Fame's* **BILLY HUFSEY** Like You've Never Seen Him On TV!

JAMIE LEE CURTIS The Wacky Life Of Hollywood's Best Body

07
0 35770
709897
FF 35
UK £2.50
GERMANY 12.50 DM
SPAIN 495 PTS

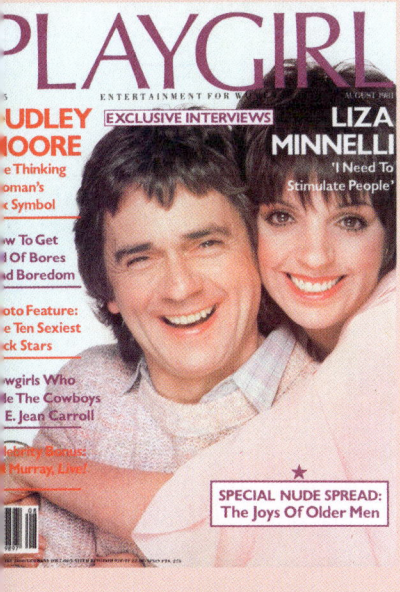

PLAYGIRL
ENTERTAINMENT FOR WOMEN
AUGUST 1981

DUDLEY MOORE
The Thinking Woman's Sex Symbol

EXCLUSIVE INTERVIEWS

LIZA MINNELLI
'I Need To Stimulate People'

How To Get Rid Of Bores And Boredom

Photo Feature: The Ten Sexiest Rock Stars

Cowgirls Who Ride The Cowboys By E. Jean Carroll

Johnny Bonus: Bill Murray, Live!

SPECIAL NUDE SPREAD: The Joys Of Older Men

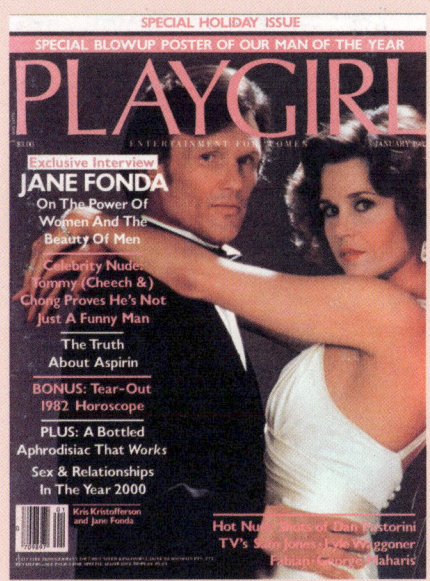

SPECIAL HOLIDAY ISSUE

SPECIAL BLOWUP POSTER OF OUR MAN OF THE YEAR

PLAYGIRL
ENTERTAINMENT FOR WOMEN
JANUARY 1982

Exclusive Interview
JANE FONDA
On The Power Of Women And The Beauty Of Men

Celebrity Nude:
Tommy (Cheech &) Chong Proves He's Not Just A Funny Man

The Truth About Aspirin

BONUS: Tear-Out 1982 Horoscope

PLUS: A Bottled Aphrodisiac That Works

Sex & Relationships In The Year 2000

Hot Nude Shots of Dan Pastorini
TV's Sam Jones, Lyle Waggoner, Famer George Maharis

Kris Kristofferson and Jane Fonda

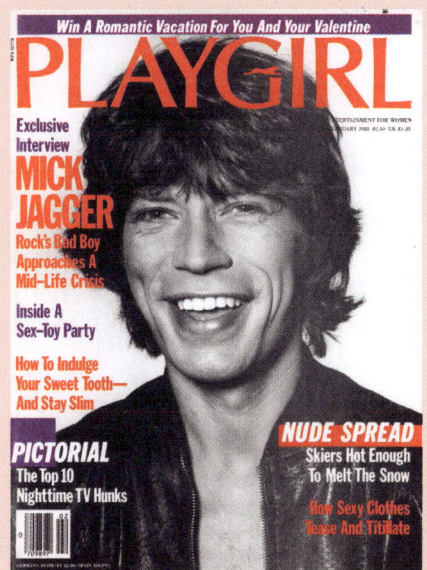

Win A Romantic Vacation For You And Your Valentine

PLAYGIRL
ENTERTAINMENT FOR WOMEN

Exclusive Interview
MICK JAGGER
Rock's Bad Boy Approaches A Mid-Life Crisis

Inside A Sex-Toy Party

How To Indulge Your Sweet Tooth— And Stay Slim

NUDE SPREAD
Skiers Hot Enough To Melt The Snow

PICTORIAL
The Top 10 Nighttime TV Hunks

How Sexy Clothes Tease And Titilate

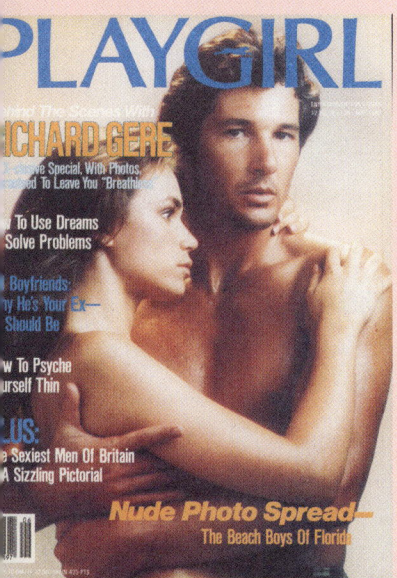

PLAYGIRL

Behind The Scenes With
RICHARD GERE
Exclusive Special, With Photos, Designed To Leave You "Breathless"

How To Use Dreams To Solve Problems

Old Boyfriends: Why He's Your Ex— Should Be

How To Psyche Yourself Thin

PLUS:
The Sexiest Men Of Britain In A Sizzling Pictorial

Nude Photo Spread— The Beach Boys Of Florida

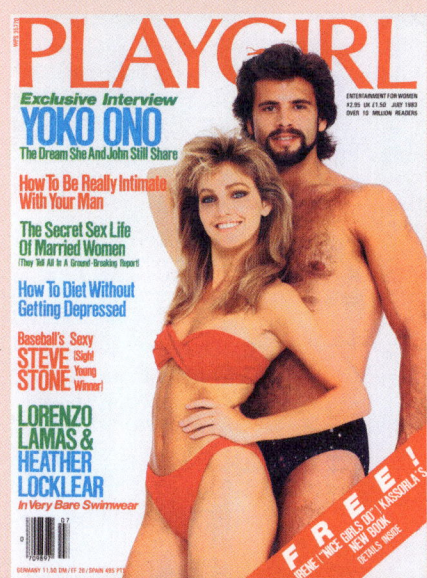

PLAYGIRL
ENTERTAINMENT FOR WOMEN
JULY 1983

Exclusive Interview
YOKO ONO
The Dream She & John Still Share

How To Be Really Intimate With Your Man

The Secret Sex Life Of Married Women
(They Tell All In A Ground-Breaking Report)

How To Diet Without Getting Depressed

Baseball's Sexy STEVE STONE (Slight Young Winner!)

LORENZO LAMAS & HEATHER LOCKLEAR In Very Bare Swimwear

FREE!
Recipe "Nice Girls Do" New Book KASSORLA'S DETAILS INSIDE

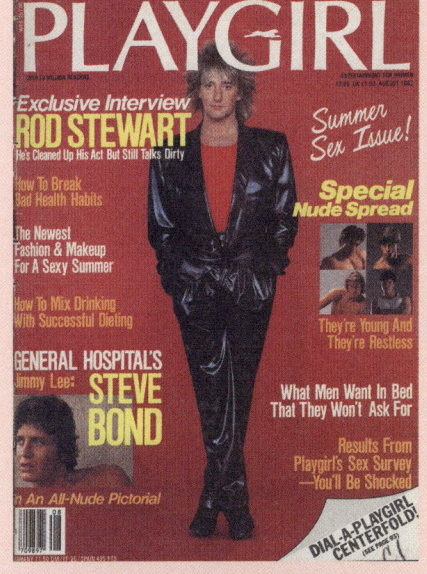

PLAYGIRL
AUGUST 1982

Exclusive Interview
ROD STEWART
He's Cleaned Up His Act But Still Talks Dirty

How To Break Bad Health Habits

The Newest Fashion & Makeup For A Sexy Summer

How To Mix Drinking With Successful Dieting

GENERAL HOSPITAL'S Jimmy Lee STEVE BOND In An All-Nude Pictorial

Summer Sex Issue!

Special Nude Spread

They're Young And They're Restless

What Men Want In Bed That They Won't Ask For

Results From Playgirl's Sex Survey —You'll Be Shocked

DIAL-A-PLAYGIRL CENTERFOLD!

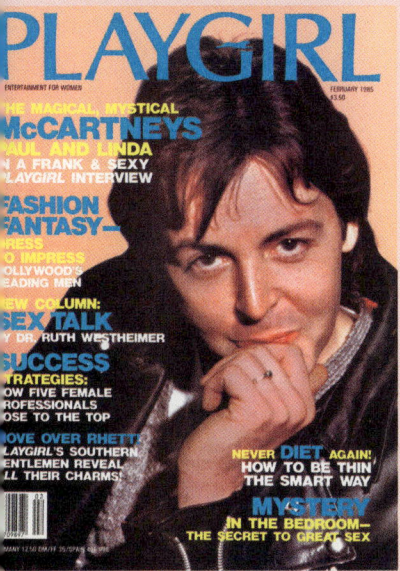

PLAYGIRL
ENTERTAINMENT FOR WOMEN
FEBRUARY 1985

THE MAGICAL, MYSTICAL McCARTNEYS
PAUL AND LINDA In A Frank & Sexy PLAYGIRL Interview

FASHION FANTASY—
DRESS TO IMPRESS Hollywood's Leading Men

NEW COLUMN:
SEX TALK By DR. RUTH WESTHEIMER

SUCCESS STRATEGIES:
How Five Female Professionals Rose To The Top

MOVE OVER RHETT:
PLAYGIRL'S Southern Gentlemen Reveal All Their Charms

NEVER DIET Again!
HOW TO BE THIN THE SMART WAY

MYSTERY IN THE BEDROOM— THE SECRET TO GREAT SEX

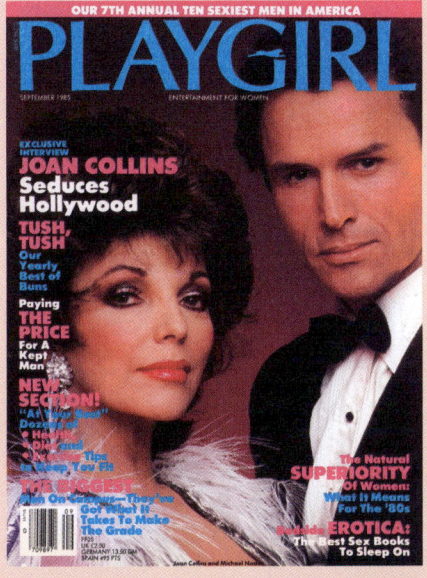

OUR 7TH ANNUAL TEN SEXIEST MEN IN AMERICA

PLAYGIRL
ENTERTAINMENT FOR WOMEN
SEPTEMBER 1985

EXCLUSIVE INTERVIEW
JOAN COLLINS
Seduces Hollywood

TUSH, TUSH
Our Yearly Best Of Buns

Paying THE PRICE For A Kept Man

NEW SECTION!
"Ask Your Best Boyfriend" Bazaar & Hottie Quiz and Tips

THE BIGGEST MEN On Campus: They've Got What It Takes To Make The Grade

The Natural SUPERIORITY Of Women: What It Means For The '80s

SEXUAL EROTICA: The Best Sex Books To Sleep On

Joan Collins and Michael Nader

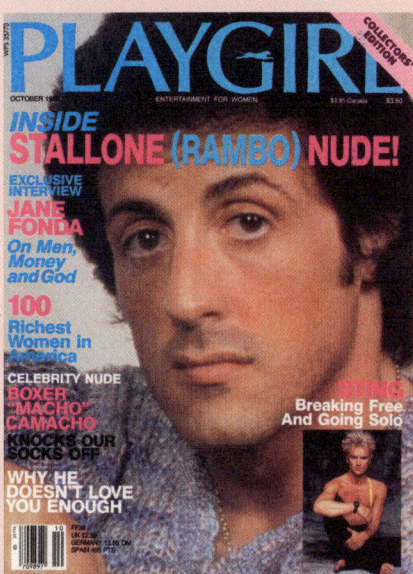

COLLECTORS' EDITION

PLAYGIRL
ENTERTAINMENT FOR WOMEN
OCTOBER 1985

INSIDE STALLONE (RAMBO) NUDE!

EXCLUSIVE INTERVIEW
JANE FONDA
On Men, Money and God

100 Richest Women in America

CELEBRITY NUDE
BOXER "MACHO" CAMACHO
KNOCKS OUR SOCKS OFF

Breaking Free And Going Solo

WHY HE DOESN'T LOVE YOU ENOUGH

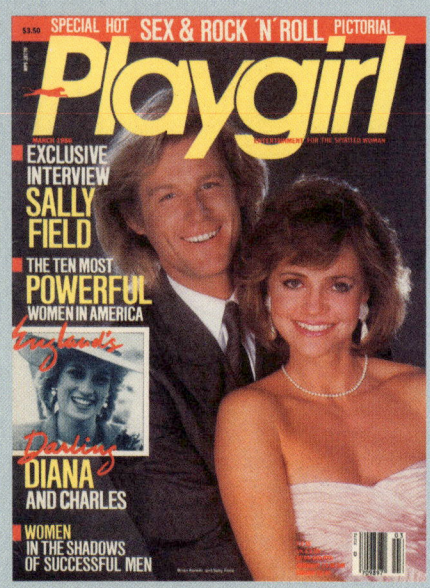

SPECIAL HOT **SEX & ROCK 'N' ROLL** PICTORIAL

Playgirl

ENTERTAINMENT FOR THE SPIRITED WOMAN

MARCH 1986

EXCLUSIVE INTERVIEW SALLY FIELD

THE TEN MOST **POWERFUL** WOMEN IN AMERICA

England's Darlings **DIANA** AND CHARLES

WOMEN IN THE SHADOWS OF SUCCESSFUL MEN

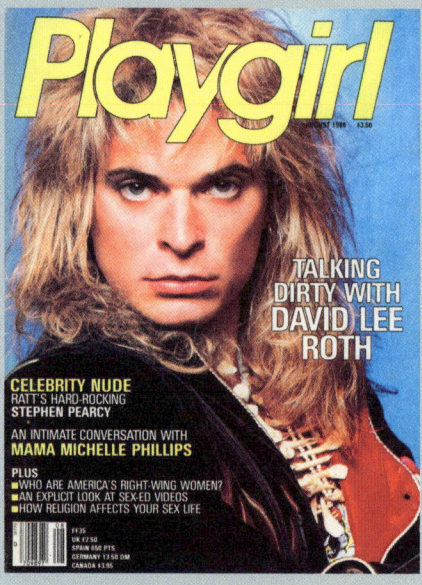

Playgirl

MARCH 1988 $3.50

TALKING DIRTY WITH DAVID LEE ROTH

CELEBRITY NUDE RATT'S HARD-ROCKING **STEPHEN PEARCY**

AN INTIMATE CONVERSATION WITH **MAMA MICHELLE PHILLIPS**

PLUS
- WHO ARE AMERICA'S RIGHT-WING WOMEN?
- AN EXPLICIT LOOK AT SEX-ED VIDEOS
- HOW RELIGION AFFECTS YOUR SEX LIFE

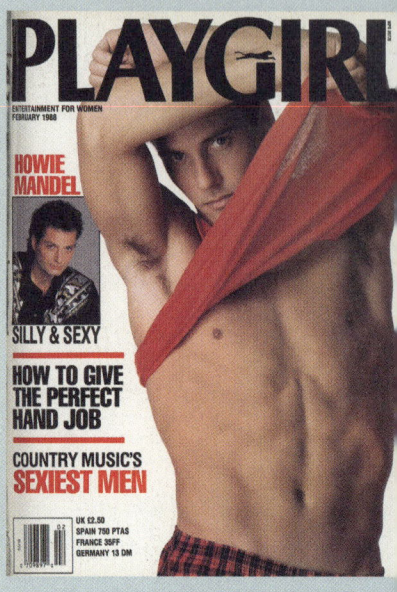

PLAYGIRL

ENTERTAINMENT FOR WOMEN   FEBRUARY 1988

HOWIE MANDEL

SILLY & SEXY

HOW TO GIVE THE PERFECT HAND JOB

COUNTRY MUSIC'S SEXIEST MEN

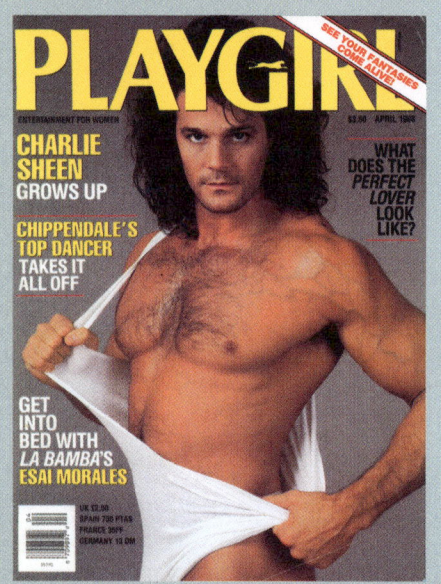

PLAYGIRL

ENTERTAINMENT FOR WOMEN $3.00   APRIL 1988

SEE YOUR FANTASIES COME ALIVE!

CHARLIE SHEEN GROWS UP

CHIPPENDALE'S TOP DANCER TAKES IT ALL OFF

GET INTO BED WITH *LA BAMBA'S* **ESAI MORALES**

WHAT DOES THE *PERFECT LOVER* **LOOK LIKE?**

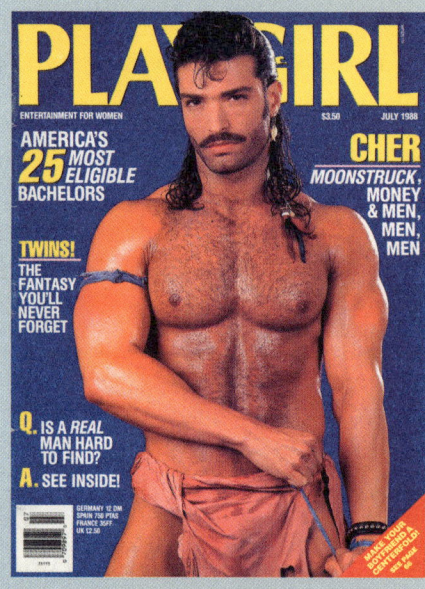

PLAYGIRL

ENTERTAINMENT FOR WOMEN $3.50   JULY 1988

AMERICA'S 25 MOST ELIGIBLE BACHELORS

CHER MOONSTRUCK, MONEY & MEN, MEN, MEN

TWINS! THE FANTASY YOU'LL NEVER FORGET

Q. IS A *REAL* MAN HARD TO FIND?

A. SEE INSIDE!

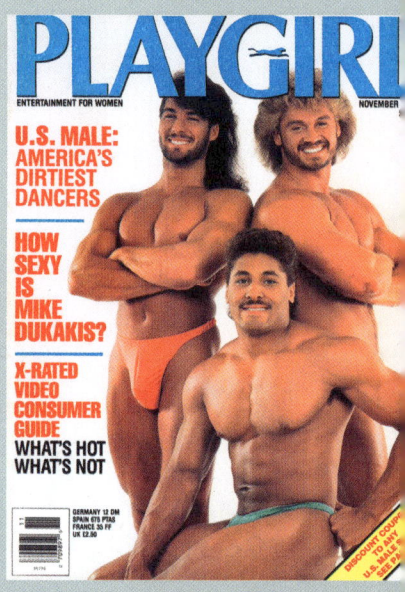

PLAYGIRL

ENTERTAINMENT FOR WOMEN   NOVEMBER

U.S. MALE: AMERICA'S DIRTIEST DANCERS

HOW SEXY IS MIKE DUKAKIS?

X-RATED VIDEO CONSUMER GUIDE WHAT'S HOT WHAT'S NOT

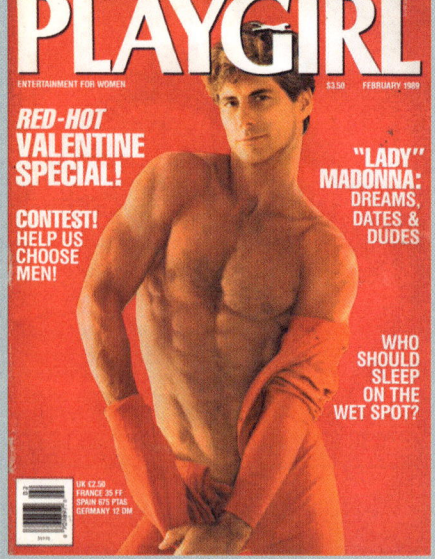

PLAYGIRL

ENTERTAINMENT FOR WOMEN $3.50   FEBRUARY 1989

RED-HOT VALENTINE SPECIAL!

CONTEST! HELP US CHOOSE MEN!

"LADY" MADONNA: DREAMS, DATES & DUDES

WHO SHOULD SLEEP ON THE WET SPOT?

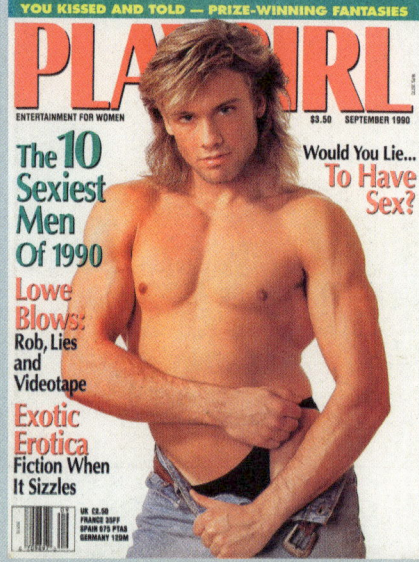

YOU KISSED AND TOLD — PRIZE-WINNING FANTASIES

PLAYGIRL

ENTERTAINMENT FOR WOMEN $3.50   SEPTEMBER 1990

The 10 Sexiest Men Of 1990

Would You Lie... To Have Sex?

Lowe Blows: Rob, Lies and Videotape

Exotic Erotica Fiction When It Sizzles

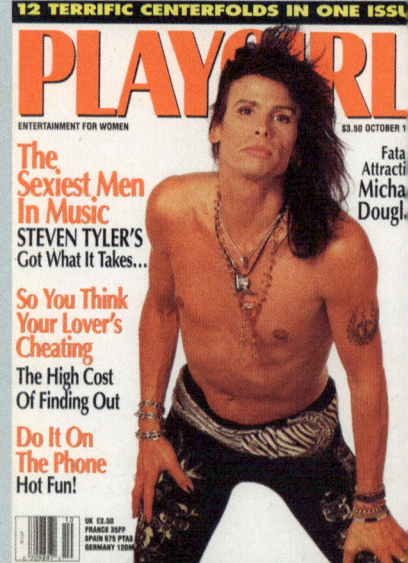

12 TERRIFIC CENTERFOLDS IN ONE ISSUE

PLAYGIRL

ENTERTAINMENT FOR WOMEN $3.50 OCTOBER 1

The Sexiest Men In Music STEVEN TYLER'S Got What It Takes...

So You Think Your Lover's Cheating The High Cost Of Finding Out

Do It On The Phone Hot Fun!

Fatal Attraction Michael Dougl...

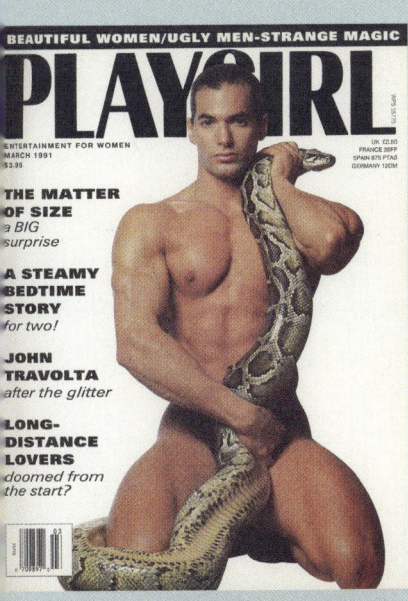

BEAUTIFUL WOMEN/UGLY MEN-STRANGE MAGIC

PLAYGIRL

ENTERTAINMENT FOR WOMEN
MARCH 1991
$3.95

THE MATTER OF SIZE
a BIG surprise!

A STEAMY BEDTIME STORY
for two!

JOHN TRAVOLTA
after the glitter

LONG-DISTANCE LOVERS
doomed from the start?

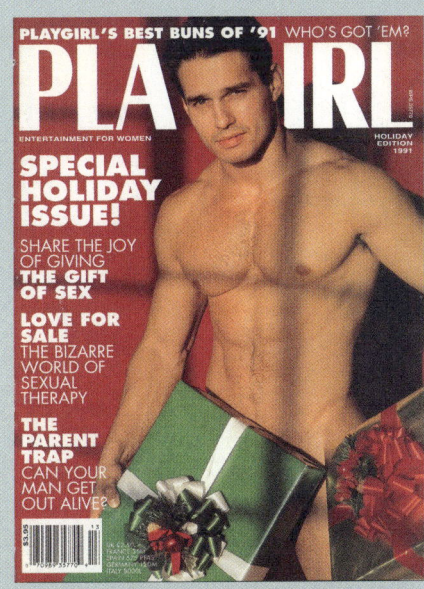

PLAYGIRL'S BEST BUNS OF '91 WHO'S GOT 'EM?

PLAYGIRL

ENTERTAINMENT FOR WOMEN
HOLIDAY EDITION 1991

SPECIAL HOLIDAY ISSUE!
SHARE THE JOY OF GIVING **THE GIFT OF SEX**

LOVE FOR SALE
THE BIZARRE WORLD OF SEXUAL THERAPY

THE PARENT TRAP
CAN YOUR MAN GET OUT ALIVE?

$3.95

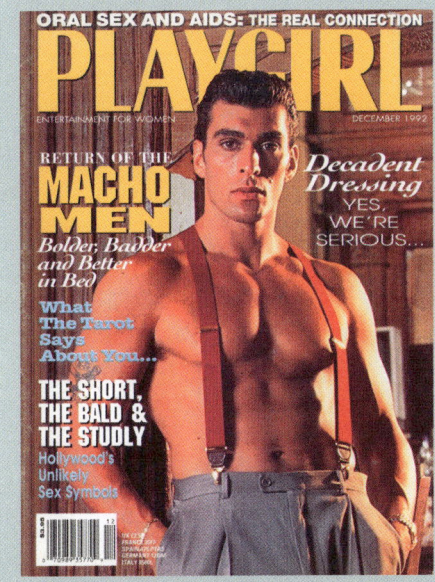

ORAL SEX AND AIDS: THE REAL CONNECTION

PLAYGIRL

ENTERTAINMENT FOR WOMEN
DECEMBER 1992

RETURN OF THE MACHO MEN
Bolder, Badder and Better in Bed

Decadent Dressing
YES, WE'RE SERIOUS...

What The Tarot Says About You...

THE SHORT, THE BALD & THE STUDLY
Hollywood's Unlikely Sex Symbols

$3.95

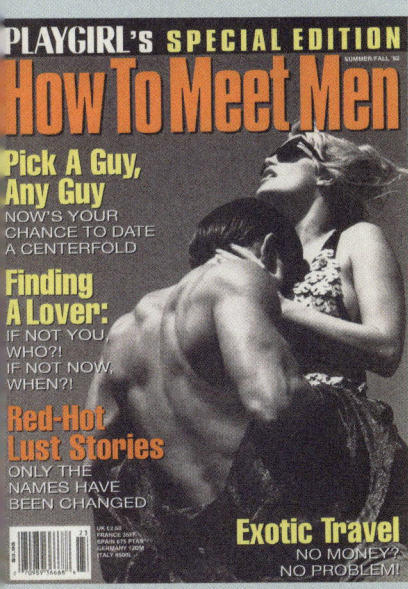

PLAYGIRL's SPECIAL EDITION

How To Meet Men

SUMMER/FALL '92

Pick A Guy, Any Guy
NOW'S YOUR CHANCE TO DATE A CENTERFOLD

Finding A Lover:
IF NOT YOU, WHO?! IF NOT NOW, WHEN?!

Red-Hot Lust Stories
ONLY THE NAMES HAVE BEEN CHANGED

Exotic Travel
NO MONEY? NO PROBLEM!

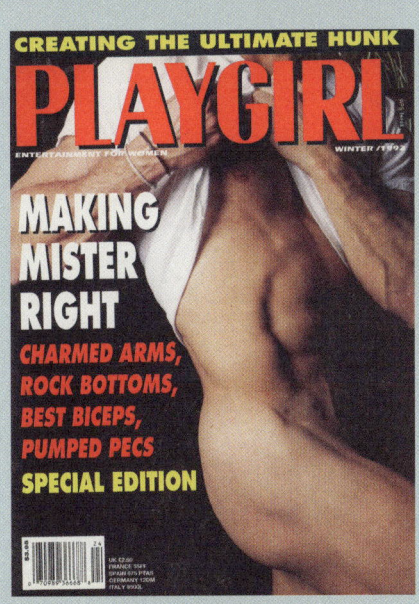

CREATING THE ULTIMATE HUNK

PLAYGIRL

ENTERTAINMENT FOR WOMEN
WINTER/1993

MAKING MISTER RIGHT

CHARMED ARMS, ROCK BOTTOMS, BEST BICEPS, PUMPED PECS

SPECIAL EDITION

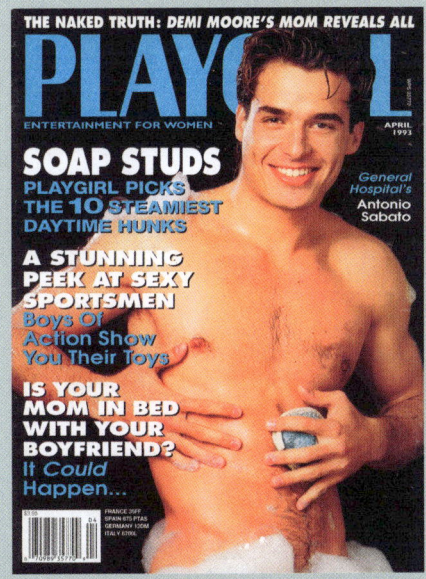

THE NAKED TRUTH: DEMI MOORE'S MOM REVEALS ALL

PLAYGIRL

ENTERTAINMENT FOR WOMEN
APRIL 1993

SOAP STUDS
PLAYGIRL PICKS THE **10** STEAMIEST DAYTIME HUNKS

General Hospital's Antonio Sabato

A STUNNING PEEK AT SEXY SPORTSMEN
Boys Of Action Show You Their Toys

IS YOUR MOM IN BED WITH YOUR BOYFRIEND?
It *Could* Happen...

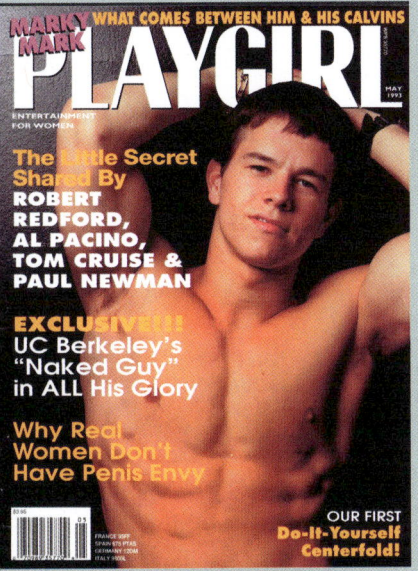

MARKY MARK WHAT COMES BETWEEN HIM & HIS CALVINS

PLAYGIRL

ENTERTAINMENT FOR WOMEN
MAY 1993

The Little Secret Shared By ROBERT REDFORD, AL PACINO, TOM CRUISE & PAUL NEWMAN

EXCLUSIVE!!!
UC Berkeley's "Naked Guy" in ALL His Glory

Why Real Women Don't Have Penis Envy

OUR FIRST **Do-It-Yourself Centerfold!**

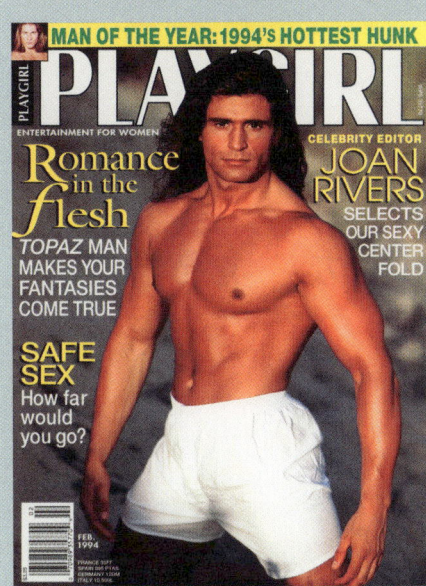

MAN OF THE YEAR: 1994'S HOTTEST HUNK

PLAYGIRL

ENTERTAINMENT FOR WOMEN

Romance in the flesh
TOPAZ MAN MAKES YOUR FANTASIES COME TRUE

CELEBRITY EDITOR JOAN RIVERS SELECTS OUR SEXY CENTER FOLD

SAFE SEX
How far would you go?

FEB. 1994

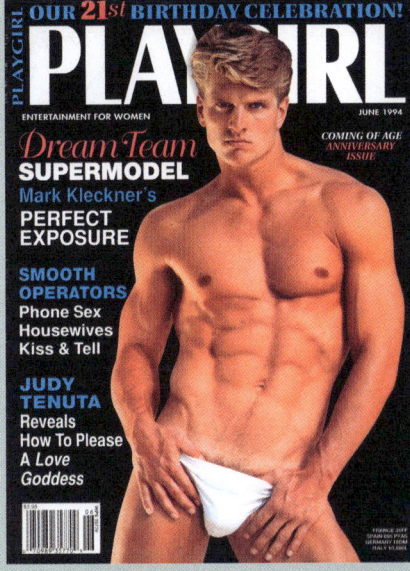

OUR 21st BIRTHDAY CELEBRATION!

PLAYGIRL

ENTERTAINMENT FOR WOMEN
JUNE 1994

COMING OF AGE ANNIVERSARY ISSUE

Dream Team SUPERMODEL
Mark Kleckner's **PERFECT EXPOSURE**

SMOOTH OPERATORS
Phone Sex Housewives Kiss & Tell

JUDY TENUTA
Reveals How To Please A Love Goddess

Ultimate Fleshfest

Canada's HARDEST NUDE Strippers

PLAYGIRL

SEPT 1999

ENTERTAINMENT FOR WOMEN
PLAYGIRL.COM

Sexy Male Supermodels
UNZIPPED
See The Men Beneath The Clothes

Runway Romeo
Our Centerfold Flashes More Than Fashion

You've Got Male
How To Find Love And Lust *Online*

King of the Catwalk
TYSON BECKFORD
He's Got Looks That Thrill

10 Ways To Save Time For Sex

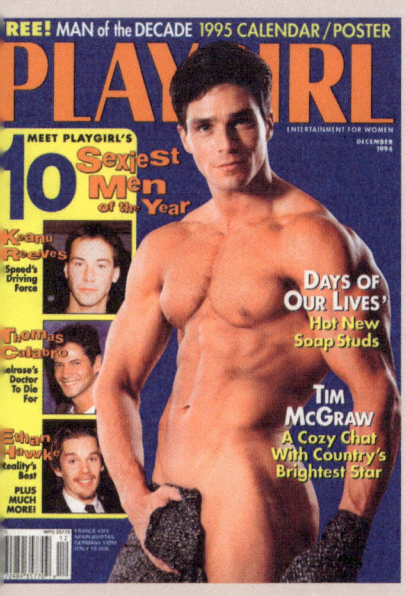

FREE! MAN of the DECADE 1995 CALENDAR / POSTER

PLAYGIRL

ENTERTAINMENT FOR WOMEN
DECEMBER 1994

MEET PLAYGIRL'S
10 Sexiest Men of the Year

Keanu Reeves
Speed's Driving Force

Thomas Calabro
Melrose's Doctor To Die For

Ethan Hawke
Reality's Best
PLUS MUCH MORE!

DAYS OF OUR LIVES'
Hot New Soap Studs

TIM McGRAW
A Cozy Chat With Country's Brightest Star

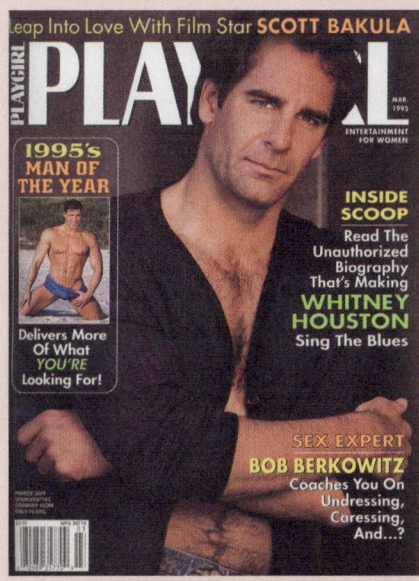

Leap Into Love With Film Star SCOTT BAKULA

PLAYGIRL

ENTERTAINMENT FOR WOMEN
MAR. 1995

1995's MAN OF THE YEAR

Delivers More Of What YOU'RE Looking For!

INSIDE SCOOP
Read The Unauthorized Biography That's Making
WHITNEY HOUSTON Sing The Blues

SEX EXPERT
BOB BERKOWITZ
Coaches You On Undressing, Caressing, And...?

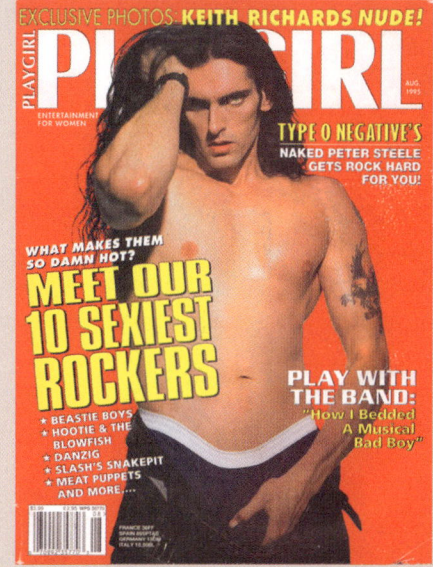

EXCLUSIVE PHOTOS: KEITH RICHARDS NUDE!

PLAYGIRL

ENTERTAINMENT FOR WOMEN
AUG. 1995

TYPE O NEGATIVE'S
NAKED PETER STEELE GETS ROCK HARD FOR YOU!

WHAT MAKES THEM SO DAMN HOT?
MEET OUR 10 SEXIEST ROCKERS
+ BEASTIE BOYS
+ HOOTIE & THE BLOWFISH
+ DANZIG
+ SLASH'S SNAKEPIT
+ MEAT PUPPETS
AND MORE...

PLAY WITH THE BAND:
"How I Bedded A Musical Bad Boy"

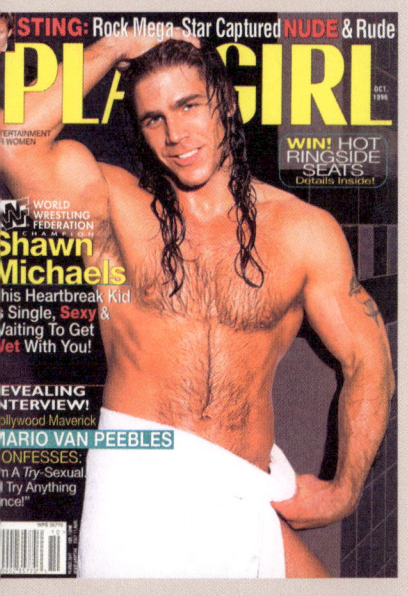

STING: Rock Mega-Star Captured NUDE & Rude

PLAYGIRL

ENTERTAINMENT FOR WOMEN
OCT. 1996

WIN! HOT RINGSIDE SEATS
Details Inside!

WORLD WRESTLING FEDERATION CHAMPION
Shawn Michaels
This Heartbreak Kid Is Single, Sexy & Waiting To Get Wet With You!

REVEALING INTERVIEW!
Hollywood Maverick
MARIO VAN PEEBLES
CONFESSES:
I'm A Try-Sexual...
I'll Try Anything Once!"

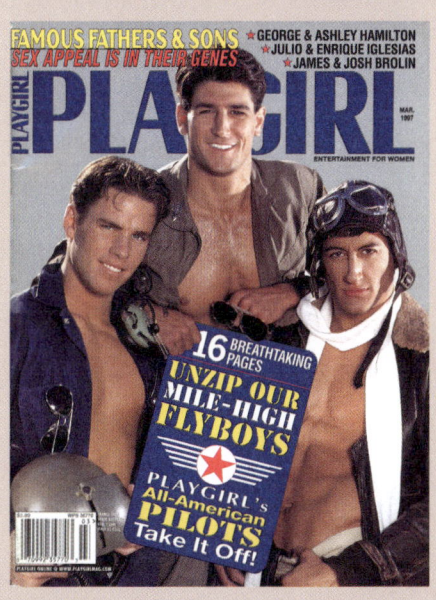

FAMOUS FATHERS & SONS
SEX APPEAL IS IN THEIR GENES
★ GEORGE & ASHLEY HAMILTON
★ JULIO & ENRIQUE IGLESIAS
★ JAMES & JOSH BROLIN

PLAYGIRL

ENTERTAINMENT FOR WOMEN
MAR. 1997

16 BREATHTAKING PAGES
UNZIP OUR MILE-HIGH FLYBOYS
PLAYGIRL'S All-American PILOTS Take It Off!

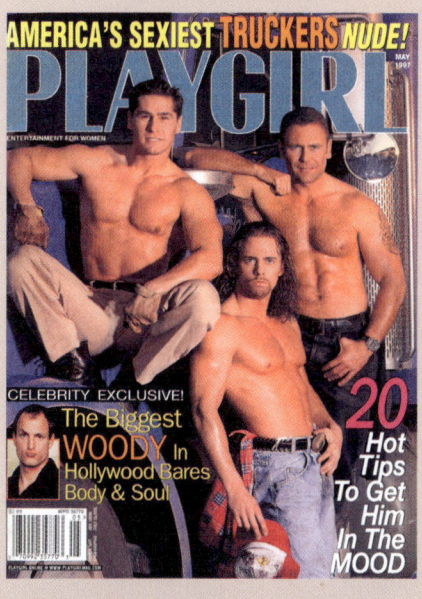

AMERICA'S SEXIEST TRUCKERS NUDE!

PLAYGIRL

ENTERTAINMENT FOR WOMEN
MAY 1997

CELEBRITY EXCLUSIVE!
The Biggest WOODY In Hollywood Bares Body & Soul

20 Hot Tips To Get Him In The MOOD

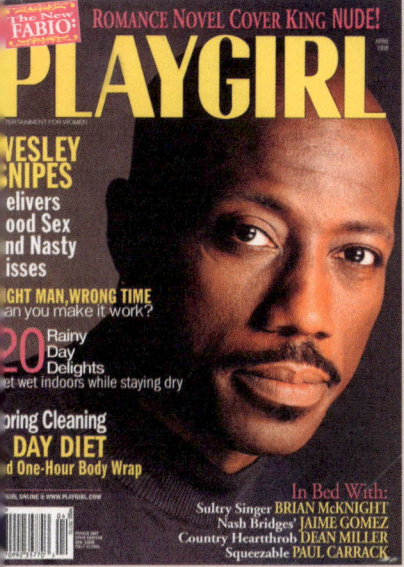

The New FABIO!
ROMANCE NOVEL COVER KING NUDE!

PLAYGIRL

ENTERTAINMENT FOR WOMEN
APRIL 1998

WESLEY SNIPES
Delivers Good Sex And Nasty Kisses

RIGHT MAN, WRONG TIME
Can you make it work?

20 Rainy Day Delights
Get wet indoors while staying dry

Spring Cleaning
3 DAY DIET and One-Hour Body Wrap

In Bed With:
Sultry Singer BRIAN McKNIGHT
Nash Bridges' JAIME GOMEZ
Country Heartthrob DEAN MILLER
Squeezable PAUL CARRACK

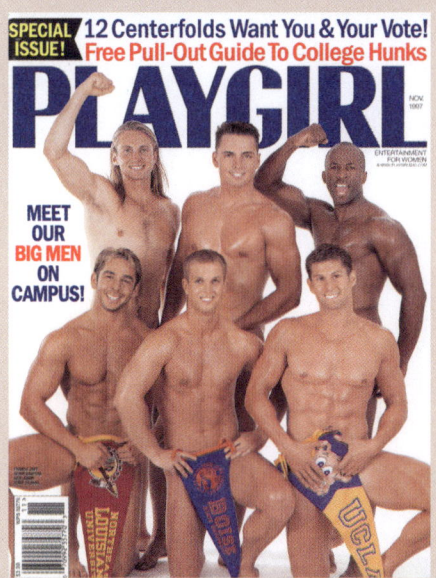

SPECIAL ISSUE!
12 Centerfolds Want You & Your Vote!
Free Pull-Out Guide To College Hunks

PLAYGIRL

ENTERTAINMENT FOR WOMEN
NOV. 1997

MEET OUR BIG MEN ON CAMPUS!

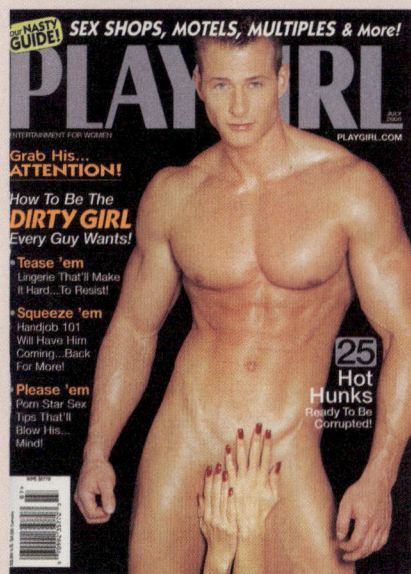

OUR NASTY GUIDE!
SEX SHOPS, MOTELS, MULTIPLES & More!

PLAYGIRL

ENTERTAINMENT FOR WOMEN
PLAYGIRL.COM
JULY 2004

Grab His... ATTENTION!
How To Be The DIRTY GIRL Every Guy Wants!

• Tease 'em
Lingerie That'll Make It Hard...To Resist!

• Squeeze 'em
Handjob 101 Will Have Him Coming...Back For More!

• Please 'em
Porn-Star Sex Tips That'll Blow His...Mind!

25 Hot Hunks Ready To Be Corrupted!

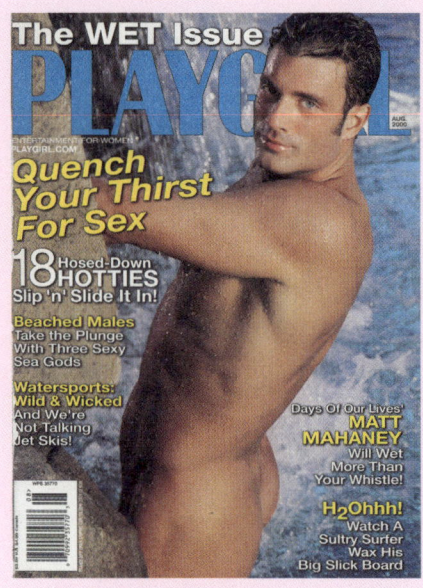

The WET Issue
PLAYGIRL
AUG 2000
PLAYGIRL.COM

Quench Your Thirst For Sex

18 Hosed-Down HOTTIES
Slip 'n' Slide It In!

Beached Males
Take the Plunge With Three Sexy Sea Gods!

Watersports: Wild & Wicked
And We're Not Talking Jet Skis!

Days Of Our Lives'
MATT MAHANEY
Will Wet More Than Your Whistle!

H₂Ohhh!
Watch A Sultry Surfer Wax His Big Slick Board

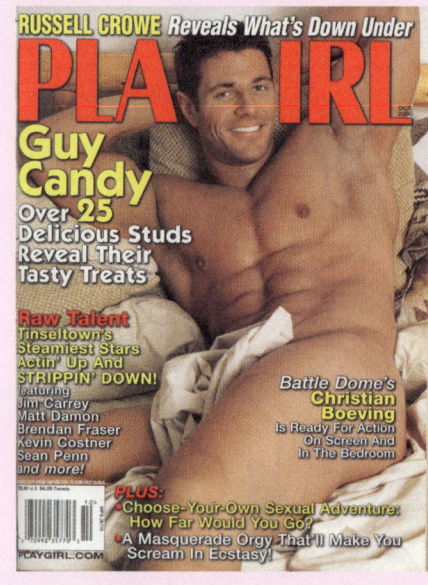

RUSSELL CROWE Reveals What's Down Under
PLAYGIRL
OCT 2000

Guy Candy
Over **25** Delicious Studs Reveal Their Tasty Treats

Raw Talent
Tinseltown's Steamiest Stars Actin' Up And STRIPPIN' DOWN!
Featuring Jim Carrey, Matt Damon, Brendan Fraser, Kevin Costner, Sean Penn and more!

Battle Dome's **Christian Boeving**
Is Ready For Action On Screen And In The Bedroom

PLUS:
• Choose-Your-Own Sexual Adventure: How Far Would You Go?
• A Masquerade Orgy That'll Make You Scream In Ecstasy!

PLAYGIRL.COM

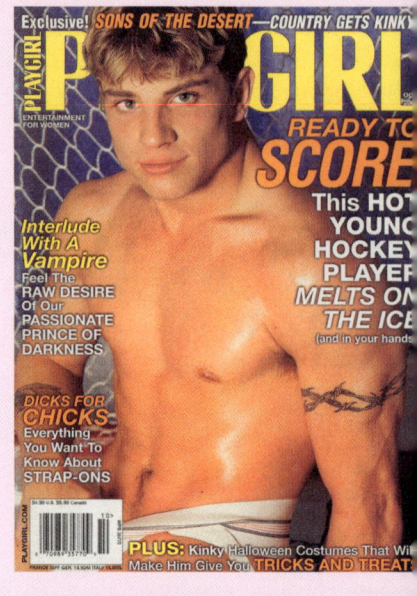

Exclusive! **SONS OF THE DESERT**—COUNTRY GETS KINKY
PLAYGIRL
ENTERTAINMENT FOR WOMEN

READY TO SCORE
THIS HOT YOUNG HOCKEY PLAYER MELTS ON THE ICE
(and in your hands)

Interlude With A Vampire
Feel The RAW DESIRE Of Our PASSIONATE Prince Of Darkness

DICKS FOR CHICKS
Everything You Want To Know About STRAP-ONS

PLAYGIRL.COM

PLUS: Kinky Halloween Costumes That Will Make Him Give You TRICKS AND TREATS

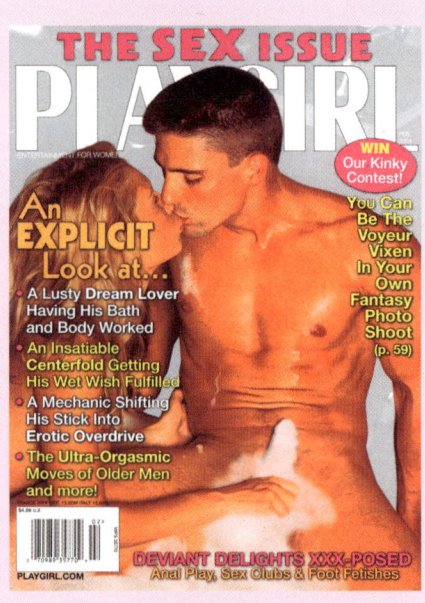

THE SEX ISSUE
PLAYGIRL
ENTERTAINMENT FOR WOMEN

WIN Our Kinky Contest!

An EXPLICIT Look at...
• A Lusty Dream Lover Having His Bath and Body Worked
• An Insatiable Centerfold Getting His Wet Wish Fulfilled
• A Mechanic Shifting His Stick Into Erotic Overdrive
• The Ultra-Orgasmic Moves of Older Men and more!

You Can Be The Voyeur Vixen In Your Own Fantasy Photo Shoot (p. 59)

DEVIANT DELIGHTS XXX-POSED
Anal Play, Sex Clubs & Foot Fetishes
PLAYGIRL.COM

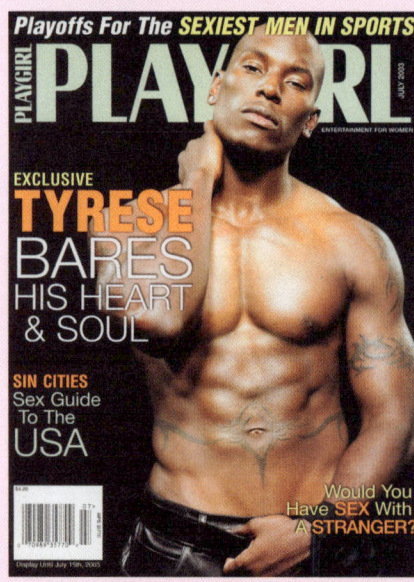

Playoffs For The SEXIEST MEN IN SPORTS
PLAYGIRL
JULY 2003
ENTERTAINMENT FOR WOMEN

EXCLUSIVE TYRESE BARES HIS HEART & SOUL

SIN CITIES
Sex Guide To The USA

Would You Have SEX With A STRANGER?

Display Until July 15th, 2003

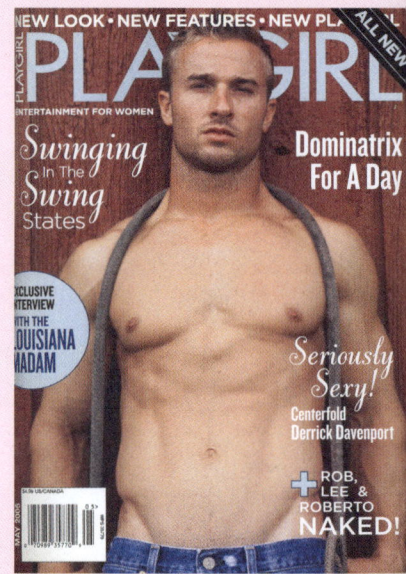

NEW LOOK • NEW FEATURES • NEW PLA... ALL NEW
PLAYGIRL
ENTERTAINMENT FOR WOMEN

Swinging In The Swing States

Dominatrix For A Day

EXCLUSIVE INTERVIEW WITH THE LOUISIANA MADAM

Seriously Sexy!
Centerfold Derrick Davenport

+ ROB, LEE & ROBERTO NAKED!

MAY 2005

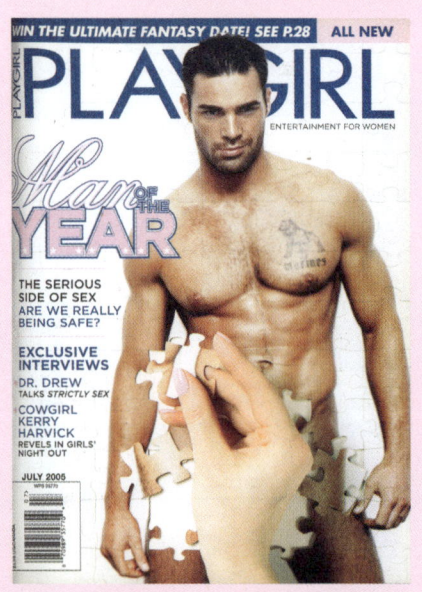

WIN THE ULTIMATE FANTASY DATE! SEE P.28   ALL NEW
PLAYGIRL
ENTERTAINMENT FOR WOMEN

Man OF THE YEAR

THE SERIOUS SIDE OF SEX
ARE WE REALLY BEING SAFE?

EXCLUSIVE INTERVIEWS
DR. DREW Talks Strictly Sex

COWGIRL KERRY HARVICK Revels In Girls' Night Out

JULY 2006

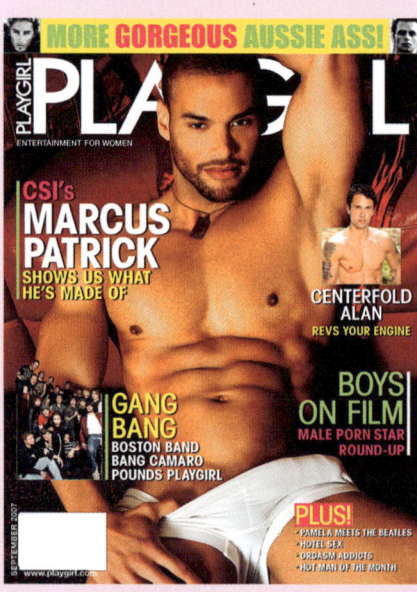

MORE GORGEOUS AUSSIE ASS!
PLAYGIRL
ENTERTAINMENT FOR WOMEN

CSI's **MARCUS PATRICK** SHOWS US WHAT HE'S MADE OF

CENTERFOLD ALAN REVS YOUR ENGINE

BOYS ON FILM
Male Porn Star ROUND-UP

GANG BANG
BOSTON BAND BANG CAMARO POUNDS PLAYGIRL

PLUS!
• PAMELA MEETS THE BEATLES
• HOTEL SEX
• ORGASM ADDICTS
• HOT MAN OF THE MONTH

SEPTEMBER 2007
www.playgirl.com

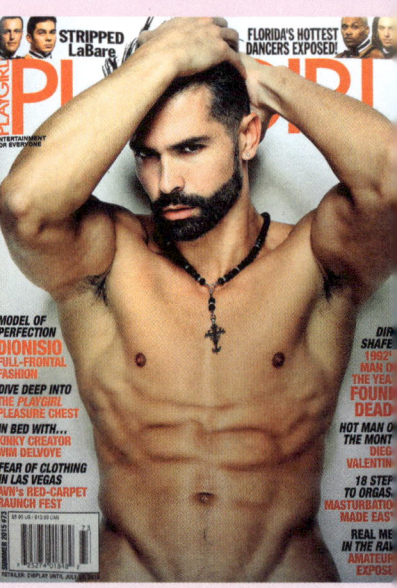

STRIPPED LaBare   FLORIDA'S HOTTEST DANCERS EXPOSED!
PLAYGIRL
ENTERTAINMENT FOR EVERYONE

MODEL OF PERFECTION
DIONISIO
FULL-FRONTAL FASHION

DIVE DEEP INTO THE PLAYGIRL PLEASURE CHEST

IN BED WITH... KINKY CREATOR WIM DELVOYE

FEAR OF CLOTHING IN LAS VEGAS
AVN's RED-CARPET RAUNCH FEST

DIR... SHAFE...
1992 MAN O... THE YEA... FOUN... DEAD...

HOT MAN O... THE MONT... DIEGO VALENTIN...

18 STEP... TO ORGAS... MASTURBATION MADE EAS...

REAL M... IN THE RA... AMATEUR... EXPOS...

SUMMER 2015 #73

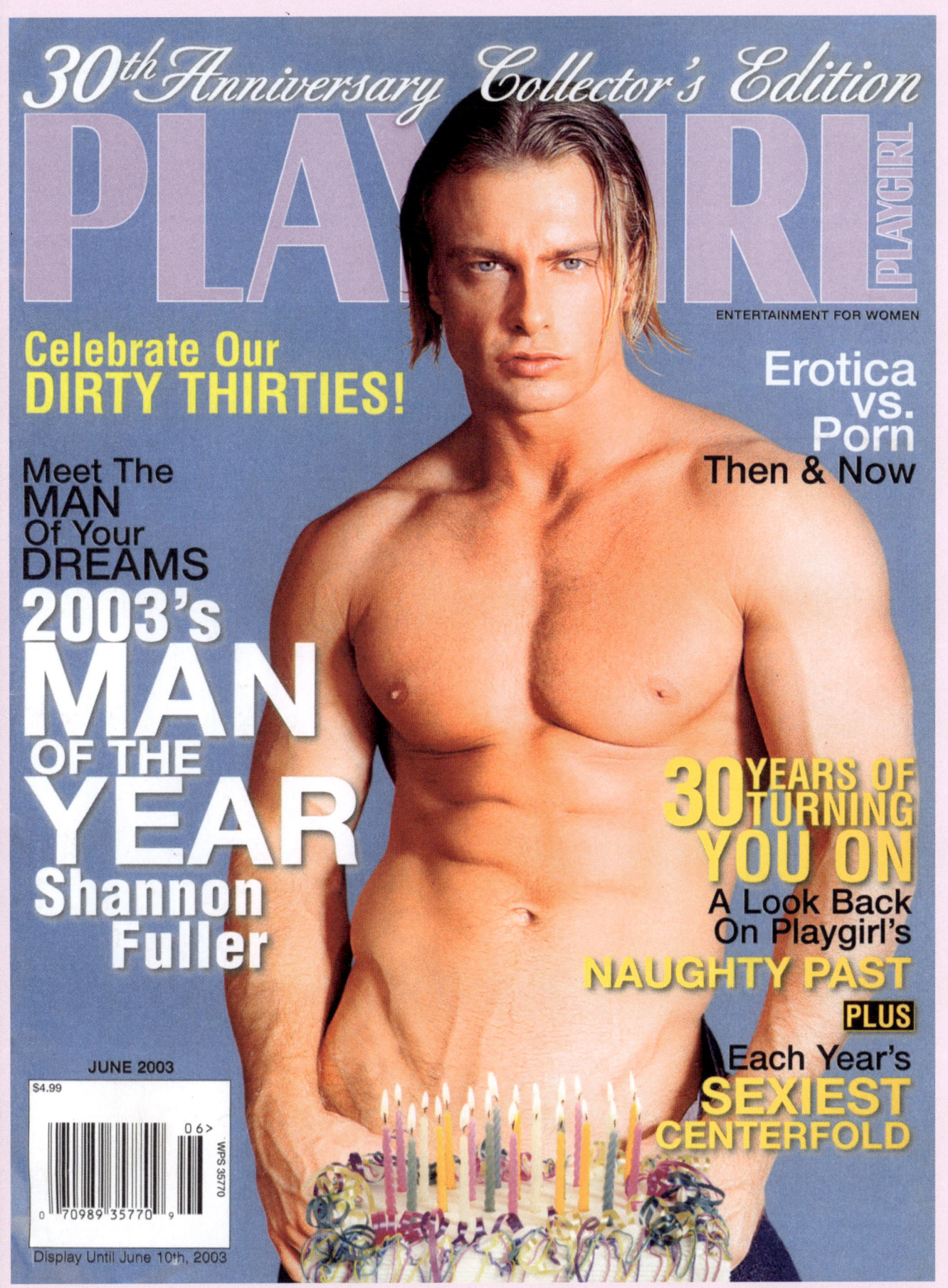

30th *Anniversary* Collector's Edition

PLAYGIRL

PLAYGIRL

ENTERTAINMENT FOR WOMEN

Celebrate Our
DIRTY THIRTIES!

Erotica
vs.
Porn
Then & Now

Meet The
MAN
Of Your
DREAMS
2003's
MAN
OF THE
YEAR
**Shannon
Fuller**

30 YEARS OF
TURNING
YOU ON
A Look Back
On Playgirl's
NAUGHTY PAST

PLUS

Each Year's
**SEXIEST
CENTERFOLD**

JUNE 2003

$4.99

WPS 35770

0 70989 35770 9

06>

Display Until June 10th, 2003

CHAPTER 2

ARTICLES

Some readers do enjoy *Playgirl* for the articles!
Our pages have been graced with many essays
by feminist luminaries, such as Anaïs Nin's
"Eroticism in Women" (1974) and Maya Angelou's
"Are Feminists Humorless?" (1975). We've also featured
provocative investigative journalism like "Anatomy
of a Live Sex Show" (1974), "I Slept with a Male Prostitute"
(1981), and "Tricks of the Trade" (1992),
as well as practical information designed to educate and
improve one's sex life, including "Voyeurism as Foreplay"
(1980) and "Both Sides of Bisexuality" (1987).
The *Playgirl* folio contains historical ponderings
that may still be reflected upon today, like
"How Movies Ruined Our Sex Lives" (1981)
and "A Decade of Female Sexuality" (1983), as well as
lighthearted contemporary musings such as "I Was an
X-Rated Novelist" (1991) and "In Praise of Penis" (2007).

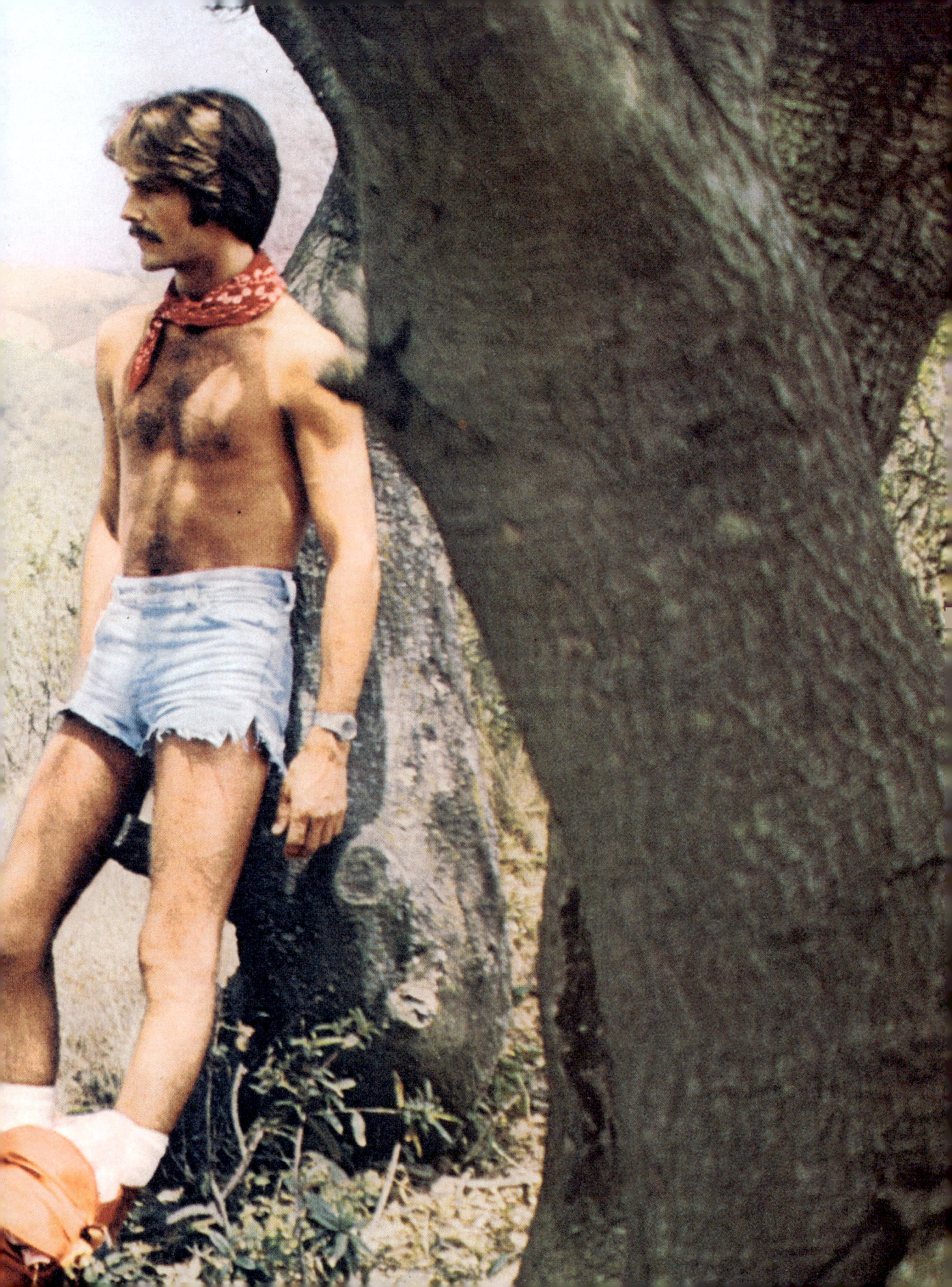

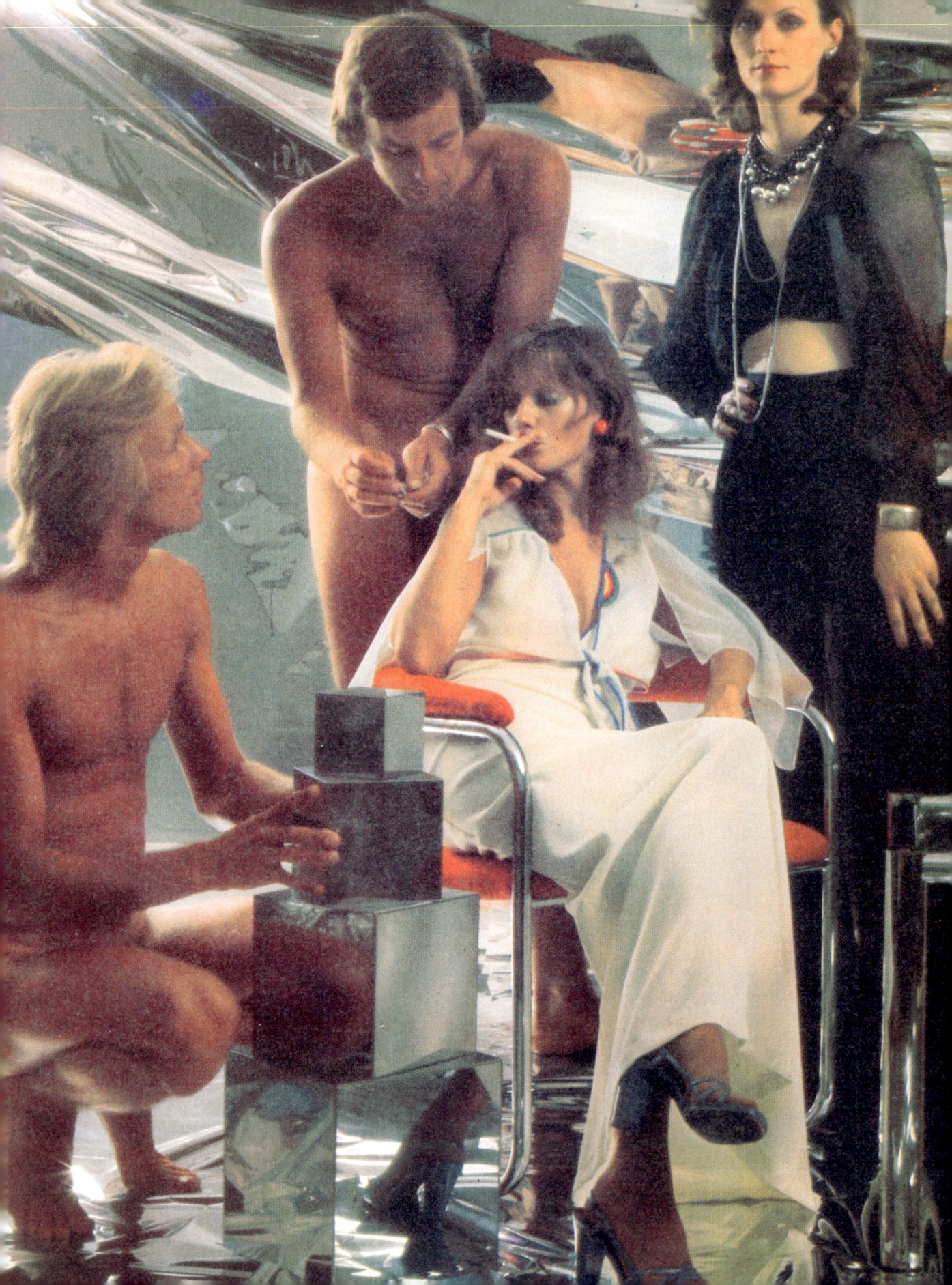

ARE FEMINISTS HUMORLESS?

MAYA ANGELOU

I distrust the humorless. Those who declare the seriousness of their cause and the sincerity of their commitment with tightened lips and stony faces lose me as a baptismal candidate at the very lip of the font.

It is said (of course, by human beings) that human beings are the only animals who laugh. I haven't had any reports from hippos or tapirs, but I do know nature has given *Homo sapiens* mental membranes which, when activated, cause sounds to titter off our lips in giggles or to roar out of our mouths in guffaws. Since we have that strange little organ, it behooves us to keep it in use or it, like the little toe and the appendix, will wither its way into extinction.

As women, as equal actors in the comedy of life, we can invent our own roles daily. We have the ability to see the truly funny aspects of our age and write our own jokes about ourselves. For our children, our husbands, lovers, and friends, but more selfishly for our own souls, we should create healthy humor and circulate it as effectively as unfair caricatures of us have been distributed for ages.

The very serious women's liberation movement, like all social struggles, has built into its skeletal body a degree of risibility that only the most clenched-teeth sexist (of any gender) can resist. There are those moments when the "new woman" confronts the "old man" and the result can be as comic as Charlie Chaplin on the run or Lucille Ball on the loose.

Playgirl ran a cartoon in an early issue which caused me to convulse in gales of laughter, and even now, as I write about it months later, I have to control myself or risk never getting to my own punch line. A worn-out, bedraggled, frightened, and exhausted wolf is shown dragging himself on all fours (or maybe fives) to a huntsman. The caption reads, more or less,

"There was this girl, all dressed in red who gave me some line like, 'Come up and see my grandmother.'"

There is a sassiness and an independence about today's young women which affords me tremendous pleasure, because it indicates that the movement for our equality will survive and, more important, survive robustly. We would make a sorry spectacle if history found us a triumphant yet puling and whining lot without a snap in our fingers or a grin to our names. Who truly wants to live in a world without gusto, love, and laughter?

I suggest that it is counterproductive if we shout about freedom, then imprison ourselves in lifeless platitudes, or exhort the imperative need for equality, yet indulge the imbalance of humorlessness.

Having looked at some of the grim, intentionally shaggy women who purport to be representing my interests for a truly brave new world, I restrain denying them openly only with the most ferocious control (meanwhile blowing kisses to the sleek Gloria Steinem). This is no encouragement for all women in the movement to ape the glamorous Ms. S., but surely there is no need for us to prove by our appearances that we are indeed only bones and hanks of hair (mostly uncombed) and dour, angry faces. That stance is unfortunate.

We deny our humanity if we withhold our humor. We must accept the challenge to construct folktales of our laughable times, of our heady triumphs and bumbling failures. If we reject our capacity and need for serious humor, we reduce our humanity to witlessness and our femininity to absurdum.

For obvious reasons, I am not encouraging a revival of the Uncle Tom shuffling model, but I do so want to be delivered from the sour Ms. Raggedy Ann.

(Originally published November 1975)

I SLEPT
WITH A MALE
PROSTITUTE

TRACY CABOT

A s a journalist, I've spent hundreds of lonely nights dutifully ensconced in a luxurious, but lonely, all-expenses-paid hotel room while chasing an elusive celebrity or an exclusive story. In glamorous resorts like Aspen and Las Vegas and in big, exciting cities like New York, Chicago, Dallas, and San Francisco, I've sat cross-legged on a sprawling, empty, king-size bed in front of a color TV, eating a solitary, room-service dinner. I've longed for anyone to share the empty hours with, but I was unable to face an unknown city at night alone.

As a woman, I have ached with horniness, even at home. Between relationships, when I felt too ugly or too fat or too depressed to risk any rejection, I have raged at the inequity that allows a man to have sex delivered like Chicken Delight, yet insists that a woman quash her desires until she is summoned.

If I were a wealthy Palm Springs widow, gigolos and fortune hunters would seek me out, would caress my wrinkled and browned alligator skin, would love me as if I were young and beautiful—in exchange for the benefits of my bounty. Unfortunately, on my writer's income, I can't afford to support a man full time, but I'd never thought about an hourly or evening rate until I met J.T.

J.T. is twenty-seven years old. He was born in Miami, Florida, where he began hustling sixty-year-old divorcees and widows when he was just eighteen. "At first," he told me, "I was repulsed by their wrinkles and old bodies, but then when I got the money, I felt so good it didn't

bother me anymore." After moving to California, J.T. has continued to support himself by "giving pleasure to women." Most of his customers are married, and many of them give him gifts and see him on a regular basis, sometimes for lunch or just to chat. He is an intimate part of their lives, like their hairdressers or manicurists.

"I never have trouble getting turned on," J.T. likes to brag. "In California, my customers have ranged from twenty-five to forty years old. Most of them just want to fool around a little without endangering their marriages. We usually go to a motel room. Some of the women I see have never made it with anyone but their old man; they're curious, but they want to play it safe. I offer a service with discretion. Most of the women are pretty foxy and wouldn't have any trouble getting laid for free, but they don't want any emotional involvement, and they don't want to get caught," J.T. explains.

I have always been fascinated by prostitutes: Why do they get paid while the rest of us scheme to give it away? What is it like to have sex for money? Why are there so many prostitutes for men, no matter what their sexual tastes, and until recently, none for women? Even the ancient ruins of Pompeii boast relics of a whorehouse—but it was only for men.

In a favorite fantasy of mine, I try to put myself in a man's place, to imagine what it would be like to go to a whorehouse—but one filled with men instead of women. There would be tough-looking ones in T-shirts with round, firm, vein-lined muscles bulging under packs of cigarettes rolled up in their sleeves. There would be young ones with pink cheeks, blond curls, and baby-soft skin rosy over a smooth white tush. There would be sensitive, poetic types who play the guitar and sing. Smooth-shaven and bearded, dressed and undressed, they would parade before me so I could choose.

In Pompeii, the price a man paid for the services of a whore was determined by weighing his penis on a scale as he entered the house. In my fantasy, the male prostitutes would be priced according to their special talents in bed and the weight and size of their equipment.

Chances of actually locating such a dream bordello are pretty slim, however. Instead, there are escort services in most large cities that will supply men for an evening's date. If you specify "open," "sexy," or a "liberal" type, the escort service will get the picture. The other way to find a male prostitute is by going to the most expensive hotel bar in town between the hours of one and three in the afternoon; you tell the maître'd or bartender that you wouldn't mind company, and it's likely that he'll recommend a "regular."

But there are no male whorehouses, per se, on record. It's only recently that men have accepted women liking sex at all, let alone wanting to buy it. Sex for money has belonged exclusively to men. Until just recently, only men had the sexual freedom and the disposable income needed to enjoy intercourse without love. Now women have the same opportunities.

The situation the night I met J.T. was in some ways like my fantasy. I was taking some friends from out of town to a local club where men dance and strip for women, but I never imagined I'd be taking one of the dancers home. The show started at eight o'clock, and by the time it was over at ten we were all a little drunk and very aroused. For two hours, men of different physical descriptions, ranging from tall and macho to slight and ethereal, had gyrated in front of us. Each one wore a different costume; one was a cowboy, one a cop, and then there was J.T., the magician.

As he twirled his tight, muscular body and thrust his buttocks, chest, arms, and hips closer and closer to our table, I felt a tightening in my stomach. His cape swirled, touching my arm, and a chill shivered through my body. I was certain I'd caught a glimpse of his cock, and had he purposely looked at me?

I watched as J.T. moved among the tables of women, who were shrieking, hooting, and pushing bills into his pants. He was getting more and more brazen, touching first this customer and then that one. Watching, I wanted him to touch me. As if he had read my mind, when he swept back to the stage, J.T. stopped to touch my neck with his lips, his hand resting for just a second on my thigh and then deliberately moving over my pubis, up my stomach, and under my breast, just missing the nipple.

The thrill I felt at the hands of this slightly sleazy stranger was a surprise. It had been four long months since my last rotten relationship had ended, and I had finally gotten used to celibacy—most of the time. In fact, I had been wondering if I would ever be jarred out of my sexual lethargy.

As J.T. removed his magician's garb piece by piece while doing tricks and waving scarves, the women roared their approval, applauded, threw money, and grabbed at him as he passed. When he had stripped down to a giant G-string, his perfect California suntan, orthodontist's-dream white teeth, baby-smooth hair, and silky, unmarked skin, were all on display.

"If any of you ladies would like to see more of J.T.," the announcer said over the loudspeaker system as the applause died down, "he'll be around to the tables after the show. J.T. is one of those lucky guys who makes a living from keeping ladies happy, so keep a tight grip on your purses." At first, I thought it was a joke. Surely my elitist sexuality hadn't been turned on by a male hooker. In any case, I never thought I'd pay for sex—that is, not until J.T. came over to our table after the show.

He was charming and delightful, making conversation with each of us, remembering our names and whether or not we were married or had kids. Casually, he managed to touch each of us, while letting us know that more intimacy would cost money.

"How much?" I wondered out loud, and my out-of-town visitors glared at me as if I had made a faux pas. Unflappable, J.T. smiled and said, "My rates start at fifty dollars and go up from there. It's all negotiable, and satisfaction's guaranteed or you don't have to pay."

J.T. knew I was interested even before I did. The truth was that my rising hormones were getting out of control, but I wasn't ready to risk another emotional involvement and possible relationship problems just because of my overactive libido. A male prostitute could be the answer, but paying for sex isn't easy to accept.

Looking at J.T., listening to him speak, I realized he wasn't much different from the female prostitutes I had met—without resources, without educations, street kids, escapees from the ghettos of poverty. While chasing his dream of becoming a movie star in Hollywood, J.T. was surviving on the only skill he had, parlaying his only assets—his looks, his tongue, and his cock—for a chance at the good life.

"Well, how much for me?" I asked.

"Depends on what you want," J.T. replied slickly. "Seeing you're an attractive lady, for $100 I'd be willing to give you the super-deluxe treatment—the royal treatment, everything that would please a woman, but slow and easy and very sensuously. I include everything from oral sex to intercourse, and basically I do it exactly the way you want."

I could see J.T. wasn't going to fall in love with me. He was no more emotionally involved than a salesman making a deal. His enthusiasm was for the pitch, for closing the bargain, for the money, but not for me. I secretly wanted him, but I didn't want to pay. There was a challenge in seeing if I could get him for nothing.

"I carry soft fur gloves," J.T. continued. "With the gloves, I give an erotic body rub, then I switch to unscented sesame oil. We could even dip into my special 'happiness case' for a little extra pleasure—speed, coke, grass, 'ludes, anything you want. I provide a service, and I have to be considerate of what the people need. If you'd like a complete evening of conversation, dinner, sex, and drugs—say, six or seven hours—it would cost about $250, including my dinner."

It was absolutely amazing how quickly J.T. had gotten around to what and how much. He had started out by simply asking if we enjoyed the show; five minutes later, he was listing his services; then he was gone. "I'll be back," he said, winking, and we ordered another round of drinks. Out of the corner of my eye I kept tabs on J.T. He was stopping at each table, sometimes staying just a brief thirty seconds, sometimes sitting down and chatting for two or three minutes. Then he was back.

"I had to check out the action," he explained offhandedly. "It's a slow night. Mostly single ladies, and they don't like to pay." (Most of his customers, I later learned, were married.) "But if they really want me, they do." Casually, he rested his hand on my thigh. Yes, I decided, I really wanted him, but no, I didn't want to pay. I knew there were lots of men who would go to bed with me for nothing.

"How does a woman know you're any good?" I teased.

"Why don't we go outside," he flirted back, "and I'll give you a free sample. Then you'll see how good I am. I'm an expert, that's why ladies pay me. Besides, I really like giving pleasure to ladies."

The offer was irresistible. It was no big surprise to find that J.T. had his own little joy wagon, a VW van, in the parking lot. Alas, I was not to be the first to get the free sample.

Inside the van there was a water bed, a stereo, and the thickest, plushest carpeting I'd ever seen. "Double padding," he said, grinning as I sank deep into the dark red rug. "Have a seat." He motioned to the fur bedspread. "How about a glass of wine? A joint?" The wine was white and the grass expensive. My head felt light, and I was a little giddy. If the sample went all the way, I was ready.

He sat down next to me and began to fondle my breasts, first around the outside edges and then closer and closer to the nipples, his touch getting firmer and firmer. Then he squeezed a nipple, gently pinching until it stood firm and puckered. Easily he slipped his hand beneath my T-shirt and lifted one of my breasts to his mouth. He bent over it as if he were about to take Holy Communion, adoring, worshipping, tonguing, and biting it. He was like a hungry child, gobbling me up inch by inch, sucking, kissing everywhere.

His lips were soft and full, his skin like velvet, and his cock rock-hard, bulging under his pants. I tingled as he kissed the back of my neck; I felt his firm-muscled thigh, the pull of his erection. One hand cupped my breast; then his other ran up my leg, high under my skirt. His fingers were tripping lightly up my inner thigh, followed by his soft lips. His warm breath wafted over my pubis.

My breathing grew louder, and I felt warm and moist between my legs. J.T.'s pants were unzipped, and his rosebud pink cock seemed about to burst out of them. "Do you think you'd like to buy some more of my time?" he asked, stopping just as I was about to come.

"No way," I muttered, hardly able to catch my breath, but I was on to his little trick.

"Well, I have an appointment," he said, smiling. "I have to go now. Come on. I'll walk you back to your table. Here's my card. Put it in your purse. Call me—I deliver."

My knees were wobbly; my heart was pounding. I couldn't believe what had happened. J.T. was straightening up the van, turning off the stereo. "I strip for private parties, but I never take money until afterwards, and then only if the ladies are satisfied. Give me a ring, but not early in the morning. You'll love it, I promise. I'll read your tarot cards. I can tell fortunes," J.T. rattled on amiably, relishing my discomfort. My libido was stuck in high gear, and he was going to leave it that way.

My friends were giggling when we went back into the club, and I don't think they believed me at first when I told them what had happened. Then they agreed that I had done the right thing, that paying for sex would ruin it forever, that J.T. was a jerk. But for the next two weeks, I couldn't stop thinking about him. I masturbated constantly and never really was satisfied. The touch of a warm body had aroused in me all the old sexual feelings, but I wasn't ready to face a possible rejection in a singles bar or to face even an emotional involvement. J.T.'s card was burning a hole in my wallet, but I wondered what the long-term effects of paying for sex would be on my psyche and just how abnormal it would be if I did hire J.T.

"For 2000 years, going to prostitutes hasn't hurt men," says Dr. Robert Reitman, director of the Valley Center for Marital and Sexual Therapy in Woodland Hills, California. "I doubt if it's going to hurt women. The exchange of sex for money is more up front, more direct than other ways we have found to get sex—with guilt, lies, manipulations, and threats, or in exchange for emotional and financial security."

His views were echoed by sex therapist Barbara M. Roberts, director of the Center for Social and Sensory Learning in Encino, California. "I work a lot with single people who have sex problems," she explained. "Often, they don't have a partner to work things out with. Besides, experiential sex therapy is the only effective kind.

"Prostitution should be legalized, both for men and for women. I believe it serves a useful purpose in our society. For a woman, going to a prostitute is a way to assert her right to have the same things men have, and it's easier to buy it than to stand around a singles bar. We live in a youth and beauty-oriented culture, and that makes even hanging out in bars an impossible pickup situation for many women. A male prostitute could be the perfect answer. When a woman is over forty, it's difficult for her to find companionship and sex any other way.

"Actually," she continued, "we pay in one way or another anyway, so why not with money? You pay a shrink for a warm, nurturing relationship that some people believe should come naturally and for free. Why not a sex partner? For a woman, it's making a choice instead of sitting around waiting to be chosen."

Indeed it does feel powerful to be able to choose a man, to be able to call him and buy his time, to ask for and get exactly what one wants. My hormones were raging the night I called J.T. "I'd like to see you," I said, wondering how explicit I should be on the phone.

"Tonight?" he asked.

"Yes."

"Since I'm not busy tonight. I'll give you the royal treatment for $100." He took my address and promised to show up quickly.

Trying to be casual, as if I hired men all the time, I greeted him in my sexiest jeans and T-shirt. He was wearing a pale blue three-piece suit with a white shirt and white shoes, like the best man at a summer wedding. He kissed me and hugged me. He said that I looked wonderful, that my house was beautiful. He loved my dogs, my cats, my intellect, my sensitivity. Obviously I was the most wonderful, perfect woman ever.

On the couch, we necked, kissed, and explored each other's bodies. J.T. took my clothes off piece by piece, admiring each newly revealed body part, kissing and stroking. Then I watched as he undressed, slowly unbuttoning his cuffs, his shirt, his pants. Watching J.T. undress in my living room, I knew I was being presented with a little performance, a show. He was aware of each movement, each muscle flex, each angle and position. He knew how he looked best.

Naked, we lay together talking. He stroked me while reading my tarot cards, predicting the most wonderful future, knowing my special qualities. He listened sympathetically to my fears and insecurities, nurturing and touching me. I felt deeply understood and knew why he had such a big clientele of married women whose husbands never talked to them.

In my bedroom, he supplied the special music, the massage oil, the sexual expertise. J.T. sensuously smoothed the unscented sesame oil on my body, between my toes and fingers and up my arms, rubbing the tension out of each muscle, gently yet firmly melting away the nerves and stress of the day. By the time he was done with the massage, I felt as if he knew every part of my body intimately, as if I could trust him to give me nothing but pleasure.

Then he touched my clit with his finger, expertly making me come. His tongue was everywhere in my most secret crevices. In the darkened room, it was easy to pretend that J.T. was the man of my dreams, that I was Brenda Starr, finally embracing the man with the eyepatch, a mysterious stranger whom I love and who has always loved me. Or he was a childhood sweetheart, returned after ten years spent yearning for me to declare his feelings, to love me forever.

"More, more," I heard myself saying. Then J.T. bore home his own orgasm after several of mine.

"Are you satisfied? Did you enjoy it?" he asked.

"Yes, yes."

"I have to go now," I heard him saying through a twilight haze of sleep and satisfaction.

"The money's in a jar on the table in the kitchen," I told J.T. sleepily, wanting to get back to my dreams and fantasies of him.

"You're beautiful," he whispered. "I'll let myself out."

In the morning, I remembered the warmth, the sex. But there was a nagging feeling. It was as if again, in my fantasy, I saw J.T. leaning over me. But for him, I was invisible: When he looked at me, he looked straight through me.

(Originally published February 1981)

EROTICISM
IN WOMEN

ANAÏS NIN

ILLUSTRATED BY MASAMI TERAOKA

From my personal observation of woman, I would say that woman has not made the separation between love and sensuality which man has made. The two are usually combined in woman; she needs either to love the man she gives herself to, or to be loved by him. After lovemaking, she seems to need the assurance that it is love and that the act of sexual possession is part of an exchange which is dictated by love. Men complain that she demands reassurance or expressions of love. The Japanese recognized this need, and in ancient times, it was an absolute rule that after a night of lovemaking, the man had to produce a poem and have it delivered to his love before she awakened. What was this but the linking of lovemaking to love?

I believe women still mind a precipitated departure, a lack of acknowledgement of the ritual which has taken place; they still need the words, the telephone call, the letter, the gestures which make the sensual act a particular one, not anonymous and purely sexual.

This may or may not disappear in modern woman, intent on denying all of her past selves, and she may achieve this separation of sex and love which to my belief, diminishes pleasure and reduces the heightened quality of lovemaking. For lovemaking is enhanced, heightened, intensified by its emotional content. You might compare the difference to a solo player and the vast reaches of an orchestra.

We are all engaged in the task of peeling off the false selves, the programmed selves, the selves created by our families, our culture, our religions. It is an enormous task because the history of woman has been as incompletely told as the history of the blacks. Facts have been obscured. Some cultures such as the Indian, Cambodian, Chinese, and Japanese have made their sensual life very accessible and familiar through their male artists. But many times, when women have wanted to reveal the facets of their sensuality they have been suppressed. Not in as obvious a way as the burning of D. H. Lawrence's works, or the banning of Henry Miller or James Joyce, but in one long, continuous disparagement by the critics such as those made about the work of Violette Leduc. Many women resorted to using men's names for their work to bypass prejudice. Only a few years ago, Violette Leduc wrote the most explicit, eloquent, moving descriptions of love between women. She was introduced to her public by Simone de Beauvoir. Yet every review I read was a moral judgment upon her openness. There was no moral judgment passed upon the behavior of Henry Miller's characters, merely an objection to language. In the case of Violette Leduc it was upon the character itself.

Violette Leduc in *La Batarde* is utterly free:

"Isabelle pulled me backwards, she laid me down on the eiderdown, she raised me up, she kept me in her arms: she was taking me out of a world where I had never lived so that she could launch me into a world I had not yet reached; the lips opened mine a little, they moistened my teeth. The too fleshy tongue frightened me; but the strange virility didn't force its way in. Absently, calmly, I waited. The lips roved over my lips. My heart was beating too hard and I wanted to prolong the sweetness of the imprint, the new experience brushing at my lips. Isabelle is kissing me, I said to myself. She was tracing a circle around my mouth, she was encircling the disturbance, she laid a cool kiss in each corner, two staccato notes of music on my lips; then her mouth pressed against mine once more, hibernating there . . . We were still hugging each other, we both wanted to be swallowed up by the other . . . As Isabelle lay crushed over my gaping heart I wanted to feel her enter it. She taught me to open into flower . . . Her tongue, her little flame, softened my muscles, my flesh . . . A flower opened in every pore of my skin . . ."

We have to shed self-consciousness. Women will have to shed their imitation of Henry Miller. It is all very well to treat sensuality with humor, with caricature, with bawdiness, but that is another way of relegating it to the casual, unimportant areas of experience.

Women were discouraged from revealing their sensual nature. When I wrote *Spy in the House of Love* in 1954 serious critics called Sabina a nymphomaniac. The story of Sabina was that in ten years of married life, she had known two lovers and one platonic friendship with a homosexual. It was the first study of a woman who tried to separate love from sensuality as man does, to seek sensual freedom. It was termed pornographic at the time. One of the "pornographic" passages: "They fled from the eyes of the world, the singer's harsh, prophetic ovarian prologue. Down the rusty bars of ladders to the undergrounds of the night propitious to the first man and woman at the beginning of the world, where there were no words by which to possess each other, no music for serenades, no presents to court with, no tournaments to impress and force a yielding, no secondary instruments, no adornments, necklaces, crowns to subdue, but only one ritual, a joyous, joyous, joyous, joyous impaling of woman on man's sensual thrust."

Another passage from *Spy*, labeled purple prose by the critics: "His caresses were so delicate that they were almost like a teasing, an evanescent challenge which she feared to respond to as it might vanish. His fingers teased her, and withdrew when they had aroused her, his mouth teased her and then eluded hers, his face and body came so near, espoused her every limb, and then slid away into darkness. He would see every curve and nook he could exert the pressure of his warm slender body against and suddenly lie still, leaving her in suspense. When he took her mouth he moved away from her hands, when she answered the pressure of his thighs, he ceased to exert it. Nowhere would he allow a long enough fusion, but tasting every embrace, every area of her body and then deserting it, as if to ignite only, and then elude the final welding. A teasing, warm, trembling, elusive short circuit of the senses as mobile and restless as he had been all day, and here at night, with the street lamp revealing their nudity but not his eyes, she was roused to an almost unbearable expectation of pleasure. He had made of her body a bush of roses of Sharon, exfoliating pollen, each prepared for delight. So long delayed, so long teased, that when possession came it avenged the waiting by a long, prolonged, deep thrusting ecstasy."

Women through their confessions reveal a persistent repression. In the diary of George Sand we come upon this incident; Zola courted her and obtained a night of lovemaking. Because she revealed herself as completely unleashed sensually, he placed money on the night table when he left, implying that a passionate woman was a prostitute.

But if you persist in the study of women's sensuality you find what lies at the end of all studies, that there are no generalizations, that there are as many types of women as there are women themselves. Only one factor is established, that the erotic writings of men do not satisfy women, that it is time we write our own, that there is a difference in erotic needs, fantasies, and attitudes. Explicit barracks or clinical language is not exciting to most women. When Henry Miller's first books came out, I predicted women would like them. I thought they would like the honest assertion of desire which was in danger of disappearing in a puritan culture. But they did not respond to the aggressive and brutal language. In the Kama Sutra, which is an Indian compendium of erotic lore, they stress the need to approach woman with sensitivity and romanticism, not to aim directly at physical possession, but to prepare her with romantic courtship. These customs, habits, mores change from one culture to another and from one country to another. In the first diary by a woman (written in the year 900), the *Tales of Gengi* by Lady Murasaki, the eroticism is extremely subtle, clothed in poetry, and focused on areas of the body which a westerner rarely

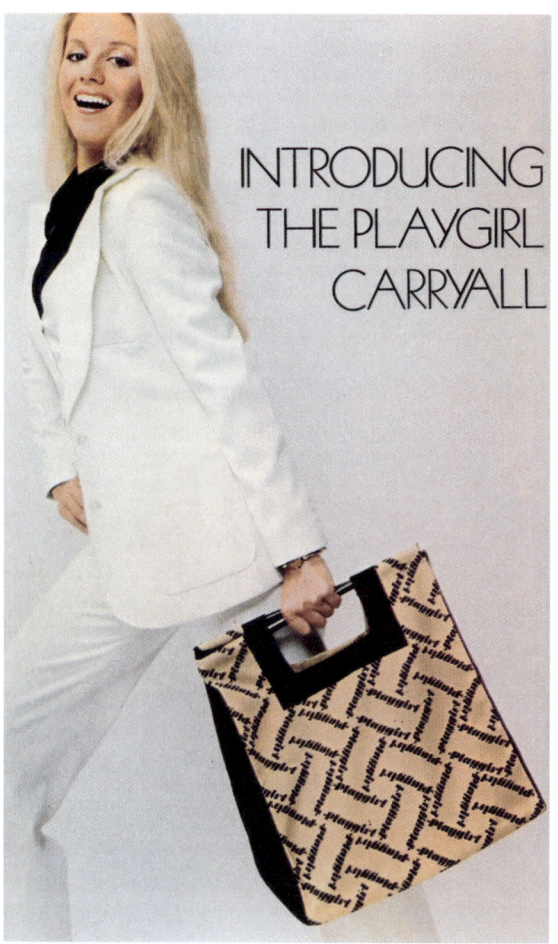

INTRODUCING THE PLAYGIRL CARRYALL

notices: the bare neck showing between the dark hair and the kimono.

Only one common factor has been stressed, and agreed upon, that woman's erogenous zones are spread all over her body, that she is more sensitive to caresses and that her sensuality is rarely as direct, as immediate as man's. There is an atmosphere of vibrations which need to be awakened and have repercussions on the final arousal.

The feminist Kate Millet is unjust to Lawrence. Whatever he asserted ideologically, she was not subtle enough to see that in his work, which is where the true self is revealed, he was very concerned with the response of woman.

My favorite passage is from *Lady Chatterley's Lover*: "Then as he began to move, in the sudden helpless orgasm, there awoke in her new strange thrills rippling inside her. Rippling, rippling, rippling, like a flapping overlapping of soft flames, soft as feathers, running to points of brilliance, exquisite, exquisite and melting her all molten inside. It was like bells rippling up and up to culmination. She lay unconscious of the wild little cries she uttered at the last . . . she felt the soft bud of him within her stirring, and strange rhythms flushing into her with a strange rhythmic growing motion, swelling and swelling till it filled all her cleaving consciousness, and then began again the unspeakable motion that was not really motion, but pure deepening whirlpools of sensation swirling deeper and deeper through all her tissue and consciousness, till she was one perfect concentric fluid of feeling, and she lay there crying in unconscious inarticulate cries. The voice out of the uttermost night, the life!"

It was a disillusion, in our modern times, to discover that women courting each other did not necessarily adopt more sensuous, more subtle ways of winning desire, but proceeded with the same aggressive, direct attack as men.

Personally this is what I believe: that brutal language such as Marlon Brando uses in *Last Tango in Paris*, far from affecting woman, repulses her. It disparages, vulgarizes sensuality, it expresses only how the puritan saw it, as low, evil, and dirty. It is a reflection of Puritanism. It does not arouse desire. It bestializes sexuality. I find most women object to that as a destruction of eroticism. Among ourselves, we made the distinction between pornography and eroticism. Pornography treats sexuality grotesquely to bring it back to the animal level. Eroticism arouses sensuality without this need to animalize it. And most of the women I have discussed this with agree they want to develop erotic writing quite distinct from man's.

The stance of male writers does not appeal to women. The hunter, the rapist, the one for whom sexuality is a thrust, nothing more.

Linking eroticism to emotion, to love, to a selection of a certain person, personalizing, individualizing, that will be the work of women. There will be more and more women writers who will write out of their own feelings and experiences.

The discovery of woman's erotic capacities and the expression of them will come as soon as women stop listing their griefs against men. If they do not like the hunt, the pursuit, it is up to them to express what they do like and to reveal to men, as they did in oriental tales, the delights of other forms of love games. For the moment their writings are negative. We only hear of what they do not like. They repudiate the role of seduction, of charm, of all the means of bringing about the atmosphere of eroticism they dream about. How can man even become aware of a woman's all-over-the-body sensitivity when it is covered by jeans, which make her body seem like those of his cronies, seemingly with only one aperture of penetration? If it is true that woman's eroticism is spread all over her body, then her way of dressing today is an absolute denial of this factor.

Now there are women who are restive with the passive role allotted to them. There are women who dream of taking, invading, possessing as man does. It is the liberating force of our awareness today that we would like to start anew and give each woman her own individual pattern, not a generalized one. I wish there were a sensitive computer which could make for each woman a pattern born of her own unconscious desires. It is the exciting adventure we are engaged in. To question all the histories, statistics, confessions, autobiographies and biographies, and to create our own individual pattern. For this we are obliged to accept what our culture has so long denied, the need of an individual introspective examination. This alone will bring out the women we are, our reflexes, likes, dislikes, and we will go forth without guilt or hesitations, towards the fulfillment of them. There is a type of man who sees lovemaking as we do, there is at least one for each woman. But first of all, we have to know who we are, what are the habits and fantasies of our bodies, the dictates of our imagination. We not only have to recognize what moves, stirs, arouses us, but how to reach it, attain it. At this point I would say woman knows very little about herself. And in the end, she has to make her own erotic pattern and fulfillment through a huge amount of half-information and half-revelations.

Puritanism hangs heavily on American literature. It is what makes the male writers write about sexuality as a low, vulgar, animalistic vice. Some women writers have imitated men, not knowing what other model to follow. All they succeeded in doing was in reversing roles: women would behave as men had, make love and leave in the morning without a word of tenderness, or any promise of continuity. Woman became the predator, the aggressor. But nothing was ultimately changed by this. We still need to know how women feel and they will have to express it in writing.

Young women are getting together to explore their sensuality, to dissipate inhibitions. A young instructor of literature, Tristine Rainier, invited several students at UCLA to discuss erotic writing, to examine why they were so inhibited in describing their feelings. The sense of taboo was strong. As soon as they were able to tell each other their fantasies, their wishes, their actual experiences, the writing, too, was liberated. These young women are seeking new patterns because they are aware that their imitation of men is not leading to freedom. The French were able to produce very beautiful erotic writing because there was no puritan taboo and the best writers would turn to erotic writing without the feeling that sensuality was something to be ashamed of and treated with contempt.

What we will have to reach, the ideal, is the recognition of woman's sensual nature, the acceptance of its needs, the knowledge of the variety of temperaments and the joyous attitude toward it as a part of nature, as natural as the growth of a flower, the tides, the movements of planets. Sensuality as nature, with possibilities of ecstasy and joy. In Zen terms, with possibility of satori. We are still under the puritan oppressive rule. The fact that women write about sexuality does not mean liberation. They write about it with the same vulgarization and lower-depths attitude as men. They do not write with pride and joy.

The true liberation of eroticism lies in accepting the fact that there are a million facets to it, a million forms of eroticism, a million objects of it, situations, atmospheres and variations. We have first of all, to dispense with guilt concerning its expansion, then remain open to its surprises, varied expressions, and (to add my personal formula for the full enjoyment of it) fuse it with individual love and passion for a particular human being, mingle it with dreams, fantasies, and emotion for it to attain its highest potency. There may have been a time of collective rituals, when sensual release attained its apogee, but we are no longer engaged in collective rituals, and the stronger the passion is for one individual, the more concentrated, intensified, and ecstatic the ritual of one to one can prove to be.

(Originally published April 1974)

HANDLE with CARE

A User-Friendly Guide to the Penis

—By S. W. Westcott—

Here's a tale of how good sex can go bad in a hurry: Imagine you're on top, making love to your man when things really start cooking. Just as you reach the brink of orgasm, the two of you thrust together and his penis misses its target. A sound something akin to a dry twig snapping echoes through the room, and suddenly the man beneath you has a look on his face that only Lorena Bobbitt could appreciate. His penis—an instant before immersed in pleasure—is now crooked, swollen and turning all sorts of peculiar colors. He's screaming in agony, and you're wondering how you're going to explain this one at the hospital emergency room.

Nightmare occurrences like this can and do happen. In fact, they happen far more often than most people think. It's estimated that more than three million American men are impotent because of intercourse-related injuries ranging from severe penile fractures that require immediate surgery to reoccurring minor "traumas" that can, over time, cause the penis to function improperly.

"The fact is that the penis is a biological structure, and it is *not* made of concrete," points out Irwin Goldstein, M.D., professor of urology at Boston University School of Medicine. "It *can* break."

The dangers of sexually transmitted diseases have been widely publicized, spawning the "safe sex" revolution, and you'd be hard-pressed to find a woman who hasn't suffered some pain or injury between the sheets, but few people realize the penis can suffer injuries—sometimes career-ending—from intercourse, oral sex, and even the old tried-and-true hand job. Although literally millions of sexual acts occur daily without any serious wounds to man or woman, injuries do happen with surprising regularity. Any experienced urologist can tell story after story that would make your man whimper.

"We see a tremendous amount of this problem," says Goldstein. Often, his patients will come in and say, "I was hav-

ing foreplay with my girlfriend. I had this great erection, but I was wearing tight jeans. My penis was pointing down instead of up, and I was too embarrassed to say, 'Wait a minute' so I could rearrange myself. She was pushing her pelvis against me in frantic foreplay, then *bam*!—end of story, and I've been impotent ever since."

"Whenever anyone walks into the office with this problem," continues Goldstein, "he can't believe that no one ever told him it was possible to injure an erect penis. The perception is that when it's hard, it can't be hurt. And that perception is just plain *wrong*."

The *up*side to all this is that as long as you're careful, there's no need to endure a life of pure vanilla sex or abstinence. In fact, experts say one of the very best ways to keep a penis in good working order is to make sure it gets regular workouts.

Through practicing what Goldstein calls "defensive sex," which includes good communication, ample lubrication and common sense, a couple can have a fulfilling and enjoyable sex life while insuring that nobody gets hurt. With this in mind, there are a few things you should probably know about the penis in your life if you want to make sure it will be there when you need it.

HARD AS A...BALLOON

Rule number one is that penises and their sidekicks, the testicles, actually require tender loving care. The average penis is simply not as tough as most men make it out to be. Although the erect penis is often described with terms such as "granite" and "rock-hard," the truth is the erect penis is more akin to a sturdy balloon. When deflated, it's flexible, rubbery and seemingly indestructible. When fully inflated, it loses that flexibility, becomes rigid, and can "pop" if subjected to too much pressure.

"Often what you hear is a cracking noise. The penis then can become swollen—like an elephant trunk," says Dr. James Elist, a Beverly Hills urologist and author of *Put Impotency In Your Past.*

HOP ON POP?

Not surprisingly, the riskiest position for intercourse-related injuries is when a woman is on top and coming down on a man's penis with her full body weight. Elist relates a case in which a woman had been going hot and heavy, when suddenly the phone rang. It must have been a pretty important call because in mid-thrust she lunged for the phone, snapping her lover's wood "like a toothpick."

In addition to letting the answering machine handle calls at inopportune moments, urologists suggest several preventative steps to avoid injuries when the woman is in a "partner-superior position." For one thing, try to refrain from movements for which there is full re-entry with every thrust. While things are usually lined up well enough for the penis to glide back into the

vagina, if it should happen to miss, kiss that erection good-bye.

"A man should literally hold onto the woman's pelvis during active intercourse when she's in a partner-superior position," says Goldstein. "The fewer complete separations there are, the more likely the man will stay in the vagina when the woman's body weight comes down."

THE PROPER WARM-UP

Lubrication is also essential. Plenty of love-juice will reduce the resistance the penis faces when entering the vagina and allow for some leeway if the man and woman are not perfectly aligned. Women should also be careful while leaning backward when they are on top, because they often bend the penis in a way that puts it at risk.

"The main thing is to make sure not to flex the penis when it is fully rigid; meaning if you like acrobatics, do them *very* carefully," says Dr. Nachum Katlowitz, the physician in charge of the unit for male sexual dysfunction at Cabrini Medical Center in New York City. "If you stress the penis when it's rigid, you can raise the pressure on it to over 1,800 pounds per square inch, which

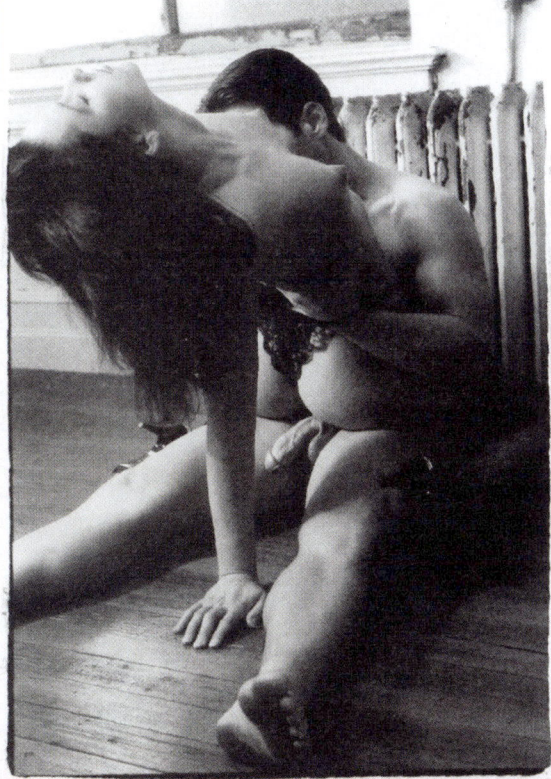

can rupture something."

If things do go amiss, swallow your pride, put on some clothes, and get to the emergency room—*fast.* Through surgery, many men can recover from a penile fracture without suffering long-term effects.

THE "BENT-SPIKE" BLUES

Even more common than severe penile fractures are repeated injuries to the penis which can take their toll over a period of months or years. Often what urologists call "minor traumas"—derived from acrobatic sex or even overzealous masturbation—can lead to breaks in the fibro-skeleton of the penis. When the body heals these small injuries, scar tissue is left behind. If enough scar tissue builds up, the penis may start leaning distinctly to one side, rather than due north.

Known as Peyronie's Disease or "bent-spike syndrome," the condition can lead to impotence, particularly when the scarring affects the artery through which the blood flows to the penis, or to the valves which play an important role in maintaining an erection. Even if the valves or arteries are not damaged, a penis with a wicked curve—besides looking somewhat peculiar—can make sex difficult, painful or impossible for everyone involved.

"Certainly a man can hurt a partner's vagina with a very curved penis," says Goldstein. "He may not be able to penetrate in any way, shape or form."

In some instances, Peyronie's Disease disappears on its own, but it can be treated medically, as well. For less severe cases, doctors often prescribe Vitamin E because of its ability to reduce or eliminate scarring. If the problem persists, surgery is also an option.

But beyond the physical problems, an unconventionally formed love-lizard can take an emotional toll as well. "Some people have incredible psychological reactions to the abnormal penis shapes," said Goldstein. "Men may harbor a perception that they are freakish or ugly, and they don't want women to see them naked. We try to stress as much as possible that what they are seeing is simply a result of an injury and nothing to be ashamed of."

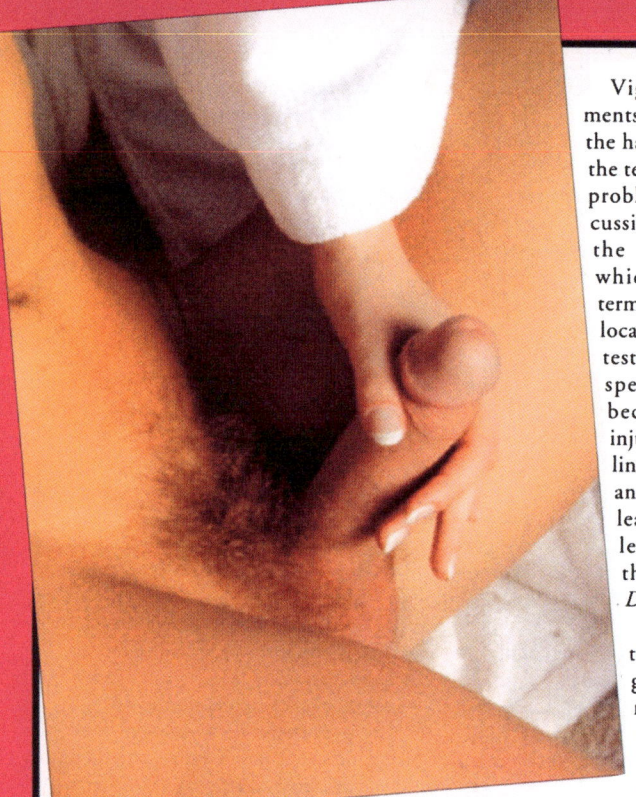

Vigorous hand movements in which the butt of the hand bangs up against the testicles can also cause problems. Repeated percussive action can injure the small epididymis, which in laywomen's terms is basically a tunnel located on the top of the testicles through which sperm must travel to become mature. The injury can cause painful, lingering inflammation, and in severe cases may lead to fertility problems. So the rule of thumb is: *Do* stroke. *Don't* squeeze.

(However, while the testicles are being gently caressed, it might be wise to take note of any lumps or bumps that seem out of the ordinary. Elist estimates that between 60 to 70% of all testicular cancers are found by men's love partners.)

WORD OF MOUTH

Oral sex also poses potential risk to the penis. If bacteria from the human mouth enters a break in the skin, it can lead to infections. Elist recalls a patient who spent five days hospitalized with an inflamed pecker. Doctors were puzzled as to what might have caused the severe infection until Elist met the man's girlfriend. She smiled, revealing gleaming braces on her teeth—braces that the patient later conceded had cut him.

Sharp teeth can do similar damage. It's important to be careful not to bite or scrape a penis with enough force to break the skin while performing oral sex. Bacteria can enter existing cuts or sores. If your lover has any of these, they can also be an indicator of certain sexually trans-

THIS SIDE UP

When it comes to manual manipulation of the penis and testicles, women should also remember to handle with care. Consider what happened to one of Dr. Goldstein's patients: In order to get her husband aroused, the wife would tightly squeeze her husband's flaccid penis. The trouble was, once he was erect, she kept right on squeezing. Much like a fully inflated balloon being pinched in the middle, something eventually had to give—and did.

> A woman needs to be aware of whether she's giving the "little guy" more action than he can handle, even if her man is carried away by the moment.

"Her over-enthusiasm actually broke his penis," Goldstein reports. "It has a large indentation in the center, and he is basically impotent. In order to have sex, this man has to inject medication directly into his penis to improve the flow of blood so an erection can be maintained. He will also likely face surgery to try to straighten his penis and improve its ability to perform sexually.

mitted diseases, so before you place yourself at risk, have him checked out by a doctor. (It may be that he's just too embarrassed to tell you how he inadvertently trapped some skin while zipping up his fly, but for your sake—and his—it's better to be safe than sorry.) "If a couple is really into oral sex, they have to be careful—especially if they tend to go wild," said Elist.

TALK IT UP

In the final analysis, the best way to avoid any sex-related injury—to either the man or the woman—is to make sure the lines of communication are open and remain open throughout sexual intimacy. Let your man know beforehand that he should speak up if something is painful or uncomfortable. Too many men would rather suffer in silence than let go of their macho self-image and concede that something which should be affording them pleasure is instead causing them pain.

In addition, drugs, alcohol and endorphins can often mask the warning signals that let a man know an activity might be questionable. So a woman needs to be aware of whether she's giving the "little guy" more action than he can handle, even if her man is carried away by the moment.

Obviously, communication is also important when a couple is changing sexual positions without separating. Him rolling in one direction and you the other is the surest way to put an abrupt stop to that lovemaking session—and potentially others for months to come.

And now for the good news. There is one prescription for keeping the penis in good working order that many couples have no trouble following. Have *lots* of sex. Research has shown that the more active the man is sexually throughout his life, the more virile and potent he will be. Just as muscles go wimpy without a regular workout, so does the penis. "The best way to keep your sex life healthy," says Elist, "is to make love as often as possible. As with any exercise—the more you do, the better you'll feel. I see a lot of patients from 60 to 70 years old who still have sex three or four times a week. The key to their success? Practice!" ♥

S. W. Westcott is an award-winning journalist whose articles on sex and relationships have appeared in such national publications as American Health, Penthouse *and* Woman's Day.

I WAS AN X-RATED NOVELIST

YONA ZELDIS McDONOUGH

The ad said, "Staff writer wanted for adult fiction."

Although I was 21 and newly minted from a classy women's college, I knew perfectly well what it meant. The question was whether I wanted to pursue it. With only a moment's hesitation, I dialed the number. I had always thought of pornography as an exclusively male province and envisioned that my call would be answered by some lecherous cross between Al Goldstein and the Big Bad Wolf. So I was surprised—and relieved—by the pleasant female voice on the other end of the line.

Fran[1] outlined a novel and told me to write the first chapter. She said that it should be about 20 pages long and take no more than four hours to complete. She also seemed very concerned with the speed and accuracy of my typing—much more than with my abilities as a writer. I was soon to learn why. The setting I was told to write about was a small Texas town; the subject, a repressed, tyrannical father who rapes his teenaged daughters—not a pretty tale. But I examined my situation: College graduation was behind me; graduate school awaited me in the fall. In between, I needed to make some money.

I could have waited tables, worked in a dreary office or peddled freshly squeezed orange juice under a blazing August sun.

Instead, I pulled out my Olivetti portable and began to write the first chapter of *Bound Daughter*. I took to the work like the proverbial duck to water. I loved creating characters and atmosphere, writing dialogue and building suspense. Even writing about sex—something I had never even imagined doing, much less tried—was an unexpected liberation. I crossed my fingers and called Fran back.

She gave me the name and address of the firm. A masterpiece of modern euphemism, the name did nothing to reveal the nature of the business; it might have been a graphic design studio or an architectural firm. And the address was entirely respectable—not the sordid Times Square hotel of my mind's eye, but the top floor of a residential building on Manhattan's East Side. While Fran read my chapter I looked around the office, which was clean, bright, and cheerful. The ivory, textured carpeting, blond wood furnishings, exposed brick, and leafy plants gave me the same sense of relief I felt when I heard a woman on the phone. Then Fran finished reading. She put down the manuscript and said with a smile, "You've got yourself a job." And that was how I came to write pornography.

My new employer was the single largest distributor of pornographic books and materials in the Tri-State area, putting out between seven and 10 new titles a week. To meet the rigorous production schedule, we had to turn out at least one and a quarter books per week, or a finished book every four days. No wonder Fran had wanted to know if I could type. Each book contained eight chapters of equal length; the finished product could run no more than 180 pages. Too long, and a hasty amputation was performed; too short, and it was returned to the writer for a quick "spin out." The book also required a provocative title, headline, fictitious author's name, and sexy blurb to entice prospective buyers.

From 8:00 every morning until 4:00 every afternoon, the first shift of five writers pounded out their fantasies of lust and libido. At the end of that time, they were replaced by another set of writers who wrote from 4:00 until 11:00. All the books were typed directly onto magnetic tape that was inserted into an IBM machine—a rudimentary form of word processing that today looks positively quaint. But in 1979 it seemed the height of high-tech productivity. The books were proofread, but not edited, so what was written the first time had to remain pretty much as it was. This gave the finished novels a curiously stream-of-consciousness quality. Apart from the obligatory sex scene in every chapter, I could write about anything I wanted, anything at all.

In three months I wrote 13 books, mostly novels with titles like *Heated Nymph, Bondage Brat, Mother Love* and *Island Virgin.* I also wrote a book of short erotic tales and a book that posed as a sociological study of S&M in the American medical profession. In this fictional land of broken taboos where parents routinely had sex with their offspring, sisters with sisters and every other combination imaginable, there were few restrictions, but those few had to be obeyed. There was to be no sex with little children. No necrophilia. And no one could die in a sexually related act. Abuse and torment were acceptable and often desired, but everyone had to emerge alive—and ready for more—in the end. Humor was frowned upon, and among the few books rejected for publication were those that were too funny. The audience was also clearly defined as straight or gay; gay male books contained only gay males, whereas straight books could include lesbianism but no eroticism between men.

Since I was the only woman writer that summer (Fran was the daytime office manager and proofreader), I was curious to know whether my books were distinct from those written by men. It turned out they were. Although I made no conscious choice to do so, I always adopted a woman's point of view; all events were filtered through a female consciousness. Once I was asked to complete a book started by a male writer who had left abruptly. The protagonist of his novel was also male, a strictly love 'em and leave 'em type. His handsome profile and prodigious sexual equipment allowed him to seduce—and abandon—everything in a pair of high heels. On a two-chapter-a-day schedule, I knew I couldn't devote a lot of time to reforming this character, but I also knew I couldn't stomach him as he was for the rest of the week. So I let my imagination roam. The result was that the poor oaf fell prey to a woman able to resist his facile appeal, was soundly trashed by her jealous boyfriend, and finally fell in love with another woman who insisted that he stop roaming and settle down. Without quite intending to, I had written a pornographic morality play.

For each book, I was paid $128. Since I had to type 125 manuscript pages to complete a book, this worked out to approximately $1 per page—which was what Anaïs Nin had earned when she wrote pornography, only that had been 50 years earlier. There were no benefits—vacation, sick days, or medical coverage—of any kind. Yet I knew that pornography was amazingly lucrative for some; according to statistics compiled by Women Against Pornography, the porn industry grosses approximately $8 billion a year in the United States alone. Clearly someone was making a bundle from doing this, and the someone wasn't me. But I wasn't doing it for the money—I knew that even then.

The simple fact was that I loved the work. The sudden immersion into a world of relentless, pulsating sexuality was more than exciting; it was a drug, and I was hooked. Part of it was the audience, which was almost exclusively male; commanding the attention of thousands of men all over New York, New Jersey, and Connecticut made me feel drunk with power. Since it was my task to write for men about women, I ended up writing about my fantasies of a man's fantasies about me. What turned men on sexually? What did they want to read? Did the same things excite me? I could experiment with all the options while incurring none of the consequences. Sex with older men, young boys, teachers, fathers, brothers, doctors, priests, women, dogs, and horses—such was grist that furnished my daily mill.

I found that I wrote instinctively, never planning a book or a plot, just letting the free associative mode take over. I'm not sure where I learned what would work, for I was pretty innocent at the time, but evidently I had learned, and learned well. Fran told me that my books were very, very good. And considering the limitations imposed by their genre and the hurried nature of their execution, they were. Evidently, I had learned how to anticipate man's sexual response, how to turn a man on.

In print, that is. My own sex life that summer was another matter entirely. While one part of me deftly spun these exotic dreams, the other part was often confused or bewildered by the potent world of sexuality that I was forced to confront. Thinking and writing about sex eight hours a day, five days a week left me pretty stimulated most of the time. Since the firm did a lively mail order business, product samples—dildos, vibrators, tubes of erectile cream, inflatable dolls with bubble-gum pink orifices—frequently found their way into the office and onto our desks, which only added to the perpetual sexual shimmer in the air; it was something you sensed the minute you walked in the door. As a result, there were a lot of heated couplings—and bitter uncouplings—that took place over the course of the summer, and I was not exempt.

Peter, who managed the night shift to which I had been assigned, was blond, green-eyed, and deeply tanned from days spent sunning at Jones Beach. Within two weeks, I developed a full-scale crush on him, but despite my constant state of arousal, nothing happened until he invited me for a drink one night after he had closed the office. Pretty soon our smoldering glances had turned to heated kisses across the tiny table. "Let's get out of here," he murmured. Leaving a handful of dollars on the table and a group of men at the bar gaping after us, he propelled me back up to the office, where we made love furiously on the ivory carpet. The next night, we didn't even bother with the drink: I simply waited downstairs in the street while he pretended to lock up and then, when everyone else had left, I ran back upstairs. It was only after a week of this thrilling—and exhausting—activity that I suggested he come back to my apartment. He hemmed and hawed before finally admitting he was married. Married! I don't know what I had thought that a romance born in a porn factory was going to yield, but I felt humiliated and heartbroken. After that, I went back to the office with him once or twice, but it wasn't the same. Something too real had intruded into the fantasy and broken its spell forever.

The experience with Peter made me wary of getting involved with the other men in the office, but it didn't mean I remained chaste. I had two more torrid flings—one with a beautiful Dutch boy who was only in New York for a week; the other with a man I met when I stopped into a neighborhood bar to wait out a summer shower. "You write what for a living?" he asked, nearly spilling his beer. "What do you do on your day off?" But in neither of these cases did the immediate lust translate into anything more lasting. Now, looking back from a vantage point of more than a decade, I can see why. It was as if the men I met while writing pornography couldn't distinguish between the brazen, two-dimensional characters of my fictions and the young woman who created them. And neither, perhaps, could I.

That may have finally been what brought my brief career as a pornographer to a close. Although my courses started in September, Fran offered to let me come in on a part-time basis, so I could have kept on writing. But by that time, I no longer wanted to. I began to find

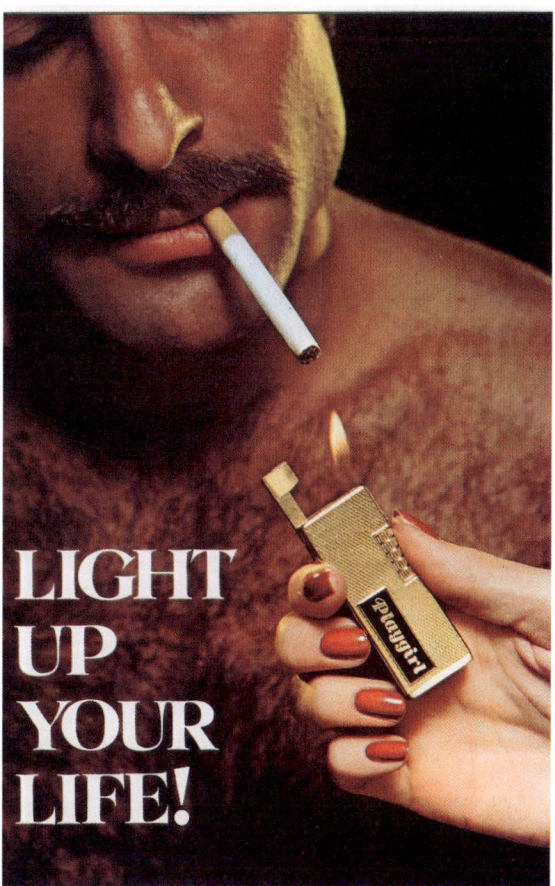

the endless four-letter words and inevitability of sex between the characters boring. Oddly enough, the pulp I was producing had given me a taste for finer forms of literature; I still wanted to write, and even to write about sex. But I wanted the sex to stem out of the particularity of my characters and their relationships to one another, not to be preordained by the genre in which they came to life.

And the shadowy blur between the sex on the page and the sex in my life had also lost its thrill. I can see now that I used the confusion to explore my own newly awakened sexual desires and feelings, and for that opportunity, I will always feel lucky. But finally I wanted something else: a more genuine grappling with sexuality that left the world of fantasy far behind, and embraced the infinitely exciting possibilities of the real.

(Originally published October 1991)

1. Names have been changed.

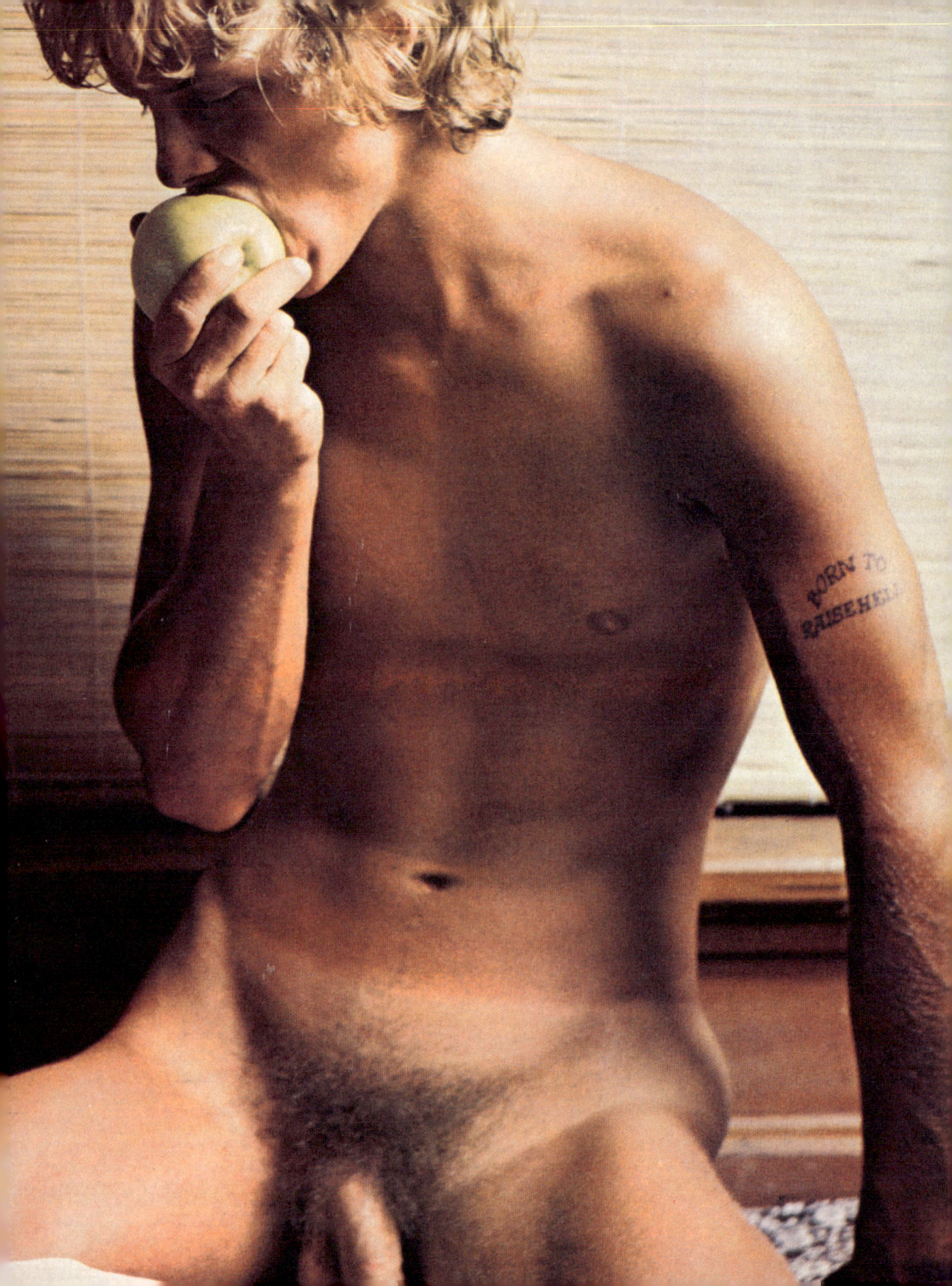

Wieners:

Not just for the gays

Writer Heather Fink

Wiener Circle

DEEP THOUGHTS ON THE ALMIGHTY APPENDAGE

THE PENIS: A BEAUTIFUL HUNK OF FLESH WHICH gives me envy, lust, and several other reveries of deadly sins. Size does not matter; it's the shape, tangible texture, color, and taste that are the rainbow in my sky.

I am not a whore, but at times I am a self-proclaimed slut. I've had hundreds of men, with penises in all shapes and sizes. I've dabbled in the unshaven, the burly, the beer-can cocks, and, of course, the growers-not-showers. These organs shrink, sometimes turtle-like, but then blossom into their beefy beauty when aroused. Smaller-built, clean-shaven men are usually the showers; they pack long rods that hang sweetly down the inner thigh, but don't get much bigger when erect. Some (mostly short and baby-faced) men can sport pudgy penises that demand all your attention to nourish. I've found that tall and lanky men shave their balls more often: They're proud to acknowl-edge their stick-straight manhood, as it comple-ments a gorgeous right angle when erect.

The face of a man can reveal so much, par-ticularly the nose. In my experience, the nose can be a true indication of penile properties—far more than hands or feet, like the story goes. Think about it. And it is pretty much a mystery which way a penis curves, if any, but a little mystery is always appreciated.

Oh, the glorious penis! That overwhelming organ with skills and ripe wonderment; the way they grow, fast as lightning and furiously solid, anxious, and playful—yet soft as a silk worm. I vow to continually worship the phallus, in all shapes and sizes, religiously on my knees, until the day I die.

THE SEXIEST THING A MAN CAN DO WHEN his head is not between my legs is very simple: stretch. Whether he is yawning, taking off his hoodie, or reaching up high for a can of beans, all it takes to drive me wild is the unexpected reve-lation of his happy trail. The happy trail is the holy grail of male sex appeal. The uniquely masculine tufts of hair reaching from his lower abdomen down to—

Wow. Describing that just made me, uh, distracted. What were we talking about? Oh yeah! Cocks! Let's be serious now.

There's a popular thought that anything with naked men in it is meant for the gays. Completely understandable. We live in a world made by men for men. The men in gay porn are often sexier than those in straight porn, since in the latter, the emphasis is on the female (for an assumed male audience). However, this does not (should not) negate a woman's desire and pleasure in seeing hot, deliciously naked men.

If women aren't visual, what are they? Audio? Tactile? Devoid of taste, desire, or art? It's an absurd conclusion that men are more "visual" than women. It is the same as asserting that men want sex more than women do. We've all been fed that gem a hundred times, but it is entirely irrelevant to the fact that we ladies fucking want it and we fucking want it now (If you're reading this magazine, I'm fairly confident you're my kind of gal).

Yes, women want it all: sex, wieners, kisses, happy trails, and we want handsome eyefuls of it, too. I should know—after all, I was once the world's most famous (only) gay porn publicist! What's that got to do with it?

As a kid I remember the excitement of unexpected bare boobies in a movie. Woah. Look at those. This must mean sexy stuff is about to happen. I empathized with those teenage boy characters when they were about to score. As they spied on some woman mysteriously showering nude in whatever coming-of-age story I was watching, my anticipation grew right along with the male viewers. It's a simple formula, really: Boobies mean sex. Female nudity means sex. Hot naked women are something for everyone to want.

It's easy to forget we chicks consume the same over-sexed hype as guys. Maybe that's why there are so many bi-curious college co-eds going wild on each other's crotches. Okay mainstream media: We get it. Naked chicks rule; seeing my own body in fancy panties is a turn-on. I like sex and all; but visually, that mess of clumsy skin and parts they call cock-and-balls wasn't something I wanted an eyeful of.

> ## What has two thumbs and loves oral? This chick right here.

Until I took my job in gay porn.

There they were: splendidly lit cock-and-balls in all their grandeur. I was daily exposed to smoldering, sparkling eyes, well-defined abs, and male genitalia shining in the warm sun.

I've always had an appetite for men. What has two thumbs and loves oral? This chick right here. I'm not whole if my beautiful flower isn't in someone's mouth with some level of frequency.

But something changed in my pursuits during this time. Suddenly, during moments of arousal, my mind filled with new thoughts: Thoughts of hard man-parts.

Hey cock, what's up? What are you doing in my brain? Wait; I know. This one is easy.

Cock, sweet cock! I am exposed to beautiful images of you all day. Of course I love you! It's you giving me a reason to get up in the morning. It's you covering my health insurance and providing prescription-drug coverage. Thank you, cock, for copay. But even more-so, thank you for looking great in a well-done portrait.

Media ignores male beauty. Women are objectified and hypersexualized while men are treated like human beings. It's about time cocks were treated like the pieces of meat they are.

So yes, naked male imagery is rarely based on what women desire. Fortunately, women have an evolving culture and self awareness. There are more female direc-tors, artists, and pho-tographers than ever before. The world is increasingly seen through the female eye, and as we step out from behind the dominant male perspective, we'll all come to understand exactly what women want: Cock.

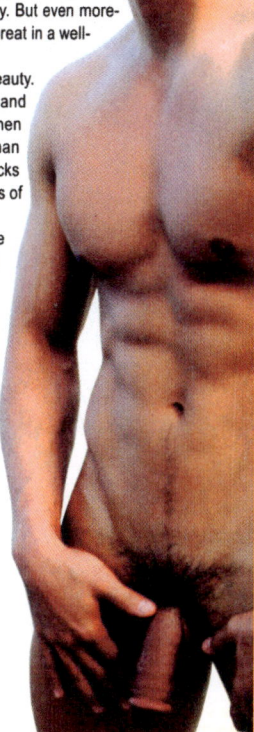

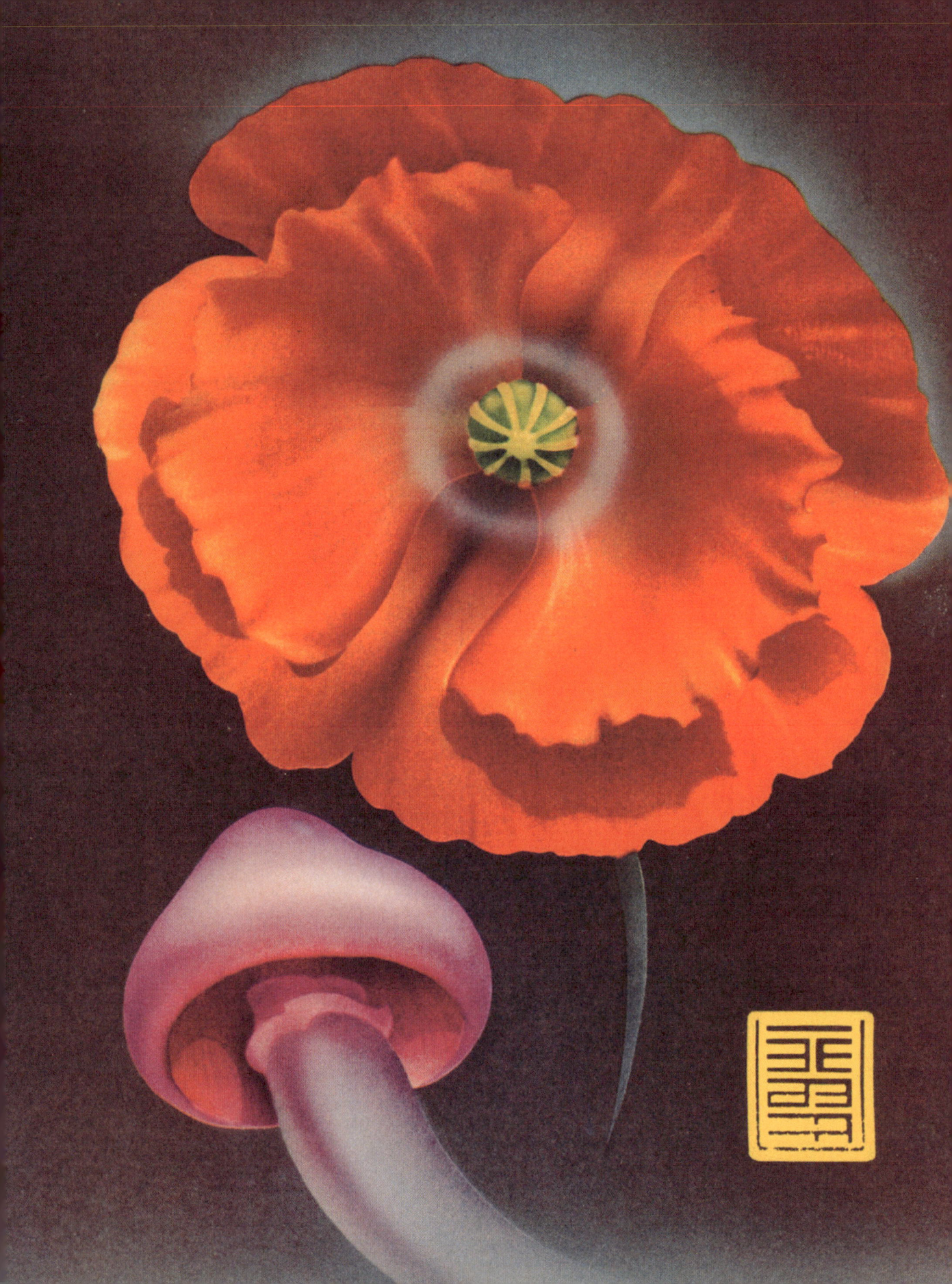

A CAUTIOUS USER'S GUIDE TO DRUGS AND SEX

JACK OWEN JARDINE

ILLUSTRATED BY BILL IMOFF

Like many other young Hollywood attorneys, Craig devotes his off-hours to sex and drugs and rock 'n' roll. If you ask him what he's doing on any weekend, his response is likely to be: "A little grass, a little coke, a little acid, a little MDA—and a cute little public defender I met in court the other day." Craig gets laid a lot and seems to consume prodigious amounts of chemicals in his quest for a better orgasm.

Nine-tenths of Linda's marijuana consumption is when she wants sex. The lover who turned her on to grass four years ago—she's now twenty-five—also bought her her first vibrator and taught her how to masturbate. It's a combination that causes her to come like a banshee.

Sid is a dedicated marriage counselor who suffers from hypertension—high blood pressure. Thanks to the medication he's taking, he hasn't had a decent erection in over a year.

Velma's prescription trip for the last six months has been Valium. She's so tranquil that she can't even remember when she last *wanted* to get laid.

Margie relies on martinis to get her in the mood, Teresa is taking testosterone, and Lenny swears by the ersatz Spanish fly he orders from an ad.

So how do drugs affect *your* sex life?

To find out, I consulted the experts, who first informed me that much research is yet to be done in this field, and that it's vital that somebody get on with it. But probably nobody will for a while for fear of being "Proxmired" out of his funding or jailed for giving research subjects illegal drugs. "So we know a lot about sex and alcohol," one sexologist complained, "but the last guy to get a grant to study sex and marijuana was shot down by Senator Proxmire."

Sex researchers William E. Hartman and Marilyn A. Fithian of the prestigious Center for Marital and Sexual Studies in Long Beach, California, told *Playgirl* they'd love to hook up volunteers to their monitoring equipment and explore the effects of a wide spectrum of substances if the legal hurdles could be overcome. "Until then, we're forced to rely on the reports of users, which is not as reliable as being able to control dosage and monitor responses electronically."

The largest body of user reports are probably at the Haight-Ashbury Free Clinic in San Francisco, where director David Smith has been gathering data since the mid-1960s, when the area was the center of the sex-and-drugs-and-rock-'n'-roll revolution. According to Smith and his coworkers, when taken in large amounts, all street drugs decrease sexuality. In small amounts they seem to enhance it.

What follows is a brief survey of the best available knowledge, on a drug-by-drug basis, of which ones do what sexually.

ALCOHOL

"It is generally accepted that low doses of alcohol may reduce social inhibitions in both sexes," writes researcher Carol Sue Carter, PhD. "Alcohol has received wide use in both modern and primitive cultures as a means of facilitating initial sexual expression." She adds that there is no direct evidence that booze actually enhances sexual pleasure. In large doses it "may inhibit or eliminate sexual performance."

Masters and Johnson cite alcohol as a major factor in some cases of secondary impotence. A man fails to achieve an erection because of fatigue, too much alcohol, or some other reason, and then turns to alcohol to relieve his anxiety about not getting it up—and fails again. Fear of failure plus anxiety plus more alcohol inevitably lead to chronic impotence.

Sex therapist Helen Singer Kaplan, MD, notes that alcohol is a general brain depressant. "It does not depress the whole brain equally and simultaneously, but rather produces a specific sequence of effects," she writes in *The New Sex Therapy*. "In its progression, it first depresses the brain centers which govern fear and so reduces anxiety and produces 'dysinhibition' before it impairs consciousness." Because its anxiety-reducing effects appear first, "small doses such as produced by social drinking release inhibitions sufficiently to often cause a temporary increase in libido in inhibited persons before they become inebriated and incapacitated."

It can also irritate the bladder and trigger urethritis in the male. "Any kind of irritating food can do this," sexologist/gynecologist Allen L. Lawrence, MD told *Playgirl*. "The old concept of Spanish fly was that it created an irritation in the urethra. Alcohol, spices, and peppers will do that."

AMPHETAMINES

Injected, amphetamines give many needle freaks prolonged or intensified sexual pleasure and/or orgasm. "Specifically described as aphrodisiacs are intravenous injections of amphetamine or MDA [an amphetamine-related hallucinogen, known as the counterculture 'love drug'], notes Dr. Carter. "Both drugs reportedly reduce inhibitions and enhance or prolong sexual experience in both sexes. Following amphetamine injection, a few females reported immediate orgasm, and more than half of the males interviewed . . . reported spontaneous erections."

Taken orally, amphetamines produce highs which are neither so immediate nor so dramatic as those brought on by injection. Dr. Kaplan reports that some users claim amphetamines "enhance their interest in sex as well as their performance, confidence, and abandonment. Indeed, some, after becoming habituated to this substance, claim they cannot function sexually without it." Amphetamines

are a stimulant going up and a depressant coming down. Caffeine has the same rebound effect.

"With amphetamines you can get very high, but it may be too high to be sexual," warns Dr. Lawrence. "You may be racy, but not very physical. Some people get very high on amphetamines, but when the depressive cycle comes, they don't want to deal with sex. Over a long period they may not see any change in their sexual life at all, but it's happening. Sometimes they're interested and sometimes they're not, but the drug changes the pattern." It programs the partner, too, he contends. "Your partner sees you high and says, 'he's too high or she's too high; it makes me anxious to be around them, they're too flighty,' so you set a new pattern of how and when it happens. You catch them when they're not high and flighty and when they're not low and depressed, and you have a new pattern."

AMYL NITRITE

"Its aficionados claim that this substance enhances the intensity and pleasure of orgasm," Kaplan reports. "This drug is a vasodilator which is sometimes prescribed to relieve the pain of angina pectoris victims. Theoretically, the drug, which is 'popped' during the height of sexual arousal, may act by increasing the vascular response of the genital organs."

Amyl speeds up the heart and thus increases blood pressure—part of what happens normally during orgasm—which users experience as a "rush." Amyl nitrite smells like glue. When banned by the FDA, amyl was quickly replaced by butyl nitrite, which does about the same thing but smells like old tennis shoes and is sold as a "room odorizer." Side effects include headaches and, in rare cases, heart attacks.

ANTIBIOTICS

"Antibiotics change the flora of the intestinal tract and vagina," observes Dr. Lawrence. "Many women use tetracycline to prevent acne and wind up with vaginal infections. This is because antibiotics kill the normal bacteria of the vagina, and allow bacteria that are pathologic to take hold and overgrow." Yeast infections quite commonly start that way, as does *Hemophilous vaginalis*, the old nonspecific vaginal infection. "At the same time, you change the acidity and the vagina's ability to heal itself. With your defense mechanisms reduced, there's more potential for a pathologic organism to grow and for you to develop an infection. You not only upset your natural immunity system, but the acid/base balance of the body and the sugar/glycogen balance of the vagina as well. All get upset, as do the bowels, which could result in diarrhea, which can lead to hemorrhoids, which can certainly affect the sexual relationship."

Also, allergic reactions to the drugs or chemicals you're taking can produce vaginal itching. "We all know about hay fever and how our noses itch, but very few people realize that the mucous membrane of the nose is very similar to the mucous membrane of the vagina."

ANTIHISTAMINES

These will do two things, Dr. Lawrence notes. "They'll tend to reverse the allergic reaction, but they'll also dry the vagina." They may also make you drowsy and prone to fall asleep in the middle of anything.

BARBITURATES

These are centrally acting nervous-system depressants which do not have a specific sexual effect, but act in the same manner as alcohol. According to Dr. Kaplan, "Small doses may temporarily release sexual behavior from inhibition, while larger doses of sedatives depress all behaviors, including sex. Chronic abuse of sedatives seems to generally diminish human sexuality."

CHOCOLATE

Once mistakenly touted as a sex turn-on, chocolate's main physiological effect comes from its caffeine content, which provides a little "lift." "I'm sure it turns on many ladies to the aesthetics of smell and taste and sugar, and the fact that somebody gave it to them helps, too," contends Lawrence. "It's also an irritant to the urethra, but it's not an aphrodisiac."

COCAINE

"Drug-induced sexual exhilaration and, less frequently, spontaneous erections have been reported following cocaine injection," notes Dr. Carter. "Amphetamines, MDA, and cocaine probably all act in part through their central-nervous-system properties."

Although the most intense results come from shooting it, most users snort it, and some apply it directly to their genitals. One of Dr. Lawrence's patients told him, "I put it on my clitoris and it was the worst thing I ever did because I couldn't feel a thing afterward." But she said the coming out was nice because it was very tingly, Lawrence relates. Psychologically, coke gives a feeling of well-being, which is essential to good sexual functioning, but used locally it's an anesthetic. "Snorting it is one thing," he observes, "but on the sex organs it's counterproductive."

CODEINE

This is a pain killer, a nervous-system depressant, so it flattens out your sexuality, reduces your interest in sex, spoils your disposition, and puts you to sleep.

COFFEE

As in chocolate, caffeine is the active ingredient and gives a heightened sense of well-being. Too much of it produces "coffee nerves," a jittery feeling which can make sex a bit cumbersome. "With men," Lawrence observes, "you'd have a higher number of premature ejaculations because the nervous system is so hyped, and with women it might create enough of a diversion to distract them so they'd be less orgasmic—or it could create enough of a high to allow them to let go, depending on the individual and the circumstances."

DEMEROL

This is a pain killer that creates an intense high. "A small amount, intravenously, probably would make a person a little more receptive because they'd lose their inhibitions," notes Lawrence. "On the other hand, it's a mood depressant, like morphine. People on morphine lose their interest in sex."

HASHISH

Like marijuana, both hashish and hash oil are immediate stimulants that dissociate conscience and morality. You tend to let things happen. "It's not like taking a diet pill, which affects you later on in the evening when you're so jittery and coming down off it that you just can't think about getting sexual," Lawrence observes. "People who use grass, hash, and hash oil do it to get high, to dissociate from their previous morality and to get into a different head space where they can be more accepting of their sexuality." Hash acts like very potent marijuana; it's easy to do too much in an effort to maintain one's interest in or capacity for sex. Some Turkish hash contains opium, which tends to make sex seem beside the point.

HEROIN

Derived from opium, this and other narcotics are interesting, according to Kaplan, "in that apart from generally depressing the central nervous system, they seem to specifically reduce the sex drive. A person who is on high doses of heroin is likely to forego sexual intercourse; if he does attempt coitus, he may experience erectile difficulties."

HORMONES

The main ingredient in the Pill, estrogen, has very little effect on the average young woman's sexuality, Dr. Lawrence reports. She already has enough. "I notice some women will tell me that on birth-control pills they have heightened libido. Some women will tell me that they have a decreased libido." Estrogen definitely increases the sexual appetite of women in the older, menopausal and premenopausal age group. Testosterone, he says, will increase it even more.

"Women in their fifties and sixties who are going through menopause will come in with a very lowered libido," Lawrence reports. "A small amount of testosterone increases it significantly. They come back and say, 'Thank you so much, I really can get off now, I can masturbate, and I have an *urge* to do these things.' But I doubt if testosterone does a whole lot for a young woman."

Researchers at Wesleyan University found that around the time of ovulation, sex activity initiated by women increases by about 20 percent—except for women on the Pill, for whom it decreases in midperiod. On the Pill you don't ovulate.

LSD

Frequently sex is impossible to accomplish—or even think about—on acid. LSD is the favorite sex drug for many experienced trippers, although they may fuck more often on grass, because getting stoned is usually more convenient than tripping, which takes up much more time. A lot of yesterday's hippies have returned to the system and thus consider their time important, so they do less acid than they used to. "Don't insist on getting laid every trip," cautions one such user, "or you'll miss the rest of what acid's there for."

A San Francisco physician and outspoken critic of government drug-enforcement policies, Joel Fort, MD, treated sex on acid in his controversial 1969 book, *The Pleasure Seekers*:

"Strong emotional bonds or positive feelings for each other, changes in time [and other sensory] perception, unusual genital sensations, diminished inhibitions and symbolic overtones can be part of an LSD experience and will in some circumstances produce a mystical or ecstatic sexual union which may seem endless . . . Such an experience would derive mainly from the underlying characters of the lovers, discriminate and experienced use of the LSD, the setting and chance factors. Many instances have been reported of lessened sexual interest and involvement while under the influence of an LSD-type drug, and no instances have been authenticated of repetitive male orgasms resulting from taking the drug."

Explaining how it works, Dr. Lawrence adds that "acid is a psychic expander. It also detaches you from your morality and previous ideas and concepts. A lot of people's view of sex is dictated by previous experiences which form a pattern, a 'set,' that you make up for yourself. Acid breaks up your customary patterns, so you can get into a sensation and spend a lot of time on it. Your sensory system starts accepting things it didn't accept before. As for sex on hallucinogens, if you want it to happen, it's more likely that it will."

Many acid users claim to have learned sexual abilities while under LSD, such as how to relax the throat muscles for deep penetration or even how to have an orgasm.

LSD normally takes about an hour to "come on" and keeps the user occupied for the next ten to twelve hours.

MARIJUANA

"Women," note Murray E. Jarvik and Edward M. Brecher, writing in the auspicious *Handbook of Sexology*, "are more likely to report an increase in desire; men are more likely to report an increase in enjoyment—but both phenomena are commonly reported by both sexes. Some women report that they were unable to have orgasm until they began using marijuana; both men and women report that orgasm is more intense and enjoyable under marijuana." They add that for sexual enhancement, dosages are usually low.

If you're smoking pot for sex, remember that it takes a few minutes to come on. With quality grass, two or three hits will be sufficient; there's no need to continue smoking till you feel the effects, because by then you may have had too much.

The reasons for pot's sex-positive effects are varied. "Perhaps marijuana, like alcohol, loosens inhibitions. Perhaps it enhances 'sensate focus,' that is, a person's attention to sensuous input in contrast with the nonsensuous content with which the mind is commonly burdened," theorize Jarvik and Brecher. "The tendency of time to seem to pass more slowly, and thus the tendency of events to seem to endure for a longer time span, may partially explain reports of more enjoyable orgasm."

One frequently satisfied user asks, "Does grass make orgasm better, or does orgasm make grass better? If I get stoned first, and then I come, I'm suddenly three times as high as I was before!"

Some people get too high on grass to be able to stay in touch, particularly if it's very potent grass and they don't get stoned very often. They feel overwhelmed and unable to control themselves. Dr. Lawrence says he's dated women who say, "Oh, I couldn't function on it. I can't have sex if I'm smoking marijuana; it makes me want to go to sleep. It makes me so high that I feel jittery. I wouldn't know whether I'm doing the right thing." Many people, he adds, "get very programmed into it and the increased intensity of sensation, so the experience is very positive and they get hooked on it. People get hooked on it for sex. They'll have to smoke before they have sex in order to get enough courage or heightened sensation or loss of inhibition." Marijuana can apparently increase the desirability of one's sex partners, too, as one sex-and-grass enthusiast reports. "I'd much rather smoke and have sex than not, because I'm not always that turned on to some women that I'm going to be sexual with. But if they're available or interested, to get past my disinterest, I'll smoke; then almost anything will stimulate me."

MDA

This is the only psychedelic drug with a clear reputation for increasing libido. MDA is an amphetamine-related hallucinogen whose reported "truly sexually stimulating effects," according to Dr. Kaplan, are not "an isolated phenomenon, but within the matrix of the total hallucinogenic experience." Unfortunately, half the MDA purchased on the street turns out to be PCP, commonly known as angel dust, which is anything but good for sex. If the MDA you buy is real, you'll probably want to do nothing but make love for the next four or five hours. If you're the only one doing it, one breathless user advises, make sure you've got a good supply of batteries because you'll be horny enough to wear out two or three lovers and then some.

METHADONE

This long-acting narcotic is used as a substitute for heroin to reduce the withdrawal cravings of addicts. Most heroin addicts would rather shoot up than fuck. "Some methadone users, also, report decreased sexual interest," notes Dr. Carter, adding that "the effects of methadone are typically less debilitating than those from heroin use, and relatively normal function is usually recovered during methadone maintenance."

NITROUS OXIDE

A stimulant in small amounts, but in larger amounts this giggly drug—also called laughing gas—will put you to sleep. But you'll wake up in two or three minutes, and the gas will be completely out of your system in ten. The sexual effects? Women who date dentists say it's a gas.

PCP

Unlike LSD and other drugs which heighten sensory awareness, PCP severs the mind from the senses. Although it releases inhibitions, few users find it does anything for sex. "Sex isn't possible behind PCP," insists one. "It's a head trip. If you could, you probably still wouldn't want to." Another explains, "When you've been dusted a lot, sex isn't the big deal it used to be. Coming isn't the only kick there is." Neurologist R. Stanley Burns and psychologist Steven Lerner, considered the nation's leading authorities on the drug, have accumulated data by keeping in touch with 1,400 chronic users, and warn of PCP's inherent unpredictability. "It doesn't matter if it's your first experience or if you've been using it for six years," says Lerner. Very few dusters have good sex experiences on PCP—even the rare one who does cautions against overconfidence, particularly in group-sex situations. "With four or more people on angel dust there are a lot of variables, and a little paranoia can really mess things up."

PEYOTE, PSILOCYBIN

These, too, are mind expanders, although they're chemically quite different from LSD. Their reputation is more for body trips than head trips, although much depends on set and setting, the individuals and their expectations. Some users say sex on these substances is great, some say it's bad. Your chances of finding either substance are very slim.

QUAALUDES

A lot of people say you just haven't balled if you haven't done it on 'ludes. Others say they don't want to be tranked to enjoy sex, they want to be speeded up. Quaalude is a brand name for methaqualone. One doctor reported, "I've had patients who have asked for 'ludes and I've given them Sopers, and they say there's no effect. Chemically they're the same thing; the only difference is the filler and the label. I tried it for myself, and all it did was put me to sleep. The more I took, the faster I went to sleep. But I didn't get any higher sex drive." The effect seems to vary with the individual.

SPANISH FLY

"This compound irritates the urogenital tract and was once used as a diuretic," writes Dr. Carter. "In large doses Spanish fly may result in priapism [abnormal, persistent and often painful erection of the penis], which probably earned for it the reputation as a sexual stimulant. There seems to be no evidence that the substance increases sexual desire in either sex."

A mail-order sex-aid merchant recently stated that he sold "an awful lot" of "placebo Spanish fly" and "ersatz aphrodisiac" pills—which could not conceivably have any effect on anyone—and defended the practice by citing letters from happily satisfied users who claimed the pills had cured their impotence and dramatically improved their sex lives. "As long as they believe the stuff works, it works," he told me.

THE DRUG CHART

CHART PREPARED WITH THE ASSISTANCE OF JOHN C. BUFFUM, PHARM. D., ASSISTANT CLINICAL PROFESSOR OF PHARMACY, UNIVERSITY OF CALIFORNIA SCHOOL OF PHARMACY, SAN FRANCISCO; STAFF CLINICAL PHARMACIST, VETERANS ADMINISTRATION MEDICAL CENTER, SAN FRANCISCO

Substance	CNS stimulant	CNS depressant	Enhances sex	Distorts senses	Relaxant	Disinhibits	Intensifies experience	Stretches time	Irritates urethra	Effect on libido	Effect on potency	Comments	Cautions
Alcohol		●			●	●				●▲	▼	Small amounts can help in first encounter, a lot gets in the way	Don't mix with other depressants
Amphetamines	●		●		●[1]					▲	▲	Prolongs orgasm	Chronic users often lose all interest in sex
Amyl Nitrite			●			● ●					▼	Prolongs orgasm but softens erection	Headache sometimes results
Antibiotics												No direct sexual effect	Can cause vaginal infection
Antihistamines		●			●							Can dry vagina	Can make you drowsy; don't mix with alcohol or other sedatives
Barbiturates		●			● ●							Like alcohol, a little helps, a lot hinders	Don't mix with alcohol or other sedatives
Betel Nuts[2]	●		● ●		●					▲	▲	Widely used in Asia as stimulant/aphrodisiac	Too much causes dizziness, vomiting and diarrhea
Butyl Nitrite			●			● ●					▼	Same as Amyl Nitrite	Same as Amyl Nitrite
Cocaine	●		●							▲	▲	Cadillac of sex drugs; injected, can take the place of sex	Don't mix with any other stimulant; deadens mucous membranes
Codeine		●								▼	▼	Pain killer; flattens sexuality	Don't mix with alcohol or any other depressant
Demerol		●								▼	▼	Pain killer; flattens sexuality	Don't mix with alcohol or any other depressant
DMT	●		● ●			● ●				▲▼	▲▼	Like LSD, some experience with the drug is needed before used for sex	Some cautions as with LSD
Hashish	●	●	●	●	●	● ●				▲		Aids in "sensate focus" (getting into your senses)	Easy to do too much to be sexually useful
Hash Oil	●	●	●	●	●	● ●						Same as hashish but stronger	Very easy to do too much to be sexually useful
Hawaiian Baby Wood Rose	●		● ●			● ●				▲▼	▲▼	Very similar to LSD	
Heroin		●								▼	▼	Some users get very horny coming down, but most lose interest in sex	Too much can be fatal
Hormones: Estrogen										▲▼	▲▼	Increases libido of older women, reverse effect for men	
Progestin										▲▼	▼	Same as estrogen	
Testosterone										▲	▲	Increases libido of both men and older women	Can activate prostate cancer in males
Inhalants (glue)		●			● ●							Giggly high; useless for sex	Very toxic to brain tissue and liver cells
Kola Nuts[2]	●				●					▲	▲	Said to be an aphrodisiac for men	
Lettuce Opium												Doesn't seem to do much of anything	It's as much like opium as catnip is like marijuana

▲ Increases for some individuals ▼ decreases for others ? Studies inconclusive or effects variable
[1] David E. Smith, MD, Sex & Drugs 1979 symposium [2] Young-Klein-Beyer, Recreational Drugs (1977)

(Continued on page 88)

Substance	CNS stimulant	CNS depressant	Enhances sex	Distorts senses	Relaxant	Disinhibits	Intensifies experience	Stretches time	Irritates urethra	Effect on libido	Effect on potency	Comments	Cautions
Librium		●			●	●				▼		Eases anxiety	Don't mix with alcohol or any other depressant
LSD	●		●	●		● ●				▲▼	▲▼	Effects depend on expectations and setting; experience with it is needed before using for sex	Sometimes sex on acid is impossible, sometimes it's great; unstable personalities should avoid it
Marijuana	●	●	●	●	●	●				▲	▲	Sexually, a little helps, a lot can get in the way	Easy to do too much to be sexually useful
MDA	●		●			● ●				▲▼	▲▼	Like LSD without the visual effects; known as the Love Drug	Unstable personalities should avoid it
Mescaline	●		● ●			●				▲▼	▲▼	More visual trip than LSD	Same as LSD
Methadone		●								▼ ▼		Makes users disinterested in sex	Same as Heroin
Methaqualone (Quaaludes) (Sopers)		●	●		● ●					▲▼		Like alcohol, a little helps, a lot hinders; impairs coordination from waist down	Don't mix with alcohol or any other depressant
Morphine		●								▼ ▼		Reduces interest in sex	Don't mix with alcohol or any other depressant
Nitrous Oxide		●	●	●	●	●						Laughing gas	Remember to take some air with it or you'll pass out; liver problems in heavy users
Opium		●		●						▼ ▼		Reduces interest in sex	Highly addictive
PCP	●	?	●	●	●	● ●				▼ ▼		A dissociative anesthetic; rarely good for "normal" sex; takes the pain out of fist fucking.[1]	Easy to OD; very unpredictable
Peyote	●		● ●			●				▲▼	▲▼	Mescaline source; sex may or may not seem appropriate	Trip involves vomiting; same cautions as LSD
Psilocybin	●		● ●							▲▼	▲▼	Same as LSD	Same as LSD
Spanish Fly							●					Good wart remover, but not an aphrodisiac	Produces world's longest blister
Placebo Spanish Fly												Actually cayenne pepper; no sexual effect	Ripoff
Saltpeter (potassium nitrate)												No sexual effect	
Strychnine	●				●							Causes painful erection	Kills with convulsions
Tobacco	●									▼		Lowers testosterone and blood-oxygen levels	Impairs general health; reduces stamina
Valium		●			● ●					▼		Like alcohol, eases anxiety	Don't mix with alcohol or any other sedative
Yohimbe[2]	●		●			●				▲▼	▲▼	West African aphrodisiac	Don't mix with antihistamines, amphetamines, tranquilizers (except Librium), narcotics or alcohol

▲ Increases for some individuals ▼ decreases for others ? Studies inconclusive or effects variable
[1] David E. Smith, MD, Sex & Drugs 1979 symposium [2] Young-Klein-Beyer, Recreational Drugs (1977)

CHART PREPARED WITH THE ASSISTANCE OF JOHN C. BUFFUM, PHARM. D., ASSISTANT CLINICAL PROFESSOR OF PHARMACY, UNIVERSITY OF CALIFORNIA SCHOOL OF PHARMACY, SAN FRANCISCO; STAFF CLINICAL PHARMACIST, VETERANS ADMINISTRATION MEDICAL CENTER, SAN FRANCISCO

STRYCHNINE

In small amounts it exaggerates the function of the central nervous system. In larger amounts this same effect is what kills, overwhelming the system, causing total contractions so you can't breathe. It both creates and increases sensation, changing your whole biochemistry in the process. Strychnine is the active ingredient in seeds of *Strychnos nux-vomica*. Painful erections are associated with strychnine poisoning. Nux-vomica is used in some contemporary preparations for impotence, such as "afrodex" and "potensanforte."

SUGAR

More is known about sugar metabolism in the human body than about all other drugs—probably because such studies are legal. "Sugar produces a sense of wellbeing," notes Dr. Lawrence, "compared to the hypoglycemic episode where the sugar burns off and you have a state of depression, shakes, nervousness. I think what happens with sugar is that people become sugar junkies. Without it they feel low, nervous, and they need more sugar just to feel good. You get high on sugar because you're running on pure fuel." The effect of all this on sex? A little can help, a lot can get in your way. "Heavy meals frequently are contrasex," notes Lawrence. "Light meals have a more positive effect on sex."

TOBACCO

It's unfashionable to say anything nice about tobacco these days. But nicotine, tobacco's major psychoactive ingredient, is a central-nervous-system stimulant, and as such "might therefore be suspected of having mildly favorable sexual effects in some people under some circumstances and at some dosage levels," according to Jarvik and Brecher. They also note that "to the extent that smoking impairs general health, it almost certainly impairs sexual response." A physician who prefers not to be named told me he thought women who smoke cigarettes probably give better head, "because they're used to putting things in their mouths"—but he could offer no documented proof.

According to Alton Ochsner, MD, whose 1954 book, *Smoking and Cancer*, drew early attention to tobacco hazards, abstainers have better sex lives and fewer cases of either impotence or low sperm count than persons addicted to nicotine. Sexual power returns to those who quit. One couple made quitting smoking a sexy experience in itself: Whenever they wanted to suck on a cigarette they'd suck on each other instead. Cigarette smoking produces carbon monoxide in the blood, which inhibits production of testosterone. People who don't smoke have higher blood-oxygen levels, resulting in more available energy for sex or anything else.

TRANQUILIZERS

In the long run, a lot of tranks are very sex-negative drugs, although a single pill may decrease inhibition. "Someone using Valium very regularly will have a low libido," states Dr. Lawrence. "A woman who takes tranquilizers and diuretics develops a dry vagina."

YOHIMBE

This ancient treatment for impotence is, at this writing, still legal in the United States, and gaining popularity as a street drug. "Yohimbe is generally used for sexual purposes," write Young, Klein, and Beyer in their popular psychopharmacological work, *Recreational Drugs*. "The drug's action, lasting from two to four hours, causes a change in the user's peripheral blood flow while, at the same time, it stimulates the spinal ganglia, which control the corpus spongiosum. What that simply means is that it will help to produce a strong male erection for men suffering from problems of psychological impotence." Females, too, claim sex-positive effects. "The drug causes pelvic tingles, mild perceptual changes, and psychic stimulation," contend Young, Klein, and Beyer, "but will result in hallucinations only if taken in extremely high and potentially toxic doses."

Yohimbe, strychnine, and methyl testosterone are combined in the medical preparations "afrodex" and "potensanforte," with what Dr. Carter terms "limited" medical effectiveness.

This list of drugs and their effects is by no means comprehensive—a book-length treatment would be needed to fully explore the topic. Although anecdotal material abounds, much hard research remains to be done. Brecher and Jarvik point out that "the inherent sexual puritanism of Western culture and of scientific and medical institutions within that culture, stands in the way of such well-controlled, double-blind trials. As a result of this antisexual bias, neither staffing nor funding has, with rare exceptions, been available for the scientific study of potentially stimulating sexual effects. Studies of depressant effects are less subject to cultural taboos; no doubt for this reason, well-controlled anaphrodisiac studies are a bit less scarce."

What we do know so far is that the effects of most of the drugs which influence human sexuality depend on the individual human beings who take them. Where you start from (how far you are from optimal functioning) determines whether or not a specific drug has a prosexual or an antisexual effect for you. If you suffer from impaired self-confidence, for instance, a drug such as cocaine, which increases self-confidence and improves the user's self-image, can materially improve your sexual performance. If you're nervous, apprehensive, or quite inhibited when it comes to sex, small amounts of a depressant such as alcohol can loosen your inhibitions and help you relax enough to enjoy sex. Jarvik and Brecher suggest that "whatever contributes to healthy human functioning generally contributes specifically to enhancing libido and sexual response, and that whatever impairs healthy human functioning impairs libido and sexual response."

(Originally published August 1979)

71

COUPLING IN THE YEAR 2000

RICHARD MELTZER

Will it be group-gropes with aliens, or what?

The future, chances are a good, solid fif-ty-fifty that we'll have one. If the Homo-sap. race doesn't get atomized by the Big One or ecologized into equally unpleasant submission, said race will keep on keepin' on the way it always has: by the making of babies. And as long as babies are made from the usual biological micro-whatsems, we'll continue to have occasional instances of at least one permutation of that grand old, age-old bugaboo, the (hetero)sexual relationship. That all-too-familiar permutation being: the one where the boy person and the girl person also play, for at least part of their sex lives together, the daddy person and the mommy person, just the way it is with most coupled and fertile raccoons, earwigs, and octopi.

All sorts of other permutations would, of course, go along for the ride—life's like that—and *geez*, we can have fun speculating from now until doomsday (the metaphoric one, of course) on all the various and sundry forms these permutations might just ultimately take. In the universe of mere idle future think, even the sky ain't much of a limit.

But (there's always a but) before we actually plunge headlong into all this delightful hokum, it proba-bly wouldn't hurt to put the whole thing in perspec-tive by noting how flawed most of this stuff tends to be, even in the short run. Heck, it wasn't too long ago that Hugh Hefner ran a "Playboy philosophy" piece dedicated to the notion that the sexual revolution (so-called) had, from a technological standpoint at least, already been fought and won. What he said was *looka here*, you can already go to your neighborhood *drugstore* and purchase: (1) an incredibly wonderful *pill* that—dig this—prevents conception; and (2) some other dandy drugs—penicillin, tetracycline, etc.—that (oh boy) will cure ya of VD. Hallelujah, he was telling us, finally technology has given us a sexuality that is all pleasure and no dues to pay—a mainstream genital get-down that is both pregnancy- and fester-free! It's guaranteed!

Well, that couldn't have been more than fourteen, fifteen years ago, and here we are, faced with the hard reality of millions of sensible, sexually active women having *had it* with the physiological harm wreaked on 'em by oral contraceptives (Back to the rubber, boys! Sorry about the decrease in, uh, pleasure!); faced with antibiotic-resistant strains of clap and syph in fact *caused* by the elimination of weaker strains by said "wonder drugs" (not to mention the ascendancy of herpes, which seems as aloof to scientific prodding right now as the much- vaunted Big C). And you might've heard the latest on vasectomies causing arterial sclerosis in lab apes . . . (Nice try, Hef, but you don't even get a Tiparillo on that one.)

All of which mainly serves to underscore one big area of doubt in the prediction biz before us, namely the role of technology in the evolution of interpersonal whoop-de-do.

Meantime, the ultimate roles to be played by feminism, gay liberation, and (even) scattergun, decadent swingerdom are just as hard to compute. For our purposes here, these unlikely bedfellows represent the avant-garde of the whole relationship ball game. Whether any of their various solutions to today's overriding *humdinger*—the siegelike impasse of conventional man-woman one-on-one (hey, let's face it, things're somewhat *fucked*)—manage to gain mainstream currency in the decades (centuries) ahead depends on at least a trio of hefty imponderables:

1. Can the mass psyche (it's kind of *massive*) come to recognize the same "need parameters" for its nervous system as do today's various lib partisans for *theirs*?

2. How far will the lib parties themselves opt to take things should it all proceed beyond what's currently just a relative dress-rehearsal stage?

3. Will the entrenched forces of who knows what *dare to allow* any of this, or will they try their darndest to co-opt, neutralize, and/or simply oppress—just as they've done with blacks, peace-creeps, and organized labor? (Like, does anybody *really* expect the Equal Rights Amendment to pass or abortion still to be legal by 1985?)

So—what the hey—let's just put on our guessing caps and guess, let the old flawed imagination run hog-wild on the theme of coupling in the year whenever. What follows is a goodly dose of projected outcomes, some whacko, some mundane, but all just as likely (or unlikely) to someday (or never) occur:

1 For starters, lots of interesting stuff is bound to float in on the wake of Lee Marvin versus Michelle Triola, lib marriage's latest parody of the Real Thing. One such something could be the elevation of contract cohabitation to the level of standard operating procedure for coupled unmarrieds with "mutual postbreakup security" on their collective mind. Should it culminate in more and more live-in mates signing their names to such and such, don't look for subsequent increases in relationship longevity, however: Recycling potential hostilities onto a piece of paper just keeps the fundamental garbage submerged a couple of seconds longer than usual.

Related side trip: Vegas will eventually make book on relationship outcomes and durations, complete with year spread, alimony/palimony odds, etc. A truly "all-American" couple will be a pair of athlete/lovers whose ongoing lives both on and off their respective playing fields can be publicly monitored and used as the raw data of multiparlay bets.

2 As unresolved hostilities reach truly epidemic proportions by the early decades of the twenty-first century, threatening to tear the very social fabric asunder, "relationship management" will finally become a crucial enough concern for the techno-state to intervene. Relationship therapists will then ascend from their present-day incidental status to a fully institutionalized role that crosses all boundaries of class, race, ideology, and sexual orientation (gay couples will be stuck with them too). For the genuinely liberated and enlightened, relational shrinks already will have seen much duty as nonmalevolent advisors on the interpersonal psyche, but the much larger subset of the future, the Terminally Married (whose motto is "Straight life or bust" and whose chief demographic function is the machine-womb spit-out of workers and consumers), will suddenly be faced with "universal family counseling," a polite euphemism for periodic visits by the local behavior police, psychology grads to the last man jack.

Instead of guns, these highly skilled neuro-oinkers will carry canisters of film, twentieth-century relationship propaganda to be screened and screened till you upchuck your din-din. Among the possible therapies Mr. and Mrs. Future America will face are Tarzan-Jane therapy, Thin Man therapy, and Neil Simon therapy. A not-so-ironic by-product of such intrusion will be the creation of a subset within the subset, a hardy group of intrafamily battlers who develop techniques to avoid detection and wait until dark to make full use of their *cherished right* to psychically maim each other.

3 With population steadily on the rise, it won't be too long before living space becomes as rare a commodity as organic food matter and non-radiation fuel. When even the one-bedroom apartment is a luxury only the ultrarich can afford, zillions of standard adults will, out of simple necessity, be living four or five to the room—er—bed. Group marriage on a mass scale could become the order of the day. By the same token, heavy-duty, one-on-one monogamy would take on an aura of cultural perversity, a minority indulgence mainly for the privileged and powerful.

4 As the acquisition of material booty gradually loses its lure, so too will the promise of the "good life," that often-illusory carrot on a stick so essential to keeping the disenchanted masses from climbing the goddamn walls. Mass deviance of the Woodstock Nation sort is likely to rear its state-choreographed head, mainly as a reliable safety valve for premeasured quotas of pent-up libidinal steam. Hyperactive teens, bored housewives, and skittish insurance executives will run off

to predesignated communes to snort lithium, run around nude, and boogie up a storm; they'll be officially viewed as going through the most benign of "phases," they'll go ape over all the pseudo free-love rapture their systems can take, and sooner or later they'll return home to the arms of similarly programmed "understanding loved ones." The actual feedback (in terms of, um, social redefinition) will be negligible, but in any event everyone will have the option of *going wanton* at least once in his/her lifetime.

One topical deviance not likely to flower in the future-world sun is the son of a gun we now know as machismo. Macho will, as quickly as in the next thirty years, come to be regarded as—above all—a rather *corny* manifestation of heterosexual arrogance; it'll probably linger a bit in boxing, football, and S&M circles before playing itself out even there and returning to the military, where it belongs.

5 Even as we close the book on gender as an out-moded all-encompassing cliché, we'll still be stuck with cocks and pussies as anatomical limits to boy-girl other-side-of-the-fence *understanding*. For the committed couple with an abiding desire to truly overcome this limitation, mutual sex change may be the only answer. The *National Enquirer* has already given us the gripping tale of Harry and Jean Reynolds—formerly Sheila and Thomas Reynolds—parents of two, who figured it might be neat to experience each other's organs at a 180-degree rotation. While their hep surgical acts are not likely to usher in a mutual-sex-change *fad* just yet, the inevitable advent of nonmessy *reversible* sex changes is bound to up the ante, even if it's no more than a dumb stopgap solution to marital doldrums.

6 Next stop is the creation of *new sexes entirely*: new organs, new secondary characteristics, new emotional chemistries, new (at least for starters) social roles. The "binary experiment" we've been operating under for umpteen thousand years has still got us thinking in terms of overly harsh dichotomies; throw some additional numbers into the configuration and our whole logic for that sort of crap goes out the window bit by bit. It would certainly take several centuries (as "mad scientists" secretly doodle with unborn fetuses and the like) for any such hogwash to come to pass, but stranger things already have happened in our mere lifetimes (e.g., an Oscar for Broderick Crawford, the Jerry Lewis telethon, Wayne Newton as a superstar, etc.).

7 OK. We may be getting to the point where all vital "sexual touchstones" of the human physical orbit can be replicated from substitute materials (plastic substances that *feel right*, or, let's say, preserved muskrat entrails that must be *refrigerated after use*). And by all, we're talking all: not just standard stuff like vaginas or a no-quit, erect *membrum virilis* but (all kinks are cool) enlarged nostrils and hairy armpits, etc., constructed "as you like 'em." Anything you want in a sex partner you'll be able to have in (artificial) spades, as the old-fashioned inflatable love doll throws in the towel and winds up in antique shops alongside Barbie and Ken.

8 But then again, even the most radical love-doll updates will probably seem—to the tastes of some—little more than an extension of your hand and/or vacuum-cleaner nozzle. What's called for in such instances is a minimal helping of *fabricated independent thought* (other than exclusively sexual), something to at least simulate the twin illusions of *challenge and transcendence*. Robots, androids, you name 'em: No matter how technologically crude the automaton (as long as it walks and talks), it's gotta have at least the *appearance* of a "mind of its own"—even if the setup is in fact closer to that of a programmable microwave oven than a 150-IQ human bean.

The impact of plastic on flesh (or vice versa) could easily become an ultimately hotter proposition than that of flesh on flesh (with all the irrational horseshit the latter all but presupposes).

9 With cloning and all the test-tube variations of the human imaginative rainbow inevitably replacing current procreative tendencies, the race could easily find itself freed from the *biological* necessity of twosomes altogether, and thus seed wastage (by the male of the species) would be disengaged at last from the sins of Onan. For the single-action good life, however, a world of self-contained masturbatory units would require something more substantial than skin mags and stroke books, and idealized sex-act holograms (vast improvements on the ones in George Lucas's *THX-1138*) might prove just what the doctor ordered. While not genuinely "solid," these three-dimensional mirages would lend invaluable assistance to the ultranifty end of universal beat-off, particularly if the technology of Odorama manages to evolve with parallel haste.

10 Let's pay our respects to *The Amazing Colossal Man* and *Attack of the Fifty-Foot Woman*, a dandy duo of radiation flicks dealing with the *negative* fantasy whereby a marriage partner is nuked into supergrowth, creating a gross marital asymmetry of sufficient dimensions as to make both victims' respective relationships

unendurable. The central (nonnuke) metaphor here is one of nonparallel *development*, the quite rational fear that, with all the "self-realization" claptrap so prevalent today (and unlikely to vanish tomorrow), one's "other half" stands a good chance of evolving into something so *fiercely individual* that coupling in conventional terms would become not just a low priority, but an almost impossible pipe dream. A sense of "radical otherhood," such as the planet has rarely—if ever—encountered, might be required to resolve the situation.

11 Come such a revolution, several related juxtapositionings would also fall into place, to wit: relations with animals, plants, and nonhumanoid machines. And we're not just talking Rover, Trigger, and Bossy, or Bo Derek and an orangutan—or even John Lilly and his dolphins—we're talking the whole kit and caboodle of subhuman life forms (with or without genetic enhancement of their capacity to love us). Jim Morrison once strutted himself as the "Lizard King"; Tim Leary has spoken of acid trips during which he was the boy ant pursuing the girl ant down through the loam; and who can ever forget Joyce Kilmer's no-holds-barred crush on a tree? It can't be too many millennia before *fornicating with fishes* and *going steady with grapefruit* become actual romantic options. We might even advance to a stage where we "think love" (like, why not?) as hordes of gonococci caress our urethras, especially if DNA engineers give them cute, little microbe faces . . .

One thing the world of flora and fauna will *not* be in a position to offer, however, is true love beamed to the deep recesses of the cerebral cortex—the ever-popular "mind fuck." Sure, we'll be able to transplant the gray matter of a loved one into the cranium of an ostrich or walrus, but for any and all *mind fucks supreme*, it'll be our old friend the computer—sure to outthink us any day now—supplying the basic thrust. If today's highly impersonal "rap girls" can tell you ultrafunctional dirty nothin's over the phone, just think what your very own IBM Z-52-S-E-X (which really *knows* you) will be able to trigger in the way of hard-core mind smut. Orgasm-inducing drugs will, of course, be readily available to provoke mind-boggling get-offs at the appropriate moment(s) without the necessity of physical contact, so you won't even have to think hygiene and keep your machine free of dust, crud, and personal sex ooze.

12 When they're not "doing" humans themselves, computers should have little trouble servicing what still remains of the human-human sphere. The real landmark moves will come in the field of computer dating.

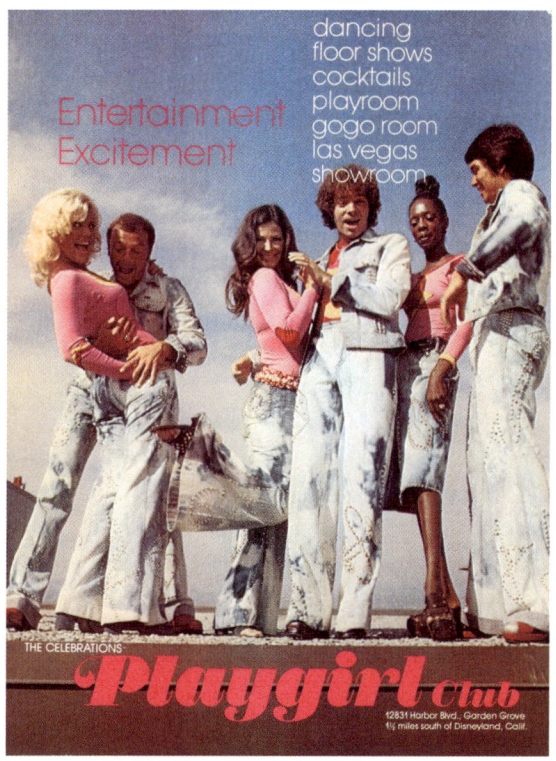

When compu-date services start asking questions like "Do you insist on forty-five minutes (or more) of cunnilingus on the first date?"—and when long-distance cunt-lappers are no longer willing to trust their instincts as to whether a would-be object of attention will assent to such an act—on that day we will begin to *scratch the surface* of technologically minimized new-love disappointment. Should a subsequent introduction of screening procedures somehow dealing *not inaccurately* (at last) with *emotional/intellectual suitability* prove a provisional success as well, a sizable segment of the dating-disenchanted public would then opt for computer selection as a substitute for their own imperfect judgments. And after that (as the system is "improved" even further), the deluge . . .

At best, the computer's bound to become a crutch, with too many rubes depending on it for the false security of companionship by exact specification; at worst, you'll get a decline in openness and spontaneity in the world at large and the rise of "couple solipsism"—trillions of momentarily satisfied elitist pairs running around operating under the *truly* grand illusion that they are each "perfectly mated." What a Great Fall these jokers are in for! (Which is where, I seem to recall, we came in . . .)

(Originally published February 1982)

PICTORIALS

Playgirl was the first magazine of its kind to objectify the male body. With a focus on the female gaze, eye contact, narrative, and the voyeuristic fantasy of a real-man encounter, the pictorials are what the magazine is most known for. Over the span of five decades, our major go-to photographers have included David Meyer, Norbert Jobst, Greg Gorman, Richard Armas, Dean Keefer, and Greg Weiner, along with contributions by Bill King, Herb Ritts (under his own name as well as, allegedly, pseudonyms), Bob Seideman, Sarah Pendergast, Silvia Pecota, Alison Morley, Suze Randall, and David Vance, to name a few. These photo sets are a seminal part of the magazine's history and are integral to putting the "play" in *Playgirl*.

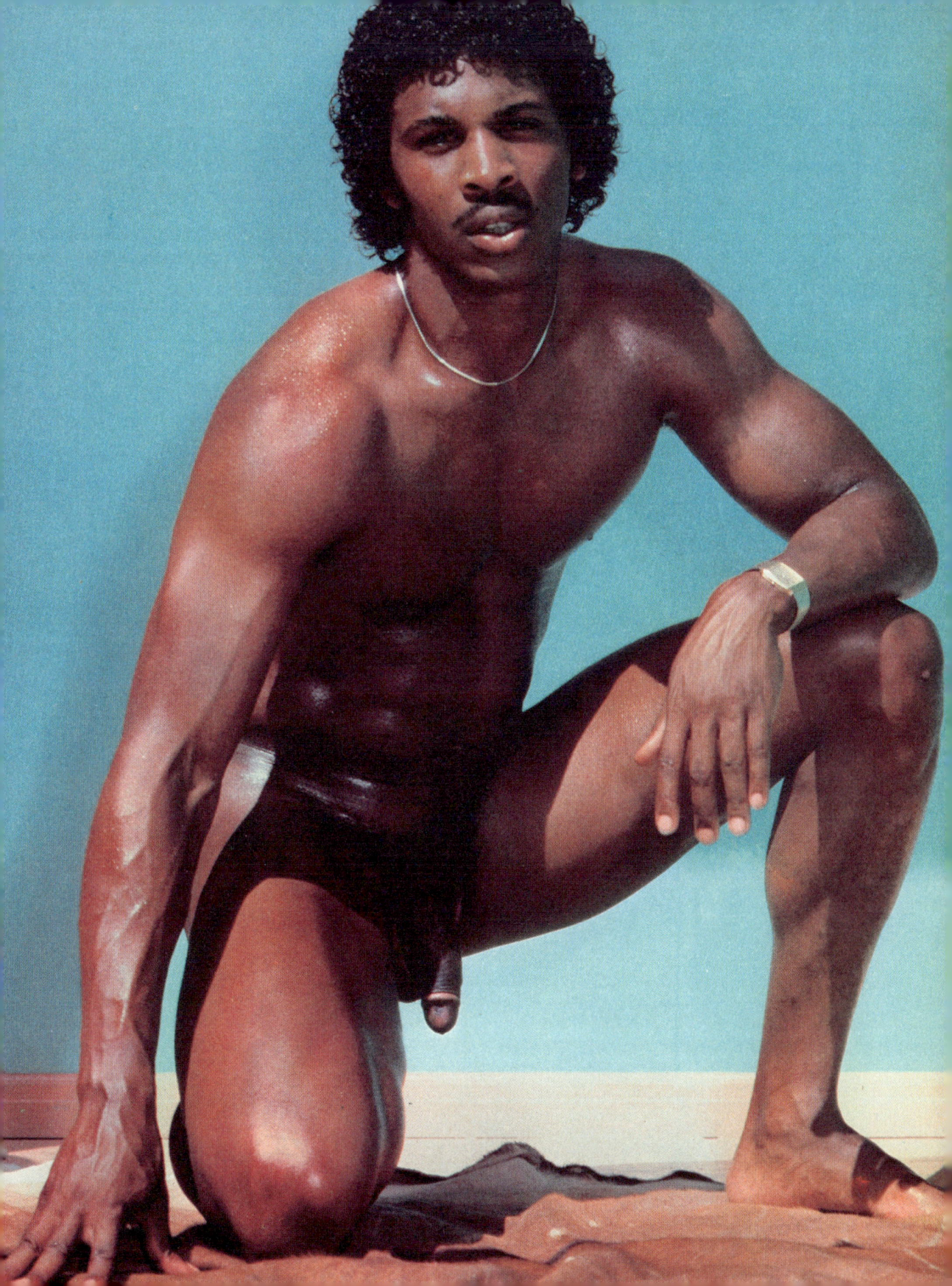

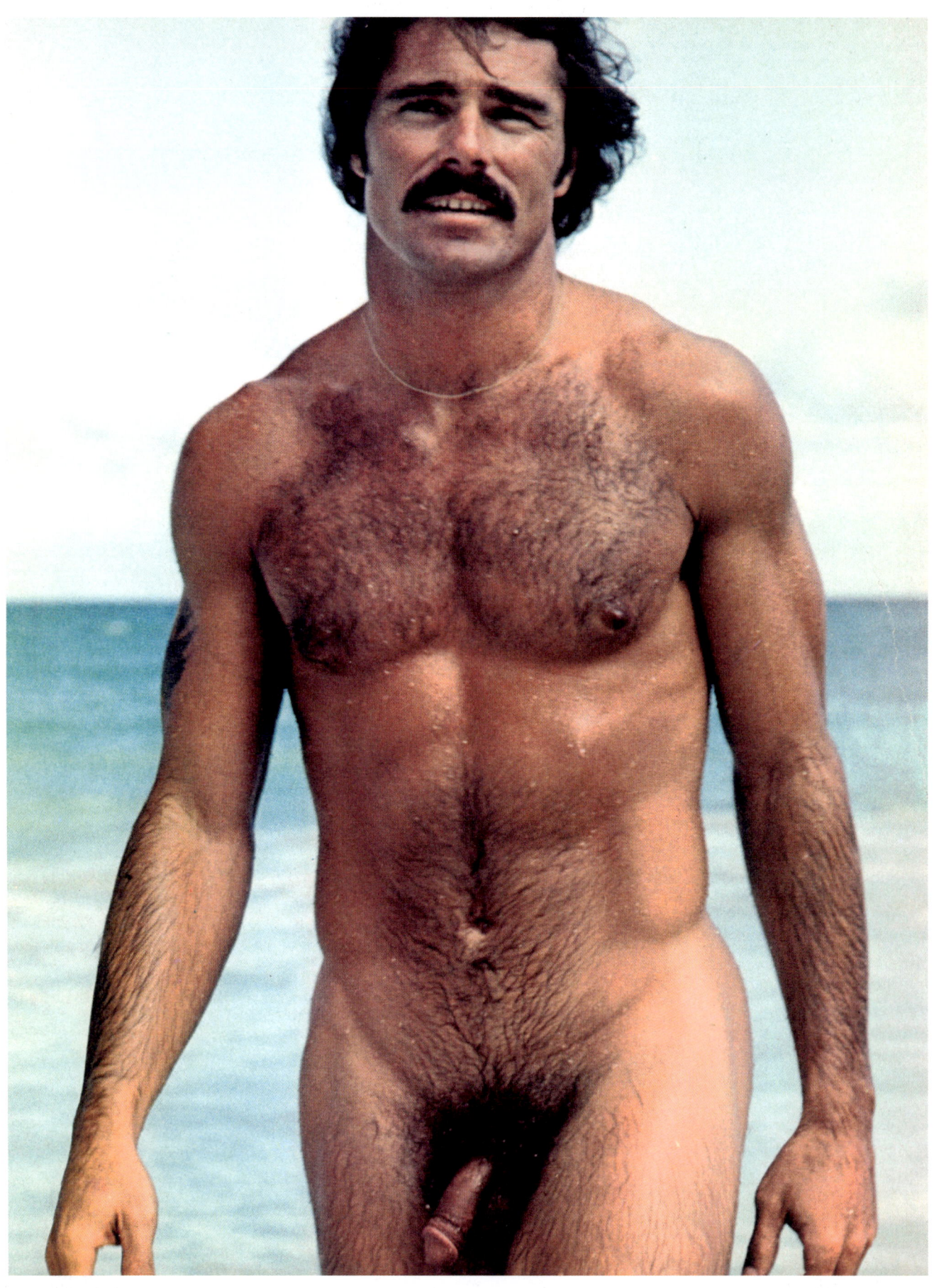

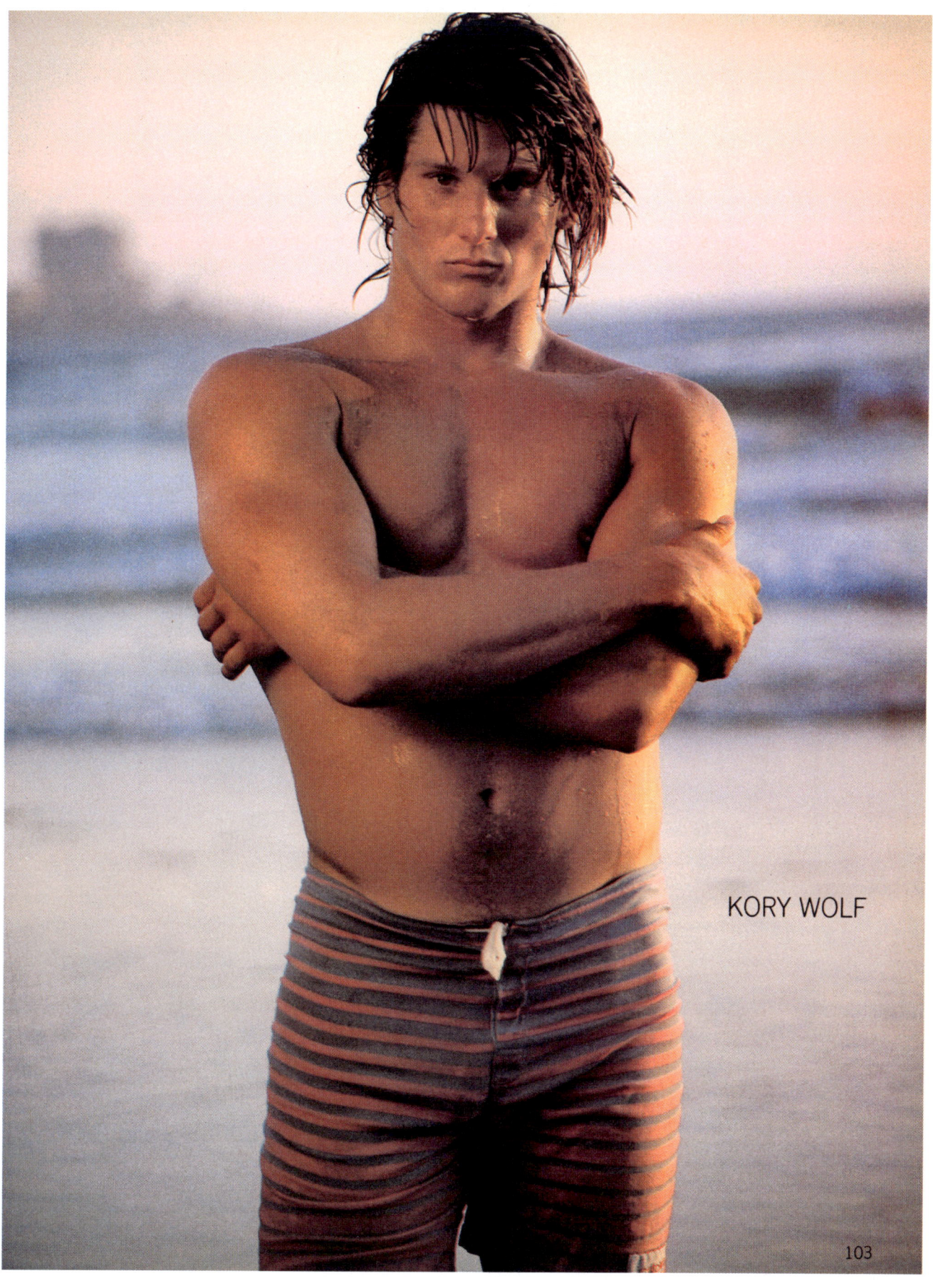

KORY WOLF

103

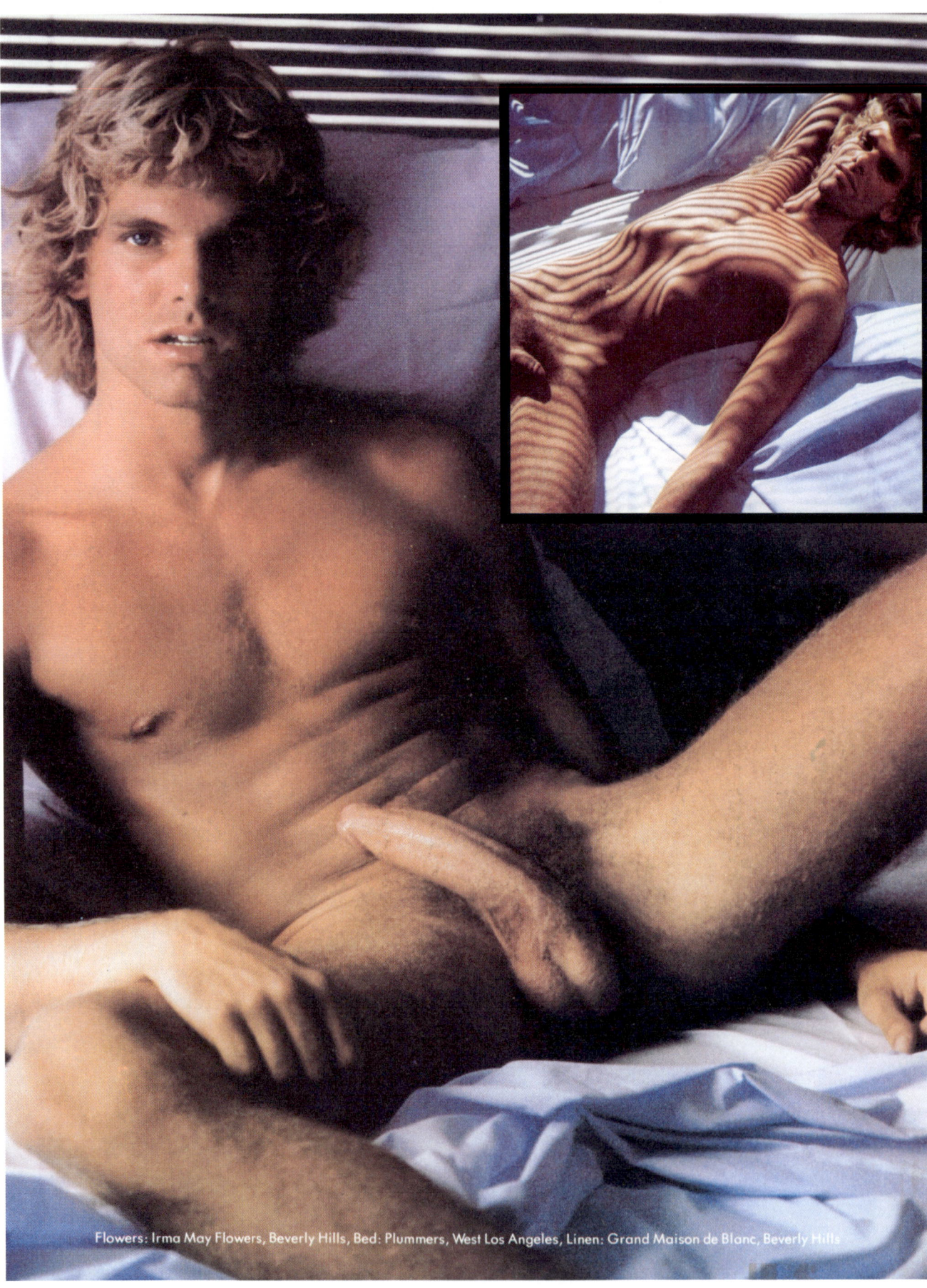

Flowers: Irma May Flowers, Beverly Hills, Bed: Plummers, West Los Angeles, Linen: Grand Maison de Blanc, Beverly Hills

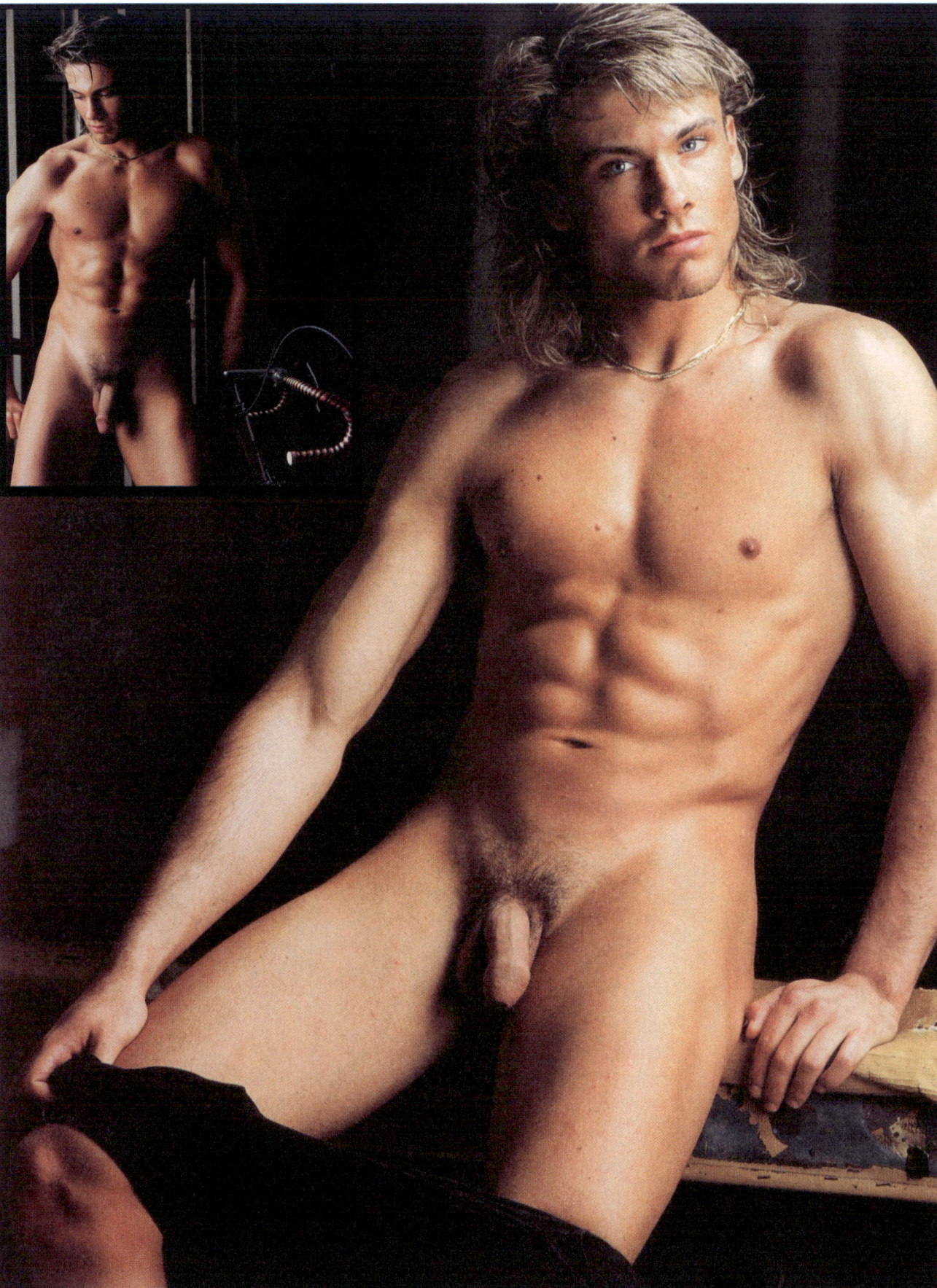

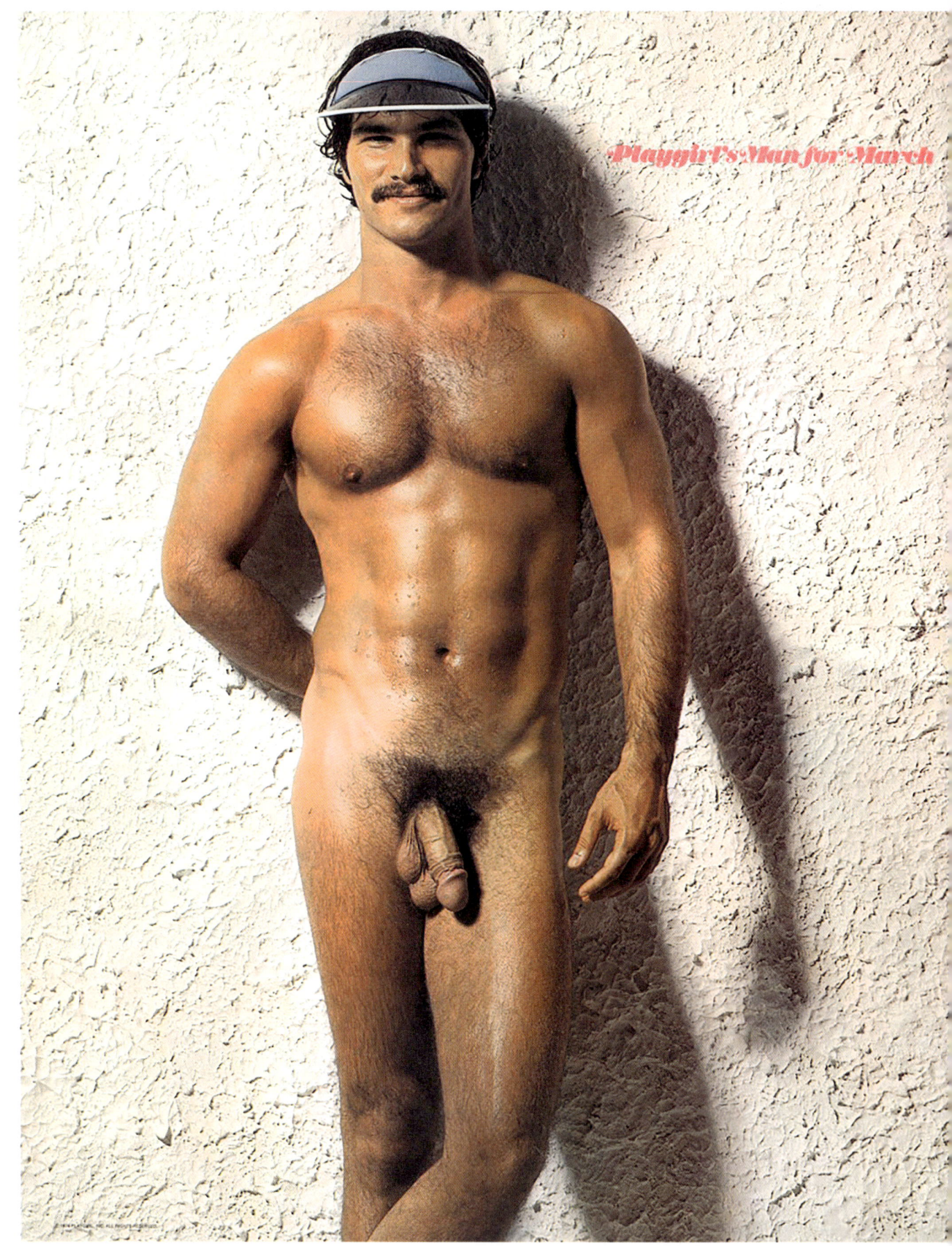

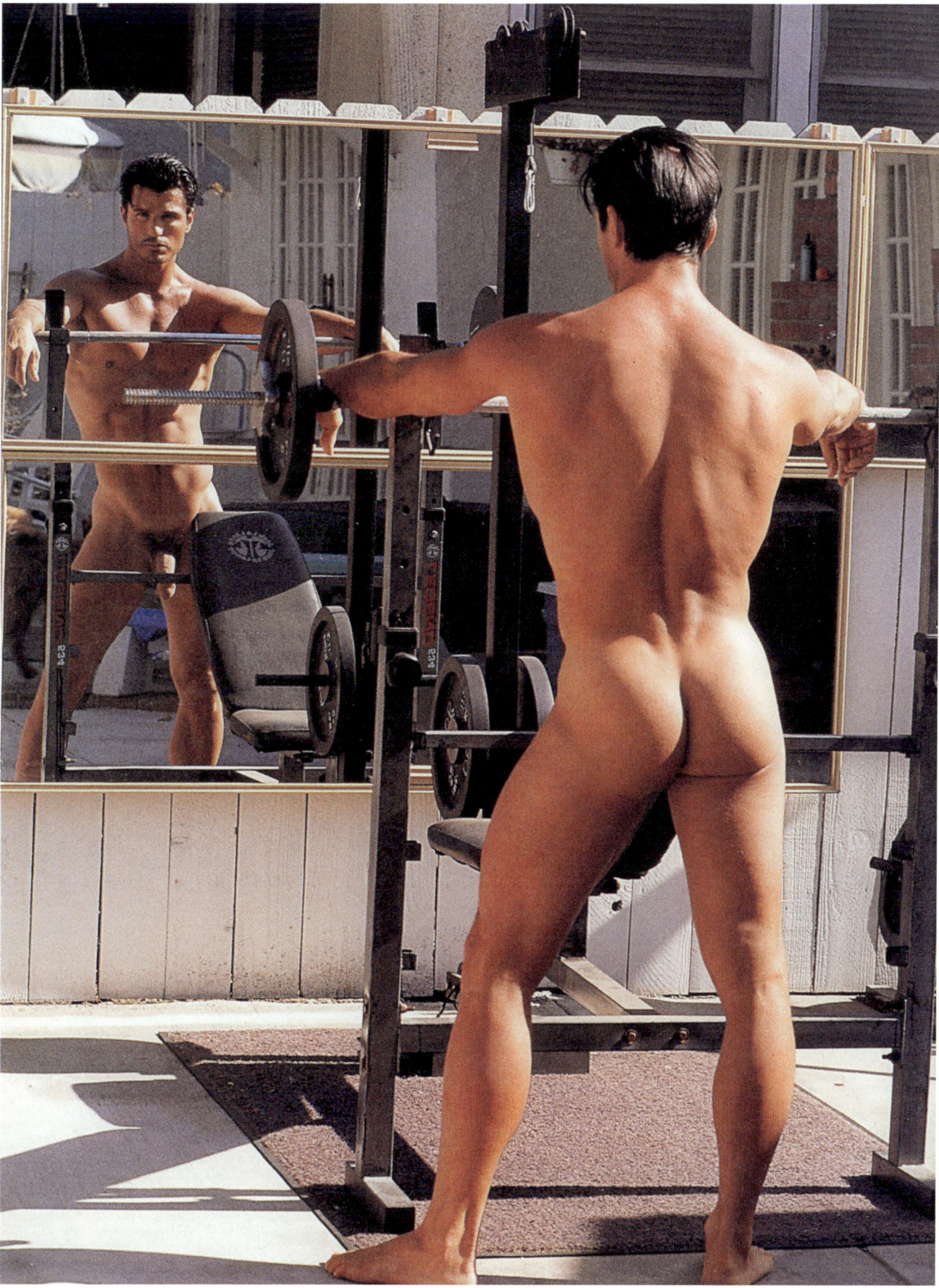

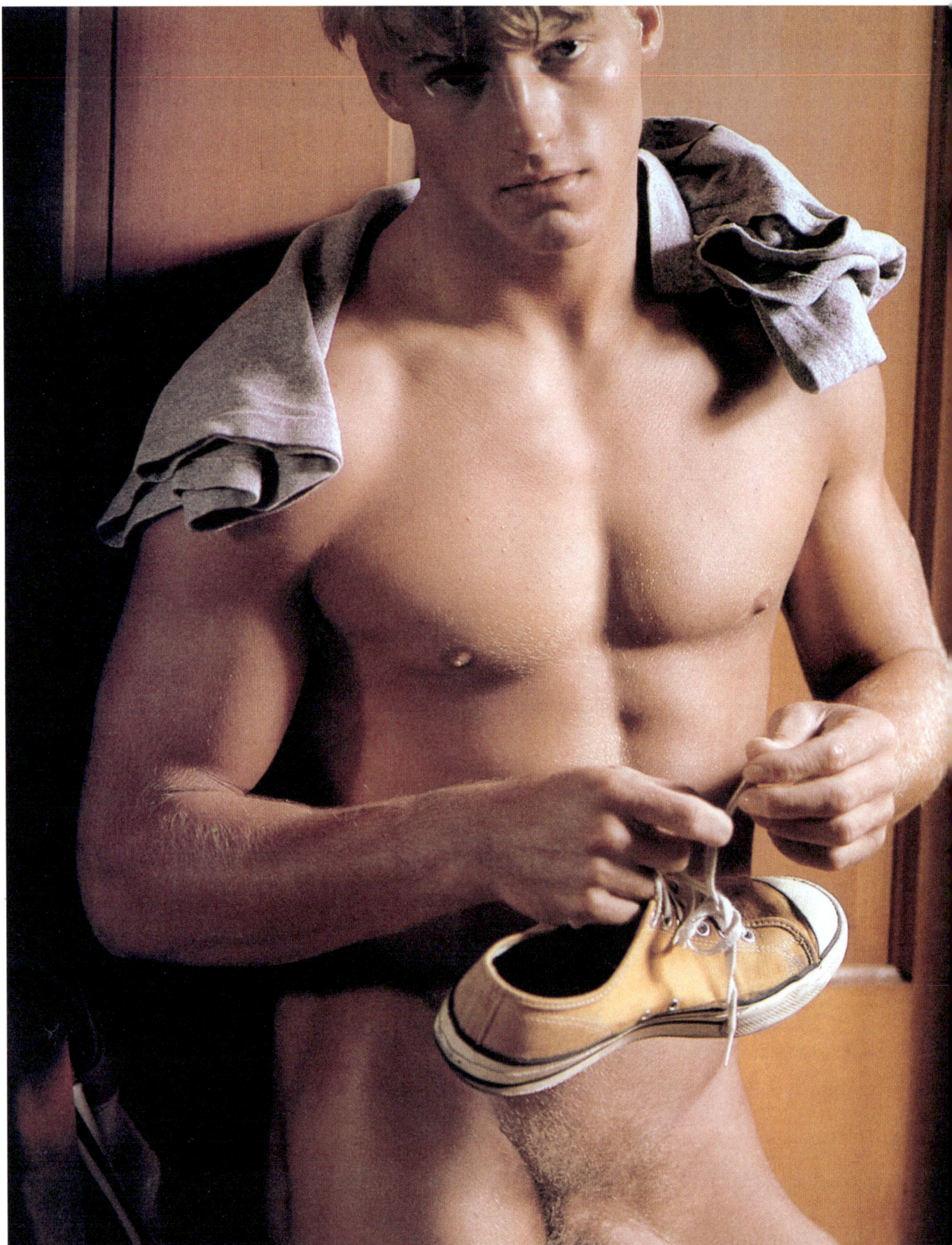

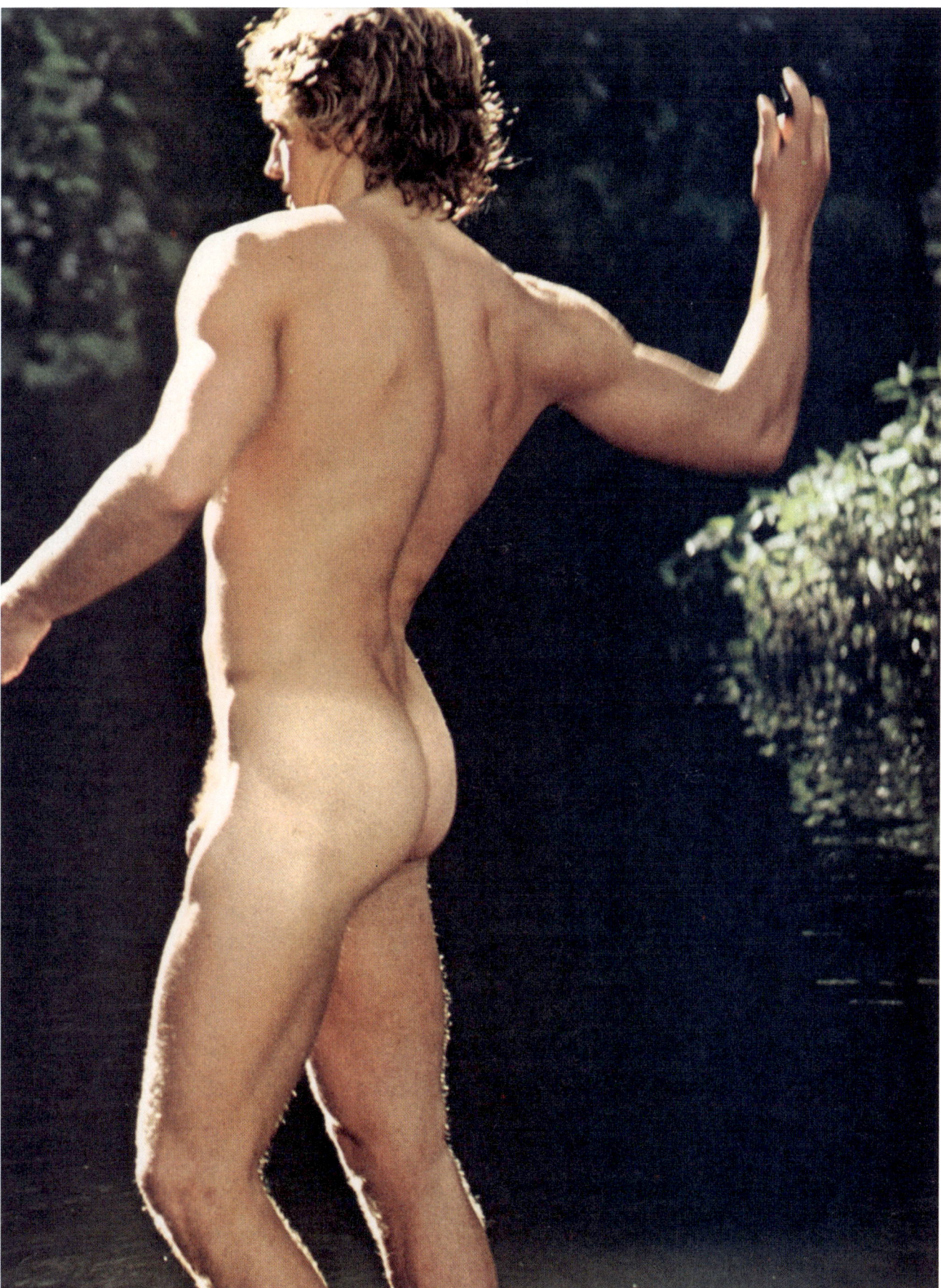

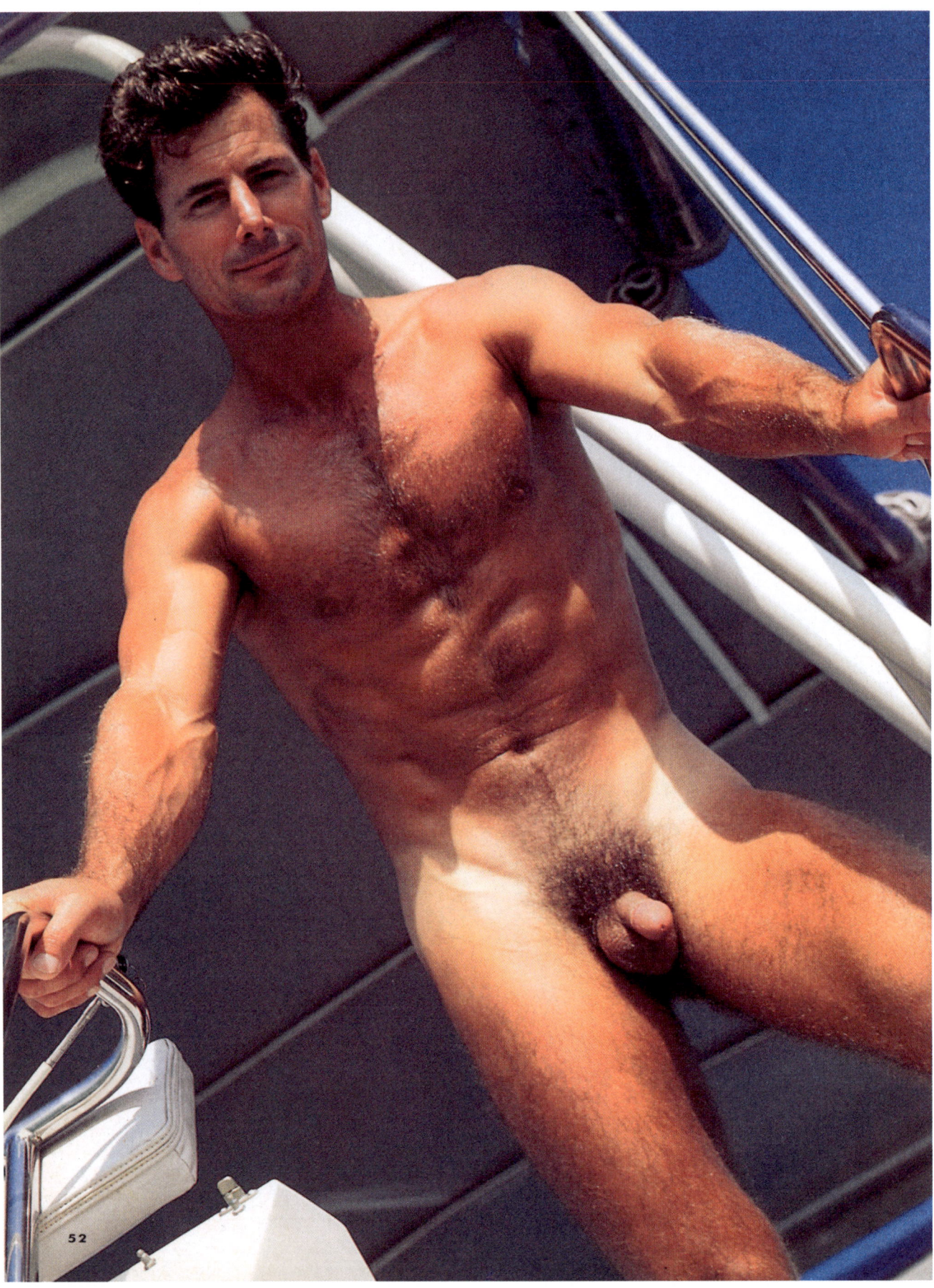

52

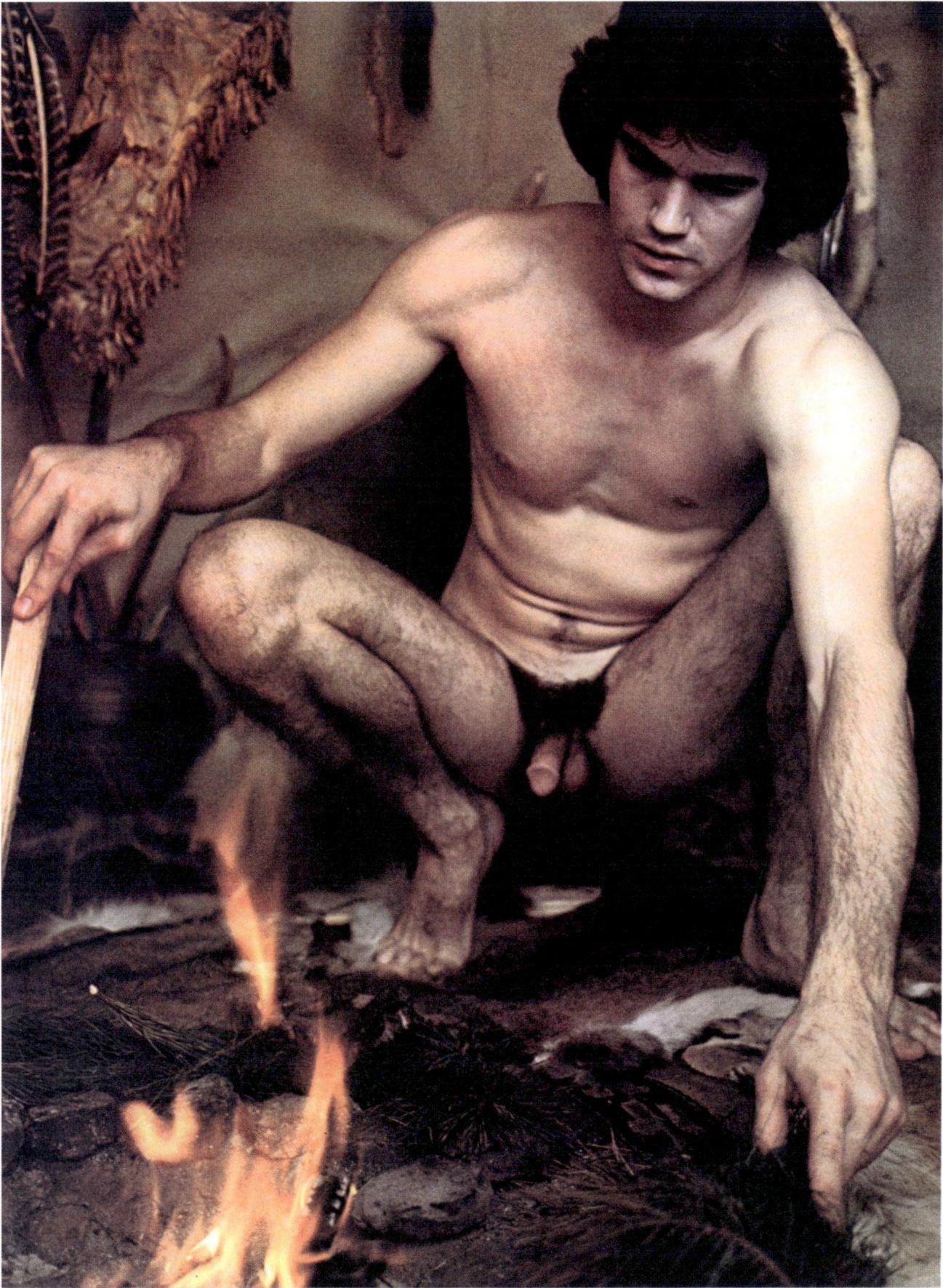

R E A R

CAPTIVATING

STIMULATING

ENTHRALLING

FASCINATING

V I E W

TITILLATING

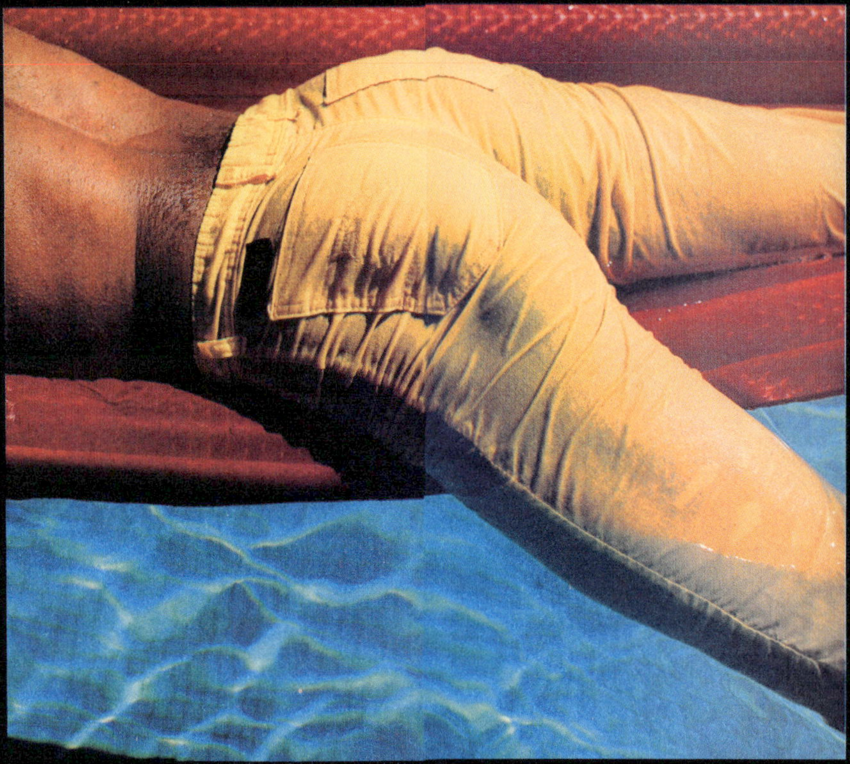

SENSATIONAL

DEVASTATING

PROVOCATIVE

PHOTOGRAPH: OLIVIER FERRAND

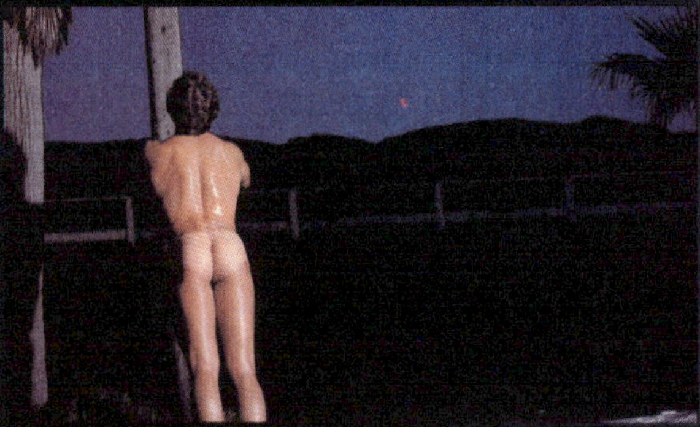

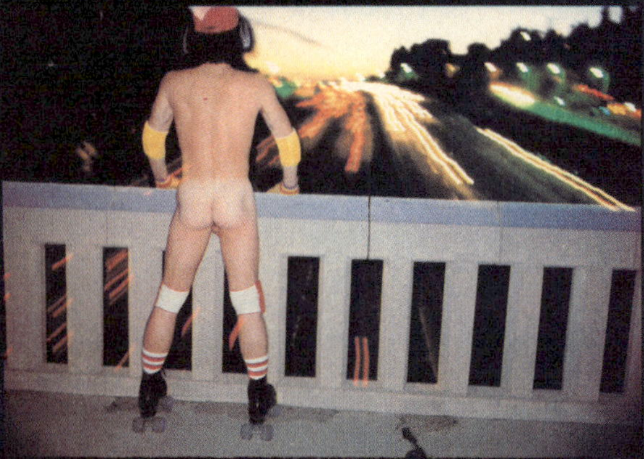

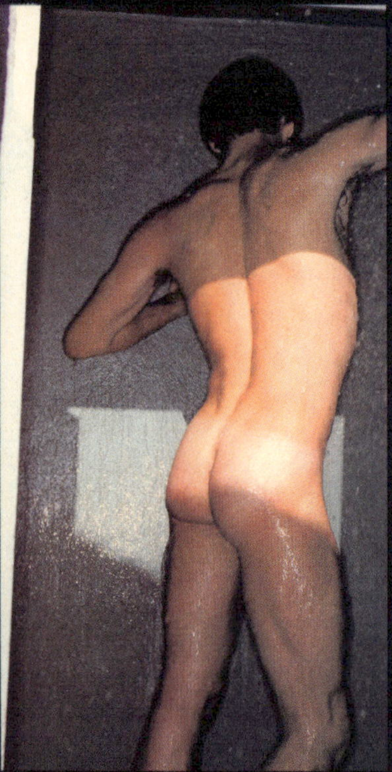

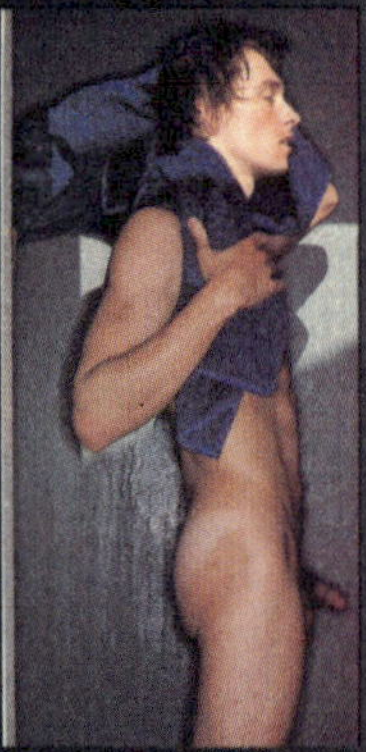

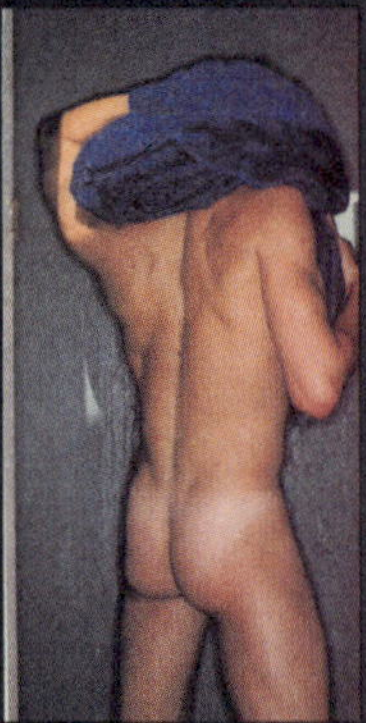

PHOTOGRAPHS: OLIVIER FERRAND

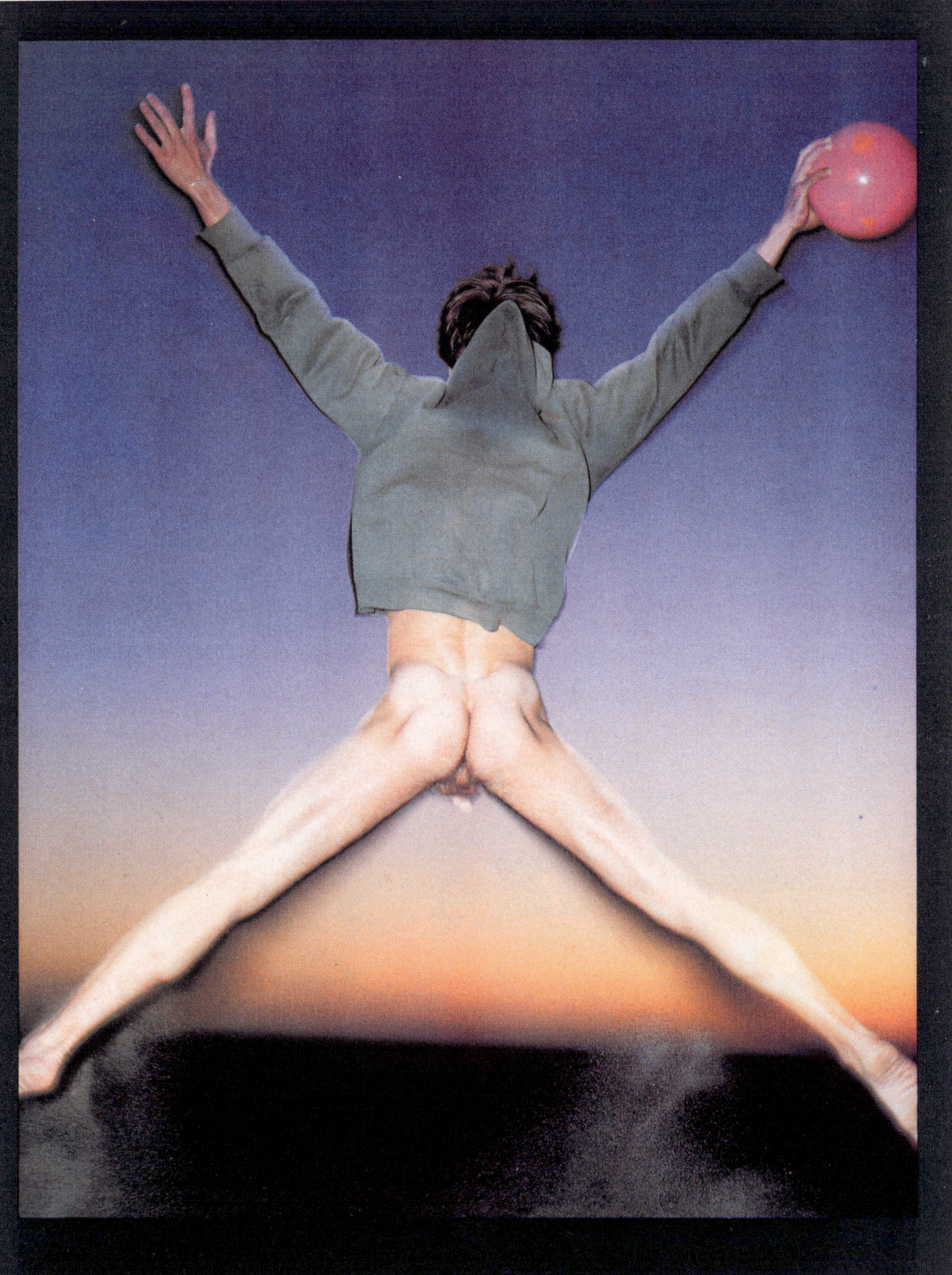

CHAPTER 4

INTERVIEWS

From the start, *Playgirl* has boasted exclusive
interviews with iconic women and has been charmed
by the likes of Dolly Parton, Jane Fonda, Bette Midler,
Cher, Yoko Ono, Gloria Steinem, Grace Jones,
and Joan Collins, as well as icons we've lost,
like Anne Rice and Joan Rivers. And the men
got their due as well. *Playgirl* has sat down with
Hollywood legends such as John Travolta, Sylvester Stallone,
Burt Reynolds, Robin Williams, and Larry Flynt.
More recent conversations have included
Sandra Bernhard, Margaret Cho, Alan Cumming,
and Shirley Manson of the band Garbage.

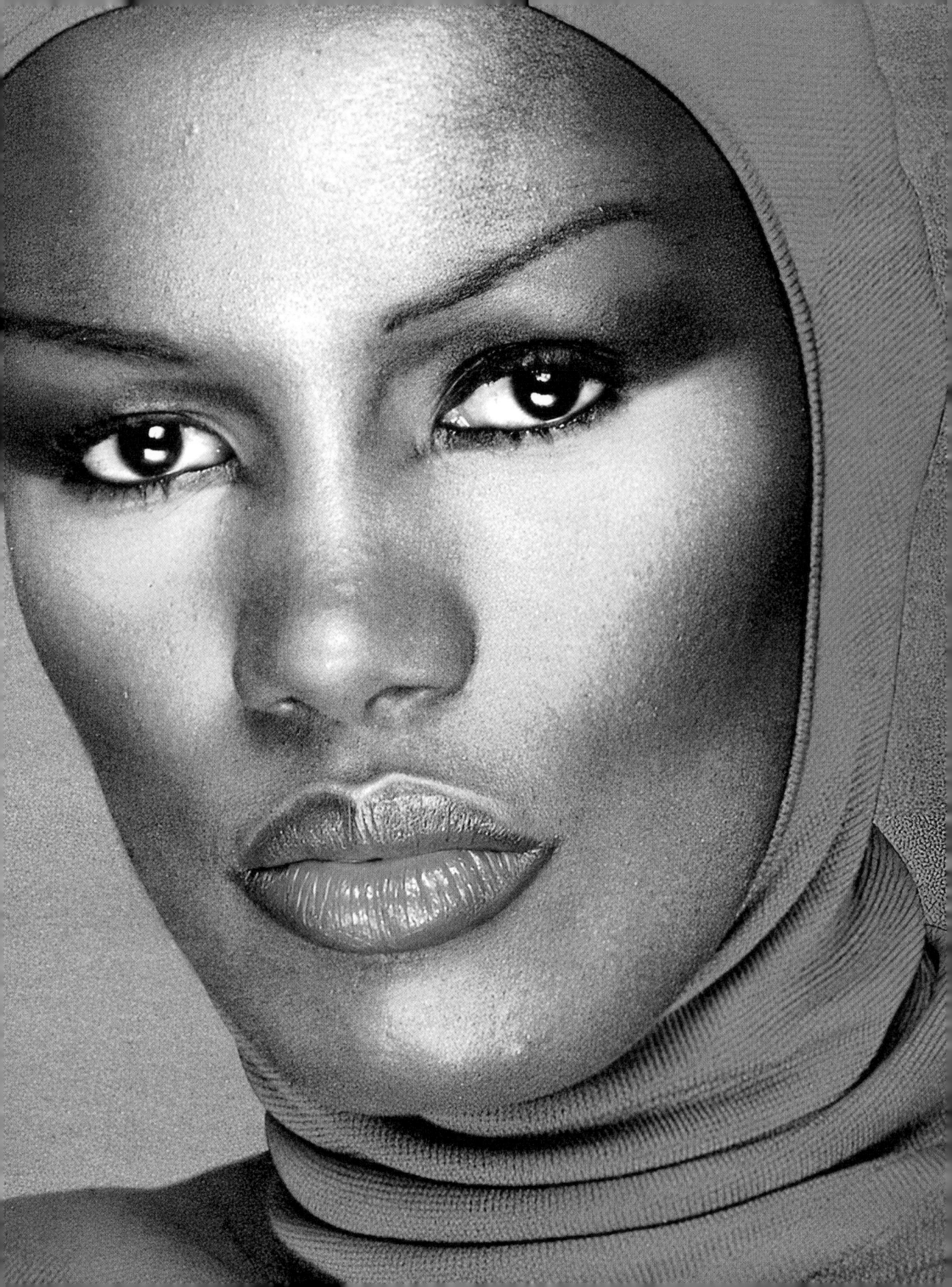

GRACE JONES

BY ALEX MICHAELS
AUGUST 1985

There's a story about you that seems to be adding to your legend—that you appeared on a TV talk show in London and actually punched out the host. Is this true? Do I have anything to fear in this interview?
No, of course not. You're not coming off at all like the way this TV guy did. One minute he was nice and the next minute he got mean and rude, like he put on a mask. I think he got intimidated because he was so impressed that his other guest was a cousin to the queen, and they are very funny about the queen there, you know. So he just ignored me through the whole interview. I had to sit there for half an hour and nothing happened. He had his back turned to me. It was awful. When I mentioned to him that I would like to walk off the show, he said, "Just calm down, darling, just relax. I'll get to you in a moment." So I got very angry and a little fidgety. Finally, I stood up and just started to hit him. He was completely shocked. He held his papers over his head and shouted, "She's crazy. Get her off me!"

How would you describe yourself?
I hate questions like that. You know why? Because for people who don't know me, I'm sure they'll all see me in so many different ways. Most of them will be very curious because there's a certain amount of mystery there.

And you want to keep that mystery as long as you can?
I think so, yeah.

Do men feel threatened by you? By your look, the persona you've created?
I think so. When men approach or make a confrontation, it's always with a certain amount of attitude attached to it. It's not just spontaneous. I think I throw them off.

Which you don't mind doing?
No.

You recently posed nude for *Playboy*. Why?
For the sake of art and because of the photographer, Helmut Newton. Helmut has a special vision. He adds a kind of humor to these photos that they don't usually have, and he creates a work of art. He could be a film director. Another attraction was that I got to work with

my lover, Dolph. That made it kind of special.

But the photos aren't completely nude. I'm showing just enough, but not everything. I think it's much more intriguing—much sexier—to leave a question mark.

You've been called a creature whose beauty transcends gender and color, someone who's almost—
No color, no sex.

Is that how you feel about yourself?
Yeah, I do. But that's more how I feel about how the world should be, rather than how I feel about myself. Because for me, I don't take it all that seriously. I don't know anyone who's been killed or injured as a result of racism or of being a woman or anything like that.

Do you feel that you are both a man and a woman?
No, that's not a feeling; that's just a fact.

Why do you feel the future is no sex?
What I mean is no sexual roleplaying. You know, the macho image, the ego of the male—which has dominated this century for I don't know how many goddamn years—that thing about a male being fabulous at 55 but a woman isn't. I think that's going to bite the dust.

DOLLY PARTON

BY LARRY GROBE
JANUARY 1981

You were reluctant to do this interview, weren't you?
Yes, I was.

Was it because the magazine offends you or because you're concerned about your image among a certain segment of your fans?
Well, I know that I'll be plastered on the covers of this and that magazine (when *9 to 5* is released), and there won't be much I can do about a lot of it, but I don't want to get on the cover of too many sex-oriented things, although I love that stuff myself. I just don't want to do 'em to a point where it looks like, here I am in Hollywood, I start wearin' low-neck clothes, I start doing *Whorehouse*, I start doin' *Playgirl* and *Playboy*, and then my image changes. It means something to me, what my family and my people think and feel. I'm still the same person I was before I ever got toHollywood.

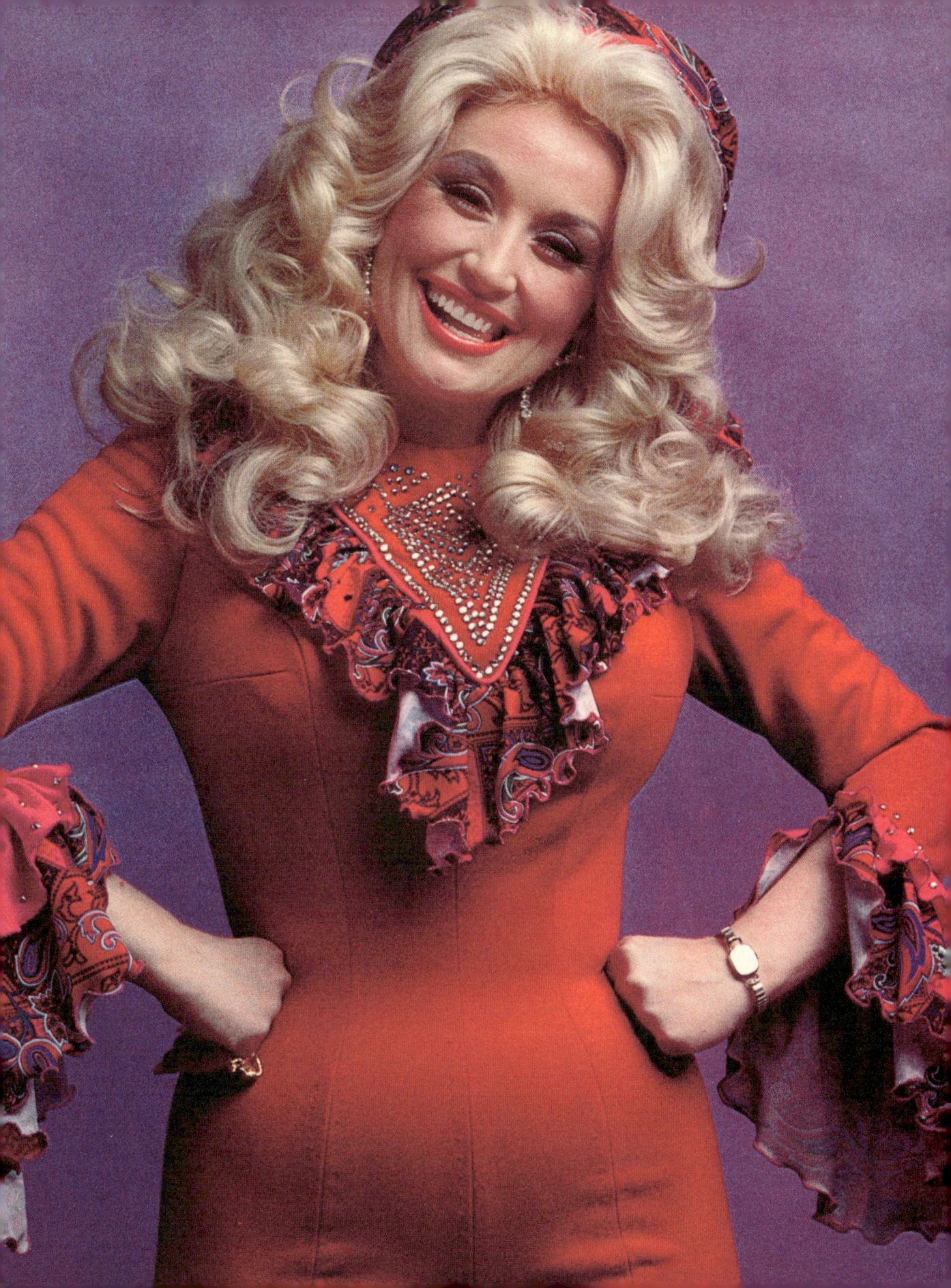

The low-neck clothing you're referring to, is that the dress you wore for the Academy Awards?

Yes. I got a lot of comments about the dress. It was very low. It was a little much for me, but it was somethin' I wanted to wear because I wanted to look like Old Hollywood, 'cause it was kind of a thrill and a fantasy for me. I went home to Nashville and somebody made the statement, "Well, hell, I'm real glad to see you; I'm surprised you're talking to us. We figured you got out there with all those people and went crazy with all of them dope heads." It kinda hit me real hard, but it was good that it did.

Are you uncomfortable in Hollywood, or have you adjusted?

I like bein' here. I like it better than I used to. I've adjusted to it more. There are a lot of wonderful people here. It could never be my home, but it's excitin'.

You are on record, though, for calling show business in general a "phony world."

I'm talking about the surroundings, all the airs people have to put on. Everybody is trying to be different, to have a gimmick. I'm just talking about all the hokey things, all the freaky people like Elton John and myself who try to come up with something to catch your attention. It's kind of a joke, what I said, but there was a great deal of truth in it as well. I take my music extremely seriously, but I'm talking about all the things that go along with it—the parties, the award shows, all the people trying to outdress the others, trying to get into *Time* magazine with their dresses cut below the tailbone or whatever.

And here you are in *Playgirl*. Do you look at magazines like this one or any of the men's magazines?

I don't usually look at either.

But if someone handed you a copy of *Playgirl* and *Playboy*, which would you thumb through first?

Well, to be honest—I don't mean it to sound strange, as if I get off on women—but *Playboy*, I think. I enjoy the stuff that's in it . . . I get embarrassed, too, really. I mean, I like naked bodies and all that. I don't have any hangups about it, but somehow it embarrasses me more when I see a naked man in pictures, totally naked, than when I see naked women.

Do you think women—or men—are exploited in these publications?

Not any more than they want to be exploited.

Do you think women and men find different things erotic?

I don't know. I can't answer for all women. I know a lot of girls who read *Playgirl*, and they look at it mostly in a joking manner, like, "Hey, look at this one" or, "Hey, did you see that one?" Although the men are beautiful, it's hard for me to take it seriously. It seems natural for women to pose and be pretty, and it just seems a bit clumsy for a man to strike so-called sexy poses. I love men, I love skin, but I can't think of it as serious. Usually, when I look at nude pictures it's with a whole crowd of girls and there's so much jokin' and laughin' going on that you don't really see the person. You just see an *it*.

LARRY FLYNT
BY BARBARA CADY
MARCH 1978

Before you came on the scene, there were already a host of skin magazines for men—*Playboy*, *Penthouse*, et cetera. Why did you start *Hustler*?

I wanted to deal with sex the way I·knew it growing up. I've served in both the Army and the Navy, I've worked in factories, washed dishes, sold encyclopedias and Bibles, and I wanted to deal with sex in a very unpretentious way. I wanted to bring it out of the locker room and write about it the way my friend on the street talked about it—four letter words and all.

Are you suggesting that *Playboy* and *Penthouse* don't present a true picture of male sexuality?

Well, you know, like Hefner says, with *Playboy* they sell the sizzle—not the steak. Hefner is very great at creating fantasies and parading his pornography as art. With *Hustler*, I've always admitted that I deal with pornography.

You've certainly got the critics—and the indictments—to prove it.

But wait a minute now. All of the sexual fantasies and fetishes that fill the pages of *Hustler* are done from more of a reporting point of view than an advocating one. And there is a big difference. When you pick up a copy of *Playboy*, it's obvious that Hefner likes blondes and big boobs. You pick up a copy of *Penthouse*, it's obvious that Guccione is a crotch man and likes brunettes. You pick up a copy of *Hustler*, and you don't really know what I am. That's because I fight to keep my own sexual preferences out of *Hustler*. I accept the reality that the sexual appetite varies so much that I may not be on a parallel with other individuals. So, we publish photographs of brunettes, redheads, blondes, skinny girls, fat girls, old girls, young girls, because we want to respond to the reader for what he is—not for what we think he is.

If there's any truth in what you say, it's rather sad, don't you think, that people have to be sexually educated by pornography?

Well, we aren't taught in the home or in school—and certainly the church plays no part at all. So while I agree that men's magazines may not necessarily be educating us in the classical way, I think that they are more helpful than they are harmful. And if we don't get it from them, where in the hell are we going to get it from. I mean, as phoney as Hefner has been about all of this pseudo-sophisticated horseshit that he has tried to dump on people, he has been extremely helpful as a pioneer in the field of human sexuality by helping us come to grips with our sexuality.

But now I would like to get back to what you were saying about *Hustler* demeaning women. There is no way that a woman can make a valid argument that publishing pictures in a magazine she feels is exploitive of women is a violation of her rights. While she may not approve of it, it is a form of expression that people are entitled to make. And I think that anytime we get involved in these real controversial issues like abortion, pornography, religion, and politics, in order for everyone who's arguing to be safe they've got to align themselves with the Constitution. Our Constitution is the basic foundation for us being able to be here and to have the forms of expression that we have today.

But how do you see women's sexual repression—as opposed to men's—related to religious repression?

This triggers something very deep in me and it's difficult to express, but the way I interpret the Bible, women are a sign of pleasure and evil. And I think this is a partial reason for many of the overt acts of violence towards women. Men actually resent women because they feel that women are making them sin. Women, therefore, make men feel guilty. The aggressive overt acts of violence toward women by men represent an act of revenge for making them sin. Of course, women have the same guilt problems based on religion, too.

But the female is much more repressed sexually than the male, and I think this has a lot to do with achieving sexual fulfillment, with achieving successful orgasms. You see, a little girl is taught really to avoid little boys, while little boys are encouraged to chase little girls. If a ten-year-old girl shows an interest in a boy, she's told

it's wrong by her parents. But now if a ten-year-old boy shows an interest in the girls, why his father smiles and stands very proud and tall, because it's a sign of his son's manhood. So we're programmed into the double standard at a very early age.

Little girls are also taught that their genitals are ugly and dirty.

Yes, and that there's one washcloth for their face and one for "down there." I think things are changing somewhat, but the biggest single dilemma I see ahead for the female is not her inferiority but her sexual superiority. She is aware of this, but the male is not—and there's the problem.

Why is she so superior?

She is capable of greater endurance, she doesn't have to perform and she can achieve multiple orgasms. Now you show me any male that falls into this category and I want to interview him for *Hustler*.

But if men aren't aware of this, where's the problem?

Well, they're starting to realize it, but most of them don't like to admit it. The result is an emasculation of the male ego, and that's the reason for the enormous rise in bisexuality among men—especially since the women's movement came into full bloom. This is because a great deal of the philosophy behind the feminist movement encourages women to get into themselves, either through masturbation or lesbianism. Now that is the radical side of it, but this factor—coupled with the fact that the female is sexually superior—results in the emasculation of the male ego and the turning to bisexuality as a form of ego protection. I think it should be made clear, however, that this trend is only among adolescent males.

Do you think this trend is statistically significant?

No one is dealing with this now because very few people know about it other than the young male coeds who are willing to admit that they are practicing bisexuals. There are private studies that show a thousand percent increase over the past five years.

Now after we're adults, our environment has really very little effect on changing our sexual mores. And that's why it's so difficult to communicate with adults about these changing attitudes and about sexuality in general. Adults have pretty much accepted their own sexuality for whatever it is—good, bad, or indifferent—and find it kind of difficult to relate to bisexuals or gays, if they are straight, or vice versa. But we are moving closer and closer to a bisexual world, and I think in generations to come we will be relating to one another as sexual beings rather than as straight, gay, or bi.

If the effect of the women's movement among young men is a turning toward bisexuality, what's been its effect on more mature males?

There's no doubt that it's been a big contributing factor to impotence. I think even the men who won't admit it are extremely self-conscious and concerned about their ability to perform and that's why the male ego is as it is. You know, I'm a firm believer in the basic Freudian principle that everything we do is motivated by sex—the way we dress, the kinds of cars we drive, the homes we live in, how we go about doing our job. Everybody wants to excel at what they do—whether they're a lawyer, a chemist or a publisher—in order to enhance their sex appeal to their mate or their would-be mate. So that's why thoughts of being impotent or not being able to perform are the biggest blow that the male ego can have. And this ego has to be fed in some way. And if men can't feed it in the bedroom it's going to be fed in the street with violence.

Specifically against women?

Violence against women and violence against other people. I mean, men have to prove their manhood. That's why a lot of men like to fight and get into barroom brawling. Many of these people, I think, are really very insecure about their sexuality. Now with regard to women—getting back to what I said about religion—she represents pleasure to the male, which, according to the Bible, is associated with immorality. And this is where male guilt feelings come in. The male really wants to punish her for this. So these feelings—coupled with the fact that the male is sexually inferior—makes him want to get even with the female. I think that's why a great deal of the sadomasochism you're seeing in the pages of a lot of men's magazines today—and the fact that this is a very common fantasy—symbolizes the male attitude toward women.

Now the women can protest about this all they want to, but the protest is not going to bring change. It may focus attention on the problem, it may define the problem, but I think only communication is going to solve it.

Isn't that a rather facile answer to a very complicated problem?

I don't think so. You know, women should never have had to fight for equal rights. They should always have had them from day one. But so should the blacks. But we are where we are now—and that's why so many women are so emotional about it. And they've got a damn right to be emotional. But we cannot make decisions out of emotion. They have to be made from knowledge. So the female must accept that the crisis exists, must accept this reality and say, "Okay, what do we do at this point?"

Exactly. What do we do?

It's very simple. The women are going to have to educate the men. After all, they're going to have to live in the world with them, they're not going to get away from them. You know, I understand more and more about the woman every day of my life, and I'm fascinated by her. Men are rather basic, but women are very complex, paradoxical creatures. And they've got a lot more on the ball than we are willing to give them credit for.

I didn't have the insight into the female five or ten years ago that I do today, but I'm able to appreciate their problems more now by having a better understanding. So, I don't think that all men should be dismissed as male chauvinist pigs. I think that's a good way of defining most of them, but I also feel that there's a way for them to be converted. If I can be converted, anybody can.

Is there anything that you consider too outrageous, too "dirty" to print in *Hustler*?

I've drawn the line in my own mind, but not legally. I think that legally there should be no obscenity laws. Because when you start drawing the line, it becomes a question of who is going to censor the censor. And I just don't think that anyone should be in the business of drawing a line where free expression is concerned.

But getting back to your question, there definitely are certain things that I would not publish in *Hustler* out of my own personal convictions and principles. *Hustler*'s not an extension of my attitudes, but a mirror that reflects the attitudes of society and the private fantasies of the readers. So I have to discipline *Hustler* to the marketplace. But by doing this, I'm not so much a censor because, number one, I wouldn't touch something in my magazine that I felt my readers would not be interested in and, number two, I wouldn't touch something that I felt was harmful or that infringed upon someone else's rights.

At the beginning of the interview, you stated that you've never made any bones about being a pornographer. What do you hope to gain by admitting this, especially in view of all the laws against obscenity?

Well, you've hit on it exactly. *Hustler* is pornographic, but it's not obscene. And that's where we have the problem. I'd have to say that our Constitution gives us absolutely no protection from obscenity, but when people try to equate obscenity with pornography, that's when we get into trouble.

There are magazines in this country that deal with a lot more explicit pornography than *Hustler* does. I deal with soft pornography, which means that we don't show erections and penetration and the consummation of the

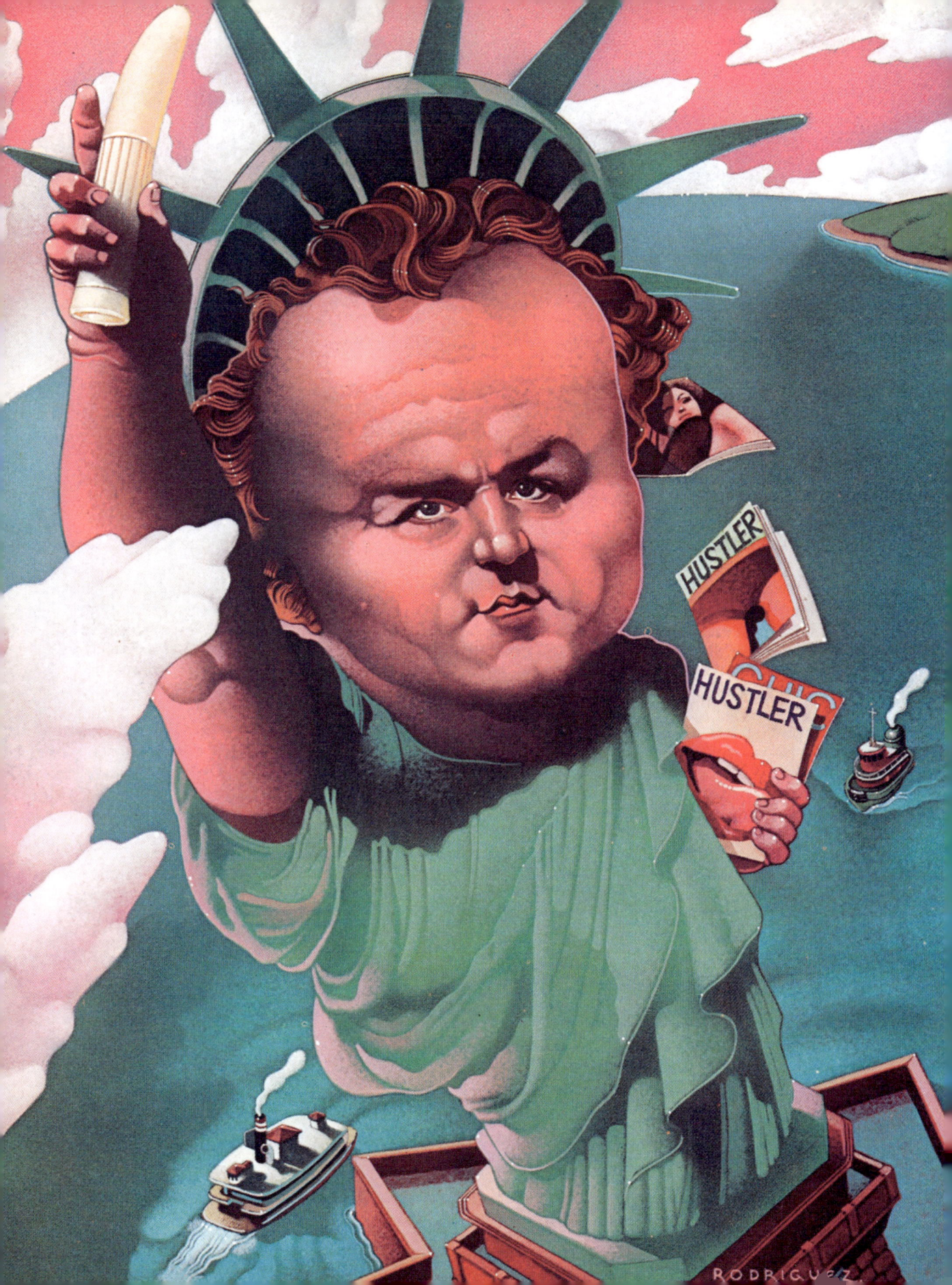

sexual act itself—which in itself is not obscene, because even the Supreme Court has said that nudity in itself is not obscene and that because you feel that something is pornographic it is not necessarily obscene. But when you say "pornography," most people think you are admitting to obscenity.

Do you feel that *Hustler* is being singled out for prosecution for any specific reason?

Yes, because of the political and social commentary that we deal with. I was indicted in Cleveland primarily because of a cartoon that I ran which showed President Ford, Rockefeller and Kissinger raping the Statue of Liberty. And certain sources in Cleveland were saying that Cleveland was a Republican city, and since we need to go to Washington to get our money we're not going to let Larry Flynt get away with this sort of thing. But Cleveland is a city that had a brothel on every street and rows and rows of adult book stores that sold hardcore pornography. And I only dealt in soft core. So you ask me!

So you're saying that your indictments are all the result of *Hustler*'s political stances.

That and questions of taste. I ran a cartoon, for example, about the time President Ford's wife had her mastectomy. It showed the silhouette of a woman in the White House with a Christmas atmosphere and the caption read, "All I want for Christmas is my two front tits." Now, we received an enormous amount of criticism about how tasteless that cartoon was. Well, my mother had a mastectomy, and you know one of the first things that I told her when they wheeled her out of surgery was, "At least you've got something in common with Betty Ford." And I brought the first smile to her lips. So the two of us accepted reality, and in publishing *Hustler* I try to take the same attitude. We try to force people to look at a side of themselves that they don't really want to.

So *Penthouse* and *Playboy* have very little censorship problems because they supposedly stay within the boundaries of good taste. But *Hustler* and magazines like *Screw* are always being prosecuted. Where *Playboy* and *Penthouse* may tiptoe through the boundaries of good taste, I might trudge through them with combat boots on. And what's the difference? You're seeing people sent to jail and prosecuted for taste.

You've been accused, as I mentioned earlier, of hiding behind the First Amendment. I don't expect you to agree with such accusations, but what are your feelings?

I'm not hiding behind it, I'm exercising it. You know, people don't really understand me when I say that society has no rights that exceed the rights of the individual. They say, "Doesn't this guy believe in majority rule?" and that sort of thing. Well, majority rule is only good in a democracy if you have the protection of the Bill of Rights, and the purpose of the Bill of Rights is to protect us from government. But people think this part of the Constitution belongs to the government.

I don't mean to get up on a soap box and give people a lesson in civics, but the First Amendment gets its meaning and vitality from the unrestricted right of free choice. And that's what I've put myself on the line for—and risked going to jail for. It's totally beyond my understanding how after some two hundred years, people still question what kind of movie you can see or what kind of book you can read. I feel very strongly about the issues involved here, and although I concede that many of my detractors may have a lot of staunch supporters, what about protecting the rights of people who want to buy my magazines—or any others—because they find something of interest in them? That's always been my argument. The Constitution is for the minority.

But you're in the minority. Do you think you'll get a fair shake?

I'm fighting to see that I do. And because of my struggle, because of my indictments and prison sentences, I've been given a forum. And I've been taking excellent advantage of it—speaking before college audiences, doing television and radio interviews all over the country, and talking about public apathy toward First Amendment rights and about society's priorities. And in doing so, I think I've contributed to exposing the extent of crimes like pedophilia and incest.

You see, I've been accused of polluting the minds of millions of people, so I've had to make more of an effort than the average person to try and understand what the First Amendment is all about, to try and come to grips with what the influence of pornography on people really is—if there's any influence at all. And I tell you, I wish everyone could experience what I've experienced, because it would result in a new awareness of what government and individual rights are all about. People would see that the government really has no business at all in legislating morality.

You know, my life has been a raunch to riches story. But now, quite frankly, I want to vindicate myself in the courts legally. I want to do more than just vindicate myself socially. It's become a question of what I can do for an encore.

ANNE RICE

BY DARYNA McKEAND
NOVEMBER 2000

What do you think about pornography?

It's fine! I think it's absolutely fine. I wrote three books of it myself.

Outside of fiction and in reality, is it OK? Incest . . . pedophilia, things like that?

Oh, gosh...what can I say? I certainly think that children have to be protected from adult sexuality. Totally and completely protected from pedophiles. And pedophiles are dangerous people . . . but at what age do you stop protecting teenage women from adult contact? That's a debatable thing. I really believe that young women of 16 and 17 years of age have a right to choose men over 18 as boyfriends. I really believe that strongly. And I don't believe that they should be condemned just to go out with teenage boys.

There's nothing worse in hell.

Exactly. We're the only society I've ever heard of that tells marriageable young women that they're supposed to go out with boys. That's silly. They have a right to men. I believe that enough to have written *Belinda* to get that point across . . . I think right now that young girls of about 12 and 13—their greatest danger lies with boys that are 14 and 15 . . . I don't know if adults are their worst threat. I mean, they're in more danger of getting raped in hallways of the schools, or things like that happening to them, or getting shot up like at Columbine.

When you were younger, how did you first learn about sex?

My mother told me about it when I was very young. She told me, and I remember asking her, "Does this take place in the bathroom or the bedroom?"

She seemed to be kind of amused by that and said, "Oh, always in the bedroom." But I mean that can show you how young I was, that I thought it would take place in the bathroom. I didn't believe her. I thought she was making it up. I didn't believe that anything like that could be true. It was kind of like the *Saturday Night Live* skit where all the kids are talking at a slumber party—I don't know if you've seen that skit—and saying, "Oh, I would never do it," and then one of them starts saying, "Yeah, I could do it" and all of them say it. So anyway, that skit is a great, classic skit, and I think I felt kind of like that. That "I would never do it."

How did you explain sex to your son?

I don't recall ever explaining it to my son. But you have to realize that my son grew up in a time that all he had to do was watch [porn channels on TV] to know what sex was about. I don't think he read my pornography. I'm sure he didn't read it. I wouldn't have encouraged a young child to read it. I guess that's the only prohibition I would put [on writing]—I don't think it's recommended for a young child to read heavy pornography of that kind because children have to develop their own fantasy life. The fantasy in [the Beauty books] is so well developed that it might crowd them a bit.

Rice published the first book of her three books of erotica, The Claiming of Sleeping Beauty, *in 1983; the other two followed over the next two years. There was no way in hell that I was going to pass up an opportunity to ask a porn-writing pro how she got so good at what she does.*

What's the best kind of foreplay? Thinking about it? Is foreplay more of a mental thing, or—

Yeah, kind of. I think—my own life is kind of dull. I'm not sure it's really worth talking about. Just the normal foreplay things that everyone enjoys: kissing, fondling, um, oral sex, you know? Things like that. I would say, exploring your bodies and taking your time . . . seeing what each other enjoys. All the old cliches—I don't have much to say that I can add to what's been said in the last 30 years.

Do you see your male vampires as gay, bisexual, or what?

I see all of my characters as transcending gender. And I think that this is pretty much the way I see the world. I see the world as beautiful. I don't think gender matters . . . To a vampire, what matters is somebody warm and beautiful. It's not that that person has to to be of any particular gender . . . I really feel that we must never condemn anybody for being homosexual or lesbian or whatever. I have always felt that way. I've never been able to feel a revulsion for homosexuality, or a disapproval of it. On the contrary, I see it as kind of romantic.

How is it more romantic than heterosexuality?

Well, I suppose heterosexuality can be seen as highly romantic, too, but a great deal of heterosexuality has to do with very practical family values. I don't see them as romantic, whereas homosexuality almost always has to do with love for love's sake. Since it is free from family values, it seems more to have to do with a real choice. A real—how shall I say?—a passionate choice.

And that always seemed rather lovely to me. You fight such a battle sometimes to be with the person you want to be with.

You just said, "choice." Do you think that homosexuality isn't genetic?

Oh, I think it is inborn. I really do. My own suspicion about that is that it'll probably be proven within a few years that it is genetic. Maybe I fantasize too much about it. It would be much easier to get married in spite of [being gay], and do your best. I've always seen it as highly romantic. I am kind of in love with Oscar Wilde . . . Maybe I see it as more romantic than it really is.

Vampires can't have sex, can they?

Vampires? I've been toying with the idea that they can get more physically intimate, but I don't know yet if they can have sex . . . they might be able to. I might work that yet.

Can they get erections?

According to my mythology, they are always almost erect. Lestat says, in *The Queen of the Damned*, that "We always look like we're prepared for sexuality."

SANDRA BERNHARD
BY LAURA FISSINGER
NOVEMBER 1989

How old were you when you lost your virginity?

Nineteen. It was horrible! I just grabbed somebody from the Hollywood Bowl (laughs) and fucked him. I only slept with him once, on a Saturday afternoon, and the sex wasn't very glamorous or romantic. (Sly, quick grin.) It's gotten better, though.

Here's a completely unanswerable question: Why are men the way they are?

(Seriously) You know, I'm one of the few women I know who really doesn't expect that much from men. I don't want anything from them. In terms of anything, I'm not very dependent on men. So subsequently, I basically like them. I think I get along better with men than almost any woman I know. Women are much more disappointing to me, because my expectations are higher. I've been hurt by women much more than by men.

Speaking of which, do you ever discuss your sex life, sexual preference, or dating situation for the record? And notice that I did not mention the name Madonna? (Both laugh).

Yeah—and I thought that would be the first question out of your mouth! But no, I don't talk about my love life in print, because it kind of dispels the mythology. I do what I do (laughs) and I do it with whom I do it—and I'm having a great time. I'm just supportive of everybody's sexuality—and I completely embrace people's happiness, however they get it. And I think that's the statement, more than using myself as an example of whatever.

About myself, I say that I've covered the waterfront. (Laughs.) So I'm not denying anything. But also I don't want to reveal people who are in my life, because it's an invasion of their privacy. And that's not right. Besides, most of them aren't even in the public life. But I'll put it this way—anything goes, as long as nobody's getting hurt.

SHIRLEY MANSON
BY JENNY HIGGONS
AUGUST 1996

What's it like to be the only girl in an all-guy band?

I don't really know there's a difference. It just feels the same as it would be in any other band. I don't find my sexuality a barrier, communicating with men at all. We just get on as people.

What's your opinion of tasteful nudity—male or female?

I love looking at naked bodies, male or female, and whenever possible! I think nudity is always tasteful.

What do you think about pornography?

Pornography is an absolute necessity. I don't condemn it in any way at all. I actively condone it. I think it's very healthy and actually helps a lot of people come to terms with their own sexuality.

They say that women are not as visually oriented as men.

I think we're equally as visual, it's just that different things turn us on. Men like very obvious sexual signs. Women are a lot more subtle.

Then how can you explain a magazine like *Playgirl* being around for 23 years?

These are sweeping generalizations. There are definitely women who get totally turned on by looking at full-frontal male nudity. But I think in general, most women are into the more subtle nature of sexuality.

I read that you also prefer large penises!

I was actually joking, although, yeah, I don't want a tiny penis. I think it's a male-perpetuated myth that women don't care. I'm not saying that they have to be enormous, but I don't think any woman wants a tiny one.

BETTE MIDLER

BY CLAUDIA DREIFUS
SEPTEMBER 1975

Bette Midler as a child—what was she like?

I was a little chubbier than I am now. I had gigantic tits and I was very plain. I wore harlequin glasses—you know those hideous glasses that ruined a lot of people's lives. I was fairly bright. I had a terrific sense of humor. I was what you would call a go-getter. Mostly I was into theater.

I understand you were never permitted to see anything "risqué."

My father was out there painting housing for the navy and he never cared. It was my mother who was into musicals. She would only see a musical or perhaps a Walt Disney adventure.

But your stage act is very bawdy.

Yes. Yes, it is. Isn't it lucky?

Is the bawdiness a reaction to all those happy, sexless musicals?

Well, I guess so. I really like to laugh, and I like a dirty joke. I guess that comes from being so cloistered as a child. I was taught to be very good, and my father hated it when I wore eye makeup.

So how did you rebel against all that cheerfulness and goodness?

We lived in this slum in the country outside of Honolulu. I was always fascinated by the local Bad Girls. And we were surrounded by these JD's—juvenile delinquents—and listen, I loved them. I used to follow them even though they wouldn't take me with them or anything. I'd go after them on their adventures, like shoplifting. I've always liked that other side of life, you see.

For instance, on Saturdays, from the time I was six years old to the time I was eighteen, my father would take me and my sister to town to go to the library. My parents would go off shopping at the local John's Bargain Store and my sister and I would either stay in the library or walk around town. When I was young, I would rush in and read all about French courtesans till it was all rushing out of my ears. Later, when I got very brave, I'd go out to the red light district and walk around. All the sailors and people in the armed forces would go there to see a dirty movie or a bawdy show or to pick up a girl. It was a real red light district, and it was so wonderful! It wasn't bullshit Forty-Second Street or bullshit Eighth Avenue. It was for real—opium dens and lots of Orientals.

DURAN DURAN

BY CHARMIAN CARL
OCTOBER 1995

Would either of you ever ponder a face lift?

I don't think so. A penis extension would be great, but you know . . .

Do you need a penis extension?

No, I don't. If I wanted to get it in my mouth, I would.

You're really on the edge, Warren.

Hey, baby, this is a woman's magazine. I think it's horrible that women feel exploited. *Playgirl* has been around for a long time. Women can look at men and watch pornography now. I love pornography. Whoever wants to derive enjoyment out of it, can. It's not just for men anymore.

What about the perception that women who enjoy sex are sluts?

If we believed in public perception, we would've stopped playing a long time ago. All that really matters is how you relate to people in your life and time. The only thing you need to know is who you are and why you do certain things.

That you can't control. At first, we thought there should be no merchandising, but if *you* don't do it, people will just bootleg it anyway. Like I okayed some of it just so I can get some of the money from it. It's like the fan magazines. If you don't talk to them, they make up an interview.

What about overexposure?

That's the only thing I worry about. I get scared that sometimes there might be so much out there that everyone gets fed up.

Well, then you're in a pretty dangerous position aren't you?

Yeah. I have to be very choosy about what I do. I've had offers that were incredible, financially phenomenal. But, it would have just wiped me out.

How did the Kotter series come about for you?

I had a feeling it was a huge hit from the very beginning. It felt right when I did the pilot. It was ABC, it was young, hip and I knew those were the three qualities it needed to go and it did.

It also needed a star.

That's right. They were very smart in the way they played me up. The pilot script went Gabe, me and then the rest. I was the leader of the Sweathogs, very clearly. Originally, the pilot was structured to how my success is now. What happened was, in order to play it safe, they wrote the first six episodes so that everyone was very equal. They wanted to let the people decide who were the favorites. Well, the structure was inevitable that I would rise out of it. I was Vinnie. I was covertly the leader. It was inevitable. I feel like no one gave me Vinnie Barbarino. I did a watered down version of Vinnie until it was obvious who the people liked. By about December, I started doing all the Elvis shit. *I* added all that. That's what the people picked up on.

Where do you want to take Vinnie?

I don't know. He's been such a natural progression for me. I have no limits for him. The new season will be totally unlike what you'd expect from him. In the past, I've kept him thick. Not real dumb, but street-wise. I love to surprise the audience. You never quite know what's gonna come out of Vinnie next.

Who is the character based on—how authentic is it?

A little of everyone. Imagination. You bring people in from your past.

Think you'd get along with Vinnie?

I'd enjoy him, but I don't know if I'd get

stimulating and intelligent.

Do you figure on leaving the series soon?

Well, I'm contracted for a while yet, but I think we're gonna be a little too old to be in that classroom soon. I know *I'm* gonna be too old soon.

How much of Vinnie's cockiness with women do you share?

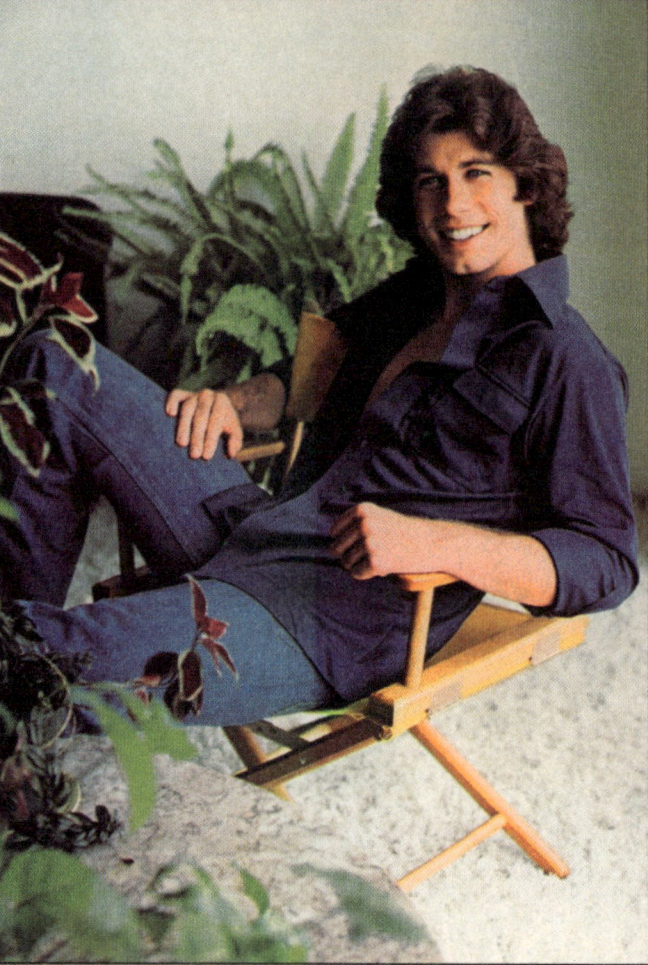

None. My attitude towards women is an attitude towards people in general. I am not a sexist. If I like girls, I like them for who they are. Do you know? Not *because* of anything. Women that I've known have had very different qualities and you can never tell with me. If there was a common denominator, though, it would be a basic goodness and warmth. I like that.

Your attitude towards women must have changed a lot. Surely women are much more aggressive with you these days.

Well, I'm finding more now than ever before that I haven't decided what I like in women. I could say there are five girls in my life that I would love to have a heavier relationship with, but yet I can't commit myself to any one because I don't know yet what I'd like forever. I would like to be around what makes me feel the best for

My tendency is to go with people who a of common magnitude, like someone el in the business who's just as successful. O my instinct is to go with someone I alread know.

Has any girl that you've been with trie to sell her story?

Not one I've been with, no. There's couple who could have, easily, but haven' As a matter of fact, they sl away from it.

Do you have someone aroun you know that could, hyp thetically, tell you if you head was getting too big?

I don't need that. No one's ev had to do it because it's not truth. If anything, it's gone t other way. I know what pow television has and what a h record does but sometimes don't feel worthy of succes Not because I'm n talented—I feel like I'm mo than talented enough to here—but sometimes press an television coverage makes bigger than what it is.

Were you a good-looking k in school?

(Travolta laughs and goes to get picture of himself at fourteen.) I always the ones that were gawl at school. Here's me at fourtee See now, I always had pret eyes. I was an adorable chil from the day I was born un ten. Then from about ten o my face was real small and I ha a big nose and big lips. My ey were always blue, very prett but it didn't seem to co-ord nate till about twenty years ol

You're into Scientology. D you spend a lot of money o Scientology training?

No more than anybody el would on any other self-help program-like analysis or medical help or the equiv lent.

Do you not like to talk about being Scientologist?

I talk about it when it's appropriate. I ju find so many people hedge on it. So ma people get upset. Only if they ask me, d talk about it. I think that it's amazing thing, that it has so much to sa It's so logical. For some reason, it got a l of bad publicity early on, in the late sixti All I know is that it helps me.

Why is it good for you?

It teaches me to know how to know. I a technology about people, what they and why they do it. Everyone's got com mon denominators, everyone does certa things under certain situations. When yo spot it, it's cool—you know it. There wonderful, basic things that help me de

JOHN TRAVOLTA

BY HENRY SCHIPPER
SEPTEMBER 1983

How important is sex in your relationship?
I'm a very sexual person, and it's a strong part.

When you say you're a sexual person, what do you mean by that?
I tune into the sexuality of others. It always entertains me on some level. I find different sexuality in different people interesting. How they approach it. Because, see, sex is simple, but how you approach sex is not. And that's what I always find interesting—how people skirt the issue, how they dive in, how they don't dive in. I love it. I'm always curious about that.

Such a rich area to be tuned into.
Oh, it is!

Because it's constantly happening, isn't it? A part of every interaction, even when it's totally disguised.
Sure, and the thing is, I've known people who block it, but it's so strong underneath the block that it seeps through every crevice, and you go, "Whoa, they are blocking a whole lot of sex, but boy is that sex there." And I plug right into it and I go, "Jesus, they are hot." They may be blocking this aspect or that, but their essence can't deny it.

Have you ever felt like a sex object?
If I ever have, I've enjoyed it [laughing]. It's not something I'm concerned about. I think that when I'm looked at as a sexual object I get a bigger kick out of it than the people who are looking at me because I can't imagine them thinking of me as your classic sex object. I always feel like I'm getting away with something.

What? You don't feel that you're sexually attractive? You must feel that.
Well, sometimes I do. Like in the trailer for *Stayin' Alive*—it's photographed well, and I have a certain presence that's exciting. But I've always approached people in terms of an affinity and intellect. The idea that people also see me as sexy is . . . interesting.

Do you use your affinity with people as a means of flirting?
If I'm in a seductive mood, I will do that. But my sexuality comes out regardless. If I am in an intellectual mood, even if I'm being really pure about my communications, the sexuality still comes out. When I want to turn it on, I can do it easily with looks or charm or whatever. But that's a whole different trip to me. I know that, physically, I move in a very sexual way, especially in dance.

When you're dancing like that, can you feel women undressing you with their eyes?
Once in a while, but I get such a kick out of it. Once I was in a public situation where a couple of women pinched me on the butt—and I liked it, I wasn't offended by it. Or when they say, "Oh, I'd really like to do this or that to you," I laugh, because I think it's great and brave of them to admit such a thing. It never has bothered me. It titillates me, if anything.

BURT REYNOLDS

BY CELESTE FREMO
JUNE 1981

OK. Let me ask you about something else. You're one of the most popular movie stars today. Women adore you. But I wonder, do you like your own looks?
That's funny. Somebody was asking me the other day about which interview questions I hate. And I said that one of them is "What is it about your looks that you like the best?"

Oh, dear, have I hit upon a touchy point?
There's no way I can come out of that question alive. [In saccharine tones] My eyebrows. I think my eyebrows are just the most wonderful! No. To tell you the truth, I honestly don't like my looks very much. I mean, I see people when I am driving home that I would rather look like. That always sounds terrible to say because I'm a star, so I sound phony or ungrateful. But I don't think there's anything different or special about my looks. I think I look an awful lot like a Cro-Magnon man. I'm hard to light because my eyebrows stick out about three inches above my eyes. You could plant corn in these furrows in my forehead. My eyes are getting narrower and smaller each year. But I don't really think about it much until somebody starts saying, "Well, take a look at yourself." I don't really. When I see a caricature done of me—like that one at the Brown Derby where I looked like a

chipmunk, that was real nice—that's when I say, "Holy God, do I look like that?" Whenever anybody does a caricature of me they always put 9,000 of these lines on my forehead. My eyebrows are enormous and my eyes are about that big [squints]. So I guess that's what I look like.

What do you consider to be good-looking in a man?

Not male models. I don't mean to denigrate them, but some male models make me cringe. There's no pain. I want a little pain, you know? I think pain is necessary to the fullness of a person's looks.

I see, the Zen of Beauty: One must suffer to have enlightenment and a good-looking face.

Yeah. But it's true! The people that haven't—you know, I grew up in Palm Beach, and there's a lot of non-sufferers around there. God, they were boring!

Has your view of sex and sensuality changed through the years?

Uh—not a great deal. I think some of the things I thought were sexy twenty years ago I still think are sexy. I think that, on the screen, anticipation is much sexier than the act. And sometimes that's true in real life. I think that romance—the romantic part of the relationship—is still the sexiest part. [Grins wildly] Usually when I've been asked about sex before, I've always said, "I like this in a woman and that in a woman and forty-four-inch boobs." But I won't do that this time. I mean, when I answer these questions, unless there is a joke at the end, people are always waiting for the other shoe to drop. But I always have and always will be a romantic. I know that sounds like Suzanne Somers. [Pauses] Let me ask you a question. Am I more aggressive or less aggressive than most people you interview?

You're not exactly passive but you're not overly combative either. Although you are fairly sensitive on a few subjects.

I just wondered. Sometimes I think I'm getting more combative. Except I was pretty open with Barbara [Walters, in an interview which aired in late 1980] because I know her well and trust her. I also know that if you make her laugh, she cuts that out of the tape.

What a pity. Getting back to what you consider to be sexy—

I still think a little slit in a long dress is sexier than a short miniskirt. A flash of leg is fabulous. Suntans are wonderful. The human shape is very important. Body language is very important. My thinking about it hasn't changed much over the years.

GLORIA STEINEM
BY LESLIE GOURSE
MAY 1985

I have the impression, from reading your book, that you have a tremendous maternal instinct toward women. Is that true?

It's not maternal. What really happened was that feminism made sense of my life. And it also helped me as a writer. Up to then, I'd been imitative, trying to write like the grownups, like male writers. I hadn't used my own experience. I had been led to believe that women's experiences were irrelevant or unusable. And the understanding that the sexual caste system, or whatever you want to call it, is not decreed by God, biology, or Freud and can be changed, helped me so much. I can't fail to explain how it helped me, and to report on women who are changing. I think I feel more like a sister than a mother.

Is it better or worse for the women's movement that it's less vociferous than it was? Is the movement stronger?

The truth is that it is *more* vociferous than it was. It's just that it doesn't seem as odd. It's more familiar. The culture has changed. People say to us this magazine has softened or become less radical. We're actually more radical than we used to be, but now there's majority support for the basic issues.

When an issue was new, say, battered women or displaced homemakers or rape or incest or abortion, we went through the necessary steps of demonstrations and speak-outs and press conferences and civil disobedience—whatever it took to bring that issue to the public. Then if it's a real issue, if it's true to people's lives and resonates with people, it will get majority support. Then you start institutionalizing. You start changing the rape laws; you start getting funds for battered women's shelters. You know, it's true that 10 years ago there weren't even words like that. It was just called life.

Each new issue will get active demonstration. For example, pornography is a relatively new issue. So you get marches. It's hard to take a historic look, because it's all so complicated. But, in general, we've had our first wave of suffragist activity and gained for women a legal identity. We had all been legally ownable and not identified by men. Now we'll spend about another century of struggle to get a legal *equality* for all women.

And even after that I'm sure there will be other movements until we have a society, or societies, however diverse they will be, that won't determine your whole future on what you were born. So let's say we are 15 years or so into this century of change. We've already gained majority support. What we're just beginning is institutional change. We have the *idea* of equal pay; but we don't yet *have* equal pay. We have the *idea* of equal parenthood; we don't *have* equal parental leave. We have to make new choices into practical, possible options for most people.

What are the most important issues between women and men now?

The umbrella issue is power. There's an imbalance of power in getting salaries, raising children. The most overwhelming issue currently is children. Young couples may get along very well, until there are children. Then women have two jobs, while men have one. At colleges where I talk, only the young women raise their hands and ask: "How can I combine a career and a family?" Young men never stand up and ask that. We won't be able to solve the problem of balance until men are willing to put in as much time as women for the children.

Now it's: You can go out so long as you don't disturb society. "*You* work it out," the men tell the women. It's putting the burden on the victim. The difference between *Ms.* and other magazines is that we're not saying you should be a superwoman, but that you have to have power to make choices and require men to be more responsive.

How do you see your future?

Ten years from now I hope I'll be writing more about feminist theory to be incorporated into political-theory courses.

You wrote, "Hope is a very unruly emotion" about hope dashed into anger in the McGovern camp. And, "The psychology of despair is a delicate thing" about former New York mayor John Lindsay's precautions to avoid a riot in Harlem the day after the King assassination. You have a philosophical turn of mind. Are you an idealistic writer?

Yes. Concepts—I like to see how things relate to each other. I can't remember what I had for breakfast, but I can remember concepts.

Outrageous Acts is filled with wry, witty views of disastrous situations. Where did you get your sense of humor?

My father loved puns. If you asked him what was on the radio, he'd say a book and a glass. My mother loved a certain kind of satire—Dorothy Parker, Stephen Leacock. Of course, I didn't come from a humor-producing background. But the contradictions of life make you cry or laugh or both. And I'm glad that comics now are into revelation, insight, and recognition rather than hostility and ethnic slurs.

Have you made any special sacrifices for the women's movement?

I have no grounds for complaint. I've sacrificed financial security. The magazine doesn't support me. But I keep all my money from my lecture circuit. And in the past year the book has been making some money. The rest I give away. It's not altruism; I like to see what the money does. The *Ms.* Foundation for Women is the only national women's fund. It supports battered women, women working in coal mines. And every once in a while, you see someone, almost always a writer, who needs a couple of thousand dollars to finish a worthy project. I tell the writer that the money never has to be paid back. "I have faith in you," I say. "And if you ever have money, pass it on." And people do. It's like a chain. I'm not a goody two-shoes, but everyone wants to be considered an individual—to matter in the world in some way. And this is most satisfying for me.

ALAN CUMMING

BY JAMYE WAXMAN
NOVEMBER 2005

How did boys in Scotland talk about sex?

Oh, we used to call erections a bricker 'cause they'd be hard as a brick. If you went for the medical at school, this man would touch your balls, and all the other boys would say, "Be careful not to get a bricker." If you did, they said that the nurse had kept a teaspoon in the freezer and if you got a hard-on she'd go "boing" and bash you on the cock.

And then there was the one where a boy would say, "Do you know the way spunk floats in the bath." And you'd say, "Yeah," and they'd go, "Wanker! Wanker!" But masturbation is good . . . Why is it an insult?

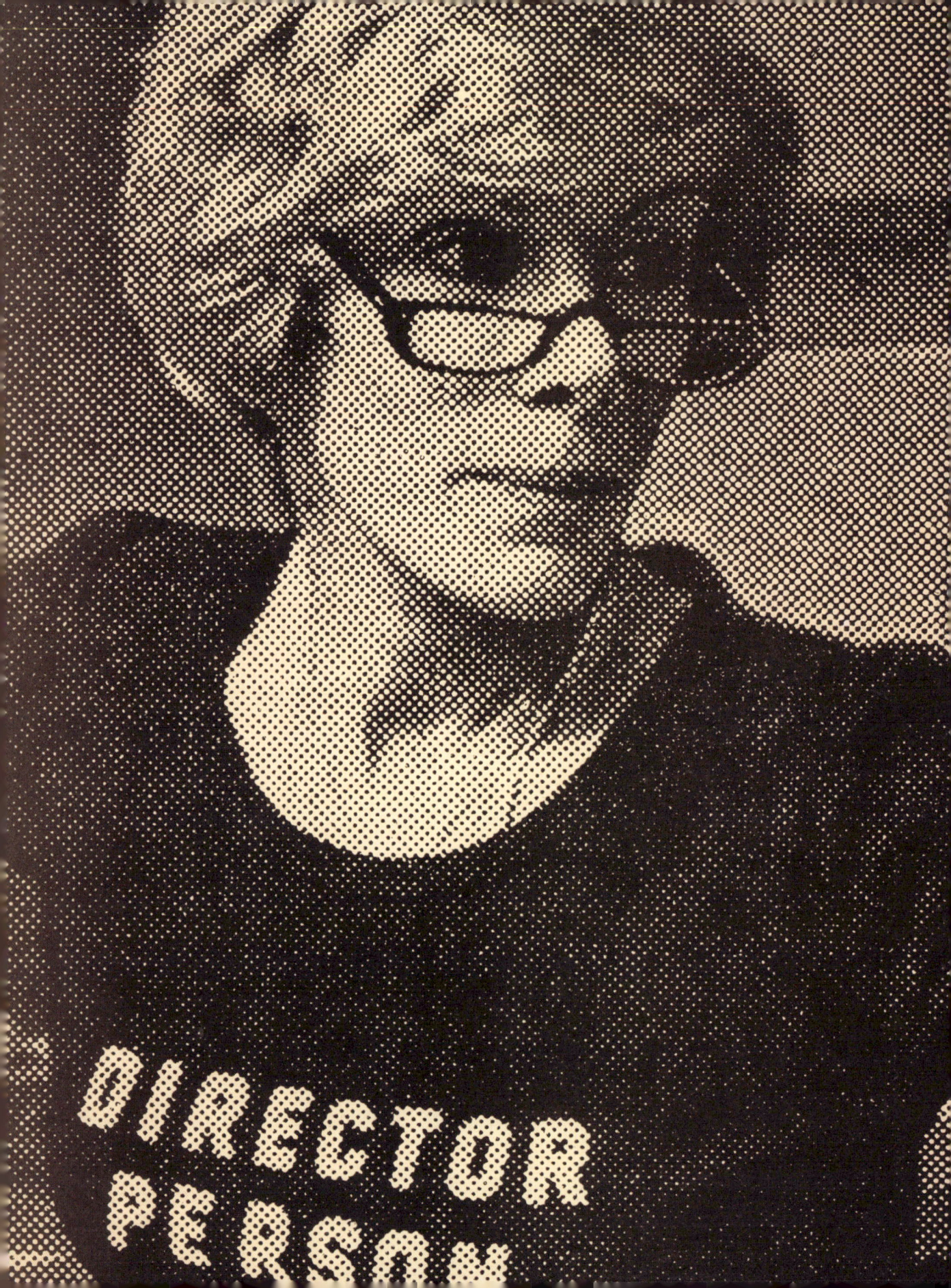

DIRECTOR PERSON

JOAN RIVERS

BY BARBARA CADY
NOVEMBER 1977

As a woman—and as a comedian who uses a lot of material about women—you've obviously given our problems a lot of consideration. Have you figured out what women want?

I know what *I* want. I would like to be very beautiful, very young and very wealthy. And I wouldn't care about being smart, because nobody would wait to see.

Do you think that's what all women want?

It's a very shallow thing to say, but I think so. Some friends and I went to dinner with a reigning sex symbol recently, and for dinner she ordered "the green things." She couldn't remember the name for peas! And her husband—and all the men—said, "Isn't that adorable? Isn't that the cutest thing?" So I tried to impress them and ordered cauliflower, a vegetable with a long name.

She didn't really say "the green things."

I swear to you on my daughter's life. Couldn't remember the name. And the men just tittered and giggled over it. So you tell me. It ain't fair.

But what about people like Gloria Steinem, who keep saying that things are changing?

Oh, look who's talking with her streaked hair and her aviator glasses. Things are changing in a good sense that we're all busy, we're all working, but Gloria Steinem wants to be very attractive. If she really didn't care, her hair would not be gorgeous and she would not be wearing aviator glasses and no bra. She would be in Earth Shoes and a nice sensible sweater, right? And if you want to keep your hair clean, just keep it short—or shave it off, if you really don't care what you look like. I don't care how liberated we are, we all want to look divine.

Is it different for men?

Yes, don't you think? First of all, a man looks better as he gets older, which kills me. Kills me! I find men in their forties and fifties with their faces craggy and their graying hair so sexy I can't begin to tell you. They've already achieved something and they know who they are. That's why when women have affairs with younger men, I say, "O-o-o-o, boring. He's 22. What has he done? Who is he?" But men just look divine right through their sixties. The suits fit well and it's all there—and it's just horrendous.

So despite the women's movement, you insist that things haven't changed.

I wish I could say to you, "Yes, it's all changing, and it doesn't matter what a woman looks like." But it still comes down to standing in the singles bar to see if the guy is going to pick you up. We pretend the game has changed, but it hasn't.

What really upsets me is that when women hit their sexual peak at 35, nobody cares! Because the men are always saying, "Give me a 17-year-old." But then I think of all these young girls that did marry all those distinguished men in their forties and fifties. I have a friend who married a very famous actor in this town 10 years ago when he was 60 and it was wonderful and romantic. Now he's 70, senile, and hard of hearing—and she's hysterical. He's become a nice old man who is having bowel movements and worrying about whether he's taken his prunes. The grand old man falls asleep after dinner and it ain't so much fun. She's taking care of a father, not a husband—and she's stuck with him now. And by the time he kicks—watch, he'll fix her and go at 96—it's too late for her. She'll be a young wife of 73.

If things are as bad for women as you say they are, what's your advice to them?

Look great. I think any lady—and I mean this—if you've got $3, fix the puss and the boobies, fix that hair, work on yourself. It's just all part of life and you can't deny it.

See, I don't understand the whole liberation thing. I never ever thought that I couldn't get where I wanted to get being a woman. And I realize, of course, that in the past there were tremendous limitations. But now, I think, it's a great advantage to be a woman. Four years ago you were hot to be Black, two years ago you were hot to be Puerto Rican—in 1977 it's got to be the obligatory woman. Ladies who shouldn't be in high positions are there only because they're ladies. But that will all equal out, too.

Also the nice thing now for women is that there's not the burden there was on me when I got out of college to get married right away. Now you can be 28 and have a wonderful career and people say, "Good, she's having a terrific life—with or without."

So all your humor about being single for so many years is straight from the heart?

Totally. My mother was hysterical that I wasn't married. I got out of college when I was 20 and was a bridesmaid nine times. And I wasn't successful in the profession of my

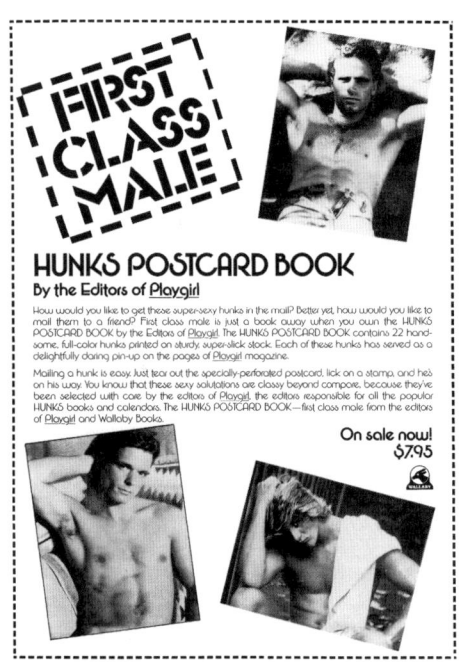

choice. When you are 26 and an office temporary, telling people what you want to be is not cute. But now, you can be a person. You can also sleep with people.

But aren't women still considered whores if they sleep around?

I don't think so, but I'm married. I know I was playing games at 27, always sneaking around.

So what do you think women these days are telling their daughters about having extramarital sex?

"Don't do it!" But I would like my daughter to live with someone for a year before they get married. That would shock my mother, if she ever heard me say that, so I know I've changed. But, also I think that because so much of the attraction is just physical, it's a good thing to get that out of the way to find out if you can live together. 'Cause living together is a whole other thing.

What about sleeping around to get ahead? Is that a dead end in your business?

Yes. All the ladies that I know who have made it have never made it because of that. I think it will get you the little part in the movie or the little job, but I don't think anybody is really going to trust anyone with anything just because you're sleeping with them.

Why do you think there are so few successful women?

Because I think that once they meet the man they like, they just stop. It's very easy to stop, easy to have a child and easy to take care of a house. All the successful women have made it because they couldn't stop. A man is obligated to go on; a woman is not.

Is there anything that's out of bounds for you with regard to sex and humor?

That's what I love to talk about—and make funny. I get very embarrassed, however, in a very beautiful love or sex scene—actually with any intimate, serious thing. So I love it when it's funny, because then you get all your tensions relieved. Of course, it's never funny when it's happening to the two people involved, but sex really is hilarious. Unfortunately, there are too many things that are being shown that are serious that shouldn't be shown.

Sex is getting too explicit for you?

Yes. I like to fantasize about it. I like it when they shut the door after Rhett carries Scarlett O'Hara up the stairs. I was embarrassed—and so was my husband—when I saw *The Sailor [Who Fell from Grace with] the Sea.* I think you've got to crack a joke eventually, because you just don't want to be there. So humor into anything is wonderful.

What about sexual jokes? Do these upset women?

Well, with sex sometimes you're really pushing into areas women don't want to go into. I'll ask a lady—maybe one that's been happily married for 24 years—if she wouldn't like to have an affair with Cary Grant. If he dies as he left the bedroom so he couldn't talk, so nobody would know. Or I'll ask, "Do you think your husband has ever cheated on you?" You find ladies in a certain age group very, very nervous about that.

I also find that a lot of ladies get very upset because I knock what they think is very sacred—the rings, and the coats and the whole Beverly Hills or New York upper class existence. They can't laugh when I tell them, "If your grandmother did not have a tennis racket in her hand when she hit Ellis Island, you should not be playing tennis now. Jews, Italians—anybody suave—you should sit in the shade and hire someone to play for you. Also, if you're a man over 40 in Beverly Hills, you should wear socks." But these silly things hit a little too close sometimes, and women—or men—don't find it amusing.

But what's the response from women when you ask them, for example, if they'd like to have an affair with Cary Grant?

Totally divided. Half the audience will go with it, and the other ladies will go into total shock. Their glasses cloud up. But I always figure that if you've got glasses and you're wearing them on a chain, you're not my group. Or if you've got a corsage and you're proud of it, you're not my group. I think religious ladies, by the way, have no sense of humor. Those kinds of women get me very nervous.

So knowing the type of people who like you, what do you do when you walk out on stage and see a roomful of glasses—on chains—and corsages?
I know I'm going to earn my money that night. And I'll go into airline jokes and a little more on cooking and cleaning. I mean, they got all dressed up and paid to see you, so you always try to hope that they'll like you. But sometimes you just think to yourself, *I've written the last housekeeping joke. There isn't another one in me.*

BY CHARMIAN CARL
FEBRUARY 1994

What men in the entertainment industry do you think have been the most helpful to women?
I think I truly have never stopped to think about it. I couldn't care less. Nobody helps you. Nobody gives you a leg up. Nobody does anything. You do it yourself.

Yet if they have power over you, they can cut you and leave you out in the cold.
So you go off and you do your own thing, just bigger and better. You know what I'm saying? "Go screw yourself." You know you're smarter, you know you can do it better, and you know if this one lets you go, somebody else will give you the money to do your own thing. I mean, men get cut, too. We must never forget, a lot of men are very cut down. Truly, my whole philosophy is about getting the job done and doing it incredibly well. If you have to fight people, you're going to fight people, and everyone's going to be there to second-guess you and say you're wrong. And, that's all part of the business, it's all part of being successful—and looking good at the same time, which you sure do.

Thank you. You don't believe the old saying that an attractive woman can't be taken seriously?
I think that's all the more wonderful, because you just surprise them all the more. That's what I think is wonderful. Surprise, surprise—Dawn Steele, surprise, surprise! All these women. Look at Sherry Lansing, so good-looking. She produced the Glenn Close movie *Fatal Attraction*. She was the head of the studio for awhile. And that's what's so great.

I read an old interview you did with *Playgirl* back in '77. You were talking about sitting next to Robert Vaughn on the plane, and you're both in tie-dyed pantsuits, and you both have Louis Vuitton luggage and gold chains around your necks. You looked at him and said, "Look, we're two old twins." And he moved to another seat.
He moved away. I remember that. "Look, we're twins!"

It's sad, isn't it?
Oh, he had no humor. No humor, that man.

One doesn't get very far without it.
No, what gets you through life is drive, some brains, and a lot of humor.

Sometimes it's hard to laugh, though. What is your secret to survival?
Survival? Just keep going. Just push through it and keep it busy. Busy work eventually makes it into something for you. Work and take everything.

BEASTIE BOYS
BY IAIN BLAIR
NOVEMBER 1987

You've had a lot of bad press. Is it justified?
MCA: No, it's fucking not.
MIKE D.: The truth is we're quiet, laid-back guys who like to stay at home and listen to Barry Manilow. All the stuff they print about us is a big lie.
AD-ROCK: Actually, it's all true.

You've been accused of being grossly sexist.
MIKE D.: 'Cause of the dancing girls in the fucking cages, right? Well, that's bullshit, man. Yeah, it was our idea, but the girls up there like it. We're not degrading and humiliating women. What do you think? That we whip 'em and force 'em to dance every night?
MCA: We're not sexist, 'cause we like to insult everyone and everything. For feminists to think they're singled out is very selfish on their part.

Where did the idea for the giant dick come from?
MIKE D.: They asked us what we wanted onstage, and we said a giant dick, a giant six-pack, and a giant cage with a dancing girl in it. We figured that'd be a pretty decent party.
MCA: It was a joke. Trouble is, most promoters just

don't get it. The guy in Kentucky banned it, but he was a pussy. He didn't say, "Your dick is banned." He just said, "The inflated prop will not be permitted." What a dickhead—it's hydraulic. He didn't know shit.

Has success spoiled you?

MIKE D.: Nah, we're still the same, it's just that we have to work a lot harder now. We used to have a lot of fun, not really work that much, and not have any money. Now we've gotta work our balls off, we're making tons of money—but we're too busy and tired to spend it. Ironic, isn't it?

MCA: The main difference is we used to stand on street corners and yell at girls. Now we drive around in limos and yell at 'em. It's more effective, 'cause everyone's more offended and we have a better time.

JANE FONDA

BY CELESTE FREMON

APRIL 1979

You get scared? Still?

Oh, I always do. I always think I'm in the wrong place, I shouldn't be in the film, they should get another actress, I'm not the right person for the part.

I remember, about a week before we started shooting *Klute*, I said to Alan Pakula, "You know, seriously, Alan. I just don't think I can do it." While I was doing the research, I would hang out at after-hours clubs with these hookers. The pimps would come around, and nobody ever tried to pick me up, to get me to be one of their girls or anything. I said to Alan, "I'm just not right for it, I mean, if nobody has propositioned me, I clearly just don't have what it takes." The same was true with *Julia.* I had nightmares.

What's your worst fear?

That I'm not good enough. I always see another actress in the part. It's better now than it used to be because I'm beginning to recognize what I can do well.

Do you consider yourself a beautiful woman?

No. I'm photogenic. A very good cameraman can make me look a lot better than I deserve. I can be ugly as hell—this morning, for example. Put it this way—when I'm healthy and happy, I'm a pretty woman. I'm not a beautiful woman. And I don't care very much. If a movie part requires my being very pretty, I will work hard to be pretty. And, frankly,

at my age, when you're doing a movie where you're supposed to look good, there are a lot of tricks. Things bouncing light off to get rid of this, get rid of that. But if a movie requires me not to be that way, I'm not going to try to pretty myself up. I just take the makeup off and be what I am. There's a thing I want to do for television that requires me to be extremely homely, so I'll just take my false tooth out—this one's false.

You've really been a genuine "sex symbol." Do you remember how you thought of yourself then?

When I was first active, a lot of women would ask, "How did you feel about being Barbarella? What do you think of the women's movement?" But I never internalized the knowledge of what I had done to myself. It wasn't till I met Tom that I began to remember coming to Hollywood for my first screen test and being told that I had to wear falsies, being told that my hair wasn't blond enough, and being told that I should have my jaw broken and these teeth removed so that my cheeks would sink in. You know, high cheekbones. And how I went along with it for fifteen years. You can't help but feel that, well, if this is what people like but it's not really me, then they can't really like me when the falsies are off and the hair is off and the eyelashes are off. So it's a feeling of terrible alienation—from yourself.

I know the feeling. You think: *If that's what they're responding to, God help me if they ever really . . .*

. . . saw me . . . You know, this doesn't feel like an interview, it feels like just talking to a pal. And that worries me. I mean, there've been so many times when I've been stabbed in the heart.

Doesn't that drive you nuts? You must be hassled constantly.

Well, not bad hassles. I mean, people talk to me a lot and ask me for my autograph, but they don't bother me very much. People actually claw Redford. Women standing next to their husbands will claw at him. I've just been amazed watching this scene of us when we're filming at the casino. Thank God it just doesn't happen to me.

Why?

I think part of it has to do with the way you look and carry yourself. If you're dressed to attract attention, you're going to get more. If your vibe says, "Hey, man, respect my being," people tend to be pretty cool.

How would you define sexuality? What attracts you in a man?

When I think how my answer to that question has changed in the last eight to ten years! I find that I'm not

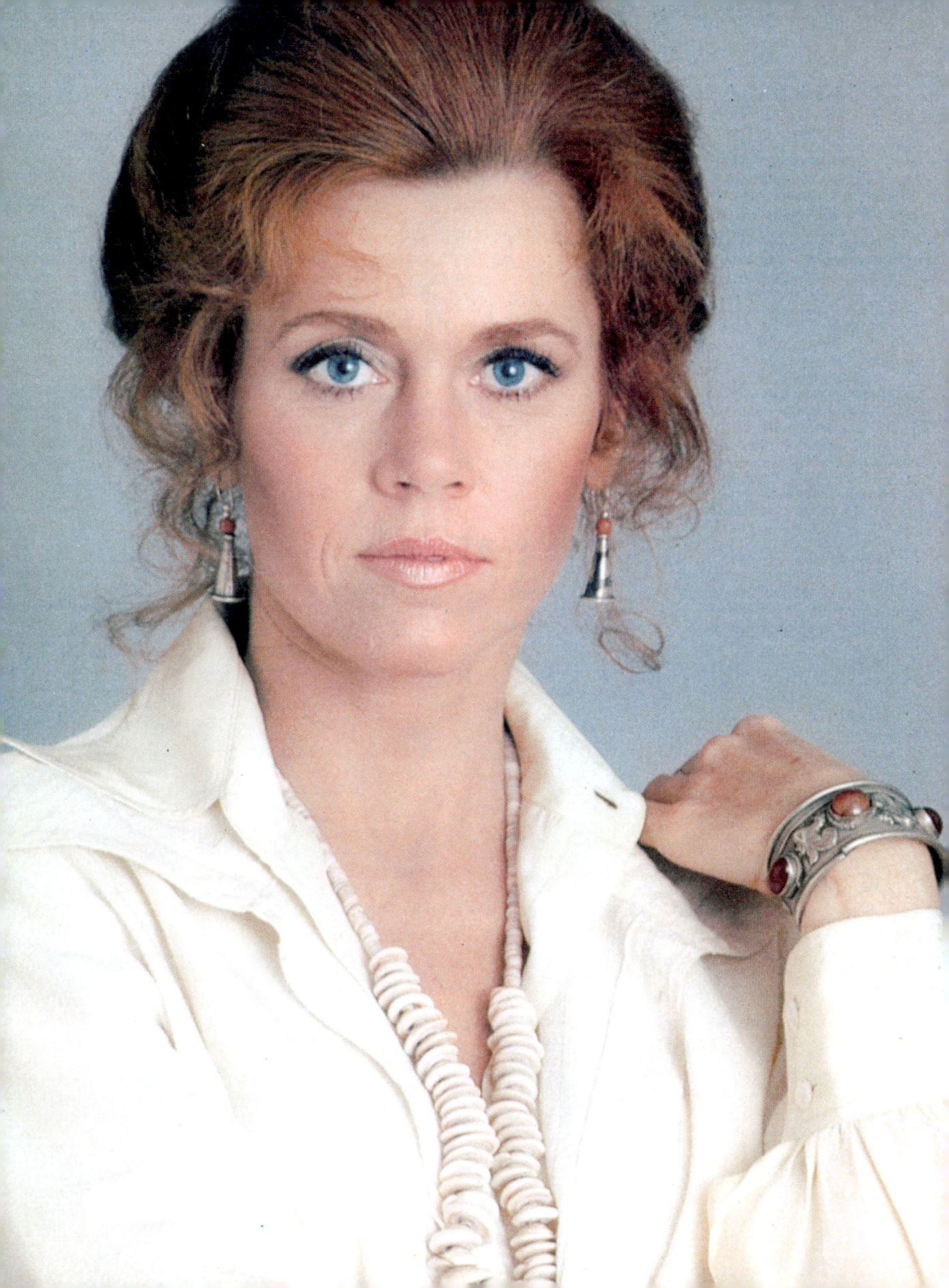

attracted anymore to men whose interests I don't share. When you share interests and when a man obviously has an inventive mind and a great deal of concentration. Did you ever read *Stranger in a Strange Land*? Well, each of the women who had a relationship with the main character said that what it was about him that made him so special was his ability to concentrate. It's like everything in the whole world is concentrated on this moment.

Do you believe in monogamy?
Monogamy is what makes me happy.

Did you go through a period of sexual experimentation that gave you the freedom, in a sense, to be monogamous?
Probably not in the way that you mean it, but I was a bachelor woman for a whole lot of my life and I didn't like it, and I don't think liberation is the same as playing around sexually.

If that's what it's not, what is liberation?
Liberation is a situation in which the real, full, human, positive potential is unleashed. That happens when you are stable and wholeheartedly involved in a happy relationship with a person whom you respect and care about. Sleeping around has to do with being neurotic, has to do with escapism, has to do with decadence. It has nothing to do with human nature. Human nature is survival; sleeping around has nothing to do with survival. Human nature has to do with being happy and being secure; sleeping around has nothing to do with being secure. There's no way you can be secure sleeping around because all you can think about is, *Whom do I love? Who loves me? Why? What's important?* There's no foundation anymore. It all goes out the window.

A lot of the women I used to know are dead; they're just dead; they killed themselves or they were murdered. It may sound glib but it's absolutely true. They were the shining stars of the sexual movement, the sexual revolution, because of their beauty and because of their youth. One of them was married to the son of a very wealthy, very well-known man. I knew her quite well. She died of an overdose, was left to die by her husband in the apartment. I won't give you the name—I might get sued by the family. Being sexy, being hip, killed them.

I don't know if it's a reaction to your Vadim/Barbarella days or it's your upbringing coming through but you still seem to have a strong puritanical streak.
Puritanical may have a negative connotation to it but I consider it healthy. For example, when jokes were going around Hollywood about Roman Polanski and that thirteen-year-old girl, people were laughing and saying thirteen is really

old. I don't even know what the jokes were. I just wanted to pretend that I didn't have anything to do with this industry. I found it shocking and extremely disturbing. And I would never go to a place like Studio 54. It just rubs against every puritanical fiber in my body. I can just feel the drugs there.

BY CELESTE FREMON
OCTOBER 1985

Actually, looking at the quotes that have been attributed to you from the time you were 18, there are some doozies. Isn't it difficult to find that so much of what you've said over the years has been recorded for posterity?
Oh, God! It's even worse when you're the child of a celebrity. It means that very early on [in life], you're quoted. Your growing-up process get's played out in the press. I always believe in looking at the positive side of it, though. People can look and see that one can make mistakes and say foolish things, and learn from one's mistakes and grow up—and that it doesn't necessarily destroy your life.

Your early anti-war quotes are well known, but there was a certain widely quoted column of Hedda Hopper's, as well.
[Groans] When I said, "Marriage is obsolete."

What would you say to that 21-year-old girl now, if you could, to make her life a little easier.
[Sighs] Probably not much. There are certain things that just have to play themselves out. I was rebelling. I mean, this was a young girl whose father had been married five times, whose friends' parents had not stayed married, whose girlfriends who'd gotten married were no longer married, and for whom there had been very little evidence that marriage leads to happiness or permanency. And because she's imaginative and independent and spunky she's turning it into a whole philosophy. And she'll outgrow it. She did.

Take my daughter. I won't even say what some of her little rebellions are. I witness them and I think to myself, *I know that some parents would get absolutely furious and jump up and down and scream and try to force some philosophy down her throat. But I know she's no fool. She's like I was, and she'll overcome it.*

You have said in the past that usually you are terrified before you begin a film. Is that still true?
Oh, I always get scared. I hope I always do. When you

stop being nervous then you might as well telephone it in because then you don't have any stake in it. You gotta stay hungry. My best work is done when I'm scared to death.

The same is true of *The Morning After*. I'm absolutely scared to death. It's very hard to play a good drunk. And I like being challenged that way. I like overcoming my fears.

How are you researching your new character?

I'm looking for her. I'm going to start hanging out in bars. I'm looking for mannerisms. I'm looking for the kind of drunk that she is. I've talked to a lot of friends of mine who are ex-alcoholics. I'm going to go to meetings. This character's a loser. She's a riot. She's in trouble. [Pause] I really like her a lot. But I'm going to have to put myself inside her skin, and that's hard.

How easy is it going to be for Jane Fonda to hang out in bars and at AA meetings?

I'll put on a disguise.

Does that work? I saw Margot Kidder do that one time and everybody around just said, "Hey, there's Margot Kidder in a weird wig!"

I haven't done it in a long time. The last time I did that kind of research was when I researched *Klute*, and this is a somewhat similar kind of movie. Before *Klute* the last film I had done was *Barbarella*. And for *Klute* I had my hair totally changed. My hair was short instead of long and I looked like a different person. I hung out with call girls, madams, streetwalkers, pimps, all kinds of prostitutes and drug pushers. It was really the underbelly of New York City. I did it through contacts that had been set up for me by the studio, and no one but my contacts knew who I was—no one!

Were you ever scared?

I never get scared. I'm a chameleon. But now, even my voice is so recognizable because of the record, it may be a problem. It's going to be a lot harder for me to become a chameleon. But emotionally, I always feel that I fit in anywhere—absolutely anywhere.

I can do it incredibly easily. I think one of the things about actors is that we don't have any tremendously strong identities. We may have strong beliefs but we don't have strong identities, so it's very easy for us to take on colors of people. It's why we're so comfortable acting—and why I'm always a little bit off kilter when I'm not acting. I mean, I'm in seventh heaven now because I know who I'm trying to become. I have a focus. I'm becoming this person. Until I know what my next person is to become, I'm just me. And I have a little bit of a vacillating identity problem.

JOAN COLLINS
BY LARRY GROBEL
SEPTEMBER 1985

Do you feel that you're in the forefront of liberated women in the eighties today?

Well, I wouldn't say I was in the forefront. I'm not a dedicated feminist in that way. What I do, hopefully, is to let women see that you're not washed up at 40, and that you haven't lost your brains or your appeal because you've reached those big milestone birthdays, and that you can also be attractive and able to think. And also, that you can have your children and let them go off to college, or whatever, and then get involved in another job. I think that's what I tried to do in posing for *Playboy:* to give a lot of women hope.

What was the reaction to that, and how do you feel about it?

The reaction was 100 percent positive, totally. I was absolutely amazed. I was terrified before it came out. I called Aaron Spelling [executive producer of *Dynasty*] and said, "Aaron, I think I've just wrecked my career." I said, "Please don't fire me when you see these pictures," because, you know, I was a bit frightened of the Middle America backlash.

But what happened was just the opposite. I mean, even my father, my son at boarding school, my daughter at college, my friends, everybody liked it. A lot of women wrote to me and said that I had become a heroine, and that what I had done was extremely brave and had opened the door for yet another step against the negative view of aging that is so prevalent in our society.

So you struck a blow for womanhood?

I think so. I felt that in some small way I was taking a step for our sisterhood.

Could you talk about your belief that less is more in the sense that you did not appear in full-frontal nudity in *Playboy*? You did it rather tastefully because you believe that by showing less, you are actually leaving more to the imagination.

Yes, I think it's much more attractive to do that. It happened on the beaches in San Tropez where 80 percent of the women of all ages walk around topless. Sitting in this little beach bistro, I observed the attitude of the men toward the women who were topless, and the attitude of the men toward the girls and the women who were either wearing bikini tops or halters. They were much more interested in the ones who were covered up—much more. OK, they'd take a look at the bare boobs, they'd seen it, so what? But the ones that they hadn't seen they were much more interested in. And I thought then, *Well, that's the male animal for you. He might think that he wants to see it all, but it's better that you don't show him all.*

How strong a woman are you? Do you feel that you are strong in relationships, in your economic situation, managing yourself, agenting yourself, looking out for your career?

I'm pretty strong. I value my own opinion now. I listen to—as Shirley MacLaine said the other day—my inner voice. Probably my least effective area is relationships. I tend to be slightly wimpish in those, I would say. I come on a bit stronger than I really am, possibly because thinking about those early years of people always telling me what to do, I feel that if I'm going to do what I want to do, I have to overassert myself. But I'm getting much better.

I realized how strong I was when my daughter had her terrible accident. I was told that she was going to die, or be a vegetable for life, and I refused to believe that. And then I realized that I was really pretty strong, and I think strength's very important. I think if you don't have strength, then life basically is very tough. That's another thing you don't learn in school—life is tough and life is not fair. And I heard that a lot in the hospital, people always saying to me, "Life isn't fair." We see that all the time, and I realize that no, life is not fair. Why should I have all this success? I mean, there are probably people out there who deserve it a lot more than I do. [Pauses] Not really.

Who were the great romances in your life?

The great romances? Whichever one is going on at the time, darling.

What do you look for in a man?

Obviously, physical attraction is very important. That's the first thing that one is attracted to and sees, the physical package. But then, sense of humor and mutual interests, and a shared liking of the same things. I like very much to go out a lot and I like to stay in a lot and do very family-oriented things. And, you know, just shlep around. I want to be with somebody who's amenable to that, who likes, say, going out to San Francisco and six parties one weekend, and the following weekend staying home and being a hermit. And I think it's necessary to be able to talk and communicate, to be able to talk about everything—not to have secrets.

I don't want to be with somebody that I have secrets with, or hide things from, or lie. I don't want any of that.

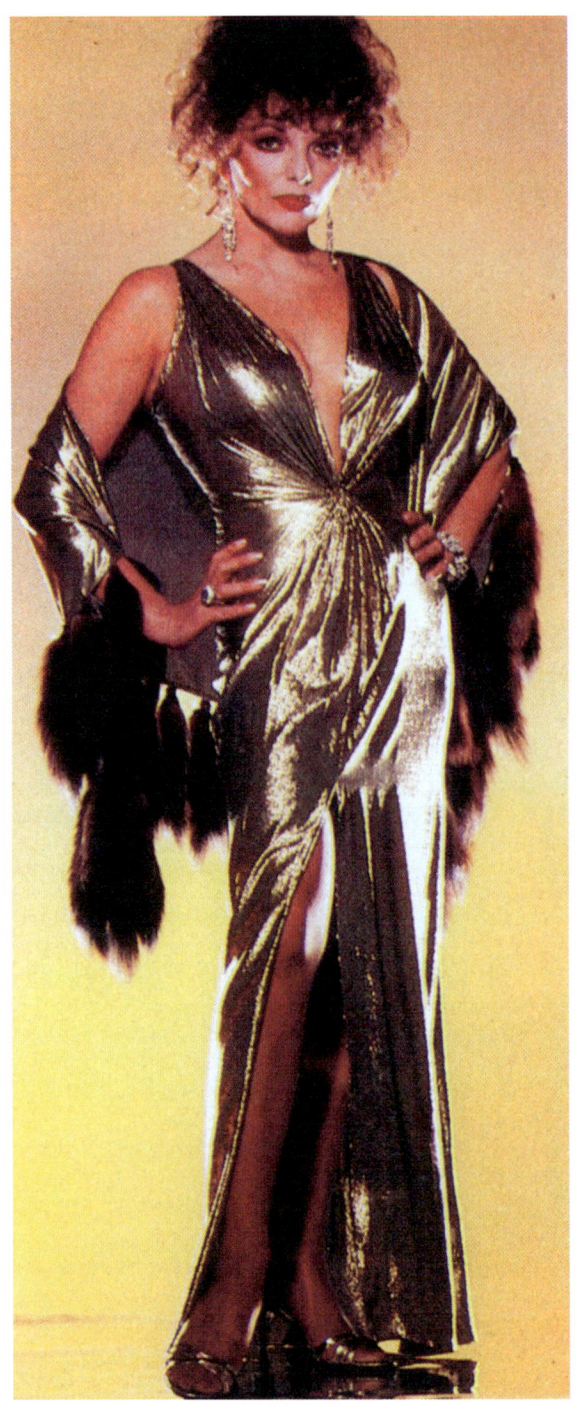

And obviously, fidelity is important in a relationship.

Your current boyfriend, Peter Holm, is 37. Are you more attracted to younger men at this time in your life?

Oh no. I think the most attractive movie star is Sean Connery. And he is older than me. Kris Kristofferson, Robert Redford, Paul Newman—no, I think that there are some very attractive men around my own age. At the time when I was going through my dating, from the time that I broke up with Ron and the time that I met Peter, the men that I came into contact with, or met at parties, or people introduced me to, were all quite a bit younger than me. So this sort of happened that way.

SYLVESTER STALLONE

BY HENRY SCHIPPER
July 1981

How important is sex in a relationship?
Of course, sex is very important, but more important than the actual act of sex is the threat of a sexual encounter at any unexpected moment, the air constantly being permeated with sexual "vibrations." The fact that the act is not consummated fifteen times a day is secondary, but the sex appeal is always there.

Sex appeal is something that can be kept alive for fifty years. Sexual encounters, as do all things, tend to fade in time, more or less hit a normal pattern. In the beginning people are hanging from the doors and chandeliers, piling into the trunk of their Volvos. You know, "Hey, let's go make it in an abandoned elevator shaft tonight." But then it gets a little serious, and one has to move on to serious living. I believe that one tempers oneself. Exhaustion sets in, problems of everyday life. The relationship becomes more mature, but from that maturity there stems an intelligence. And in that intelligence comes what I would call sexual attractiveness. You click into, you might say, seducing each other's minds, and that is the most erotic of all. That is the greatest turn-on, the mental turn-on. That's what keeps men more aroused than any plastic contraption, any movie, any skin magazine, anything. To me, the mental arousal is Vesuvian. It's the most explosive kind of arousal.

Have you ever been totally orgasmically satisfied? You know, the black-out orgasm?
Yeah, that happens. But let's face it, if it happened too often, I think one's brain would fry right in the shell.

But you've had experiences that have been totally—
Yeah, black-outish. What is the word, dare I say it—religious? You know, a mystical aura, feeling like I was in Camelot.

Did that have anything to do with love?
Yes, absolutely. That's love. And it's strange, you can fall in love with a person for twenty-five minutes, you really can. I mean desperately, passionately, hopelessly in love, and then during the thirtieth minute, the love affair's over. No pains, no hurts, no guilts, no sense of abuse. It's just that certain things seem to have a time period, a life expectancy. So be it. It's hard for some people to comprehend that. But there's a difference between getting laid and really having love made to you. When you have love made to you, and that person really digs you, loves you, is all consumed by you, that's wonderful. But it may only last one night.

Do you remember the first time you got laid?
Yeah, I do. It was in a Corvair. It was a traumatic experience because the girl was going out with the toughest guy in the school, one of those kids that weigh about 285 pounds at birth. We had just finished, and then a flashlight hit me, and it was him. He says, "You and I have something to settle." So I had to get out of the car naked and get into a punch-out with this guy. I was so scared, and so embarrassed, from being naked that I was doin' great, until the police took us away. And, man, it's very hard to explain that to your mother—"Where are your clothes?" "Well, it was a little warm tonight, I thought I'd dress lightly, Ma." After that, I figured, hey, sex is really exciting.

Really, if I didn't look at it with a sense of humor I'd be Freudian today.

You have a reputation of taking your characters home with you. If you're really into a role, does it ever affect the way you make love?
It does. It certainly does. Absolutely. Specifically, with Johnny Kovak [from *F.I.S.T.*], the character was so consumed with his problems that sex was almost an intrusion, you might say, into the world of unionism and men. When I was doing *Rocky*, sex was always very, very good; it was kind of like sensitive time, very sensitive. With *Paradise Alley*, it was, you know, sneak attack. [Laughs] "Get it when you can. Hey, take it or leave it, baby." Really, it was gross. I didn't particularly like that character. He was extremely crude, and it affected my lovemaking terribly. He was doin' the world a favor by taking his clothes off. My wife was happy to see that fellow bite the dust.

Rocky must have been her favorite.
She loves *Rocky*. If she had one wish, I would walk around with boxing gloves on for the rest of my life.

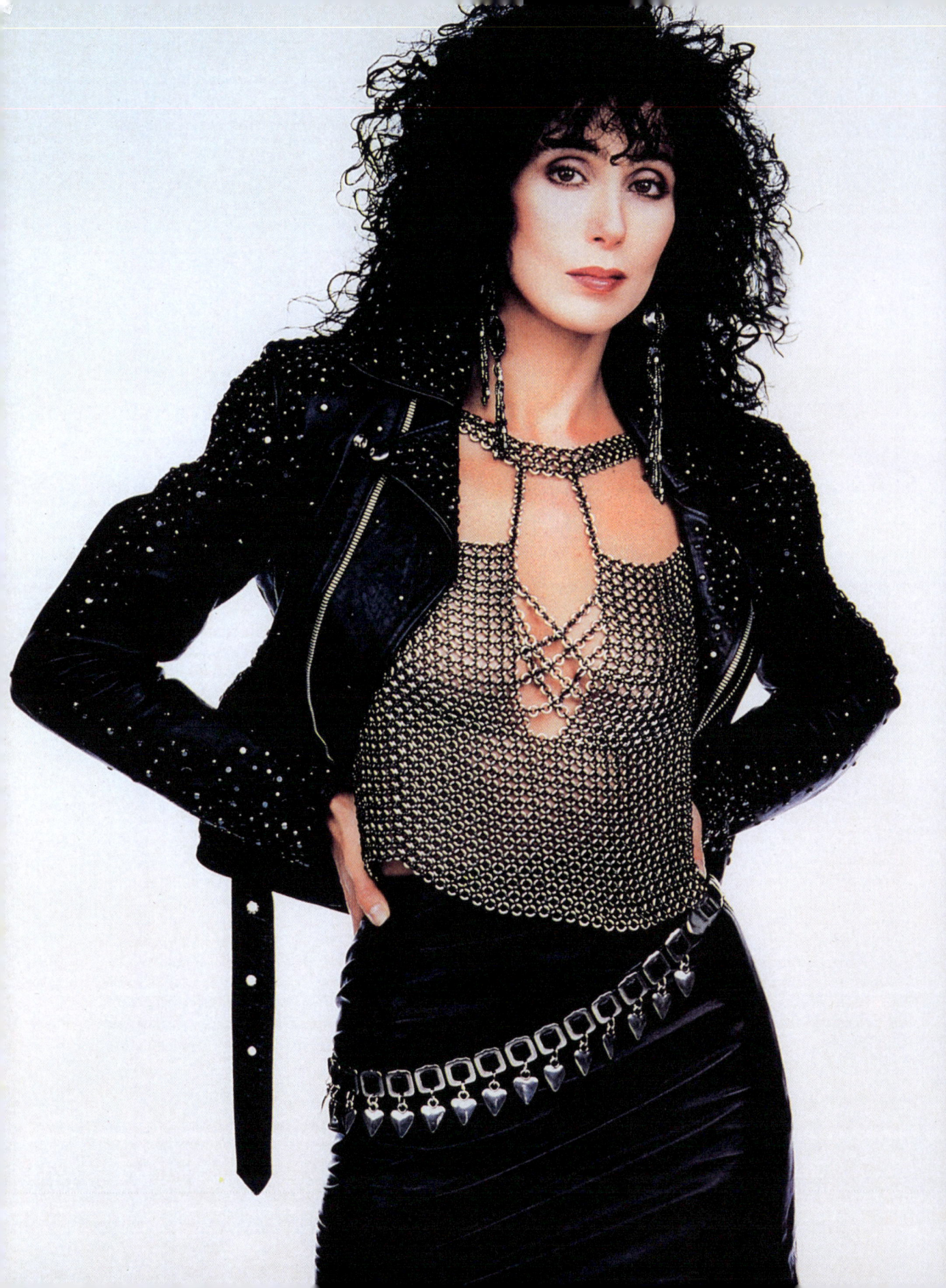

CHER

BY IAIN BLAIR
JULY 1988

You seem to be pretty tough and demanding.

Hey, you can't afford to be soft, 'cause this business eats its young. A man is admired for being tough, but if you're a woman, you're a bitch. And if you're sweet, they walk all over you, so I'd rather be a bitch. Actually, I'm real soft too, but almost nobody sees that side of me.

What about your boyfriend, Robert Camilletti?

Oh, he sees both sides. He's only 23, but he's real understanding and very protective of me. We've been together since my fortieth birthday, and he's a very calming, peaceful influence on me.

There's been a lot of gossip about you and younger men.

Yeah, but what's the big deal? I like to play, and go dancing and to rock-and-roll shows, and most older men aren't interested. They're boring old farts who fall asleep after a hard day at the office. I don't want that.

Will you ever marry again?

Never. I shouldn't say that 'cause it'll probably be the next thing I do. But having been married twice now, I don't think so. I have a very rebellious nature, and I'm afraid the moment I was married, I'd leave.

You look better than a lot of twenty-year-olds. What's your secret?

Hey, I keep expecting it all to fall to shit, and when it does I'll have it lifted or whatever. Basically I don't do drugs, I eat well, and I work out, but this is the worst shape I've been in years. It gets harder as you get older.

You're a bigger star in 1988 than ever. Are you surprised?

Oh, yeah! You know, sometimes I feel like an old hooker. Stay around long enough and people start to respect you.

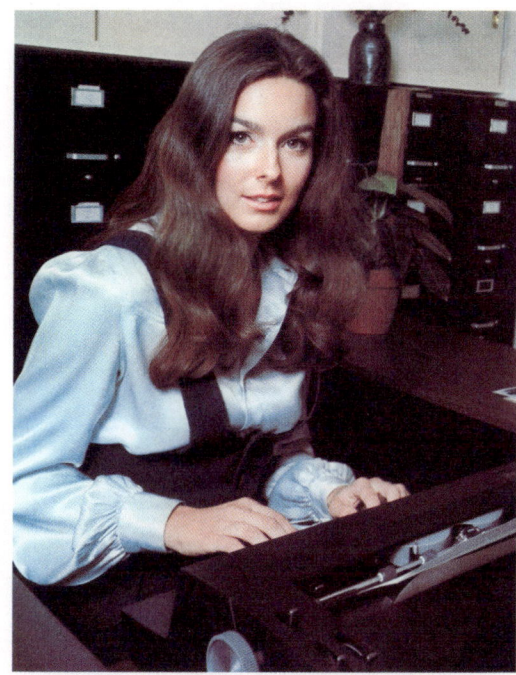

What Kind of Woman Reads Playgirl?

MARGARET CHO

BY COLLEEN KANE
AUGUST 2007

Are you a fan of porn for women?

I think it's really great. All women are interested in sex, and I think it's a perfect thing. I'm also on the board of directors for Good Vibrations, one of the founders of that whole [sex toy] business catering to women. We need to be able to take control of our sexuality and be able to feel good, be empowered that way.

Do you get lots of sex toys from them?

Well, they give me a lot. And I'm sort of a purist, like I only like the Hitachi Magic Wand . . . I tend to be monogamous in terms of sex toys.

Female ejaculation: friend or foe?

To me it's, I'm drinking a lot of water, and I'm gonna do it someday. The depictions I've seen of it seem ridiculous, like, oh no, they can't do that, there's a hose somewhere, there's a trick. But it's possible, I suppose.

CENTER-FOLDS

This is a curation of some of our best centerfolds,
which have been a "staple"
of the magazine's legacy since its inception.

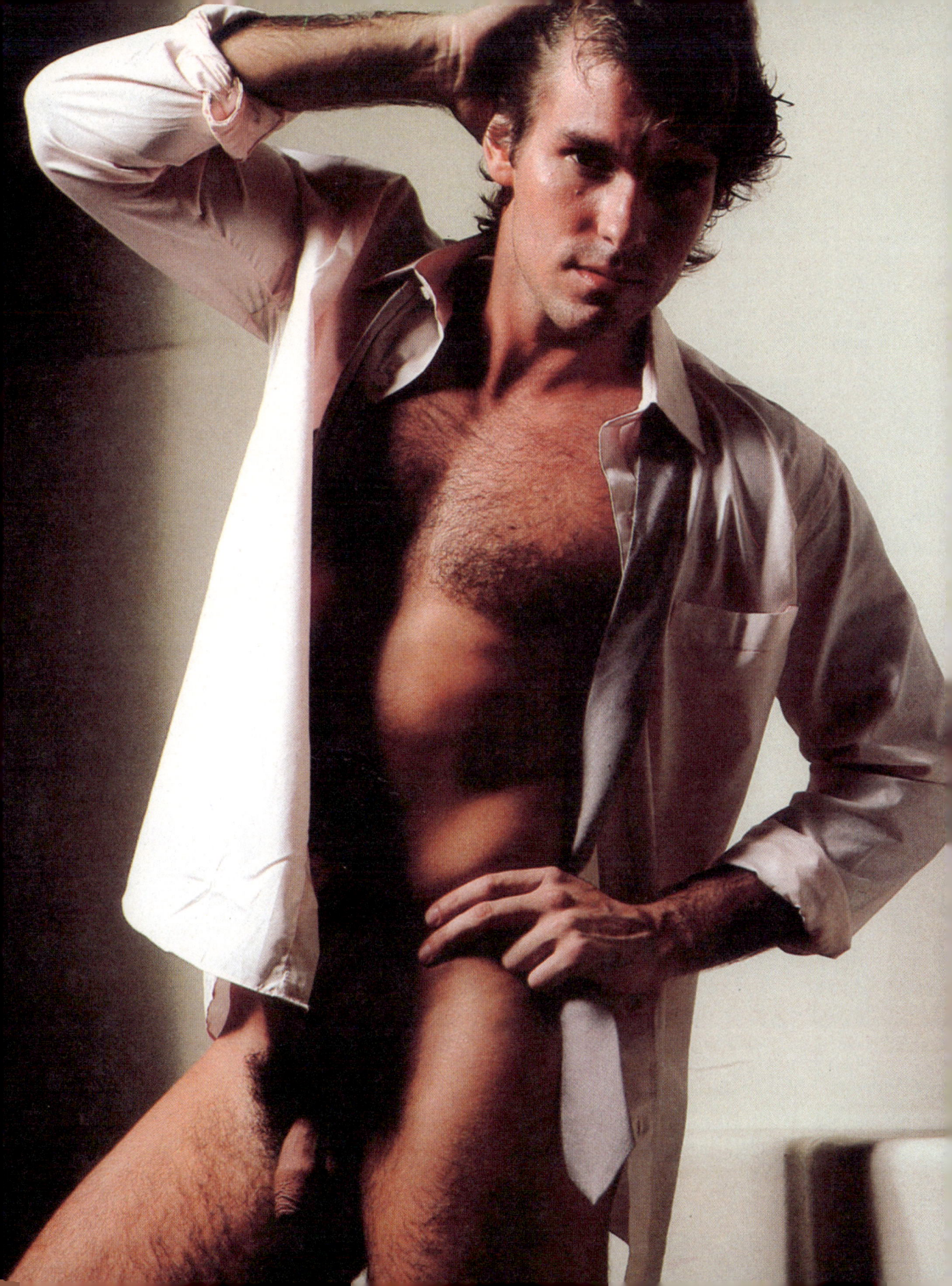

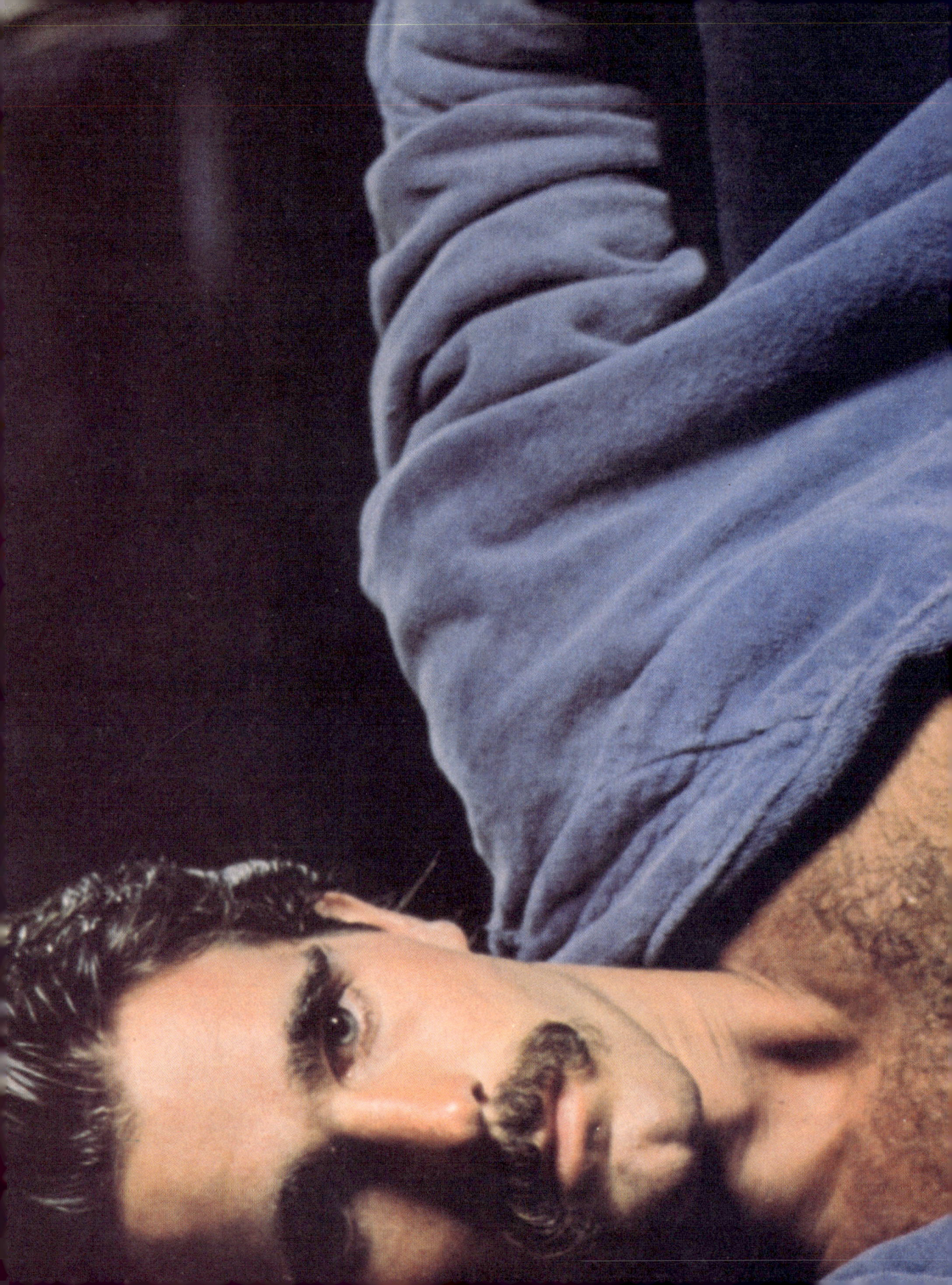

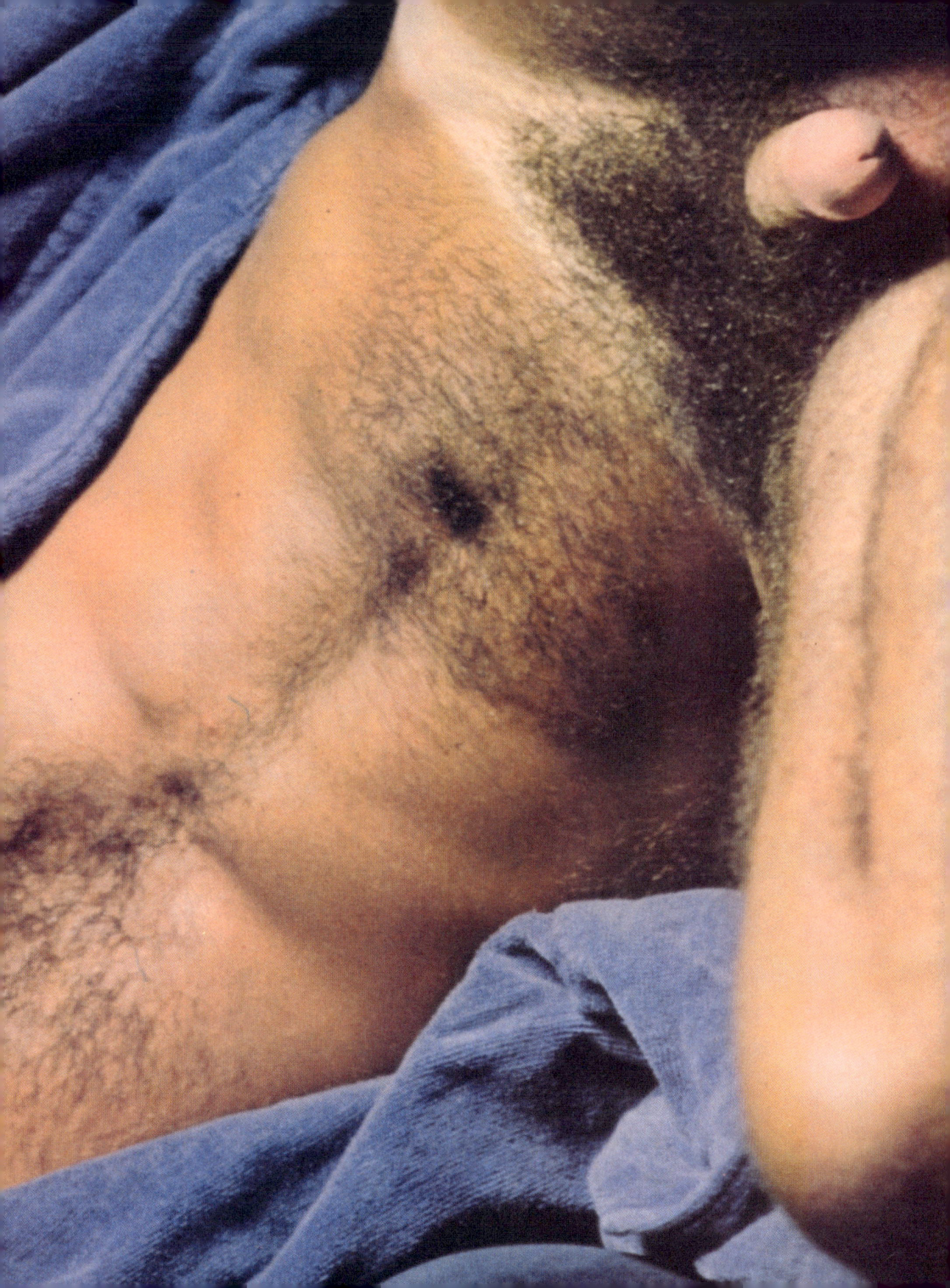

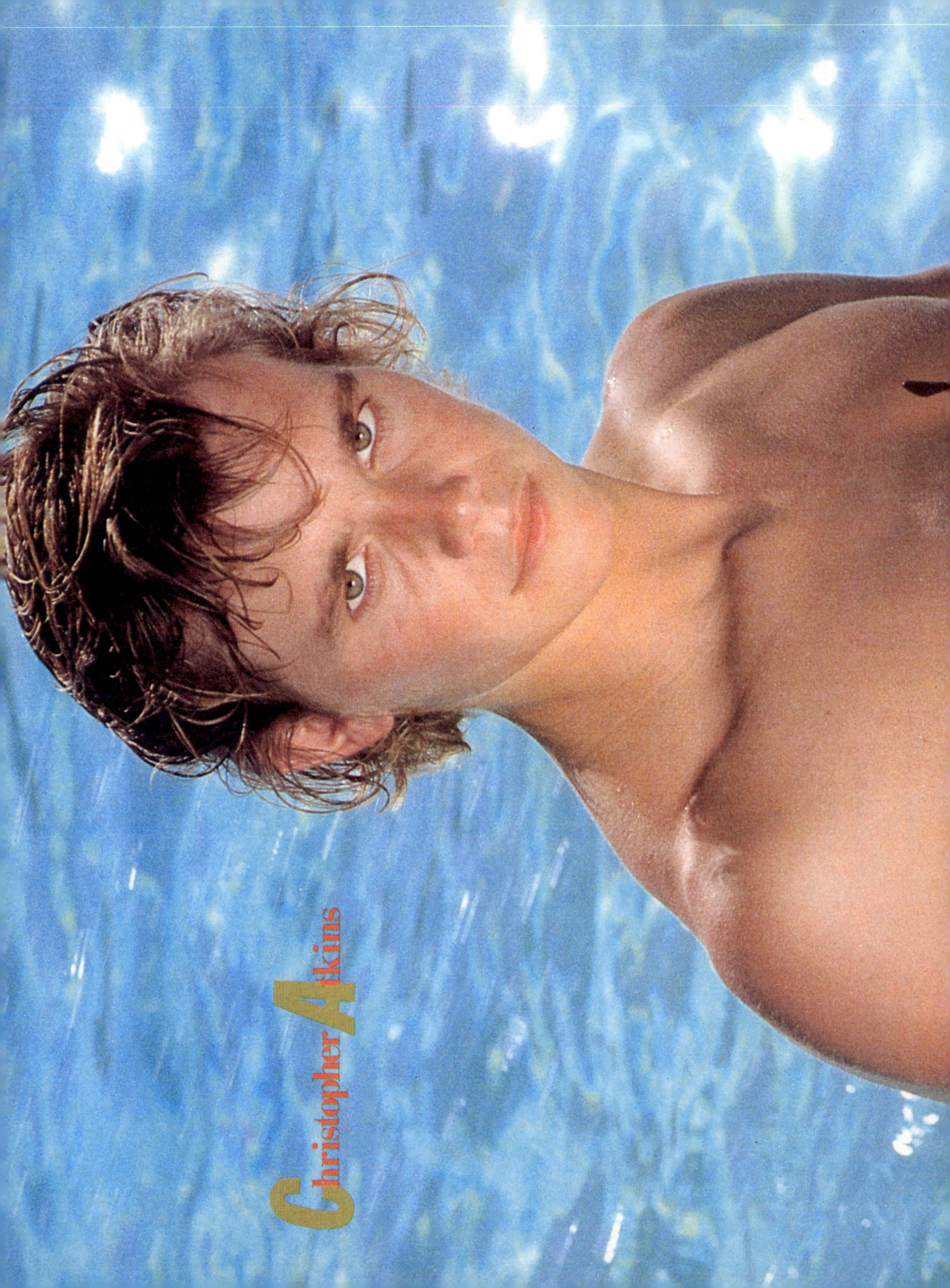

Christopher Atkins

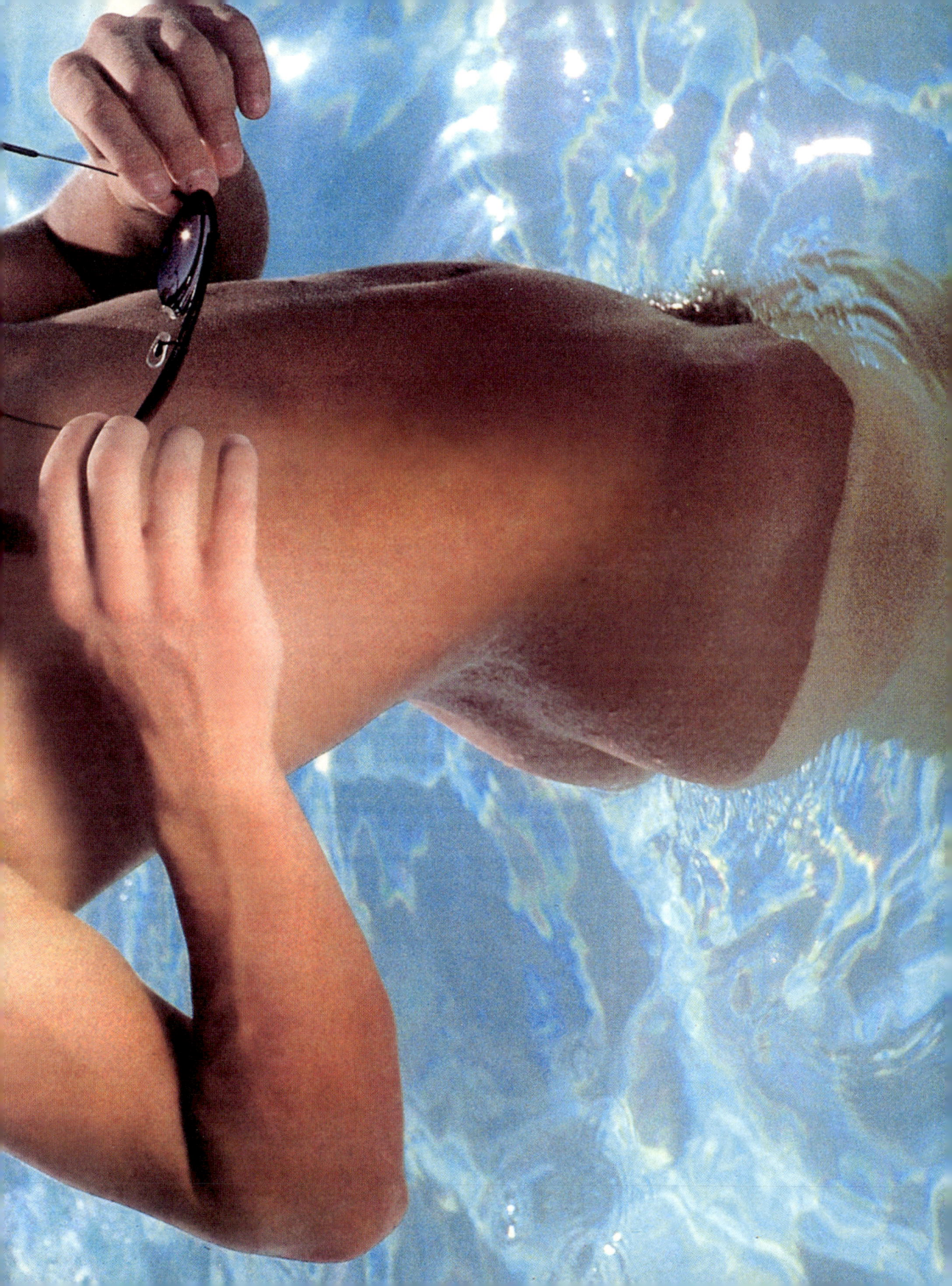

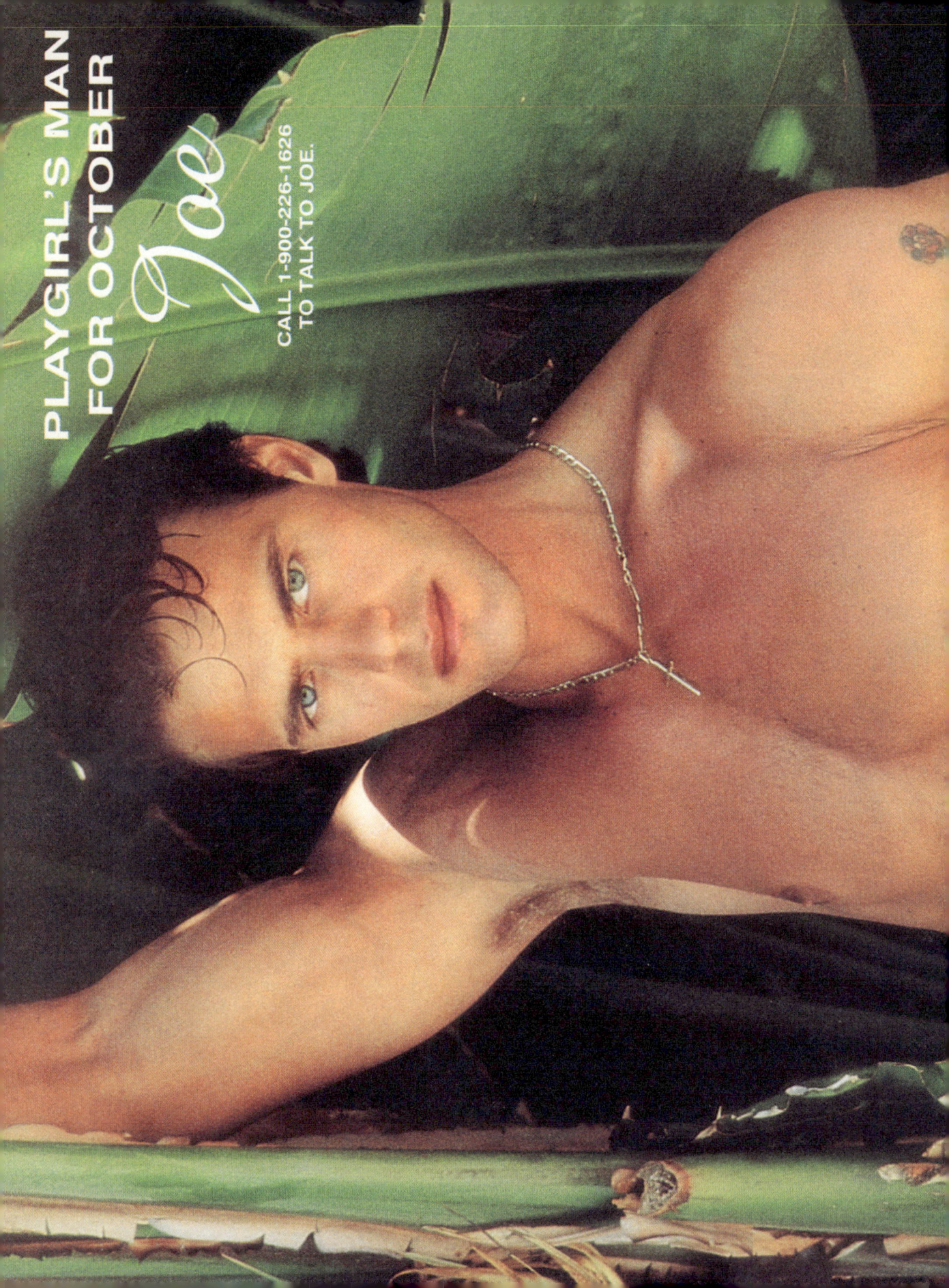

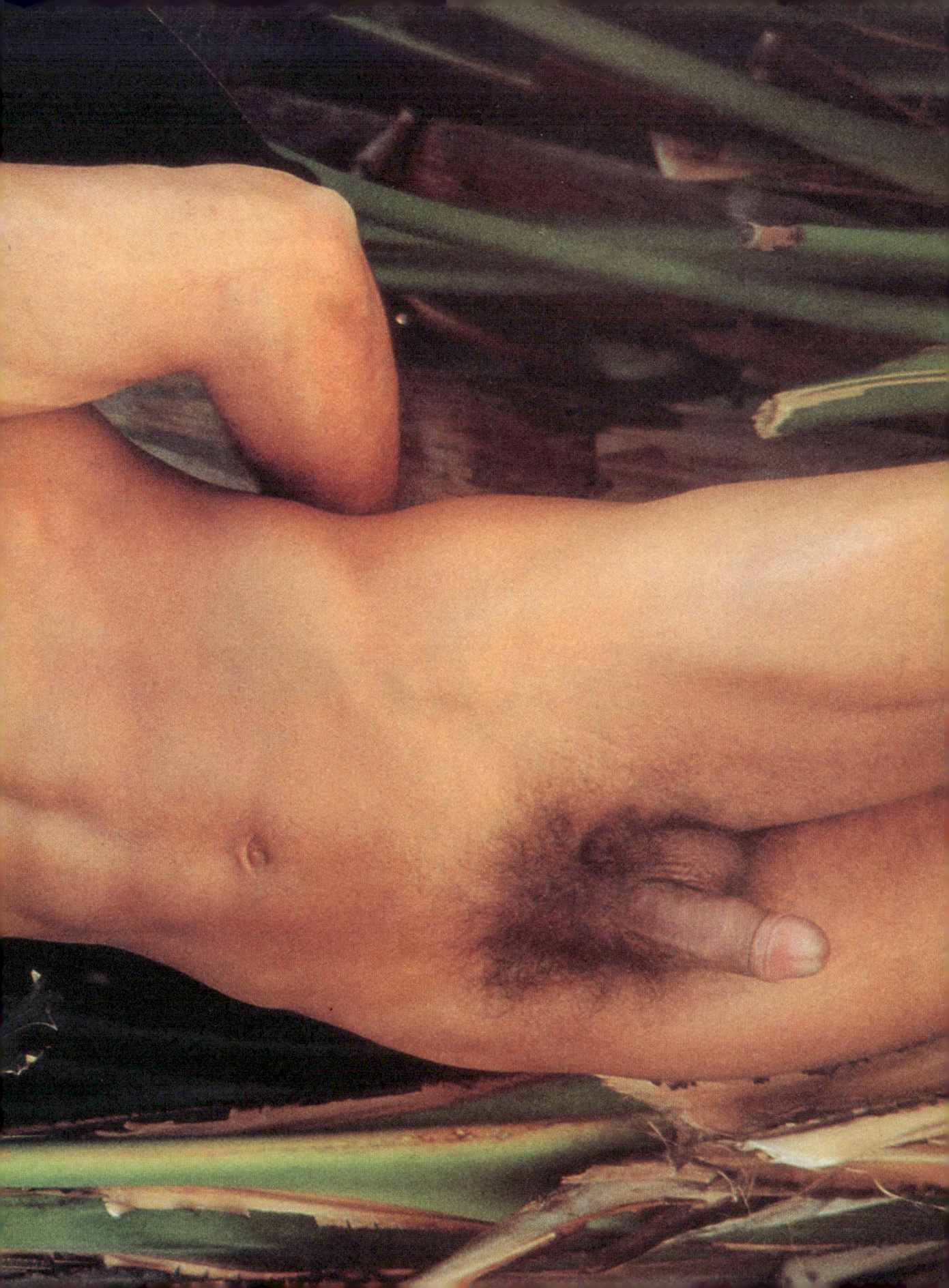

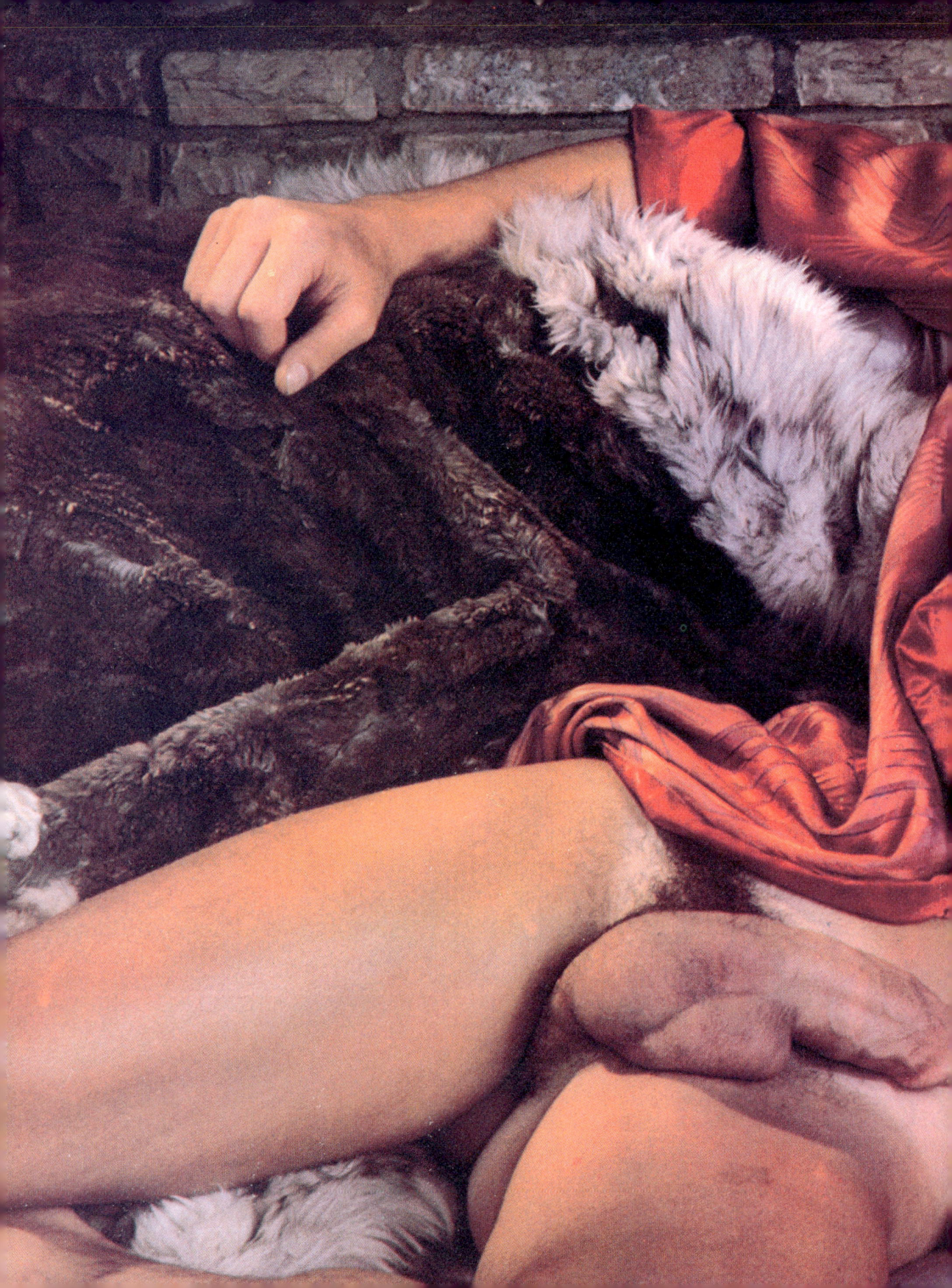

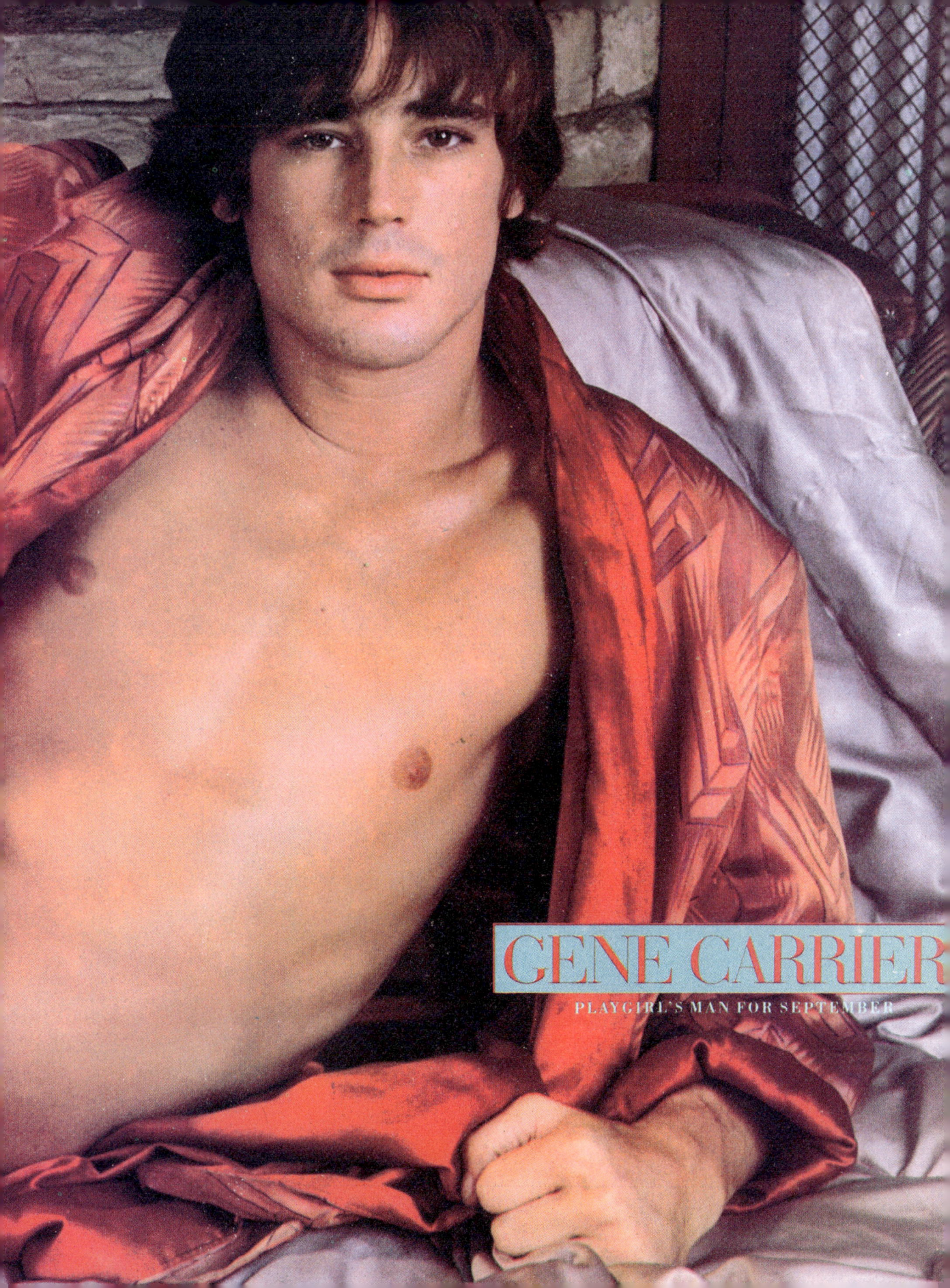

GENE CARRIER

PLAYGIRL'S MAN FOR SEPTEMBER

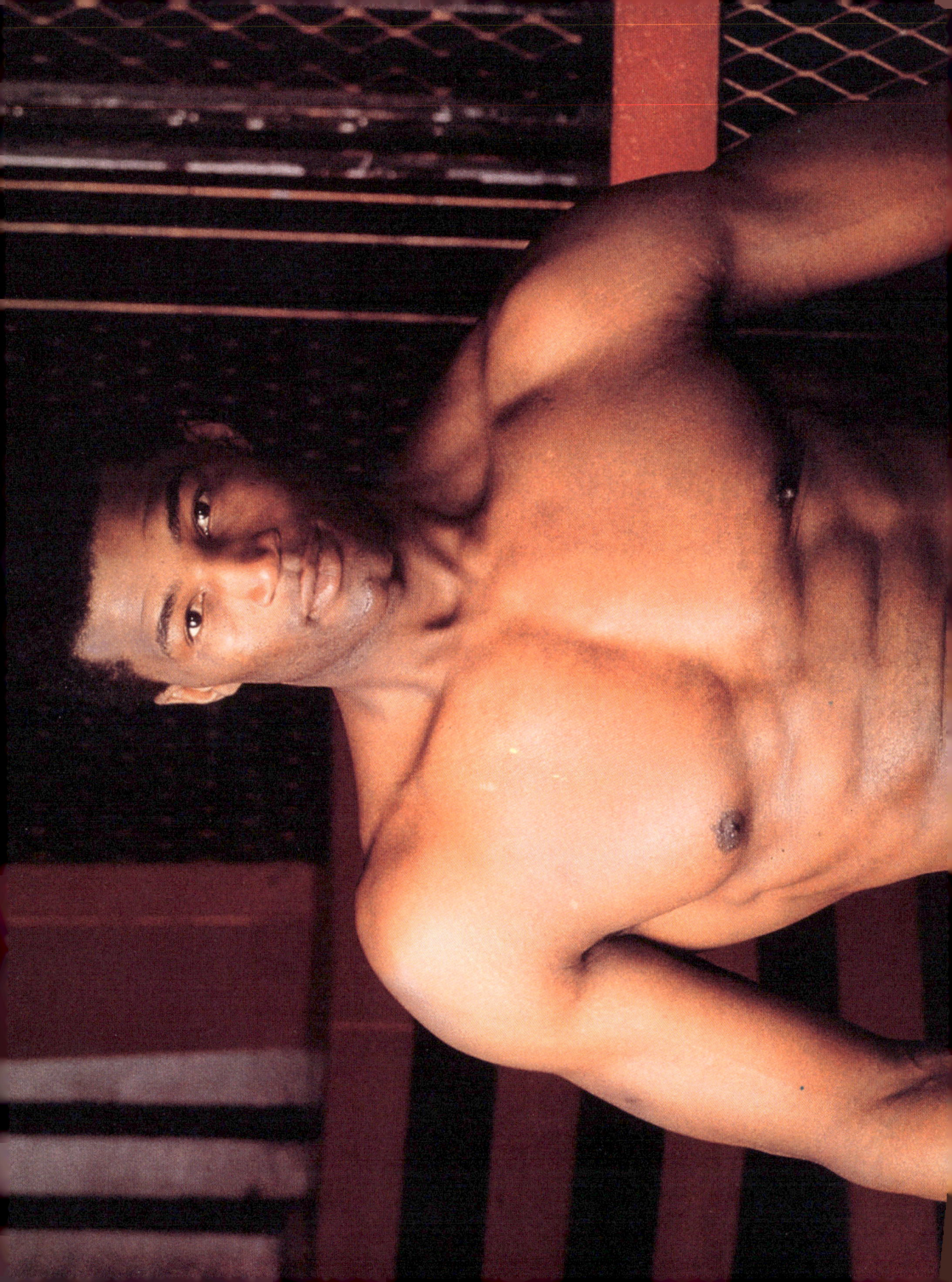

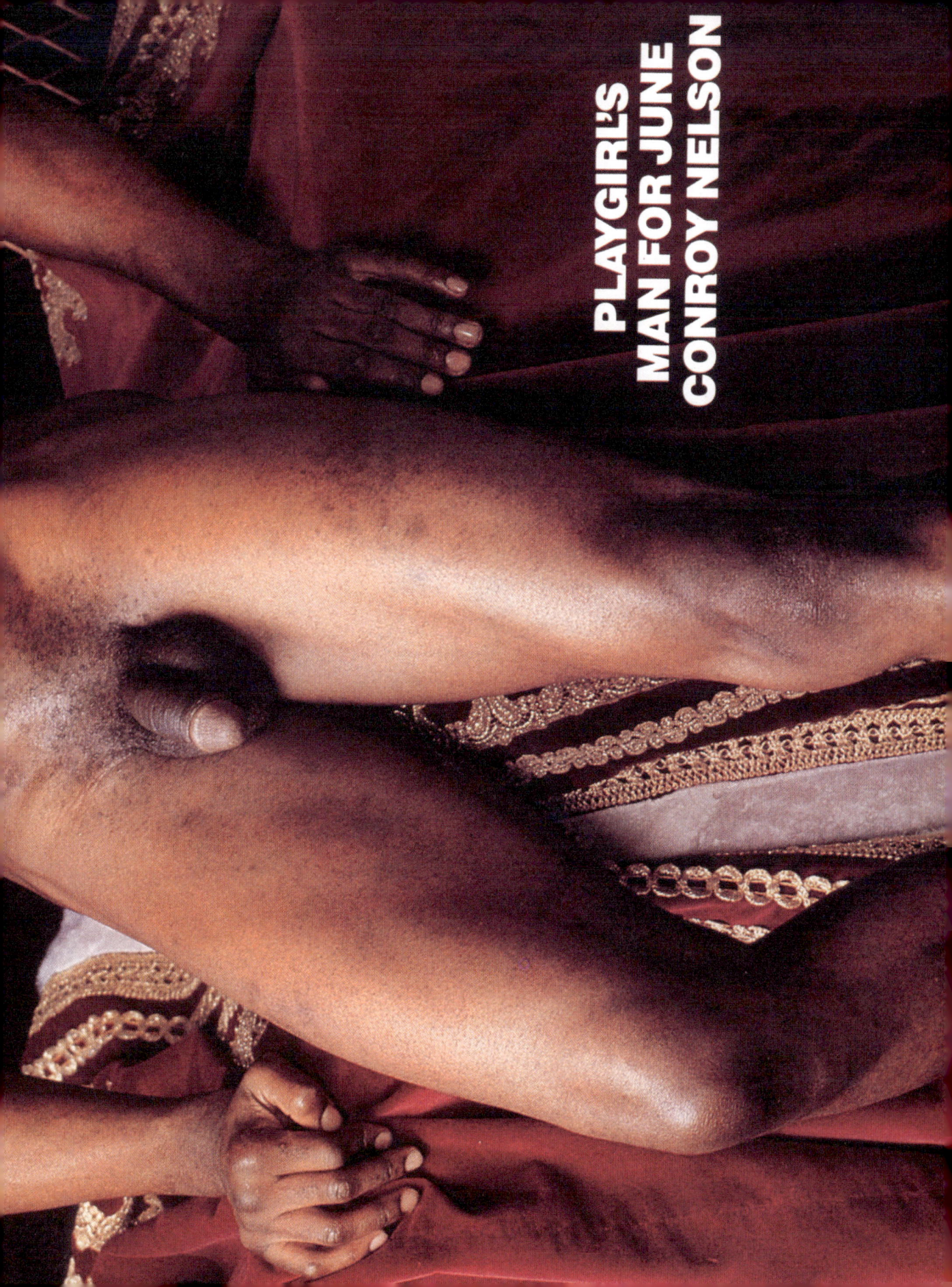

PLAYGIRL'S
MAN FOR JUNE
CONROY NELSON

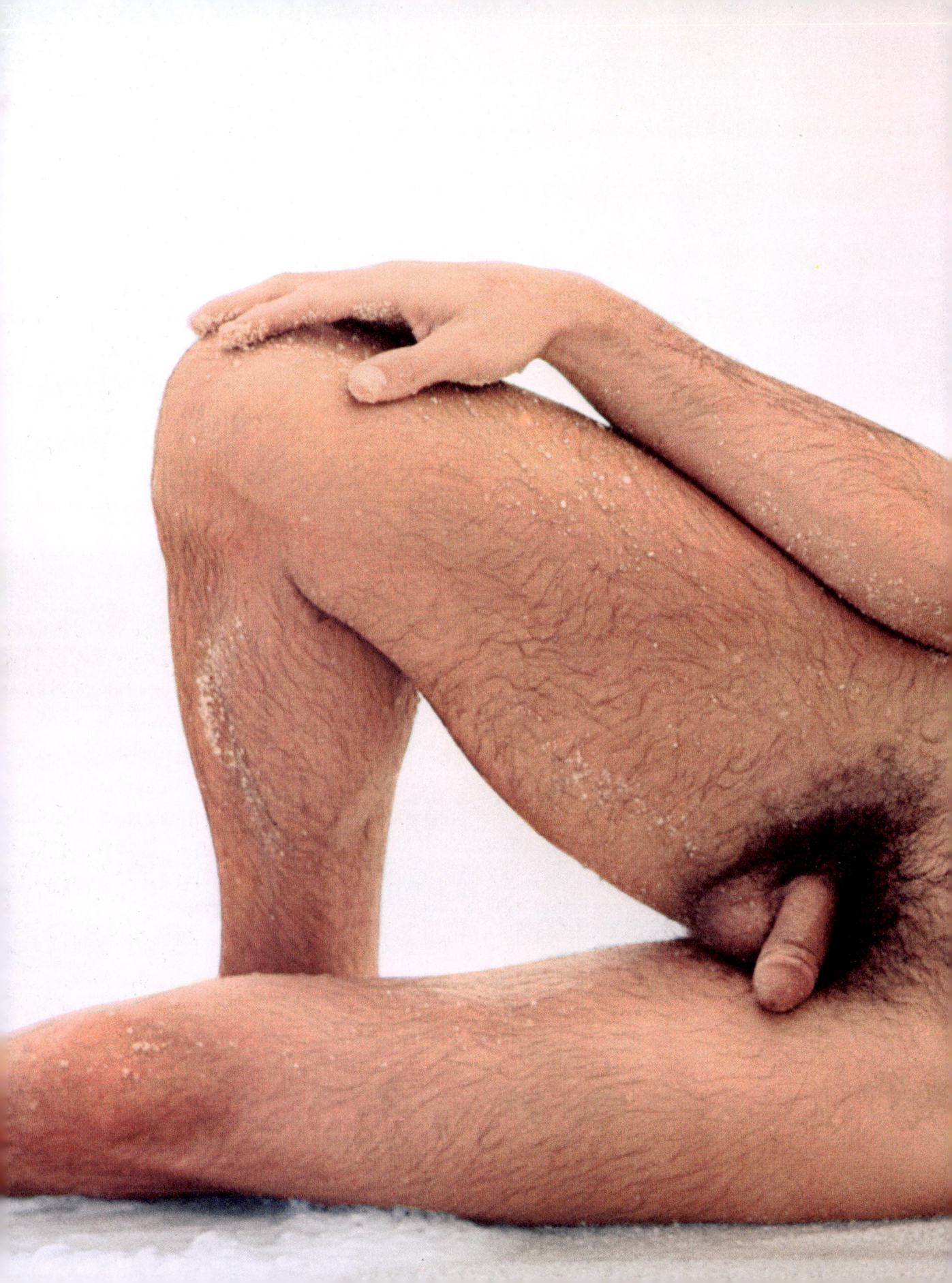

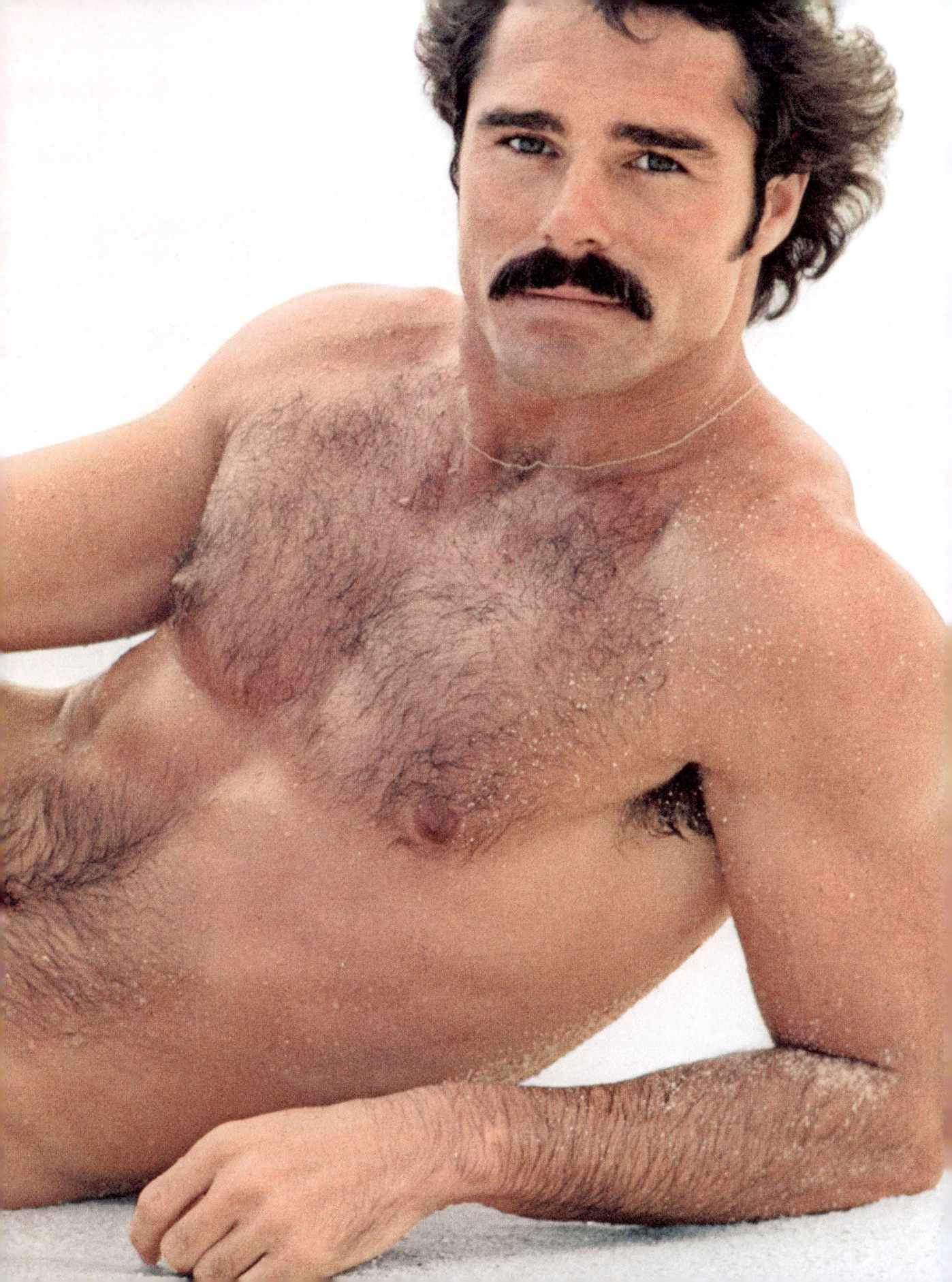

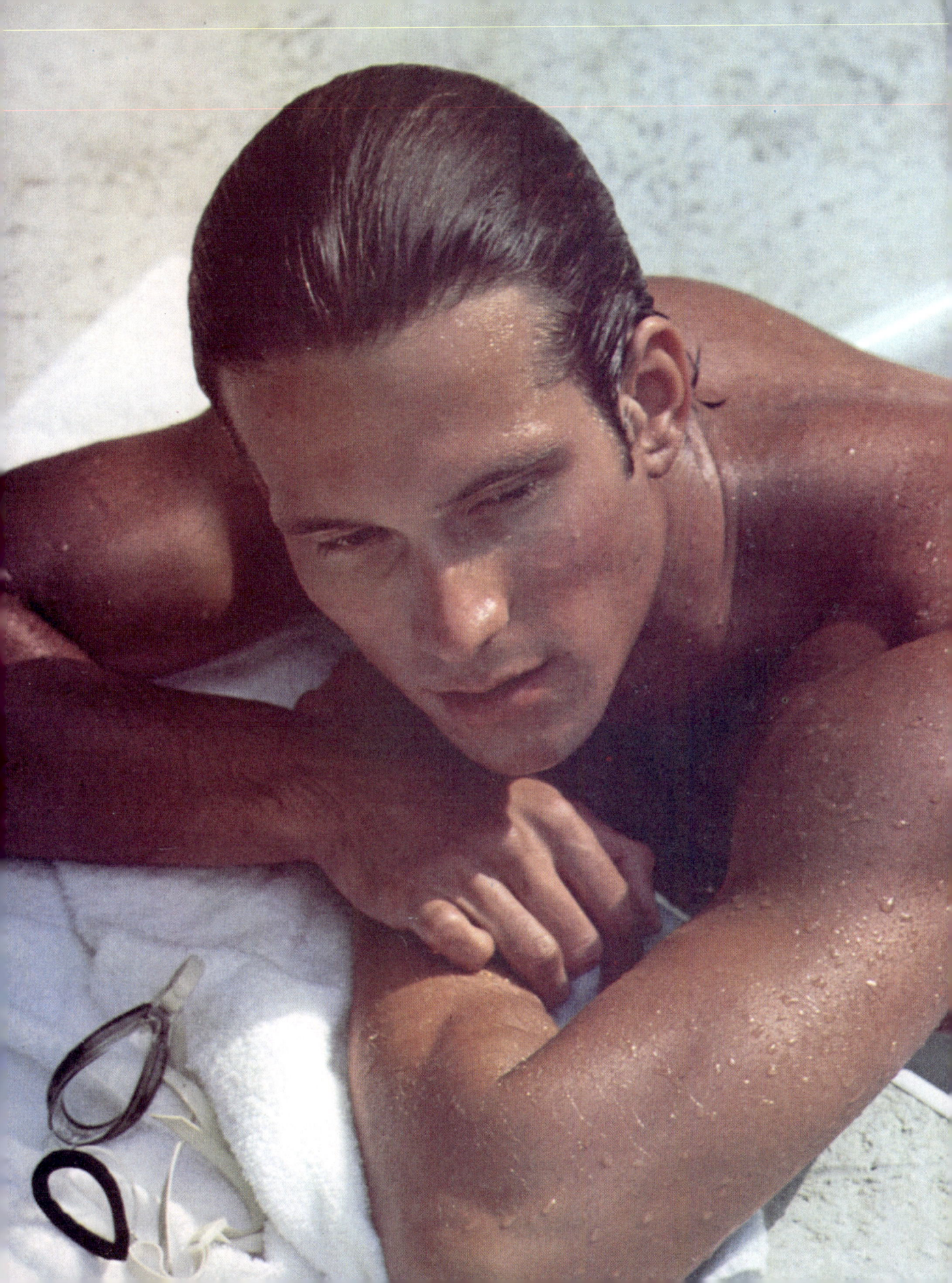

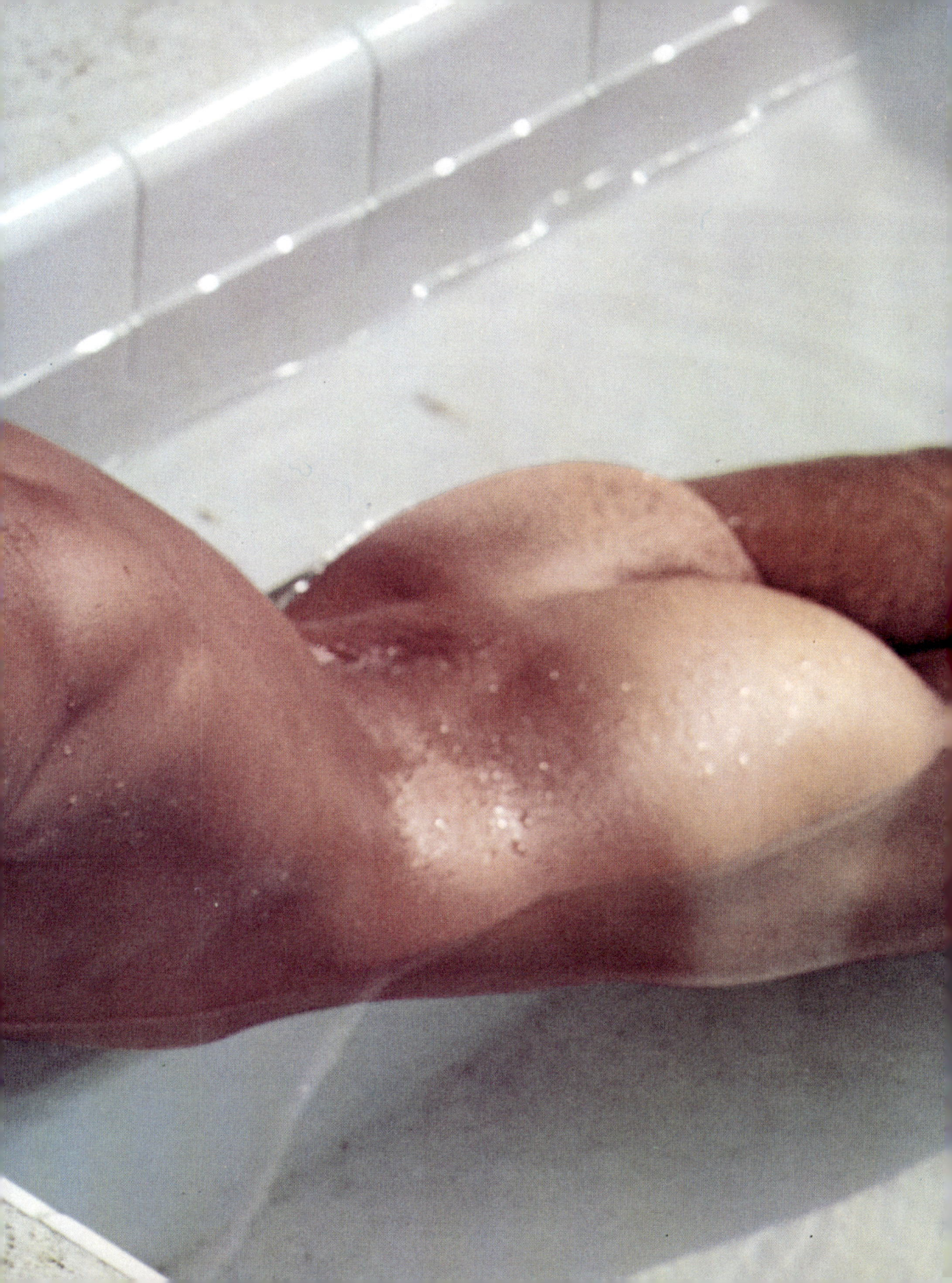

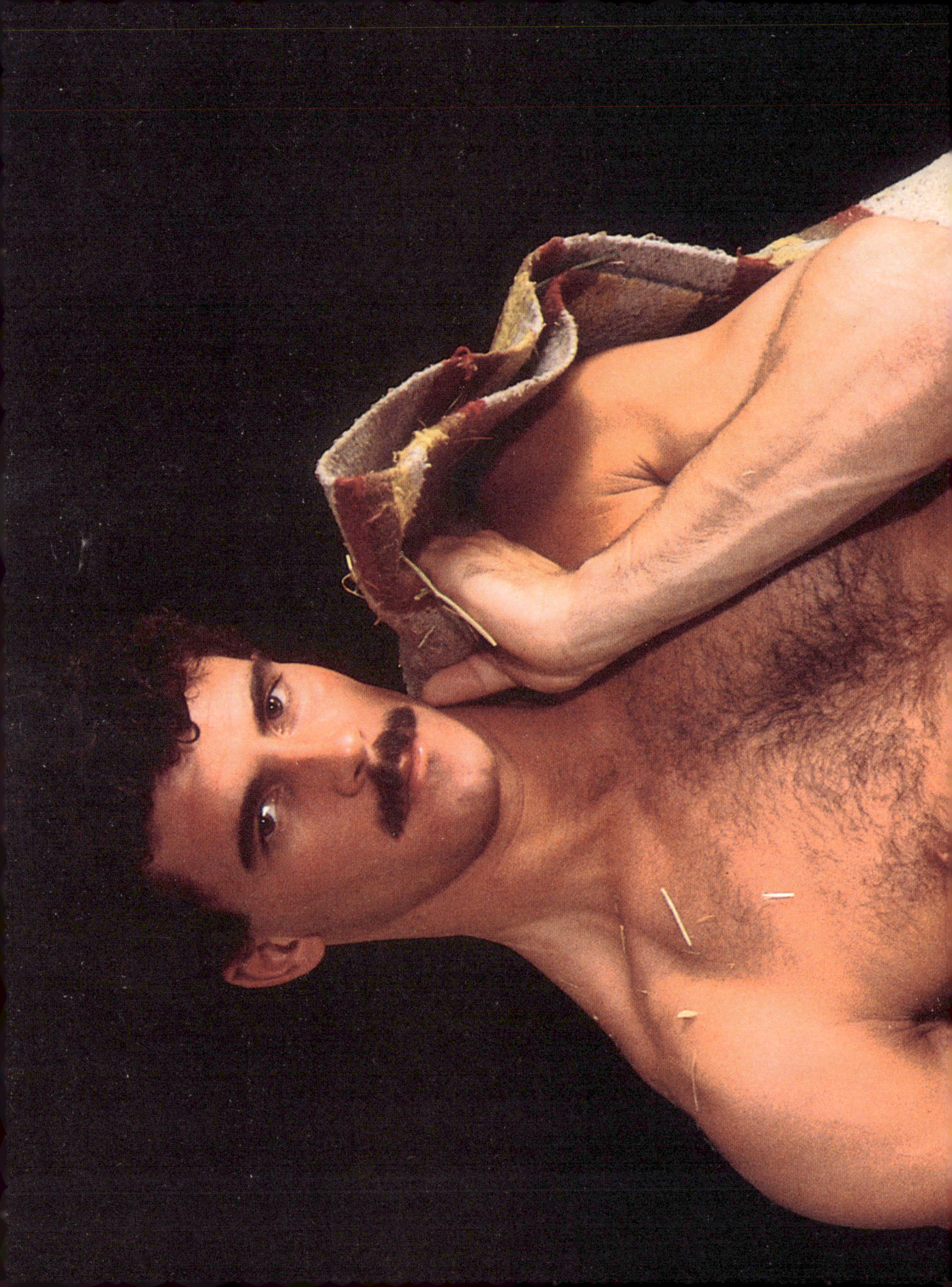

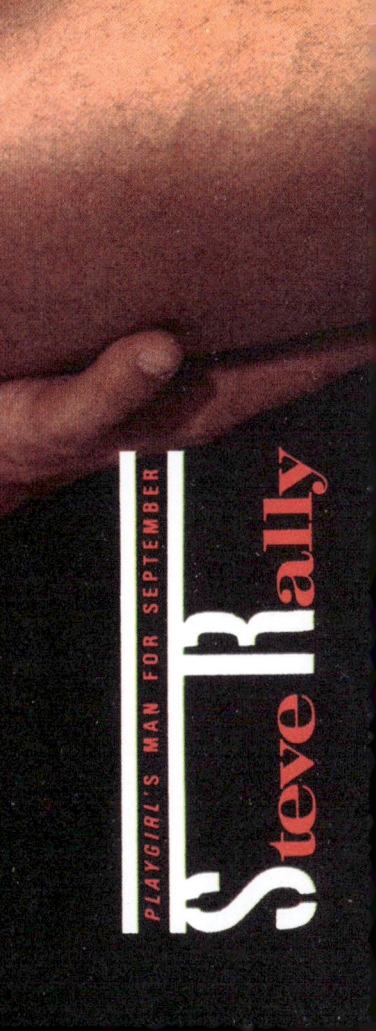

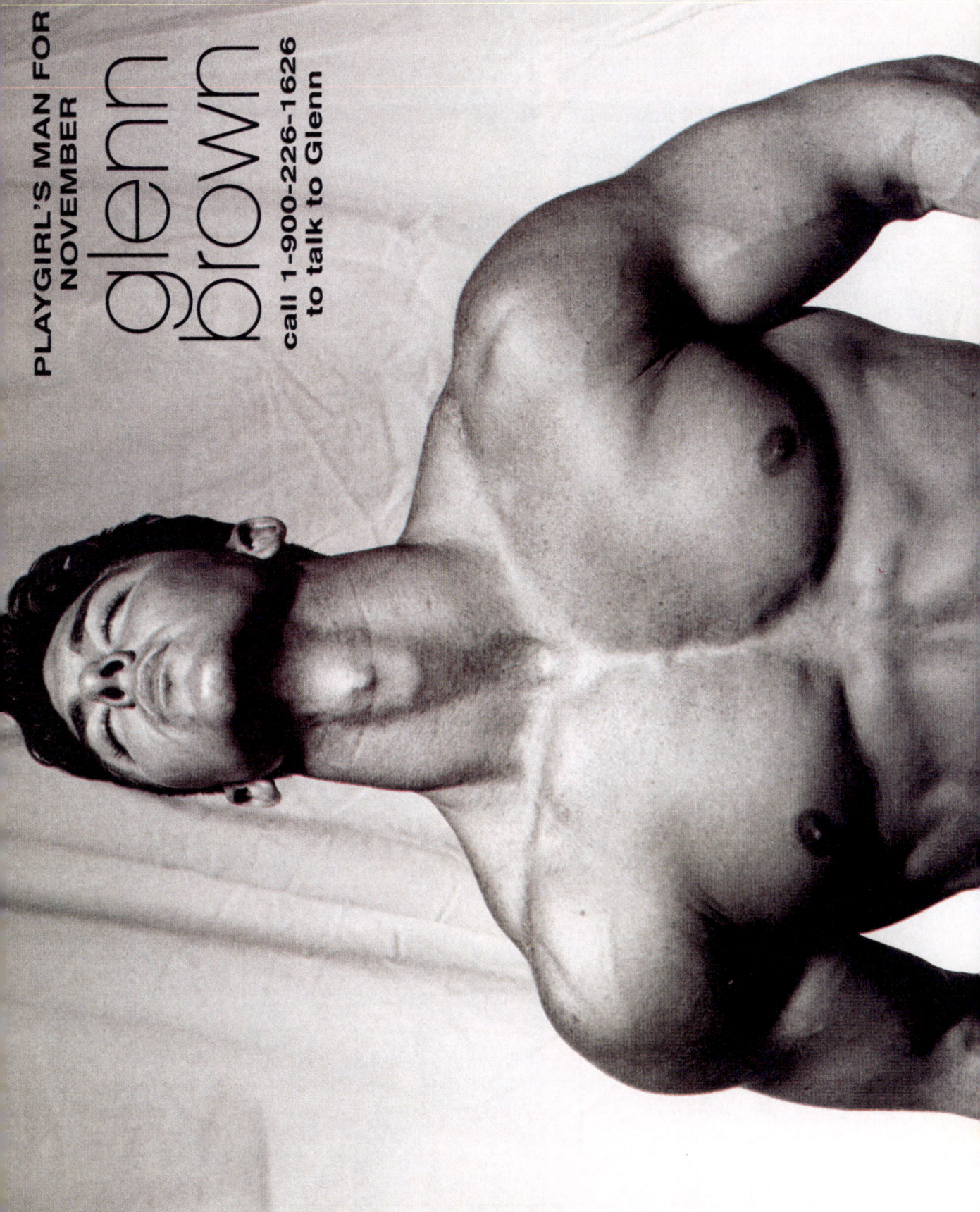

PLAYGIRL'S MAN FOR
NOVEMBER

glenn
brown

call 1-900-226-1626
to talk to Glenn

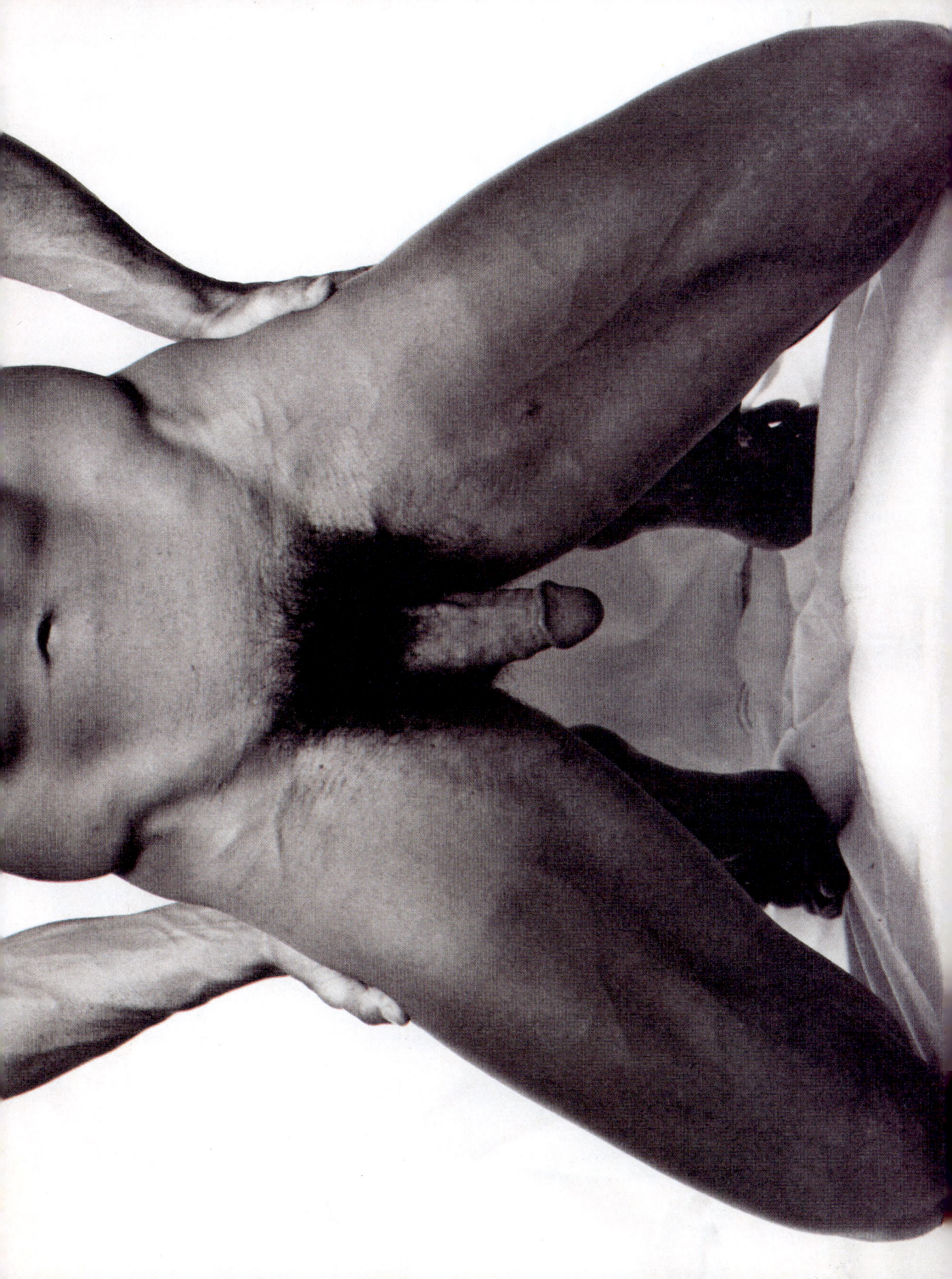

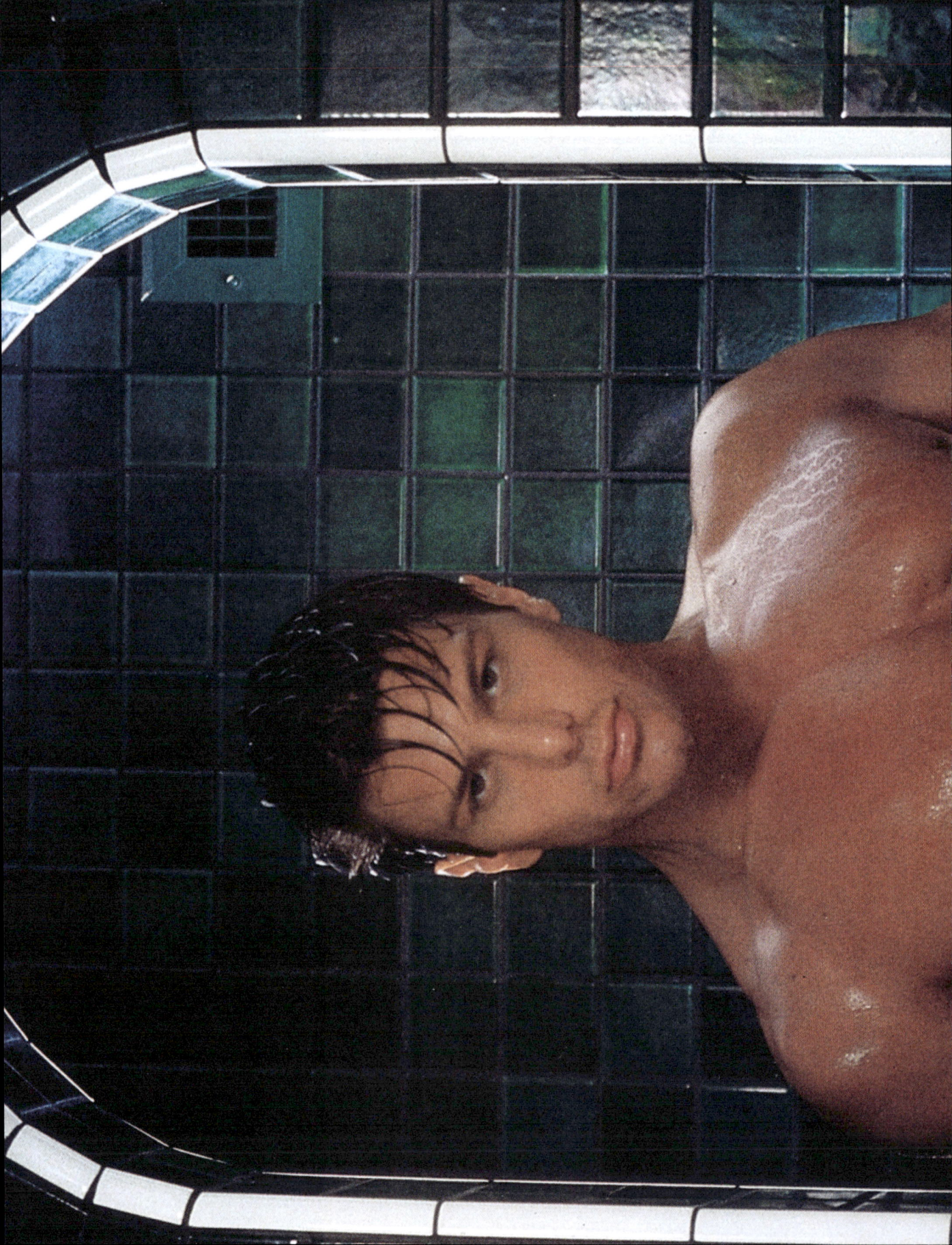

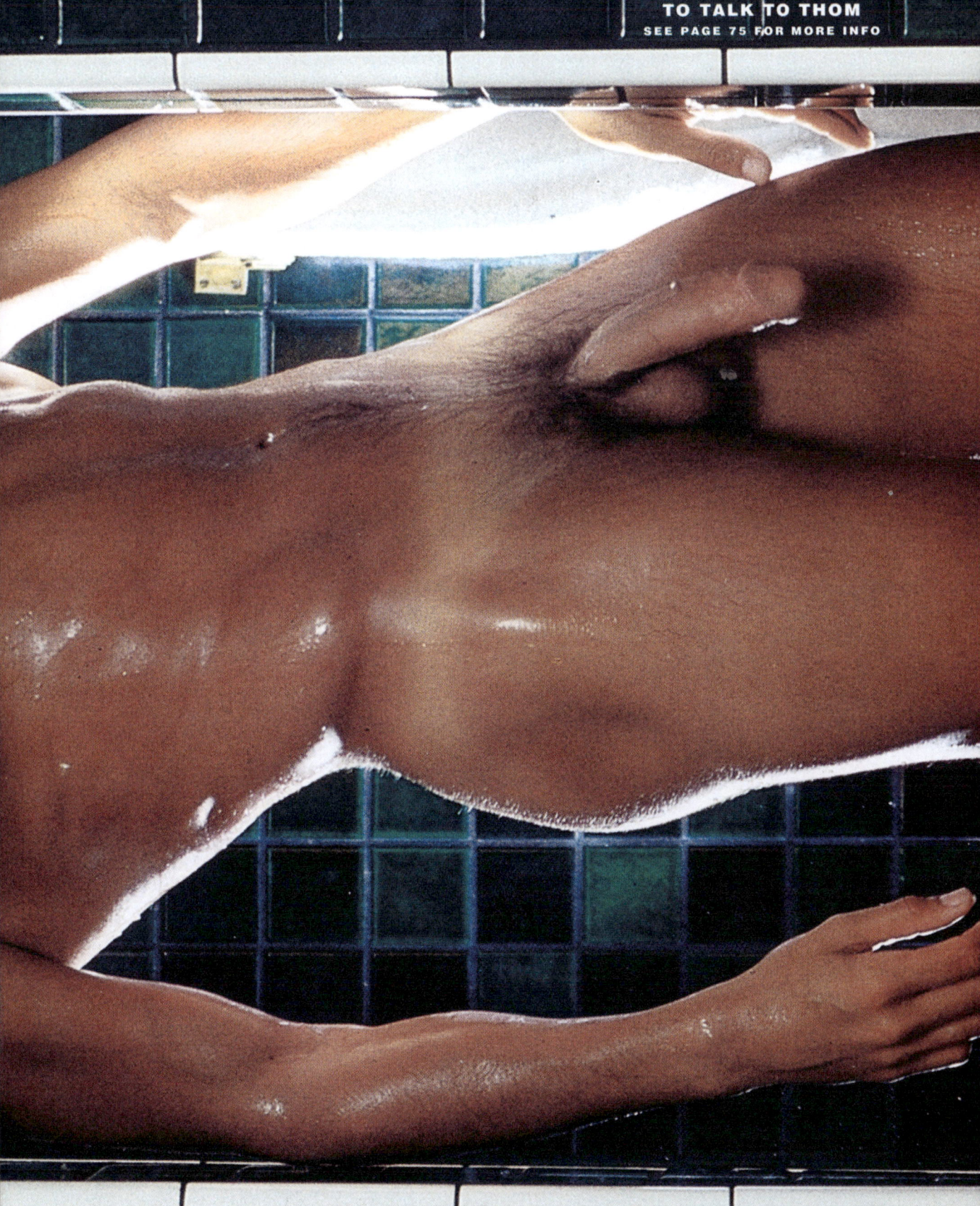

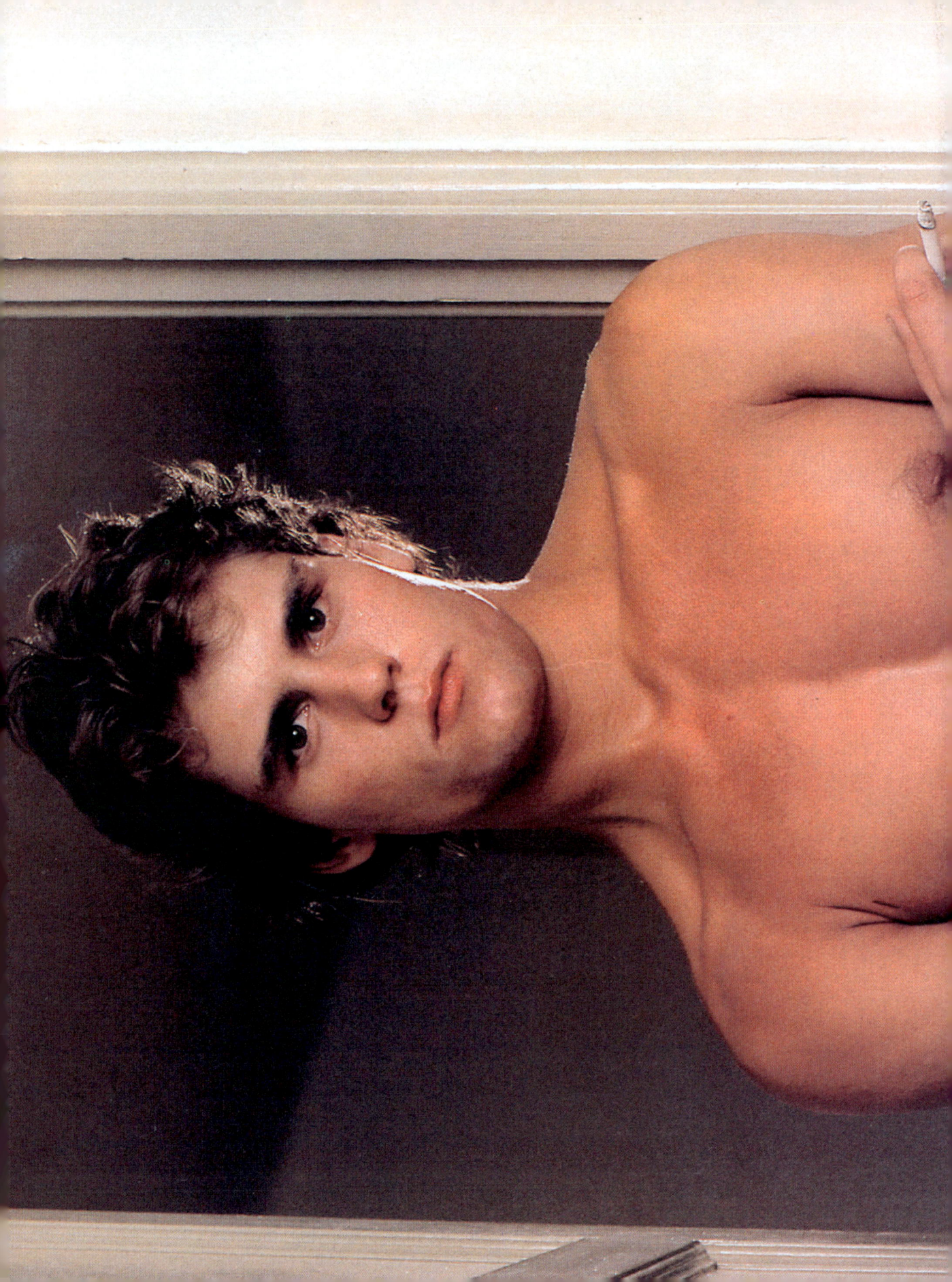

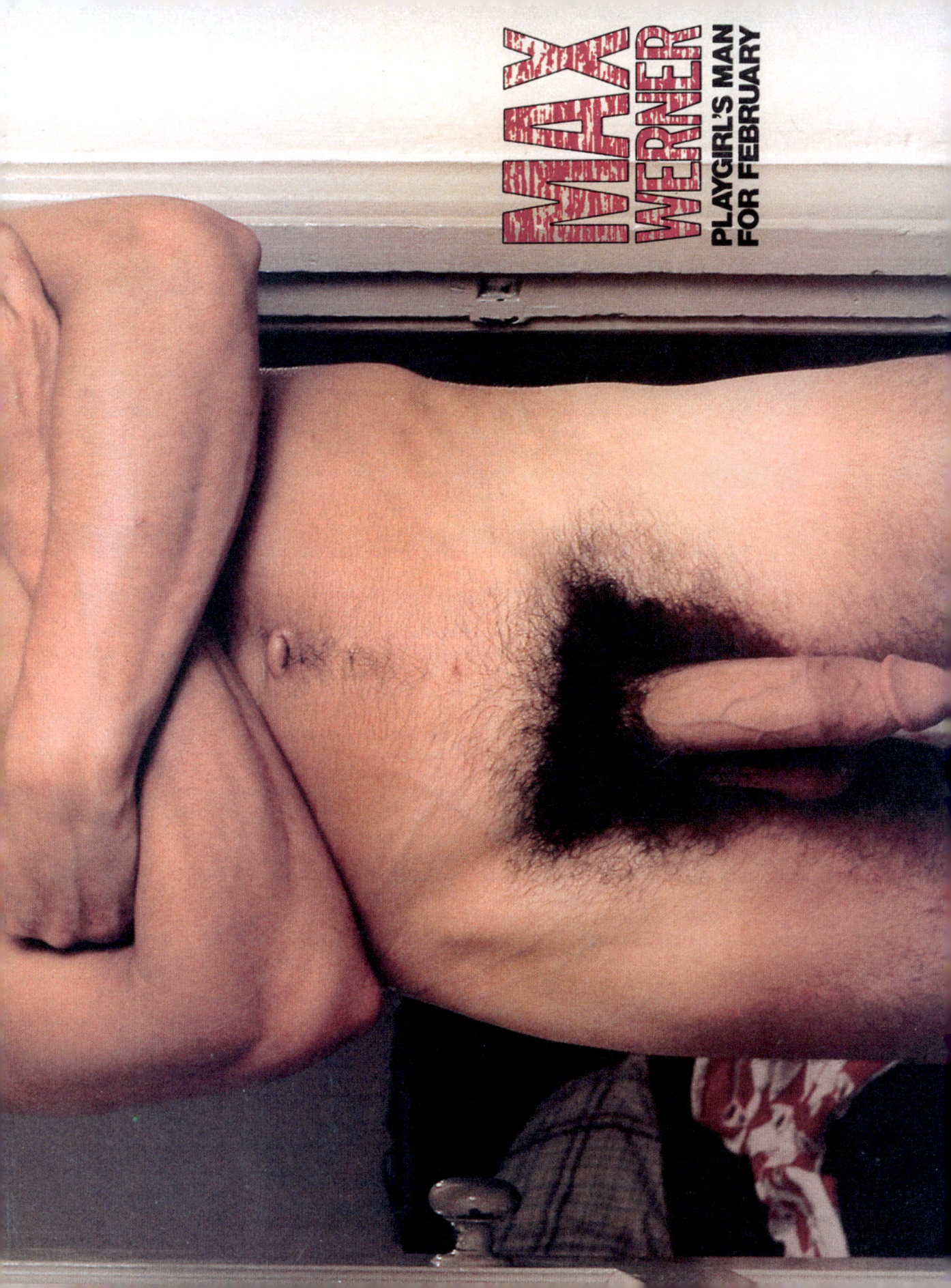

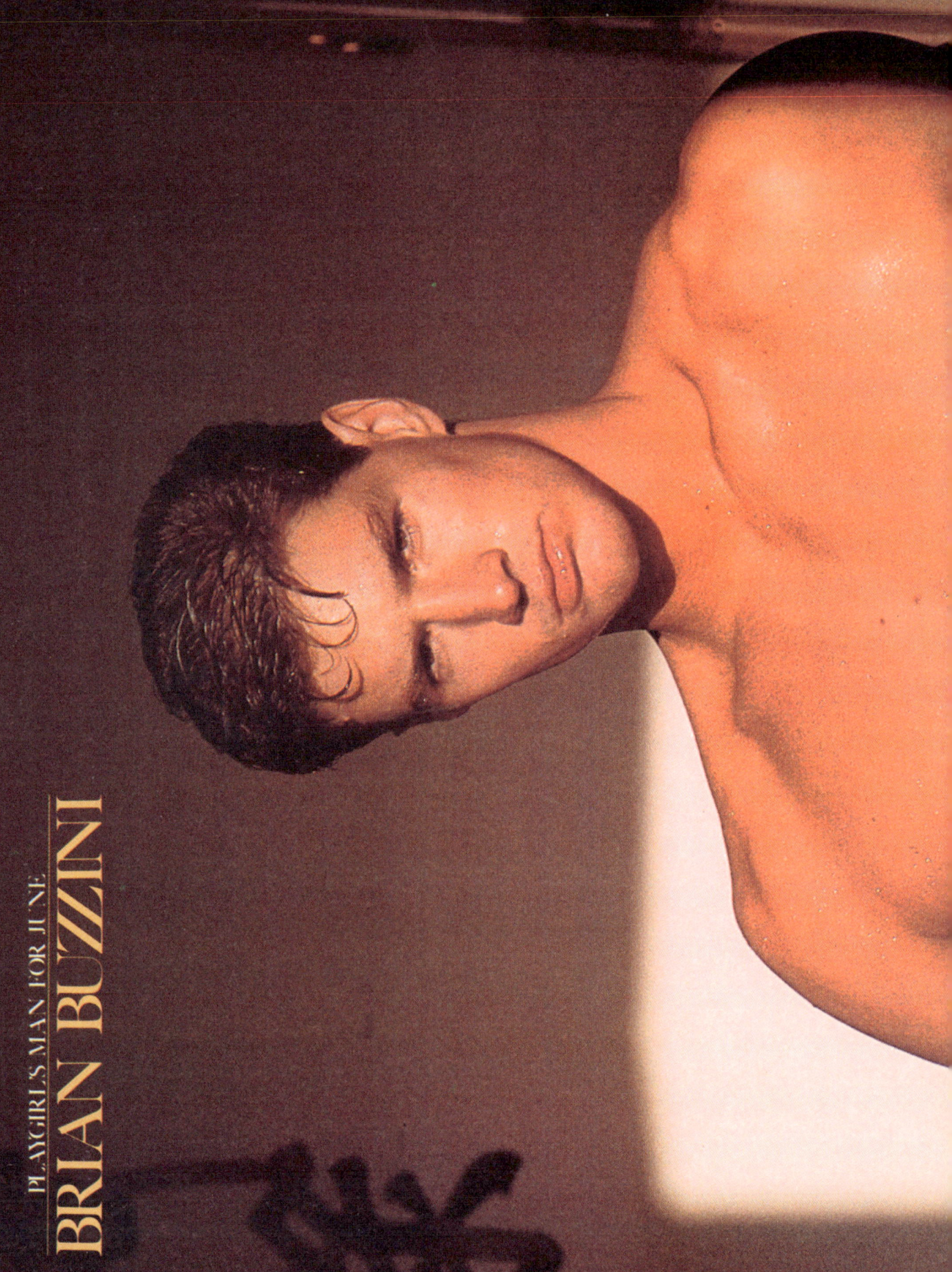

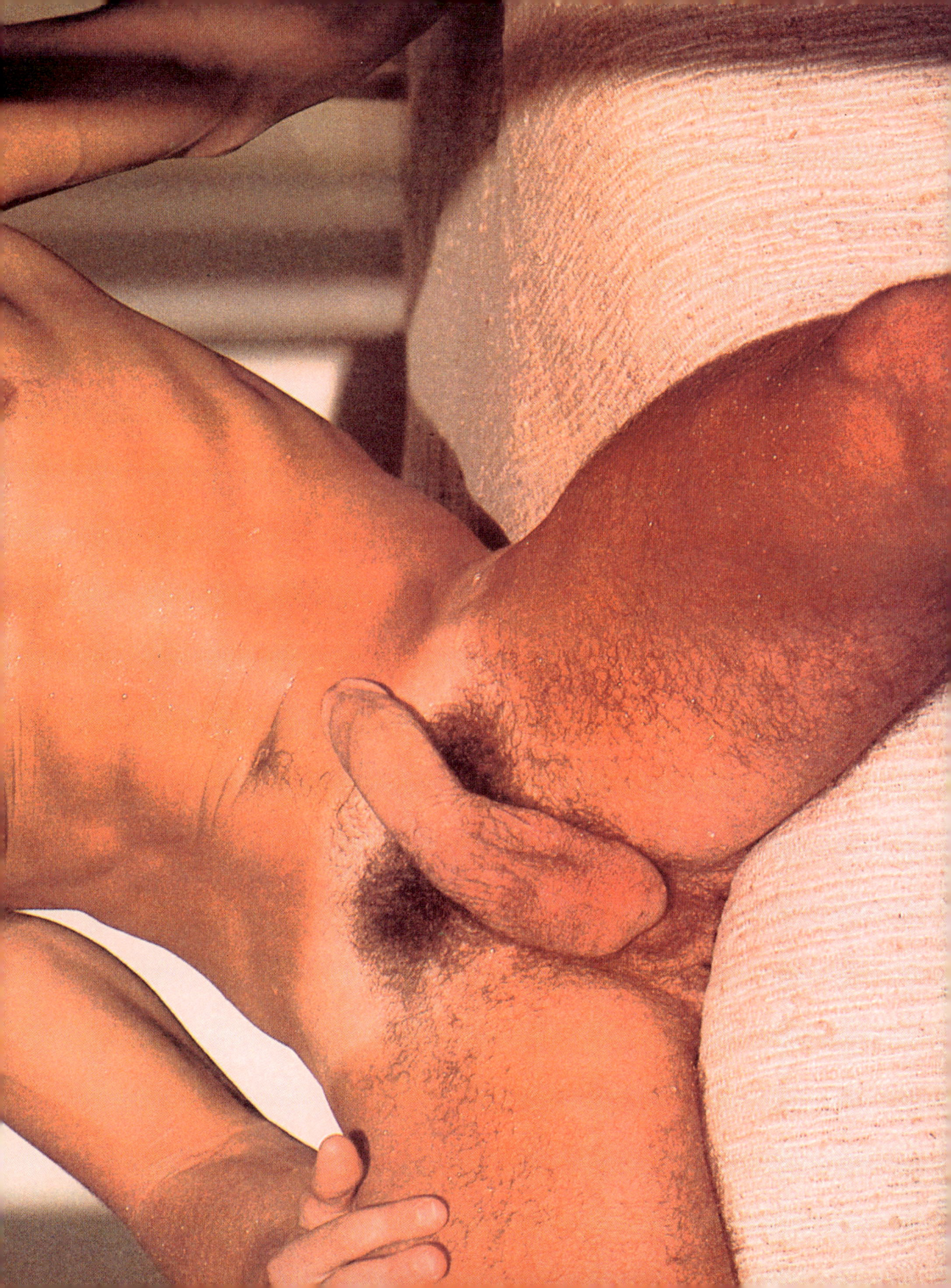

CHAPTER 6

BEST OF THE
1970s

Playgirl was founded in 1973, and the "golden years" contain much of the brand's greatest photography, which laid the groundwork for the iconic *Playgirl* aesthetic. The magazine often featured celebrities as the centerfolds, with some of the decade's most famous to get unrobed, including singer Fabian, NFL all-pro Jim Brown, and actors George Maharis and Sam Jones (a.k.a. Flash Gordon), while others like musicians Rod Stewart and Randy Jones of the Village People got steamy but stopped short of baring all. Beyond the flesh, the magazine's early years also featured exclusive articles and interviews with feminist forces like Joan Baez, Joan Rivers, Maya Angelou, and Anaïs Nin. On the other hand—and prior to cancel culture—a boldly misogynistic William S. Burroughs piece appeared in March 1978, entitled "Women: A Biological Mistake?" Articles like "Taking Care of Business: The Women's Movement Moves On" (1978), "Hiring a Man for Sex" (1975), and "The Male as Sexual Object" (1978), which featured Catherine Deneuve, backlit this decade of disco, economic struggle, and cultural change.

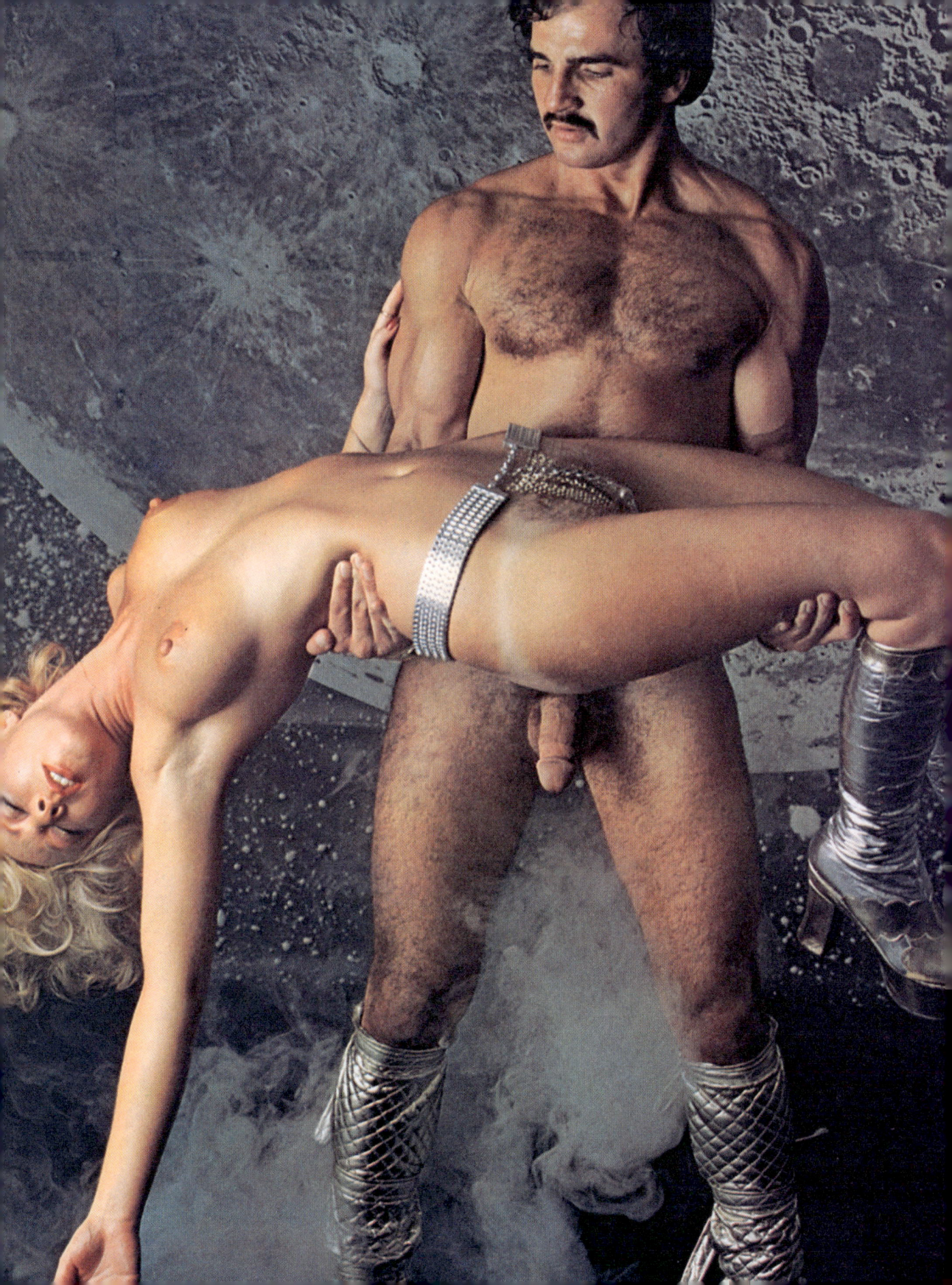

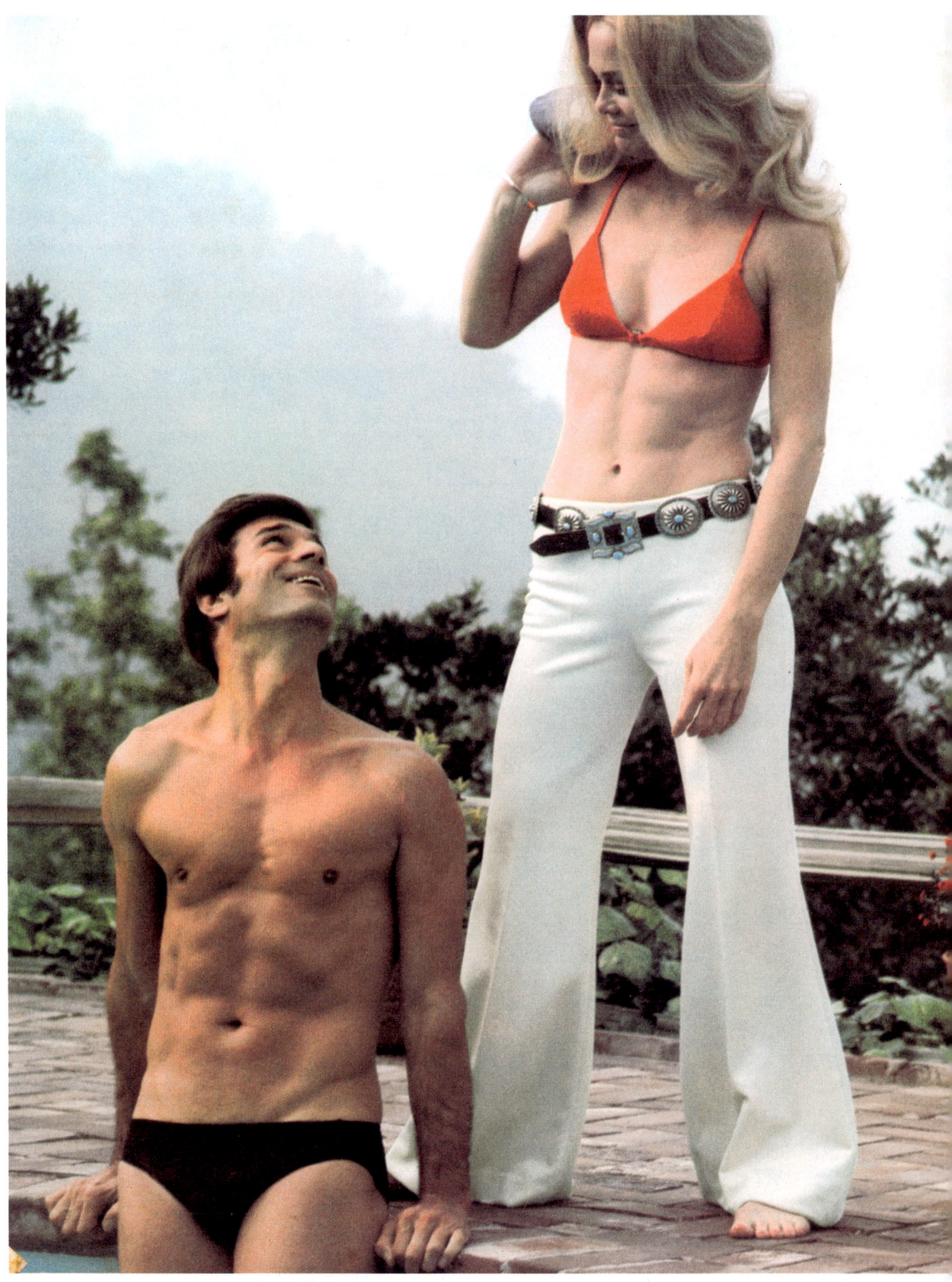

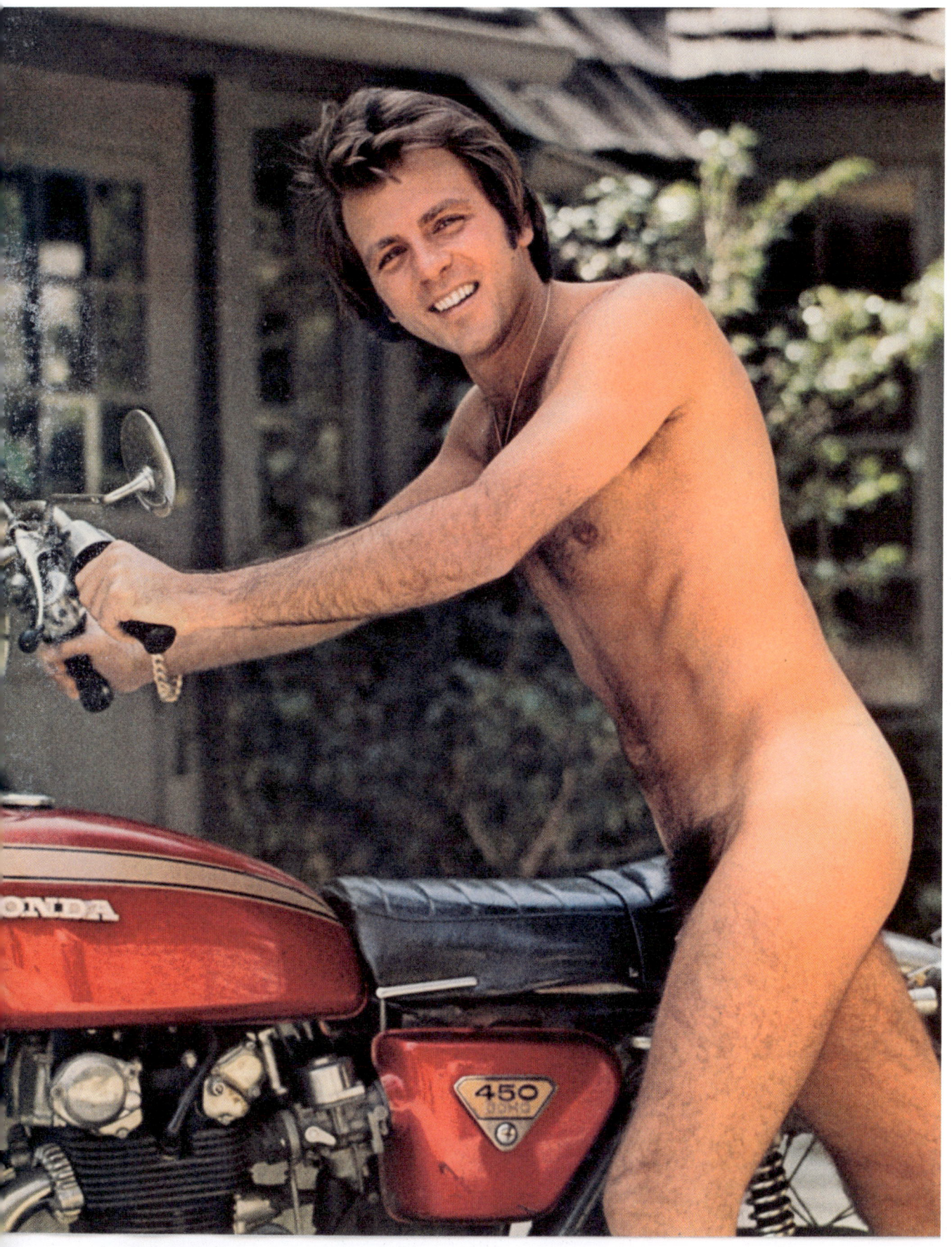

TO
BED
WITH...

Ever wish you could sneak a peak into your
favorite fantasy man's bedroom? Here's
your chance as *Playgirl* takes a look
through the keyhole at some of stardom's
most seductive sleeping habitats.

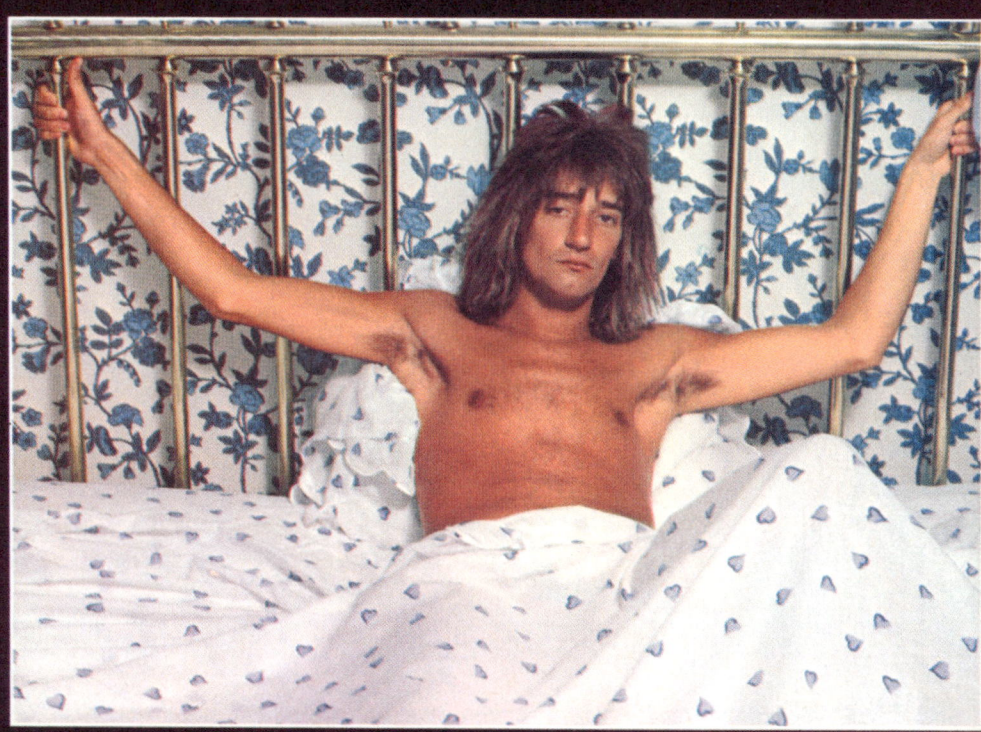

DAVID STEEN

Rockstar Rod Stewart spends a lot of time in his bedroom "writing
lyrics, watching television—and drinking Bacardi and Coke in the
early hours of the morning." No singing, Rod?

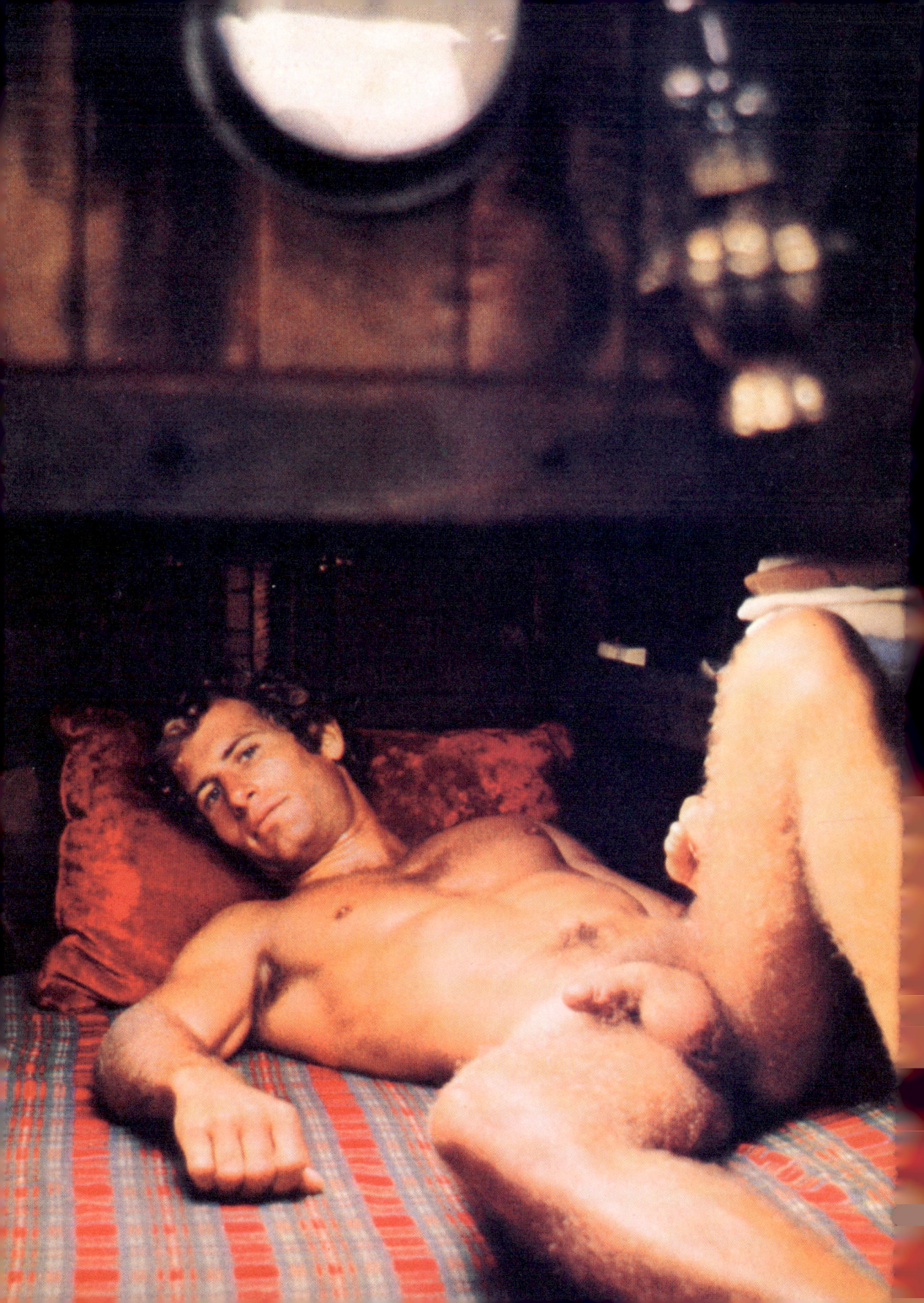

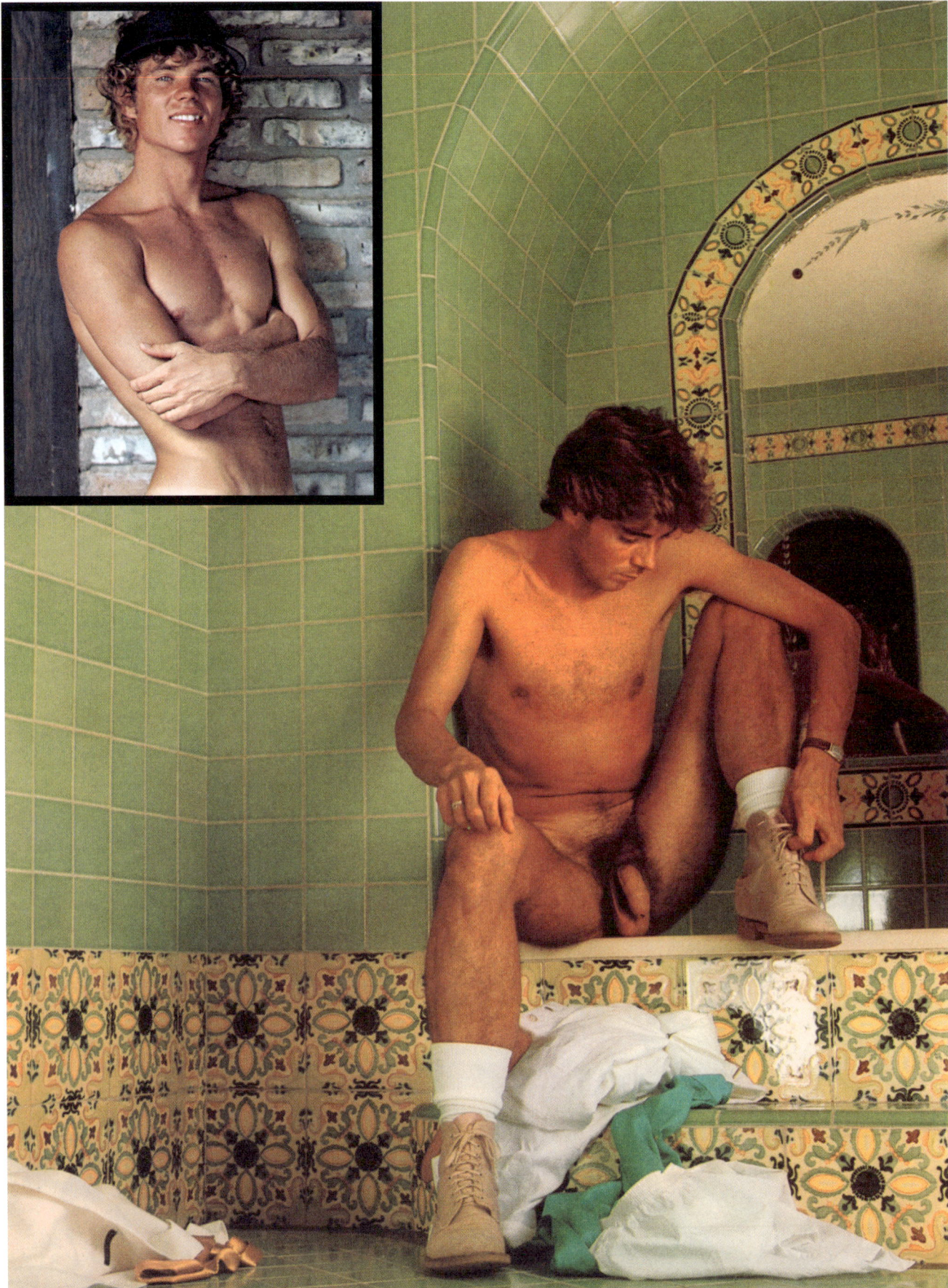

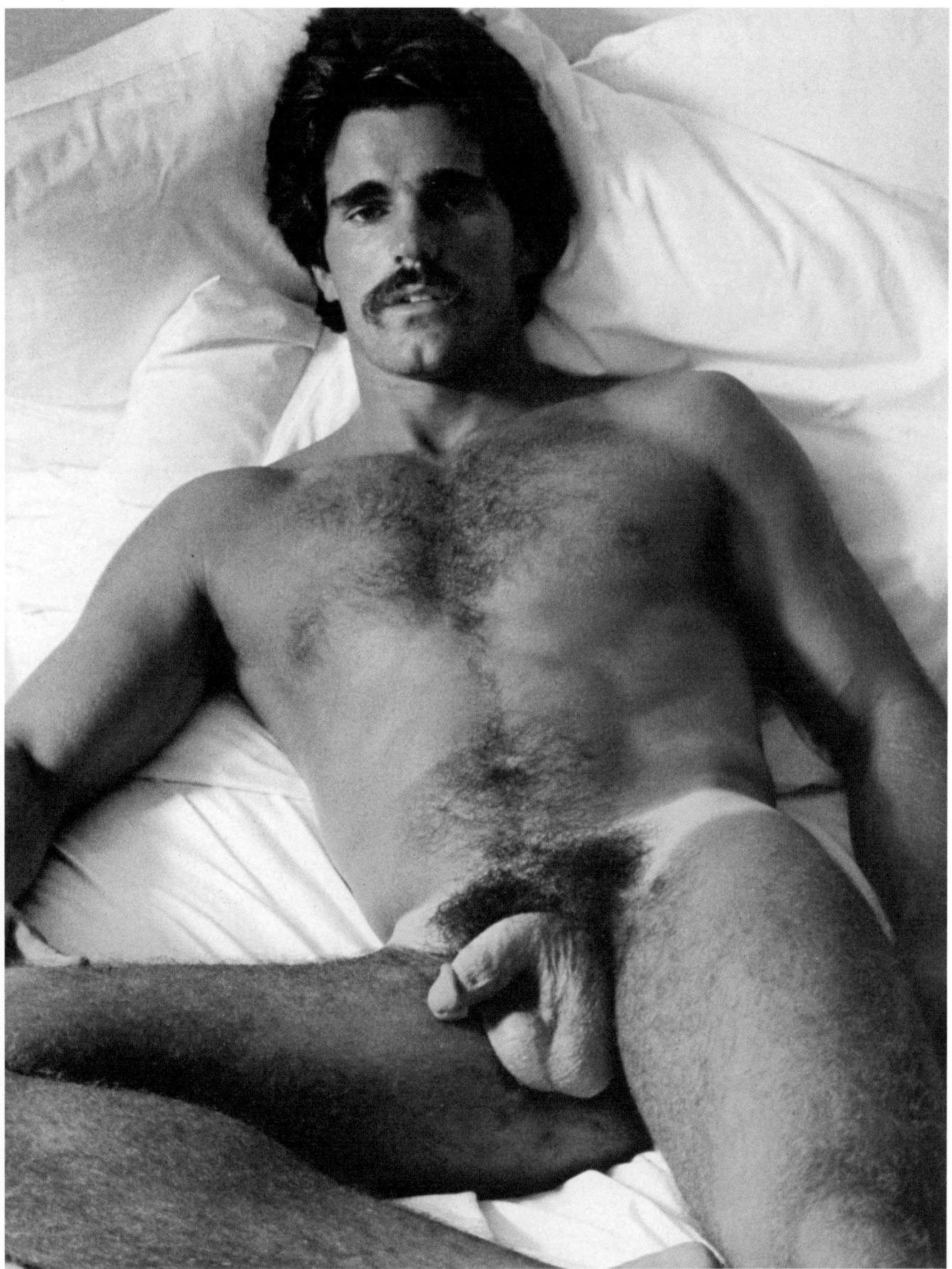

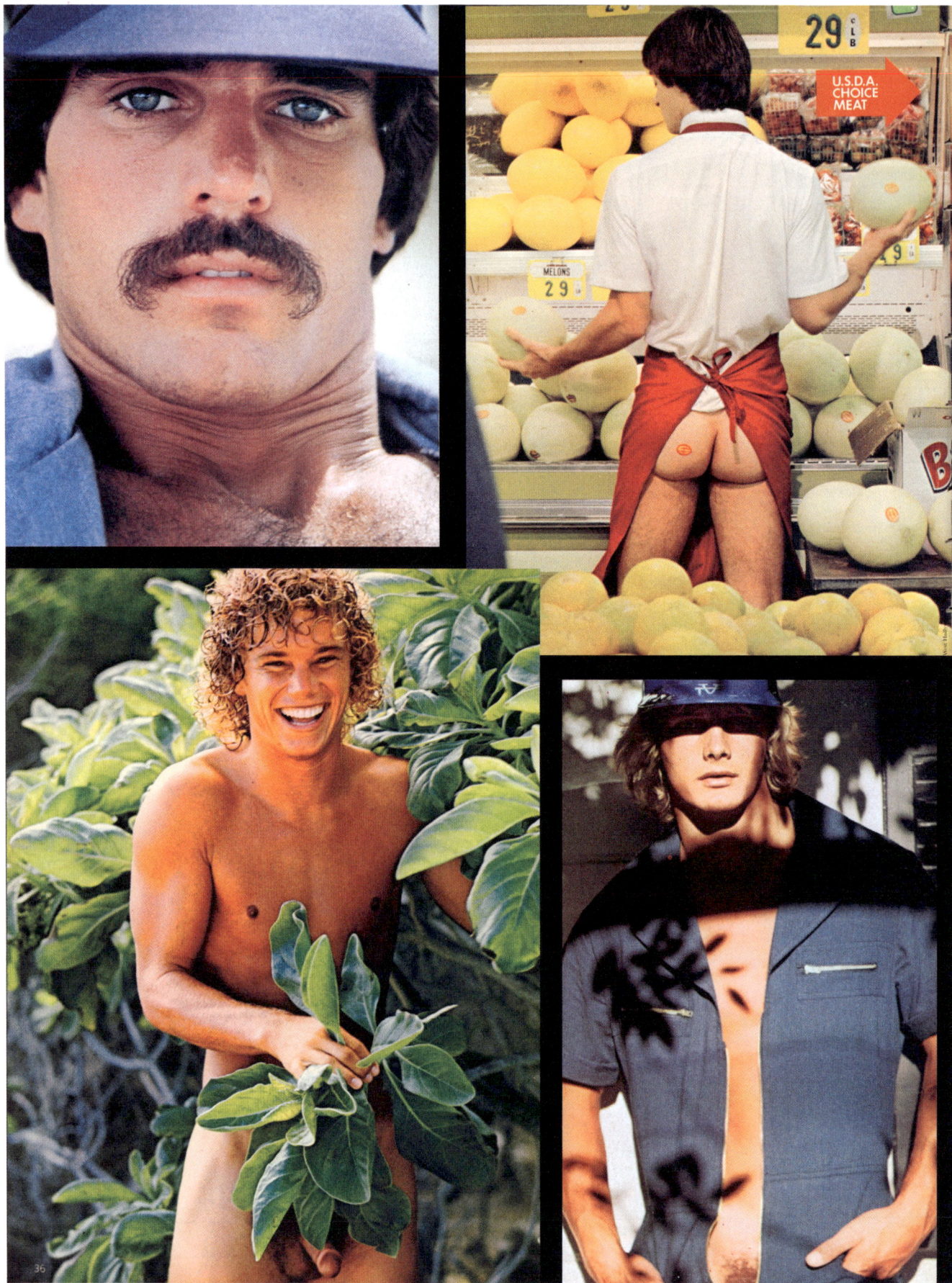

29 C LB

MELONS
29 LB

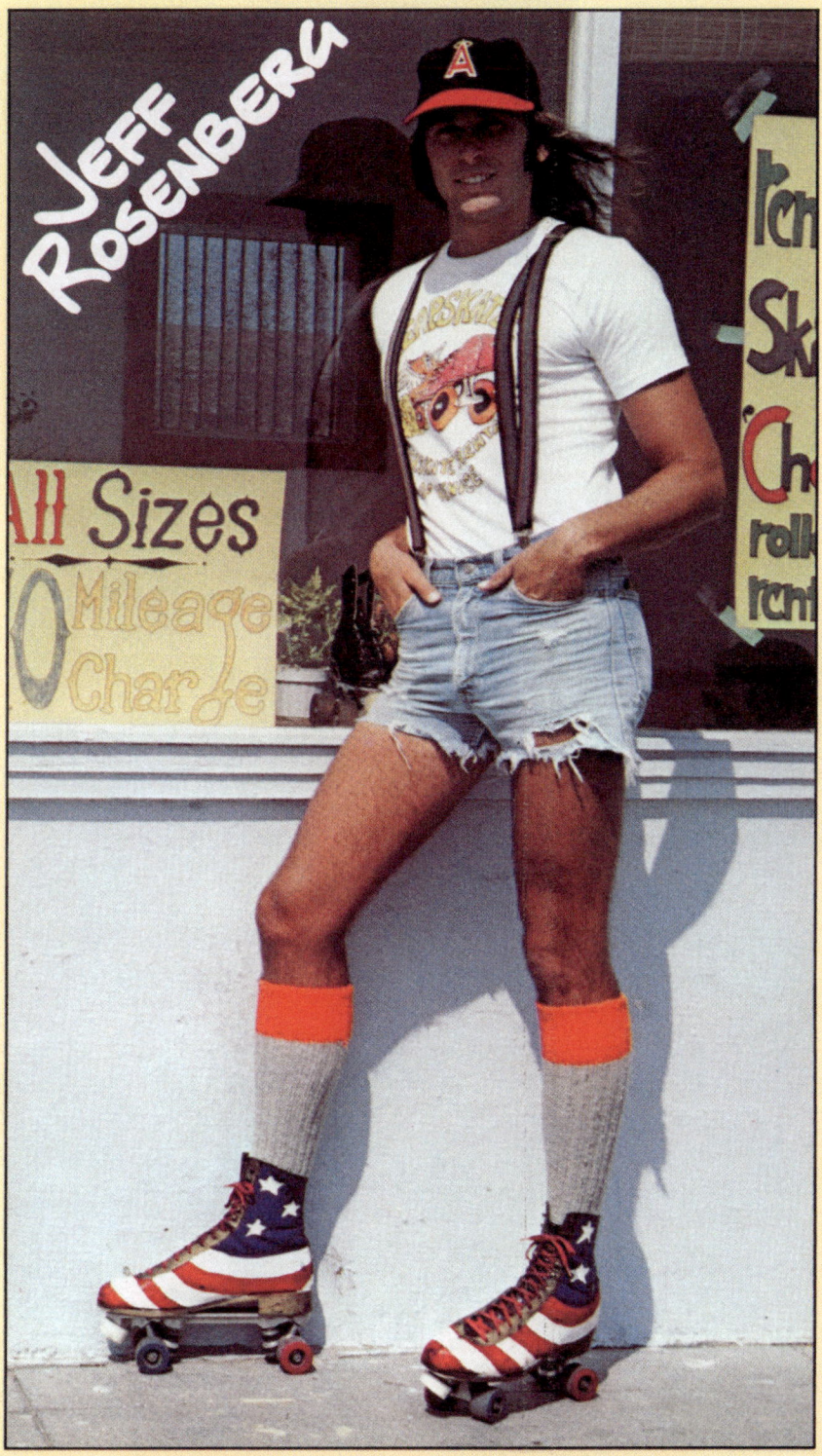

Jeff Rosenberg has been chosen as a finalist in the *Playgirl* Natural Man contest, which will be held in Los Angeles in the fall of 1977.

NATURAL MAN CONTESTANT

Photographed by LAURA BERGMAN

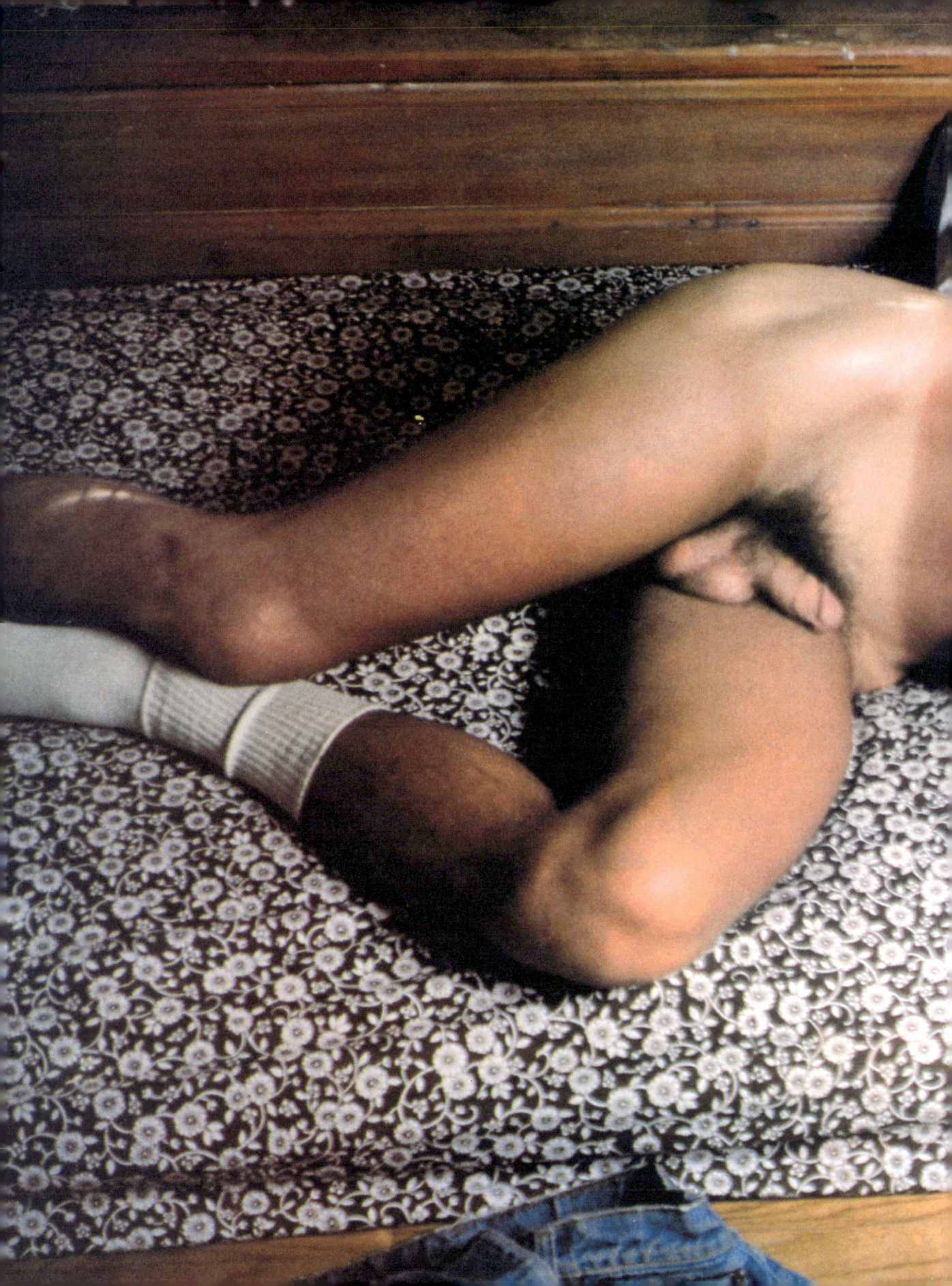

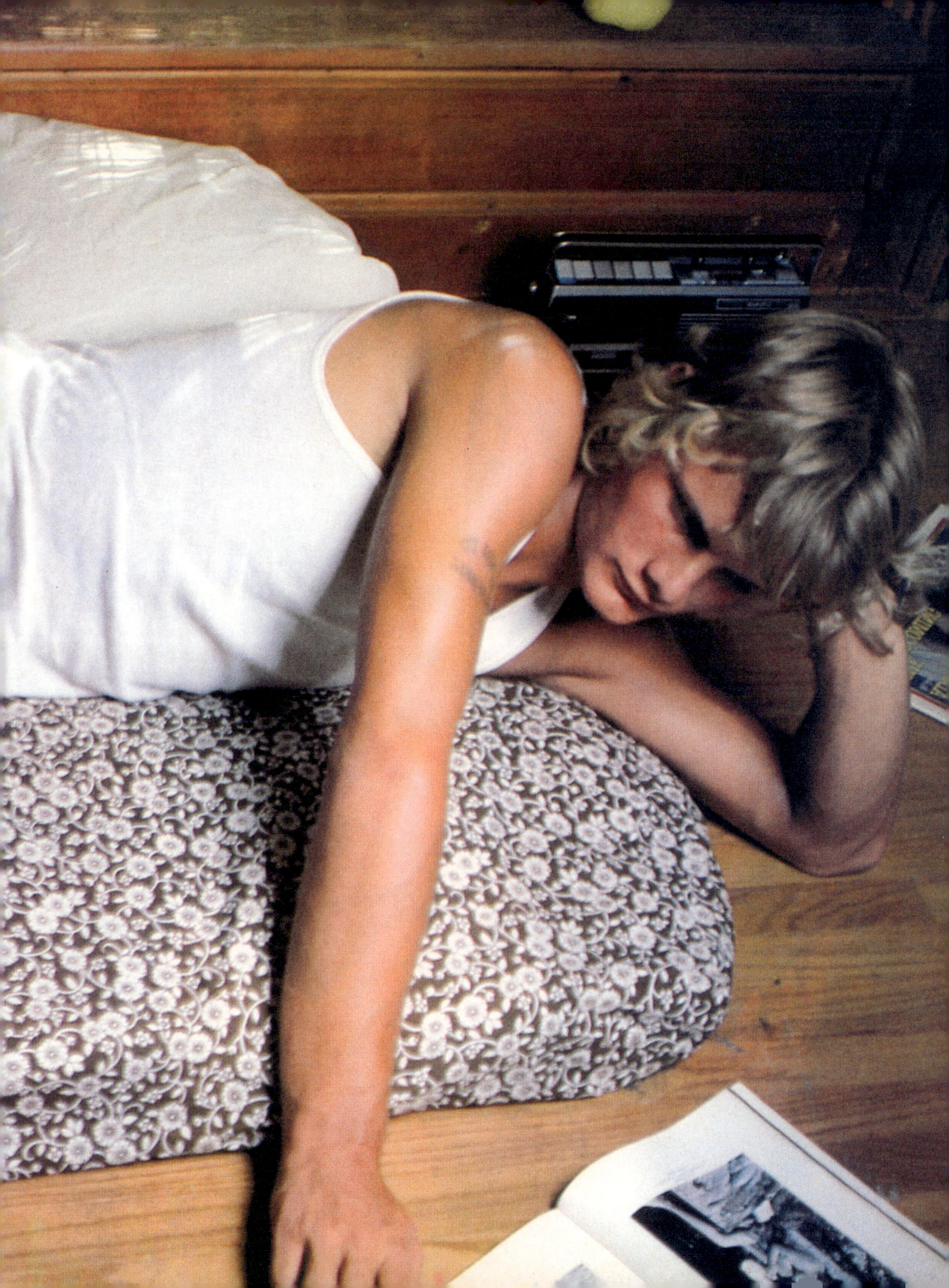

BEST OF THE
1980s

This collection serves as a time capsule of all that is totally eighties: bright neon colors, big hair, and the advent of MTV culture. Some bodacious babes featured—with or without their knowledge— in the buff include Christopher Atkins, Bob Chandler, Arnold Schwarzenegger, and Sylvester Stallone. Iconic interviews of the decade include Johnny Depp, Richard Gere, John Travolta, and the late River Phoenix. Not everything, however, ages so well: in the September 1986 issue, *Playgirl* ranked Donald Trump amongst the year's "Top 10 Sexiest Men"—gag me with a spoon! Articles of the era, like "AIDS: Can You Believe Your Doctor?" (1988), "The Feminization of the Workplace" (1986), and "Coupling in the Year 2000" (as imagined in 1982), as well as a bitchin' fashion spread featuring Heather Locklear, exemplify the age of materialism and technological revolution on the dawn of deadly disease.

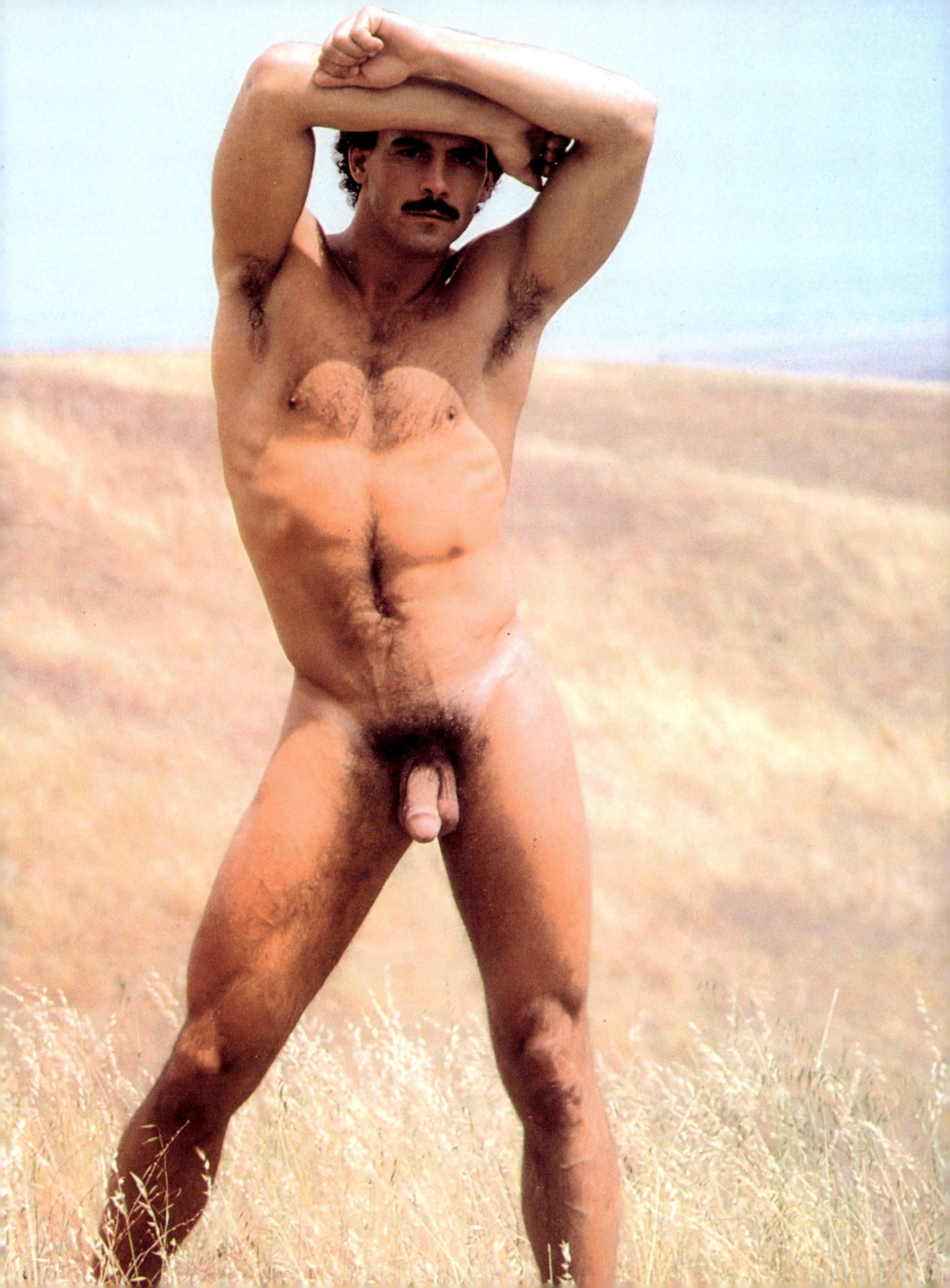

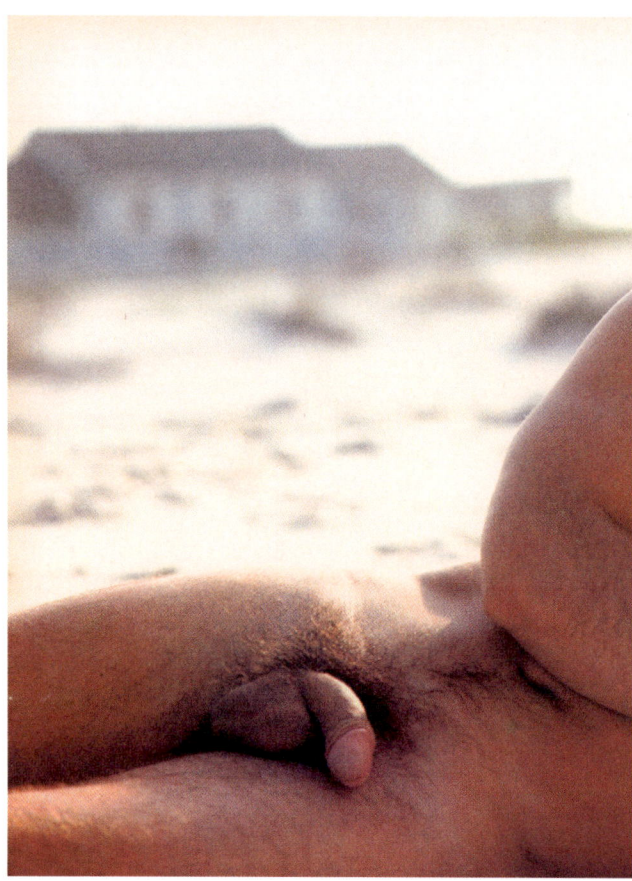

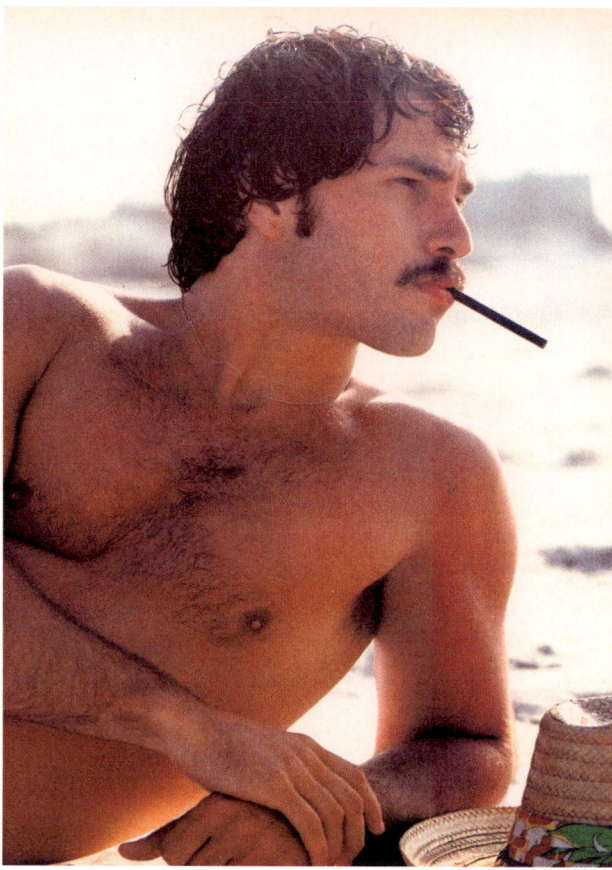

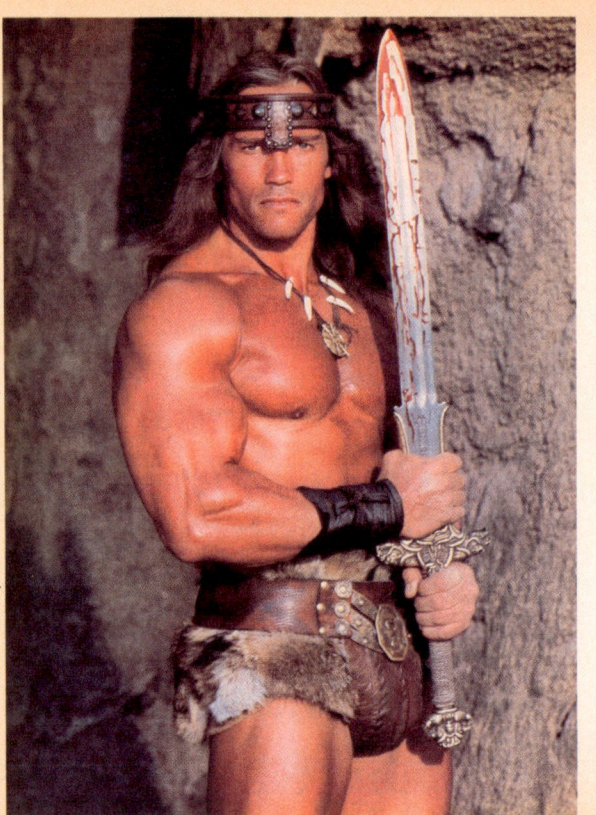

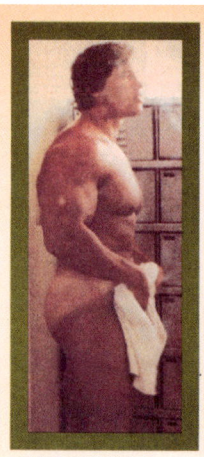

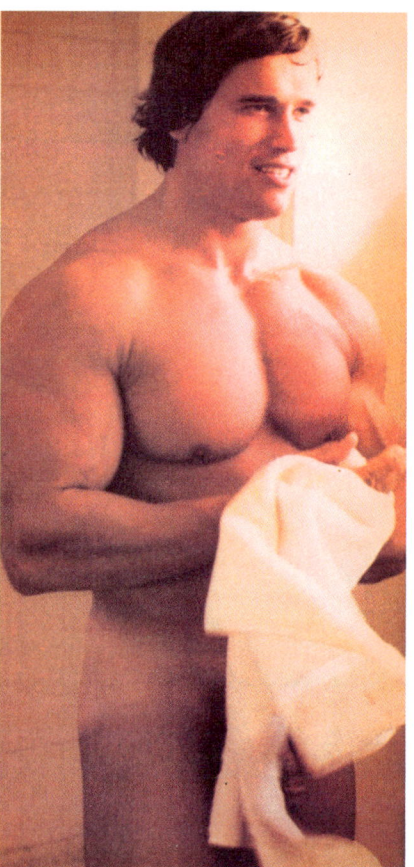

Arnold Now and Then: (Left) As Conan the Barbarian, box-office champ. (Right) Before the films and fame, during his bodybuilding days.

"In some ways we are opposites," muses the reactionary Reaganite of his liberal love, "but that just makes things spicy. Our relationship, I always say, is spicy."

His views on sex ("the best workout") were articulated openly and often on the Tonight Show in the mid-'70s, a public stance he now says was calculated to sell his sport. "If you tell people that pumping up feels as good as sex," Arnold told Rolling Stone last year, "that you can eat all the cake you want, get stoned, have a good time and everybody will love you—well, those are sell statements. Sex is something everybody understands, so I compared bodybuilding with sex. My job was to sell bodybuilding to the general public. And I did." ∎

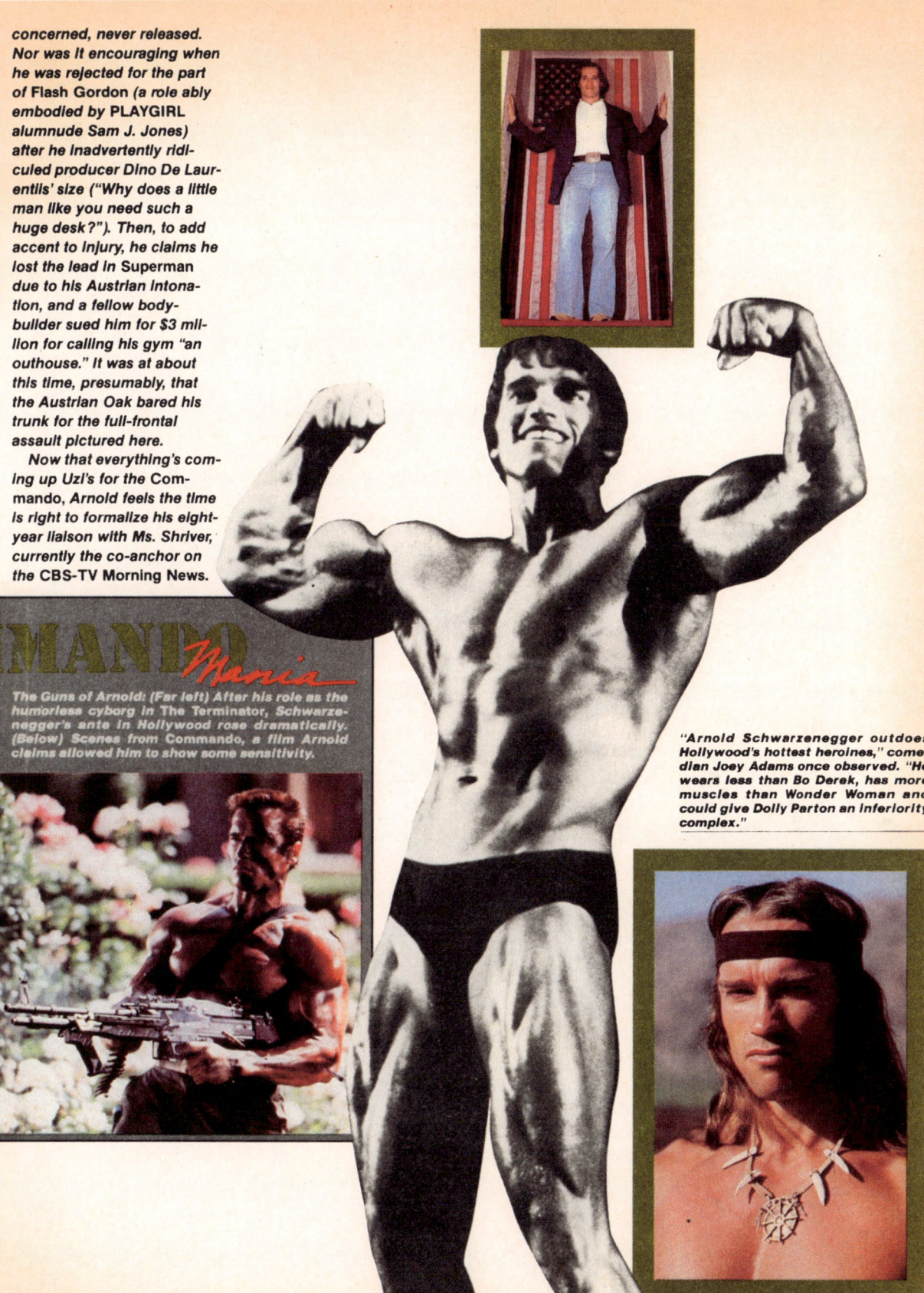

concerned, never released. Nor was it encouraging when he was rejected for the part of Flash Gordon (a role ably embodied by PLAYGIRL alumnude Sam J. Jones) after he inadvertently ridiculed producer Dino De Laurentiis' size ("Why does a little man like you need such a huge desk?"). Then, to add accent to injury, he claims he lost the lead in Superman due to his Austrian intonation, and a fellow bodybuilder sued him for $3 million for calling his gym "an outhouse." It was at about this time, presumably, that the Austrian Oak bared his trunk for the full-frontal assault pictured here.

Now that everything's coming up Uzi's for the Commando, Arnold feels the time is right to formalize his eight-year liaison with Ms. Shriver, currently the co-anchor on the CBS-TV Morning News.

COMMANDO *Mania*

The Guns of Arnold: (Far left) After his role as the humorless cyborg in The Terminator, Schwarzenegger's ante in Hollywood rose dramatically. (Below) Scenes from Commando, a film Arnold claims allowed him to show some sensitivity.

"Arnold Schwarzenegger outdoes Hollywood's hottest heroines," comedian Joey Adams once observed. "He wears less than Bo Derek, has more muscles than Wonder Woman and could give Dolly Parton an inferiority complex."

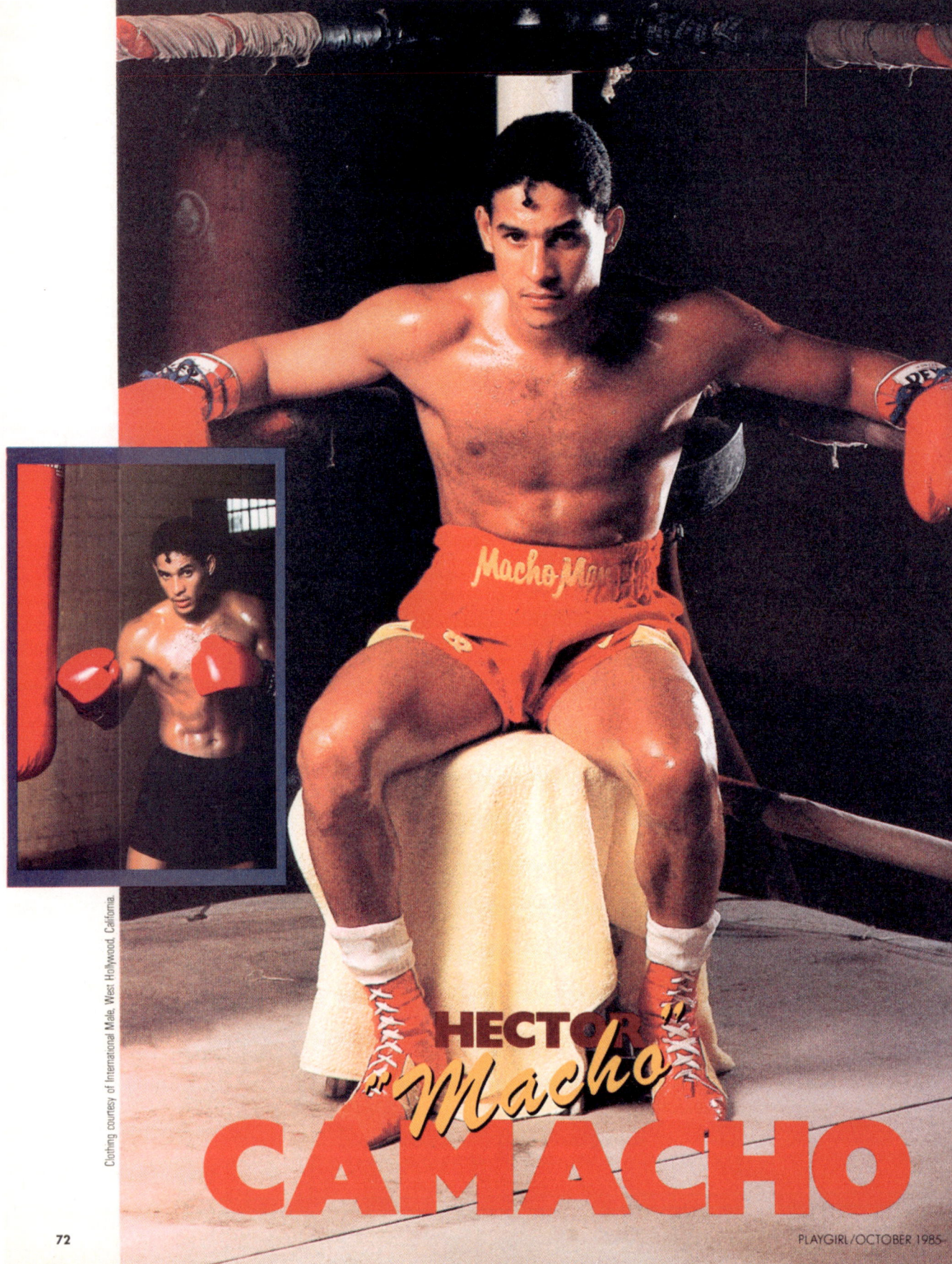

HECTOR "Macho" CAMACHO

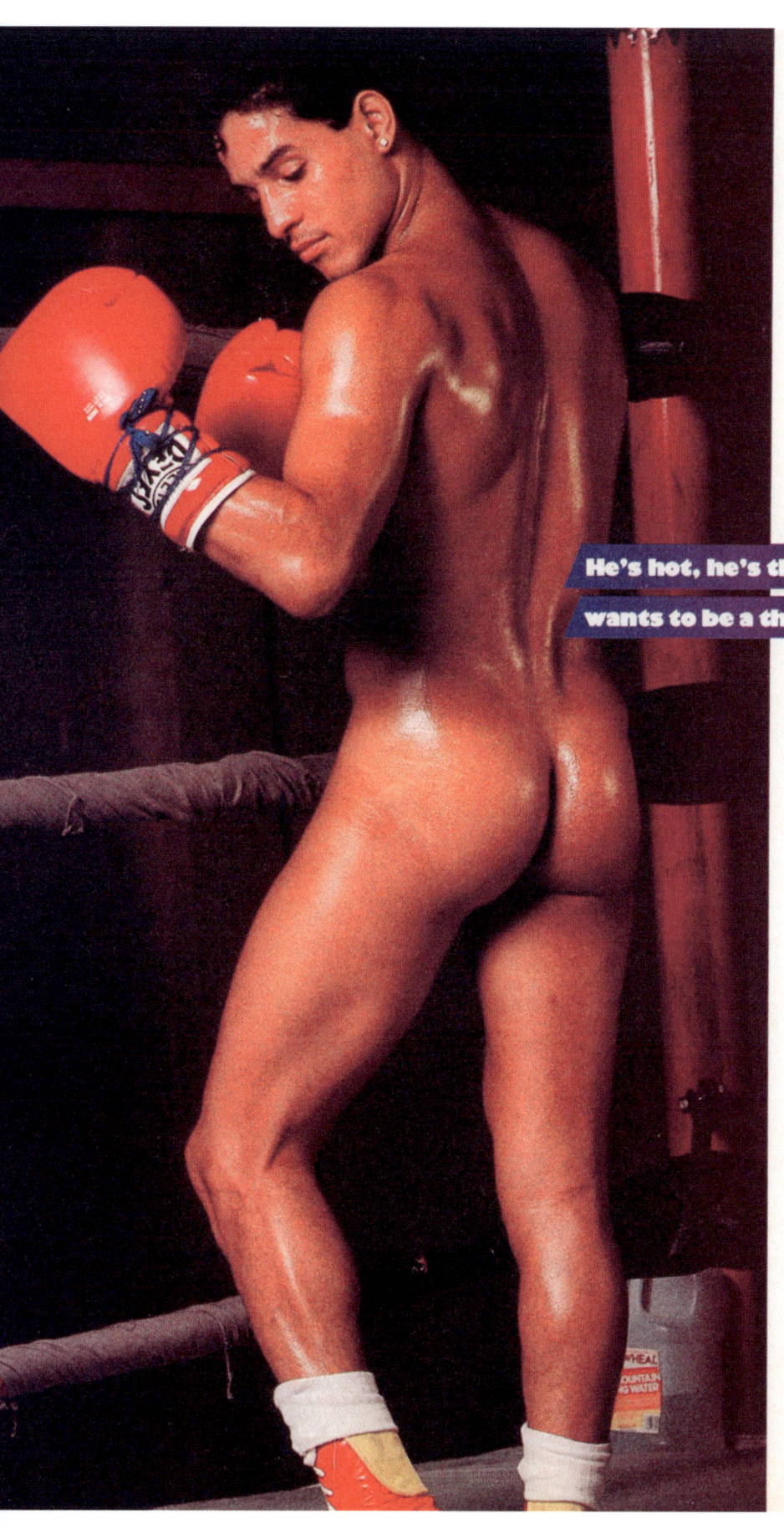

THEY CALL THIS 5-FOOT-6-INCH, 135-pound man with the brilliant brown eyes and killer grin "Macho." For once, the name fits. As Hector Camacho will tell you a dozen times, he was *born* to be a boxer, "the way Ali was born to be Ali and Sugar Ray was born to be Sugar Ray." Of course, fate helped out a little by giving him the perfect surname, one that rhymes with a word that instantly connotes temper, strength and raw power. Fate also made sure that he grew up in a mean neighborhood—Spanish Harlem—where the quickest way out of the Latin ghetto was through spectacular displays of fistic prowess.

Hector, 23, became a boxer at age 10, but he's been battling adversity for as long as he can remember.

"I grew up raising hell in the streets. I got caught shoplifting and stealing a couple of cars when I was 14 or 15. I didn't really hurt nobody, you know, unless I got in a fight, and it was never the way some people describe it. I was

He's hot, he's the greatest and he wants to be a three-time world champ.

also a father at the age of 15. I've got a seven-year-old son. But I'm not ashamed of anything I've done in the past. I may not be happy with everything, but I'm not ashamed of it, either."

Instead, this native of Bayamon, Puerto Rico, who immigrated to the United States with his parents at the tender age of three, is proud of other accomplishments that came after years of roughhousing.

"I was thrown out of six schools for fighting. I didn't finish high school, just dropped out in 10th grade. That's when I dedicated myself to boxing."

Since 1980, when he turned pro, "Macho" Camacho has fought 27 opponents in the ring. He has lost to *none* of them. Sixteen of the contests ended in straight knockouts, earning him a reputation for invincibility. He is the former world super featherweight champion (WBC) and as of this writing is preparing for a shot at the lightweight title in August. After that he plans to shoot for the welterweight crown.

"Go ahead and say I won the lightweight fight, because I will," he says. Odds are, he's absolutely right. Along with his renown as a stinging hit man, Hector is notorious for being brash, flashy and a lot of other rude things.

But as former welterweight champ Sugar Ray Leonard says, "When 'Macho' brags, he's not trying to convince you of anything; he's just telling you what's going to happen."

Of his boxing style Hector says, "A lot of people say that the sign of a good fighter is the guy who's all marked up.

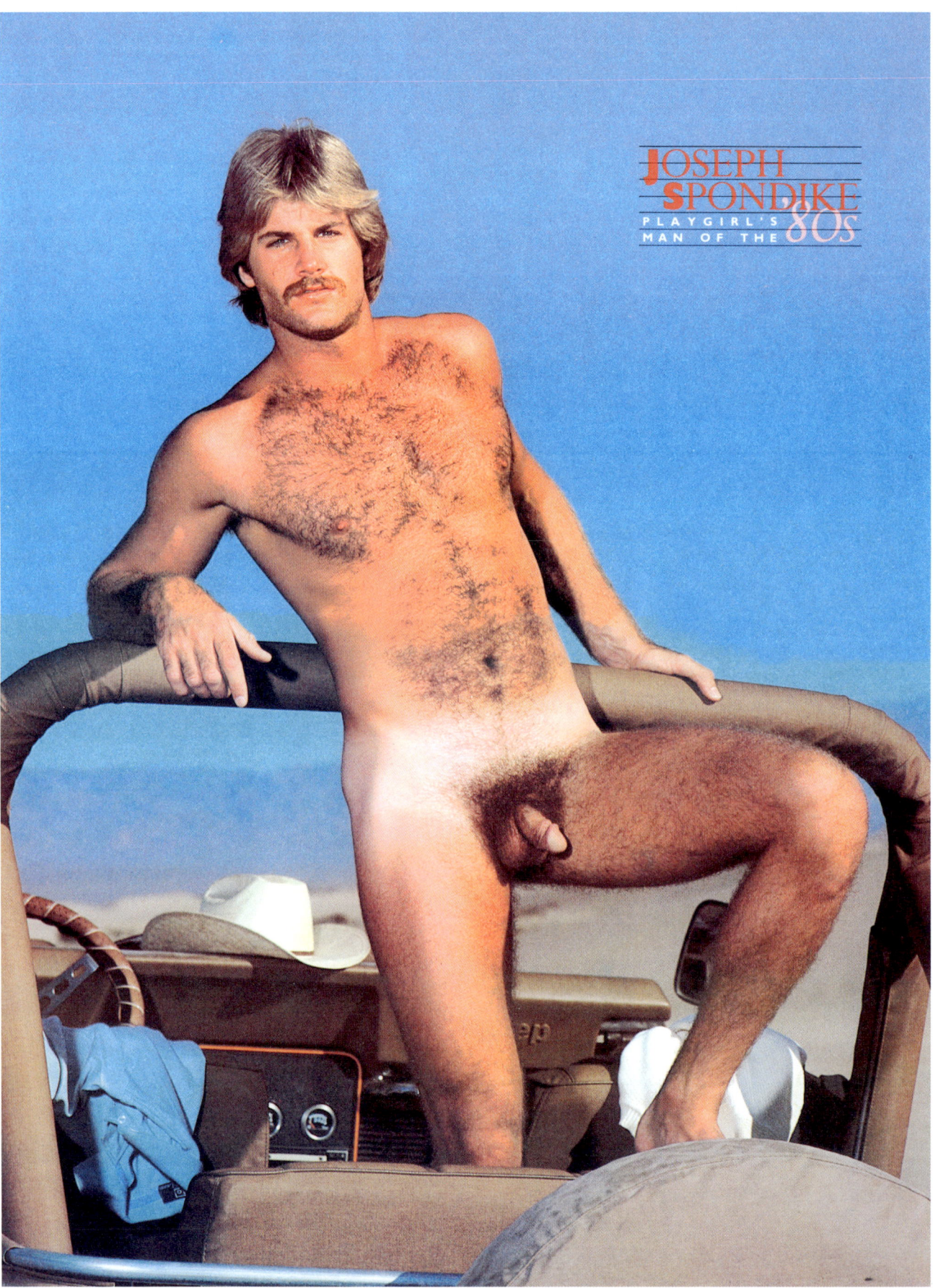

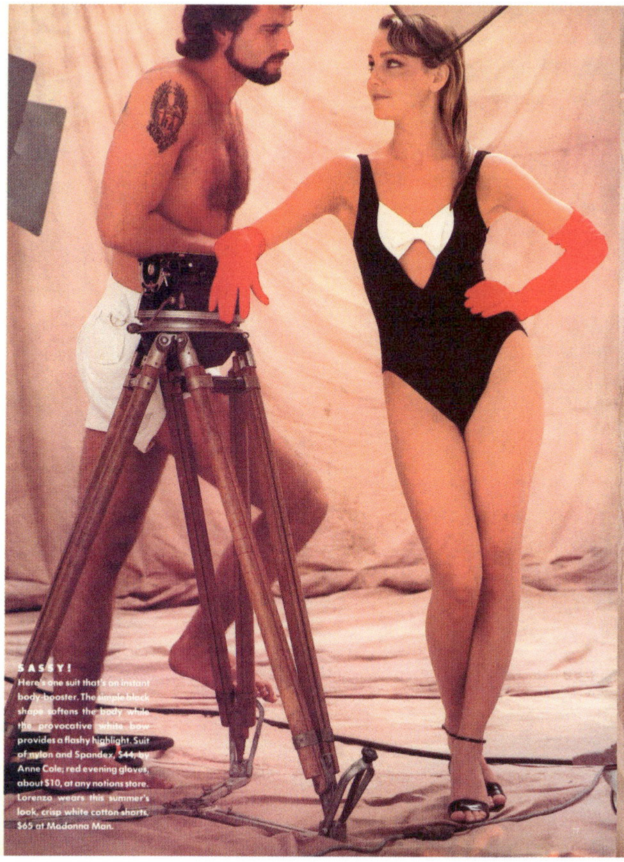

SASSY!
Here's one suit that's an instant
body-booster. The simple black
shape softens the body while
the provocative white bow
provides a flashy highlight. Suit
of nylon and Spandex, $44, by
Anne Cole, red evening gloves,
about $10, at any nations store.
Lorenzo wears this summer's
look, crisp white cotton shorts,
$65 at Madonna Man.

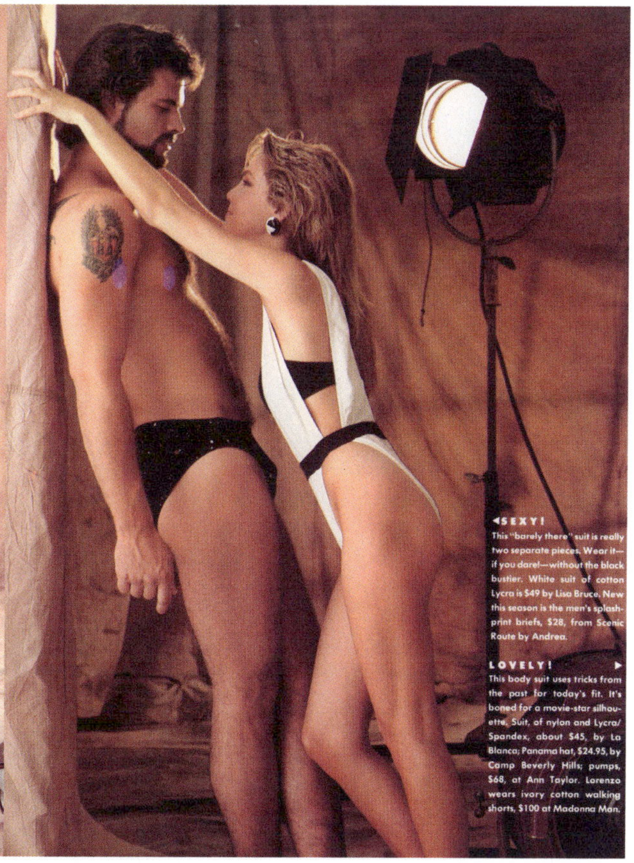

◄SEXY!
This "barely there" suit is really
two separate pieces. Wear it—
if you dare!—without the black
bustier. White suit of cotton
Lycra is $49 by Lisa Bruce. New
this season is the men's splash-
print briefs, $28, from Scenic
Route by Andrea.

LOVELY! ►
This body suit uses tricks from
the past for today's fit. It's
boned for a movie-star silhouette. Suit, of nylon and Lycra/
Spandex, about $45, by La
Blanca; Panama hat, $24.95, by
Camp Beverly Hills; pumps,
$68, at Ann Taylor. Lorenzo
wears ivory cotton walking
shorts, $100 at Madonna Man.

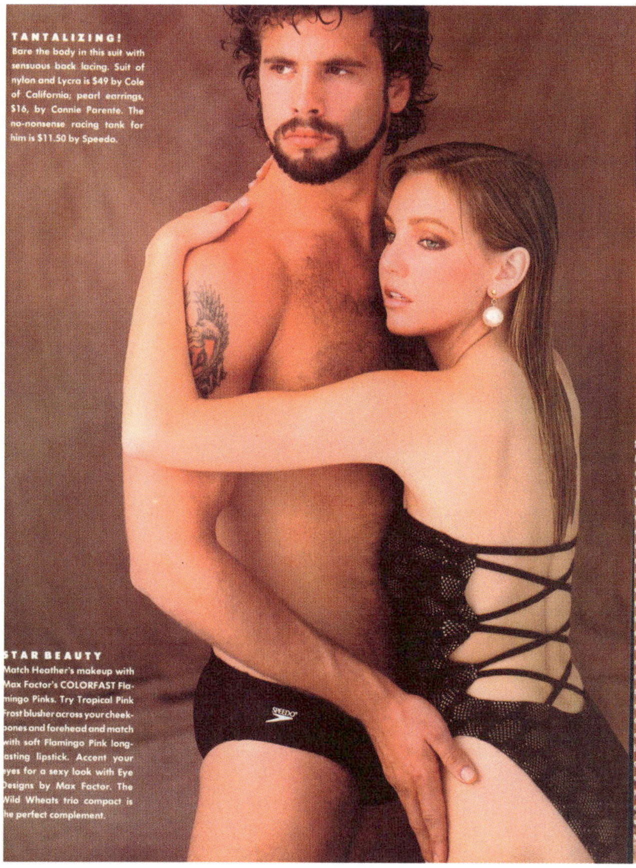

TANTALIZING!
Bare the body in this suit with
sensuous back lacing. Suit of
nylon and Lycra is $49 by Cole
of California, pearl earrings,
$16, by Connie Parente. The
no-nonsense racing tank for
him is $11.50 by Speedo.

STAR BEAUTY
Match Heather's makeup with
Max Factor's COLORFAST Flamingo Pinks. Try Tropical Pink
Frost blusher across your cheekbones and forehead and match
with soft Flamingo Pink long-
lasting lipstick. Accent your
eyes for a sexy look with Eye
Designs by Max Factor. The
Wild Wheats trio compact is
the perfect complement.

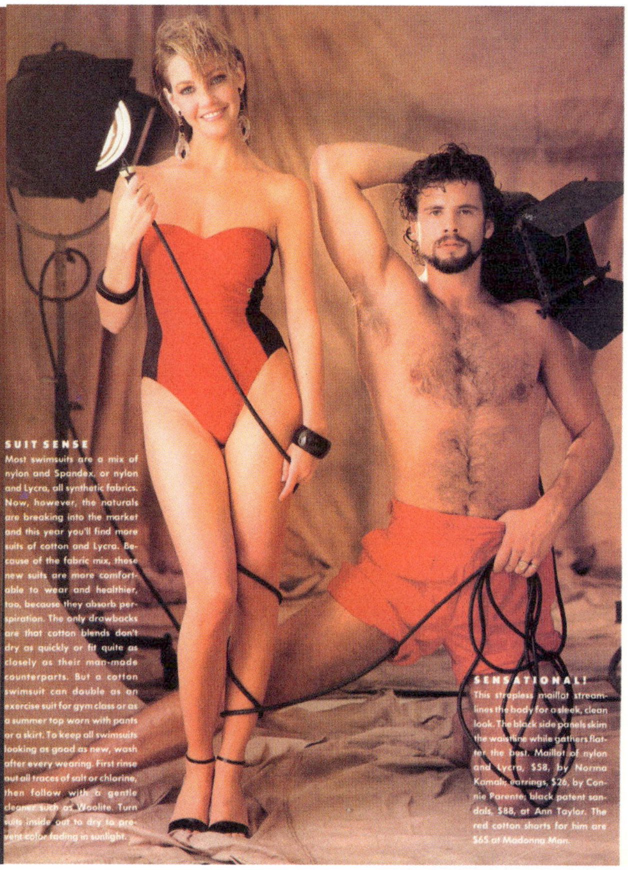

SUIT SENSE
Most swimsuits are a mix of
nylon and Spandex, or nylon
and Lycra, all synthetic fabrics.
Now, however, the naturals
are breaking into the market
and this year you'll find more
suits of cotton and Lycra. Because of the fabric mix, these
new suits are more comfortable to wear and healthier,
too, because they absorb perspiration. The only drawbacks
are that cotton blends don't
dry as quickly or fit quite as
closely as their man-made
counterparts. But a cotton
swimsuit can double as an
exercise suit for gym class or as
a summer top worn with pants
or a skirt. To keep all swimsuits
looking as good as new, wash
after every wearing. First rinse
out all traces of salt or chlorine,
then follow with a gentle
cleaner, such as Woolite. Turn
suit inside out to dry to prevent color fading in sunlight.

SENSATIONAL!
This strapless maillot stream-
lines the body for a sleek, clean
look. The black side panels skim
the waistline while garters flat-
ter the bust. Maillot of nylon
and Lycra, $58, by Norma
Kamali; earrings, $26, by Con-
nie Parente; black patent san-
dals, $88, at Ann Taylor. The
red cotton shorts for him are
$65 at Madonna Man.

CLOSE UP

UP FROM THE DEPPS

After a less-than-perfect childhood that included a broken home and drugs, 21 Jump Street's Johnny Depp is using his life experience and pouty good looks to win ratings—and hearts

BY JAMES A. BAGGETT

As undercover cop Tom Hanson on *Jump Street*, Johnny Depp is perhaps the brightest star in the Fox Network's line-up. But speaking with the 25-year-old actor, you'd never know it. In fact, Depp is so unimpressed with his celebrity status that he denies he is the star of the top-rated detective series. He'd rather refer to his character as the "strong center" of the show.

Born in Owensboro, Kentucky, and raised in Miramar, Florida, Depp is the youngest of four children. After experimenting with drugs at age 11, sex at 13, and petty crime, Depp was a high-school dropout by the time he was 16—"kind of a big mistake," he now admits. By the time he was 19, he had a job in construction and had formed and was playing guitar in a local band called the Kids.

Hoping to find fame, fortune and a record deal, Johnny and the Kids packed their bags and moved to Los Angeles. Eventually, they landed gigs with such heavy hitters as Los Lobos, Billy Idol, the Pretenders and Talking Heads. While the band waited for their chance, Depp sold ballpoint pens over the phone to make enough money to live and play in L.A. Before they could find a label that would sign the band, Depp got lucky—but not in the way he had planned.

A friend had introduced him to actor Nicolas (*Moonstruck*) Cage, who was a fan of the Kids. Cage suggested that Depp try his hand at acting. Depp met with Cage's agent, who agreed and convinced him to audition for *A Nightmare on Elm Street*. Five hours after the audition, director Wes Craven gave Depp the part. "I was devastated," he says now, with a sly grin.

Despite his lack of experience, Depp's acting career took off. A role in *Private Resort*, a flop, followed. But his third film, Oliver Stone's Academy Award-winning *Platoon*, proved to be his lucky charm. As Lerner, the Army unit's interpreter, Depp caught the attention of Hollywood casting directors and was offered his now-famous role on *21 Jump Street*.

As Hanson, a member of a special squad of baby-faced cops who work undercover in high schools, Depp is now facing life—much to his chagrin—as a certifiable prime-time sex symbol. Sporting a gold-hoop earring in his left ear (both are pierced) and a trademark long white scarf, which he wraps Indian-style around his head, Depp is the very definition of cool. With his high, chiseled cheekbones—a legacy of the Cherokee heritage on both sides of his family—and his stylishly scruffy clothes, he exudes a rock-and-roll sexuality that is steaming up TV screens across the land.

> "I am going to do everything I can to avoid being put in some teen-idol category."

PLAYGIRL: Why haven't you done a feature film since you started on *Jump Street*?

DEPP: Coming off the show and looking at features definitely changes the films I would want to do. I'm going to do everything I can—I will fight tooth and nail—to avoid being put in some teen-idol category. I don't want somebody who's writing the checks to limit me, to place me in a herd of people who can only do one thing. I don't want to be limited by other peoples' opinions. I want to play roles where I'm not necessarily the leading man. I'd like to shave my head, sew my eyeballs shut—all kinds of things. I would feel very shortchanged and it would be a terrible thing if I could do only teen-exploitation films. It just wouldn't be worth it.

PLAYGIRL: How did you land the role of Lerner in *Platoon*?

DEPP: I found out about *Platoon* in January of 1986, when my agent sent me over the script. I read it, and I was just blown away! It was so right on the money as far as truth and honesty goes. I met Oliver Stone and he said, "I want you to read this. Go out in the hall and study it." So I studied it and came back in and read for him. He said, "Okay, let's call your agent." That's how it happened. Actually, before Orion did their cut [of the film], I had a nicer part. My part really got chopped up.

PLAYGIRL: Tell me about the training you went through for the film.

DEPP: We went through two weeks of training in the jungle in the Philippines. I gotta tell you, man, it was highly emotional. You put thirty guys in the jungle and leave them there to stay together for two weeks—just like a real platoon—and you build a real tightness. It's almost like a family. We *became* a military unit, a platoon. To this day, whenever I talk to Charlie [Sheen] or any of the other guys, it's just like the same deal. We still get together all the time and try to hang out as much as possible, and it takes us right back to the platoon.

PLAYGIRL: How do you feel about your bad-boy image—you know, "former hood makes good"?

DEPP: Jesus, that has gotten a little out of hand! I run into people who think I've done time [in jail] or something. When I was a kid, I was just like any other boy. Boys are very curious. I wasn't the best kid in the world, but I wasn't an ax murderer either. As a kid, I went through experimenting with drugs and stuff early. But I got out of it by the time I was fourteen or fifteen. I saw that it was getting me nowhere. I saw the kids around me, not doing anything, not wanting to change their lives. I didn't want to be like that. I wanted to continue with my music, and I knew that drugs were holding me back. I'd seen a lot of ugly things. People fall down bad hills with drugs. It's just not worth it.

PLAYGIRL: How did you stop?

DEPP: I was very lucky. I had a lot of older friends who gave me advice, who said, "Look, really look at what's happening. This may feel kind of good, but man, there's so much more out there. There's so much you need to learn. This thing is going to take control eventually. Instead of you enjoying something, it's going to enjoy you. It'll run your life." I was lucky to have a lot of great friends.

PLAYGIRL: How did you get started in music?

DEPP: I always loved music. When I was little, my brother would listen to Bob Dylan and stuff. Also, my uncle's a preacher, and he used to have this group called the Gospel Sunlighters. When I was about twelve, I thought they were the greatest thing in the world, so I went out and bought an electric guitar for twenty-five dollars. Immediately, I locked myself in my room and started playing. I bought a chord book to figure out where to put my fingers and then started learning from records. I started playing in bands when I was thirteen, but we were horrible. We played a lot of backyard parties.

PLAYGIRL: Do you ever still play?

DEPP: I still play, but when I got my first movie, *A Nightmare on Elm Street*, things just sort of fell apart for the band. They weren't real happy that I'd gone off to do this film. It was difficult for them to stomach. We split up, and everyone went their own way.

PLAYGIRL: Would you ever consider making an album?

DEPP: I would love to play. But people know me now as an actor. I'd do anything to be on stage again, but I've got to be careful. I don't want people to say, "Oh, great, another actor is going to do a record." I'm trying to fight the teen-idol image, so if I did a record, it would make it that much more difficult. Somebody somewhere puts labels on people, and it stops them from doing certain things they love.

PLAYGIRL: What sparked your acting career?

DEPP: It was really a fluke. It was divine intervention. God said, "OK, he's been hungry long enough. Let me give him a little something." When I moved out here [to L.A.], one of my buddies introduced me to Nicolas Cage. I was walking down Melrose one day filling out job applications and Nick said, "I think you should see my agent." I did, and she sent me to read for *Nightmare*. It was very strange. I'd never done drama before. Nothing in high school. Nothing. I was

(continued on page 85)

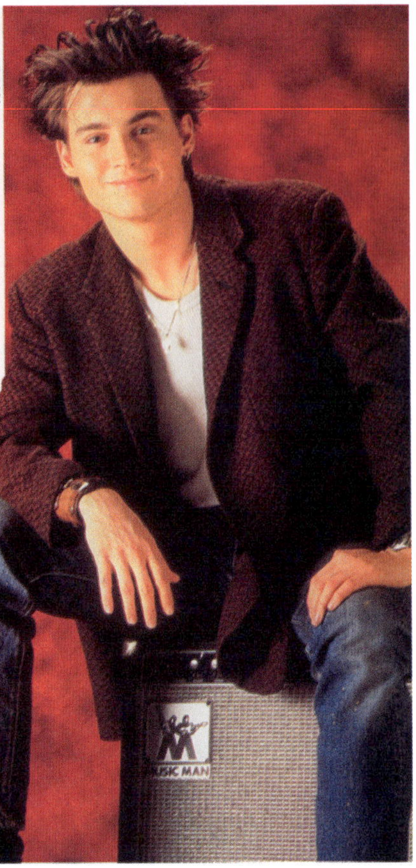

P. SALTONSTALL/ONYX

JAMES A. BAGGETT is a freelance entertainment writer who lives in Manhattan.

CLOSE UP

RIVER PHOENIX—RISING FAST

A bright new star comes of age

BY IAIN BLAIR

Hollywood's Bel Age hotel is exactly the sort of place you might expect to meet a movie star, even if the star in question is a precociously talented 18 year old rather than a 78-year-old legend. Its opulent suites, adorned with original, expensive artwork and invisibly serviced by an attentive staff that outnumbers the guests, reek of pampered luxury.

So it's quite a relief when River Phoenix, looking boyish and distinctly unglamorous in a black T-shirt and jeans, bounds into the room and onto the sofa. Slighter and even more handsome than he appears on screen, Phoenix, who most recently appeared opposite Sidney Poitier in the spy drama *Little Nikita*, seems out of place, but not uncomfortable, in his temporary high-class lodgings.

"This is the side of showbiz that I'm still trying to come to terms with," he confesses, with the look of a kid who's been let loose in a candy store, but who also realizes instinctively that too much of a good thing might be bad for him.

"All this kind of stuff—all the room service—is fine, but I'm not very good at playing this game," he points out simply. "I really don't know how to eat at one of these fancy restaurants, and I have the *worst* table manners."

Honest and refreshingly unspoiled by all the trappings of stardom despite his meteoric career, Hollywood's hottest teenage property may be slightly embarrassed by his sudden entrance into the lifestyle of the rich and famous—entirely understandable, when one learns of a childhood spent roaming the poorer streets of South America with his missionary parents.

But if the glitz of showbiz is less alluring to Phoenix than a night with pals at the local burger stand, the serious business of making movies is another matter altogether.

Mention the films that catapulted him to international stardom, *Stand By Me* and *The Mosquito Coast*, or *Little Nikita*, *A Night in the Life of Jimmy Reardon* and *Running On Empty* (the three pictures he'll be seen in this year), and this 18 year old is intense, focused, and strikingly candid about his own abilities.

PLAYGIRL: Has there been a lot of pressure to live up to the rave reviews you received for *Stand By Me*?

PHOENIX: Yeah, it's hard, especially since *Stand By Me* took everyone by surprise. I was shocked at how well it did. I felt it was a quality piece of work, but I never dreamed it'd find such a wide audience. And when that happens, you start worrying about what roles you should choose next.

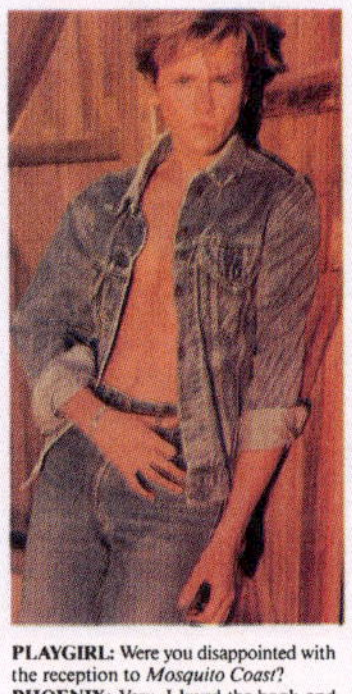

PLAYGIRL: Were you disappointed with the reception to *Mosquito Coast*?

PHOENIX: Very. I loved the book and thought the film was very faithful to it. Harrison Ford did a great job, but most people expected another Indiana Jones-type hero. They didn't want to see an anti-hero. It was disappointing 'cause everyone worked so hard on that shoot, and I felt better about my work than I did about my performance in *Stand By Me*.

PLAYGIRL: There were stories of heavy drug and alcohol abuse on the set.

PHOENIX: How do you know that? I suppose it's common knowledge—it was mentioned in *Premiere* magazine. It was like living in the drug capital of the Northern hemisphere. I know drugs were rampant everywhere in town, but as far as on the set was concerned, I don't know who was mixed up in that. I don't think it affected the creative elements, but the crew. . .if anything, it probably helped them move all the lights (laughs). It's nothing new in this business. There's a lot of temptation, and you learn from experience, "Hey, I don't want to get mixed up in this shit."

PLAYGIRL: Your real-life childhood seems to bear a striking resemblance to the one portrayed in *Mosquito Coast*.

PHOENIX: Yeah. I was born in Oregon, but my parents, who were missionaries, moved to South America, and I grew up there until I was seven. Actually, we lived all over the place, partly in Venezuela, and partly in Central America and Mexico. We kept moving!

PLAYGIRL: Was it a happy childhood?

PHOENIX: Happy? Well, it was very interesting, with a kind of day-to-day existence and reality that hasn't changed much. I've played guitar since I was five, and I was very involved in that with my sister. When we were younger, we used to sing religious songs on the streets wherever we happened to be at the time.

PLAYGIRL: Was that your start in showbiz?

PHOENIX: Yeah! It was really a novelty to sing in the streets, but we also had a whole act, with my brother Leaf, and my sisters Rainbow and Summer Joy. We entered talent contests and were pretty popular in Latin America.

PLAYGIRL: Are all your family names symbolic?

PHOENIX: I guess so. My parents named me after the river of life in Herman Hesse's *Siddhartha*, and our surname was adopted when we left Latin America and returned to the States when I was about nine.

PLAYGIRL: What happened?

PHOENIX: They were part of an organization called "The Children of God," and they were also like children of the '60s. My father was a carpenter, and then he decided to drop out and become a missionary, and he moved us all down south. But then he became disillusioned with the guy running the organization, and we all moved back—to L.A., in fact.

PLAYGIRL: It must have been quite a culture shock.

PHOENIX: No kidding. When we arrived, we were very naive and sheltered in many ways, and then suddenly we were exposed to all this information. It was like a brainstorm. I mean, we had a TV for the first time. And naturally my parents worried that we'd all be corrupted.

PLAYGIRL: Are they still missionaries?

PHOENIX: No, but they still have a strong code of ethics that they're very loyal to, and it's one that we all share. They're very spiritual, but it's not organized religion like it was before. My father still reads the Bible a lot and applies it to everyday life. He's a very practical, logical man, and then there's this other side of him that's completely way out. He's an interesting character.

PLAYGIRL: Were you raised in a very religious atmosphere?

PHOENIX: Oh, yes. I knew the Bible very well. I memorized whole chapters in Spanish when I was five and six.

PLAYGIRL: Are you still very religious?

PHOENIX: Not in the same way. I think the Bible is an incredible history book, but I feel organized religion is bullshit. It's caused more wars and bloodshed than anything else. But I do feel secure in being able to draw from it. I think there'll be a stage in my life where I'll get into it more, and try moving off into the jungle like the guy in *Mosquito Coast*, to find myself and all that stuff (laughs). But right now, I'm eighteen, and I don't want to spend a lot of time thinking about it. I already live by a code of ethics, so I'm an all-right person. I'm not messed up.

PLAYGIRL: Do your parents worry about the effects of stardom on you and your brother and sisters who are also in the business?

PHOENIX: They manage us, thank God, so we're all still very close. But my father is worried that we could be ruined by this business. It's got a lot of pitfalls and temptations, and he doesn't want us to become materialistic and lose all the values we were brought up believing in. So yes, he's pleased we're doing well, but in a way, he's almost reached a point in his life where he could just drop out again like he did in the '60s, and move to a farm and get close to the earth.

PLAYGIRL: Does that appeal to you?

PHOENIX: Yes, to one part of me. But what I've been explaining to him is that there's also this other part of me that has to fulfill myself and push myself, and find out just what I'm really capable of.

PLAYGIRL: Has this caused tension?

PHOENIX: Not tension. It'd be tension if we both held it in. But we have a very open, honest relationship; we discuss everything till we come to an understanding. Basically, whatever happens with my career, I know I'll always have a bed at home and a place I can retreat to.

PLAYGIRL: Are you close to your brothers and sisters?

PHOENIX: We're a very tight-knit family and everyone's supportive. There's no rivalry, 'cause we're all so different, both in age and character.

PLAYGIRL: Do you hang out with other young actors?

PHOENIX: Not really. I'm in my family circle most of the time.

PLAYGIRL: What do you like doing when you're not working?

PHOENIX: I'm a real music lover. I just bought this guitar, and I play a lot and I like to write songs—they're kind of "progressive ethereal folk-rock" I guess (laughs hard). Then I have this other side that's very hyper and athletic, though I'm not really into organized sports. It's more just like jumping on the trampoline and playing tag with my brothers and sisters. That's been a lot of fun, getting to know my kids—I call 'em my kids.

PLAYGIRL: Do you feel like the older brother in the family?

PHOENIX: Yeah, but sometimes I feel like the younger kid too, 'cause they're all very mature. I can talk to Summer, who's ten, just the way I've been talking now.

PLAYGIRL: Do you have a girlfriend?

PHOENIX: (Laughs) I've always hated that term, but yes, I have someone I'm very close to, though we've got no plans to get married or anything like that. But we're soulmates.

PLAYGIRL: Do you ever feel that because of your unusual childhood you don't feel the normal teenage need to rebel against your parents?

PHOENIX: Definitely. They're far more out there than I am! It's more like I'm rebelling against the mainstream of "Yeah, let's party!" To me, that's a shallow reality, and I can't find happiness in it.

PLAYGIRL: You have three films out this year. What else is in the works?

PHOENIX: Nothing. I don't plan my career years ahead. Everything's very spontaneous, like the way I've grown up. That's how I'm comfortable, and how I like to live. ■

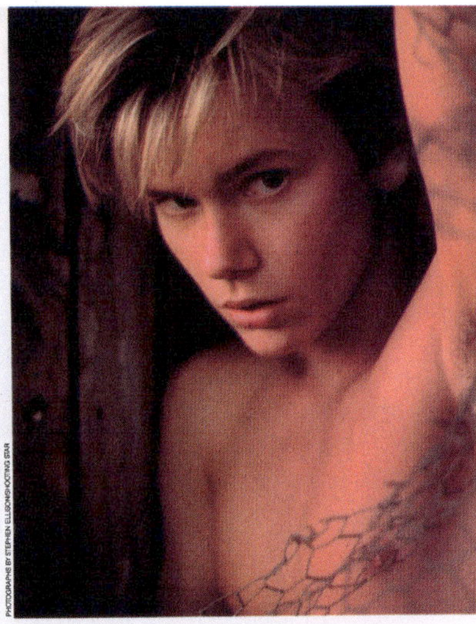

PHOTOGRAPHS BY STEPHEN ELLISON/SHOOTING STAR

"COUNT" IAIN BLAIR is a writer/musician who lives in Los Angeles.

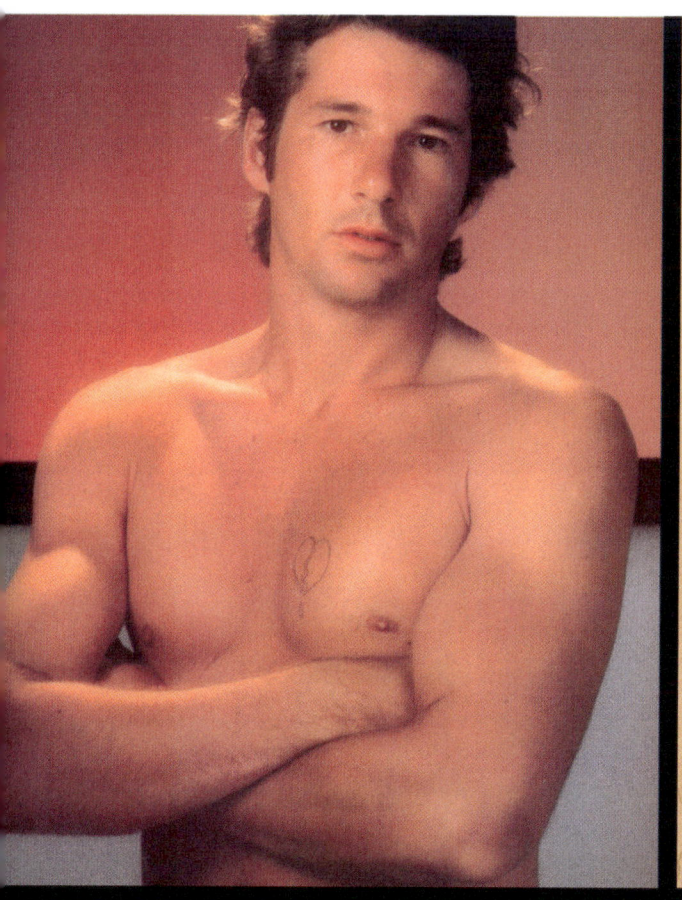

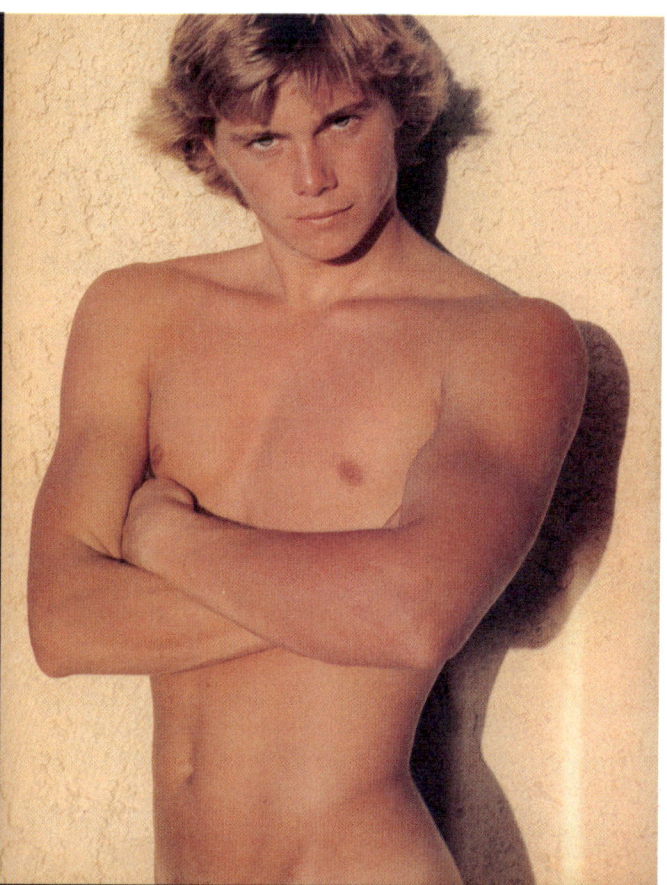

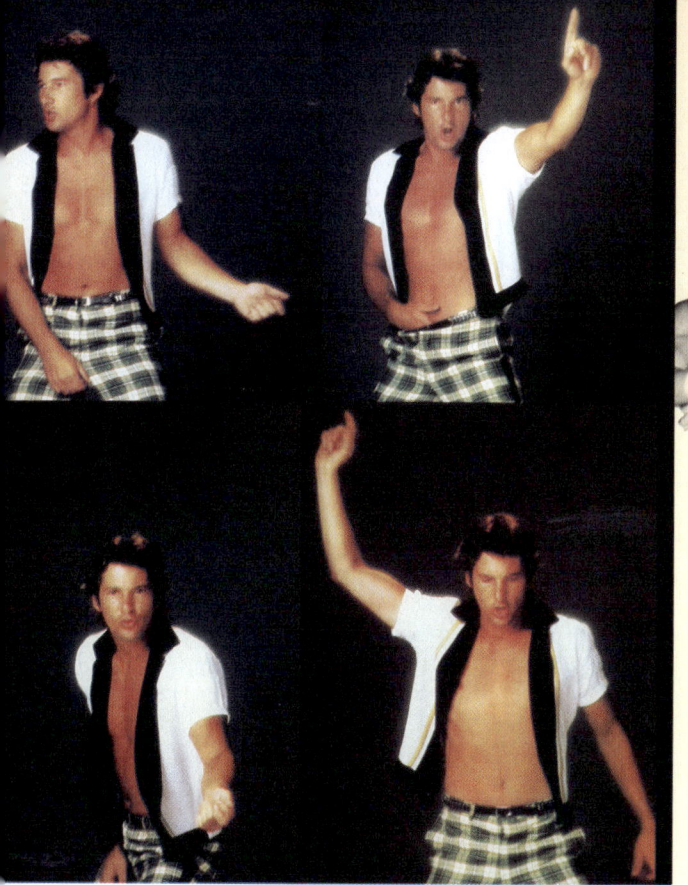

PLAYGIRL MAGAZINE PRESENTS

ROCKY

VS

SLY

STALLONE

THIRD CHAMPIONSHIP MATCH

AN EXISTENTIAL BOUT
WITH HIMSELF

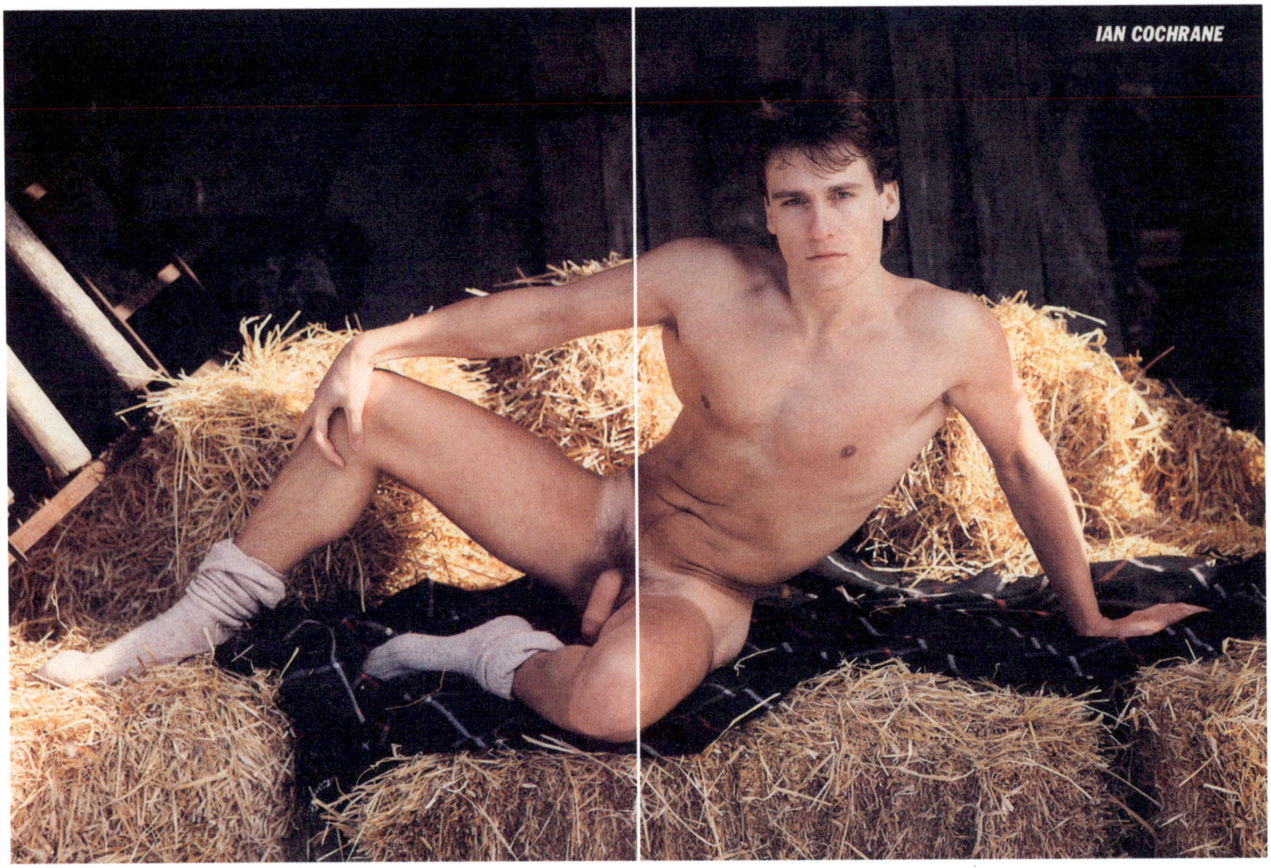

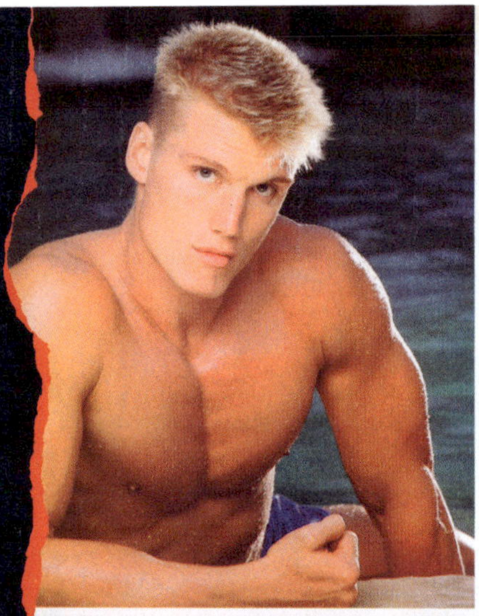

strictly routine. He has a joint degree from the Royal Institute of Technology in Stockholm and the University of Sydney in Australia. He's also fluent in four languages, has a black belt in karate and can play both the trombone and percussion instruments.

Up to now, Dolph's main claim to fame has been as the photogenic paramour to boisterous model-actress Grace Jones. Thanks to the exposure *Rocky IV* has now given him, though, it's patently obvious Lundgren packs a wallop all his own.

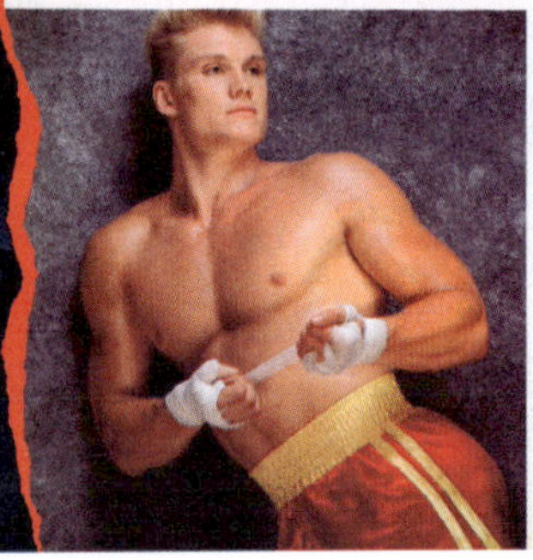

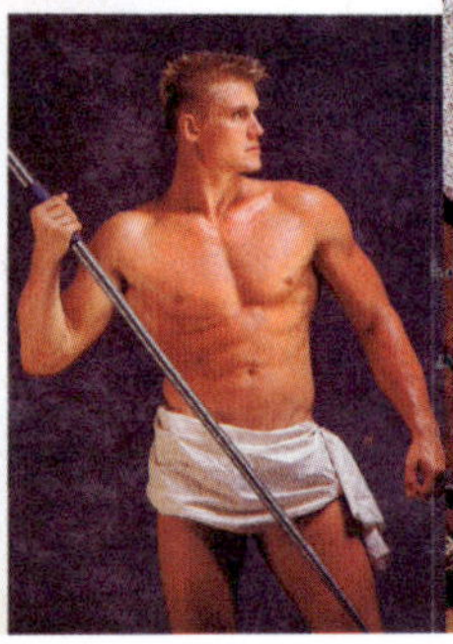

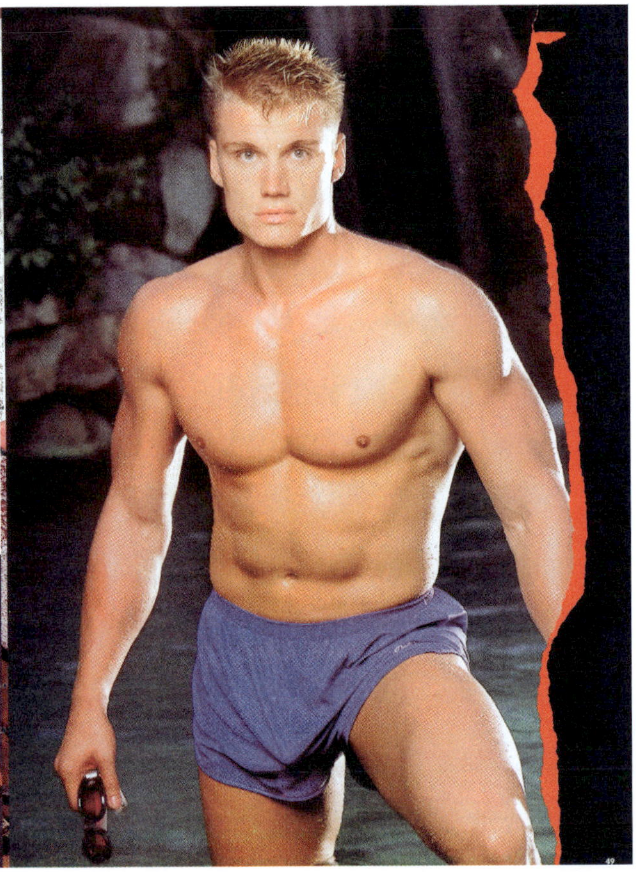

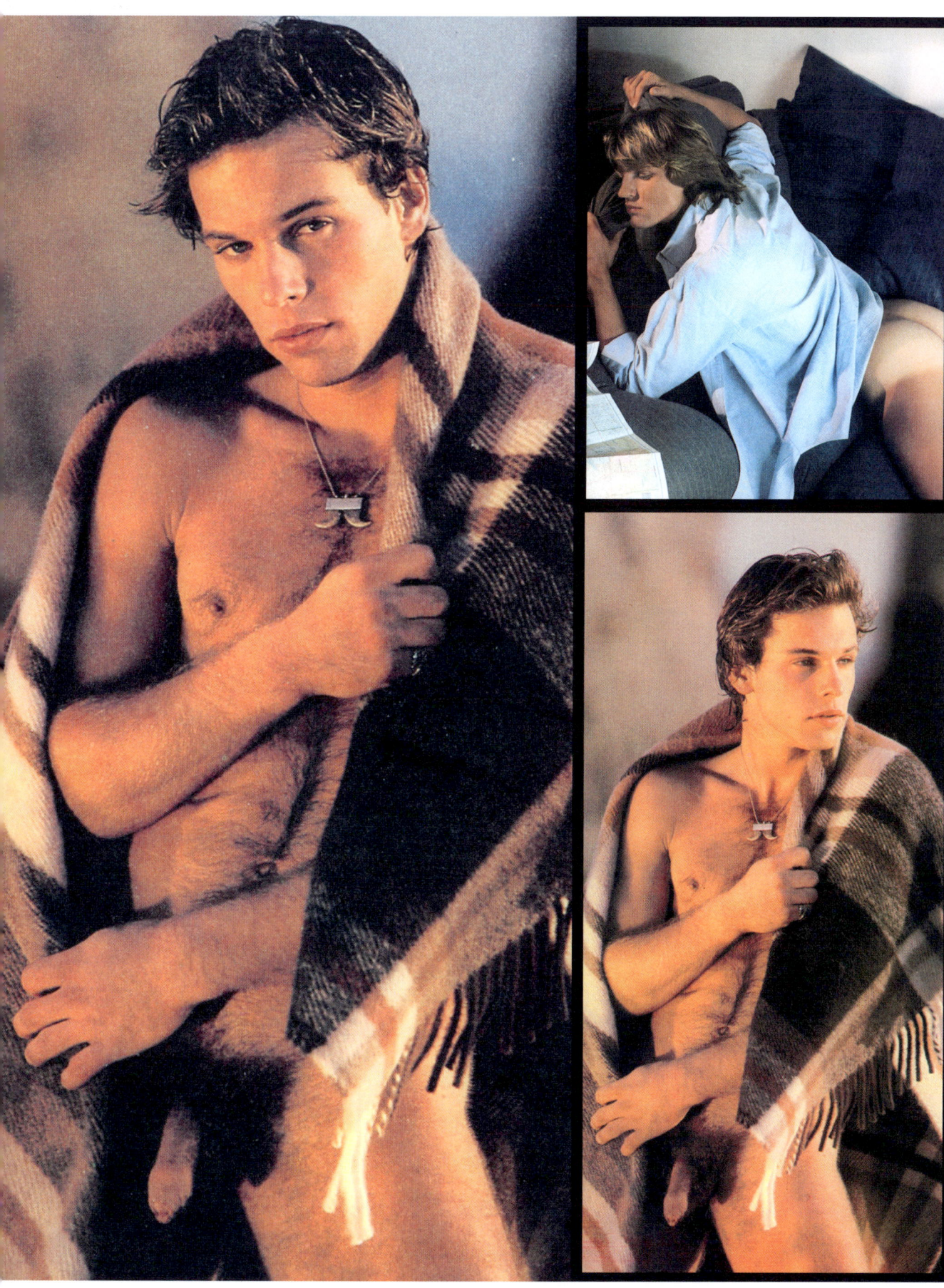

CHAPTER 8

BEST OF THE
1990s

The 1990s brought an all-out explosion of pop culture
as shown in exclusive celebrity interviews with Aerosmith's Steven
Tyler (pictured licking a *Playgirl* editor in October 1990),
Rob Lowe, *Beverly Hills 90210*'s Brian Austin Green,
Saved by the Bell's Mario Lopez, and "Marky" Mark Wahlberg
in nothing but his Calvins. In February 1994, Joan Rivers
served as the magazine's campy Editor-for-the-Day.
This decade saw several stars strip down just for the pages
of *Playgirl*: boxer Oscar De La Hoya, wrestler Shawn Michaels,
Baywatch's Jaason Simmons, and the infamous August 1995
photospread with the late Peter Steele of goth metal band
Type O Negative—fully erect!—to this day one of the most collectible
issues on the internet. And—file this under "should we really
admit to this?"—in August 1990, *Playgirl* even held a contest
to win an opportunity to "Sleep with Donald Trump"—as if!
Articles like "Sucking in the Nineties" (1993)
and "A User-Friendly Guide to the Penis" (1996)
serve as mementos of a sexy new internet-obsessed world
before the inevitable introduction of Playgirl.com in 1998.

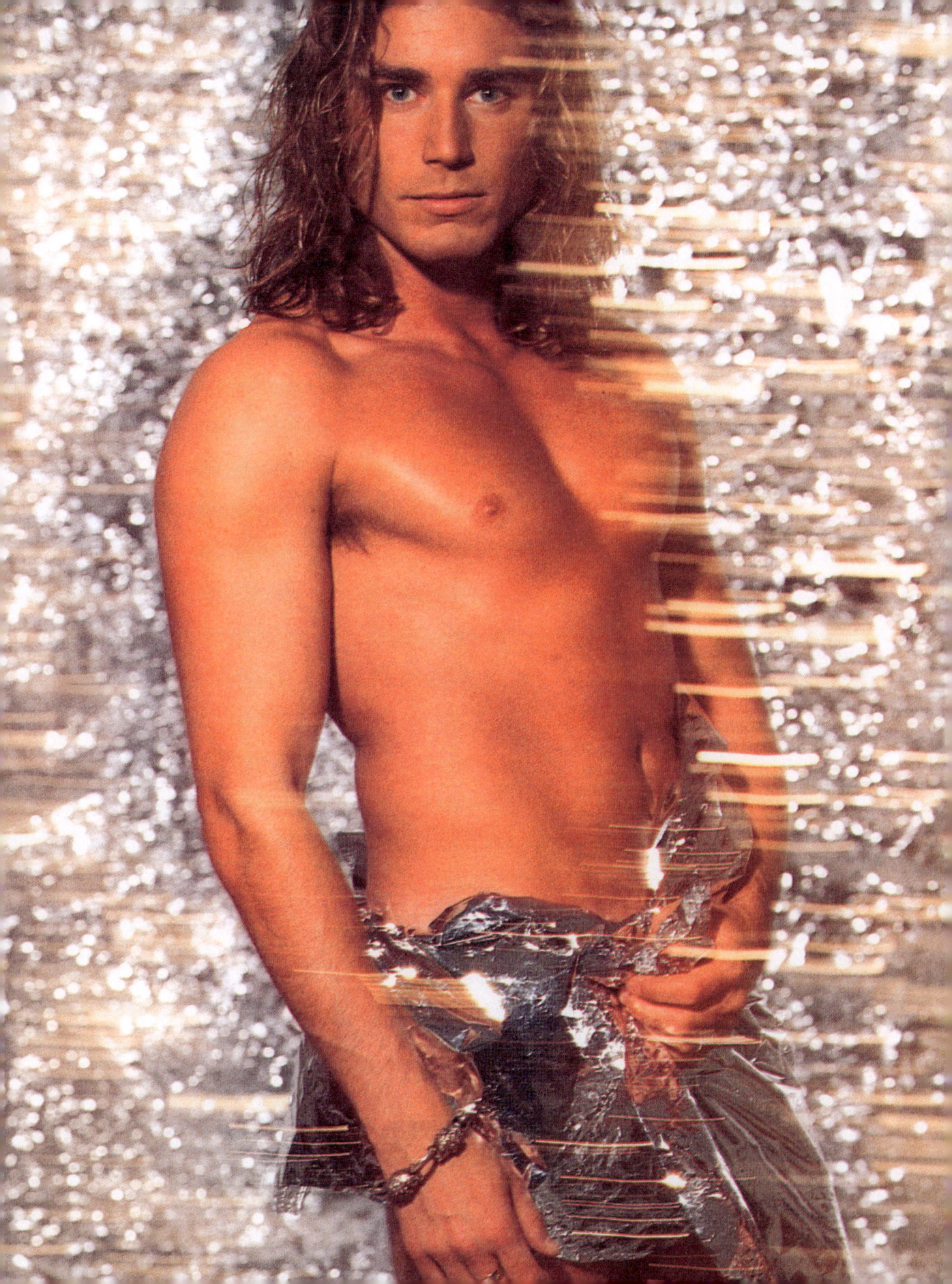

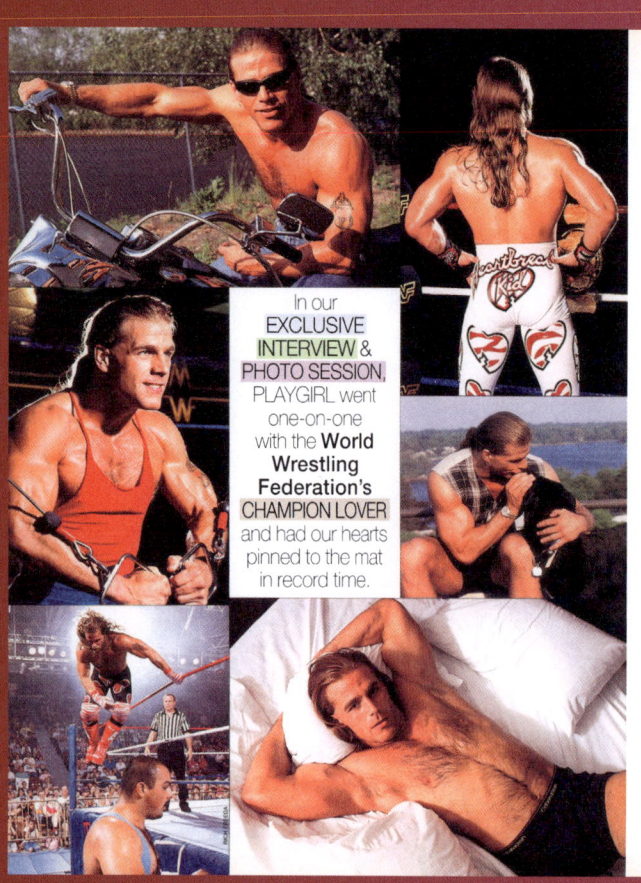

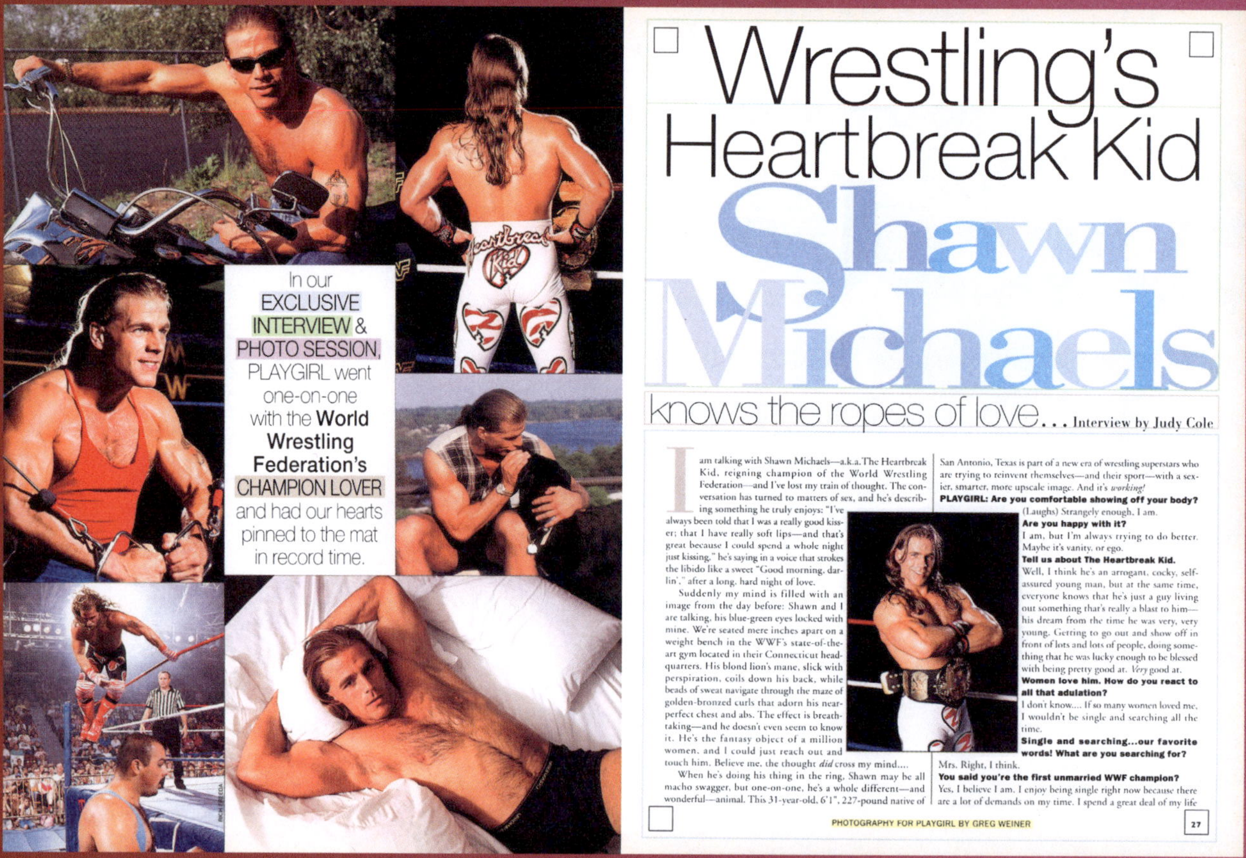

Wrestling's Heartbreak Kid

Shawn Michaels

knows the ropes of love… Interview by Judy Cole

I am talking with Shawn Michaels—a.k.a. The Heartbreak Kid, reigning champion of the World Wrestling Federation—and I've lost my train of thought. The conversation has turned to matters of sex, and he's describing something he truly enjoys: "I've always been told that I was a really good kisser; that I have really soft lips—and that's great because I could spend a whole night just kissing," he's saying in a voice that strokes the libido like a sweet "Good morning, darlin'," after a long, hard night of love.

Suddenly my mind is filled with an image from the day before: Shawn and I are talking, his blue-green eyes locked with mine. We're seated mere inches apart on a weight bench in the WWF's state-of-the-art gym located in their Connecticut headquarters. His blond lion's mane, slick with perspiration, coils down his back, while beads of sweat navigate through the maze of golden-bronzed curls that adorn his near-perfect chest and abs. The effect is breathtaking—and he doesn't even seem to know it. He's the fantasy object of a million women, and I could just reach out and touch him. Believe me, the thought *did* cross my mind….

When he's doing his thing in the ring, Shawn may be all macho swagger, but one-on-one, he's a whole different—and wonderful—animal. This 31-year-old, 6'1", 227-pound native of San Antonio, Texas is part of a new era of wrestling superstars who are trying to reinvent themselves—and their sport—with a sexier, smarter, more upscale image. And it's *working!*

PLAYGIRL: Are you comfortable showing off your body?
(Laughs) Strangely enough, I am.

Are you happy with it?
I am, but I'm always trying to do better. Maybe it's vanity, or ego.

Tell us about The Heartbreak Kid.
Well, I think he's an arrogant, cocky, self-assured young man, but at the same time, everyone knows that he's just a guy living out something that's really a blast to him—his dream from the time he was very, very young. Getting to go out and show off in front of lots and lots of people, doing something that he was lucky enough to be blessed with being pretty good at. *Very* good at.

Women love him. How do you react to all that adulation?
I don't know…. If so many women loved me, I wouldn't be single and searching all the time.

Single and searching…our favorite words! What are you searching for?
Mrs. Right, I think.

You said you're the first unmarried WWF champion?
Yes. I believe I am. I enjoy being single right now because there are a lot of demands on my time. I spend a great deal of my life

27

> "**I** tend to find **beauty** in all **girls.**"

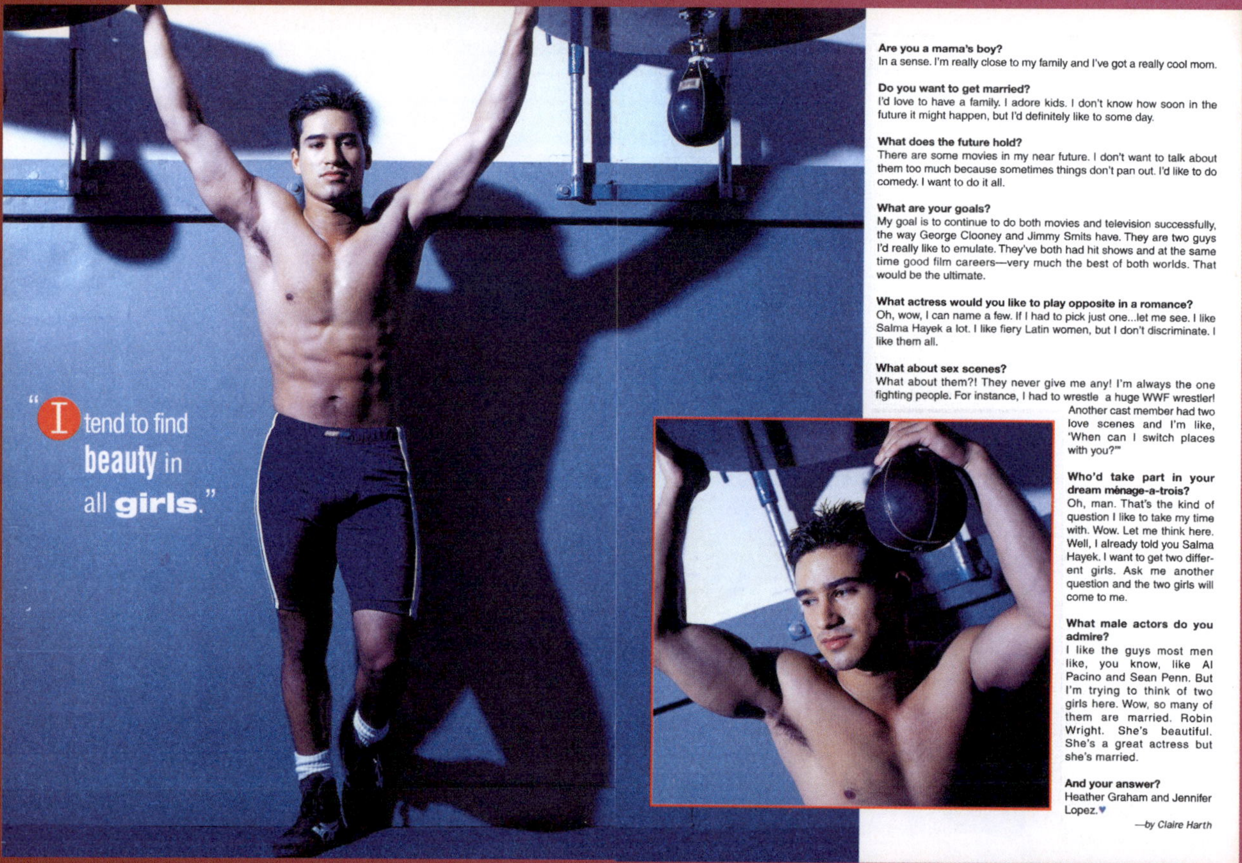

Are you a mama's boy?
In a sense. I'm really close to my family and I've got a really cool mom.

Do you want to get married?
I'd love to have a family. I adore kids. I don't know how soon in the future it might happen, but I'd definitely like to some day.

What does the future hold?
There are some movies in my near future. I don't want to talk about them too much because sometimes things don't pan out. I'd like to do comedy. I want to do it all.

What are your goals?
My goal is to continue to do both movies and television successfully, the way George Clooney and Jimmy Smits have. They are two guys I'd really like to emulate. They've both had hit shows and at the same time good film careers—very much the best of both worlds. That would be the ultimate.

What actress would you like to play opposite in a romance?
Oh, wow, I can name a few. If I had to pick just one…let me see. I like Salma Hayek a lot. I like fiery Latin women, but I don't discriminate. I like them all.

What about sex scenes?
What about them?! They never give me any! I'm always the one fighting people. For instance, I had to wrestle a huge WWF wrestler! Another cast member had two love scenes and I'm like, 'When can I switch places with you?'"

Who'd take part in your dream ménage-a-trois?
Oh, man. That's the kind of question I like to take my time with. Wow. Let me think here. Well, I already told you Salma Hayek. I want to get two different girls. Ask me another question and the two girls will come to me.

What male actors do you admire?
I like the guys most men like, you know, like Al Pacino and Sean Penn. But I'm trying to think of two girls here. Wow, so many of them are married. Robin Wright. She's beautiful. She's a great actress but she's married.

And your answer?
Heather Graham and Jennifer Lopez. ♥

—by Claire Harth

OSCAR DE LA HOYA

INTERVIEW BY JOAN TARSHIS
PHOTOGRAPHY BY JEFF KATZ

The day I arrived for our interview, he was in the ring sparring with a partner—his body covered with a thin layer of sweat, his breathing short and swift, his movements quick, almost feline. Being so close to the fighter I had watched move up through the ranks to win the gold medal at the 1992 Summer Olympics made my own breath quicken and heart race.

After a few more instructions from his trainer, Oscar jumped down from the ring and put on his robe. "Hello," he purred in his soft, bedroom voice. At 5'11", he gazed down at me with his deep brown eyes. Even more handsome up close, not only does he look like a movie star, his life reads like a film script.

De La Hoya was born in East Los Angeles 26 years ago to immigrant parents. He was a quiet child who never joined a street gang or took drugs. Instead, his fists were aimed at amateur boxing competitions and filled with awards.

While growing up, his biggest supporter was his mother, Cecilia, who died of breast cancer two years before she could see her son accomplish her fondest dream—winning the gold medal at the Olympics. When Oscar got back to the States, he placed his prized award on her tombstone in a touching memorial. With such loving devotion, it's clear that this prize fighter's warmth and gracious manner is a living tribute to his mother.

PLAYGIRL DECEMBER 1997

PLAYGIRL: Since you're a boxer, the obvious question is, did you get into fights a lot when you were a kid?
OSCAR DE LA HOYA: Actually, my brothers and my cousins used to make me fight in the street. I must have been six or seven years old. I always ended up crying and running away. They would hit me one time and that was it—it was over. I would be scared. It was always like that.
Then how did you finally get into the ring?
One day we were at my uncle's house, in the garage, just having a good time. All my cousins were boxing, and it was my turn to go up against my cousin. My gloves came up to my elbows

and my shorts went down to my ankles. My cousin got a good one in between those two huge gloves. Pow! I just started crying. I ran to my father, who was telling everybody, "Just wait and see. I'm going to take him to the gym and in a

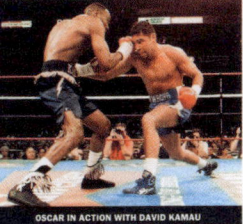

OSCAR IN ACTION WITH DAVID KAMAU

25

STYLING BY SAMANTHA DELEN/CLOUTIER • GROOMING BY CHISTA FOLEY/CLOUTIER

90210 OH, BABY!

BRIAN Austin GREEN

This sexy TV heartthrob loves hip-hop, women and long, hot baths....

• INTERVIEW BY CHARMIAN CARL •

The approach to Brian Austin Green's Spanish-style house in North Hollywood is a steep incline. At the end of the drive hangs a well-used basketball hoop resting like a shrine above the garage door. As I pull in, he greets me with a warm, infectious smile and invites me inside, where I'm treated to an enthusiastic welcome from his two dogs, Alik, an imposing but docile Rottweiler, and Bailey, a rambunctious one-year-old Golden Retriever.

This serene domestic setting reflects Brian's early successes. His career has been going non-stop since he was 10, starting with a four-year stint as Brian Cunningham on *Knots Landing*, then as David Silver on the groundbreaking night-time soap *Beverly Hills, 90210*, which after a healthy six-year run is in its final season.

Before the acting bug bit Brian, his father's successful career as a professional drummer helped him discover his love of music. Country was his dad's specialty, but it was far from this city boy's taste. Says Brian, "I've always loved rap

music, and having grown up in L.A., I was exposed to many different hip-hop flavors. Groups like the Pharcyde had a very big impact on me. They're original, diverse, hardcore and poetically on point. That's how I hear my music, too." With his new CD *One Stop Carnival* and its hit song "You Send Me," he is well on his way to yet another career path.

After a brief tour of Brian's home, we settle in the living room to chat, while Alik and Bailey do their best to capture our attention with their amusing antics.
PLAYGIRL: How did you get started in this crazy business?
Brian Austin Green: I was going to a performing arts school and was in jazz class and the band, playing music and the drums. A lot of student directors used to pick other students to be in their graduate films, so I ended up doing a couple of them just for fun. Eventually, I got an agent through a friend and I did some commercials; then I got *Knots Landing*.... Alik, stop that! (Alik drops a large rubber toy from the upper floor, which lands inches from our heads.)
What did you do after that?
I did some commercials and a couple of B movies, then a few pilots that didn't go anywhere. Eventually I did the pilot for *Beverly Hills, 90210*. The rest is history.
Were you excited about getting 90210?
No, because I had done three pilots before and knew its chances of becoming a series were slim. It didn't seem like

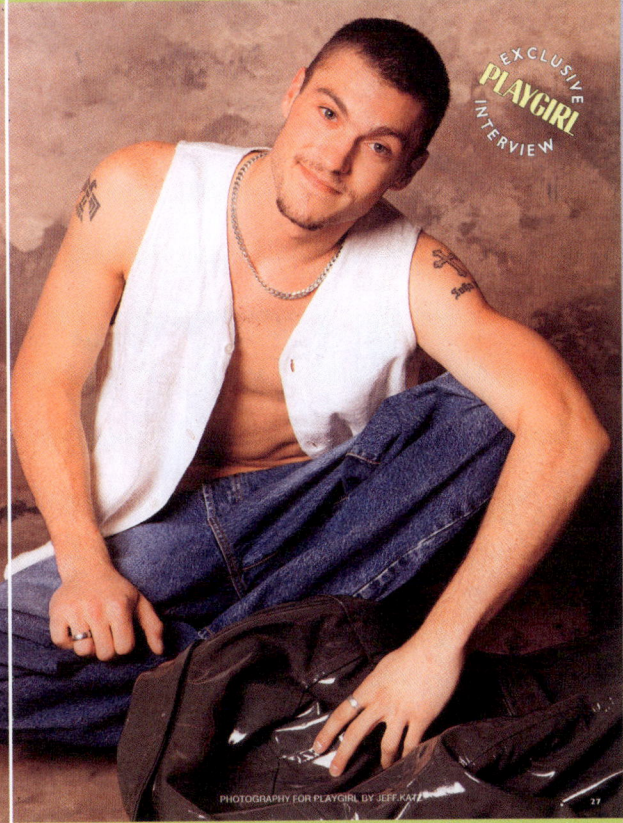

Beverly Hills, 90210's graduating class.

PLAYGIRL NOVEMBER 1996

PHOTOGRAPHY FOR PLAYGIRL BY JEFF KATZ

27

MAN of the DECADE

DARREN FOX

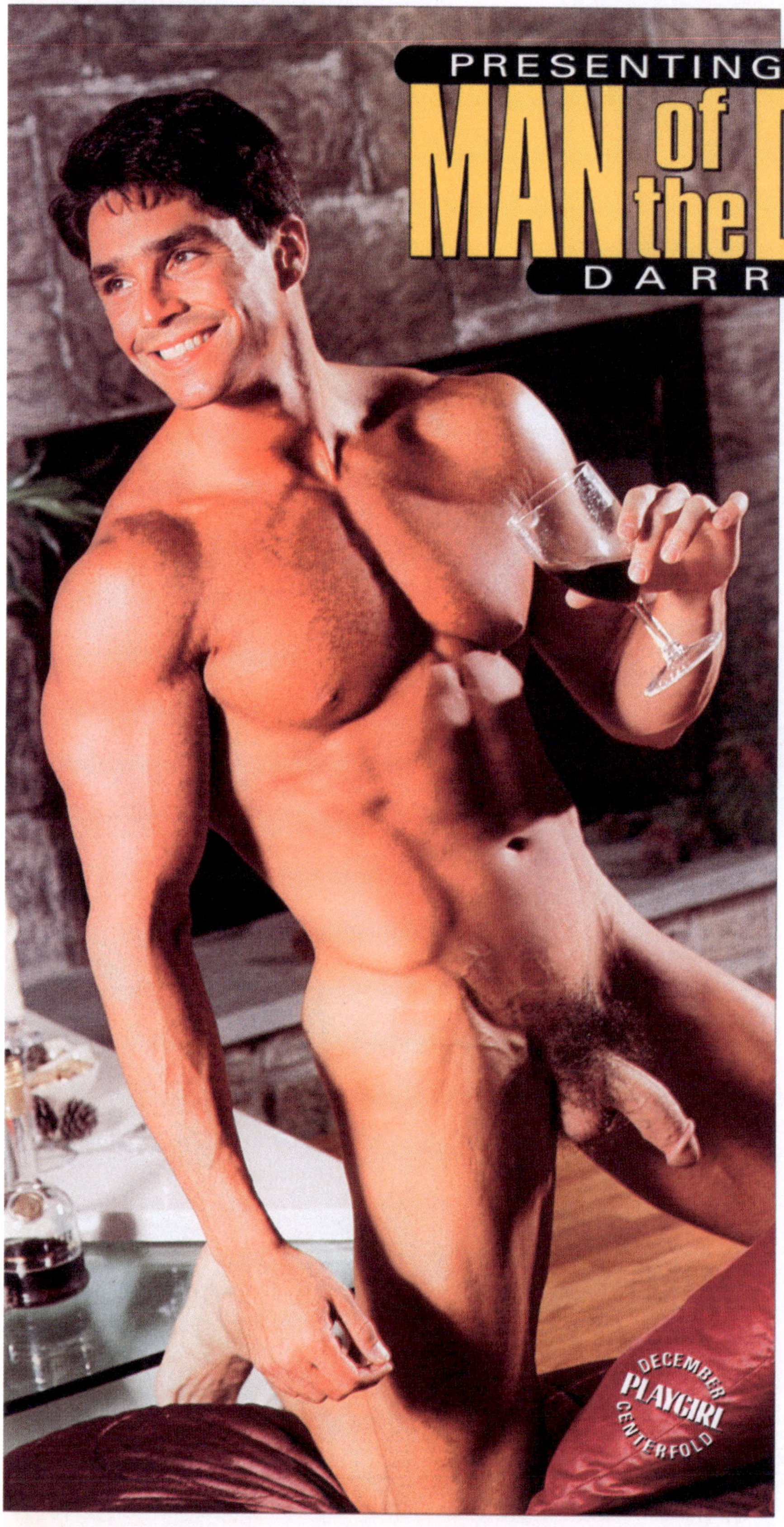

A man of steel made of flesh and pure heaven

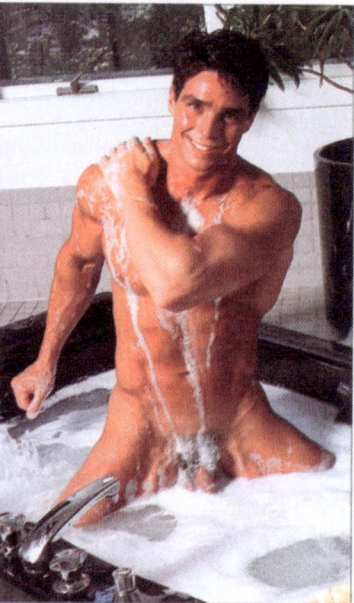

DECEMBER
PLAYGIRL
CENTERFOLD

There are men. There are models...and then there's Darren Fox. Wherever he goes, heads snap to attention. His next-to-flawless presence electrifies any room into which he enters. Men want to be him. Women just want him. And once we saw him, we were more than impressed, we knew he was destined for greatness.

At 30, Darren is busy working on a modeling and acting career, and spends seven days a week working out to maintain his breathtaking physique. "I know I'm obsessed," he admits with a laugh, "but right now, my looks are my livelihood, and once I put my mind to doing something, I won't settle for anything less than perfection."

PHOTOGRAPHY BY NATALIA KYIVSKA

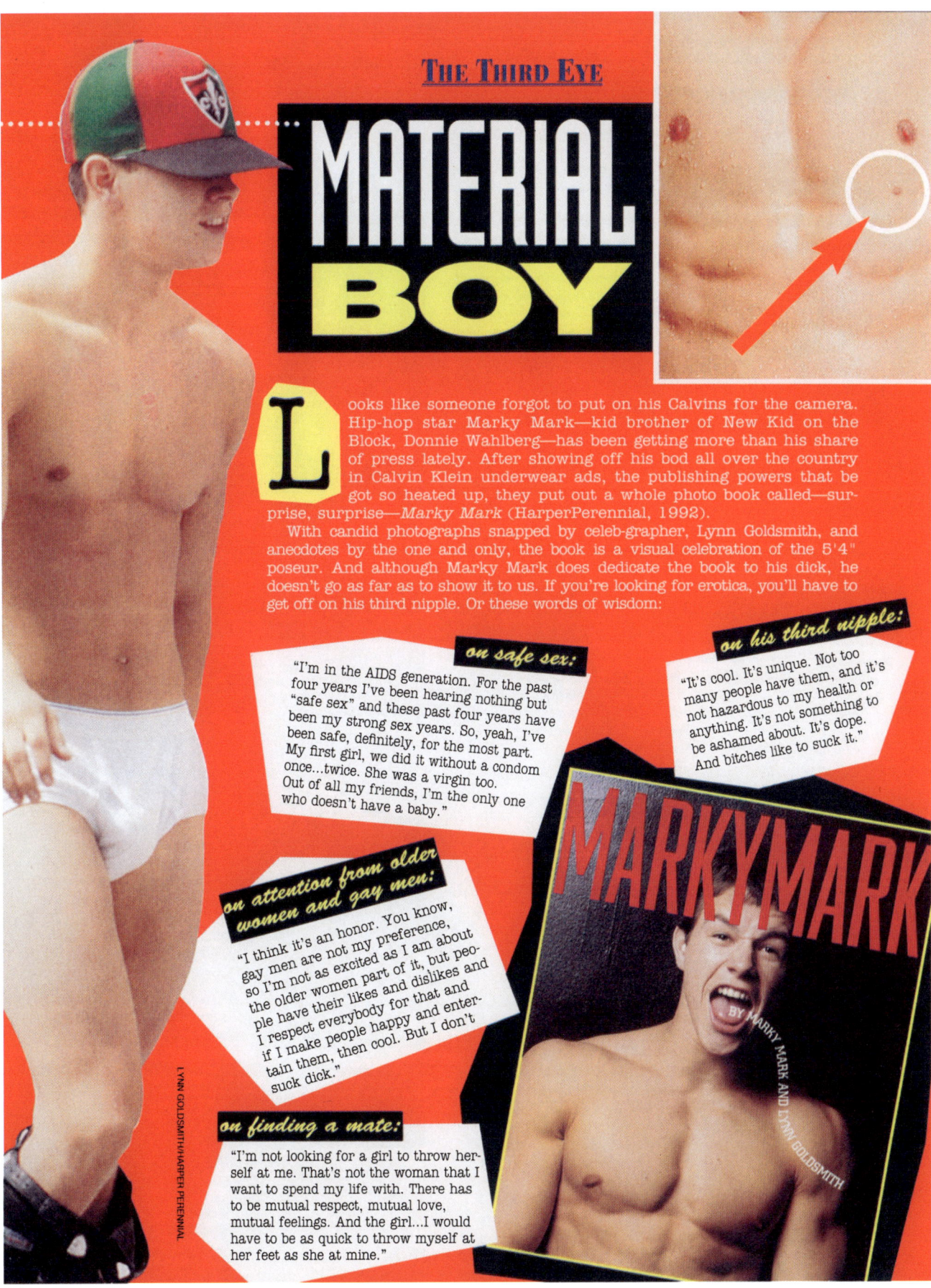

MATERIAL BOY

Looks like someone forgot to put on his Calvins for the camera. Hip-hop star Marky Mark—kid brother of New Kid on the Block, Donnie Wahlberg—has been getting more than his share of press lately. After showing off his bod all over the country in Calvin Klein underwear ads, the publishing powers that be got so heated up, they put out a whole photo book called—surprise, surprise—*Marky Mark* (HarperPerennial, 1992).

With candid photographs snapped by celeb-grapher, Lynn Goldsmith, and anecdotes by the one and only, the book is a visual celebration of the 5'4" poseur. And although Marky Mark does dedicate the book to his dick, he doesn't go as far as to show it to us. If you're looking for erotica, you'll have to get off on his third nipple. Or these words of wisdom:

on safe sex:

"I'm in the AIDS generation. For the past four years I've been hearing nothing but "safe sex" and these past four years have been my strong sex years. So, yeah, I've been safe, definitely, for the most part. My first girl, we did it without a condom once...twice. She was a virgin too. Out of all my friends, I'm the only one who doesn't have a baby."

on his third nipple:

"It's cool. It's unique. Not too many people have them, and it's not hazardous to my health or anything. It's not something to be ashamed about. It's dope. And bitches like to suck it."

on attention from older women and gay men:

"I think it's an honor. You know, gay men are not my preference, so I'm not as excited as I am about the older women part of it, but people have their likes and dislikes and I respect everybody for that and if I make people happy and entertain them, then cool. But I don't suck dick."

on finding a mate:

"I'm not looking for a girl to throw herself at me. That's not the woman that I want to spend my life with. There has to be mutual respect, mutual love, mutual feelings. And the girl...I would have to be as quick to throw myself at her feet as she at mine."

MARKYMARK

BY MARKY MARK AND LYNN GOLDSMITH

LYNN GOLDSMITH/HARPER PERENNIAL

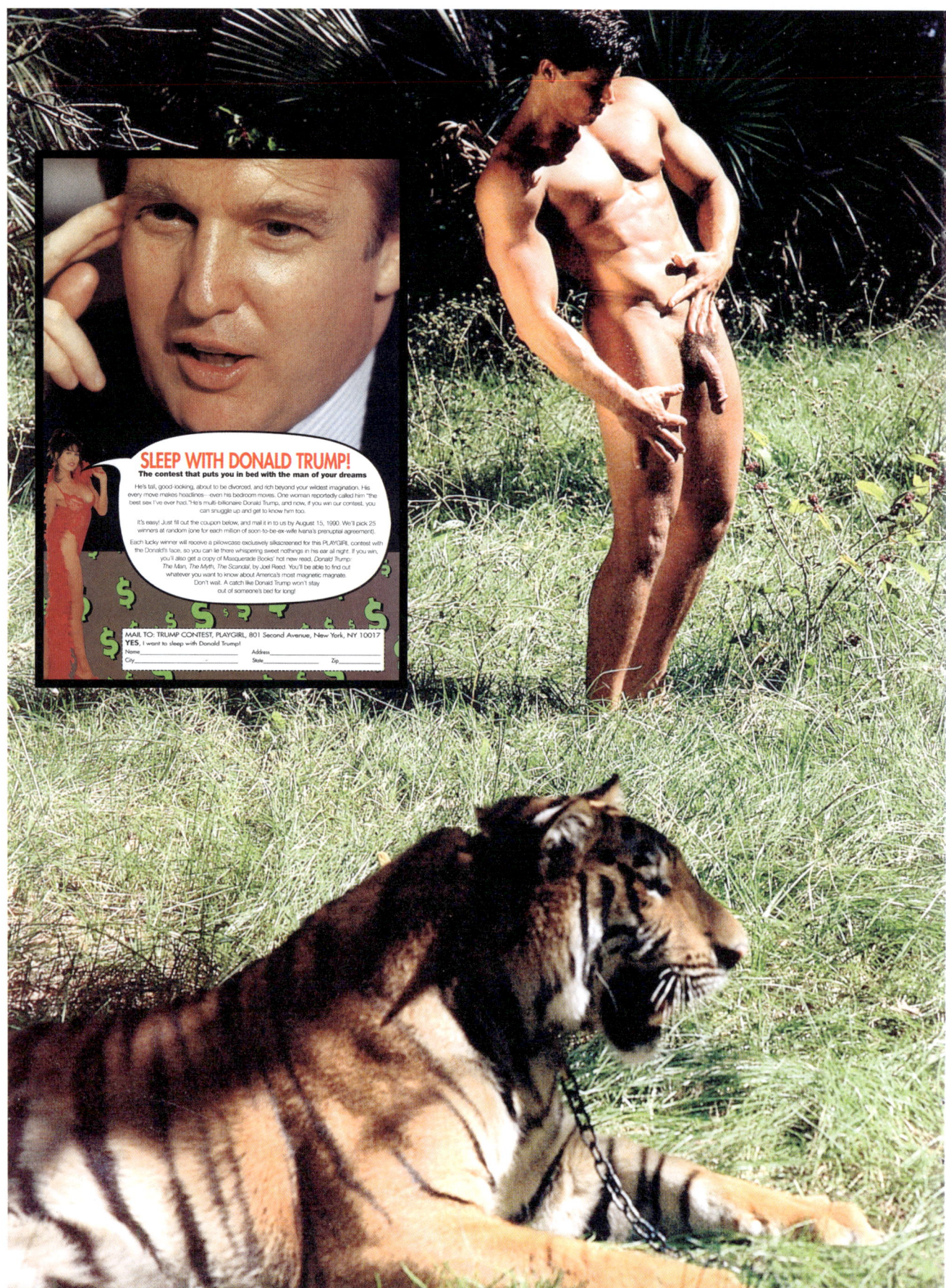

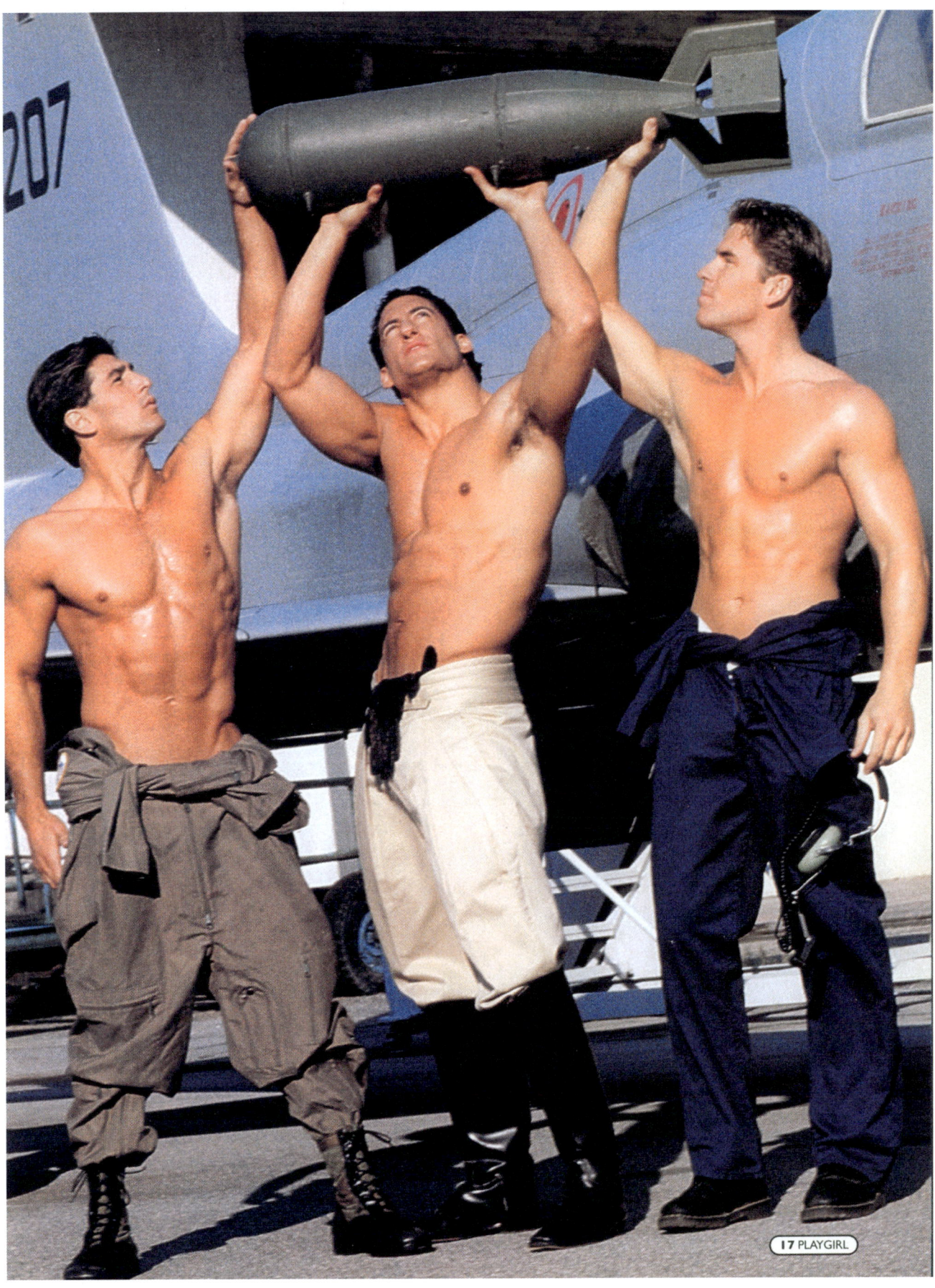

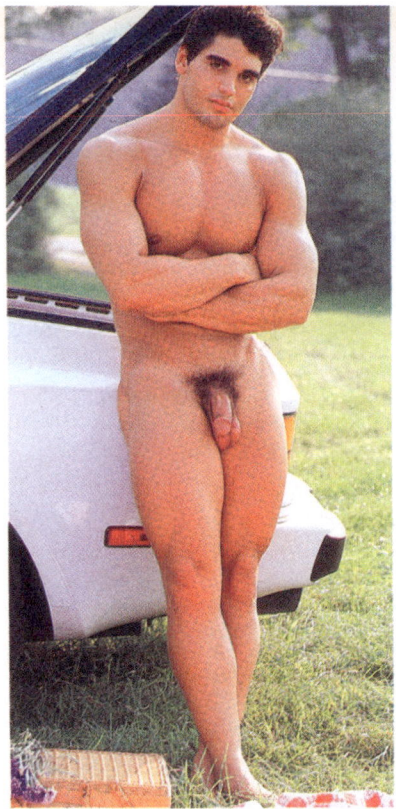

"There's a lot you don't know about me, then," Joe replies, with just a hint of a smile crossing his handsome face. "What did you think I drove—a four-door sedan?"

And then he's slowly pulling off his trousers, revealing all you've ever wondered about him. Could this really be the dark-suited loner from across the aisle in class?

Suddenly, it doesn't matter at all. From the looks of his Porsche—and his body—he's going to take you on a one-way trip to ecstasy. ■

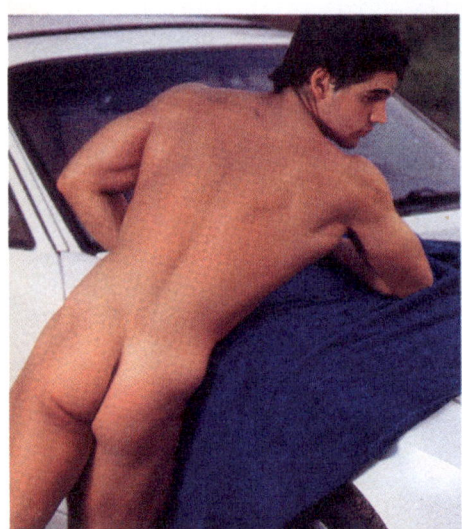

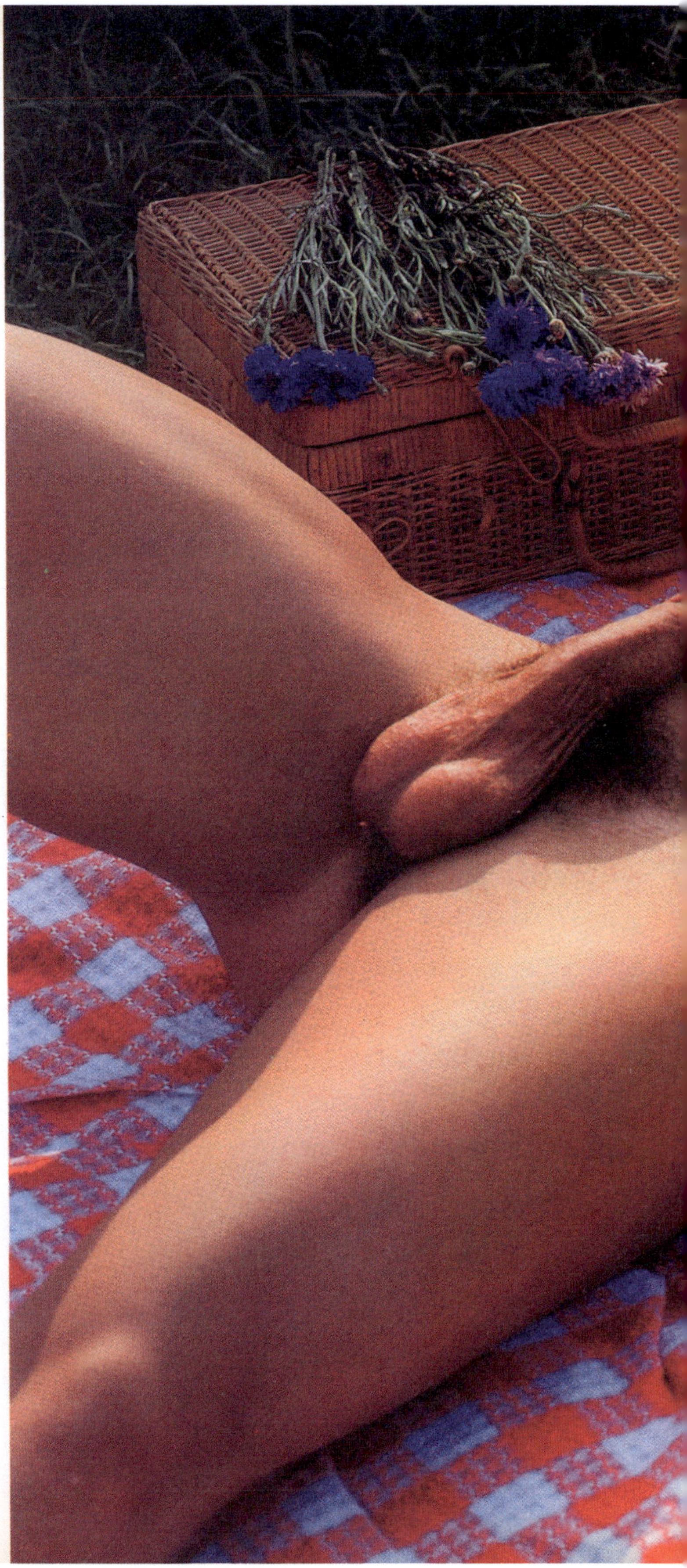

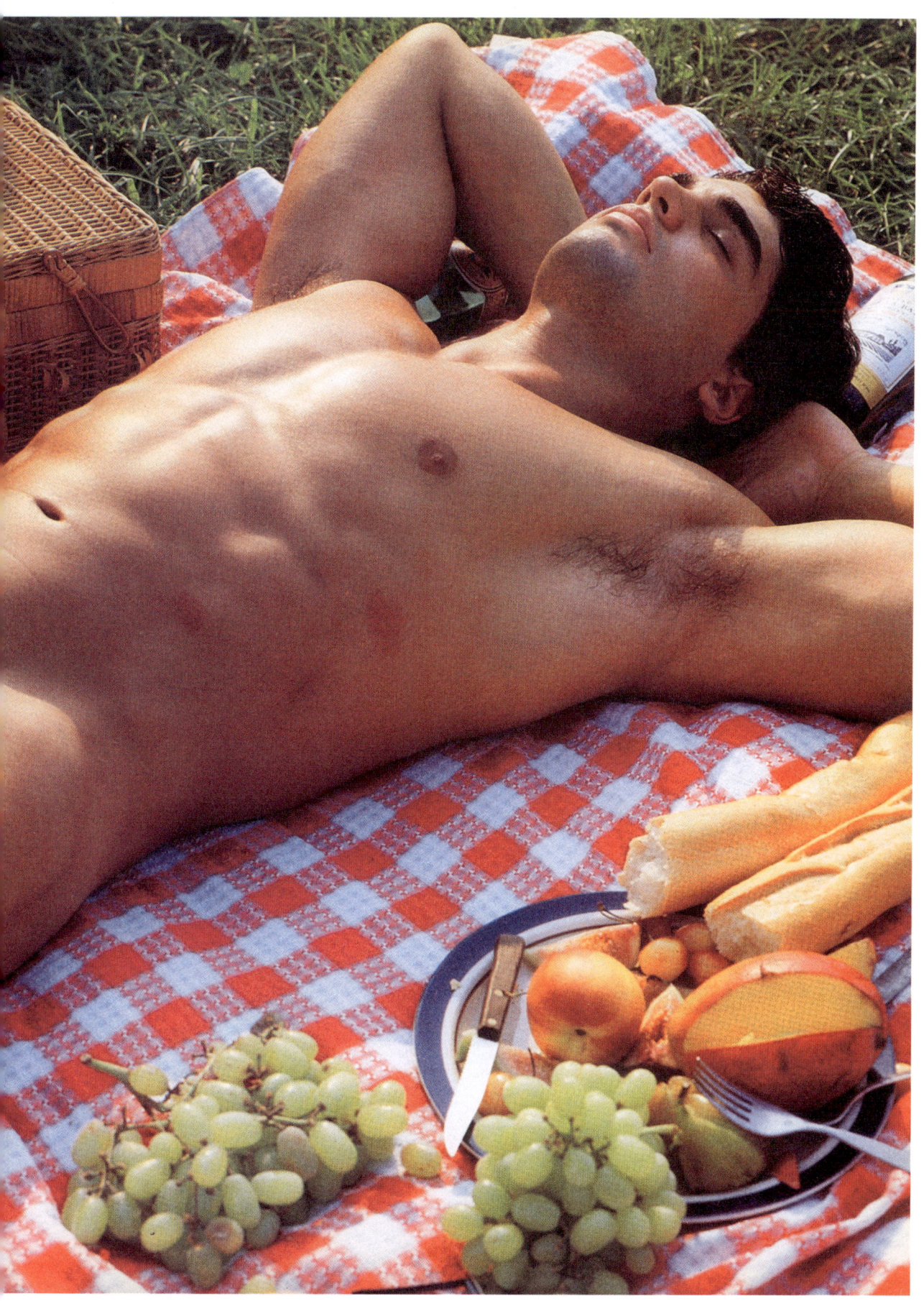

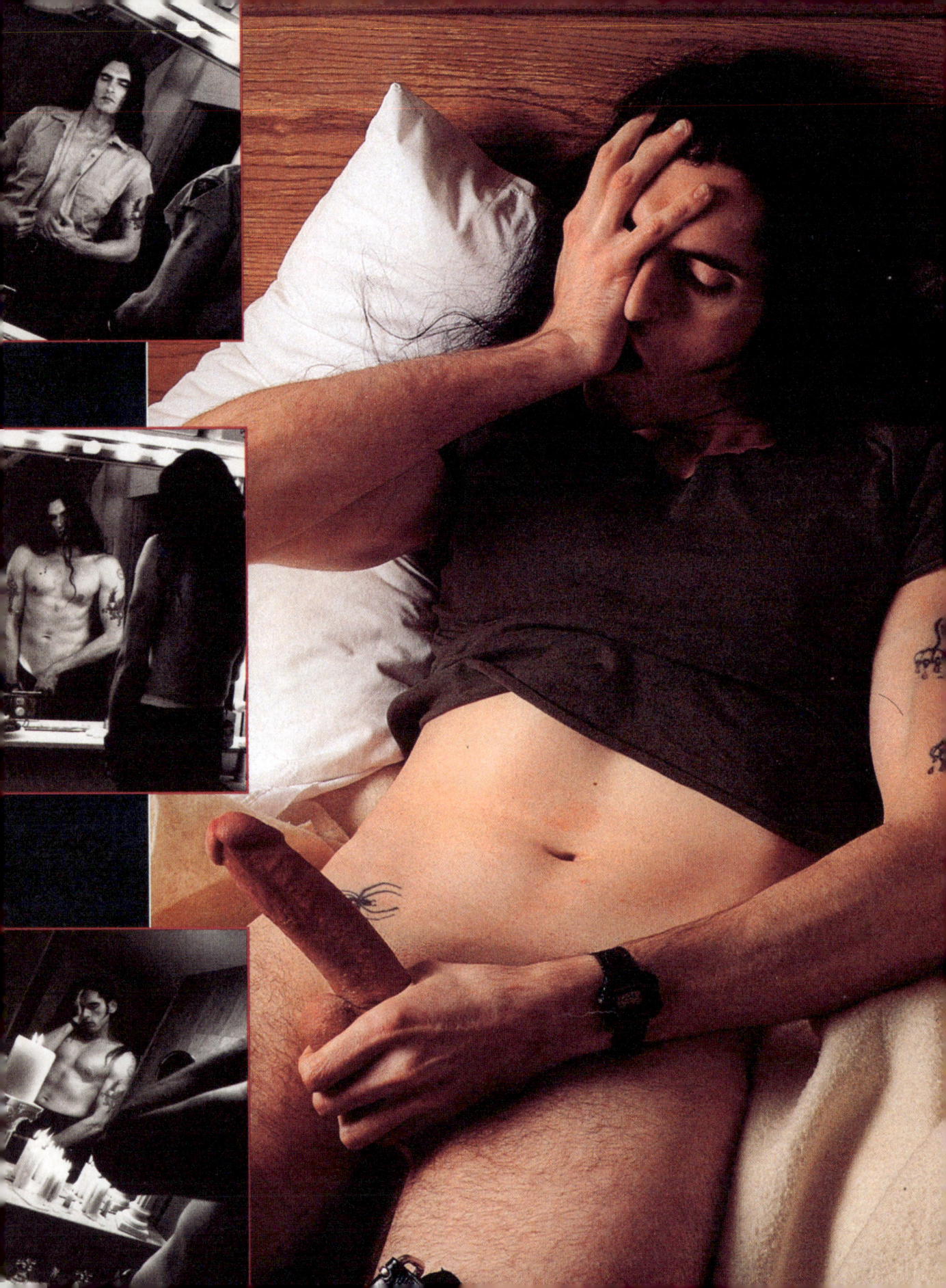

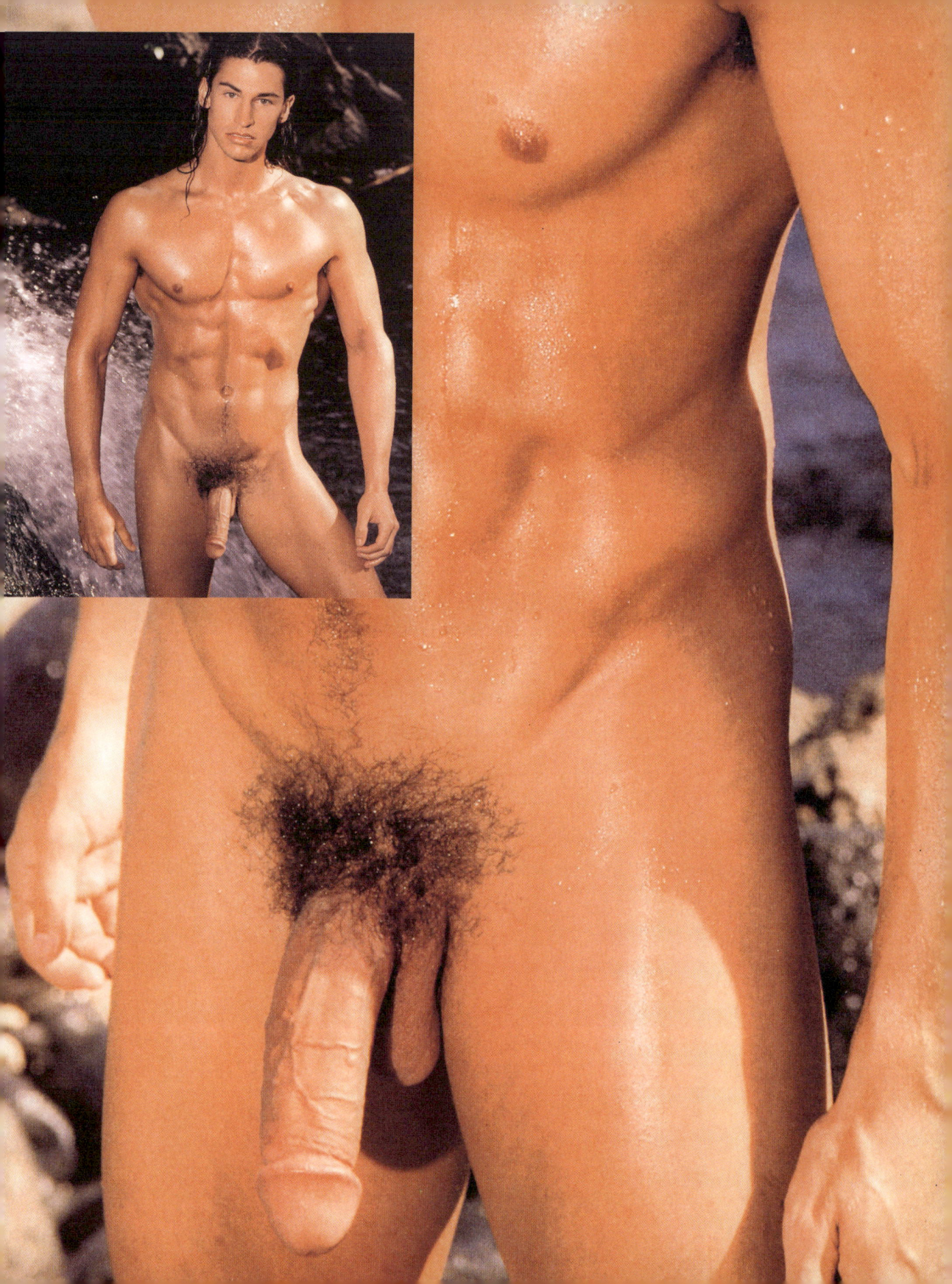

CHAPTER 9

BEST OF THE
2000s

The aughts for the magazine are what we affectionately
refer to as "the mimbo years." Still, we managed
to score some high-profile skin in exclusive risqué photoshoots
with Keith Urban, Tyrese Gibson, and actor Marcus Patrick.
In 2010, when Sarah Palin was John McCain's running
mate against Barack Obama, *Playgirl* masterminded the political
PR troll of a nude shoot with Levi Johnston, baby daddy
to Palin's grandchild. Campus Hunks, Chippendales,
Mr. Nude World and Mr. Nude Universe, and the *Playgirl*
Pin-Ups dominated the pages of the magazine,
along with no shortage of dildo reviews and phone-sex ads.
The focus turned to retrospective self-reflection and the timeline
of *Playgirl*'s legacy in various anniversary issues
before the magazine ultimately folded as a print entity in 2016.

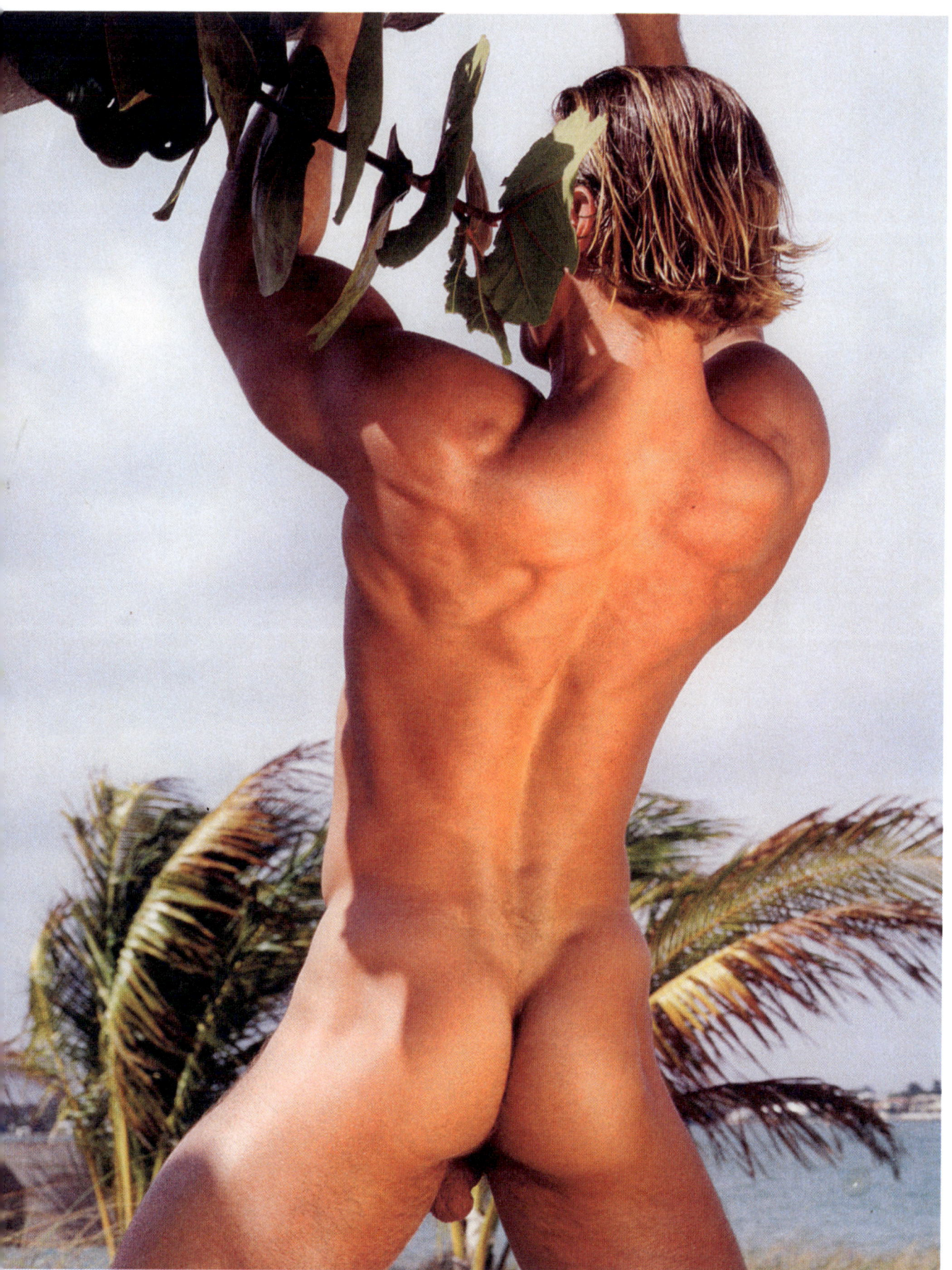

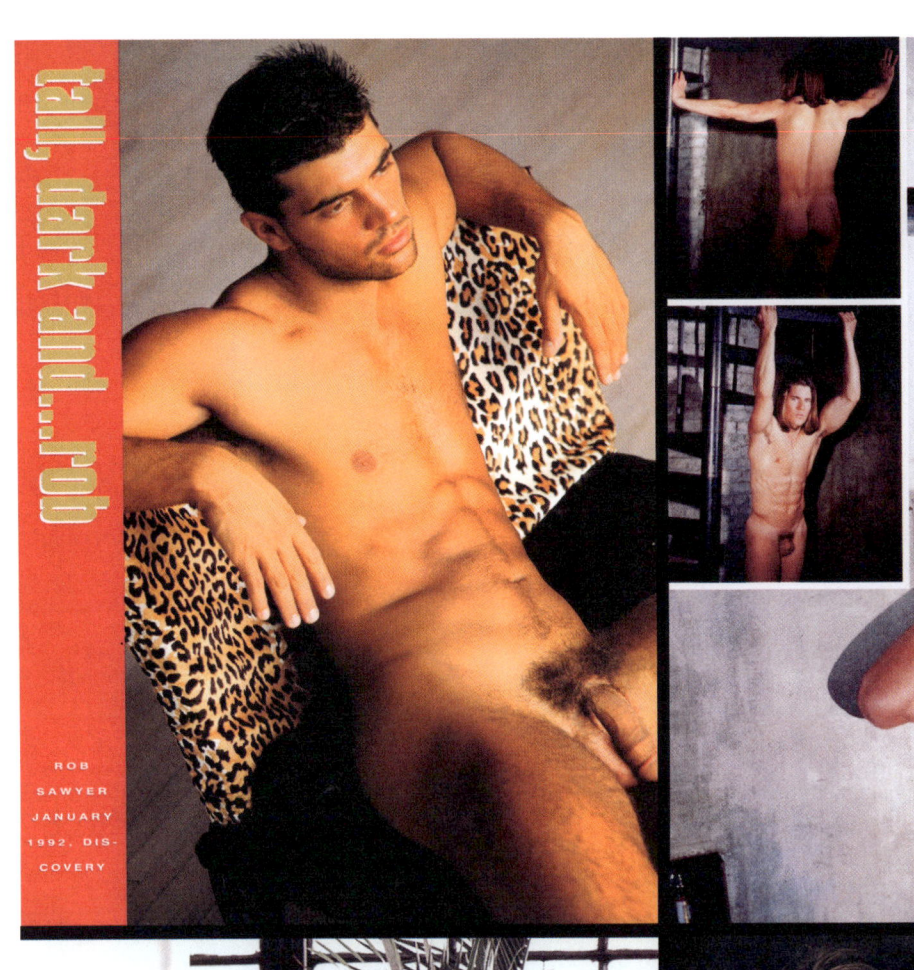

ROB
SAWYER
JANUARY
1992, DIS-
COVERY

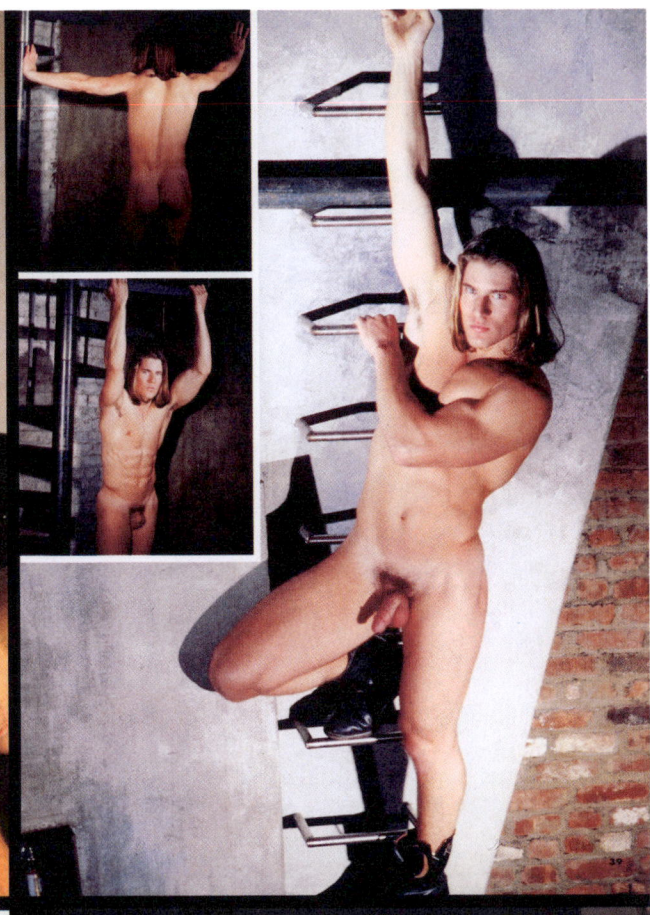

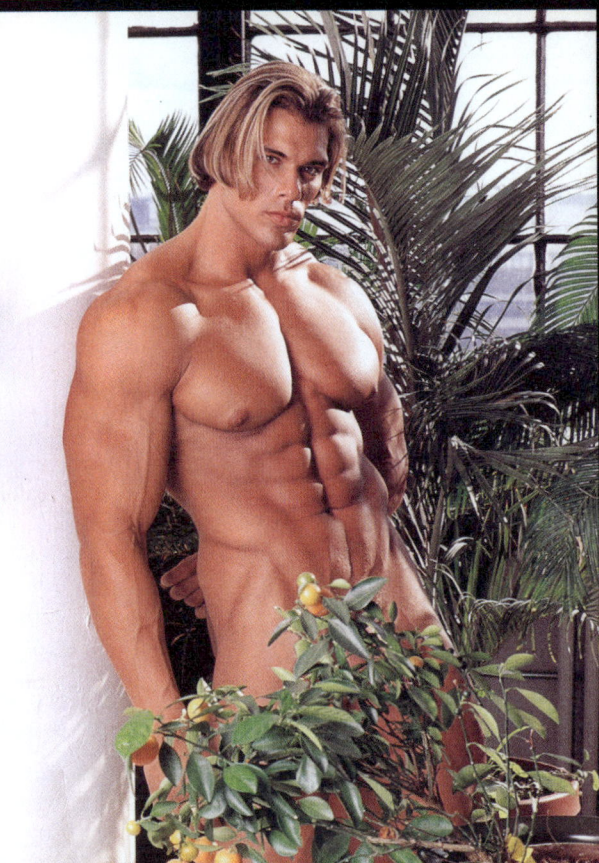

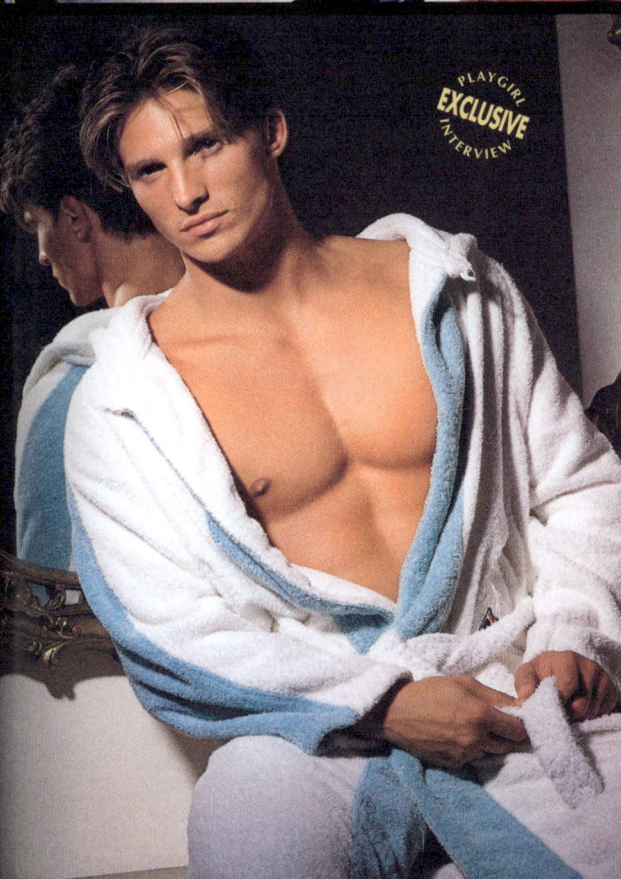

PLAYGIRL
EXCLUSIVE
INTERVIEW

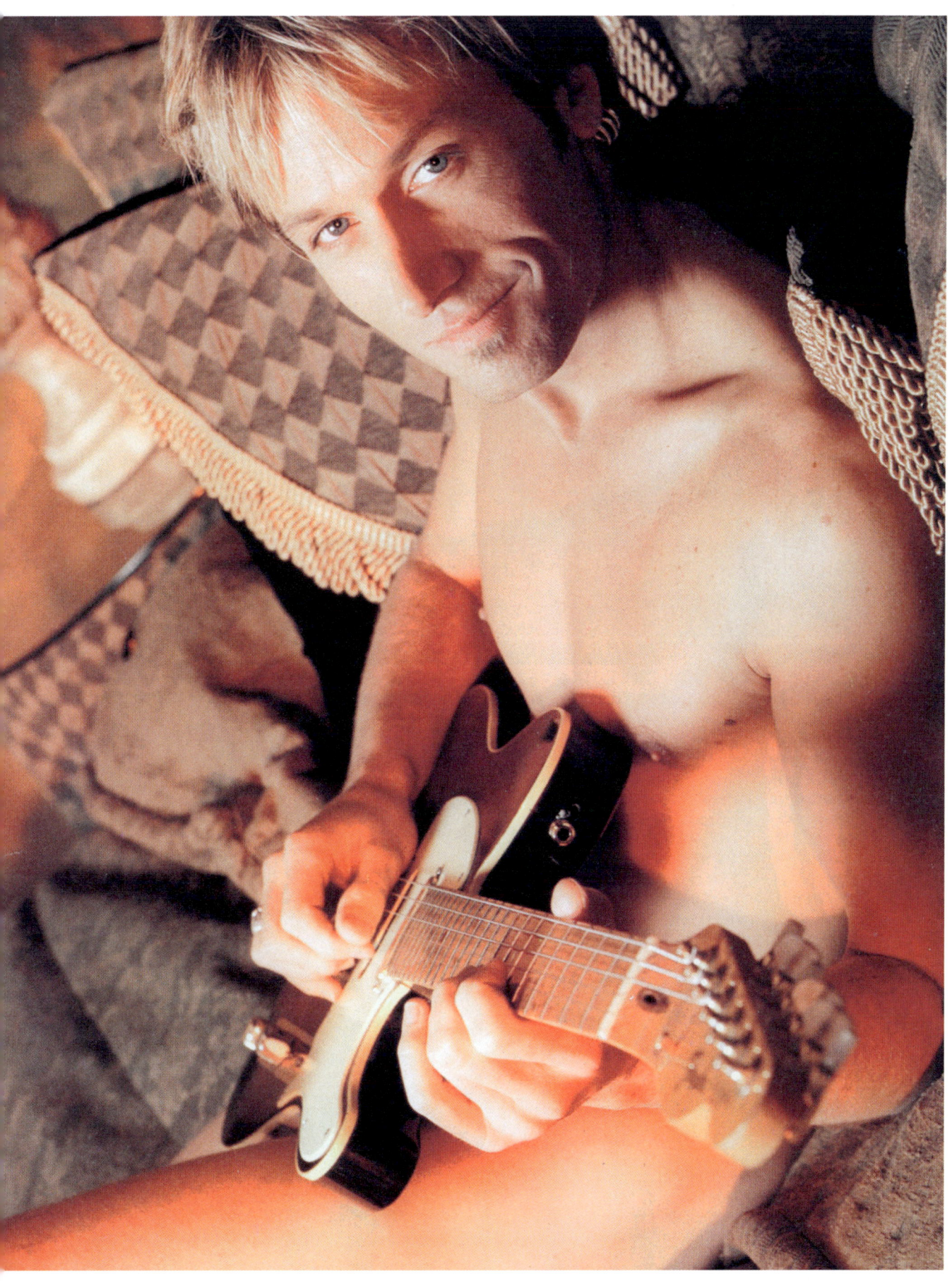

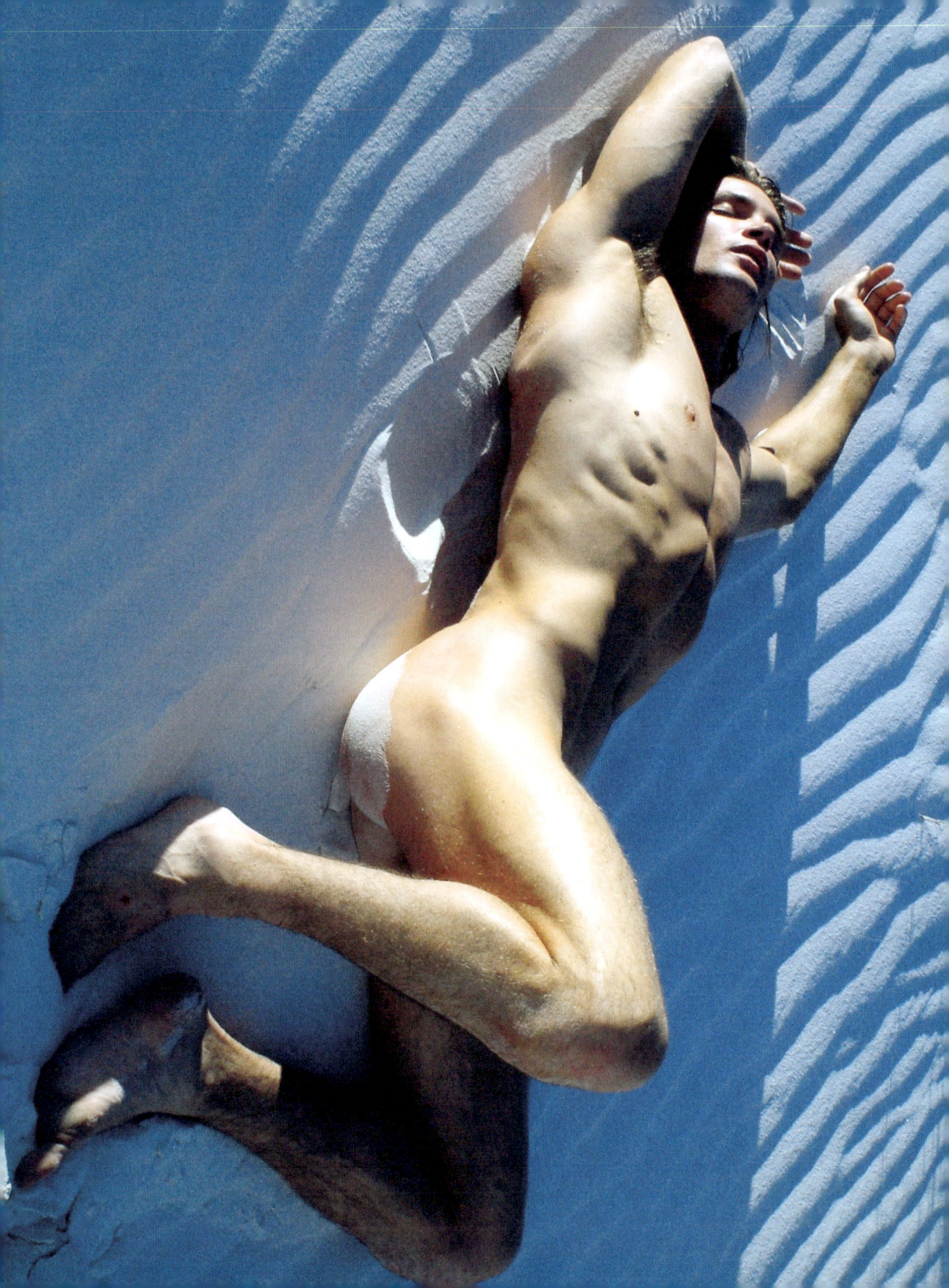

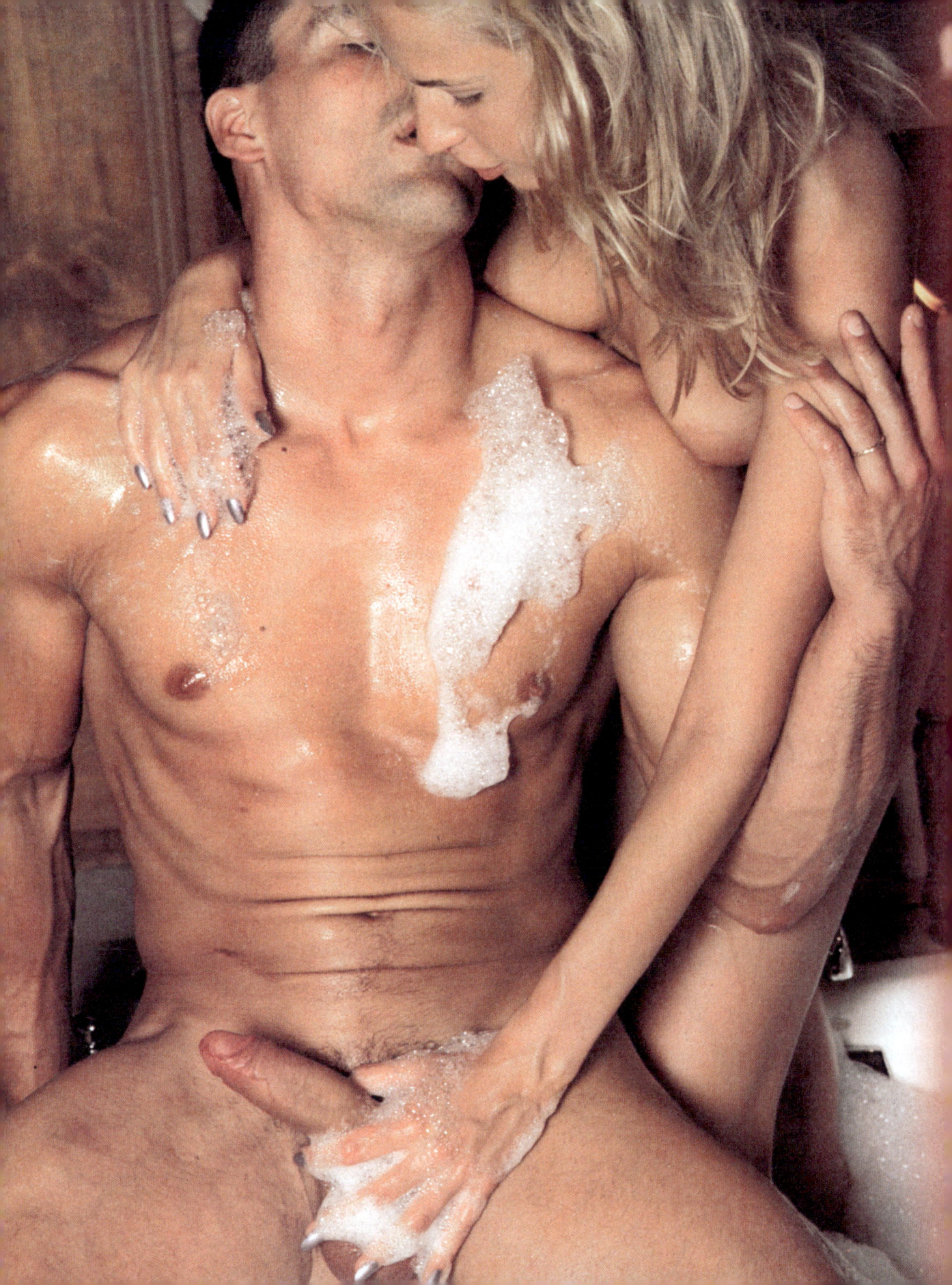

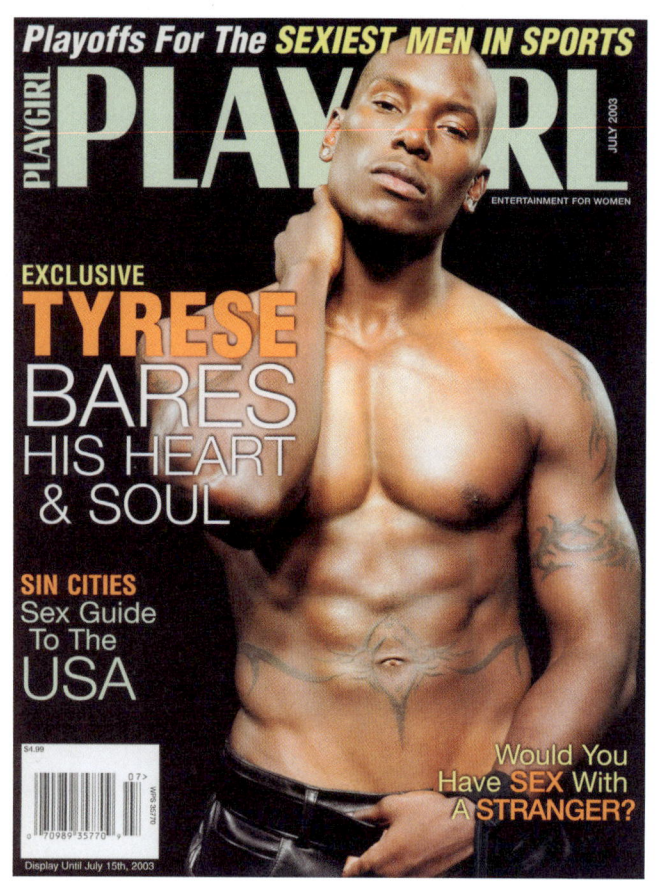

Playoffs For The **SEXIEST MEN IN SPORTS**

PLAYGIRL

JULY 2003

ENTERTAINMENT FOR WOMEN

EXCLUSIVE
TYRESE
BARES
HIS HEART
& SOUL

SIN CITIES
Sex Guide
To The
USA

$4.99

Would You
Have **SEX** With
A **STRANGER?**

Display Until July 15th, 2003

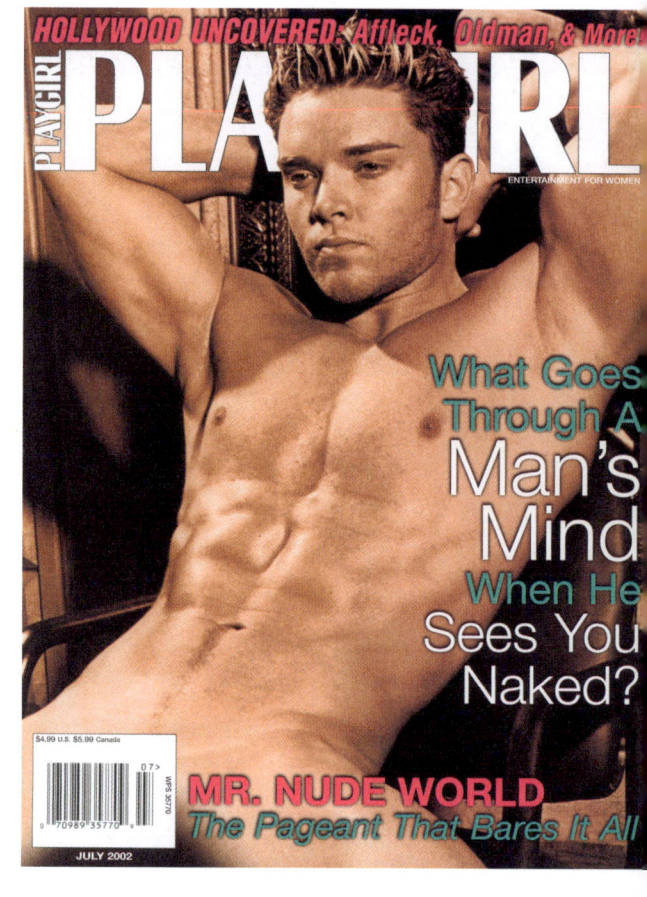

HOLLYWOOD UNCOVERED: Affleck, Oldman, & More!

PLAYGIRL

ENTERTAINMENT FOR WOMEN

What Goes
Through A
Man's
Mind
When He
Sees You
Naked?

$4.99 U.S. $5.99 Canada

MR. NUDE WORLD
The Pageant That Bares It All

JULY 2002

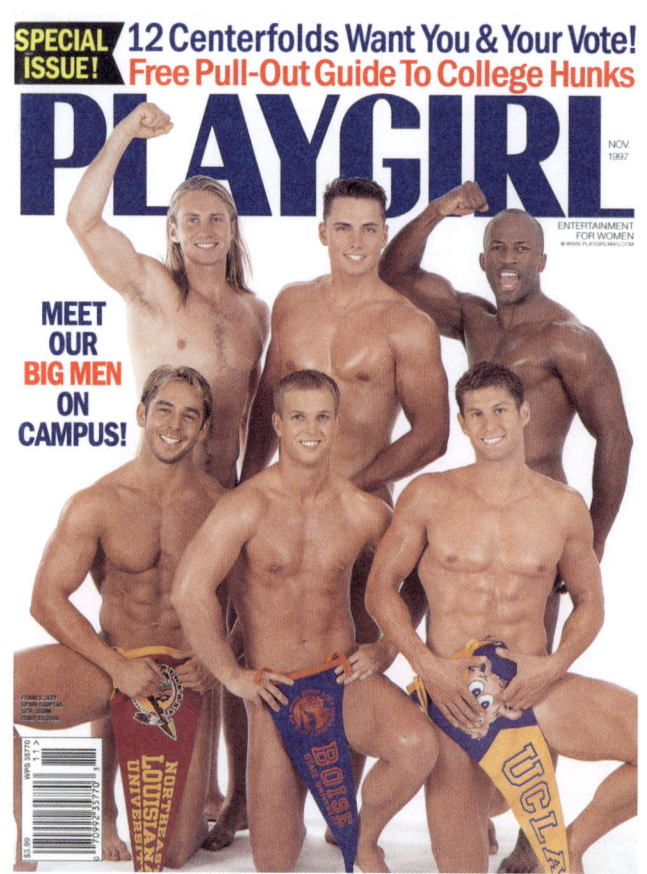

SPECIAL ISSUE! 12 Centerfolds Want You & Your Vote!
Free Pull-Out Guide To College Hunks

PLAYGIRL

NOV.
1997

ENTERTAINMENT
FOR WOMEN
WWW.PLAYGIRL.COM

MEET
OUR
BIG MEN
ON
CAMPUS!

NORTHEAST LOUISIANA UNIVERSITY
BOISE STATE UNIVERSITY
UCLA

$3.99

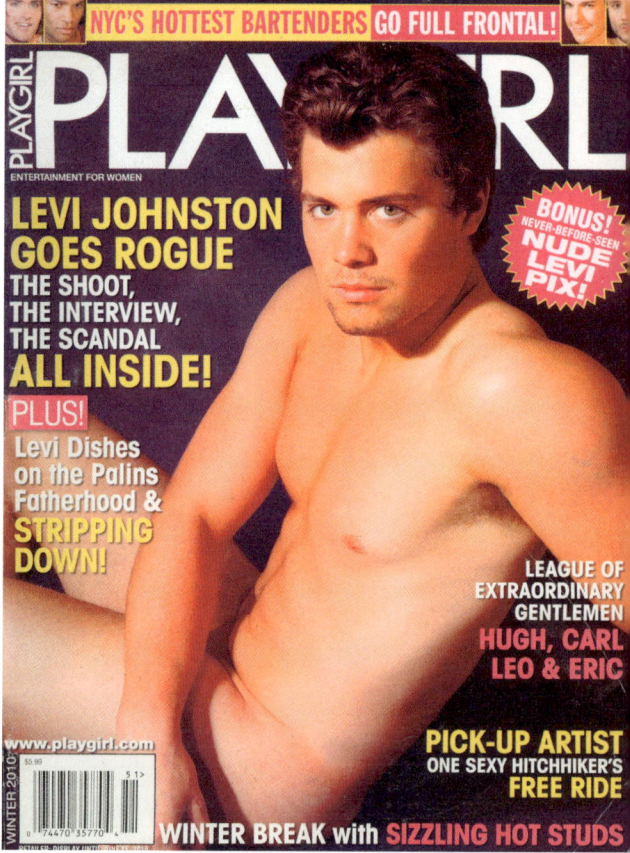

NYC'S HOTTEST BARTENDERS GO FULL FRONTAL!

PLAYGIRL

ENTERTAINMENT FOR WOMEN

**LEVI JOHNSTON
GOES ROGUE**
THE SHOOT,
THE INTERVIEW,
THE SCANDAL
ALL INSIDE!

PLUS!
Levi Dishes
on the Palins
Fatherhood &
**STRIPPING
DOWN!**

BONUS!
NEVER-BEFORE-SEEN
**NUDE
LEVI
PIX!**

**LEAGUE OF
EXTRAORDINARY
GENTLEMEN**
**HUGH, CARL
LEO & ERIC**

PICK-UP ARTIST
ONE SEXY HITCHHIKER'S
FREE RIDE

www.playgirl.com
$5.99

WINTER 2010

WINTER BREAK with **SIZZLING HOT STUDS**

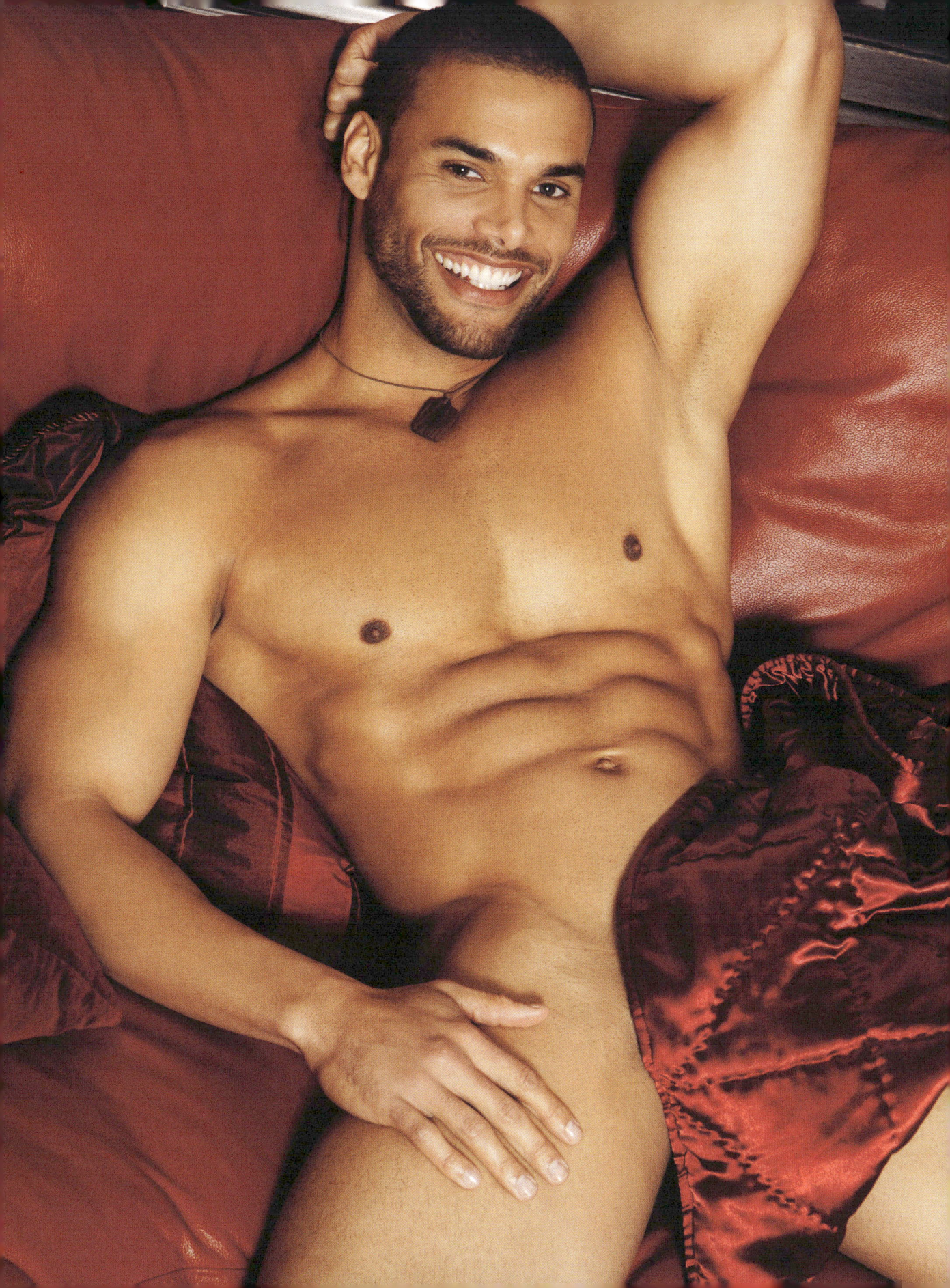

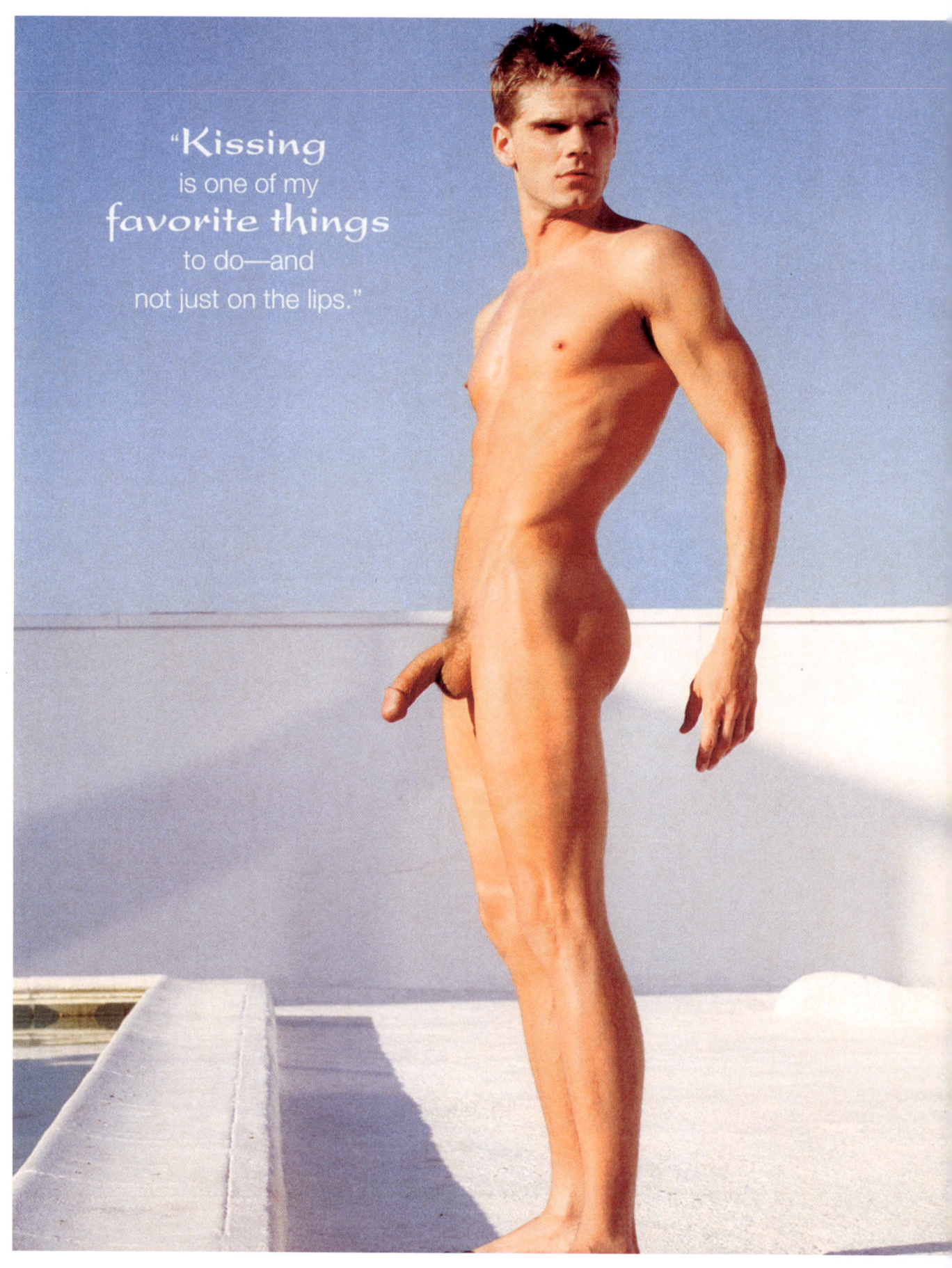

"Kissing is one of my favorite things to do—and not just on the lips."

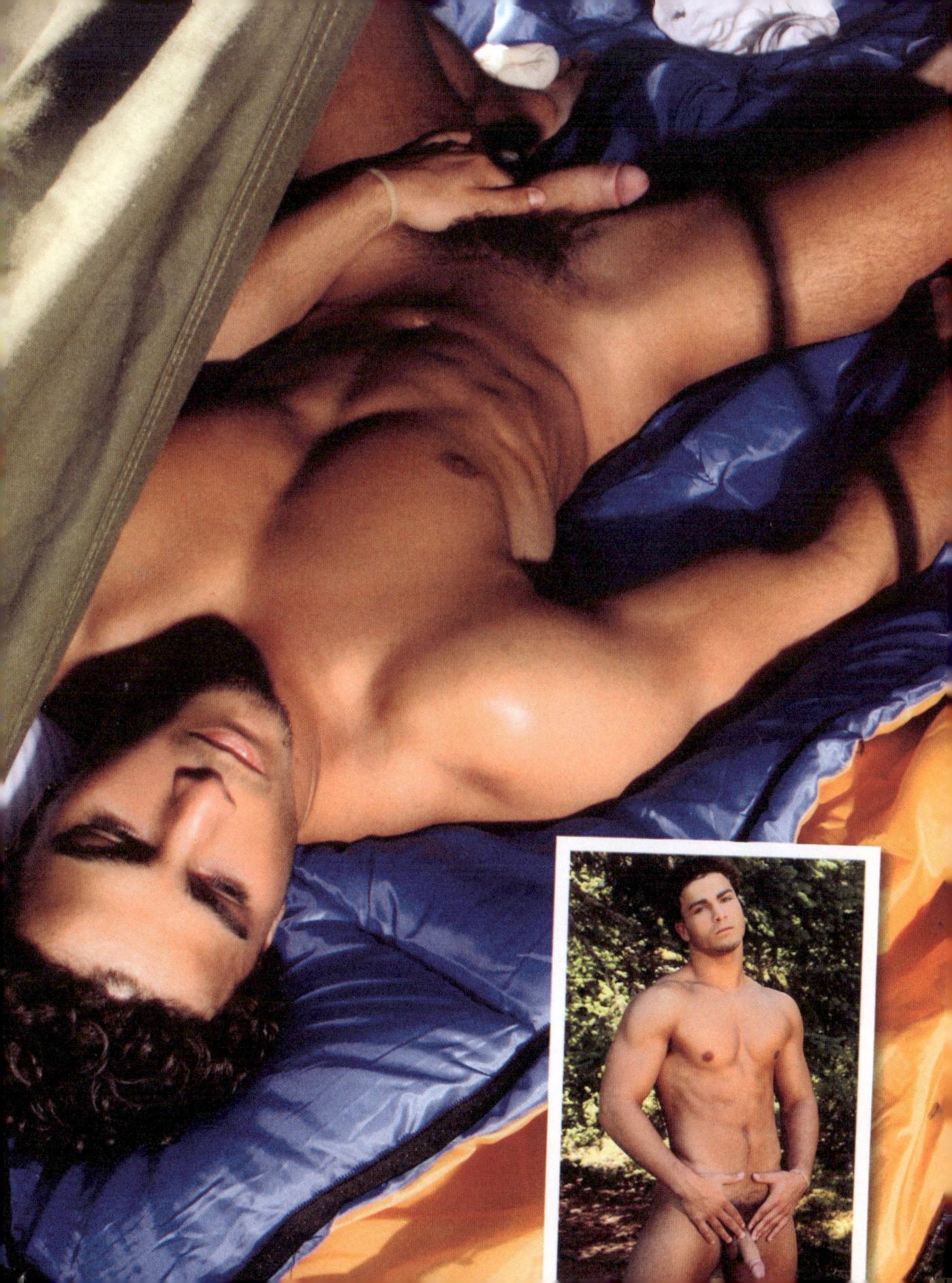

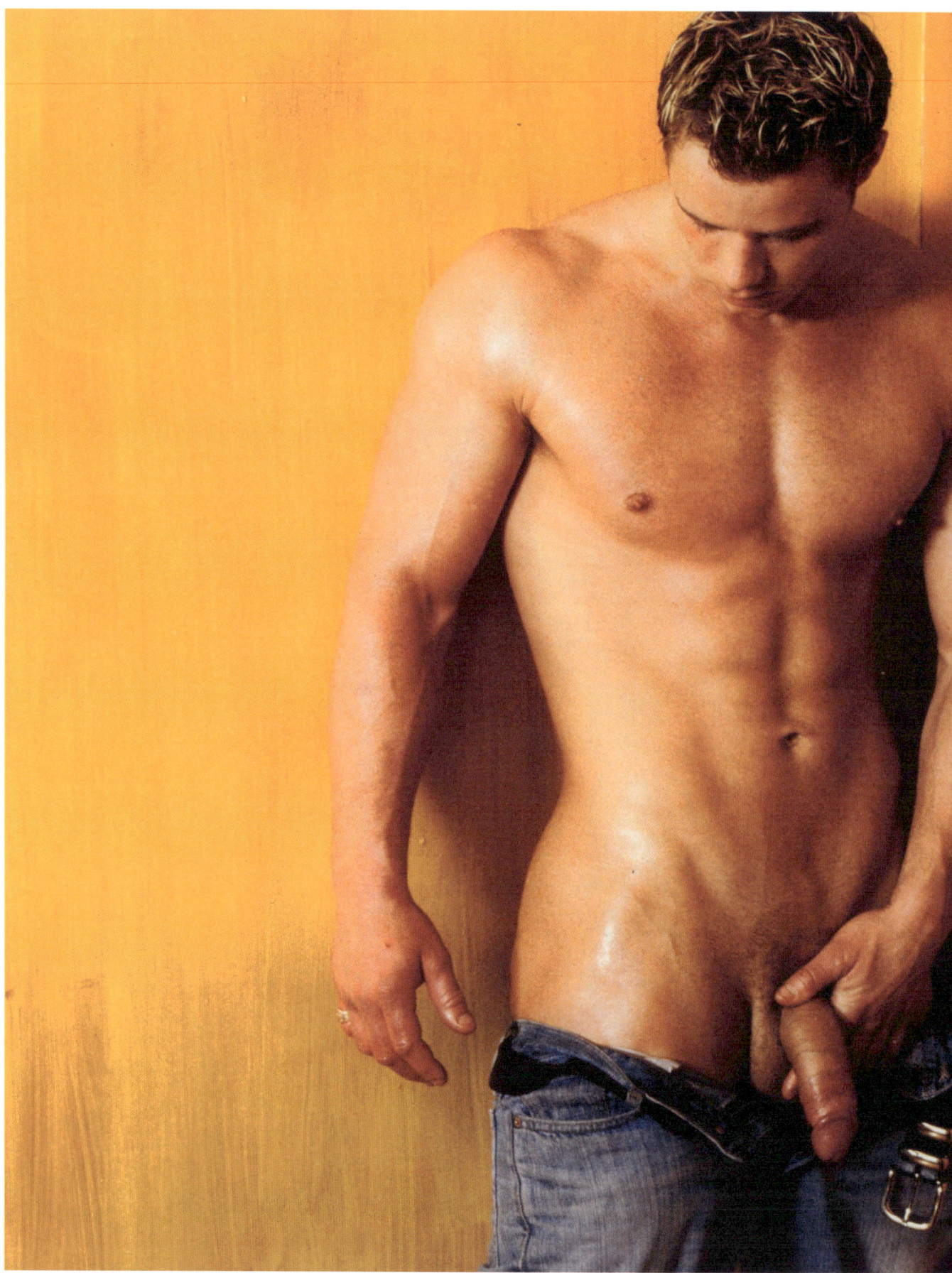

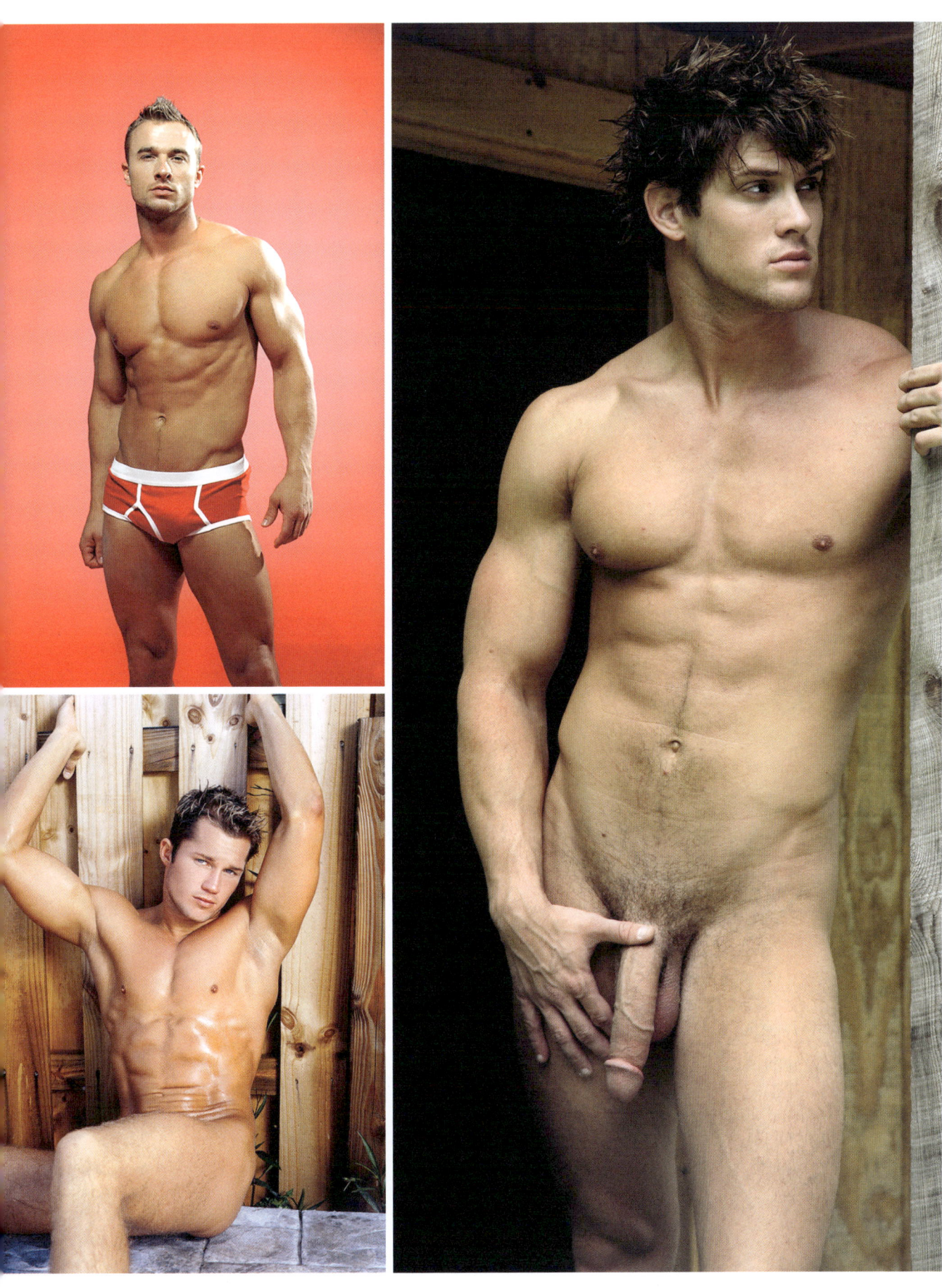

CHAPTER 10

PLAYGIRL FUNNIES

Cartoons of a uniquely adult nature—unlike any comic strips you've ever seen! From vulgar to sexually suggestive to crudely indecent, these humorous gems were an integral part of the magazine's history.

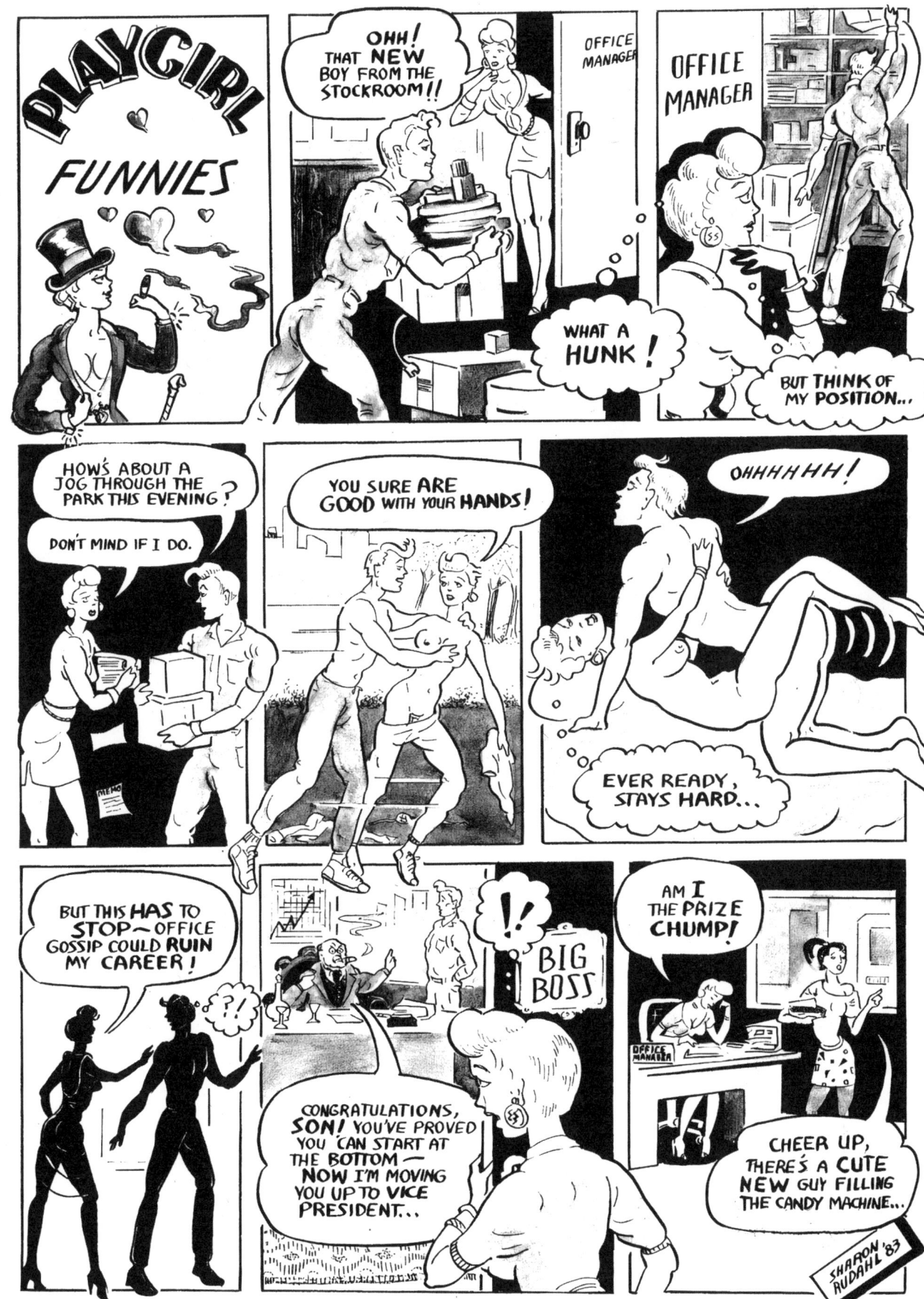

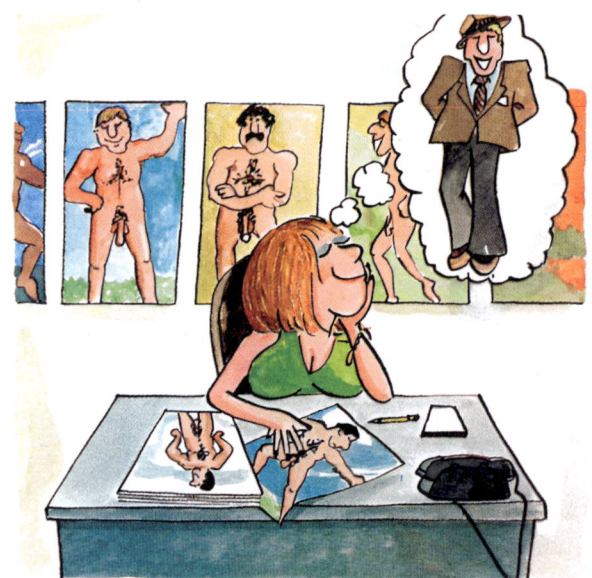

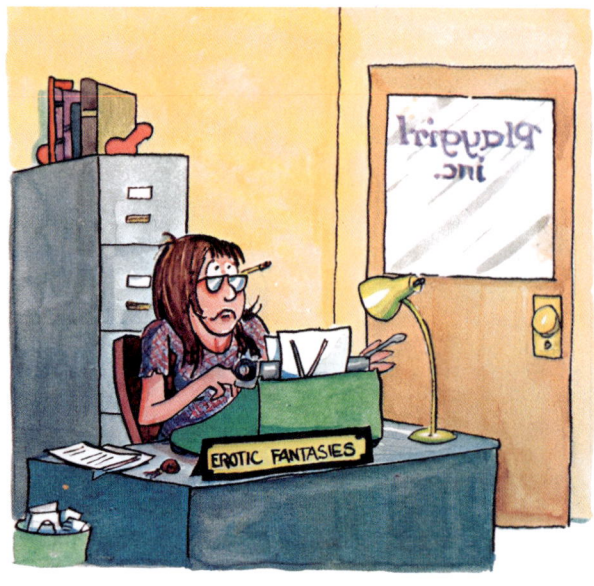

"Dear J.G:, It is quite normal to fantasize about cars and sex, but not about a gear shift . . ."

INSIDE Playgirl

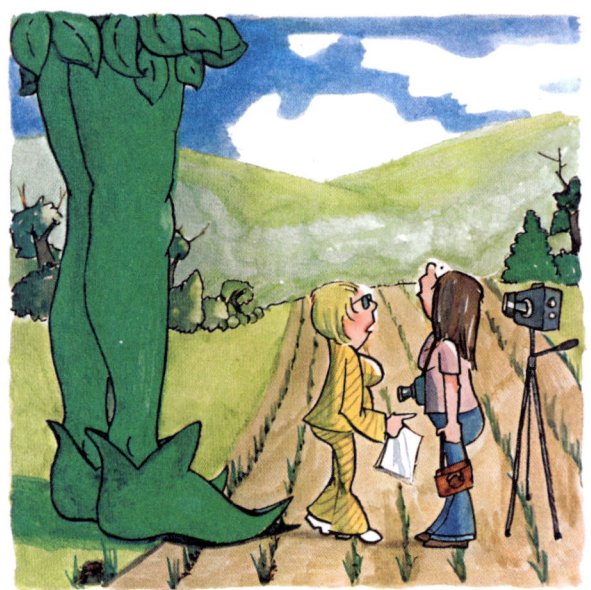

"It'll be a special issue: no ads, no fiction, no cartoons . . . nothing except a 98 page fold-out and a small article on vegetarians."

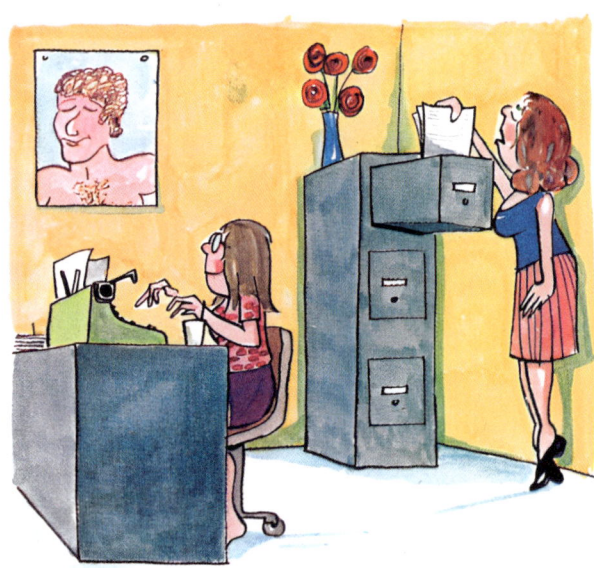

"Who filed this article on Erogenous Zones under travel?"

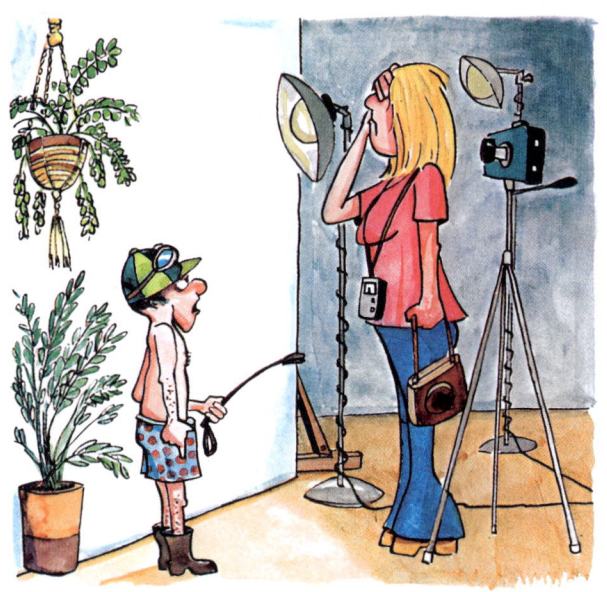

"Don't blame me, lady. The agency that sent me over said the magazine was doing a fashion feature on jockey shorts."

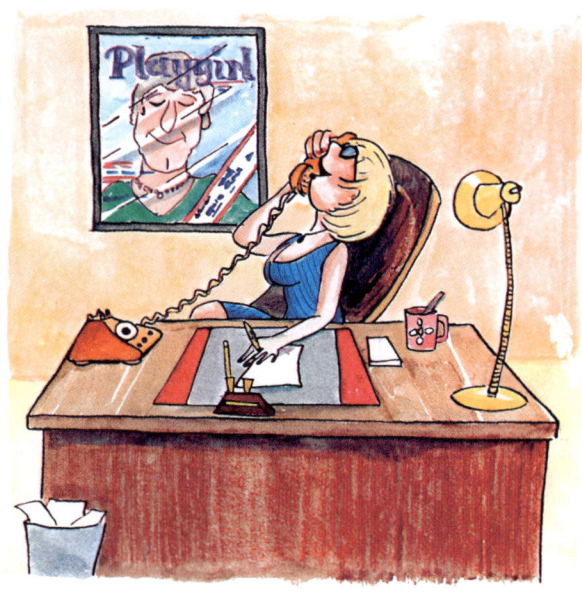

"It's settled then, Gerry. We'll shoot in the oval office and everything goes except the football helmet."

Cartoonist Tom Stratton takes advantage of the occasion of <u>Playgirl</u>'s Third Anniversary to look behind-the-scenes of the magazine's offices. Is this the way things <u>really</u> are?

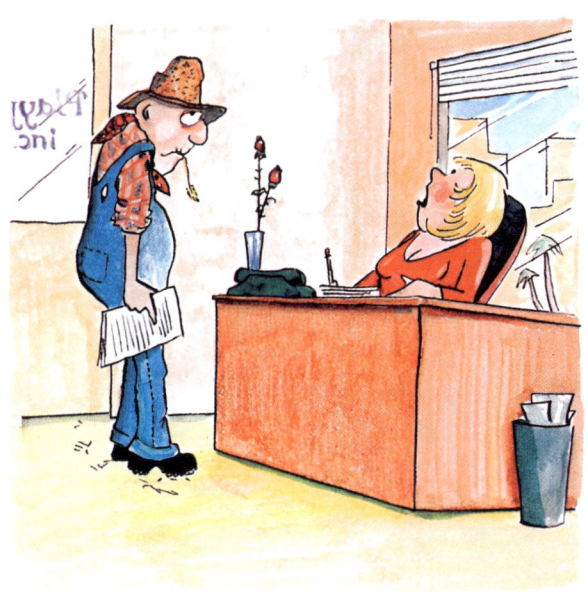

"Someone may have told you we're cock crazy around here but we just wouldn't be interested in an article on raising roosters."

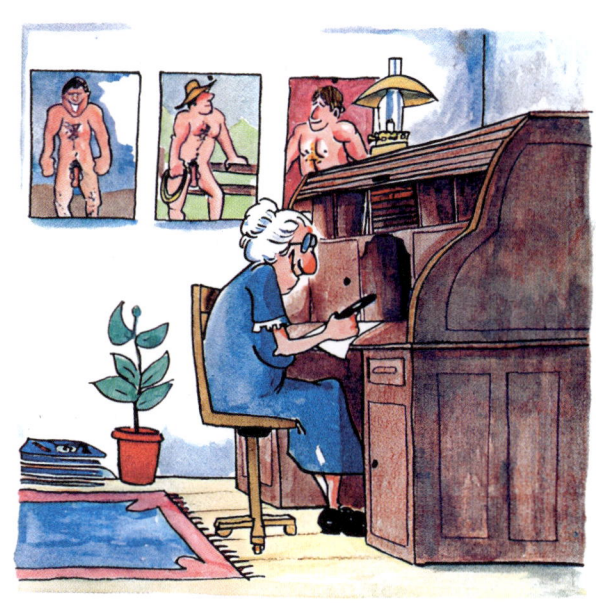

"Dear Playgirl: I picked up a copy of your magazine today and found it catering to prurient interests, without any redeeming social value and as disgusting as the last twenty-four issues."

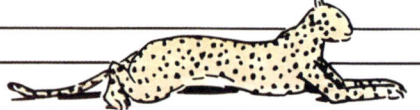

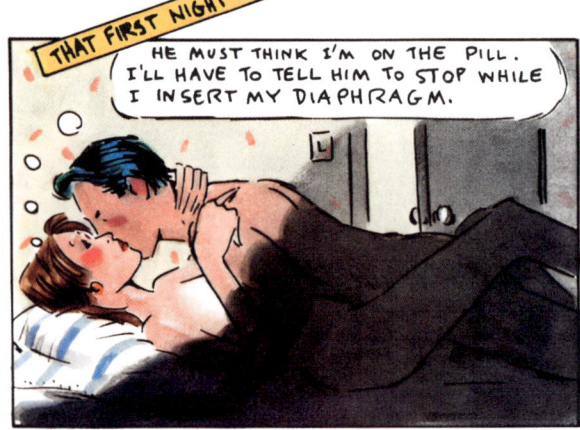

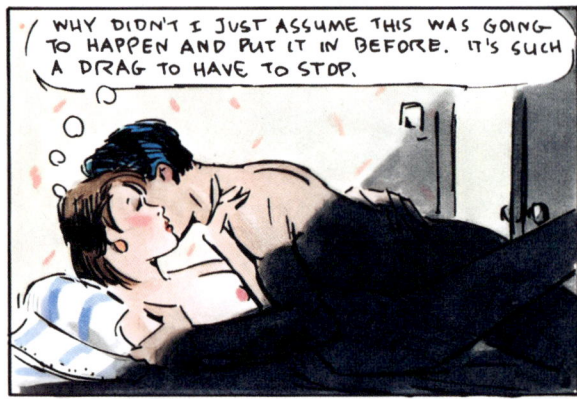

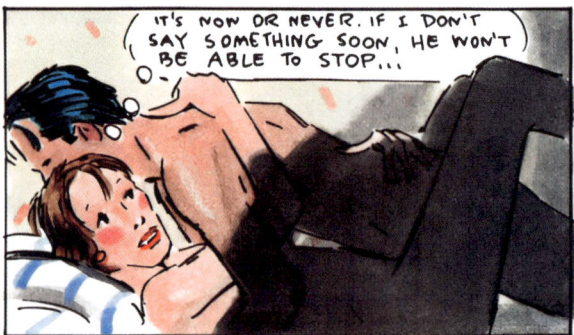

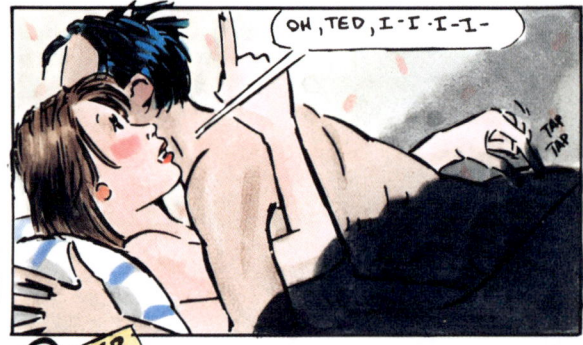

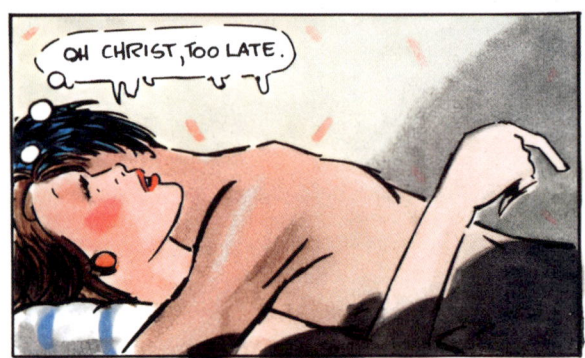

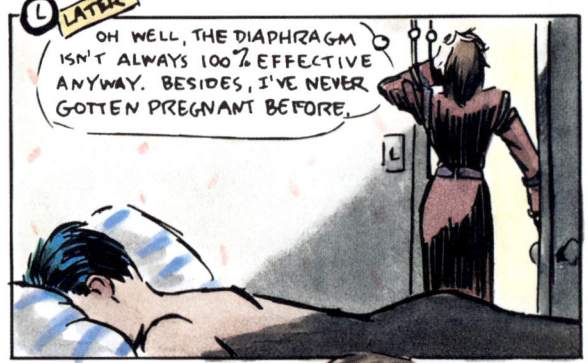

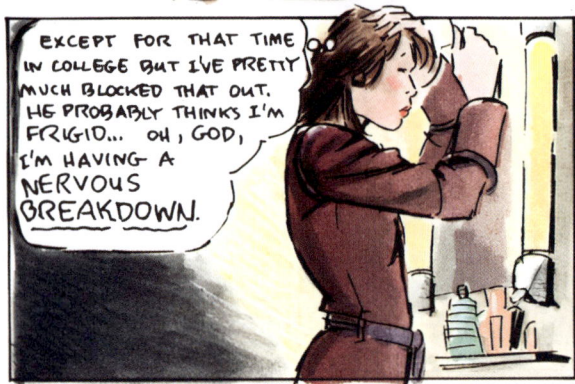

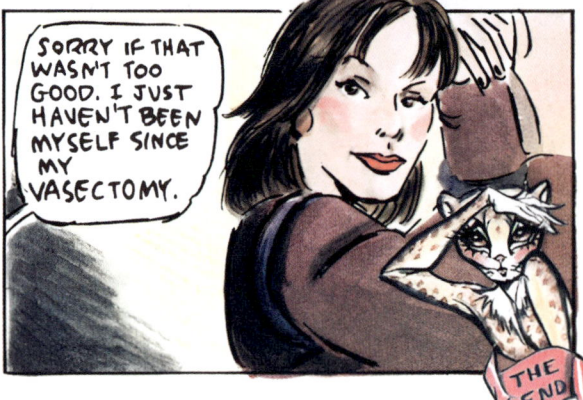

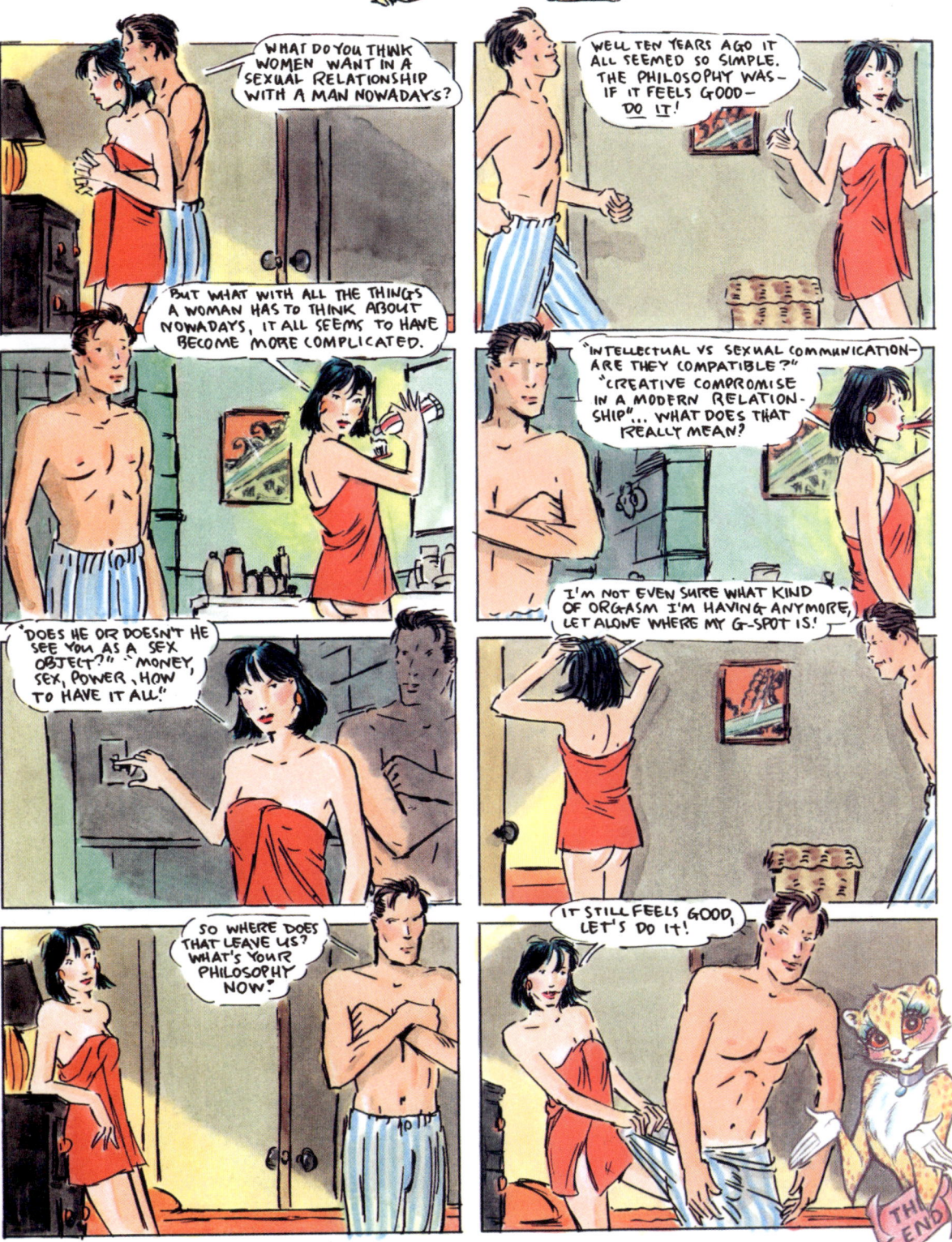

197

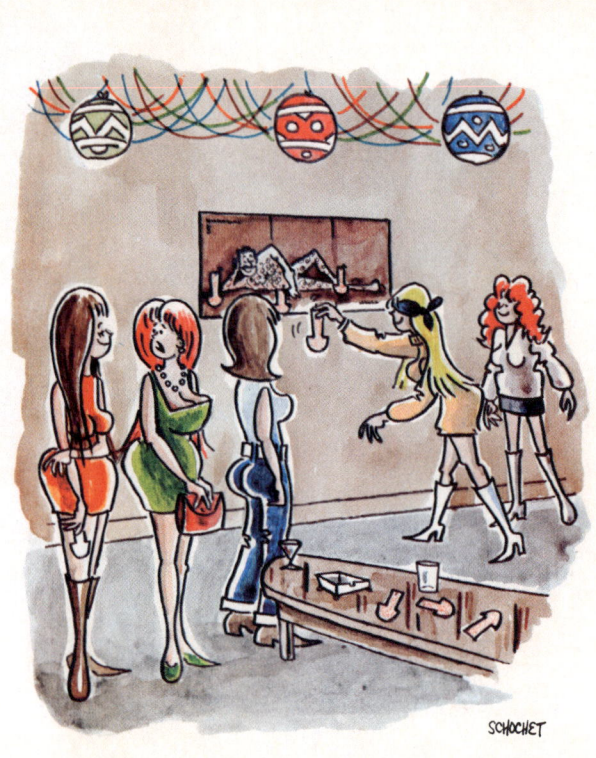

"You call it pin the what on Burt Reynolds?"

SCHOCHET

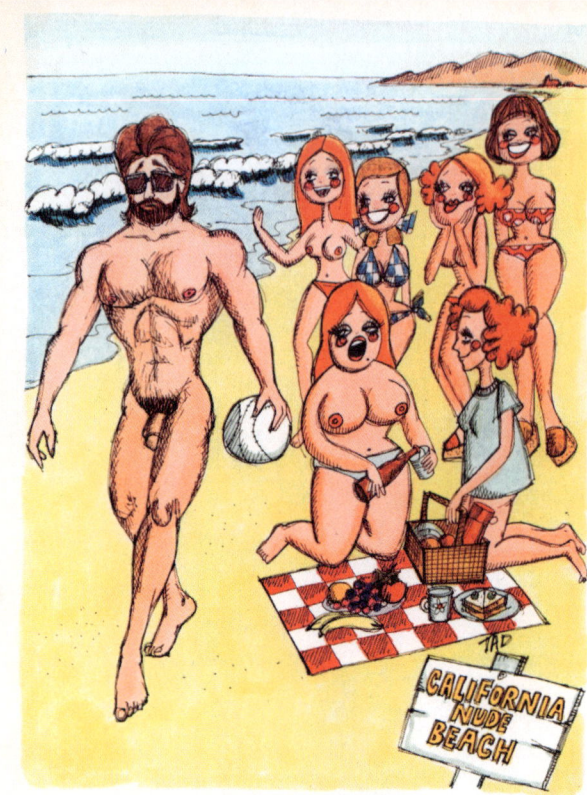

"I'VE ALWAYS BEEN A FACE WOMAN MYSELF."

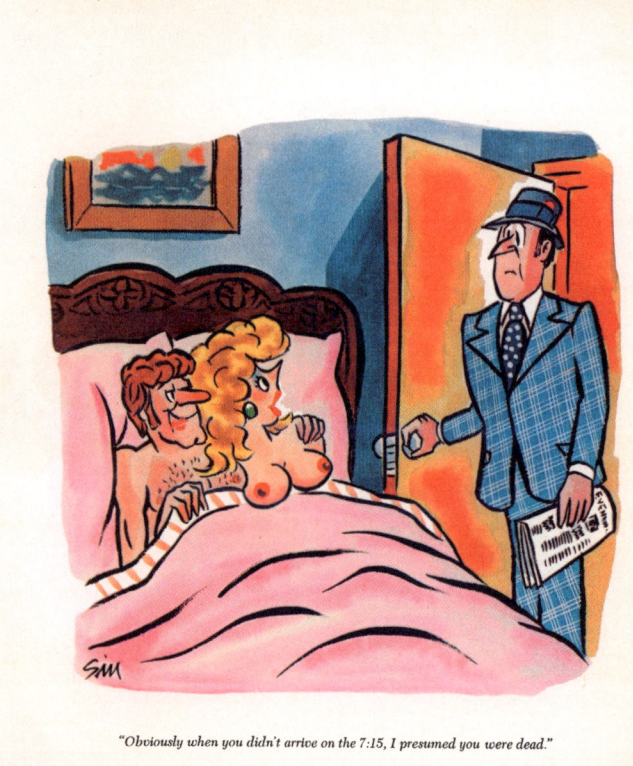

"Obviously when you didn't arrive on the 7:15, I presumed you were dead."

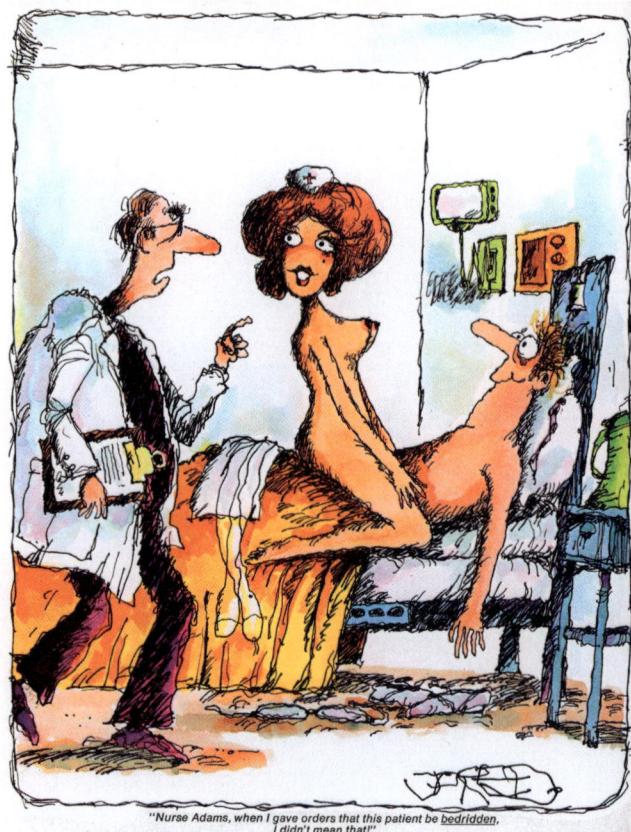

"Nurse Adams, when I gave orders that this patient be bedridden, I didn't mean that!"

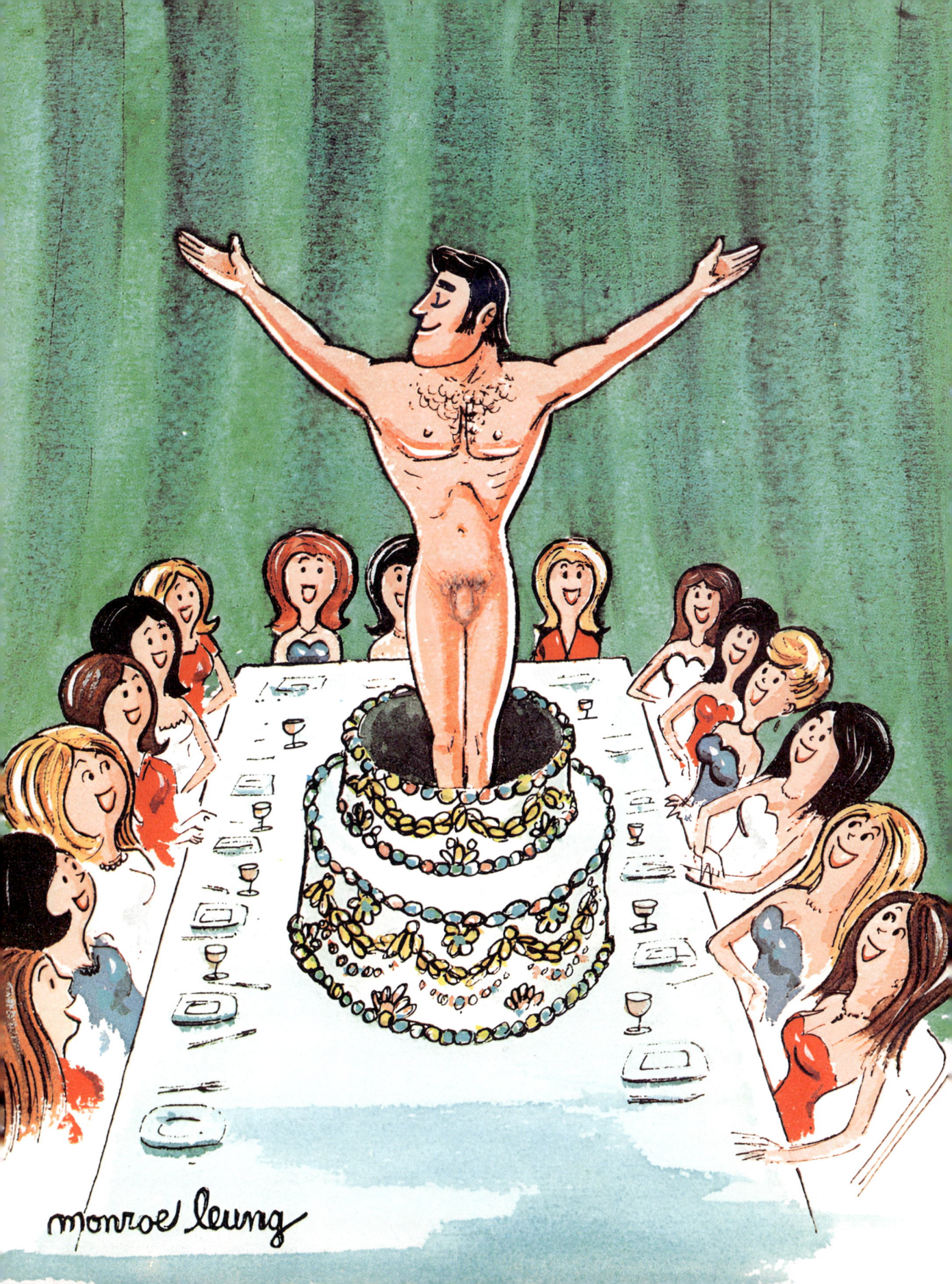

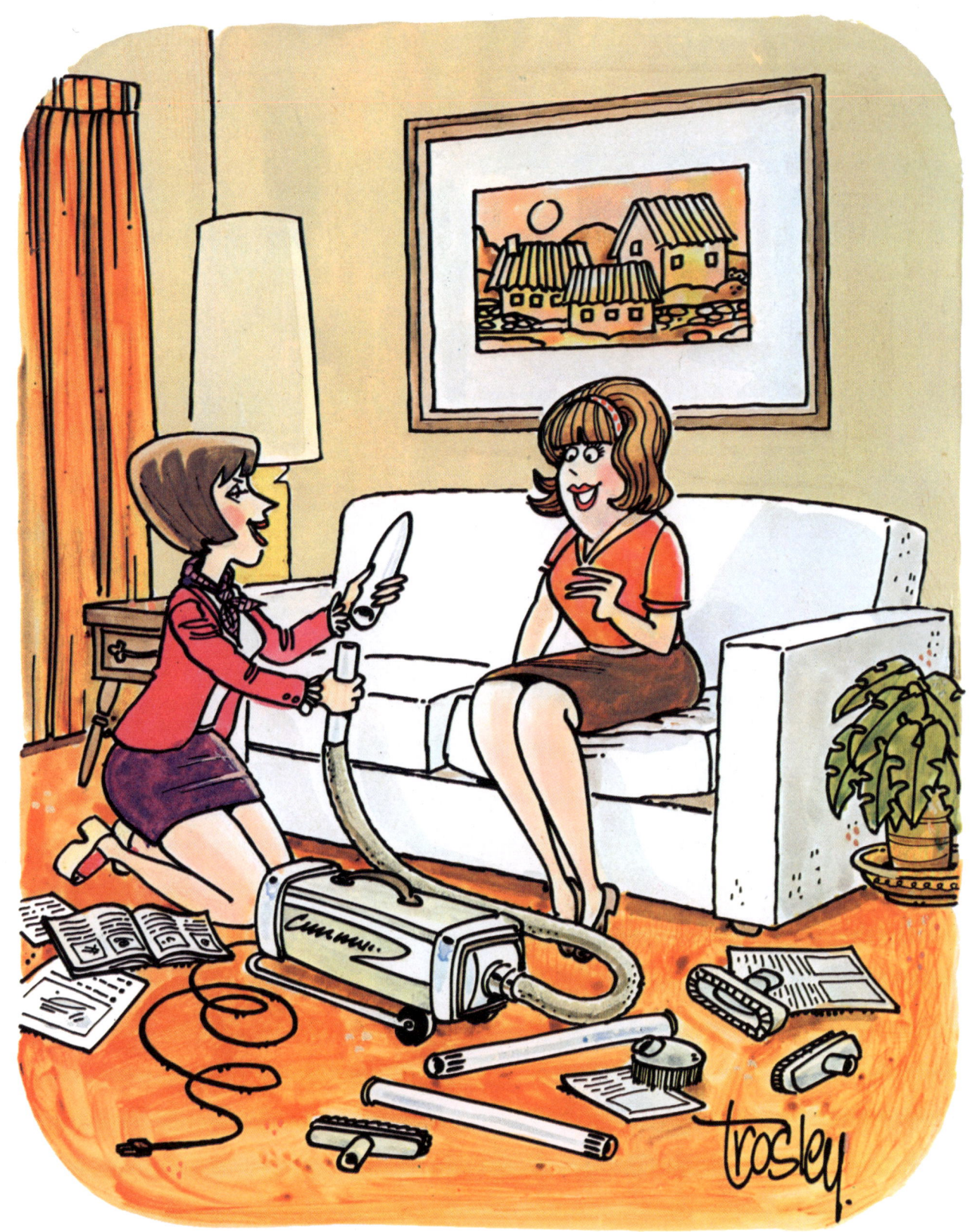

"*And with each machine purchased we are including this very handy attachment . . .*"

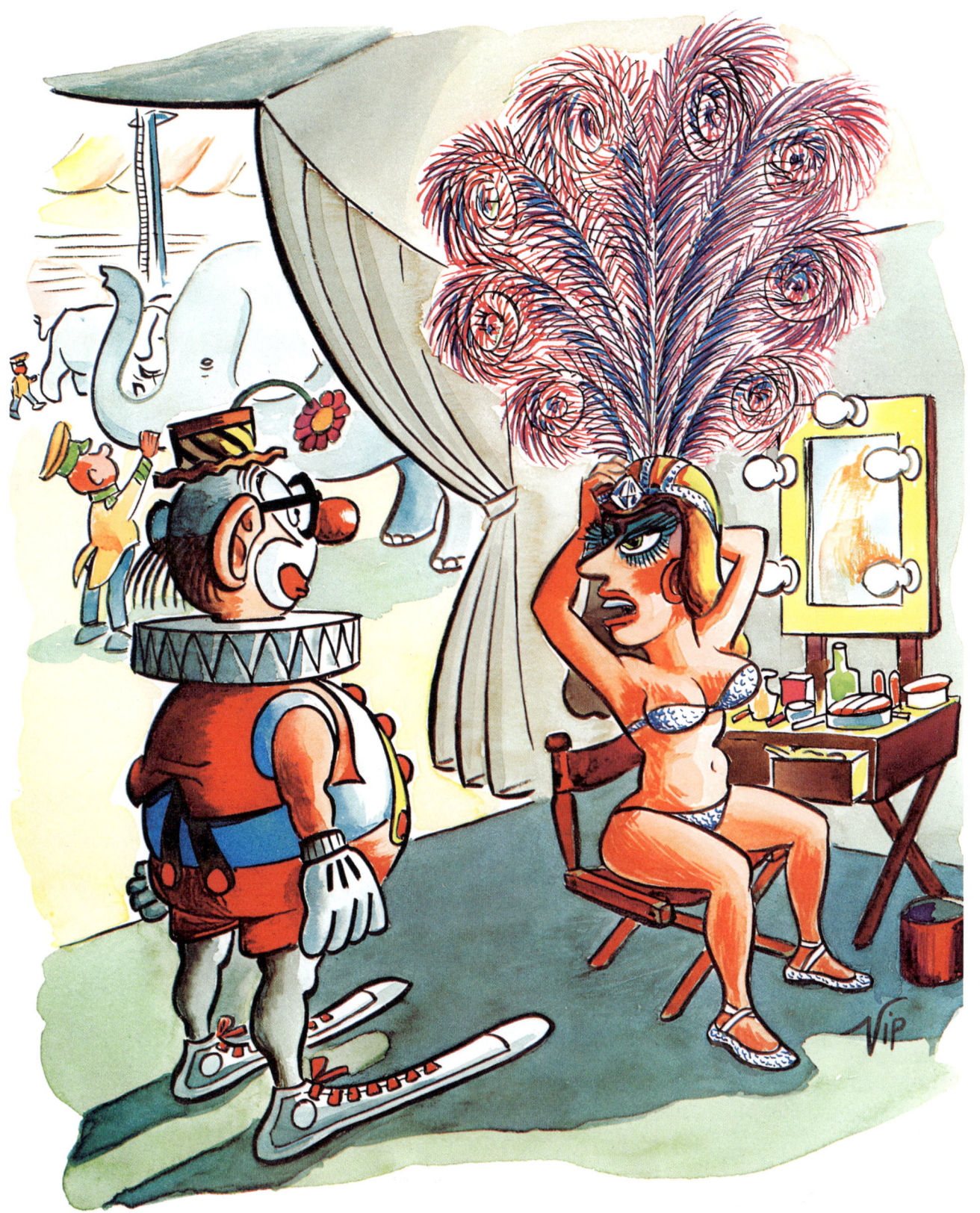

"No, I don't want to see your stupid funny bone!"

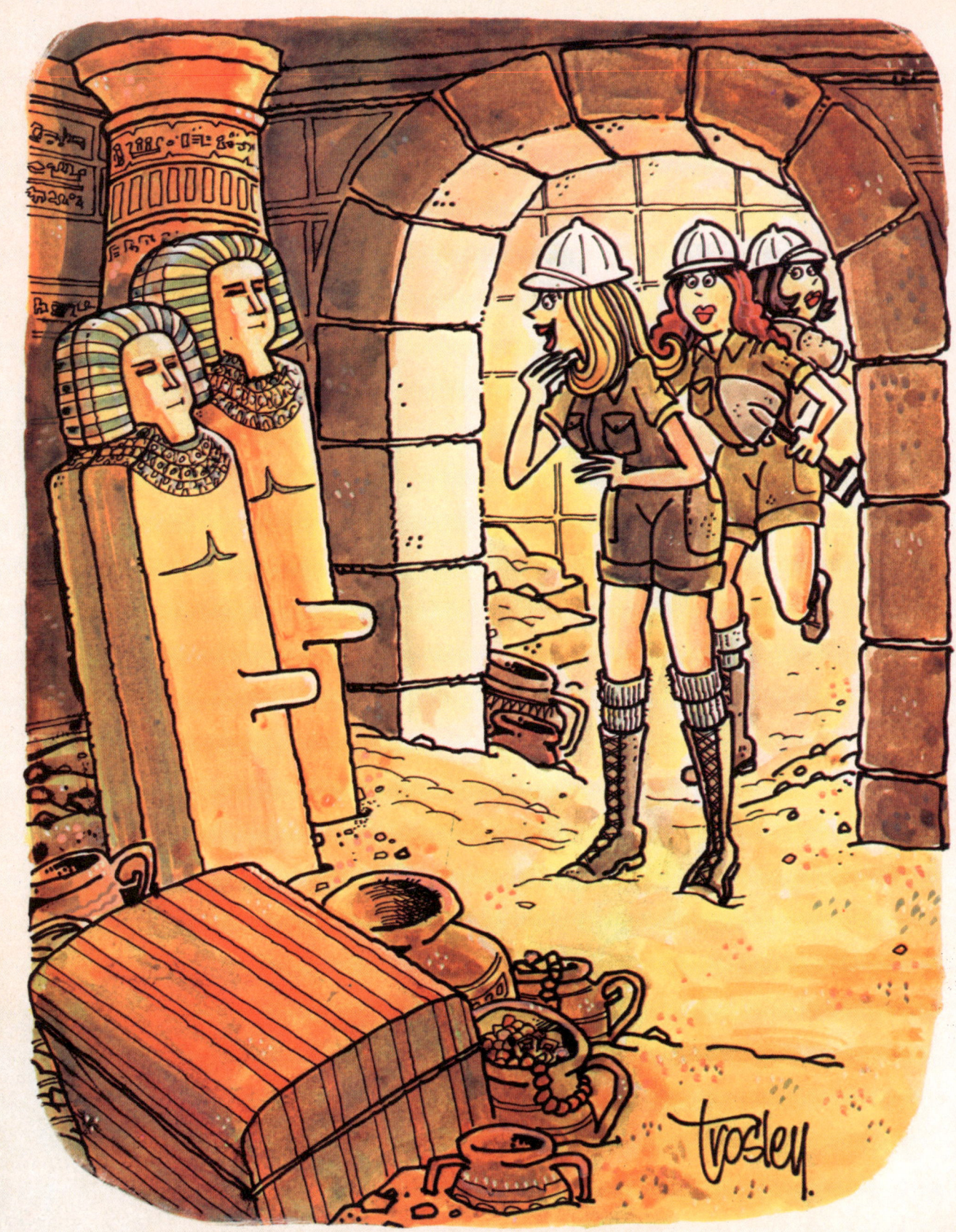

"Quick girls . . . in here!!"

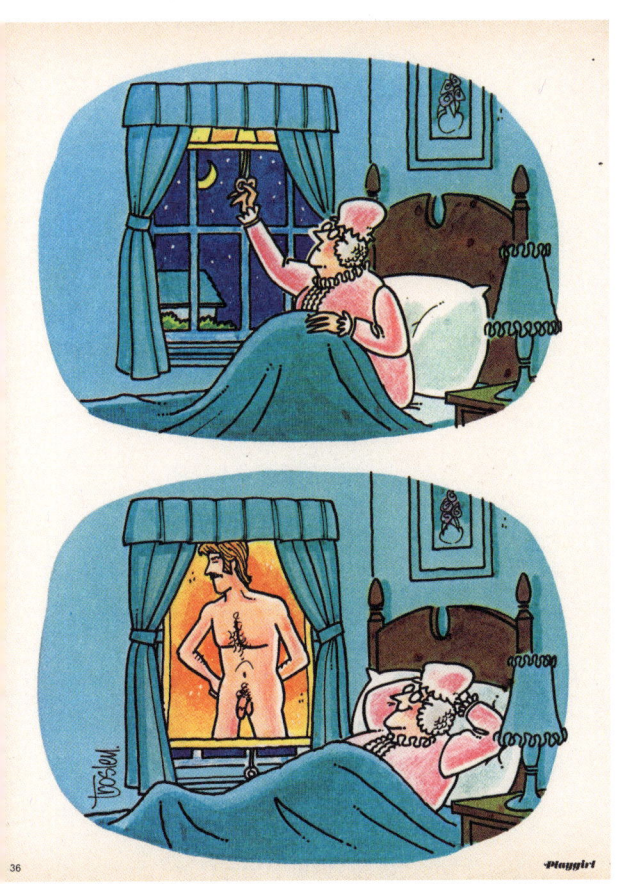

Playgirl

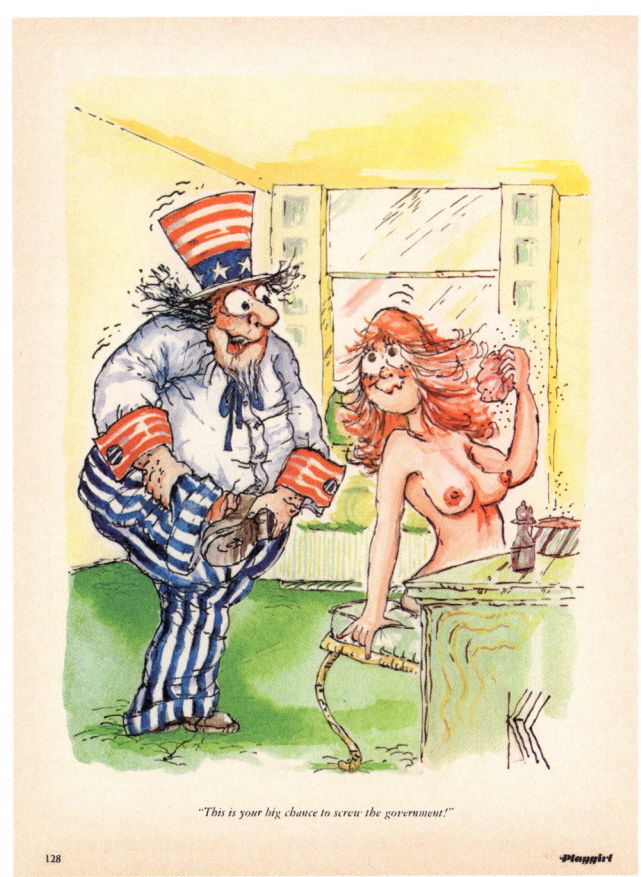

"This is your big chance to screw the government!"

Playgirl

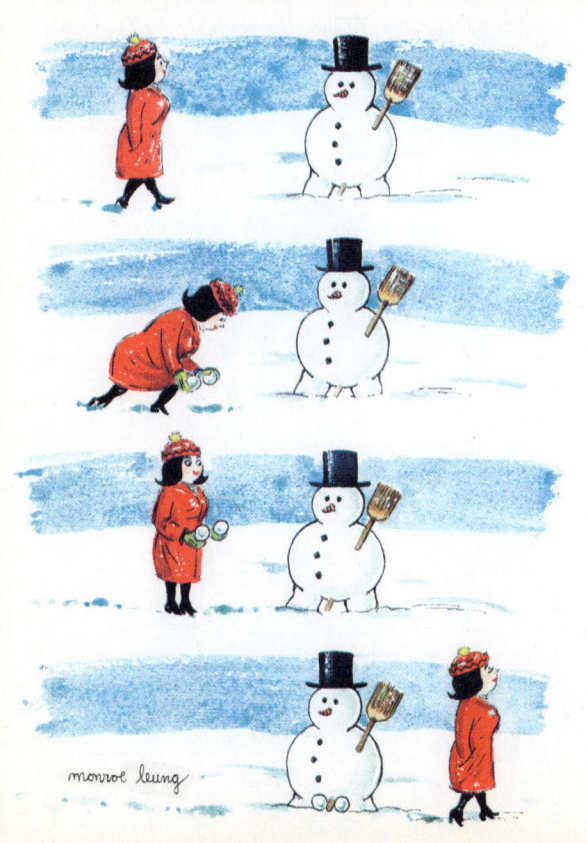

monroe leung

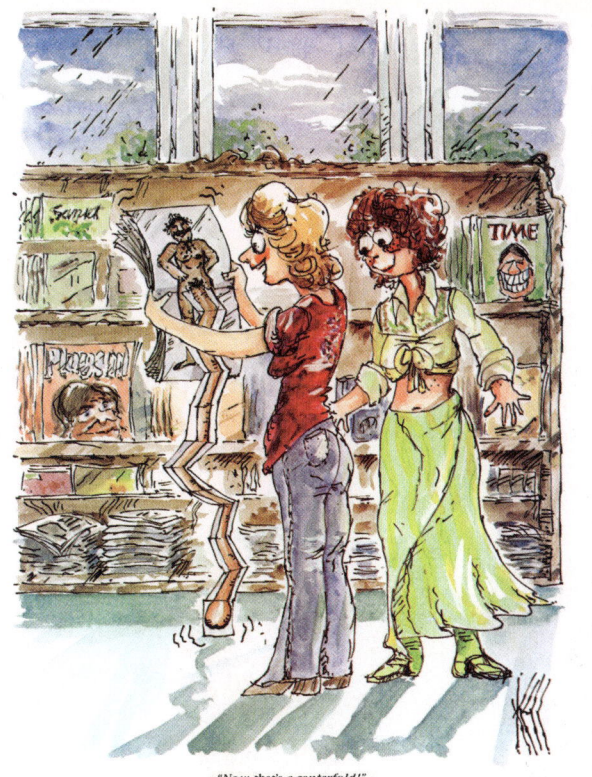

"Now that's a centerfold!"

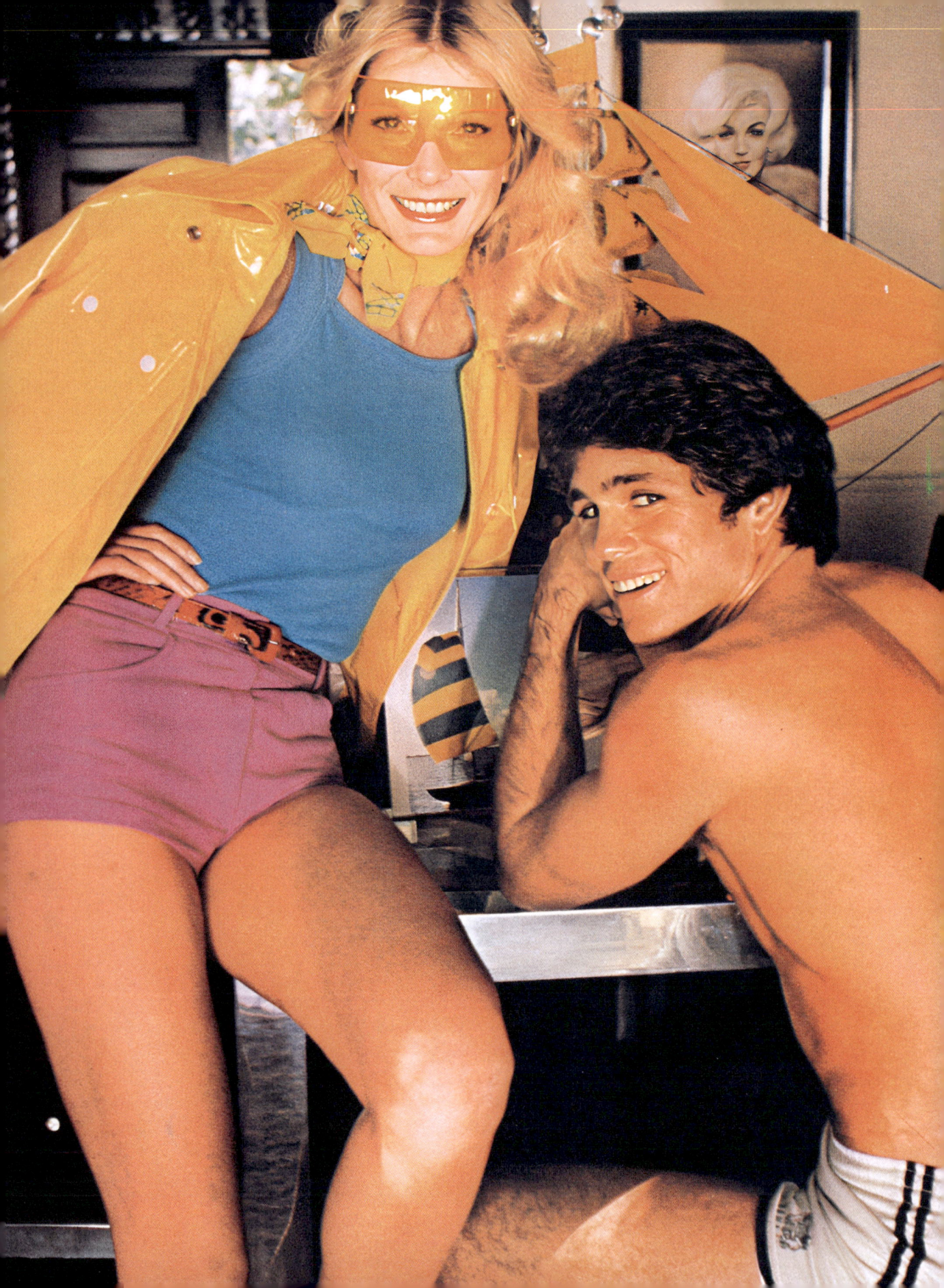

CHAPTER 11

SEX TALK

Some of the most outrageous mail, letters
to the editor, and sex advice questions sent to *Playgirl*
magazine over the past fifty years. Featuring firsthand advice
from the legendary Dr. Ruth Westheimer,
as well as our longest-standing sex advice columnist,
Dr. Theresa L. Crenshaw, MD, and most recently,
sexplorer Jamye Waxman. Readers wrote in voicing their
opinions and concerns about all aspects of the magazine,
from its newsstand availability (or lack thereof) to
the models' body hair and circumcisions, highlighting
the history of *Playgirl* and capturing a high level
of audience interaction spanning decades.
Side-splittingly hilarious and informative
at the same time: Sex Talk!

SEPTEMBER 1973

Well, we enthusiastically purchased our first edition of OUR magazine. We must admit that it is very well put together—many of the articles are interesting and some even highly amusing!

BUT, we very definitely wish to voice our unanimous complaint. Which is:

"WE WANT EQUAL EXPO-SURE" with regards to the centerfolds and various other pictures involved.

We assume and look forward to this misconception being corrected.

"THE GIRLS" of Parke, Davis & Co. Laboratories, Ann Arbor, Michigan

DECEMBER 1973

NO, NO

A pox on everyone connected with your magazine. It is not the youth of today one has to worry about, but the adults in our society like you who are spreading to, and encouraging, the minds of our young people the idea that sex is the only important thing in life.

How you will be able to justify yourselves at the Last Judgment is more than I can figure. How you can justify yourselves now to yourselves and to society is also a mystery.

God help you.

Disgusted in D.C.

Bravo! At last the women of America have a magazine of our own that deals with something else besides how to decorate an odd room. I'm only nineteen and I do not enjoy these magazines. Sure, they are nice once in a while, but *Playgirl* is the kind of magazine I'll enjoy reading all the time.

Alexine R. O'Neil,l Amenia, New York
(With all due respect to our Designs In Living, *of course. And thank you. —Ed.)*

I have never written a letter to any magazine, but I must thank you for finally giving us women an interesting magazine to read, namely *Playgirl*.

I am a twenty-five-year-old housewife, married eight years, and have three children. I am not an active women's libber, although I do agree with some of the goals they hope to attain.

On the other hand, I think it's high time for a magazine such as *Playgirl* for women. Although I must say my husband reads it, also. In fact, he bought me my first issue

I enjoy the articles, fiction, etc., but when it comes to centerfolds, Nude Discovery, and astrology pages, you really have it all.

Wow!

The only complaint I have as I mentioned on the *Playgirl* questionnaire, is that these good-looking dudes are posed too modestly.

There is nothing obscene about a man's nude body, unless it is in the mind of the individual, and that's their hang-up.

So far, you have showed us some very groovy-looking guys. In closing, I say thank you, *Playgirl*, and please give us more!

Midge Carlisle, Sarasota, Florida

MAY 1974

Thank you for a magazine that doesn't put me in the kitchen constantly or down at the laundromat gossiping.

I work and enjoy life, and while I do not mind housework, it's time someone realized my life doesn't revolve around ironing and grocery shopping.

The world is finally realizing women exist and contribute more to society than ever before.

Unsigned

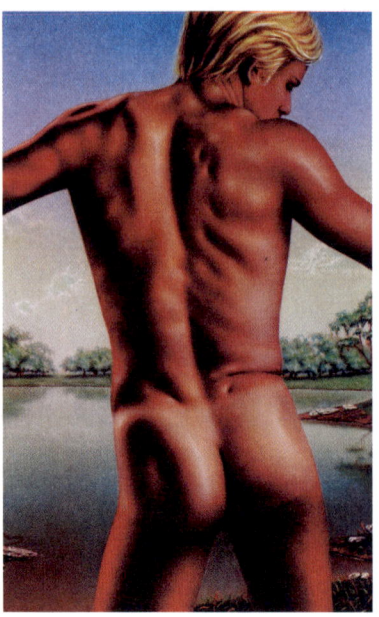

"THE DEVIL IN MS. MILAM"

I found this piece of trash left at my house, and I decided to fill out your questionnaire just to let you know that not all of America is as sick as you.

There is a time and a place for activities such as you suggest, and those people participating in them must be hard up or sick—like you.

Unsigned

(I wouldn't think of challenging you. I respect your right to your opinion, to your lifestyle, to your philosophy. But if you have the power of your convictions, why not sign your letter? —Ed.)

I believe women should challenge each and every comment made by owners, managers, and clerks of groceries, drugstores, and newsstands, that could be considered phony, invalid, or chauvinistic excuses for not having *Playgirl* readily available to those women desiring it.

I gladly buy *Playgirl* for my wife, and I'm sure other men do the same for their wives, girlfriends, lovers, etc.

Kenneth Cheney, El Cajon, California

NOVEMBER 1974

Q: My boyfriend is very considerate and attentive and tells me he loves me. He has wanted sex, but I have been reluctant to go along with this. Recently, he asked me to simply pose for him in a provocative manner so that he could masturbate to satisfy himself. I raised my dress and parted my legs, and as I watched him, I got the impression that he got more out of it than he could by actual intercourse. It stimulated me so much that I had an orgasm myself.

A: *The ability to become aroused by looking at another or being viewed by another is quite common and also quite normal, provided you feel comfortable about doing this.*

NOVEMBER 1976

ENGAGING SEX

Thanks for wiping out all my fears about what's okay to do in bed with my man. I'm nineteen and my boyfriend is 27. We've been having sex for a year and love each other very much, but about a month ago, I finally started thinking differently, and last night I went down on him. He got off four times, and this morning he went out and bought me a diamond ring. I don't think I'd be engaged right now if I hadn't read some of your articles on what people are really doing in bed. What a difference a happy head can make.

Eve H., Lubbock, Texas

DECEMBER 1976

FROM *PLAYGIRL*'S MALE READERS

I'm an eighteen-year-old guy who is one of *Playgirl*'s avid readers. Just to set you straight, I'm not homosexual. Sometimes I fantasize about being a centerfold, and this makes

my swinging hetero life even better. *Playgirl* articles are always top quality and interesting. Many are helpful because I realize more of what a female wants and am better able to understand the girls in my life. I have a lot of respect for Marin Milam and her awareness of what is happening today.

1 *Playgirl* Fan

JANUARY 1977

WANTS OLDER MEN

I'm beginning to think *Playgirl* should be labeled "Entertainment for Girls" instead of "for Women." I am very disappointed in the "boys" you have been featuring, for example, Ron Yarbrough in the July 1976 issue. What happened to the older, more mature men—broad shoulders and hairy chests. There is more to being a man than having a big penis. I wonder if these thin, hairless young men would know what to do with their endowments—maybe that is why they boast they're "free as a breeze" in their relationships with "all their women." A man is more than a man who admits he loves *one* woman and can handle a permanent relationship.

Thank God I have found such a man.

Diane Shallash, Bronx, New York
(To the contrary, we have had more "men" (as you would describe them) than boys in Playgirl *in the past three-and-a-half years. Ron Yarbrough is, in fact, 22 years old. Furthermore, according to more than one young lady of his acquaintance, he knows exactly what to do with his "endowment." —Ed.)*

FEBRUARY 1977

INCOMPATIBLE DESIRES

Q: My husband has three sexual desires—fellatio, S/M, and ejaculation on my breasts—that are causing a lot of problems. I don't

perform fellatio on him, although I've enjoyed it, because of the way he demands it. I have tried S/M with him (tying and being tied) but felt very repulsed, especially after being drilled in a very unloving way. I can't help but feel that these things have become particularly important only as a way to badger me. He never compliments me sexually or physically anymore, I only hear how I'm depriving him. I feel obligated to perform because I'm his wife and yet cannot respond naturally at my own rate anymore. Tell me, am I sexually uptight or is he unreasonable?

A: *Neither—and maybe both! The issue could be aggravated by your difficulty in asserting yourself and standing up for your rights. Just "because you're his wife" is not a good enough reason to continue to do distasteful acts. A feeling of obligation can lead to resentment and decreased mutual enjoyment, which has apparently already happened. Your husband likewise seems insensitive to you and more interested in power than lovemaking. You would probably benefit from some counseling, with him if he is willing, without if he is not.*

JULY 1977

MEN ONLY

Q: Why do you keep hiding your centerfolds behind their girlfriends? I like my men uncovered and *alone*. Can you imagine the *Playboy* bunnies with men draped around their bodies? Why, the men readers would never stand for it!

The girls who appear in men's magazines hardly ever have a guy with them, but in *Playgirl*, a lot of the men appear with women. We would appreciate it if the men were alone. We want to see them, not women.

A: *Not too long ago we were getting lots of letters asking to see women in the centerfold section. Now the trend seems to be going the other way. So, when you mail that postcard, why not also give me your pro or con vote on women in the centerfold section!*

SEPTEMBER 1977

MASTURBATION VS. INTERCOURSE

Q: My husband is 30 and I am 23. We've been married three years and my husband has masturbated an average of one to three times daily. We generally have sexual intercourse three times *monthly*. Is this normal for other men of his age or just for him?

A: *It's unusual for a man to masturbate that often for that long a period of time after marriage. With the information you've given, I can only speculate about the causes for this unconventional behavior.*

Perhaps he doesn't enjoy sexual intercourse with you. Perhaps he doesn't enjoy heterosexual intercourse, period. Perhaps there's something about intercourse that frightens him or makes him anxious.

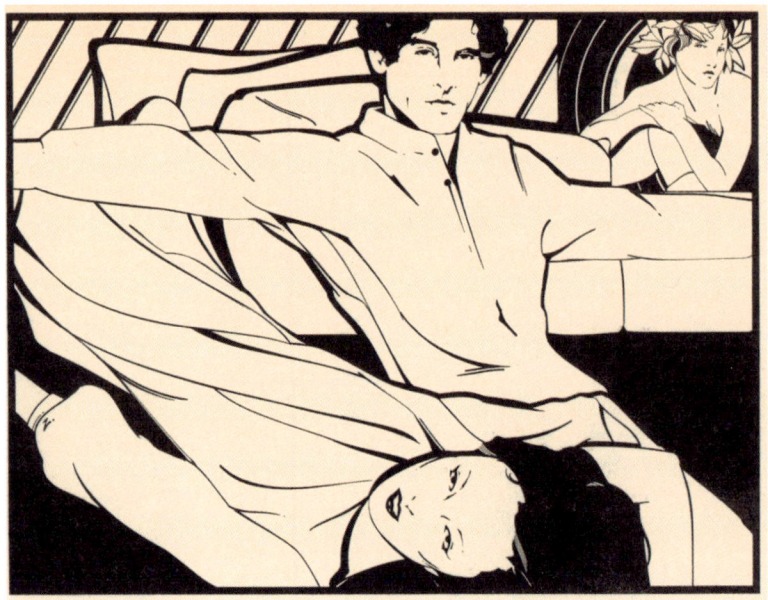

How do you feel about this situation, other than your curiosity as to its normalcy? If the frequency of intercourse is satisfactory to you, then there would seem to be no problem. If you want intercourse more frequently, then you and he will have to talk openly about possible compromises.

There's no automatic relationship between frequency of masturbation and frequency of intercourse, although in practice the two often seem to be related. He's probably capable of increasing his intercourse activity without interfering with his masturbatory activity.

DECEMBER 1977

MORNING COFFEE AND SEX

My husband, Phil, and I often swap partners with our best friends, Ken and Angela. One night at their house, when we were getting into bed in the dark, we found that as a joke the guys had switched places—Phil was with Ken and I was with Angela. At first I was embarrassed, but when I saw Phil and Ken getting off on each other, I gave in to Angela's gentle

insistence. We began to explore each other's bodies and my embarrassment turned to surging pleasure.

Angie used to come over twice a week for coffee and conversation. Now she comes over more frequently, and after we finish exchanging the latest gossip, we go upstairs.

My husband approves wholeheartedly. I understand his role in lovemaking more fully now and my new knowledge and responsiveness really gets him off.

I'm writing this letter so your readers will realize that there is nothing wrong in a natural, loving relationship with female friends.

Regina Cox, Kansas City, Missouri

GUTSY LADY

Q: First of all, let me say that I really enjoy your magazine. There is only one problem with *Playgirl*—a lot of women are afraid to purchase it!

They keep *Playgirl* magazine behind the counter at the store I usually go to. So I have to ask for it. When I bought the latest issue, the cashier at the store responded to my request with an "Oh, yeah, not many women come in for it. They're so afraid to ask for a copy. You're the only one around with any guts." Are you surprised? I was. Can't you reach these women and let them know what they are missing? Maybe someday they'll wake up. You can only hope.

Georgan Deka, Brooklyn, Ohio

A: *It doesn't come as a surprise to us that many females are afraid to buy* Playgirl. *We see it and hear it all the time. Unfortunately, sexual repression has made some women feel like perverts if they're "caught" gawking at a nude centerfold. Looking at the photographs is an open admission of a woman's sexuality and some feel embarrassed by this—maybe men will think you're a sex-crazed nymphomaniac, why else would you be looking at* that *magazine! Not every woman* is as comfortable with sexuality as you are, but this is changing by leaps and bounds. Hopefully, in time all women will be able to pick up a copy of Playgirl with the same ease that men pick up a copy of Playboy. —Eds.

AN EARFUL

Q: My boyfriend and I enjoy sex in many different ways. He likes masturbating in my ear. Well, if he likes it, why not! Now I'm having second thoughts since I've developed a little ear trouble. I heard that any infection above the nose line could cause brain damage. If my ears are infected, could my brain be too?

W.D.

A: *Don't worry. The way to a woman's brain is not through the ear. Bacteria which thrive in the uro-genital tract don't take very well to the drier climate upstairs. So forge ahead. Antibiotics can deafen even a clap in the ear.*

SEPTEMBER 1978

CHOCOLATE-FLAVORED SEMEN

Q: Somewhere I read about a pill that a man can take to make his semen taste like chocolate, vanilla, strawberry, etc. Is this feasible? If so, could you help me locate a source for these pills?

T.B., Big Springs, Texas

A: *While it is feasible that pills could influence the taste of semen, I know of none that are available. But if any of our dear readers know of such an item, please write and advise us of its properties and whereabouts.*

What I can tell you about the taste of semen is that it varies from man to man. Just as each man has a unique smell, each also has a unique taste. Some taste bitter, others sweet, and the same one can smell and taste differently, depending on what he's had for dinner. Which leads us to a little home experimentation: Feed him carrots, garlic, or asparagus and you can taste the difference.

FEBRUARY 1979

OUT OF THE CLOSET

I recently brought my copy of the October *Playgirl* into the office. Since I work for a very "straitlaced" company, I decided it was best if I kept the magazine in a plain brown envelope.

At break time, I took my copy out and sat with my close friends apart from the rest of the girls. We were talking about some of the articles and those fantastic photos of "Man of the Month" Lenny Thompson, who is really quite a man from any point of view! One of the other girls overheard us talking and asked what we were looking at. Then one girl saw the book and Lenny and the next thing we knew, all of them had moved over by us. One girl exclaimed, "I didn't realize they finally came out with a book for us women!"

By lunchtime, forty-seven women had asked where I bought my magazine and indicated they too are going to buy *Playgirl* from now on. The highlight of the day came when Mom and I were looking at the magazine and Dad said, "I never thought I'd see the day when my daughter and wife were reading something like that!" I said, "Dad, you've been reading *Playboy* for years, saying you liked the 'articles.' Well, *Playgirl* has terrific articles and the photography is very good. Face it, the time has come and we're out of the closet for good!" To this my "old-fashioned" mother replied, "Right on!" As I said, "out of the closet." Thanks for *Playgirl*.

Ann L. Brodo, Mt. Ephraim, New Jersey

UNCUT VERSION

I know this has been asked before, but can't we see a few more uncircumcised cocks? I know that the majority of the males in this country have been clipped, but in the November issue there were nineteen pricks and out of those nineteen all were circumcised (or the three I suspect of not being circumcised had their foreskins retracted). The ratio in this country of clipped penises to unclipped is about seventy percent to thirty percent, so out of approximately twenty cocks, you should be able to find five or six that are uncut.

Angie Holbrook, Salt Lake City, Utah

MARCH 1979

CALORIE COUNT OF "CUM"

Q: I am a student at Kean College in New Jersey, and would like to reply to a letter in the "Personal From *Playgirl*" column in the November 1978 issue in which a reader asked if "cum" is fattening. Ms. Zuckerman replied that she didn't know the exact calorie count in each ejaculation.

Well, I am taking a course in human sexuality this semester and have learned that there are only thirty-six calories in each ejaculation. Just thought everyone might like to know.

M.P., Carteret, New Jersey

A: *Thank you, M.P. However, since we already know that "cum" is composed of sugar and protein in a basal solution,* the more you swallow, the greater your consumption of calories. Therefore, dieters might want to take this into consideration while planning their daily calorie intake. —Eds.

OCTOBER 1981

LOOKS ARE EVERYTHING

Your June and July centerfolds were both very good-looking men. However, they shared one terrible problem: ugly peters.

I'm sure that the majority of *Playgirl* readers would agree that the uncircumcised look is decades behind the times.

Many more centerfolds like these, and you will lose a loyal and faithful reader. I am tired of looking at foreskins.

F. Wilson, Baton Rouge, Louisiana

JANUARY 1982

ONE-A-DAY

Thanks for your article about semen (November 1981 issue). My boyfriend has been trying to convince me to swallow. He keeps saying that it won't hurt me and that it's actually good for me—"high in protein," he says. I thought it was just a line.

Now I know that semen really is chock-full of vitamins, minerals, and protein. Maybe I won't need to take my vitamin tablets every day—with my new dietary supplement.

Amy Roland, Cleveland, Ohio

DECEMBER 1982

PLAYING WITH A BAND

Q: After last night, I feel like a tramp! I went to a club, got smashed, and ended up with the band. We all went back to a motel and had sex, and I shared my body with seven guys! But honestly, I loved it! It was

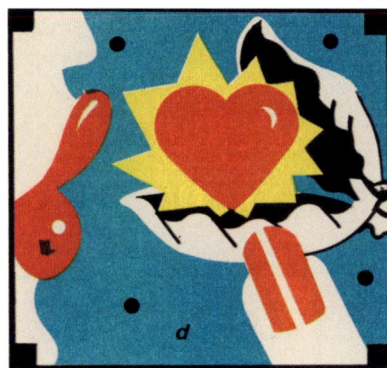

one of the most fun nights of my life. But today, I am ashamed and wondering whether it was right or wrong. I would like to do it again but I am afraid of someone finding out and calling me a slut. Is it so wrong to have the urge to go to bed with a dozen beautiful men at the same time? Am I a sex maniac?

D.O., Canada

A: *It sounds like your experience was fun for you—and for the seven band members—and no one was hurt by it. What may be disturbing you is a discrepancy between your actions and your beliefs about the way "respectable women" behave. There are many actions that inherently are neither right nor wrong. You are the only one who can decide what sexual behavior is right for you.*

FEBRUARY 1986

INSIDE STORY

Q: My husband and I like to have oral sex. I love it when he comes in my mouth. Recently I heard that swallowing a man's ejaculate can cause problems with one's stomach and general health. Is this true?

S.C., Boston, Massachusetts

A: *Where on earth did you hear that? The best information I have from medical authorities is that swallowing ejaculate is harmless. If you have acquired a fear of swallowing sperm—many women*

have—confide in your husband. Tell him that you'd like him to tell you when he is about to come.

Dr. Ruth Westheimer

MARCH 1993

Q: Frequently, after making love, my husband will perform oral sex on me and lick up his own semen. I find this very kinky and exciting. Lately, I have been fantasizing about watching my husband suck another man's penis.

Although he is hesitant, my husband has told me that if he were aroused enough, he could bring himself to suck another man for me. How should we approach a possible threesome?

Should we include a close friend who we trust, or seek out someone else?

L.S., Toronto, Canada

A: *I suggest you continue to enjoy your husband and keep fantasizing about threesomes. In this age of AIDS and other sexually transmitted diseases, it's an unhealthy and potentially dangerous idea to turn your fantasy into reality.*

However, if you are determined to pursue it, you should definitely plan in advance to have all three of you tested for HIV infection. The antibody test alone is not enough; there is now a test you can request directly for the virus, and you should get them both.

Don't choose a close friend to help act out your fantasy unless you're willing to lose him. While he may enjoy it at the time, he'll disappear if he feels guilty or uncomfortable about it afterward.

Still, strangers are hard to test or trust, so I suggest you select someone you know fairly well. The relationship will either get better or worse, but it won't remain the same.

MAY 1993

NOW IT'S OUR TURN

When I purchase *Playgirl*, it is my way of fighting back. I'm fed up with the entertainment industry, and so are a lot of other women I know. Whose idea was it to rate a woman's nude body "R" and a man's "X"? (Probably a man's!) Every woman knows that a man's body is beautiful to look at, and women outnumber men in America, so why doesn't the movie industry get it? Men have lots to look at; we ladies need more options.

Cindy Shaw, Fort Worth, Texas

I want to express my gratitude to *Playgirl*. I have received your magazine for a year now, and I plan to be a subscriber for a long time to come. What pleases me most is that *Playgirl* is a real *woman's* magazine. I think women are complex (an understatement), but the media has not fully explored our wonderful sexuality. How many subscriptions of *Vogue* can we go through before we realize there is something more to being female? That's where you come in!

S.M., Chicago, Illinois

JANUARY 1998

THE MOST FUN ALLOWED BY LAW

To reduce stress from deadlines and demanding bosses, seven paralegals and I initiated a "*Playgirl* Break" every Friday, where we sit down and pore over the current issue. We all love this break because it gives us something to look forward to at the end of the week and leaves us with exciting thoughts for the weekend. Our only suggestion is to add even more hunky Adonises. That way we can make our "*Playgirl* Breaks" daily . . .

Patricia S., Miami, Florida

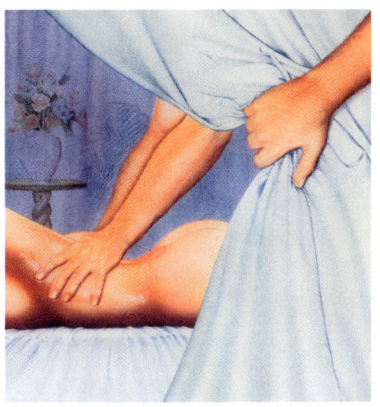

JULY 1998

DOUBLE VISION

I have been subscribing to *Playgirl* for years and have always found it enjoyable and entertaining. So when I was checking out your Real Men feature in the February/March issue, I couldn't believe you would feature a man with two penises. It was very unsettling to me. I know there are many informative articles in your magazine, but it's sad that you're resorting to this type of crazy coverage. I am sure there are many women who'll agree with me.

Grace I.V., Beaver Dam, Wisconsin

Editor's Reply: It's impossible to please all our readers. We're sorry you didn't enjoy Kamal's unique attributes, but many women did. Each month we feature extraordinary men of different colors and sizes, and Kamal is certainly one of them! To ignore his stand-out trait(s) would be closed-minded of us!

MAY 2001

I had a crush on the busboy at my local diner, so one night I decided to make my fantasies come true. I waited until it was late, and the only people left in the place were a customer reading a book, the waitress, and him. I waited until I caught his eye, and then I went behind the counter and pulled up my skirt,

revealing my pantiless coochie. A look of shock went across the busboy's face, and then he looked at the waitress. She proceeded to call me a whore and throw me out of the restaurant. The busboy came around to the parking lot where I was getting into my car to go home and told me he was sorry that his wife couldn't take a joke!

Jane D., Burlington, Vermont

JUNE 2003
FALL ISSUE

This is concerning the article "Straight Chicks, Gay Dicks"—thank goodness! I was getting a little worried about myself. The fascination with gay male sex only recently started. I read and write romantic erotic fiction and have bought several books over the past year that included male/male sex scenes. For me, I notice I get more excited when the encounter is unexpected. If it is something the men do all the time, while sexy, it is not nearly as hot as when the men have never before considered having sex with other men and just can't help themselves. The men have to be big, deep-voiced: someone I would want in my bed. Thank you for such a great article, and for helping this girl feel a little more normal.

Shannon R., via email, March 2007

JANUARY 2009

THE STRAIGHT STORY

I don't mean to sound rude, but why do all the guys look gay? In fact, I know some of them are gay porn stars. Is *Playgirl* meant for women or men? I'm a very sexual, visual woman who wants to see beautiful naked men, but I want them to be straight. Is it that you can't find straight guys that will pose nude for these kinds of magazines? It's a little disappointing . . .

Joanna D., via email

CHAPTER 12

MISCEL-LANEOUS

Various ads from the past five decades include those for the original Playgirl Club (in Garden Grove, California, 1.5 miles south of Disneyland, 1973), *Playgirl* apparel and branded clothing, the Las Vegas "Men of *Playgirl*" all-male revue (2005), and mail-in subscription coupons of yesteryear, all of which hark back to our rich history. From collectibles like Playgirl Club membership cards and VHS tapes such as the *Hunkercise* aerobic workout (1985) and the retro "video magazine" *Playgirl on the Air Vol. 1 & 2* (1984 and 1986), this collection of long-out-of-print and all-but-forgotten memorabilia is a trip down memory lane. Presenting exclusive *Playgirl* merchandise such as pillows, puzzles, bags, beach towels, mugs, playing cards, cigarette cases, lighters, keychains, board games, and more!

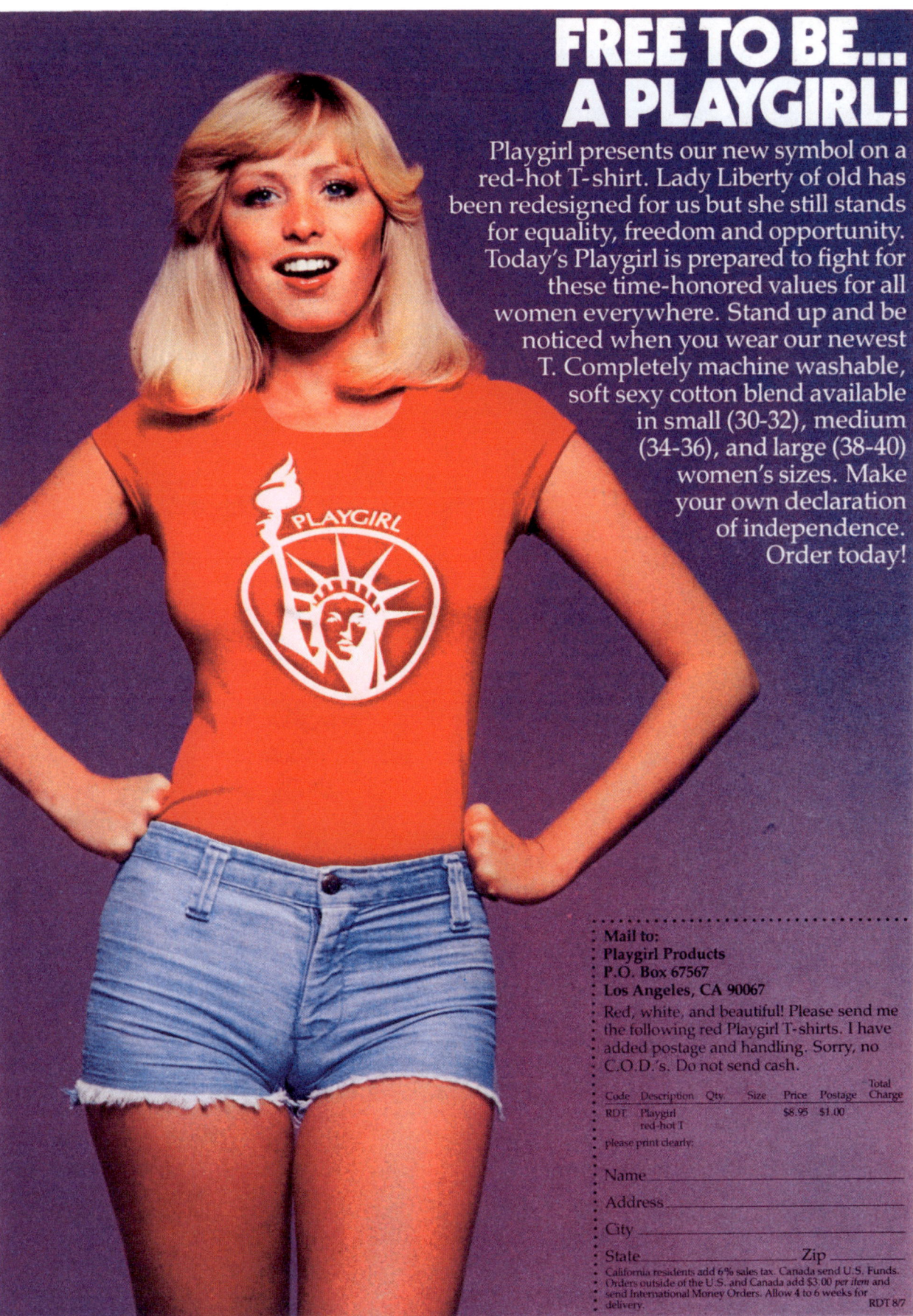

PLAYGIRL

on the air

VOLUME 2

CALIFORNIA
DREAMIN'
**AN EROTIC
FANTASY
POOLSIDE
DIP**

Exclusive Interview
**SYBIL
DANNING**
HOST OF ADVENTURE VIDEO

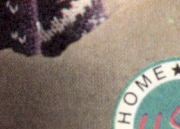

Nude Centerfold
**ALL-AMERICAN
DISCOVERY**
**SCOTT
PETERSON**

FOR MORE
BRAWNY BEEFCAKE
DON'T FORGET...
VOLUME 1

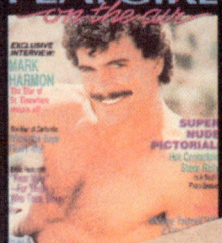

PLAYGIRL
on the air
EXCLUSIVE INTERVIEW
MARK HARMON

PHOTO: AMY ETRA

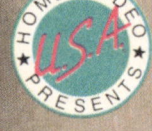
HOME ★ VIDEO
USA
PRESENTS

$39⁹⁵ EACH

FIRST CLASS U.S. MALE
ON VIDEOCASSETTE

TWIN ARTS
PRODUCTIONS

U.S.A. HOME VIDEO / A DIVISION OF INTERNATIONAL VIDEO ENTERTAINMENT, INC. / AN NCB ENTERTAINMENT GROUP COMPANY

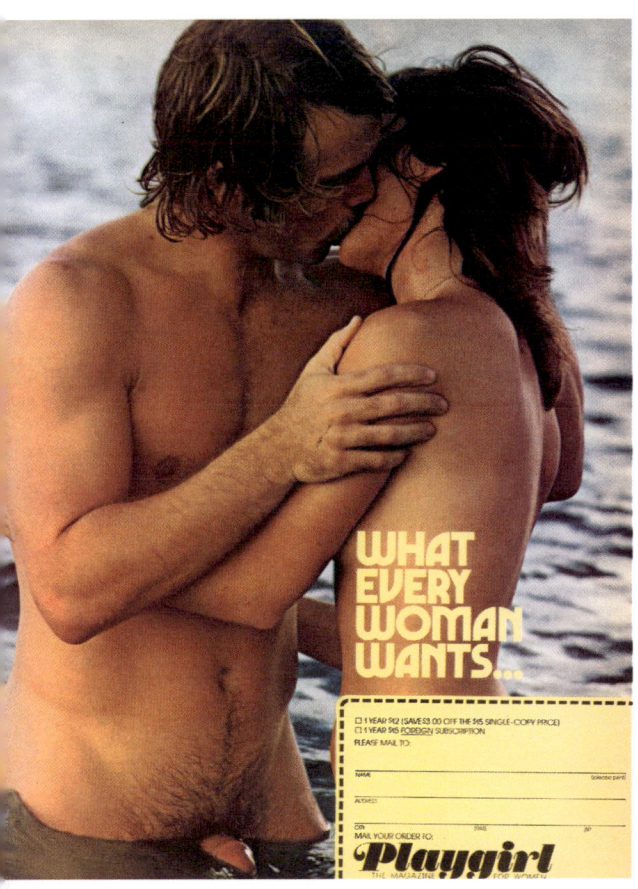

WHAT EVERY WOMAN WANTS...

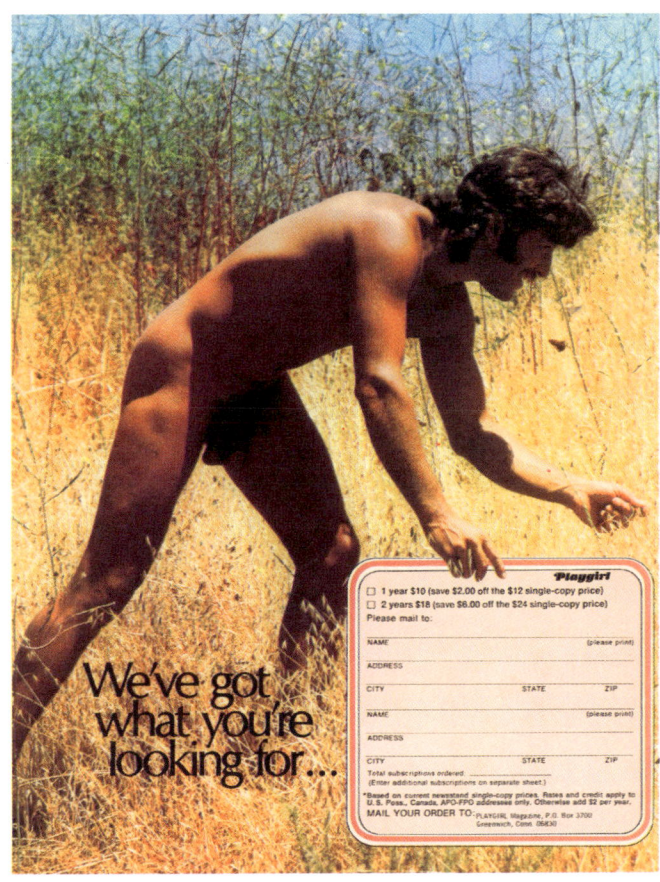

We've got what you're looking for...

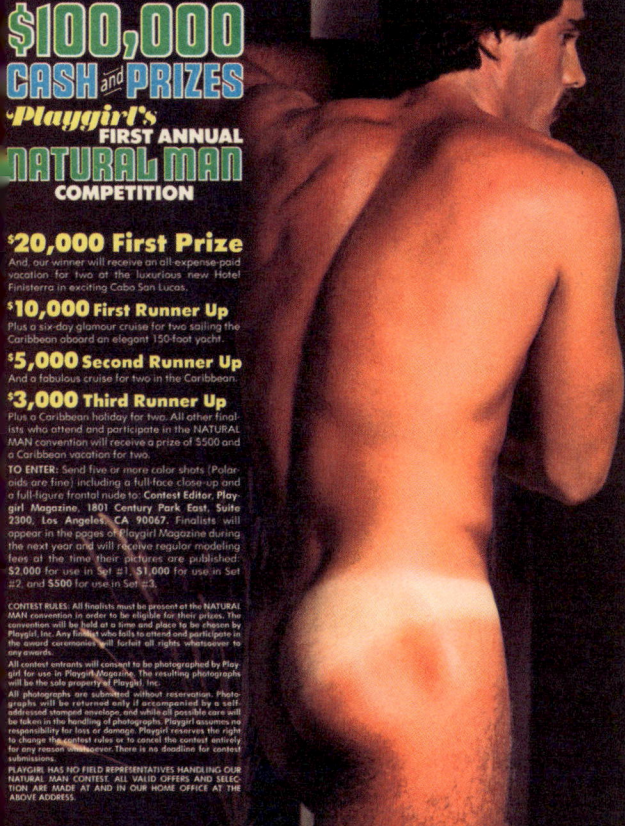

$100,000 CASH and PRIZES

Playgirl's FIRST ANNUAL NATURAL MAN COMPETITION

$20,000 First Prize
And, our winner will receive an all-expense-paid vacation for two at the luxurious new Hotel Finisterra in exciting Cabo San Lucas.

$10,000 First Runner Up
Plus a six-day glamour cruise for two sailing the Caribbean aboard an elegant 150-foot yacht.

$5,000 Second Runner Up
And a fabulous cruise for two in the Caribbean.

$3,000 Third Runner Up
Plus a Caribbean holiday for two. All other finalists who attend and participate in the NATURAL MAN convention will receive a prize of $500 and a Caribbean vacation for two.

TO ENTER: Send five or more color shots (Polaroids are fine) including a full-face close-up and a full-figure frontal nude to: Contest Editor, Playgirl Magazine, 1801 Century Park East, Suite 2300, Los Angeles, CA 90067. Finalists will appear in the pages of Playgirl Magazine during the next year and will receive regular modeling fees at the time their pictures are published. $2,000 for use in Set #1, $1,000 for use in Set #2, and $500 for use in Set #3.

CONTEST RULES: All finalists must be present at the NATURAL MAN convention in order to be eligible for their prizes. The convention will be held at a time and place to be chosen by Playgirl, Inc. Any finalist who fails to attend and participate in the convention at the place and time chosen forfeits all rights whatsoever to any awards.

All contest entrants will consent to be photographed by Playgirl for use in Playgirl Magazine. The resulting photographs will be the sole property of Playgirl, Inc.

All photographs are submitted without reservation. Photographs will be returned only if accompanied by a self-addressed stamped envelope, and while all possible care will be taken in the handling of photographs, Playgirl assumes no responsibility for loss or damage. Playgirl reserves the right to change the contest rules or to cancel the contest entirely for any reason whatsoever. There is no deadline for contest submissions.

PLAYGIRL HAS NO FIELD REPRESENTATIVES HANDLING OUR NATURAL MAN CONTEST. ALL VALID OFFERS AND SELECTIONS ARE MADE AT AND IN OUR HOME OFFICE AT THE ABOVE ADDRESS.

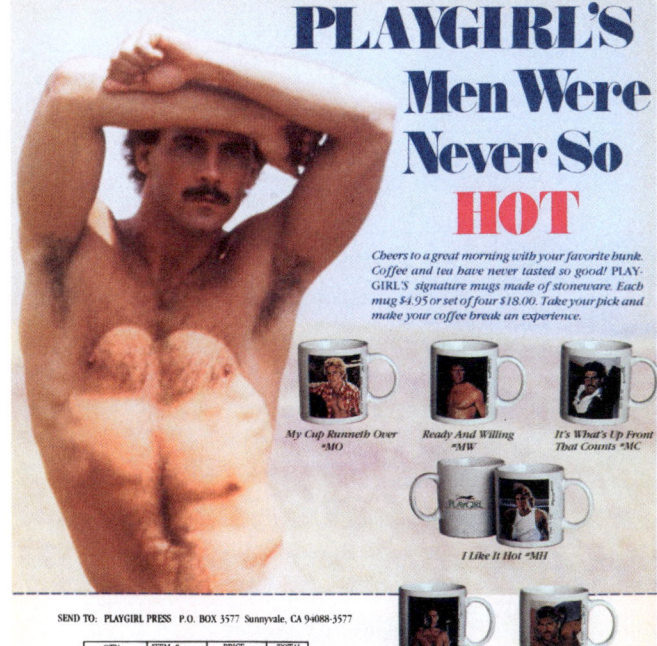

PLAYGIRL'S Men Were Never So HOT

Cheers to a great morning with your favorite hunk. Coffee and tea have never tasted so good! PLAYGIRL'S signature mugs made of stoneware. Each mug $4.95 or set of four $18.00. Take your pick and make your coffee break an experience.

*My Cup Runneth Over *MO*

*Ready And Willing *MW*

*It's What's Up Front That Counts *MC*

*I Like It Hot *MH*

*Seeing Is Believing *MB*

*I'm Good *MG*

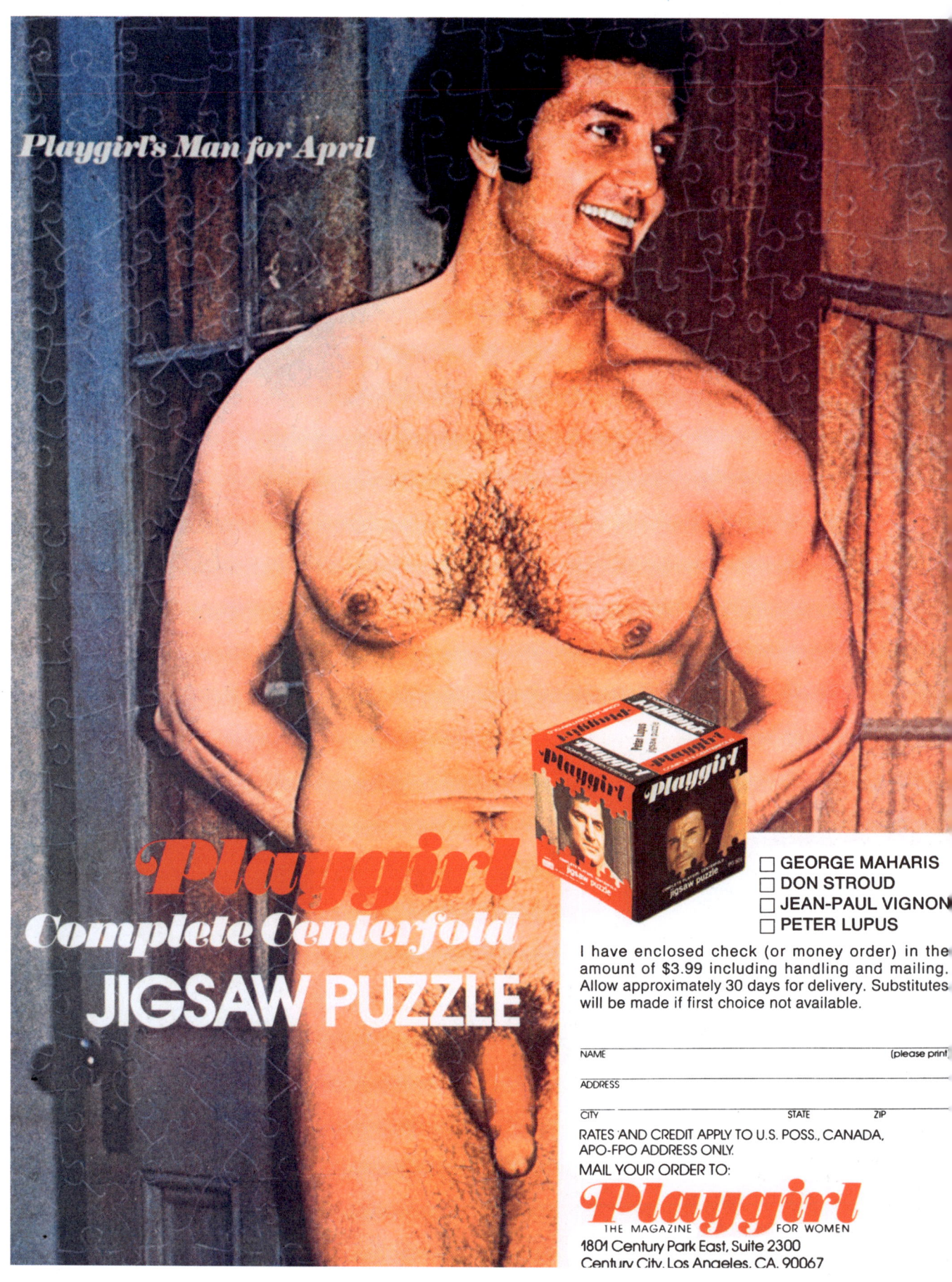

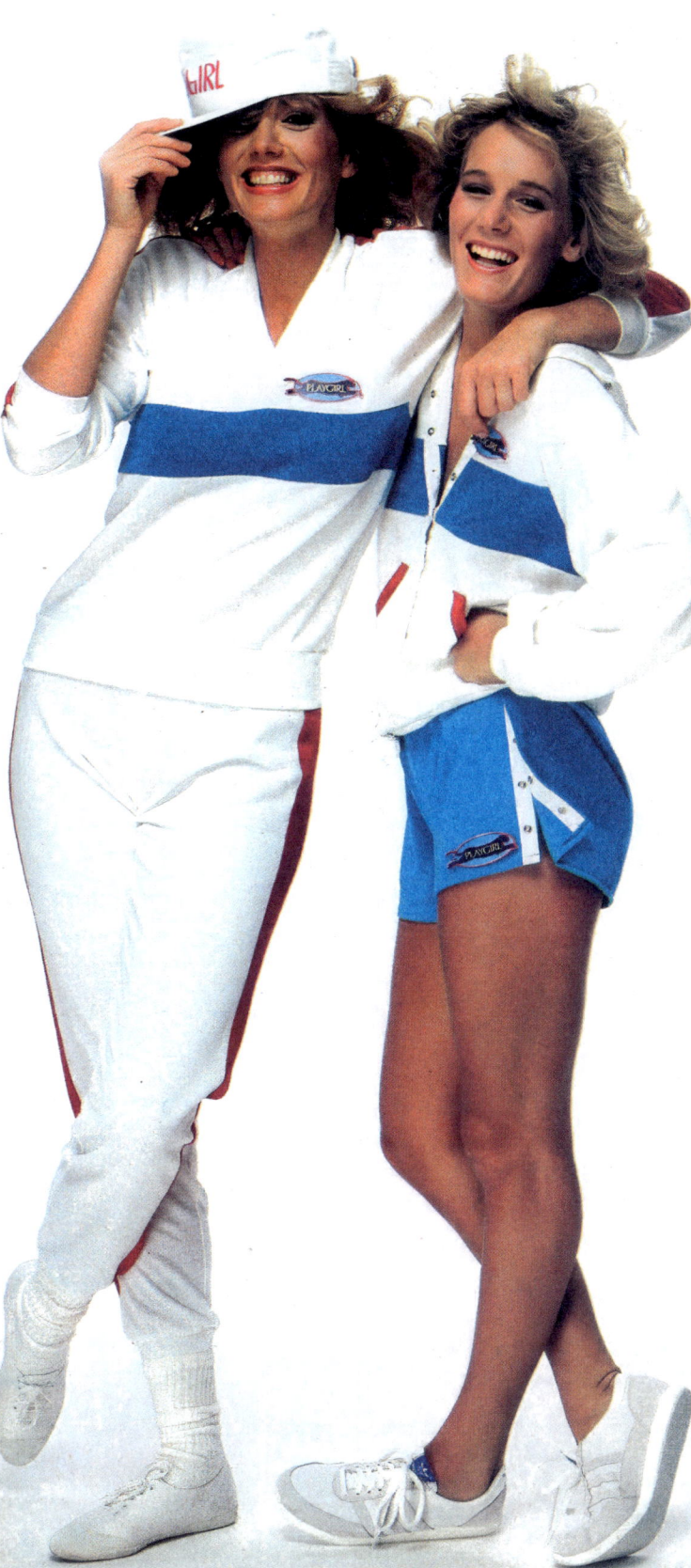

LIVE THE PLAYGIRL LIFE

PLAYGIRL doesn't have to end for you when you turn that last page of the magazine and realize you have to wait for a whole month to enjoy more of the particular pleasures that PLAYGIRL affords you. Now you can wear PLAYGIRL exercise fashions, and use PLAYGIRL gear, to create more spice in your day-to-day life. Live the PLAYGIRL Life—our sweatwear can help you remember throughout the month that you're one of our outrageous, fun-loving, pleasure-seeking readers.

ITEM #	DESCRIPTION	SIZE	QTY.	PRICE	TOTAL
A70	POLY/COTTON SWEATSUIT			29.95	
A79	POLY/COTTON SWEATSHIRT			21.95	
A76	POLY/COTTON TURQUOISE SHORTS			14.95	
A77	POLY/COTTON WHITE SHORTS			14.95	
A78	POLY/COTTON FUCHSIA SHORTS			14.95	
A80	ALL SWEATSUIT GEAR (THE SHORTS FREE!)			52.95	

POSTAGE & HANDLING: 1 ITEM ADD $1.50 _____
2 ITEMS OR MORE ADD $3.50 _____
FOREIGN ORDERS ADD $8 PER ITEM _____
SUBTOTAL _____
ADD 8¼% TAX IF DELIVERED IN N.Y. _____
GRAND TOTAL _____

NAME (PLEASE PRINT) _____
ADDRESS _____ APT. NO. _____
CITY _____ STATE _____ ZIP _____

PAYMENT INFORMATION:
PAID BY:
CHECK ___ MONEY ORDER ___ VISA ___ MASTERCARD ___
CARD # _____
EXP. DATE _____ SIGNATURE _____
(REQUIRED IF CHARGING)   PGRS-1

ORDERING INFORMATION:
PLEASE FILL IN THE SIZE, QUANTITY, SUBTOTALS AND GRAND TOTAL. PUT YOUR NAME AND ADDRESS IN THE SPACES PROVIDED. **THEN SEND THIS FORM WITH YOUR CHECK OR MONEY ORDER TO:**

PLAYGIRL PRODUCTS
801 2ND AVENUE
NEW YORK, NY 10017

Please allow 4 to 6 weeks for delivery. Items may be shipped separately. Foreign orders remit in U.S. funds, and add $8 per item for postage. The Cheetah is the trademark of Playgirl Key Club, inc. Used with permission.

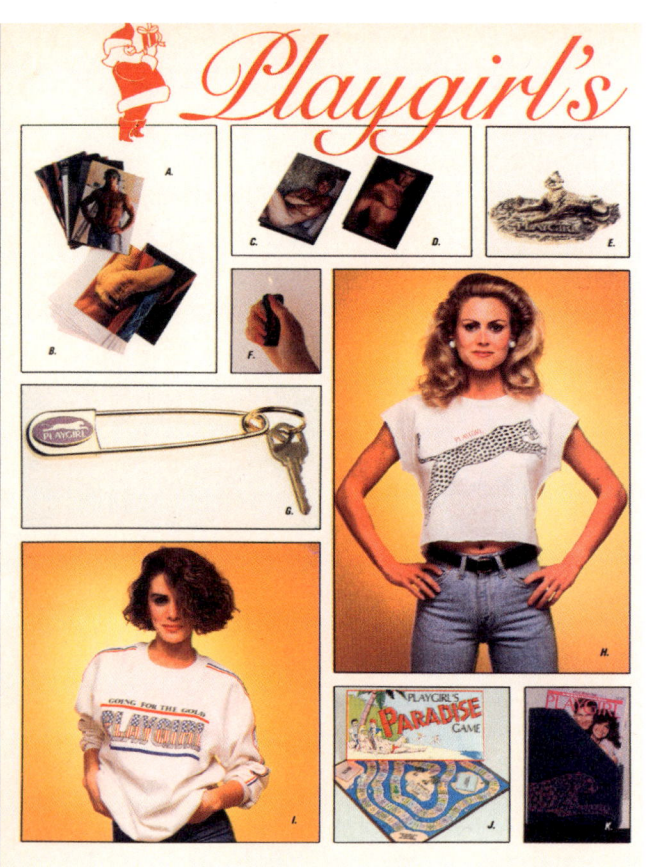
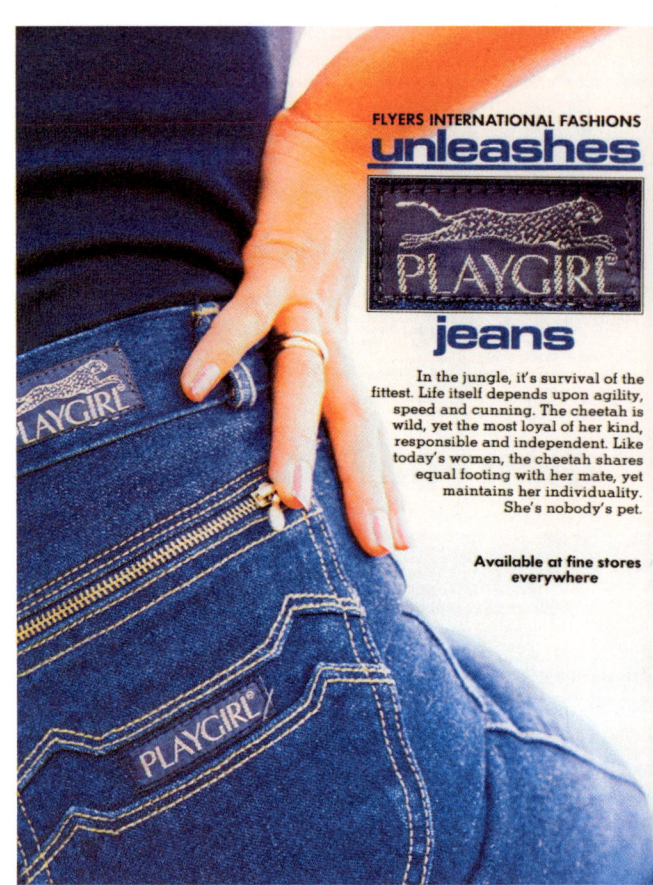

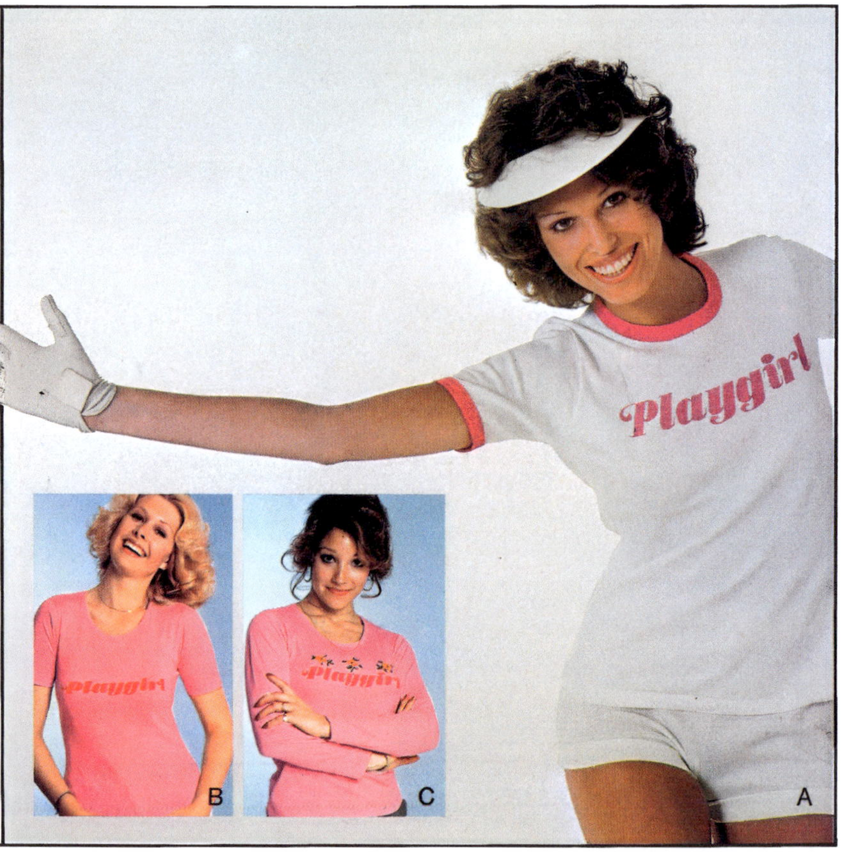

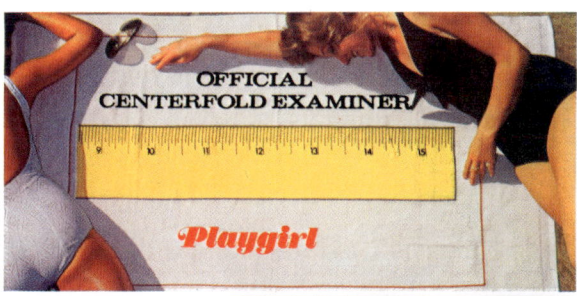
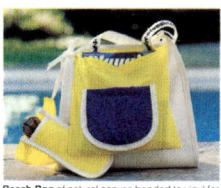
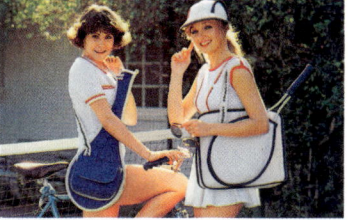
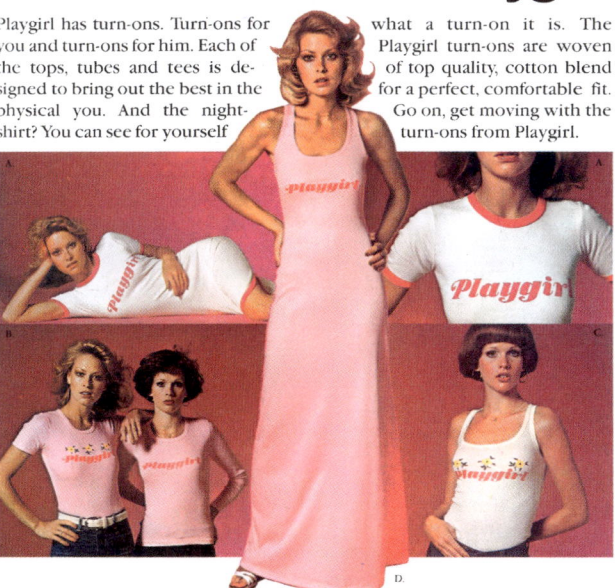
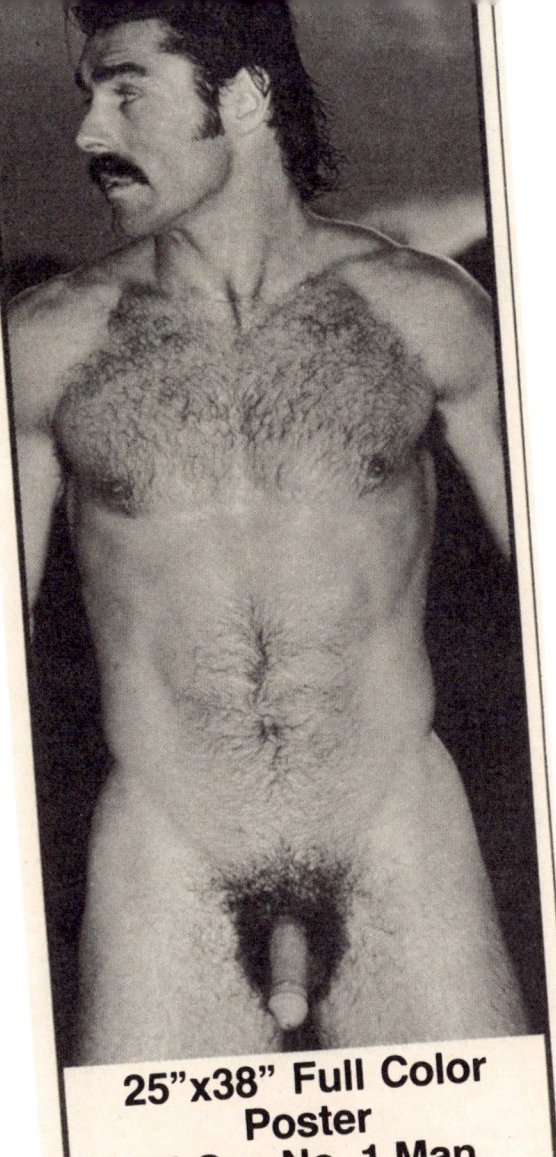

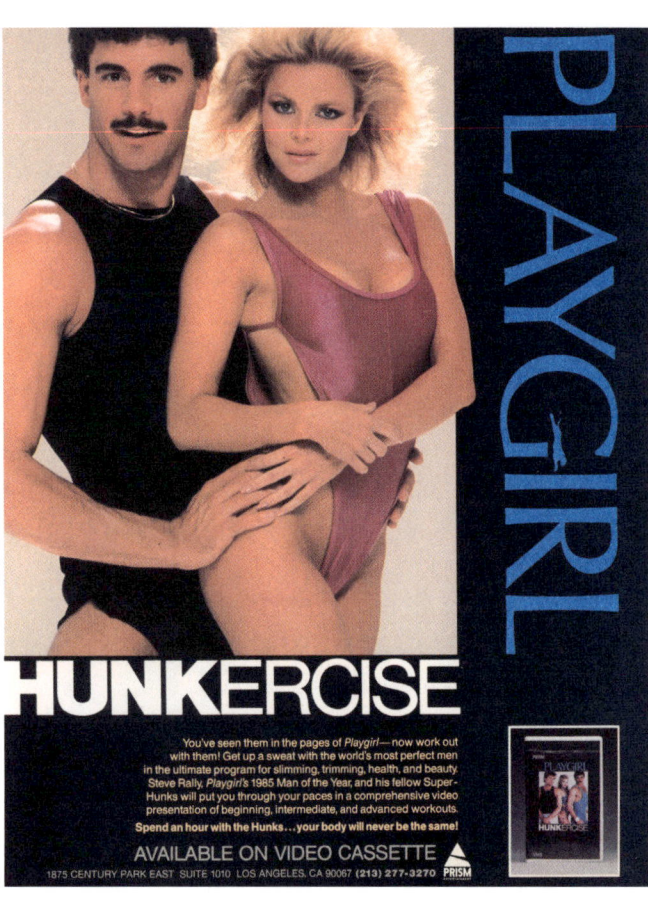

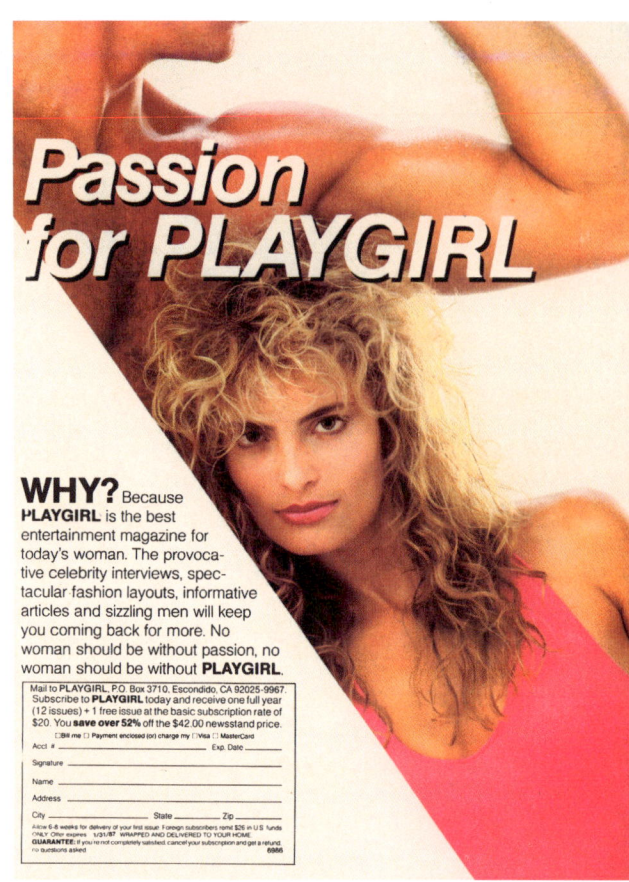

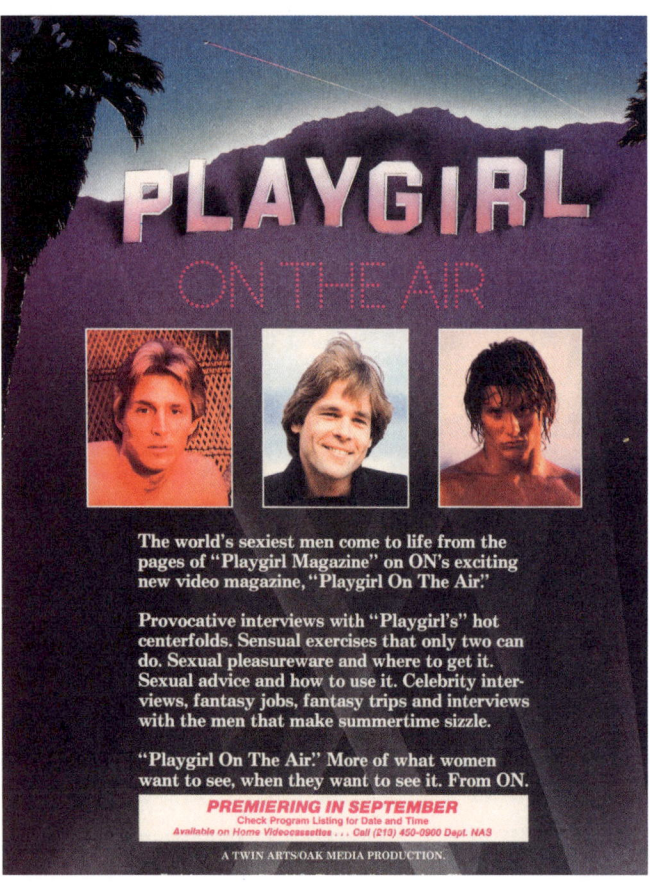

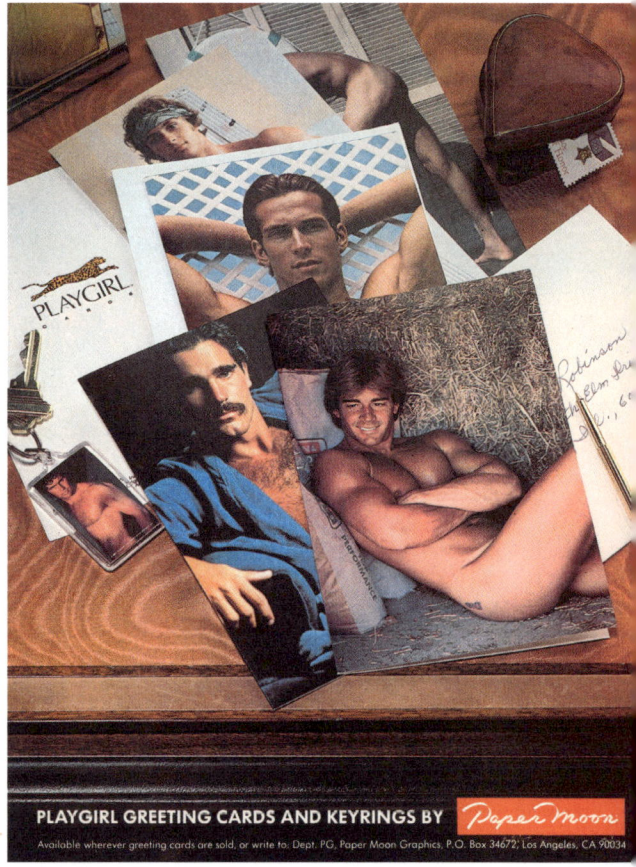

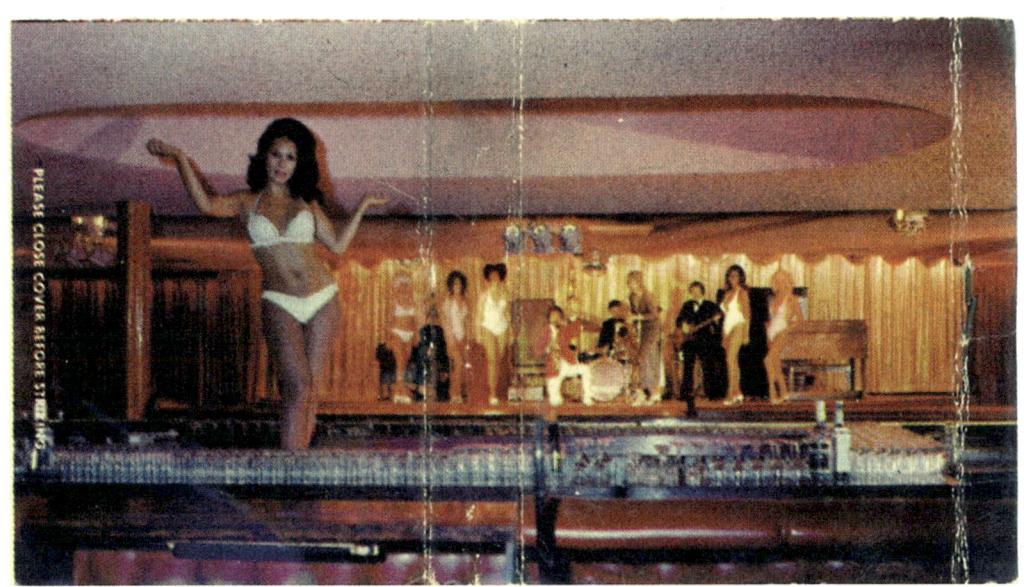

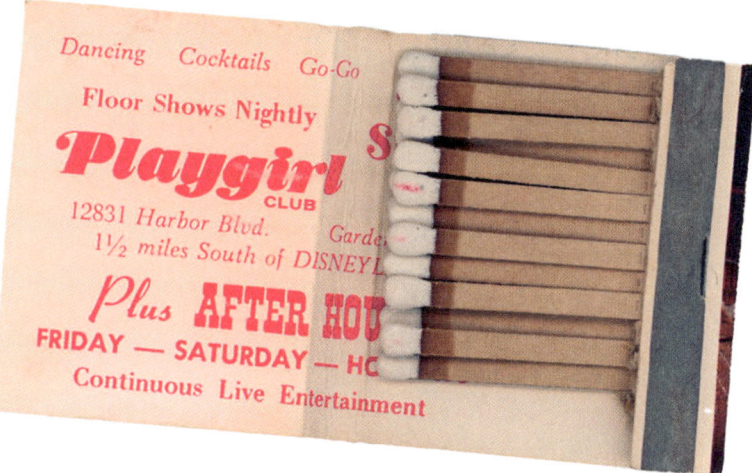

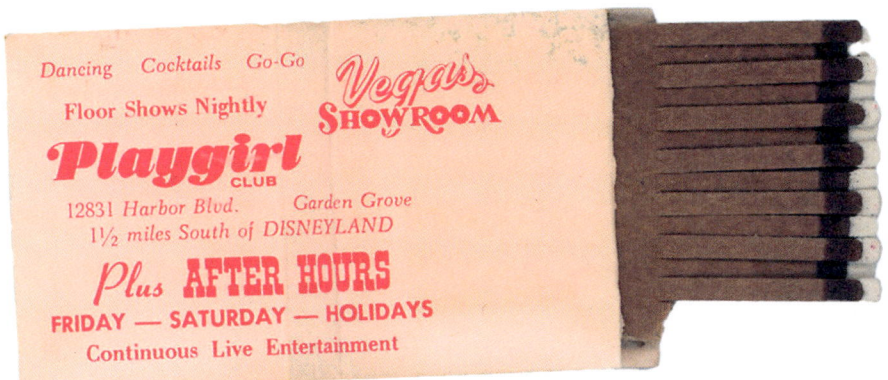

Dancing   Cocktails   Go-Go
Floor Shows Nightly   Vegas SHOWROOM
Playgirl CLUB
12831 Harbor Blvd.   Garden Grove
1½ miles South of DISNEYLAND
Plus **AFTER HOURS**
FRIDAY — SATURDAY — HOLIDAYS
Continuous Live Entertainment

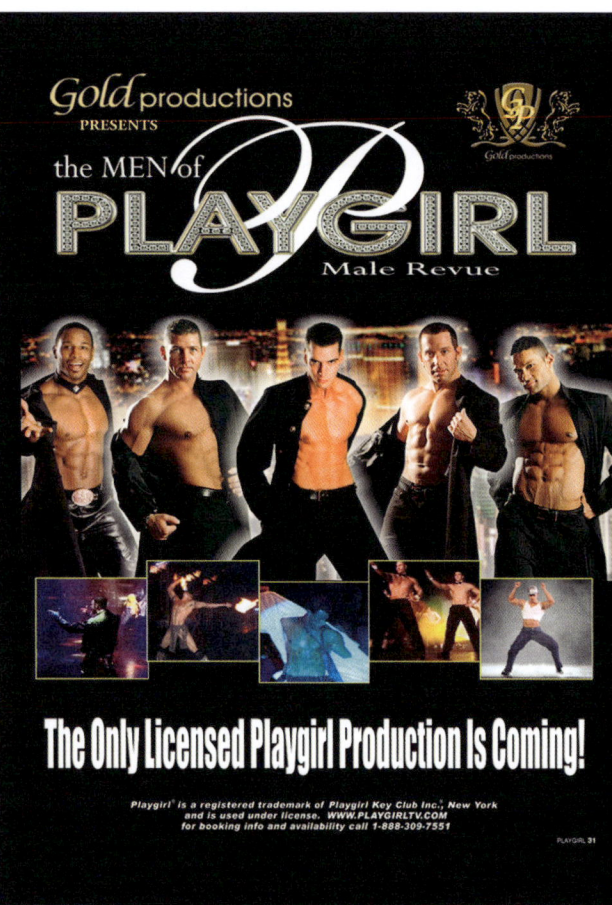
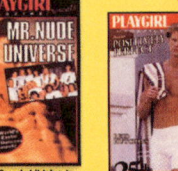
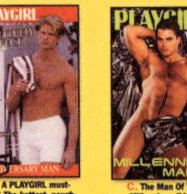
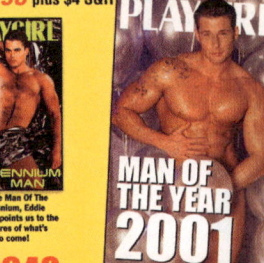
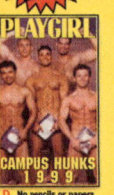
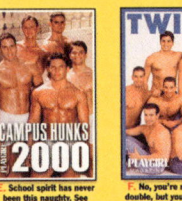
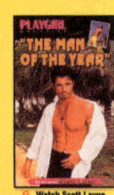
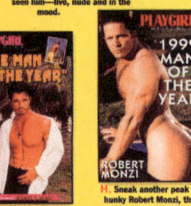
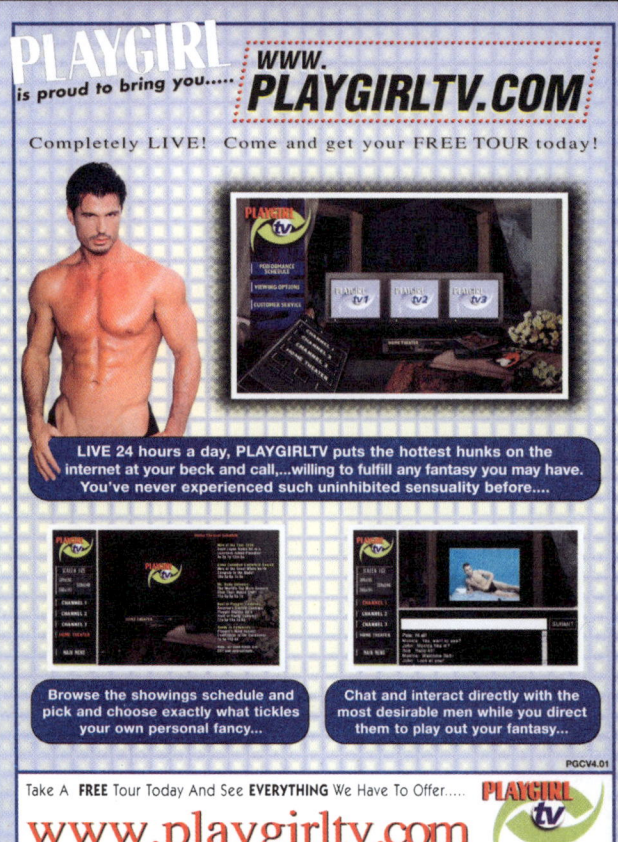
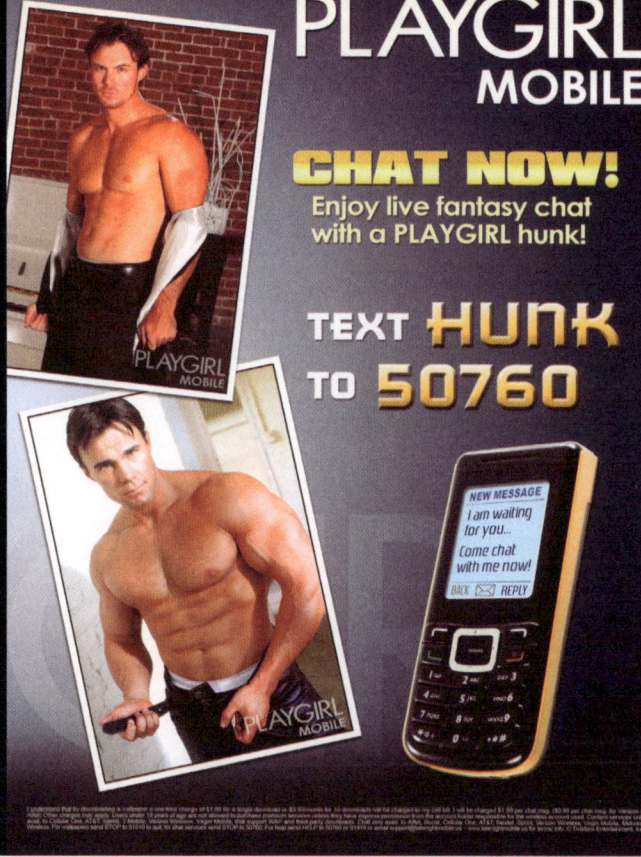

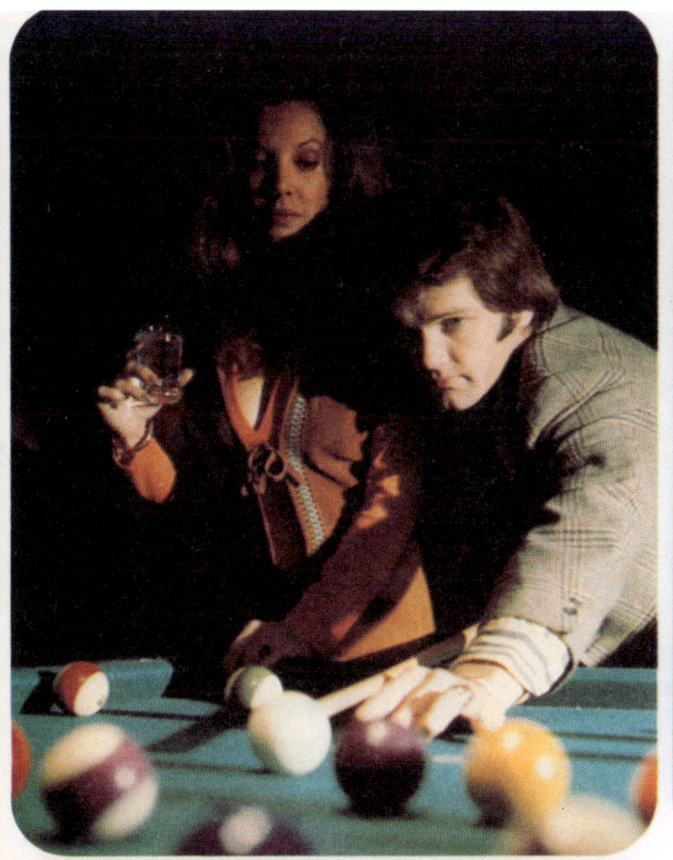

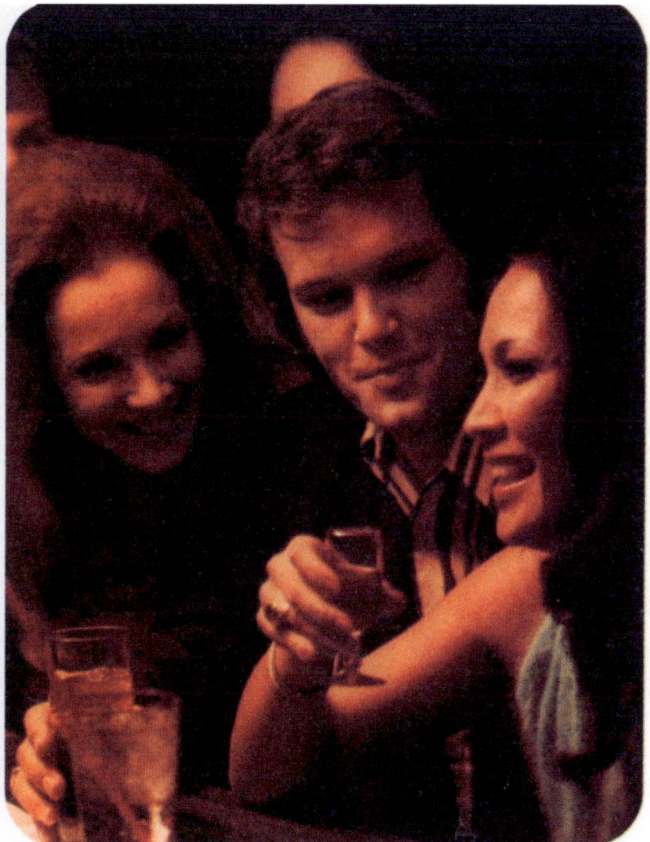

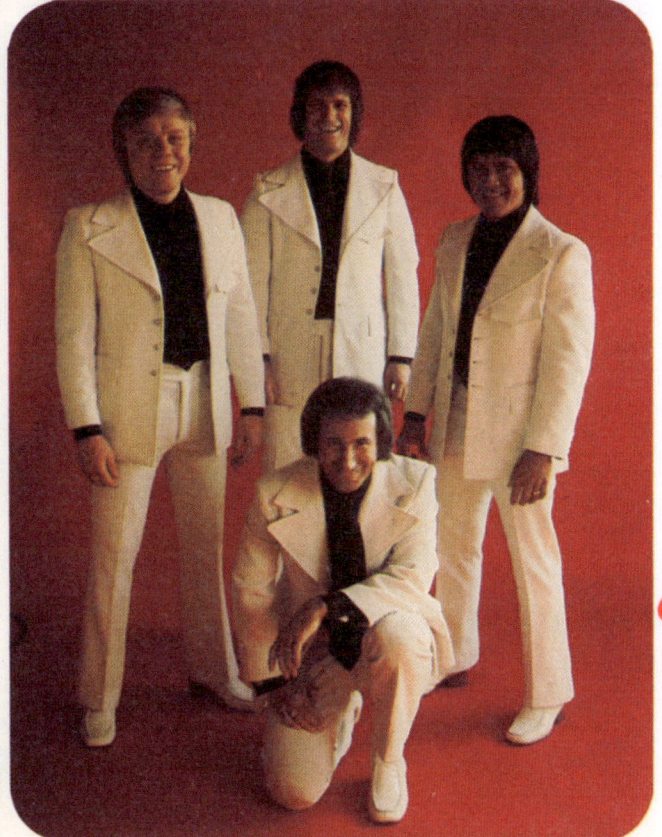

Welcome to the world of PLAYGIRL. Here you will enjoy the glamour, the glitter, and the fun of one`of America's most exciting clubs.

Featuring entertainment, dancing, floor shows, cocktails, playroom, GOGORoom, after hours and Las Vegas showroom . . . unequaled anywhere!

Appearing: THE LELAND FOUR

Playgirl Club

**12831 HARBOR BLVD., GARDEN GROVE
1½ MILES SOUTH OF DISNEYLAND.**

CHAPTER 13

PLAYGIRL TODAY

After a brief hiatus, production resumed in February 2022 for the revival of the "Man of the Month," complete with the 2024 calendar: *Playgirl Men.* The most recent *Playgirl* print edition, published in 2020, featured Oscar-nominated and Golden Globe–winning actress Chloë Sevigny and her baby bump on the cover, shot nude by famed fashion photographer Mario Sorrenti. Present-day *Playgirl* celebrates its fiftieth anniversary by commemorating the archives at long last, making them available online at PlaygirlPlus.com. In March 2024, a digital-only magazine premiered an exclusive interview and photo spread of Grammy-nominated global superstar Maluma with the return of former editors in chief on the all-new Playgirl.com.

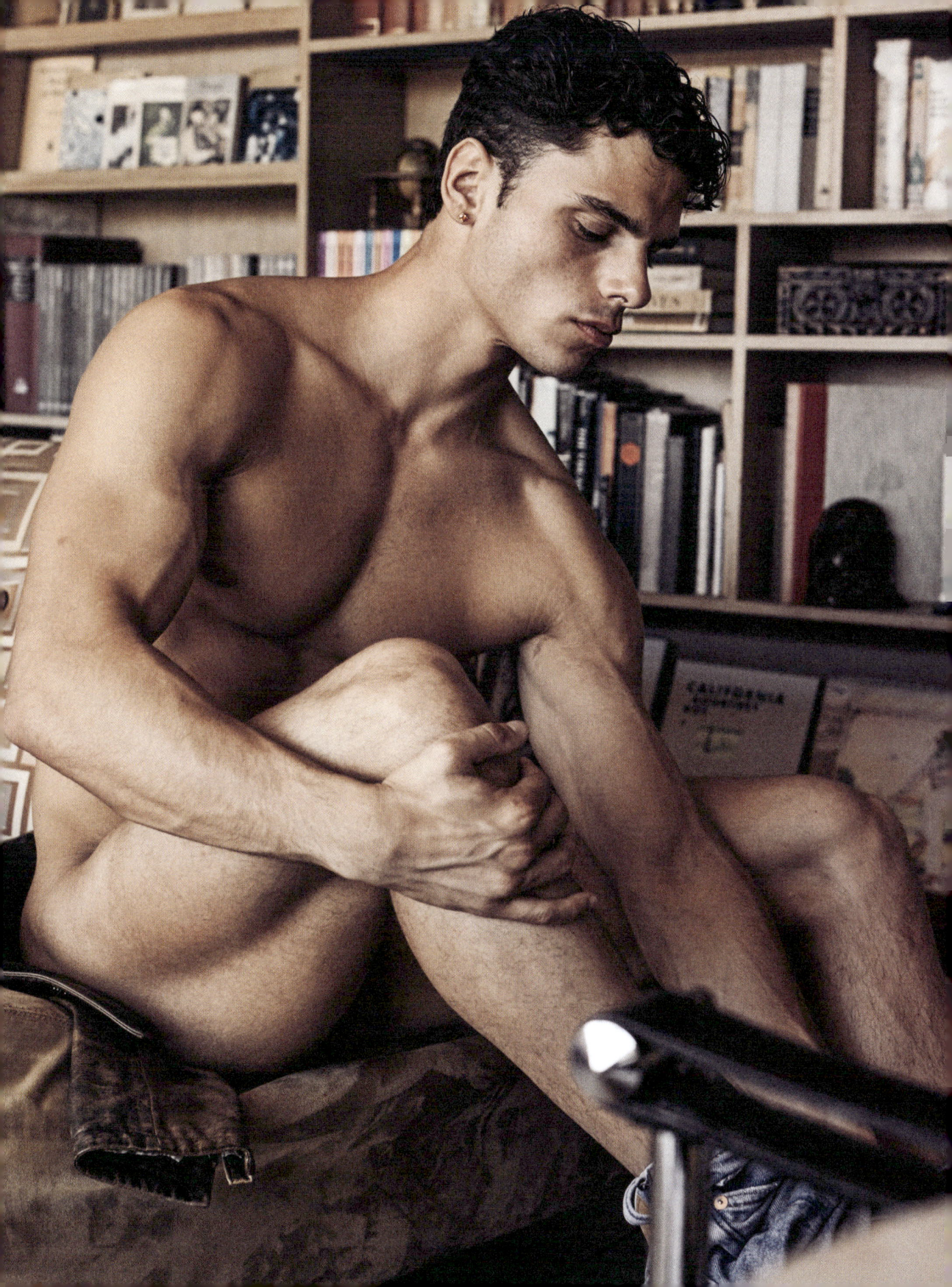

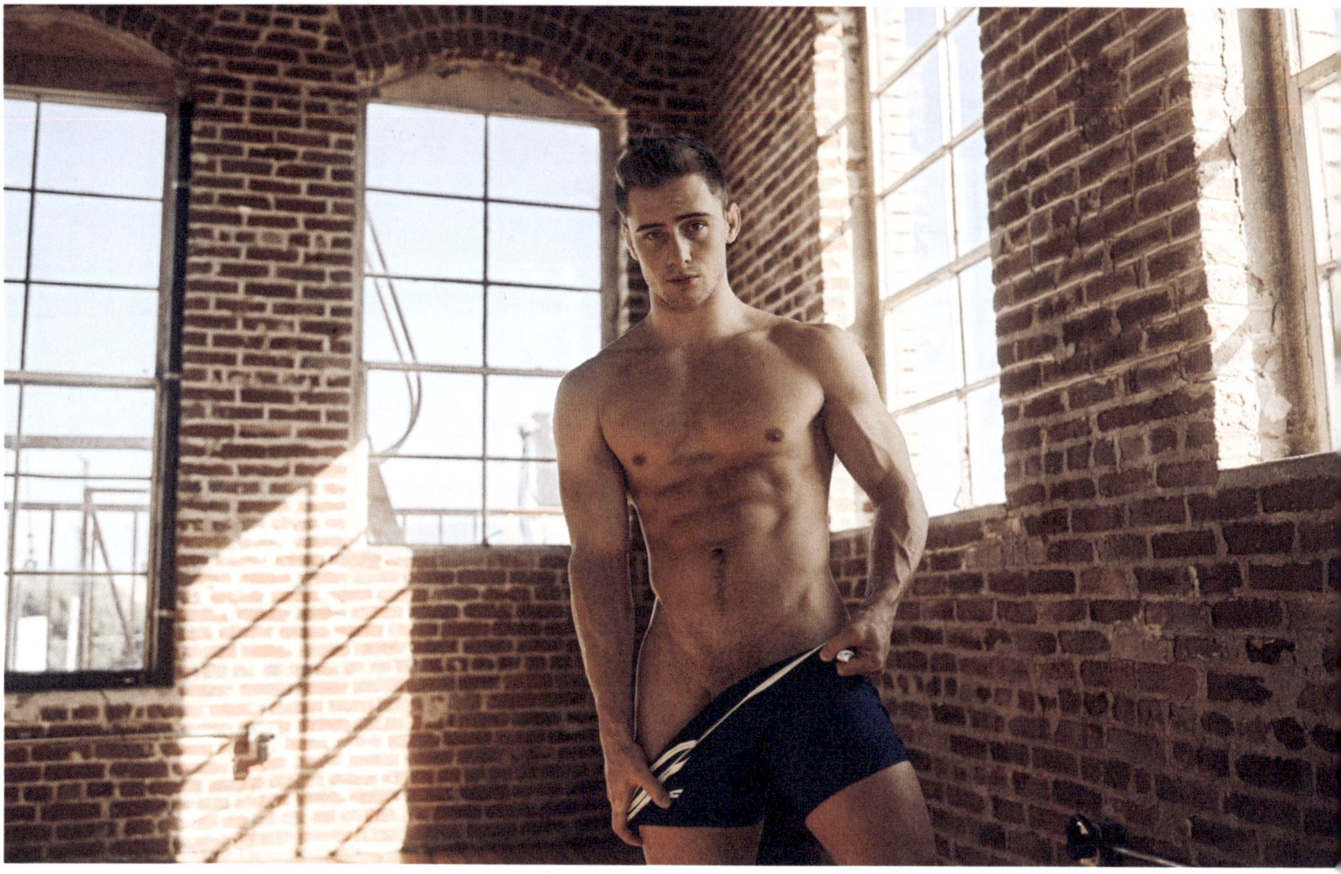

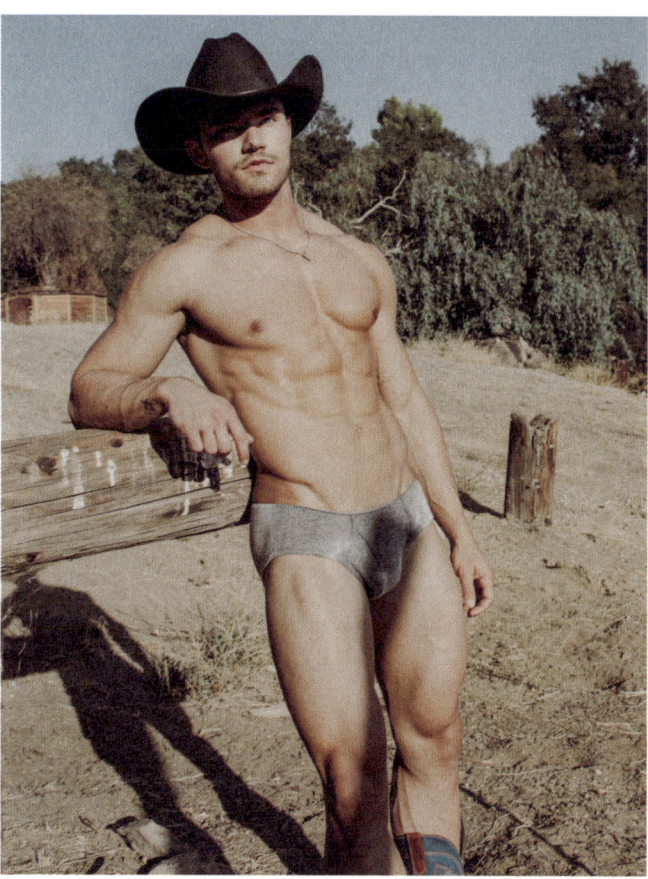
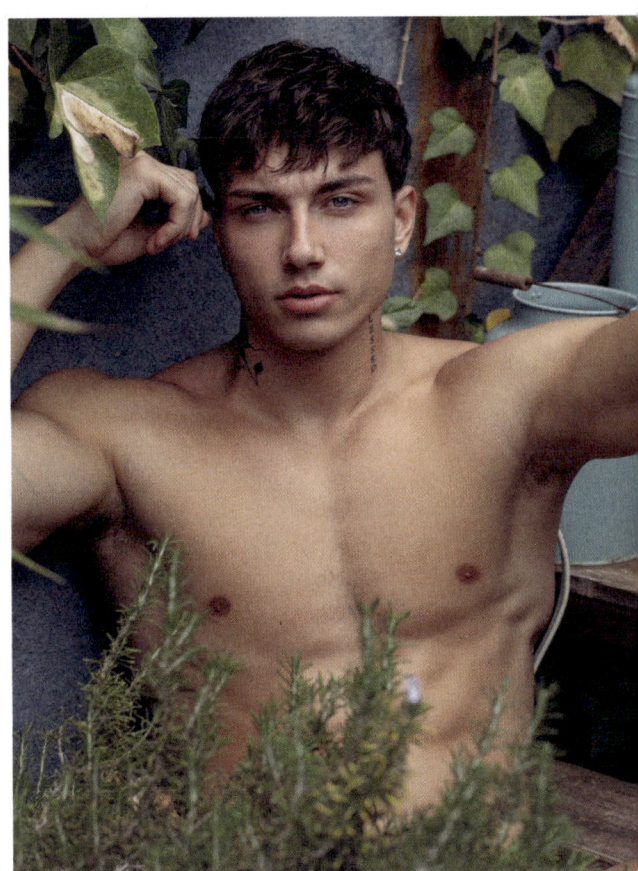

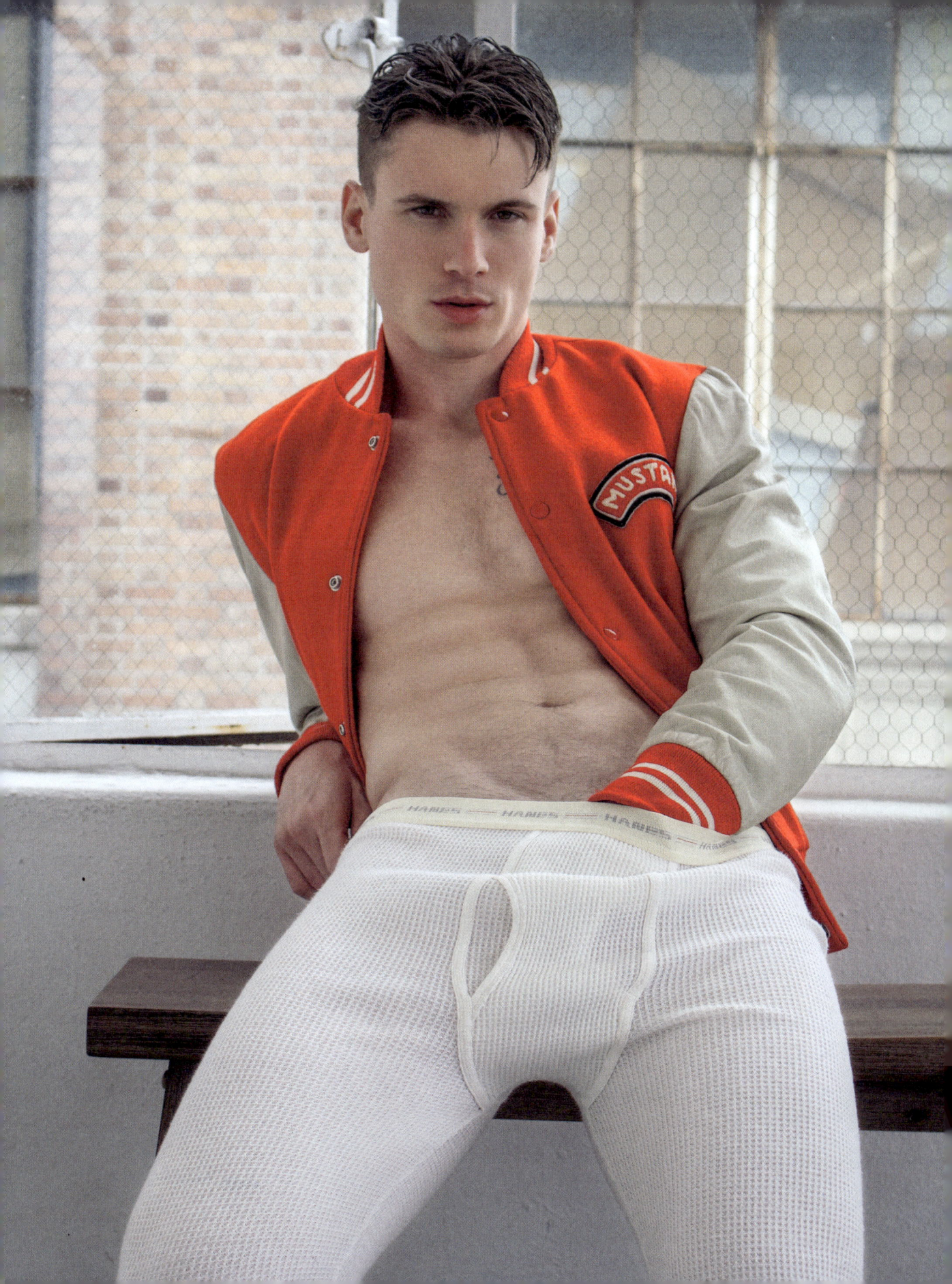

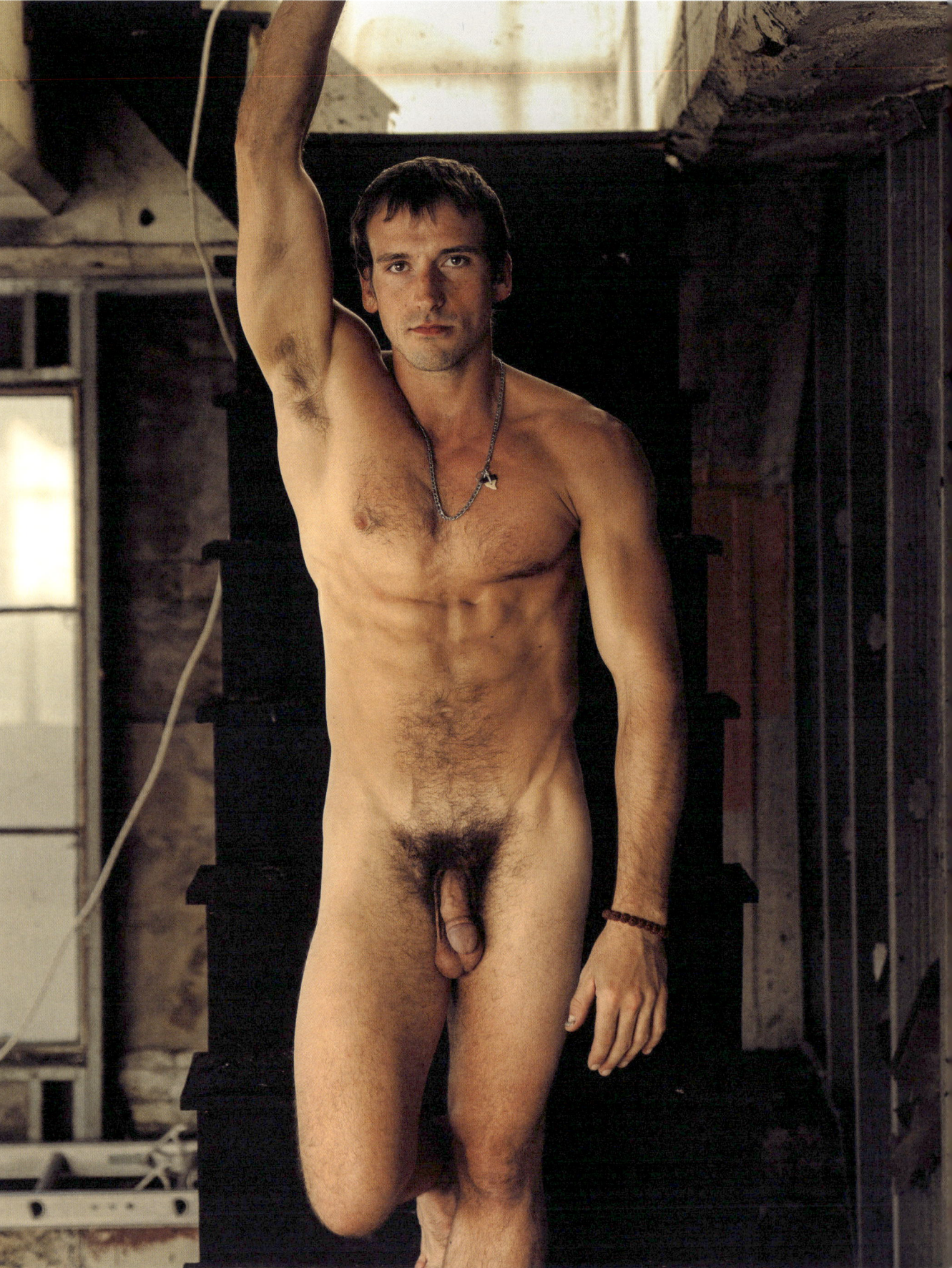

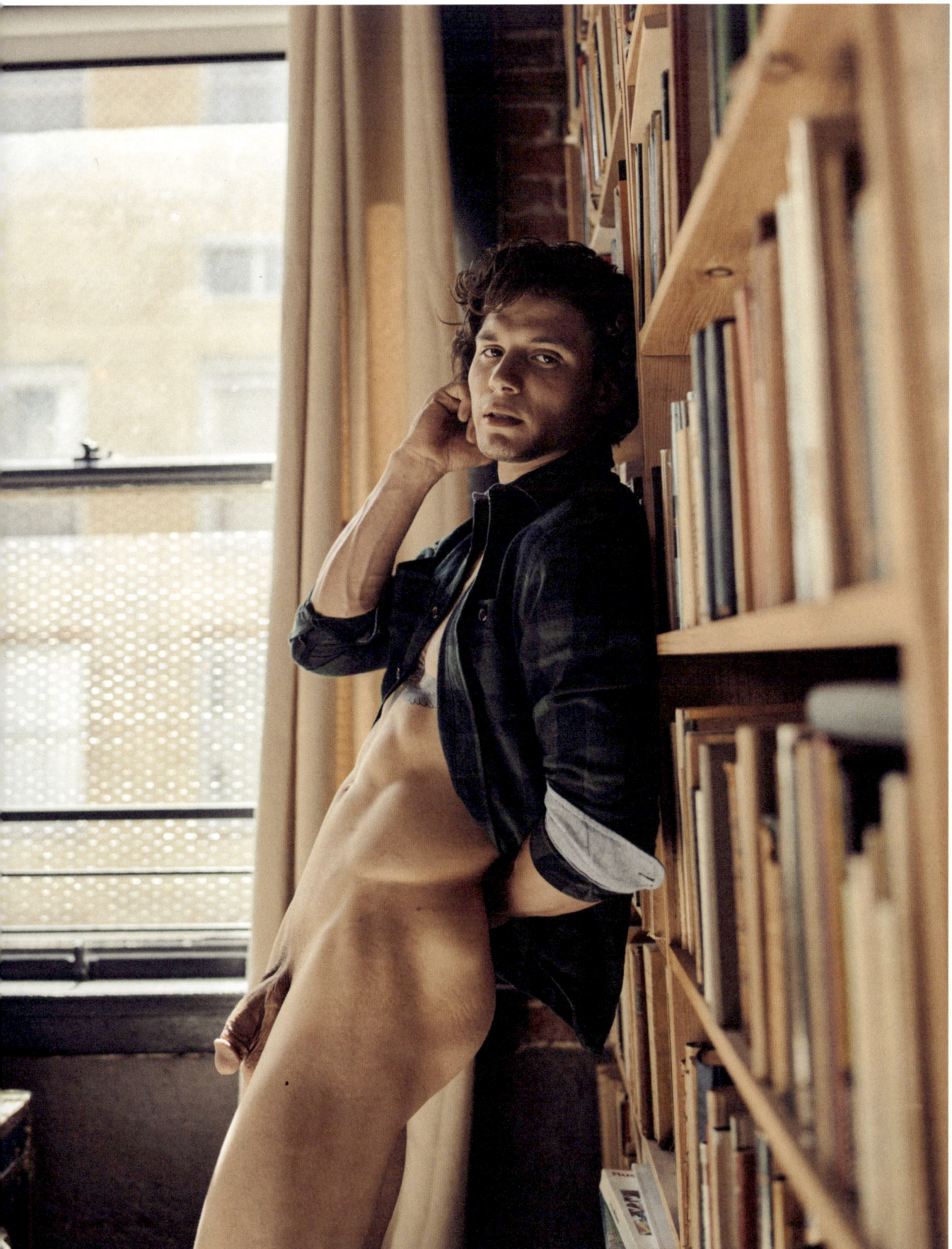

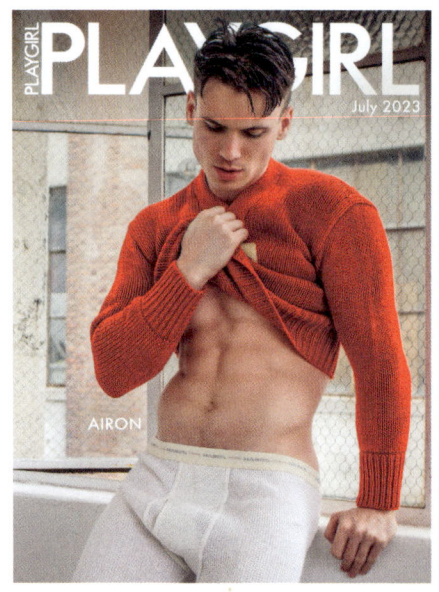

PLAYGIRL

July 2023

AIRON

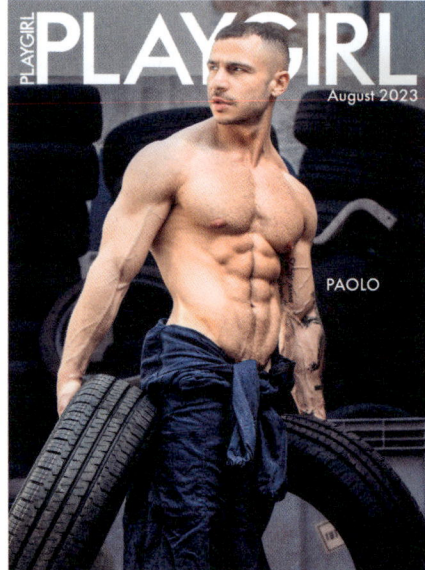

PLAYGIRL

August 2023

PAOLO

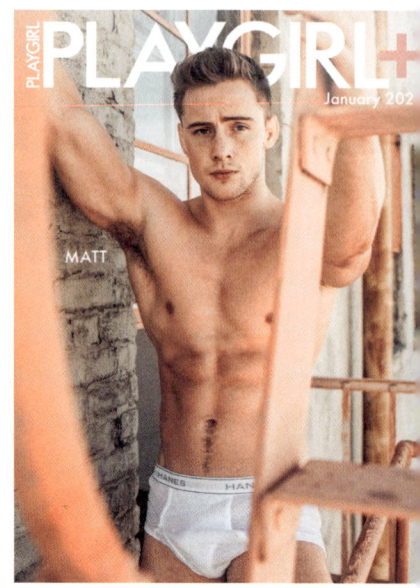

PLAYGIRL+

January 202

MATT

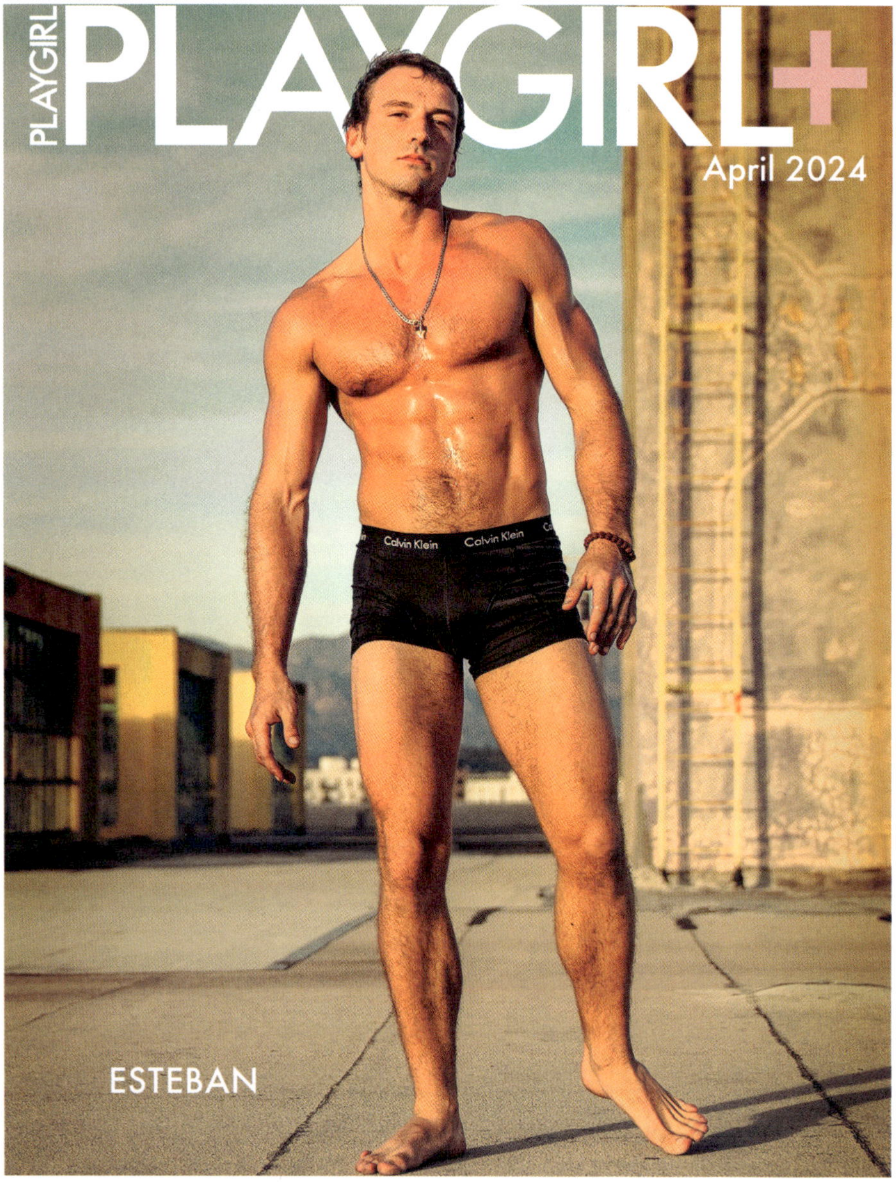

PLAYGIRL+

April 2024

ESTEBAN

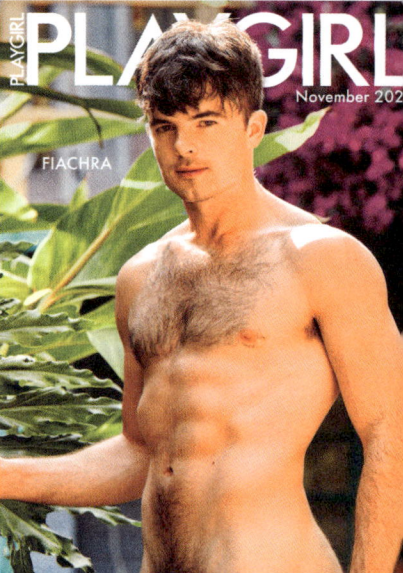

PLAYGIRL

November 202

FIACHRA

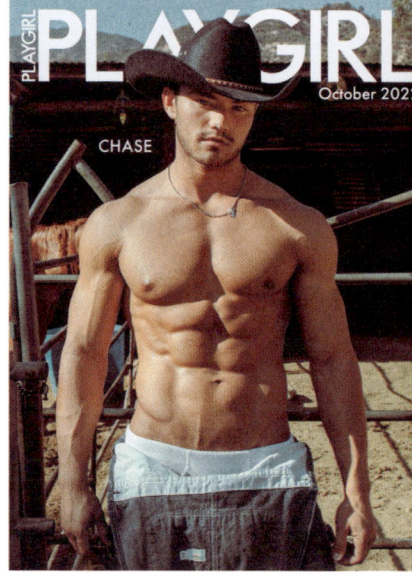

PLAYGIRL

October 2022

CHASE

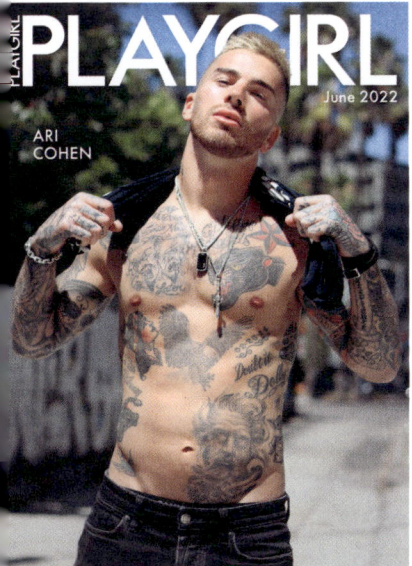

PLAYGIRL
June 2022
ARI COHEN

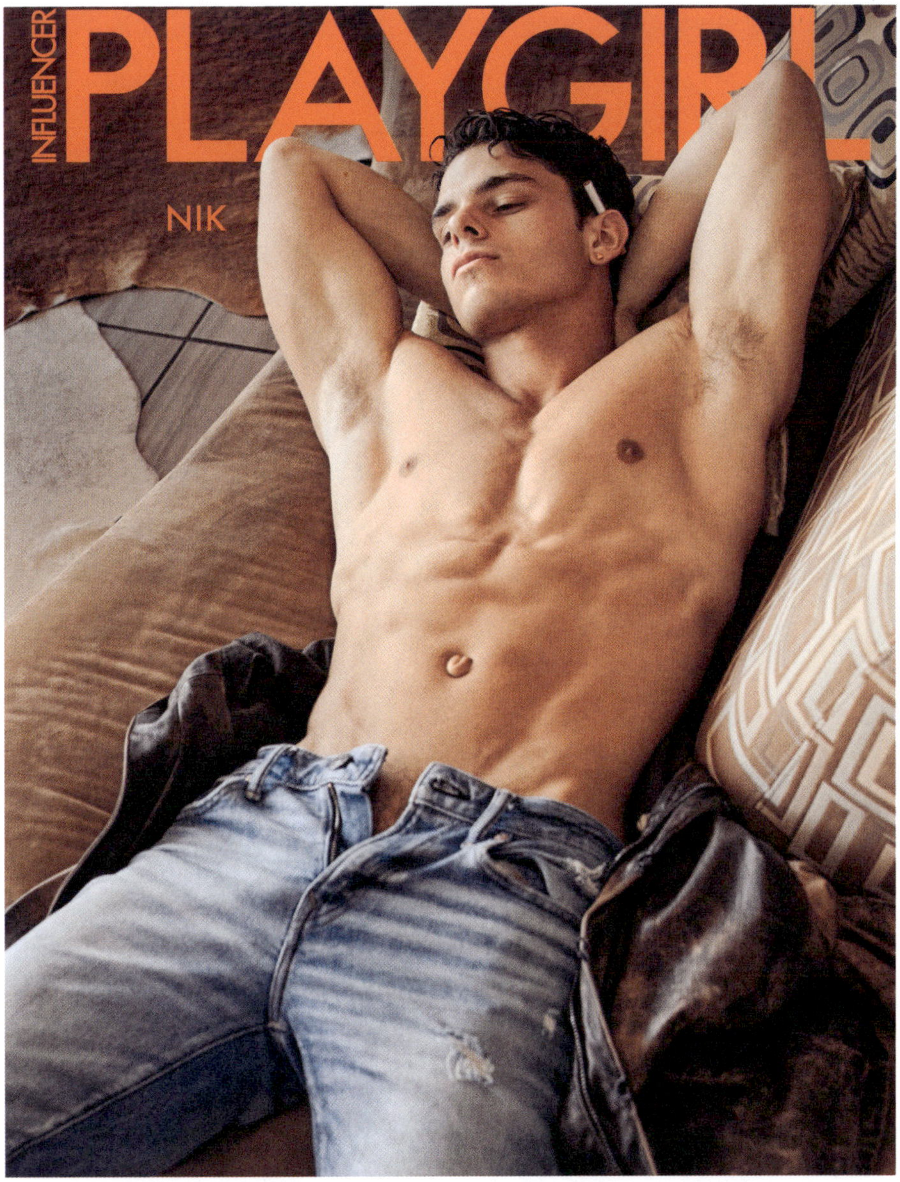

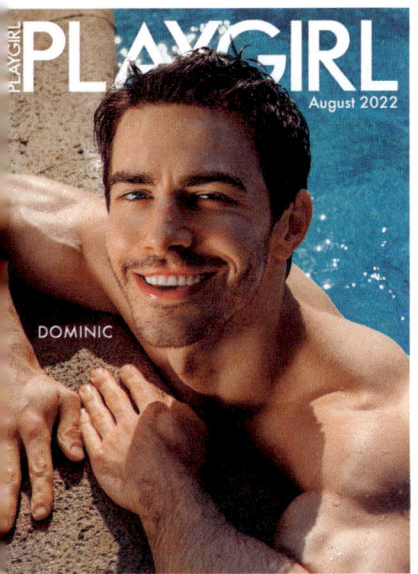

PLAYGIRL
August 2022
DOMINIC

INFLUENCER PLAYGIRL
NIK

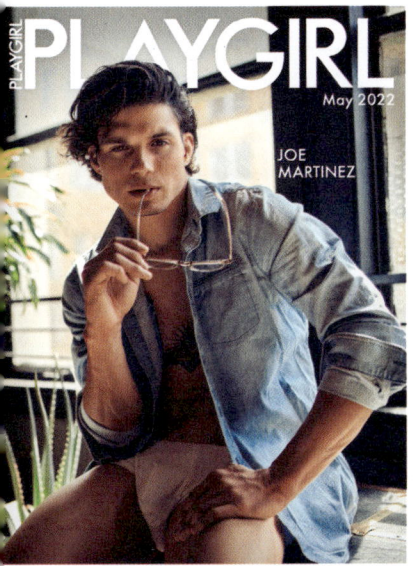

PLAYGIRL
May 2022
JOE MARTINEZ

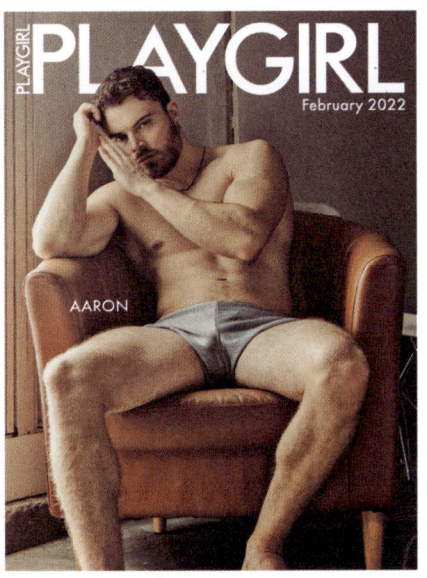

PLAYGIRL
February 2022
AARON

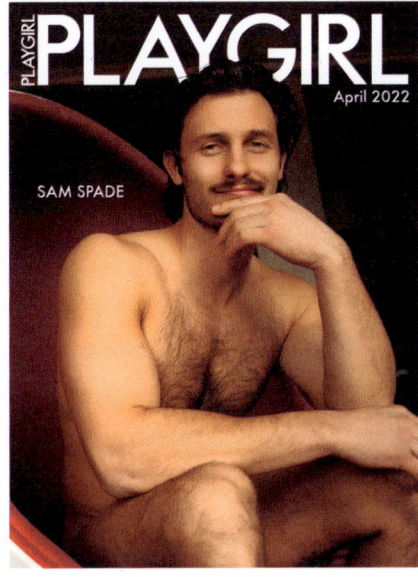

PLAYGIRL
April 2022
SAM SPADE

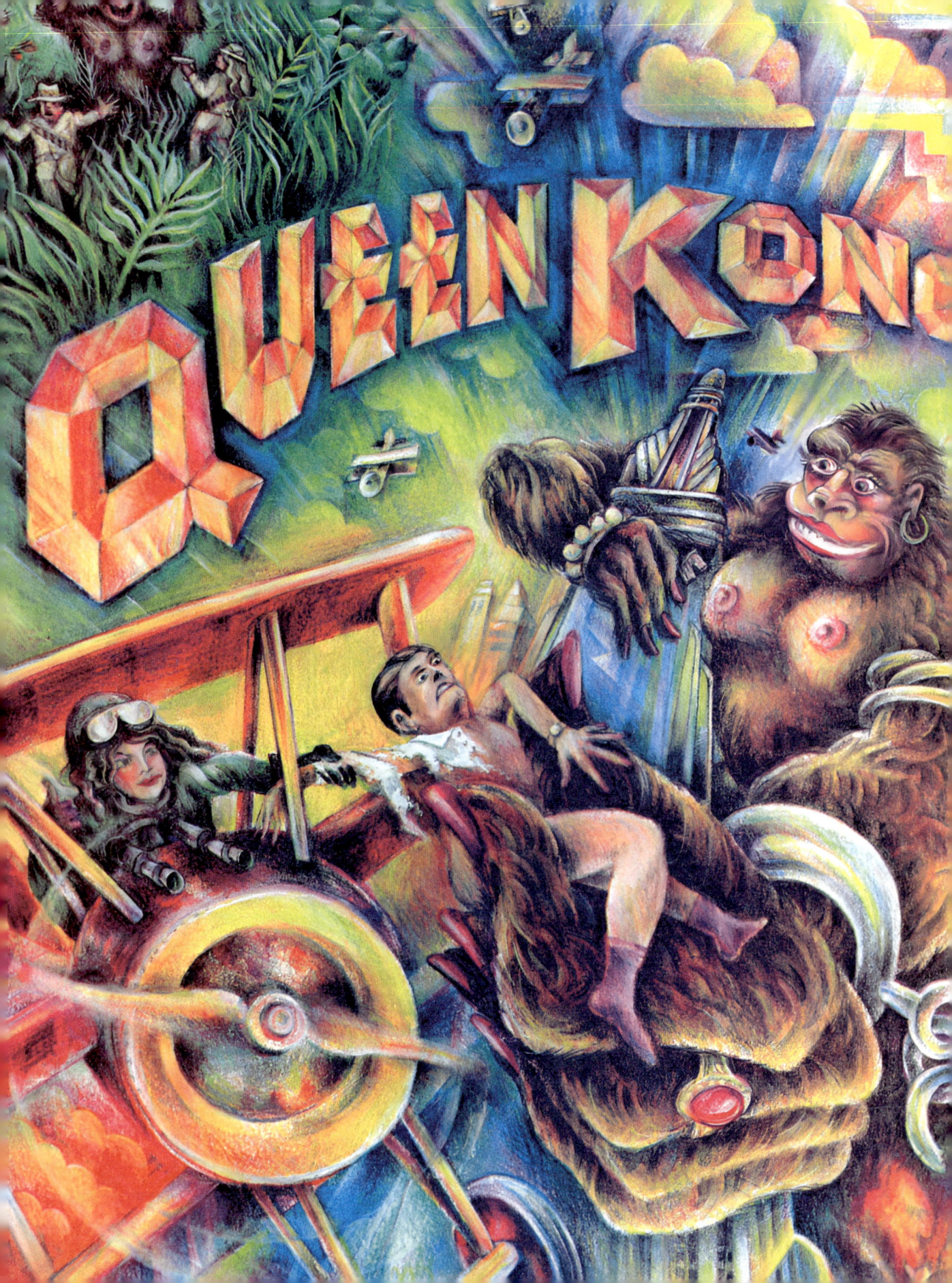

ACKNOWLEDGMENTS

Eric Alexander, Robert Azzarello, Nik Ball, Annie Bandez, Mickey Boardman, Justin Vivian Bond, Ossian Brown, Nicole Caldwell, Ari Cohen, Bruno Coviello, Stuart Davis, Davyd Dixon, Kelly Drummond, Mischa Gawronski, Dan Gibson, Stephen Grzemkowski, Sam Houston, Lanning Janosov, Channing Joseph, Brian Kaminski, Daniil Kartashov, Erika Keck, Amy Kehoe, Jonas Klabin, Chris Kohlhof, Jack Lindley Kuhns, Bruce LaBruce, Andrew Lahman, Sophia Lamar, Matt Lambert, Ean Landry, Charlie Li, Efraín López, Murphy Maxwell, Emily Mei-Mei, Sue McKernan, Colin McKinnon, Slava Mogutin, Brittany Monahan, Simeon Morales, David Moyer, Daniel Nardicio, Luca Norcen, John Norris, Danila Osipov, Jeff Pastorek, Michael Pedraza, Frankie Rice, Toni & Colin Ross, Francis Schichtel, Julie Schumacher, Eric Stevens, Jonathan Smith, Ned Stresen-Reuter, Zach Taylor, Loagan Thompson, Tim Valenti, Jamye Waxman, Timothy Woods Palma, Kameron Zane, Michele Zipp, Colin Zug-Moore, and Naida Zukic.

CONTRIBUTORS

Anneli Adolfsson, Richard Armas, Laura Bergman, Peter Brill, E. J. Camp, Roberto Chiovitti, Douglas Cloutier, Robert Cunningham, Norman Eales, Olivier Ferrand, David Glomb, Nigel Gomez, Greg Gorman, Dimitri Halkidis, Steve Henry, James & James, Rick Jason, Norbert Jobst, Sean Kahlil, Brian Kaminski, Jeff Katz, Dean Keefer, Bill King, Attila Kiss, Frank Kolleogy, Natalia Kyivska, Annie Leibovitz, Monica Levin, Brett Lopez, Robert Mapplethorpe, Maxine Elliot Martin, Kathie McGinty, David Meyer, Slava Mogutin, Alison Morley, NF Photography, Trevor Paul, Silvia Pecota, Sarah Pendergast, Toby Piggott-Brown, Suze Randall, Herb Ritts, Don Saban, Bob Seidemann, Mazi Shams, David Steen, Mark Van Dulman, David Vance, Lester Villarama, Christopher Voelker, Adam Washington, Thoas Watkins, Bob Watson, Greg Weiner, Jacky Winter, and Kal Yee.

Playgirl

The Official History
of a Cult Magazine

Library of Congress Control Number: 2024937328
ISBN: 978-1-4197-7492-8

Cernunnos logo design: Mark Ryden
Book design: Claude-Olivier Four
Editor: Rodolphe Lachat and Ruby Pucillo

Printed and bound in Italy
10 9 8 7 6 5 4 3 2 1

Cernunnos books are available at special discounts
when purchased in quantity for premiums and promotions
as well as fundraising or educational use. Special editions
an also be created to specification. For details,
contact specialsales@abramsbooks.com or the address below.

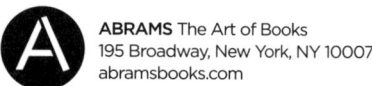

ABRAMS The Art of Books
195 Broadway, New York, NY 10007
abramsbooks.com

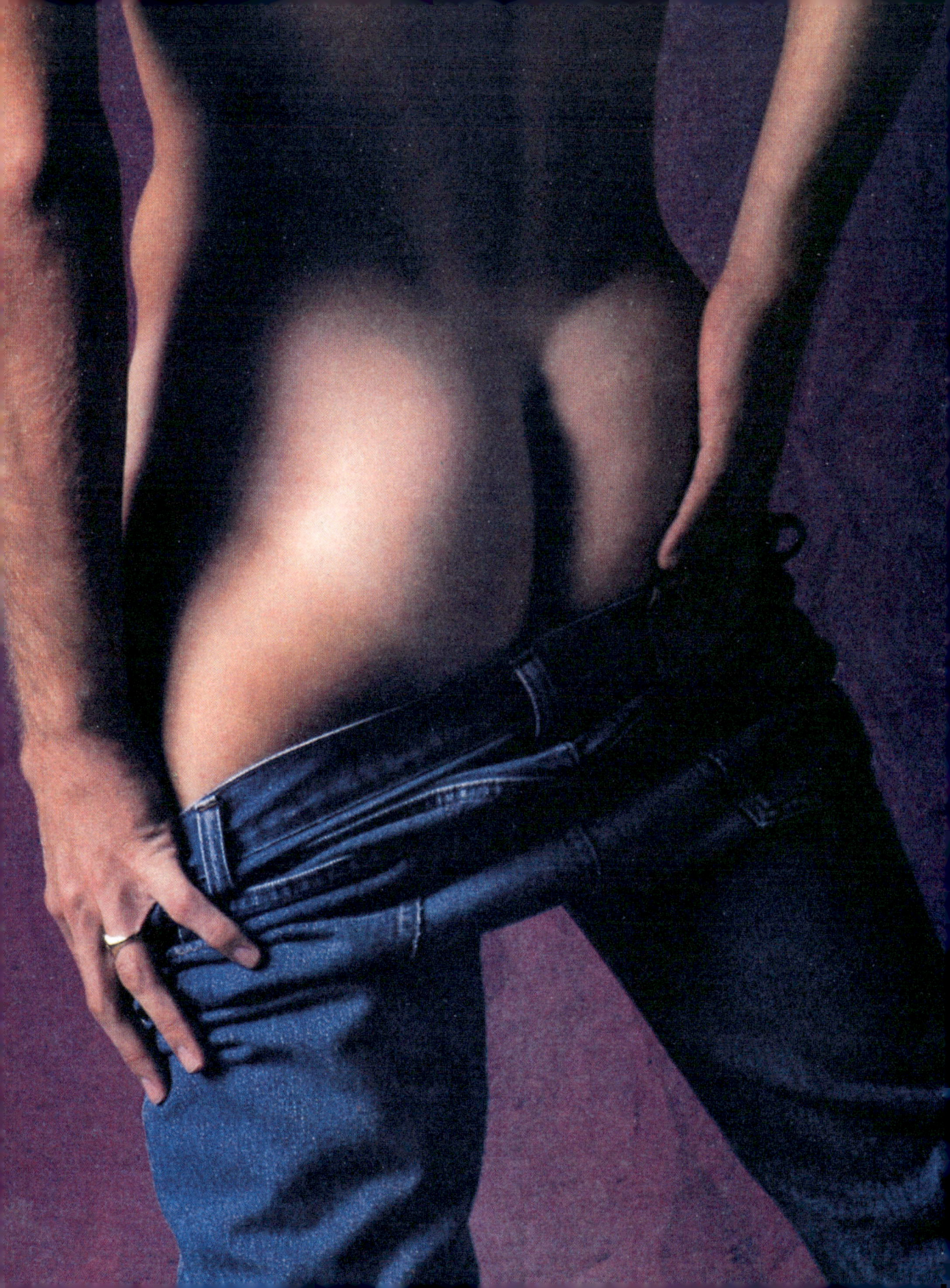

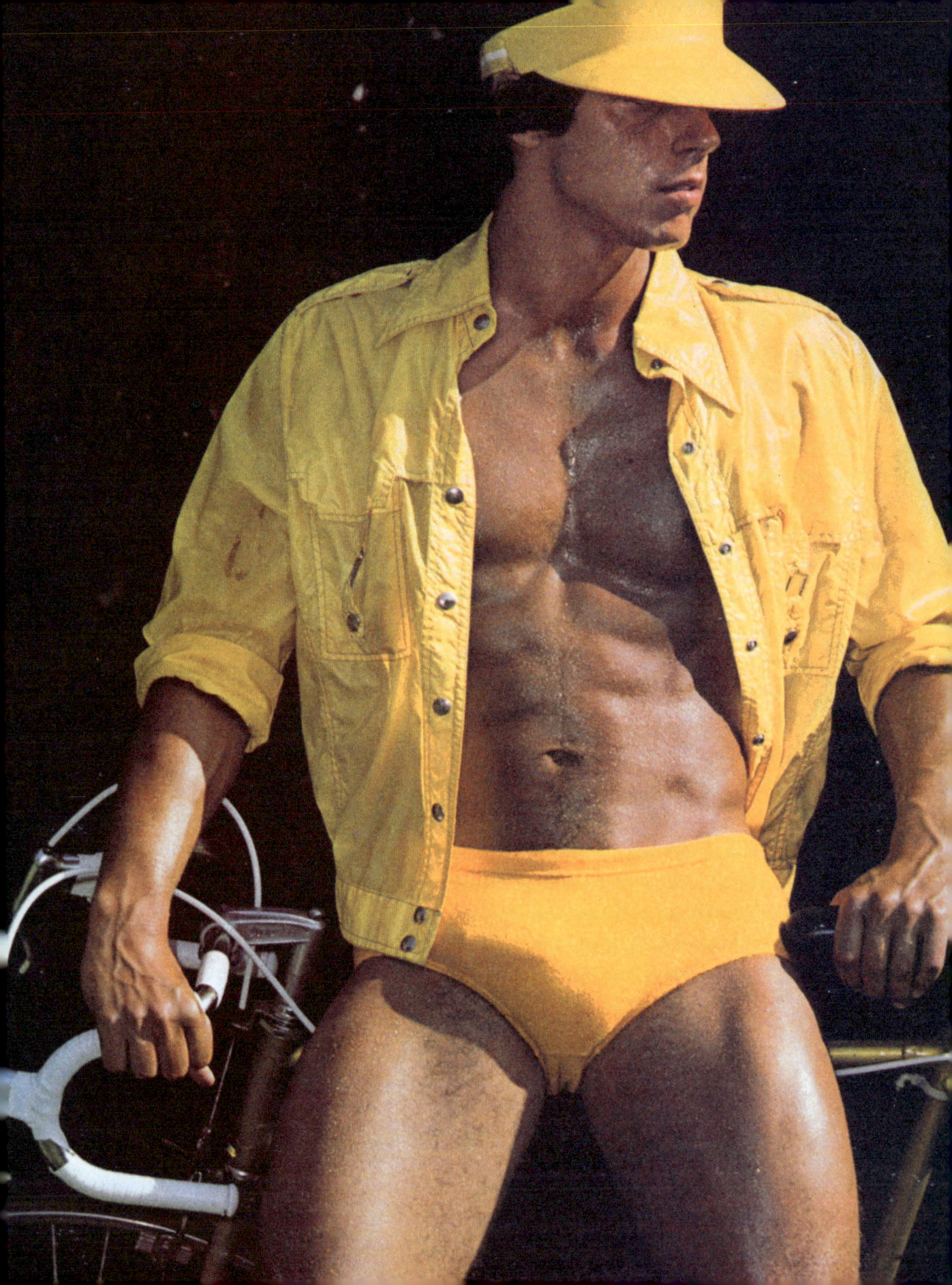

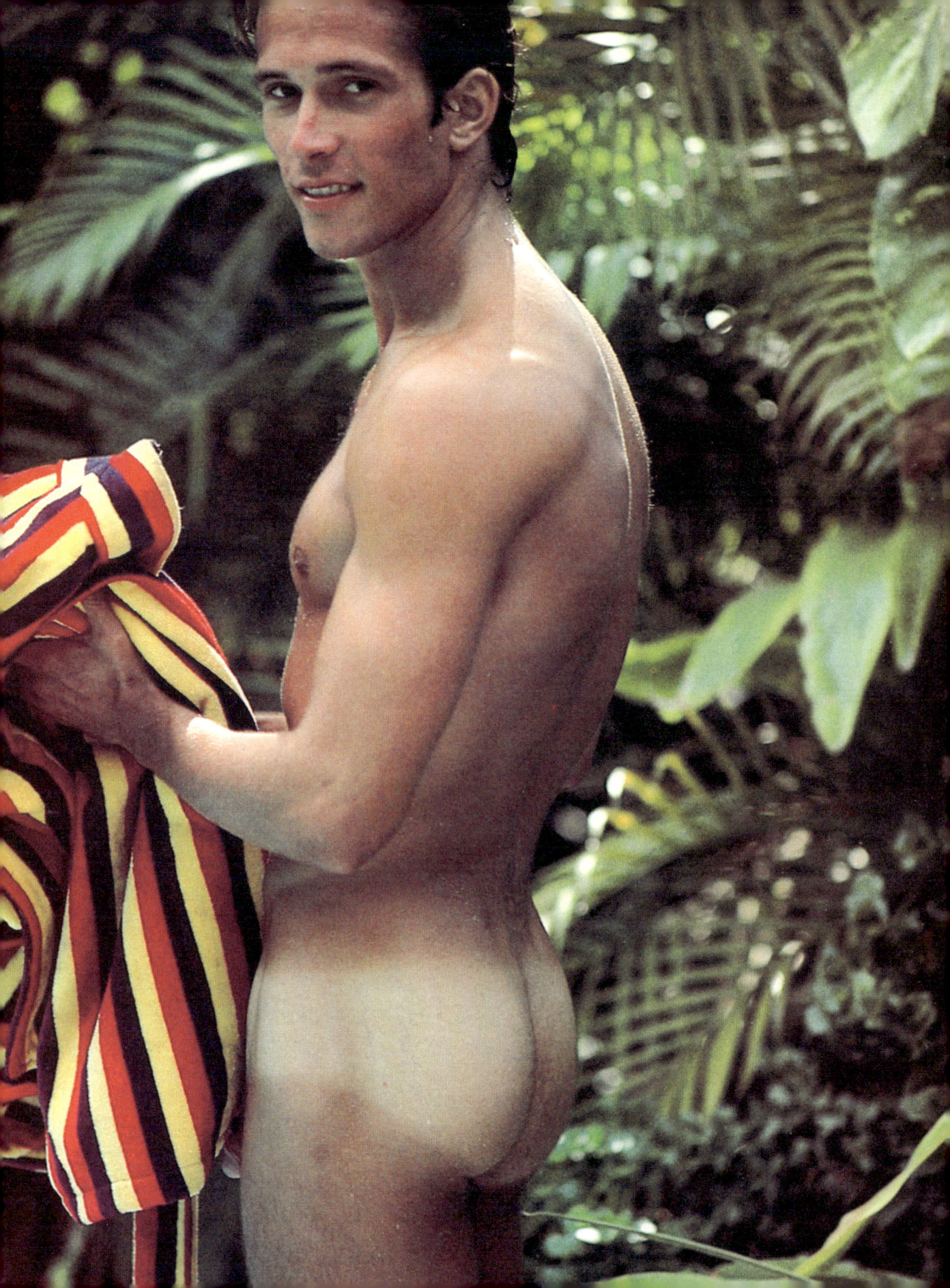

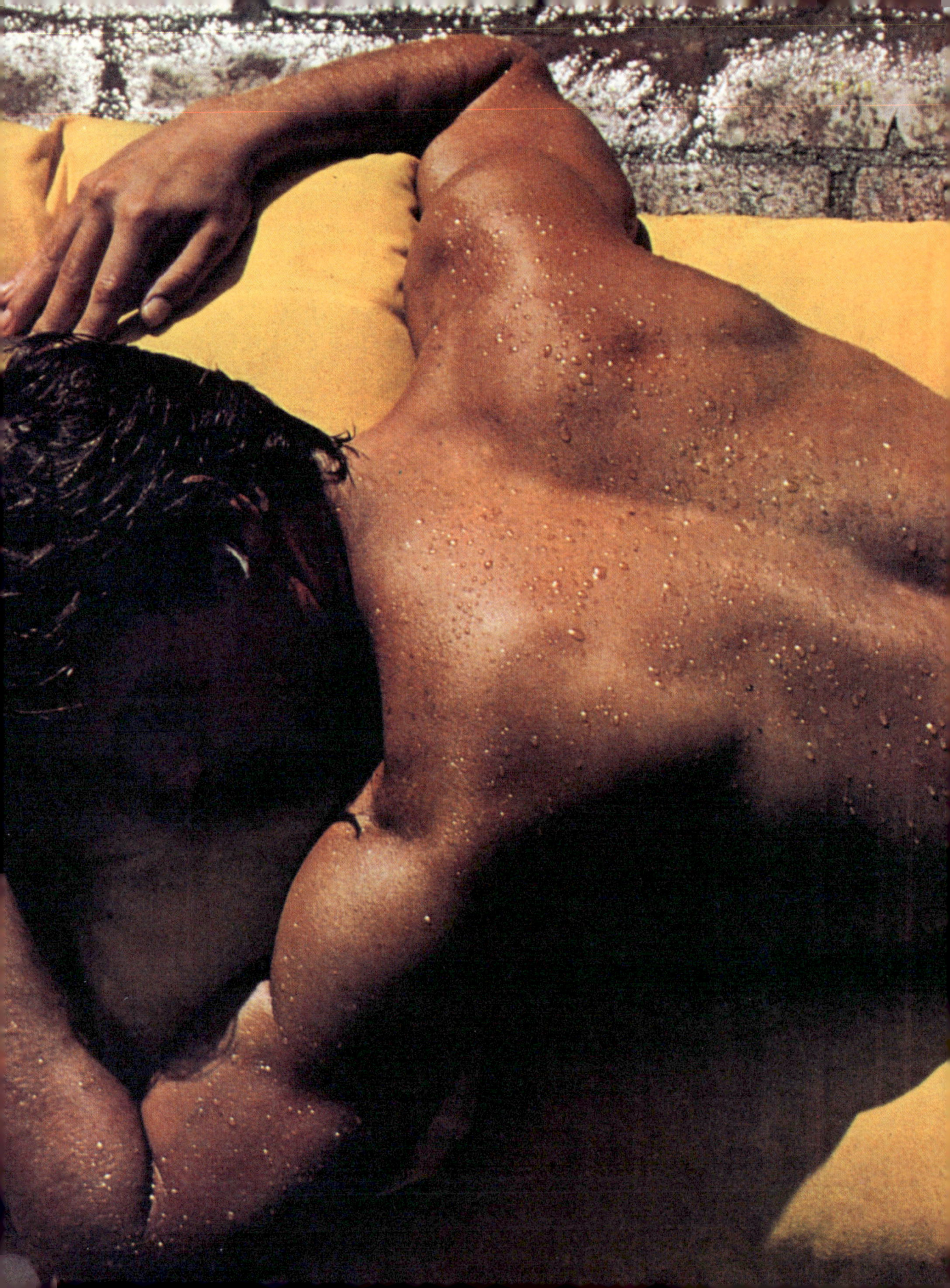

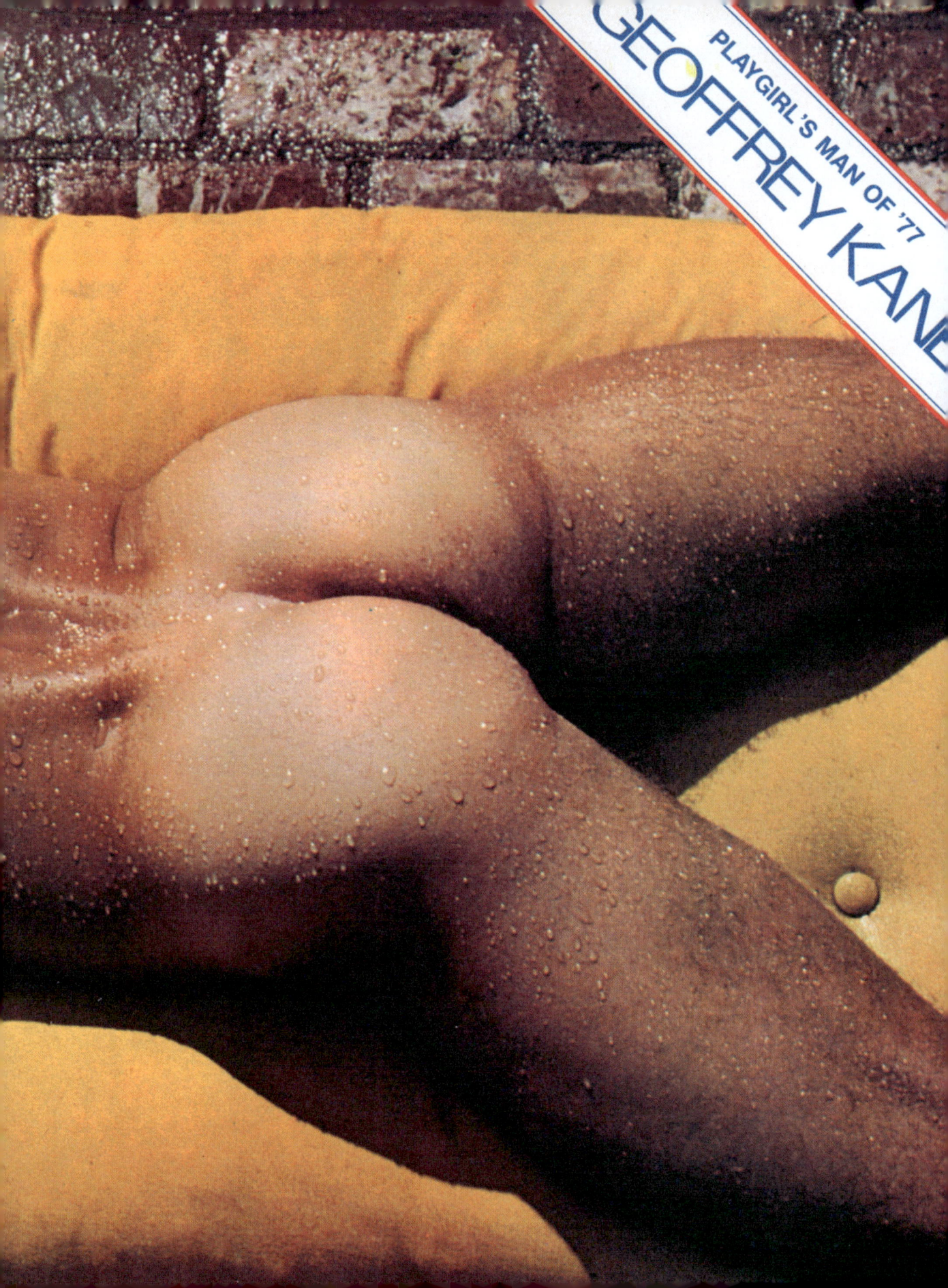

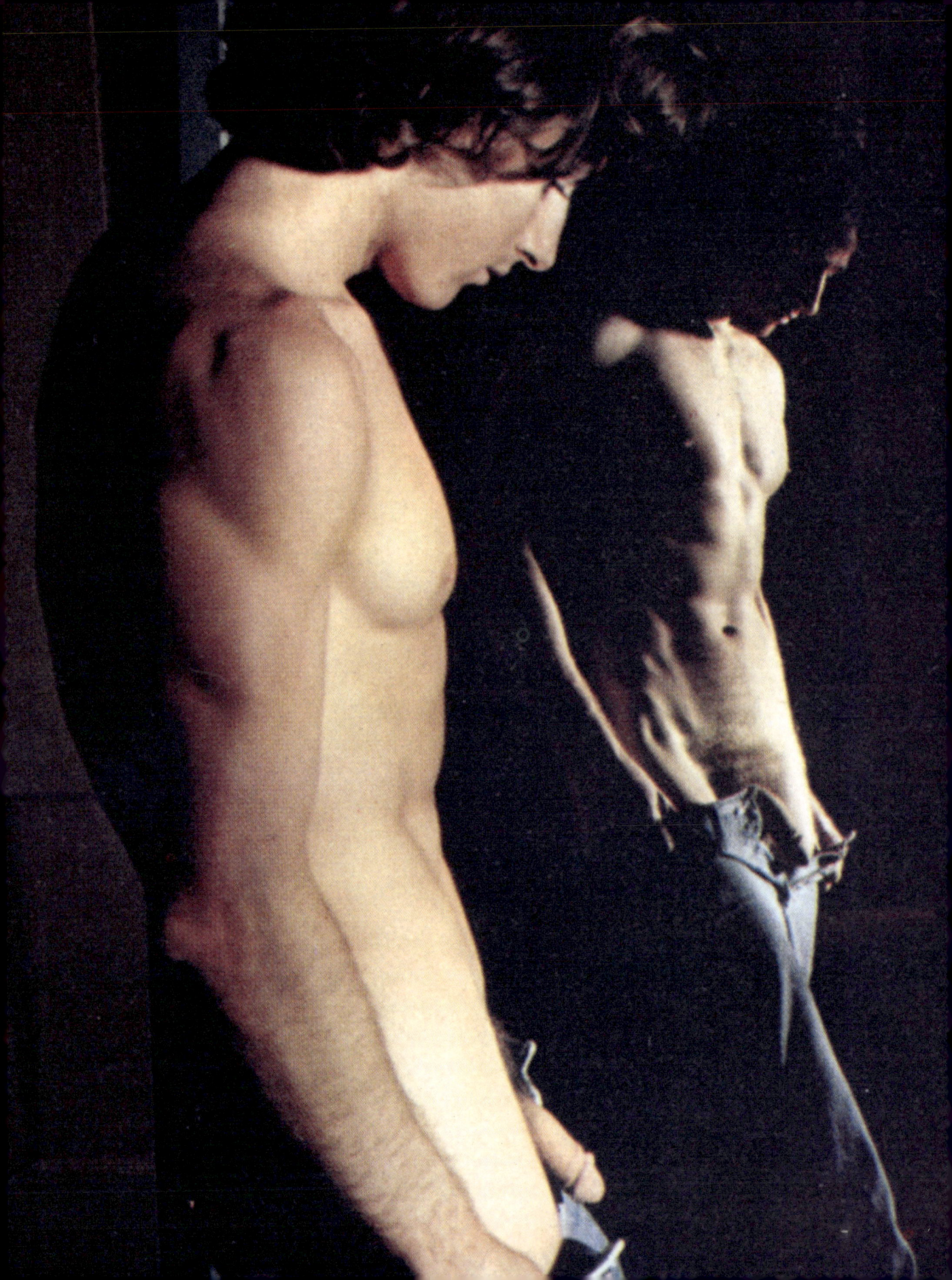